OXFORD MONOGRAPHS ON MUSIC

The Service-Books of the Royal Abbey of Saint-Denis

The Service-Books of the Royal Abbey of Saint-Denis

Images of Ritual and Music in the Middle Ages

ANNE WALTERS ROBERTSON

CLARENDON PRESS · OXFORD
1991

Oxford University Press, Walton Street, Oxford OX2 6DP
Oxford New York Toronto
Delhi Bombay Calcutta Madras Karachi
Petaling Jaya Singapore Hong Kong Tokyo
Nairobi Dar es Salaam Cape Town
Melbourne Auckland
and associated companies in
Berlin Ibadan

Oxford is a trade mark of Oxford University Press

Published in the United States
by Oxford University Press, New York

British Library Cataloguing in Publication Data
Robertson, Anne Walters
The service-books of the Royal Abbey of Saint-Denis:
images of ritual and music in the Middle Ages.—
(Oxford monographs on music).
1. France. Christian music, history
I. Title II. Series
781.7100944
ISBN 0–19–315254–1

Library of Congress Cataloging in Publication Data
data available

Typeset by Hope Services (Abingdon) Ltd
Printed in Great Britain by
Biddles Ltd., Guildford and King's Lynn

FOR ROBBY

PREFACE

This book is the result of the kindness and support of many colleagues, friends, and agencies, and I welcome the opportunity to acknowledge them here. Generous grants from the Fulbright Commission (1981–2) and from the Martha Baird Rockefeller Fund for Music (1982–3) subsidized the research I conducted for my Yale dissertation (1984) in France, England, and Italy. A Fellowship for Independent Study and Research from the National Endowment for the Humanities in 1986–7 allowed me thoroughly to rework the original text and to add vital new material. I am grateful to the staffs of all the libraries that I visited during these years, and particularly to François Avril and Patricia Stirnemann of the Bibliothèque Nationale.

Many musicologists answered my countless queries and offered useful suggestions, and I would especially like to thank Charles Atkinson, Rebecca Baltzer, Margot Fassler, David Hiley, Peter Jeffery, Thomas Kelly, Peter Lefferts, Christopher Page, Claude Palisca, Thomas Payne, Alejandro Planchart, Norman Smith, Pamela Starr, Ruth Steiner, Reinhard Strohm, Andrew Tomasello, and Nancy van Deusen. I am also indebted to my Chicago colleagues Howard Brown, Peter Dembowski, Philip Gossett, Hans Lenneberg, and Bernard McGinn. Time and again Standley Howell and the staff of the Inter-Library Loan Service of Regenstein Library provided me with materials that I thought unobtainable. Scholars of Saint-Denis in other disciplines likewise shared their wisdom with me both in printed work and in unpublished writings and personal correspondence, and I am pleased to recognize Caroline Bruzelius, Madeline Caviness, William Clark, the late Sumner Crosby, the Revd Edward Foley, O.F.M. Cap., David Ganz, Paula Gerson, Donatella Nebbiai-Dalla Guarda, the late Niels Rasmussen, Gabrielle Spiegel, Harvey Stahl, and Jean Vezin. I would also like to thank the editorial staff at Oxford University Press.

Four people deserve special thanks. Michel Huglo gave generously of his time and of his unpublished notes during my sojourns in France, and Craig Wright advised my original dissertation with discerning judgement and a keen editorial eye. Andrew Hughes and an anonymous reader for Oxford University Press read the manuscript of this book with great astuteness, and their suggestions improved it immeasurably. The credit for much of what is useful is theirs, the responsibility for accuracy my own.

Finally, I would like to acknowledge those whose help actually made this book a reality. My parents, Henry and Wanda Walters, were always a mainstay, and I owe them more than I can repay for their constant encouragement. My husband Robby and, more recently, our daughter Caroline enlisted in the campaign with great enthusiasm. Robby saw to it that the work stayed as close to schedule as possible, and he never wavered in his dedication to the project. To him I offer this book in gratitude.

A.W.R.

Chicago
1990

CONTENTS

ABBREVIATIONS AND CONVENTIONS

BIBLIOGRAPHICAL ABBREVIATIONS

AASS	*Acta Sanctorum*
AfL	*Archiv für Liturgiewissenschaft*
AH	*Analecta Hymnica Medii Aevi*
AM	*Acta Musicologica*
AMS	*Antiphonale Missarum Sextuplex*
Auct. Ant.	*Auctores Antiquissimi*
BEC	*Bibliothèque de l'école des chartes*
CAO	*Corpus Antiphonalium Officii*
CC	Corpus Christianorum
CCM	Corpus Consuetudinum Monasticarum, gen. ed. Kassius Hallinger
CE	*The Catholic Encyclopedia*
ChLA	*Chartæ Latinæ Antiquiores*, ed. A. Bruckner and R. Marichal
CLA	*Codices Latini Antiquiores*
CLLA	*Codices Liturgici Latini Antiquiores*
CT	Corpus Troporum
DACL	*Dictionnaire d'archéologie chrétienne et de liturgie*
DMA	*Dictionary of the Middle Ages*
EG	*Études grégoriennes*
EL	Ephemerides Liturgicae
EMH	*Early Music History*
GC	*Gallia Christiana*
GR	*Le Graduel romain*
HBS	Henry Bradshaw Society
JAMS	*Journal of the American Musicological Society*
JM	*The Journal of Musicology*
JPMMS	*Journal of the Plainsong and Mediæval Music Society*
JTS	*Journal of Theological Studies*
JWCI	*Journal of the Warburg and Courtauld Institutes*
LQF	Liturgiewissenschaftliche Quellen und Forschungen
LU	*Liber Usualis*
MBMRF	Münchener Beiträge zur Mediävistik und Renaissance-Forschung
MD	*Musica Disciplina*
MGG	*Die Musik in Geschichte und Gegenwart*
MGH	Monumenta Germanicae Historiae
ML	*Music and Letters*
MQ	*The Musical Quarterly*
MuS	Musicological Studies

NCE	*The New Catholic Encyclopedia*
NGD	*The New Grove Dictionary of Music and Musicians*
NGDMI	*The New Grove Dictionary of Musical Instruments*
NOHM	New Oxford History of Music
OTM	Oxford Theological Monographs
PJ	*Pièces justificatives* (from Félibien, *Histoire*)
PL	*Patrologia Latina*
PM	*Paléographie Musicale*
PMFC	Polyphonic Music of the Fourteenth Century, gen. ed. Kurt von Fischer
PMMM	Publications of Mediaeval Musical Manuscripts
PRMA	*Proceedings of the Royal Musical Association*
RB	*Revue bénédictine*
RdM	*Revue de musicologie*
RED	Rerum Ecclesiasticarum Documenta
RG	*Revue grégorienne*
RH	*Repertorium Hymnologicum*
RISM	*Répertoire International des Sources Musicales*
RM	*Revue Mabillon*
SC	Sources chrétiennes
SE	*Sacris Erudiri*
SeT	Studi e Testi
SF	Spicilegium Friburgense
SLS	Studia Latina Stockholmiensia
SM	*Studi Medievali*
SS. Rer. Mer.	*Scriptores Rerum Merovingicarum*
VSB	*Vies des saints et des bienheureux*
ZfK	*Zeitschrift für Kirchengeschichte*

OTHER ABBREVIATIONS

Alle.	Alleluia
Ant.	Antiphon
C.	*circa*
ch.	chapter(s)
col(s).	column(s)
Comm.	Communion
conc.	concilium
corr.	correspondence
d.	died.
Ex.	Example
fo(s).	folio(s)
Grad.	Gradual
Hy.	Hymn
Intr.	Introit
Inv.	Invitatory

l(l).	line(s)
MS(S)	manuscript(s)
N(n).	footnote(s)
n.g.	not given
No(s).	Number(s)
n.s.	new series, *nouvelle série*
Offer.	Offertory
Ora.	Oration
p(p).	page(s)
pl(s).	plate(s)
Ps.	Psalm
reg.	reigned
Resp.	Responsory
Seq.	Sequence
Tr.	Tract
V.	Versicle
Ver.	Verse
vol(s).	volume(s)

MANUSCRIPT ABBREVIATIONS (AS USED IN *THE NEW GROVE DICTIONARY*)

A:KN	Klosterneuburg, Augustiner-Chorherrenstift Wilten
CH:BEsu	Berne, Stadt- und Universitätsbibliothek
CH:Fcu	Fribourg, Bibliothèque Cantonale et Universitaire
CH:SGs	Saint-Gall, Stiftsbibliothek
D:BAa	Bamberg, BDR, Staatsarchiv
D:DÜl	Düsseldorf, BDR, Landes- und Stadtbibliothek
D:Mbs	Munich, BDR, Bayerische Staatsbibliothek
D:W	Wolfenbüttel, BDR, Herzog August Bibliothek
E:Gm	Gerona, Biblioteca Catedralicia
F:AM	Amiens, Bibliothèque Municipale
F:AN	Angers, Bibliothèque Municipale
F:AUT	Autun, Bibliothèque Municipale
F:B	Besançon, Bibliothèque Municipale
F:CA	Cambrai, Bibliothèque Municipale
F:LA	Laon, Bibliothèque Municipale
F:ML	Moulin, Bibliothèque Municipale
F:MO	Montpellier, Faculté de Médicine de l'Université
F:MZ	Metz, Bibliothèque Municipale
F:O	Orléans, Bibliothèque Municipale
F:Pa	Paris, Bibliothèque de l'Arsenal
F:Pan	Paris, Archives Nationales
F:Pm	Paris, Bibliothèque Mazarine
F:Pn, franç.	Paris, Bibliothèque Nationale, MS français
F:Pn, grec.	Paris, Bibliothèque Nationale, MS grecque

F:Pn, lat.	Paris, Bibliothèque, MS latin
F:Pn, n.a.f.	Paris, Bibliothèque Nationale, MS nouvelles acquisitions françaises
F:Pn, n.a.l.	Paris, Bibliothèque Nationale, MS nouvelles acquisitions latines
F:Pn, Rés.	Paris, Bibliothèque Nationale, Réserve
F:Psg	Paris, Bibliothèque Sainte-Geneviève
F:R(m)	Rouen, Bibliothèque Municipale
F:RSc	Reims, Bibliothèque de la Cathédrale
F:T	Troyes, Bibliothèque Municipale
F:TO	Tours, Bibliothèque Municipale
GB:Cjc	Cambridge, St John's College
GB:Cu	Cambridge, University Library
GB:Lbm	London, British Library, Reference Division (formerly British Museum)
GB:Lva	London, Victoria and Albert Museum
GB:Lwa	London, Westminster Abbey
GB:Mr	Manchester, John Rylands Library
GB:Ob	Oxford, Bodleian Library
GB:WO	Worcester, Cathedral
I:Ac	Assisi, Biblioteca Communale
I:BV	Benevento, Archivio Capitolare
I:CFm	Cividale, Museo Archeologico Nazionale
I:Fl	Florence, Biblioteca Medicea–Laurenziana
I:Rc	Rome, Biblioteca Casanatense
I:Rvat	Rome, Biblioteca Apostolica Vaticana
I:VEcap	Verona, Biblioteca Capitolare (Cattedrale)
NL:Lu	Leiden, Biblioteek der Rijksuniversiteit
S:Sk	Stockholm, Kungliga Biblioteket
USSR:Lsc	Leningrad, Gosudarstvennaya Ordena Trudovovo Krasnovo Znameni Publichnaya Biblioteka imeni M. E. Saltikova-Shchedrina

CONVENTIONS

I use the following spellings to distinguish between the abbey, Saint-Denis; the saint, Saint Denis (without hyphen); and the town, St Denis. This convention is a modified version of the one employed by the late Sumner Crosby in his studies of the abbey, and I have extended it to encompass other institutions, geographical locations, and saints, respectively. The designations of places and establishments are in the original languages (e.g. Saint-Germain-des-Prés), whereas all saints' names, except Saint Denis, have been anglicized (e.g. Saint Germanus) according to the spelling used in the fourth and fifth editions of the Benedictine *Book of Saints*. Liturgical and musical genres (e.g. Benedicamus) are considered to be English words not requiring italicization, so that incipits of texts can be italicized without confusion with the names of genres (e.g. Benedicamus Domino *Flos filius*). All words in names of genres are capitalized (e.g. Benedicamus Domino), but only the first word in incipits is capitalized (e.g. *Flos filius*). 'Octave' with a capital letter refers to the eighth day after a major feast, while 'octave' signifies the entire eight-day period. Designations for manuscripts and printed sources are drawn from the table of library sigla in *The New Grove Dictionary*, except for F:Pan (= Paris, Archives Nationales). For abbreviations not found in *The New Grove*, I have cited the sources in full (e.g., Vendôme, Bibl. Mun. 17C). Unless otherwise stated, all brackets found in quotations indicate my own interpolation. Works listed in the Bibliography are cited in the footnotes in the form of author's surname and abbreviated title.

LIST OF PLATES

between pp. 268–269

LIST OF MUSICAL EXAMPLES

LIST OF TABLES

Introduction

In April 1981 the Metropolitan Museum of Art in New York City mounted a major exhibition at The Cloisters, 'The Royal Abbey of Saint-Denis in the Time of Abbot Suger (1122–1151)'.[1] In conjunction with this, an international symposium on Saint-Denis and Abbot Suger was held at Columbia University. The papers presented there focused upon this brilliant period in the history of the abbey from the vantage points of monastic life, political and social history, art, architecture, and literature.[2] As always, the participants acknowledged the central position of Saint-Denis in French history as the first Gothic abbey, royal necropolis, and place of origin of the chronicles of the kings. The successful collaboration of so many scholars from diverse fields only reaffirmed that Saint-Denis, perhaps more than any other medieval institution, richly rewards careful study in a wide variety of disciplines.

Yet, as the late Niels Rasmussen pointed out in his communication, little had been done to investigate the liturgy of Saint-Denis,[3] and this was equally true of the music of the abbey. Ironically, an awareness of the special musico-liturgical practice at Saint-Denis began at least as early as 1625, when Jacques Doublet spoke of the striking ceremonies and the beauty of the singing in the church.[4] Until recently, though, only a handful of essays on the Greek Mass of Saint-Denis discussed part of the ritual in any detail.[5] Happily, the conference in New York seems to have awakened an interest, and my own dissertation,[6] along with two subsequent dissertations on individual manuscripts[7] and a few articles,[8] have appeared since 1984. The present book aims to help fill the void by providing for the first time an overview of the most important aspects of ritual and music at Saint-Denis.

The liturgical books on which to base such an enquiry do exist—indeed, for a single medieval house, they fairly abound. These manuscripts have been known only imperfectly, however, probably because an astonishingly small number of them could be positively linked to

[1] The catalogue of the exhibition was edited in Crosby *et al.*, *The Royal Abbey of Saint-Denis in the Time of Abbot Suger (1122–1151)*.

[2] The papers have recently been published in Gerson (ed.), *Abbot Suger and Saint Denis*.

[3] Rasmussen, 'Liturgy'.

[4] Doublet, *Histoire*, 353.

[5] See Huglo, 'Chants'; Omont, 'Messe'; Vincent, 'Note'.

[6] Walters [Robertson], 'Music'.

[7] Udovich, 'Modality'; Foley, 'Ordinary'.

[8] E.g. Walters [Robertson], 'Reconstruction'; Crocker, 'Matins'; Robertson, '*Benedicamus*'.

Saint-Denis by external features.[9] Partial listings of the liturgical books were made by Henri Leclercq in the *Dictionnaire d'archéologie chrétienne et de liturgie*,[10] and by Michel Huglo in *The New Grove Dictionary*,[11] and a fuller inventory appears in Donatella Nebbiai-Dalla Guarda's recent study of the library of Saint-Denis.[12] I have enlarged these lists in the catalogues in Chapters 6 and 7, which treat questions of origin, provenance, dating, and the interrelationships between sources.

If the surviving manuscripts are plentiful, the archival sources relating to the liturgy of Saint-Denis are at once less numerous and less informative than those from other places. Isolated documents sometimes provide useful information on when a feast was established or discontinued, and the records of individual endowments and the account books of the abbey witness, for example, the foundation of special services for the Virgin Mary, of a confraternity for Saint Denis, and of anniversaries for royalty. But these sources offer few details on the music that may have been sung at these events. The history of music and of the Divine Office in general at Saint-Denis is largely the story of the surviving service-books, and these are the principal focus here.

From these sources we can glean the most prominent features of ritual and music at Saint-Denis. Among other topics, Chapters 3 and 4 treat the proper tropes, sequences, Benedicamus Domino, Ite Missa Est, and Offices for Saint Denis, items mentioned only in passing, if at all, in previous literature. Chapter 5 provides information on performance practices, the organ, musicians, and liturgists from the abbey, and Chapter 1 gives a narrative account of the history of the liturgy from the Council of Tours in 567 to the pillage of the abbey by the Huguenots in 1567, a millennium that encompasses most of the extant liturgical codices from Saint-Denis. The feasts, endowed services, anniversaries, and royal celebrations that were observed at Saint-Denis are discussed in Chapter 2.

The abundant scholarship on Saint-Denis in other disciplines is the impetus for Chapter 4, a discussion of music and liturgy in the church in the light of what we already know about other aspects of the abbey. There, the connection between the reconstructions of Saint-Denis and the liturgy that was celebrated in the successive buildings is treated. Similarly, we will see that the decoration of the church is often mirrored in the music and ceremony of the monastery. Even the monks' ambitions and the ways in which they tried to achieve their political ends are portrayed in their ritual, which thus serves as a forum for their philosophy.

[9] Only 4 liturgical MSS contain shelf-marks from the library of Saint-Denis; see the discussion in Ch. 6.

[10] iv/l. 588–642.

[11] xvi. 385–6.

[12] *Bibliothèque*, 313–17.

Certainly the extensive work on Saint-Denis in other areas alone might have prompted the examination of ceremony and music in the abbey. But the unique aspects of the celebration of the Divine Office likewise make this investigation imperative. The goal of this introduction to the musico-liturgical tradition of Saint-Denis is to focus on those aspects, to offer a new chapter in the history of the abbey. It is hoped, too, that this study will serve as a point of departure for those interested in all facets—liturgical and otherwise—of this extraordinary institution.

1

Survey of the Liturgical History of Saint-Denis

A band of seven missionaries from Rome arrived in Gaul around 250. They could not have known that Christianity would prevail in these western reaches of the empire only a few decades later.[1] As it happened, the new religious tolerance came too late for one of the evangelists in the party, a bishop named Dionysius. Assigned to convert the heathen in the region of Paris, Dionysius laboured to carry out his holy charge, only to be executed for his trouble.

But his influence did not end here. Like so many early martyrs, Saint Denis, as the French would call him, accomplished more in death than he had in life. The monastery that was established in his honour grew to be one of the most powerful in Western Christendom, a renowned pilgrimage site, the preferred abbey of French monarchs up to the Revolution. By the thirteenth century the devoted monks of Saint-Denis had immortalized their beloved patron in numerous panegyrics, many of them similar to the opening of this sequence (see Ex. 4.3, pp. 279–80):

> Hail, father Dionysius,
> Light and beauty of paradise,
> Glory and honour of Gaul,
> Herald of life, trumpet of heaven,
> Flame of love, furnace of zeal
> Fountain and river of grace.

MARTYR, FIRST CHURCH, EARLY COMMUNITY

The first persons who worshipped in the church at Saint-Denis at the end of the fifth century had little in common with the Benedictine monks who composed these lyrics. They had not yet heard of the Rule of Saint Benedict (*c*.480–547), for this code that governed their late medieval counterparts took hold at Saint-Denis only in the ninth century. Saint Denis himself was no monk at all, but the first bishop of

[1] The conversion of Gaul began in the late 2nd c.; see Griffe, *Gaule*, i. 19–157; Latouche, *Caesar*, 119–47. On the history of the western Roman empire to the mid-3rd c., see the recent study in Drinkwater, *Gaul*; and the brief summary of the period of Roman rule in Gaul to the end of the 4th c. in James, *Origins*, 13–15.

Paris. In short, the earliest services at Saint-Denis were not those of a monastic community, but rather of a church answering to the episcopal seat at Paris.[2]

The life of Saint Denis and the nature of the church founded in his memory are first known through sixth-century sources.[3] The *Historia Francorum* of Gregory of Tours reports that Bishop Dionysius was sent, along with six others, to preach in Gaul in the third century.[4] Dionysius served as bishop of Paris, and there was martyred by decapitation during the persecution that took place around 250 under the Roman consuls Decius and Gratus. The story of his bloody execution is embellished in manuscript illumination of the late Middle Ages and Renaissance to include two co-martyrs with Dionysius: Rusticus and Eleutherius.[5] In fact the artists did not invent Dionysius' two friends; they simply relied on a late sixth-century tradition, which slightly post-dates the accounts of Gregory of Tours and others who do not mention the companions. The legend of Rusticus and Eleutherius caught on, however, and these two figures were firmly implanted in the *vita* of Saint Denis by the end of the eighth century.[6]

The first church was built as a basilica over the tomb of Saint Denis around 475 by Geneviève (later patron Saint Geneviève of Paris) with the aid of the Parisian clergy.[7] This type of structure was designed to

[2] The cult of Saint Denis at the cathedral of Paris was always a vital part of its liturgy; see Baltzer, 'Look', 2.

[3] Some of the early texts are reliable, others questionable, and scholars have spent much of this century distinguishing truth from fiction in these questions. See the pioneering study from the 1890s in Havet, 'Questions', 1–62; the landmark revisions and additions of Levillain in his 'Études' (1921, 1925, 1926, 1930); the results of more recent excavations by Formigé, *Abbaye*, 2–17; and the new synthesis in Crosby, *Abbey*, to name only the most important. Many 17th- and 18th.-c. authors also wrote about Saint-Denis, and 3 full-scale histories of the abbey by Doublet (1625), Félibien (1706), and d'Ayzac (1860–1) appeared prior to the late 19th c. Félibien makes the best use of primary sources and is by far the most reliable, although Doublet and Ayzac occasionally provide useful, if unverifiable, information.

[4] Gregory's trustworthy history of the Franks is edited in Krusch, *Gregorii* i. 23, ch. 30; and translated in Thorpe, *Gregory*, 87. See also Crosby, *Abbey*, 3–6.

[5] See e.g. the historiated initials at the beginning of the Mass for the feast of Saint Denis in the 3 13th- and 14th-c. missals F:Pm 414, fo. 242^v; F:Pn, lat. 1107, fo. 271^v; and GB:Lva 1346–1891, fo. 296.

[6] Levillain, 'Études' (1921), 14–19; Crosby, *Abbey*, 5. None of the extant liturgical or musical MSS from Saint-Denis, which date from as early as the 8th. c., omits Dionysius' saintly companions. Later taken for granted in other churches, they were often linked to the saint anonymously as '(Dionysii) sociorumque ejus' (see the Parisian calendar in F:Pn, lat. 5185cc, 9 Oct.)

[7] 'Such was the devotion of Geneviève that she [wanted to] build a basilica in honour of the bishop Saint Denis, but she lacked the strength [to do it herself]. When some of the presbyters met her in the usual course of things, she said to them: "My holy fathers and elders, beloved in Christ, I ask that each of you give your encouragement so that a basilica might be constructed in honour of Saint Denis"' ('Devotio erat Genovesae, ut in honore sancti Dionisi episcopi et martiris basilicam construeret, sed virtus deerat. Cui cum solito presbiteri occurrissent, ait ad eos: "Venerabiles in Christo sancti patres ac seniores mei, obsecro vos, ut faciat unusquisque vestrum consolationem,

contain a saint's relics,[8] and it typically comprised a group of buildings at the centre of which was the church itself. Such a cluster, or *domus basilicae*, was not a *monasterium*. Many early charters differentiate between these two terms, and we can safely assume that any religious house called a basilica before the seventh century did not begin as a monastery. Saint-Denis was a rural basilica because of its location on the outskirts of Paris proper. Later, owing to its age and dignity, it would become a *basilica senior*, a privileged rank shared with other important churches outside the city.[9] This first church at Saint-Denis began to function in the last quarter of the fifth century under the direct control of the church of Paris, which, after all, had helped build it.

The site of this church and of all its later reconstructions appears to be the same as that of Saint Denis's martyrdom and burial.[10] The *Vita Genovesae* states that Dionysius died in a village called *Catulacum*,[11] and modern studies of coins found in the area demonstrate that *Catulacum* is probably the town St Denis, just to the north of present-day Paris.[12] Excavating at the present church of Saint-Denis, Sumner Crosby found the remains of a chapel which he identifies as the one built by Saint Geneviève. In addition, a cemetery containing coins from the first through to the mid-fourth centuries and some intact sarcophagi from the Merovingian era were uncovered beneath and next to the church. These findings weakened an erstwhile popular theory that Saint Denis had been buried and first venerated at another church in the town, Saint-Denis-de-l'Estrée (Pl. 1). The present location of the abbey, Crosby concludes, is most likely the one and only site of the edifices built to commemorate Saint Denis.

One aspect of the liturgy likewise suggests that the martyr always rested at the location of the once and future churches: there is no 'feast

et edificetur in sancti Dionisi honore basilica"'); Krusch, *Genovesae*, 222–4. On Geneviève (later, patron Saint Geneviève of Paris), see also Dubois and Beaumont-Maillet, *Geneviève*. The following discussion draws on the following sources which Levillain and others have deemed authoritative for the history of Saint-Denis: Gregory of Tours (Krusch, *Gregorii* [6th c.]); Fredegarius (Krusch, *Fredegarii* [7th c.], 1–193); Krusch, *Francorum* [*c*.727], 215–328; the life of Saint Geneviève (Krusch, *Genovesae* [*c*.520]); the life of Saint Eligius (Krusch, *Eligii* [original text *c*.665], 634–761; and *PL*, lxxxvii. 477–594); and the life of Saint Bathildis (Krusch, *Balthildis* (*c*.660 or 670), 475–508). The various aspects of the first church and the religious community have been thoroughly studied in Levillain, 'Études' (1925), 44–97.

[8] Most 6th-c. authors distinguish carefully between the words *ecclesia* and *basilica*, and both the *Vita Genovesae* and Gregory of Tours consistently apply the word *basilica* to Saint-Denis; see n. 9, and Krusch, *Gregorii*, 237, ch. 32.

[9] See Levillain's study of these terms, 'Études' (1925), 44–7, 78–84, 98; and Duchesne, *Origines*, 420–4.

[10] The following information on the Merovingian church at Saint-Denis is drawn from Crosby, *Abbey*, 13–27.

[11] 'Catulacensum vicum, in quó sanctus Dionisius et passus est et sepultus'; Krusch, *Genovesae*, 221, ch. 17.

[12] Crosby, *Abbey*, 5.

of the Translation' of Saint Denis—probably because no Translation ever happened.[13] This is powerful testimony, since the five most important events in the life of the saint and of his church were systematically incorporated into the ritual. The martyrdom of Saint Denis was celebrated from time immemorial on 9 October. The feast of the consecration of the altar on 28 July was thought to date from 754, when Pope Stephen II crowned Pepin the Short and his two sons Charles (later, Charlemagne) and Carloman in the abbey, and at the same time supposedly consecrated the main altar of the church. The Dedication of the church first took place in the presence of Charlemagne in 775 and was re-enacted thereafter on 24 February. The festival of the Detection of Saint Denis on 9 June, inspired by the opening of the reliquary of the saint around 1053, probably entered the ritual in the eleventh or twelfth century. A fifth event, the Invention of Saint Denis, was the occasion confused with a Translation. Solemnized on 22 April, the Invention commemorates the finding, or discovery, of the bodies of Dionysius, Rusticus, and Eleutherius by a woman named Catulla. This service is not the same as a Translation, that is, the *movement* of relics from one place to another,[14] and for this reason the feast of the Invention does not witness the construction of a church on a different site from the place where the relics lay.

The supposed *Translatio* was apparently concocted around 834 by Hincmar of Reims, then a monk of Saint-Denis, in his *Miracula sancti Dionysii*.[15] Shortly thereafter the *Gesta Dagoberti*,[16] co-authored by Hincmar and Abbot Hilduin (814–40) of Saint-Denis, repeated the story to further the false claim that King Dagobert I (629–*c*.639) had built an entirely new church on the location of the original one.[17] To

[13] Levillain, 'Études' (1925), 18.

[14] There were, e.g., at least 2 slightly different translations of the relics of Saint Benedict. They were brought first from Monte Cassino to Fleury in 672, a translation which was celebrated throughout most of Western Europe on 11 July. When the old basilica was rebuilt in 882, the relics were again 'carried in' as the name of this 4 Dec. feast, the *Illatio*, implies. Only then did the monastery receive its new name, Saint-Benoît-sur-Loire; *Dictionnaire d'histoire et de géographie ecclésiastiques*, viii, cols. 229–30, s.v. 'Benoît, abbé du Mont-Cassin, No. 3. Reliques'; Cottineau, *Répertoire*, ii, col. 2610, s.v. 'St.-Benoît-sur-Loire'. Unlike Saint-Benoît, the dedication of the church of Saint-Denis was never other than to the saint himself.

[15] The portion in question of the *Miracula* comes from its preface, which is found in 2 12th-c. MSS: I:Rvat, Reg. lat. 571 and F:Pn, lat. 2445A. Jean Mabillon, not knowing of the existence of a preface, edited only the main text of the *Miracula* in *AASS Ordinis Sancti Benedicti*, Saec. iii/2, 343–64. On the life of Hincmar and his involvement with Hilduin of Saint-Denis, see Devisse, *Hincmar*, esp. ii, 1092–5.

[16] Krusch, *Dagoberti*, 396–425. For the dates of the *Miracula* and the *Gesta*, see Crosby, *Abbey*, 5, 30.

[17] Levillain, 'Études' (1925), 18–27. While Dagobert did shower favours on the abbey, he did not install a monastic order there, and he only added to the original basilica, without reconstructing it altogether, as reported in the *Gesta* and the *Miracula*. Dagobert's refurbishments are described in Ch. 4.

lend credence to their tale, monk and abbot chose 22 April for the Translation,[18] borrowing the date from the Invention while ignoring the event. But they dared not alter the actual name of the feast in liturgical calendars and books, probably because it had already existed for some time as the *Inventio* in the liturgy of both Saint-Denis and elsewhere.[19]

To fabricate the events of this Translation, the *Miracula* and the *Gesta* cited the authority of the fifth- or sixth-century *Passio sanctorum Dionisii, Rustici et Eleutherii*. Although the *Passio* gives the presumably correct version of the Invention of Saint Denis by Catulla, it does not provide a date for the event: 'The aforementioned woman [Catulla] . . ., when first she saw that the fervour of the persecution had abated, sought with a certain amount of trepidation the place which guarded the bones of the holy martyrs. She marked [this place] which she found [*inventum*] by the building of an honorable tomb.'[20] Hincmar and Hilduin, in reworking this account to their own ends, divested the *Passio* of virtually everything but the relics and the new church. Then they wrote their own version of a Translation under Dagobert. To add an air of authenticity, they gave it the date of the Invention of Saint Denis, 22 April, which the contemporaneous liturgical calendars of the abbey were no doubt recording. But despite the efforts of Hincmar and Hilduin, the liturgy of Saint-Denis disputes the legend that Dagobert built a new church by including an Invention and not a Translation.

The precise nature of the pre-monastic establishment at Saint-Denis is difficult to define, because certain Merovingian terms are hard to interpret. The use of two words in particular, *abbas* and *monachus*,

[18] 'Summa cum veneratione decimo kalendas maias transtulit eorumque memorias'; Krusch, *Dagoberti*, 406, ch. 17.

[19] Levillain's side-by-side comparison of the *Miracula* and the *Gesta* shows that both texts transmit identical reports of a Translation on 22 Apr.; Levillain, 'Études' (1921), 74. On the other hand, 2 early books for the Mass written at Saint-Denis (F:Pn, lat. 2290, and F:Psg 111), dating from the last quarter of the 9th c., record the feast of the *Invention* of Saint Denis on this date. Since this festival was called *Inventio* in these early sources from the abbey, less than 50 years after the composition of the *Miracula* and the *Gesta*, there is good reason to believe that it was celebrated earlier as well. In the first place, it is doubtful that a feast of the *Translatio* of a presumably present Saint Denis on 22 Apr. was changed into an *Inventio* of Saint Denis, that is, the sudden finding of him, 4 decades later (Levillain, Études [1925], 16–18)! Secondly, the works of Hincmar and Hilduin are not completely reliable and were composed in order to advance the abbey of Saint-Denis in the eyes of the monarchy, and these 2 sources are the only extant testimony of the Translation. It is very likely that any sacramentary from the abbey from the early 9th c. would show that the feast on 22 Apr. was the *Inventio*.

[20] 'Antedicta tamen materfamilias [Catulla] . . . cum primum persecutionis vidit tempuisse fervorem, locum sanctorum martyrum ossa servantem qua oportuit sollicitudine requisivit atque *inventum* eminentis mausolei constructione signavit'; Krusch, *Passio*, 104. Like the *Miracula* and the *Gesta*, the *Passio* is of dubious value as an historical source. The work no longer exists in its original 5th- or 6th-c. form, and none of the later recensions pre-dates the ninth century; see Levillain, 'Études' (1921), 4–28.

once led scholars to conclude that a monastery existed by the seventh century.[21] Levillain, however, demonstrates that an *abbas* in the sixth century was most often a member of the secular clergy and the head of a basilica.[22] The rest of the community consisted of several other levels of inhabitants. The *custodes* signified in a general way all those who were connected with the basilica, including the abbot. The *clerici* were persons in greater or lesser orders. *Fratres* and *pauperes* are words which appear to have no consistent meaning and can refer to almost anyone in the establishment. The *monachi*, or lay brothers, could also function as *clerici*. The important element of poverty, evidently lacking in the *monachi* of these establishments, distinguishes them from persons who were bound to regular monastic orders.[23]

In all likelihood, the early community at Saint-Denis lived according to an unwritten rule which Saint Martin had transported into Gaul from the Orient.[24] Martin's biographer Sulpicius Severus describes this early monastic custom but gives no details about singing or the liturgy. He does outline the basic regime as one of communal living in which the participants, not obligated by oath, worked, took meals, and prayed together.[25] This form of organization was probably in effect at Saint-Denis until the introduction of monastic rule in the middle of the seventh century.

DIVINE OFFICE IN THE EARLY CENTURIES

The liturgy in Gaul took many forms in the early centuries. Differences in practice were due in part to barriers of language and customs, to the geographical isolation of portions of this vast territory, to local influences, and to the work of missionaries, who tended to affect discrete areas. Only two liturgical books from Saint-Denis have survived from the Merovingian era (F:Pn, lat. 256; I:Rvat, Reg. lat. 257), and neither sheds light on rites that might have been particular to the church. And whereas the historical documents provide some information about the daily round of prayer, also known as the Hours, at Saint-Denis, there

[21] 'Ideo vir venerabelis [*sic*], pater noster Dodo, abba', and later: 'cum Dei et nostra gracia [*sic*] ad ipsa basilica, vel monachis ibidem deservientebus [*sic*]; charter of 625 from Clothair II to Saint-Denis, published in Tardif, *Monuments*, 4, No. 4 (original = F:Pan, K 1, No. 7; facsimile in Bruckner and Marichal, *ChLA*, xiii. 16–9 [No. 552]). Havet, for one, based his conjecture of the date 623–5 for the establishment of a monastic rule at Saint-Denis on this ancient document; 'Questions', 13.

[22] Levillain, 'Études' (1925), 61–2.

[23] Ibid. 52–70.

[24] Ibid. 75.

[25] Fontaine, *Sulpice* i. 274–5. On the influence of Saint Martin in Gaul, see also Besse, *Moines*, 1–33; Prinz, *Mönchtum*, 19–46.

are no direct references to the celebration of the eucharistic sacrifice, or Mass, from Merovingian times.

It is fair to assume, however, that Saint-Denis employed some form of what we now call the Gallican Mass, a collective name for the traditions which prevailed in Gaul until the Carolingian reforms of the late eighth and ninth centuries. Both the liturgy and the music of the Gallican ritual differed markedly from the so-called Roman or Gregorian repertory which supplanted it. Details of one version of the Gallican liturgy are known from two anonymous Merovingian letters once attributed to Saint Germanus, but now thought to have come from the Burgundian region of France in the eighth century.[26] Although perhaps not entirely accurate with respect to the Gallican Mass at Saint-Denis, the broad outlines of the Pseudo-Germanus description give a rough idea of how the service might have been celebrated in the abbey.

According to these documents, the Mass began with an *Antiphona ad prelegendum*, which corresponds to the introit of the Roman Mass. Like an early Carolingian introit, the *Antiphona ad prelegendum* had psalm verses. Next came the call for silence, a brief melody sung on a reciting tone, followed by the greeting, its response, and an oration. The subsequent musical item was the *Aius*, or *Trisagion*, chanted both in Greek and in Latin before the Kyrie. The *Benedictus*,[27] or during Lent the Ant. *Sanctus deus archangelorum*, preceded a collect, and the Hymn of the Three Boys (*Benedicite*) was sung between the Old and New Testament readings. Another *Aius* was then performed, and an antiphon before the gospel (*Antiphona ante evangelium*) was heard as the person assigned to chant the gospel walked to his appointed spot. After the gospel, a *Sanctus post evangelium* was sung while the reader returned to his place, and then a patristic homily was read. There followed a Litany or *Preces* for the needs of the people; each verse of this concluded with a brief congregational response.[28] The dismissal of the catechumens ensued, and an elaborate *Sonus*, roughly the equivalent of the Roman offertory, was chanted during the procession of the oblations. After the prayer which corresponded to the Roman preface the Sanctus was sung, and the transitional oration was heard. The fraction antiphon, akin to the Roman Communion, was chanted before the Lord's Prayer, following which an episcopal benediction was sung. The community responded to each verse of this prayer with *Amen*.

[26] Ed. in *PL*, lxxii. 89–98; and in modern edn. in Gamber, *Ordo* and Ratcliff, *Expositio*. The secondary literature on the Gallican Mass includes the summaries on which this paragraph is based: Stäblein, 'Gallikanische' and Huglo, 'Gallican'. See also Van Dam's recent reflections on the public mass in Gaul in his *Leadership*, 279–83, and *passim*.

[27] Canticle of Zachariah (Luke 1: 68–79).

[28] For a discussion of the Gallican *preces*, also known as the 'prayer of the faithful', see De Clerck, '*Prière*', 187–205.

During the Communion of the faithful the *Trecanum* was chanted, after which the post-communion oration and the dismissal ended the Mass.

To what extent the community at Saint-Denis celebrated Mass in this way is not known, but antiphons before the gospel, a *Preces*, and other remnants survive in later manuscripts from the abbey. There is likewise evidence that the monks deliberately preserved certain Gallican chants into the late Middle Ages for political reasons. What these chants were and how they were intertwined with politics will be described in Chapter 4.

Although no first-hand reports of the early Mass at Saint-Denis exist, a few mentions of the Gallican Office and perhaps indirectly of the Mass in the basilica have survived. Gregory of Tours reports a judgement by ordeal which took place around 579, during the reign of Chilperic I. A woman accused of adultery was to be tried by the swearing of oaths upon the tomb of Saint Denis. The brawl which followed took the lives of both the accuser and the advocate of the woman, wounded many others, and left the basilica covered with human blood. In the aftermath,

> Peace was restored with great difficulty, but services [*officium*] could not be held in the church until what had happened was brought to the notice of the King. Both parties rushed off to court, but Chilperic refused to exonerate any of them. He sent them to the local bishop [of the region around Saint-Denis] with orders that only if they were found not guilty were they to be admitted to communion. They paid a fine for their offences, and so were readmitted to communion by Bishop Ragnemod, who had charge of the church in Paris.[29]

Gregory's brief mention of the *officium* at Saint-Denis implies that organized worship had been going on there for some time, long enough at least to be taken for granted. The unusual feature—that which required rectification—was the suspension of the regular round of services. The other salient point of the passage is that the basilica was clearly under the jurisdiction of the church of Paris. The king initially referred the case back to the person in charge of the rural area around Saint-Denis, whom Gregory calls *episcopus*, that is, a deputy to the bishop of Paris. While this man set forth the conditions for the reinstatement of the offenders, it was Ragnemod who, as head of the Paris diocese, pronounced the final absolution.[30]

[29] Translation from Thorpe, *Gregory*, 294–5; original text in Krusch, *Gregorii*, 237, ch. 32.

[30] The name Ragnemod appears on a list of names of Paris bishops found in F:Pn, lat. 2291, a 9th-c. sacramentary from Saint-Amand (later adapted for Saint-Germain-des-Prés), which was in the Saint-Denis library in the 12th c. (see Ch. 7). Duchesne gives a short biographical notice for Ragnemod in *Fastes*, ii. 471; and Guérard lists him as the 21st bishop of Paris (reg. 576–91) in *Cartulaire*, iv. 213.

Almost a century later, the *Vita Eligii* describes a service at Saint-Denis during which Eligius (later, Saint Eligius) healed a crippled man. The mention of the Vigil of Saint Denis at the beginning of this passage is the earliest evidence of this service: 'on one occasion, during the celebration of the anniversary of the passion of the martyr Saint Denis in Paris, while the Vigil was being sung in the choir by the clergy [*a clero*], Eligius left the church and was walking in the portico when, from a distance, he saw a man with contracted limbs lying on the stone floor against the tomb of the saint.'[31]

Eligius' lifetime spanned the introduction of monastic rule at Saint-Denis around 650, and the event described here may therefore pre-date the establishment of the monastery. On the other hand, because the secular community continued to coexist for some time at Saint-Denis with the monastic one,[32] it is possible that either a secular or regular *clerus* could have officiated. Félibien speculates that the *clerus* may have come from the church at Paris to do the honours on the Vigil of the saint's day. The very fact that this Vigil commemorated the patron saint of a *basilica senior* lent it sufficient liturgical importance to warrant the presence of visiting clergy.[33]

[31] 'Denique quodam tempore cum anniversaria Parisiis sancti Dionysii martyris celebraretur passio, dum Vigilia a clero caneretur in choro, egressus Eligius templo deambulabat in atrio, viditque eminus virum cunctis membris contractum contra sancti sepulcrum jacere in pavimento'; *PL*, lxxxvii. 499, ch. 23. Krusch omits this portion and many other chapters in his edition of the text, evidently due to a lack of sufficient numbers of MSS to construct an adequate critical apparatus; Krusch, *Eligii*, 657–62. The context of the whole passage makes it clear that *Parisiis* here refers to 'the Paris region', and not simply to the city proper. Since the word is not limited specifically to the cathedral, it can therefore also comprise the basilica of Saint-Denis, situated in the area of Paris, and this meaning is consistent with the repeated mentions of Saint Denis in the story. Later in the chapter, Saint Eligius asks the paralytic if he truly believes that *iste sanctus* [Saint Denis] can heal him, and at the end of the account the author writes: 'nisi quod Dominus Jesus *per sanctum Dionysium* eum sanasset.' In ch. 32, he situates Saint-Denis in *Parisiis civitate*, and throughout the *Vita* the author begins chapters with *Parisiis* to indicate simply the general area.

[32] Levillain, 'Études' (1925), 77–8. In any case the rule of Saint Benedict, introduced later at Saint-Denis, permitted a priest to live and to say Mass in a monastery: 'He [the priest] should, however, be allowed to stand next to the abbot, to give blessings and to celebrate Mass, provided that the abbot bids him'; Fry, *Rule*, 272–3, ch. 60. But it does relegate clerics to a lower station: 'Any clerics who similarly wish to join the community should be ranked somewhere in the middle, but only if they, too, promise to keep the rule and observe stability'; ibid. 274–5.

[33] Félibien, *Histoire*, 'Dissertation préliminaire', (unnumbered pp.) 6. While Félibien's idea is sound, his ultimate conclusion is not. In believing that the monastic rule had been imposed long before the reign of Dagobert, Félibien tries to explain why a priest would be officiating at Saint-Denis at all. It is significant, however, that he recognized at the beginning of the 18th-c. that Dagobert had not established monastic rule in the church, for his 17th-c. predecessor in Sandionysian historiography, Jacques Doublet, did not (cf. Doublet, *Histoire*, 165). Levillain discusses the celebration of vigils of feasts in the *basilicae seniores* in the Paris area; 'Études' (1925), 82. This reference to a Vigil for the feast of Saint Denis is the earliest we have, although it must have existed prior to the 7th c.

To judge from the surviving sources, the most important development for music and liturgy at Saint-Denis during the Merovingian era was King Dagobert's institution of perpetual psalmody. It is not Dagobert himself but a charter of his son Clovis II from 654 which reports the event:

It was thought that we [Clovis] were responsible for this privilege at that holy place [Saint-Denis], namely the procedure that, just as in the time of our lord and father [Dagobert] psalmody by 'shifts' [*per turmas*] was established there, and just as it is still being done day and night at the monastery of Saint-Maurice-en-Valais, it should likewise be practised in that place [Saint-Denis].[34]

The mid-seventh-century chronicler Fredegarius likewise records: 'A few days later Dagobert died and was buried in the church of Saint-Denis . . . He had commanded the institution there of psalmody according to the model of the Valais saints [Saint Maurice and companions], but it is known that *Abbas* Aigulph, because of his laxness, opposed its institution.'[35] And a number of later sources, of which the ninth-century *Gesta Dabogerti* is one of the first, also relate the story: '[Dagobert] ordered that they should sing psalms in shifts [*per turmas*] according to the example of the Valais monastery or of Saint-Martin.'[36]

In the first document above, Clovis informs us that the practice of psalmody *per turmas* at Saint-Denis was initiated by his father Dagobert, but he implies that it was later suspended.[37] Fredegarius' version refines the date by adding that the ritual fell out of use under the *Abbas* Aigulph

[34] [All spellings *sic*] 'nos . . . hunc beneficium ad locum ipsum sanctum . . . vise fuemus prestetisse, eo scilicet ordene ut, sicut tempore domni et genetoris nostri ibidem psallencius per turmas fuit instetutus, vel sicut ad monasthirium Sancti Mauricii Agaunis, die noctoque, tenetur, ita in loco ipso celebretur'; Tardif, *Monuments*, 10, No. 11 (original = F:Pan, K2, No. 3 [22 June 654]; facsimiles in *DACL*, iii, cols. 931–3, and in Bruckner and Marichal, *ChLA*, xiii. 36–43 [No. 558]).

[35] [All spellings *sic*] 'post pauciis dies Dagobertus amisit spiritum, sepultusque est in ecclesia sancti Dionensis . . . Sallencium ibidem ad instar monastiriae sanctorum agauninsium instetuere jusserat; sed facilletas abbatis Aigulfi eadem instetucionem nuscetur refragasse'; Krusch, *Fredegarii*, 161, lib. iv, ch. 79.

[36] 'eos [fratres] turmatim ad instar monasterii Acaunensium sive sancti Martini Turonis psallare instituit'; Krusch, *Dagoberti*, 414, ch. 35. Among the later sources to repeat this version are Aimoin, *Libri*, 138, 179; Viard, *Chroniques*, ii. 181.

[37] The dates of these 3 passages are important, since the words *per turmas* appear both in Clovis's mid-17th-c. charter and in the later sources. Gindele, ignoring the date of Clovis's document, wrongly attributes the expression *per turmas* to a later period; Gindele, 'Laus', 42–4. He cites 3 instances of the use of the phrase *per turmas*, the first of which is in fact Clovis's charter, but he seems to confuse the 1st citation with his 2nd and 3rd quotations, both of which come from the 9th-c. *Gesta Dagoberti*. As a result he claims that the expression *per turmas* was a later, Carolingian depiction of perpetual psalmody in the 7th c., when, in fact, it was the current Merovingian term. Although it is true that many of the documents written to confirm Dagobert's supposed largesse to Saint-Denis are later forgeries, the present charter of Clovis is not; see Levillain, 'Études' (1926), 21 ff. Levillain uses this charter as a basis for comparison with several 8th-c. documents to sort out what is true in them.

(643–47)—before 644, according to Mabillon.[38] Although Fredegarius omits the qualifier *per turmas*, he too likens the psalmody to a ritual which could be heard in the famous monastery Saint-Maurice-en-Valais, located in southern Switzerland on the Rhône. Accounts from the ninth century and later usually add Saint-Martin of Tours to the list of places in which psalmody *per turmas* was practised. This small emendation, however, belies the authority of these later documents, for perpetual psalmody evidently did not exist at Saint-Martin in Merovingian times. It is probably Alcuin of York (*c.*730–804) who introduced it there around 800.[39] The facts seem to be that Dagobert established psalmody *per turmas* at Saint-Denis before 639, that it was modelled on the same practice at Saint-Maurice-en-Valais, that it was suspended under Aigulph perhaps before 644, and that it was reinstated by Clovis II by 654. If this timetable is correct, the reinstatement of this psalmody at Saint-Denis would have occurred after the introduction of monastic rule in about 650.

The model for psalmody *per turmas* at Saint-Denis in the seventh century was the perpetual psalmody of Saint-Maurice-en-Valais. A description of this practice is found in a document attributed to the founder of Saint-Maurice, King Sigismund. Legend had it that the king supposedly wrote this charter in 515, but the surviving document was actually forged in the late eighth or ninth century.[40] Instead of the term *per turmas*, Pseudo-Sigismund uses the word *norma*:

> It seems right to me that . . . concerning the methods of psalm-singing, eight *norme* should be done, that is, the Granensian, Insolanan, Jurensian, and Melvensian, and so forth. These should follow one another according to the Canonical Hours, namely, Nocturns, Matins, Prima, Secunda, Tercia, Sexta, Nona, and Vespers, and in peace let [the monks] serve God unceasingly day and night.[41]

[38] Mabillon, *Œuvrages*, ii. 350. On the disputed dates of Aigulph, see Ayzac, *Histoire*, vol. i, p. cxxiii. As we have seen, his position as *abbas* does not necessarily imply that monastic rule had been imposed.

[39] Krusch, 'Über', 189; Prinz, *Mönchtum*, 106–7. Alcuin's term of residence at Saint-Martin (796–804) falls shortly before the composition of the *Gesta Dagoberti*, which claims that perpetual psalmody existed at Saint-Martin in the 7th c.

[40] See Reymond, 'Charte'; Theurillat, 'Abbaye', 1–84. Theurillat rejects Reymond's idea that an original 6th-c. MS establishing Saint-Maurice-en-Valais by Sigismund exists. On the foundation of Saint-Maurice, see Besson, *Monasterium*; Theurillat, 'Abbaye'; Wood, 'Prelude', 15–18.

[41] 'Recte mihi videtur ut . . . de psallendi institucionibus fiant VIII norme, id est Granensis, Islana, Jurensis et Melvensis et cetere; et succedentes sibi in officiis canonicis id est Nocturnis, Matutinis, Prima, Secunda, Tercia, Sexta, Nona, Vespertina, et cum pace die noctuque indesinenter Domino famulentur'; Theurillat, 'Abbaye', 78. An independent copy of this document from the 12th c. specifies 5 *norme*: 'fiant quinque norme, id est Granensis, Insolana, Jurensis, Melvensis seu domni Probi'; ibid.

These *norme*, synonymous with *turme*,[42] refer to different methods of psalmody which the monks of Saint-Maurice were to solicit from the surrounding region. The various practices would fill the time between the Hours so that a state of perpetual psalmody, also called *laus perennis*, would result.[43] As for their content, the *norme* must have been a continuous succession of psalms, such that in performing *norme* in conjunction with the Hours, the Psalter was sung through once each day or at least several times per week, instead of only once a week, as Saint Benedict prescribed. The *norme* were not merely inserted abruptly between the Offices, they were integrated into the Hours so that the person who finished the last psalm of a *norma* showed his successor where in the psalter to begin the first psalm for the next Hour.[44] Evidently a certain amount of local pride and even renown for prowess in psalm-singing had developed at various locations near Saint-Maurice by the beginning of the sixth century, since the forged charter specifies the *norme* that the abbey was to include.[45]

At this point one might ask: which of the three types of psalmody is implied in *laus perennis*? In responsorial psalmody a soloist sings psalm verses, while the choir sings a respond before, after, and sometimes between the verses. In antiphonal psalmody a soloist and the choir sing an antiphon before, after, and sometimes between the solo verses, and by the ninth century, two choirs may alternate on the verses. In direct psalmody there is neither alternation nor refrain. The psalm verses were evidently executed by individual monks in order of seniority in the period between the fourth to the early eighth century.[46] The earliest psalmody in Gaul was responsorial, but it was gradually supplanted by antiphonal singing.[47] Under Saint Caesarius, for example, the church of Arles had adopted antiphonal psalmody by the sixth century. At Avignon, however, the responsorial practice persisted until the beginning of the eighth century,[48] while Amalarius of Metz, a liturgical commentator of the ninth century, implies that the antiphonal performance of psalms was the norm in Gaul at that time.[49] Clearly, psalmodic practices in Gaul were diverse for at least 200 years, a period which

[42] For a discussion of these 2 terms, see Masai, 'Vita', 64–5, n. 83.

[43] See Reymond, 'Charte', 47–8; Gindele, 'Laus', 32–4; also Mabillon's description of perpetual psalmody and its relationship to the established Offices; *Annales*, i. 28–9.

[44] Gindele, 'Laus', 34–5.

[45] See n. 41 above. The Granensian and Insolanan refer to the monasteries of Grigny and Île-Barbe, respectively, the Jurensian recalls either the Jura monastery of Condat or perhaps Romainmôtier, while the Melvensian almost certainly refers to Romainmôtier. See the interpretation of these locations in Masai, 'Vita' 66–8; Wood, 'Prelude', 16–17.

[46] Dyer, 'Psalmody', 43–74.

[47] Huglo, 'Gallican', 119–20; idem, *Livres*, 61–2; Dyer, 'Psalmody', 51.

[48] Anglès, 'Chant', 74.

[49] Hanssens, *Amalarii*, ii. 432–3; see also Dyer, 'Psalmody', 68–9.

encompassed the establishments of perpetual psalmody at Saint-Maurice and at Saint-Denis.

Whatever the method of chanting the psalms, the organization of perpetual psalmody at Saint-Denis was probably as follows. The basic *officium* consisted of the eight Offices that are named in the forged charter of Saint-Maurice. Between two given Hours, groups of monks (*turmae*) would sing the psalms, probably taking turns as soloists, beginning in the psalter where the preceding Office had just ended. The next Hour would take up where the preceding inter-hour had stopped. In terms of sheer numbers, all 150 psalms could well have been sung each day, whether the singing was direct, or whether some or all of the psalms were prolonged by the use of antiphons between verses.[50] This soloistic method of executing the psalms would have been the most efficient means, since the burden of singing is more equally shared under this system.

Dagobert opted for perpetual psalmody at Saint-Denis a decade before the establishment of monastic rule around 650. What, then, was the nature of the Divine Office that existed at Saint-Denis at the time *laus perennis* was imposed? From all indications, it was probably the order established by the Council of Tours in 567 that governed the psalmodic arrangement of the canonical Hours. Saint-Denis, as noted earlier, appears to have subscribed to the Martinian Custom with respect to its organization as a *domus basilicae*. The section of the conciliar document which discusses psalmody states 'this *ordo psallendi* should be followed in this basilica [Saint-Martin's] as well as in our churches'.[51] By 'our churches' the authors must have meant not only the immediate dependencies of Saint-Martin but also the churches of the dioceses whose bishops attended the council, and who subscribed to the Martinian code in terms of their administration.[52] Several bishops signed the conciliar decree, and the second name is Germanus, bishop of Paris, who soon after his death was canonized as Saint Germanus.[53] It is likely, then, that the basilica of Saint-Denis, whose internal life was regulated generally by the Martinian Custom and even more immedi-

[50] Gregory of Tours gives an idea of the amount of time that would be needed to sing psalms by these 2 methods [emphasis mine]: 'Martius . . . Quando stella est in hor. 2 diei, si surgas, dicis nocturnus et galli canto, quae dupliciter, ut superius diximus, hoc est *in directis* 60 psalmos. Quibus expeditis, psallis *in antyphanis* 20 psal. et stilla illa venit ad horam 5. diei. Quod si sic inchoas matutinus, 30 decantatis *cum antyphana* psalmis, luciscit'; Krusch, *Ratio*, 871. If 60 psalms *in directum* and 20 psalms with antiphons could be chanted in 3 hours, it is likely that the entire psalter could be sung in 24 hours, even if antiphons accompanied all the psalms.

[51] 'ut tam in ipsa basilica sancta quam in ecclesiabus nostris iste psallendi ordo servetur'; De Clercq, *Concilia*, 182–3; Maassen, *Concilia*, 127, ch. 19.

[52] Besse, *Moines*, 237–8; Levillain, 'Études' (1925), 75–6.

[53] De Clercq, *Concilia*, 194; Maassen, *Concilia*, 135, ch. 19. Germanus' name also appears on the list of bishops contained in F:Pn, lat. 2291 (see Duchesne, *Fastes*, ii. 470–1).

ately by Bishop Germanus, would have felt the effects of the council's instructions concerning psalmody during this period.

The Martinian regimen provides liturgical information only for the Offices of *Matutina*, *Sexta* (midday), and *Duodecima* (evening).[54] The psalms and antiphons for *Matutina* varied in number, according to the time of year and the length of the nights. There were six antiphons each with pairs of psalms in the summer (except for August), whereas from December until Easter these numbers gradually increased to ten antiphons with groups of three psalms each. *Sexta* contained six psalms with alleluias, and *Duodecima* twelve psalms also with alleluias.[55] A minimum of twelve psalms for every service of *Matutina* was obligatory, and failure to comply with this stipulation was a punishable offense. Because of the plethora of feasts and Masses during the month of August, the psalmody was suspended and replaced by services called *Manicationes*.[56]

This relatively light formula for the Offices was probably the one in use at Saint-Denis when King Dagobert added the burden of perpetual psalmody. Small wonder, then, that the practice of Saint-Maurice, with its *norme*, was short-lived at the basilica. It would be interesting to know if Dagobert intended perpetual psalmody at Saint-Denis to be every bit as rigorous as at Saint-Maurice. Actually, this probably was his wish, since Clovis's charter, although not specific, in no way compromises the description from Saint-Maurice, and Clovis, moreover, does mention this monastery by name.[57]

There were of course other regimes alive in Gaul in the seventh century, and Dagobert could have emulated one which, though not a true *laus perennis* form, was at least substantially more stringent than the *Ordo* which came out of the Council of Tours. The monastery of Luxeuil, founded around 590 by Saint Columbanus, lay physically

[54] De Clercq, *Concilia*, 182–3; Maassen, *Concilia*, 127, ch. 19. See also the discussion of the liturgical day in Gaul in Van Dam, *Leadership*, 283–9.

[55] The council did not reserve the alleluias for Easter season, and it appears that they could be sung year-round, as the rules of Saint Caesarius and Saint Aurelian also allowed (see Gindele, 'Alleluiaticus', 316–17).

[56] 'Toto Augusto manicationes fiant, quia festivitates sunt et missae'; De Clercq, *Concilia*, 183; Maassen, *Concilia*, 127, ch. 19. The implications of *manicatio* are not clear. Aimoin glosses this passage: 'Porro toto Augusto, propter crebras festivitates, manicationes fiebant. Manicare autem mane surgere'; *Libri*, iii. 138, ch. 80. Mabillon postulates that the word might refer to the saints' feasts for August which, because of the already overcrowded roster of high feasts in this month, had to be relegated to the early morning hours and thus replaced the nocturnal psalmody; *Cursu*, ch. 54, col. 406. Gastoué proposes that *manicationes* were ornate responsories sung by boys for the Sundays in August; 'Origines' (1903/4), 33. De Clercq (*Concilia*, 183) and Du Cange (*Glossarium*, v. 220, s.v. 'manicare') suggest that they were accelerations or abbreviations of Matins.

[57] 'vel sicut ad monasthirium Sancti Mauricii Agaunis die nocteque tenetur, ita in loco ipso celebretur'; Tardif, *Monuments*, 10, No. 11 (original = F:Pan, K 2, No. 3: 22 June 654; facsimile in *DACL*, iii. cols. 931–3).

closer to Dagobert than Saint-Maurice-en-Valais.[58] The original *Ordo* of this monastery had much in common with the regimen of *laus perennis* in terms of sheer numbers of psalms. It called for up to seventy-five psalms in the course of the three night watches, while prescribing only three at each of the three day hours, due to the interruption of work.[59] Dagobert certainly knew this code, for the monastic rule soon to be adopted at Saint-Denis and throughout Gaul was not that of Saint Benedict alone, but rather a mixture of the rules of Benedict and Columbanus.

Nevertheless, Dagobert preferred to implement the most exalted of psalmodic rituals, *laus perennis*, at Saint-Denis. Perhaps he hoped to marshal the diverse community into one which could keep the cult of the saint with a reverence equal to the splendour of the basilica he had just enlarged and decorated with the help of Eligius.[60] The severity of the regimen, however, was next to intolerable for a house unaccustomed even to a written code. As a result, after the death of its chief advocate Dagobert and during the careless custody of the irresolute *Abbas* Aigulph, perpetual psalmody at Saint-Denis foundered.

Dagobert's call for perpetual psalmody at Saint-Denis was none the less significant, for it led to the introduction of the *Ordo regularis* which could ensure its performance. He did not live to see *laus perennis* dropped in such short order. But his son Clovis must have viewed the inability of the community to sustain this most arduous form of divine celebration as a threat to the salvation of the souls of those royalty who had rested there since the late sixth century, among whom were his own parents Dagobert and Nanthilde.[61] Through these and other burials, Saint-Denis was gradually becoming the traditional royal burial place, an auspicious role for the abbey.[62] Clearly, therefore, the failure of perpetual psalmody at Saint-Denis played no small role in bringing Clovis to the realization that it was time to organize the life of the basilica in a manner worthy both of the sacred relics and of the royal bodies it guarded.

[58] On the impact of Saint Columbanus in Gaul, see Prinz, *Mönchtum*, 121; idem, 'Columbanus'; Riché, 'Columbanus'. The works of Saint Columbanus are edited in Walker, *Columbani*.

[59] Walker, *Columbani*, ii. 130–2, ch. 7. See also Gindele, 'Laus', 35, 38, 46.

[60] On the enlargement of Saint-Denis under Dagobert, see Crosby, *Abbey*, 29–50, and the discussion in Ch. 4 below. Whereas the *Gesta Dagoberti* provides no evidence that Dagobert held Saint-Maurice in special devotion, the abbey was known throughout Europe for its intense piety, and it is not surprising that Dagobert looked to it as an archetype; see Besse, *Moines*, 448–9; Prinz, *Mönchtum*, 102–8.

[61] See Erlande–Brandenburg, *Roi*, 69–70. The author also assumes that Clovis was buried at Saint-Denis, but there is no record of the event.

[62] On the status of Saint-Denis as royal abbey, see the discussions (with bibliography) in Erlande-Brandenburg, *Roi*; Brown, 'Ceremonial'; Spiegel, *Chronicle*, 18–37; Crosby, *Abbey*, 9–12; Beaune, *Naissance*, 83–125.

MONASTIC COMMUNITY

In the end, it was not Clovis at all but his wife Bathildis (later Saint Bathildis) who established monastic rule at Saint-Denis and in five other *seniores basilicae:*

> We must not forget that [Bathildis], for the love of God and through her persuasion of the bishops and abbots, ordained for the major basilicas, Saint-Denis, Saint-Germain [Auxerre], Saint-Médard [Soissons], Saint-Pierre-le-Vif [Sens], Saint-Aignan [Orléans], Saint-Martin [Tours], and wherever the familiarity with this latter has encompassed, and sent them letters to the effect that the brothers residing in these places should live under a holy regular order.[63]

This undated announcement, which forms part of a recitation of Bathildis's good deeds, cannot be later than the letters of the Parisian Bishop Landericus in 653 and of Clovis II in 654, which granted and recognized certain privileges for the abbey. These acts presume the previous existence of an actual monastery at Saint-Denis, although the first original charters to use the term *monasterium* date from 658.[64] It appears then that Bathildis's establishment of monastic rule in the six basilicas, including Saint-Denis, happened slightly earlier, around 650.[65]

Still, it is unclear from the *Vita Sanctae Balthildis* exactly which *Ordo regularis* the basilicas were to adopt. The seventh and eighth centuries were a veritable crucible for the monastic rules, and it was not uncommon to find as many as three at one time in a single house.[66] The hardiest and most appealing form, which appeared in the first quarter of the seventh century, was a fusion of two rules, those of Saints Columbanus and Benedict. The Columbanan abbey of Luxeuil was first to use both *regulae*, beginning in 629 under the abbacy of

[63] 'Preterire enim non debemus, quod [Balthildis] per seniores basilicas sanctorum domni Dionisii et domni Germani vel domni Medardi et sancti Petri vel domni Aniani seu et sancti Martini, vel ubicumque eius perstrinxit notitia, ad pontifices seu abbates suadendo pro zelo Dei praecepit et epistolas pro hoc eis direxit, ut sub sancto regulari ordine fratres infra ipsa loca consistentes vivere deberent'; Krusch, *Balthildis*, 493, ch. 9, rédaction A. Levillain believes that the phrase *vel ubicumque eius perstrinxit notitia* refers in passing to the churches, including Saint-Denis, which lived under the Martinian Custom; 'Études' (1925), 74–5; see also Folz, 'Tradition', 372–3. Saint Bathildis is lauded throughout the *Vita* for her generosity toward monastic institutions. She founded an *Ordo regularis* before 646 at Chelles, and later retired there (see Krusch, *Balthildis*, 495–6; Cottineau, *Répertoire*, i, cols. 753–5, s.v. 'Chelles'; Prinz, *Mönchtum*, 174–7, and *passim*).

[64] Levillain, 'Études', (1925), 77. These charters of Clothair III are F:Pan, K 2, Nos. 6, 7. See Tardif, *Monuments*, 12–13, Nos. 14, 15 (facsimiles in Bruckner and Marichal, *ChLA*, xiii. 50–9 [Nos. 561, 562]).

[65] Levillain, 'Études', (1925), 77.

[66] See Butler, *Monachism*, 355.

Walbert.[67] Among the other houses which are known to have followed suit was Saint-Pierre-le-Vif of Sens, one of the *seniores basilicae* in which Saint Bathildis imposed monastic rule.[68] Her knowledge of the Columbanan–Benedictine combination is clear from the role she played in selecting Abbot Theodfrid for the monastery of Corbie, who established the dual system there as well.[69] While the Benedictine rule did govern the monasteries in Gaul by the ninth century, the presence of both *regulae* in one house was a distinctive feature of the seventh and eighth centuries.[70] From the examples of Saint-Pierre-le-Vif and from the involvement of Queen Bathildis with Corbie, it is likely that Saint-Denis replaced its Martinian Custom with an amalgam of the rules of Saints Columbanus and Benedict.[71]

As to the singing of psalms, the burden during the day Hours was approximately the same under both rules. However, while the entire psalter could be recited in as little as two days under the *regula* of Columbanus, the four evening and night Hours (Vespers, Compline, Matins, and Lauds) never contained more than 30 psalms under the Benedictine formula, and the entire psalter was sung only once a week.[72] A final advantage of the Benedictine prescription was that Matins proceeded directly to Lauds from Easter until mid-November,

[67] Besse, *Moines*, 291; Prinz, *Mönchtum*, 271. Walbert may also have written a mixed rule for the abbey of Faremoutiers a few years earlier, *c*.620, but the date is in question; Prinz, *Mönchtum*, 286–7; Moyse, 'Monachisme', 7, 14. See the discussion of the mixed rule and its replacement by the Benedictine rule in Prinz, *Mönchtum*, 271–92; also Fry, *Rule*, 113–20; Moyse, 'Monachisme'. On the diffusion of the Benedictine rule in Gaul, see Moyse, 'Monachisme'; Vogüé and Neufville, *Benoît*, i. 162–9; Prinz, *Mönchtum*, 263–92.

[68] A charter from 659 attests the use of the 2 rules at Saint–Pierre; see Pardessus and Bréquiny, *Diplomata*, ii. 114, No. 335.

[69] Levillain, *Examen*, 225, 228. A charter of Bishop Bertfrid of Amiens from 664 mentions the 2 rules at Corbie; see Pardessus and Bréquiny, *Diplomata*, ii. 128, No. 345. Saint-Pierre of Corbie had a particularly close rapport with Saint-Denis from the time of its foundation before 667.

[70] Malnory, *Luxovienses*, 34; Prinz, *Mönchtum*, 289–90.

[71] See ibid. 274–5. But in terms of the Office, there are several indications that the less stringent Benedictine formulas would have been preferred by houses under the dual rule. As transmitted in the extant MSS, the fluctuating contents of the *regula* of Saint Columbanus suggest that this rule was never set down in a definite form; rather, it seems to have been composed sporadically, increasing in text without regard for unity in terms of literary style and even of logical continuity (Walker, *Columbani*, vol. ii, pp. xliv–xlv). The earliest surviving sources of this rule are from the 9th c. Vogüé and Neufville have demonstrated that portions of the Columbanan rule, not including the chapter on psalmody, were influenced by the rule of Saint Benedict; *Benoît*, i, prologue to ch. 7, 163–6. (Vogüé and Neufville likewise proved the entire dependence of the Benedictine rule on the earlier *Rule of the Master*; ibid. 7; also Fry, *Rule*, 79–83. See the edn. of the *Rule of the Master* in Vogüé, *Maître*, and the translation in Eberle, *Rule*.) Many extant sources for the Columbanan rule even omit the 7th chapter, *De cursu*, which deals with the liturgy (Walker, *Columbani*, vol. ii, p. xlv). On the other hand, the extant MSS of Benedict's rule, the earliest of which come from the 8th c. (Vogüé and Neufville, *Benoît*, i. 317–18), include the chapters on psalmody, and variants between sources consist in different spellings and occasional phrase omissions (ibid. iii. 258–91).

[72] Ibid. 103; cf. Walker, *Columbani*, ii. 130–2. See also Malnory, *Luxovienses*, 39.

and was separated from it by a time for reading and meditation in winter. Under the Columbanan rule, on the other hand, the night was interrupted by two distinct times for waking.[73]

In spite of its attractiveness, however, the Benedictine *cursus* was formally introduced in France only at the end of the eighth century, and no monastery seems to have adopted this liturgy exclusively until the early ninth century.[74] Clovis's re-establishment of perpetual psalmody in the abbey only four years after the institution of monastic rule around 650 already suggests that the Benedictine formula had not taken hold. Other Columbanan–Benedictine houses founded around this time opted for *laus perennis* as well, notably, the convents of Remiremont and Sainte-Salaberge.[75] The Rule for Virgins by the Columbanan monk Saint Donatus of Besançon borrows parts of the rule of Saint Benedict but eschews the section on psalmody, drawing instead on the Columbanan liturgy.[76] And a privilege of Bishop Drauscius of 667 for Notre Dame of Soissons demonstrates that the *cursus* for the Hours might be considered separate from the other administrative aspects of the rule that a monastery might follow: 'that within the walls of the monastery the virgins and chaste recluses should serve God according to the vow of those who are fearful of the oft-repeated words of God, and who put together the *regula* and the *cursus* of Saint Benedict . . . They should endeavour in all things to keep the *regula* in the manner of Luxeuil . . . for the profit of their souls.'[77] From this and other documents,[78] it is clear that a house might follow the mixed

[73] Ibid.; see also Fry, *Rule*, 202–3, ch. 8.

[74] As late as 767, a document known as the *Ratio de cursus qui fuerunt eius auctores* attests the knowledge of both the Columbanan and Benedictine formulas, among others; see Hallinger, *Initia*, 90–1, and his commentary in ibid. xlii. 79.

[75] On the diffusion of perpetual psalmody, see Prinz, *Mönchtum*, 102–7. Saint Romaric founded Remiremont as a Columbanan house around 625; ibid. 105; Cottineau, *Répertoire*, ii. 2442–3. Sainte-Salaberge (Saint-Jean-Baptiste) of Laon was established according to both rules *c.*641; ibid. i. 1559–60, s.v. 'Laon'; Prinz, *Mönchtum*, 106. See also *DACL*, ii/1, cols. 863–4, s.v. 'Agaune', and Gindele, 'Laus', 40.

[76] Donatus, *Regula*, ch. 75, col. 296. On the similarities between Saint Donatus' *Ordo officii* and that of the Columbanan rule, see Gindele, 'Überlieferung', 173, 183–4.

[77] 'ut infra septa monasterii virgines et caste reclausae debeant Domino militare, secundum votum saepe dictorum Deo timentium qui construxerunt regulam et cursum sancti Benedicti . . . et ad modum Luxoviensis monasterii . . . regulam ad profectum animarum earum studeant in omnibus custodire'; Pardessus, *Diplomata*, 138, No. 355; *PL*, lxxxviii. 1184, charta XIV; see also Prinz, *Mönchtum*, 280.

[78] The Office of Prime in Gaul, whose diffusion in the 2nd quarter of the 7th c. was a result of the growing acceptance of the Benedictine rule which called for its recitation, likewise demonstrates the knowledge of the psalmodic chapters of the rule (Fry, *Rule*, 210–11, ch. 16). On the origin of Prime, see Froger, *Origines*, 61–2; Taft, 'Quaestiones', 156. The Council of Autun around 670 stated 'that [the abbots and monks] should both fulfil and observe in all things that canon which the *Ordo* and *regula* of Saint Benedict teaches' ('ut [abbati vel monachi] quicquid canonum ordo vel regula sancti Benedicti edocet, et implere et custodire in omnibus debeant'); De Clercq, *Concilia*, 319; Maassen, *Concilia*, 221.

Columbanan–Benedictine rule in terms of administrative organization and still practise *laus perennis* at the same time. Such appears to have been the case at Saint-Denis from about 654.

Just as the community at Saint-Denis had overthrown the practice of perpetual psalmody a few years earlier, this diverse group, suddenly transformed into monks by Queen Bathildis, likewise must have chafed under the formal rule. Bathildis therefore took steps to ensure its palatability: 'And so that they would acquiesce [to an *Ordo regularis*] more willingly, she ordered that a privilege be affirmed for them, and she also granted immunities, so that they would be more inclined to entreat the mercy of Christ the highest king for the [temporal] king and for peace.'[79] The privilege mentioned here had been granted to Saint-Denis by Bishop Landericus of Paris on 1 July 653.[80] His charter, since lost, was supplanted between 1060 and 1065 by an eleventh-century forgery.[81] Levillain demonstrates that the original document defined the legal condition of Saint-Denis with respect to the church of Paris. It affirmed the rights of the monastery to administer property as well as precious possessions, including sacred books. It also forbade the presence of outside ecclesiastics, the bishop included, who were not expressly invited by the abbot to enter the confines of the monastery. On the other hand, Landericus reserved the rights of consecration of church and altar, of the annual gift of holy oil to the abbey, and of ordination or elevation of members of the community, including the abbot, who could in fact be elected by the monks by permission of the king.[82] Thus in matters of temporal administration the basilica of Saint-Denis was independent of episcopal control from Paris by 653. The charter, however, is silent on spiritual matters, and it must be assumed that there was no break with the liturgical influence that Paris must have exerted on its dependencies, and that the Divine Office continued in its pre-monastic state until 654.

In the act of 22 June of that year, Clovis II confirmed many of the bishop's intentions. He also added the special clause mentioned earlier: the restoration of perpetual psalmody in the abbey.[83] Since Clovis's charter cites Landericus' act of 653, which assumes the foundation of a monastery at Saint-Denis, it follows that his call for *laus perennis* came at a time when the abbey had been regimented, spiritually at least, according to the combined rules of Saints Columbanus and Benedict.

[79] 'Et ut hoc libenter adquiescerent, priviligium eis firmare jussit, vel etiam emunitates concessit, ut melius eis delectaret pro rege et pace summi regis Christi clementiam exorare'; Krusch, *Balthildis*, ch. 9, 493–4, rédaction A.

[80] See Levillain's detailed treatment of the privilege; 'Études' (1926), 21–53; also Crosby, *Abbey*, 10, esp. n. 459.

[81] Levillain, 'Études' (1926), 35–48, 339.

[82] Ibid. 340–1.

[83] See above, p. 13.

And so, once again, the herculean task of singing the entire Psalter at least once each day was shouldered, this time by the monks of Saint-Denis. The sources reveal nothing about Clovis's motivation for the re-establishment of perpetual psalmody nor about its subsequent longevity. To judge from the account of Saint Bathildis that even an *Ordo regularis* was distasteful to the basilical communities, we can assume that the revival of *laus perennis* at Saint-Denis would have been most unwelcome, and Félibien speculates that it did not endure.[84] Levillain summarizes the rights that Saint Bathildis accorded the abbey as bait to the trap in which the chagrined Sandionysians also found themselves under monastic rule.[85] If this is the case, then Clovis II's reimposition of perpetual psalmody was an even more bitter pill.

In spite of some reverses over the next century, the prestige of the abbey increased while its ever more intimate bond with the monarchy strengthened. This resulted not only from the ecclesiastical privileges that were conferred on the abbey but also from a grant of royal immunity which came between 657 and 664.[86] These favours only added to the economic boons which King Dagobert had conferred earlier.[87] Of Dagobert's munificence, the most important part was his concession around 635 of an annual fair which took place on days surrounding the feast of Saint Denis on 9 October.[88] The first of its kind in Gaul, the fair of Saint-Denis enriched the royal treasury as it enhanced the cult of the saint. As for the liturgy, the very fact that the fair came into being demonstrates the high rank that the remembrance of the martyrdom of Saint Denis had attained by the first half of the seventh century, for fairs were born of important religious celebrations, being designed to accommodate the hordes of pilgrims that such feasts always attracted.[89] The miracle of Eligius corroborates the seventh-century existence of a Vigil for this feast, but there is no direct evidence

[84] Félibien, *Histoire*, 25. The author mentions that subsequent monarchs, Thierry (III, presumably) and Pepin, tried without success to reinstitute the practice, but the charters containing this information are not original acts.

[85] Levillain, 'Études' (1926), 346.

[86] This charter of immunity dates from Bathildis's regency, during the minority of Clothair III. For discussion of the document, which assimilated Saint-Denis into the lands of the royal fisc and gave it sole jurisdiction over its inhabitants, see Levillain, 'Études' (1926), 53–97, 342–6.

[87] A more detailed account of the economic situation at Saint-Denis is given in Levillain, 'Études' (1930).

[88] 'In ipso quoque tempore annuale mercatum, quod fit post festivitatem ipsorum excellentissimorum martyrum prope idem monasterium, eidem sancto loco et fratribus Deo et sanctis martyribus ibidem deserventibus concessit'; Krusch, *Dagoberti*, ch. 34, 413; see Levillain, 'Études' (1930), 7–65.

[89] Huvelin, 'Essai', 40. By the 12th c. the duration of the fair was 7 weeks; Crosby, *Abbey*, 458–9, n. 61.

that an Octave, which first appears in extant sources from the eleventh century, was celebrated at this time.[90]

The early fortunes of Saint-Denis just described coincide roughly with what historians now call the Merovingian period in the history of Gaul. During these early years, as we have seen, the church of Saint-Denis was founded and supervised by the cathedral of Paris, and initially housed a more or less secular community whose liturgy was modelled on that of the parent church. The ritual in Gaul at this time was differentiated along geographical lines, and in 567 the church of Paris, as well as its dependency Saint-Denis, came under the jurisdiction of the Council of Tours, no doubt enforcing the rites that it dictated. On two occasions in the first half of the seventh century, the instructions for psalmody in this regimen, involving the daily recitation of 30–54 psalms, were drastically increased to encompass the singing of the entire psalter at least once each day, when Dagobert and Clovis tried to introduce perpetual psalmody at Saint-Denis. Clovis even had at his disposal the presumably more disciplined inhabitants of the newly founded *monasterium*, but the practice of *laus perennis* did not survive. Nor did the establishment of a fusion of the monastic rules of Saints Columbanus and Benedict around 650 seem to have much effect on the liturgy of the abbey. The community continued a mixture of monks, clerics, an abbot (who was often a member of the secular clergy), and even a local bishop. Furthermore, it remained under the spiritual, and no doubt liturgical, direction of Paris. When Carolingian kings ascended the throne, the major liturgical feasts of the year were probably celebrated at Saint-Denis in approximately the same manner as in the non-monastic church at Paris. The feast of Saint-Denis with its Vigil was perhaps the only one that could be called 'proper' to the abbey. But that Vigil service might be heard at Paris as well, for it was not yet a monastic, Benedictine Office with twelve lessons and responsories at Matins. Only slowly did the monks of Saint-Denis, as elsewhere in the France, come to a strict observance of the Benedictine rule and its ritual. How this transition came about in the abbey is a case in point.[91]

[90] Octaves of feasts other than Christmas, Epiphany, Easter, and Pentecost were virtually unknown before the Carolingian era.

[91] By examining the earliest *consuetudines* from the 8th and 9th cs., K. Hallinger has investigated the progressive adoption of the Benedictine rule, including the chapters on the Divine Ritual; see his *Initia*, esp. the introd. See also Le Roux, 'Guillaume', i. 466–9; Fry, *Rule*, 113–25.

ABBOT FULRAD (750–84) AND THE EARLY REFORMS OF THE CAROLINGIAN LITURGISTS

Together with the instauration of the Carolingian dynasty in the mid-eighth century came a far-reaching liturgical reform that set out to restructure the Gallican liturgy according to the Roman model. It was fortuitous for Saint-Denis that Fulrad, abbot from 750 to 784, played major roles in both of these events as well as in the reconstruction of the church.[92] His political activities[93] include a mission as co-ambassador with the bishop of Würzburg to Pope Zachary in 749. This trip prepared the way both for the deposition of the Merovingian *rois fainéants* and for the elevation of a line of 'mayors of the palace' who had in effect been ruling for some time.[94] As a result, the current mayor Pepin the Short was anointed in 751, and a second consecration took place at Saint-Denis in 754 during Pope Stephen II's sojourn in the abbey.[95] In recognition of Fulrad's services to the crown, Pepin conferred on him the title *capellanus* of the royal chapel, having already made him abbot of Saint-Denis in 750. Among other duties, Fulrad's new post required him to direct the court clerics.[96] Given the importance of this position, his role in the subsequent liturgical reform can hardly be overestimated. As *capellanus* and confidant of Pepin, Fulrad was the chief mediator between king and clergy. On a larger scale, his voyages to Italy established him likewise as principal intercessor between Pepin and Stephen II.[97] His functions, moreover, were not simply administrative and diplomatic: both Pepin and Pope Hadrian I called him *archipresbiter*, and the latter used the impressive designation *archipresbiter Franciae*.[98]

[92] On Fulrad, see Dubruel, *Moines*; Fleckenstein, 'Fulrad', 9–39; on the Carolingian church at Saint-Denis, see Crosby, *Abbey*, 51–84; and the discussion in Ch. 4.

[93] Fulrad's administration is well documented by Carolingian historians and by extant letters of kings, popes, and the abbot himself. The principal primary sources for the study of the history of the monarchy and the abbey during this period are listed in Crosby, *Abbey*, 51, esp. n. 1. In the 19th c. Félibien also copied many pertinent letters, bulls, and testaments which no longer exist; see Félibien, *Histoire*, 42–113, and his *PJ*, i, pp. xxiii–lxxxi, Nos. xxxiii–cvii.

[94] See Einhard's biography of Charlemagne, translated in Thorpe, *Einhard*, 55–7. For recent general introductions to the Frankish realm under the Carolingians, see McKitterick, *Kingdoms*; James, *Origins*, 123–87.

[95] Documentation for all aspects of the coronation except the date (28 July) is given in Duchesne, *Liber pontificalis*, i. 448. The precise date first appears in the 9th c. in identical readings from the calendars of the sacramentaries F:Pn, lat. 2290 and F:Psg 111 (see Ch. 2). For secondary bibliography on the 2 consecrations of Pepin, see Folz, *Coronation*, 27–30; Vogel, *Liturgy*, 185.

[96] Fleckenstein, *Hofkapelle*, 45–8.

[97] Ibid. 48. Fulrad accompanied Pope Stephen on his return to Rome in 754 and served as Pepin's ambassador to Italy in 755; Félibien, *Histoire*, 48–9.

[98] Fleckenstein, *Hofkapelle*, 46. For Pepin's confirmation charter of 23 Sept. 768, see Tardif, *Monuments*, 49, No. 60 (original = F:Pan, K 5, No. 8; see also Mühlbacher, *Urkunden*, i. 38,

In the prolonged history of the transmission of Roman practices from the Holy City to the Frankish lands, Pope Stephen's visit to France in 753–4 was but a brief moment.[99] The process of liturgical exportation from Rome, which had begun much earlier, is evident in the work of missionaries from the sixth to the eighth centuries and in the evolution of the Roman and Romano-Frankish sacramentaries, *ordines*, and other service books that circulated in Gaul. Indeed, those few months during which Stephen and Pepin the Short met on Frankish soil hardly mark the final phase of the romanization of the Franks. It took another three-quarters of a century effectively to complete the task. Only the persistence of the second and third generations of monarchs, Charlemagne and Louis the Pious, with the assistance of such ardent councillors as the aforementioned Alcuin of York and Benedict of Aniane (*c*.747–821), could finally begin to bring some kind of uniformity to liturgical practice in Gaul.

And yet sources imply that Stephen's sojourn with Pepin was a real turning point in the process. Charlemagne, in his *Admonitio generalis* of 789, stipulates 'that Roman *cantus* be performed . . . in accordance with that which our highly esteemed father King Pepin ordained'.[100] Soon afterwards, in 794, Charlemagne specifically connects his father's reformative measures with the pope's visit:

> The church [in Gaul], while it stood united with the [Roman] church in terms of holy religion from the earliest days of faith, and differed but little from it in the celebration of the Offices—which nevertheless is not contrary to faith—was united with it in terms of the *Ordo psallendi* through the attention of our most renowned, excellent and well-remembered father King Pepin and by the activity and arrival in Gaul of the most reverend and holy Pope Stephen from Rome. [This was done] so that the *Ordo psallendi* would not differ for those for whom the *Ordo* of believing was alike.[101]

No. 27; and the facsimile in Bruckner and Marichal, *ChLA*, xv. 34–7 [No. 602]). Pope Hadrian's epistle appears in Heller and Waitz, *Flodoardi*, 463, lib. ii, ch. 17.

[99] Scholars recognized early on the importance of the meetings between Stephen and Pepin the Short as primary forces behind the Carolingian reform; see e.g. H. Netzer, *Introduction*, 32–4; Klauser, 'Austauschbeziehungen', 169–77. More recent scholarship on the subject of the liturgical exchanges includes Vogel, 'Échanges'; idem, 'Chrodegang', 91–5; idem, *Liturgy*, 61, 76, 358, and *passim*. For general background on the reform of other aspects of the church as a whole, see McKitterick, *Church*.

[100] Boretius, *Capitularia*, i. 58. A similar letter from Mar. 789 contains about the same wording; see ibid. 61.

[101] 'Quae dum a primis fidei temporibus cum ea perstaret in sacrae religionis unione, et ab ea paulo distaret, quod tamen contra fidem non est, in officiorum celebratione, venerandae memoriae genitoris nostri illustrissimi atque excellentissimi viri Pipini regis cura, et industria sive adventu in Gallias reverentissimi et sanctissimi viri Stephani Romanae urbis antistitis, est ei etiam in psallendi ordine copulata, ut non esset dispar ordo psallendi quibus erat compar credendi'; Bastgen, *Carolini*, 21; *PL*, xcviii. 1021.

A few decades later, the liturgical commentator Walafrid Strabo likewise reports: 'Pope Stephen, when he had come to Pepin the father of Charlemagne, the chiefest in France, to seek justice on behalf of Saint Peter from the Lombards, brought in by means of his clerics, at the request of Pepin, the most perfect [i.e. Roman] knowledge of singing [*cantilena*], which continued in use far and wide.'[102] And finally, Charlemagne's grandson Charles the Bald (840–77) notes that native Gallican and Hispanic liturgical usages had prevailed in their respective regions 'up until the time of our ancestor Pepin'.[103]

These supposed witnesses of regal and papal activities with regard to the liturgy in the mid-eighth century are none the less all after the fact. One might suspect that the emphasis later writers placed on the roles of Stephen and Pepin in the reform was something akin to the exaggerated credit given Pope Gregory the Great (590–604) for the codification of plainchant.[104] Perhaps Charlemagne and his followers, wishing to legitimize their own efforts to impose a standard Roman ritual, simply harked back to this favourable but brief coming together of pope and king as authority. Certainly their motives were political: they wanted to demonstrate both the internal unity of Gaul and their close ties with Rome. And if these latter-day reformers were still clamouring for adherence to Roman usages almost 75 years after Pepin's and Stephen's efforts, then the mid-eighth-century attempts to which they referred could not have had a particularly lasting effect.

There were, nevertheless, several serious efforts at liturgical reform around this time in Gaul in places such as Rouen[105] and Metz.[106] Pepin's brother Remedius, bishop of Rouen, had brought a Roman cantor to his city in 760. Just a few years earlier in 753, Bishop Chrodegang of Metz had accompanied Pope Stephen to France at the bidding of King Pepin who, mindful of an imminent Lombard threat to the pontiff, dispatched Chrodegang to Rome to assure the pope of his support. The bishop no doubt had ample opportunity to observe Roman liturgical practices during the course of this mission. Chrodegang's involvement in the reform movement only increased in subsequent years. He became archbishop of the realm in 754, introduced Roman *cantilena* and customs at Metz shortly thereafter, wrote a rule

[102] 'Cantilenae vero perfectiorem scientiam, quam pene jam tota Francia diligit, Stephanus papa, cum ad Pippinum patrem Caroli Magni (in primis in Franciam) pro justitia sancti Petri a Longobardis expetenda, venisset, per suos clericos, petente eodem Pippino, invexit, indeque usus ejus longe lateque convaluit'; Walafrid Strabo, *Ecclesiasticarum*, col. 957, ch. 25.

[103] Mansi, *Collectio*, 18B, col. 730.

[104] See Hucke, 'Gregory'; Treitler, 'Homer', 334–44.

[105] See Vogel, *Liturgy*, 76; 119, n. 194; Van Dijk, 'Schola', 23.

[106] The participation of the church of Metz is the subject of Vogel's 'Chrodegang'; see also Carpe, 'Chrodegang', 51–9.

for the canons at Metz[107] and probably a stational list for his church which follows closely the Roman model, and founded a school of singing under the direction of a Rome-trained master.[108] The energetic archbishop likewise presided over the reform-minded Council of Attigny in 762.[109]

Clearly, Chrodegang and Remedius were prominent players among the first generation of reformers, that is, among those who actually witnessed Pope Stephen's visit. But while they carried out most of their work at Metz and Rouen, the encounter between Pepin and Stephen was happening in the environs of Paris. Stephen had arrived from Rome just at the start of winter, and Pepin decided in January 754 to install the Italians at Saint-Denis, where they remained for some time.[110] As temporary residence of the pope and his retinue, the abbey must therefore have been caught up in the reforming activities that occurred during those six or seven months.

The passage from Walafrid Strabo cited above notes that Stephen's clerics taught the Franks the art of Roman *cantilena*; and the *Liber pontificalis* not only verifies that they wintered at Saint-Denis with the pope[111] but also provides the names, ranks, and in some cases the places of origin of 13 of those who accompanied him:

> Of the priests and clergy of this holy church of God, [Pope Stephen] took with him Georgius, Bishop of Saint-Paul's; Wilcharius, Bishop of Nomentum; the Presbyters Leo, Philippus, Georgius and Stephanus; Archdeacon Theophylactus; the Deacons Pardus and Gemmulus; the *Primicerius* Ambrosius; the *Secundicerius* Boniface; and the Regionaries Leo and Christopher, along with others. On 15 November [753] he set out from the Holy City with them and headed for France.[112]

[107] Carpe presents a corrected version of two earlier texts of the *Regula canonicorum* in ibid. 236–300.

[108] Ibid. 99–100; *DACL*, xi/1, cols. 864–5, s.v. 'Metz, XXIII ("Le Chant romain á Metz")'; and Ewig, 'Chrodegang', 31.

[109] Ibid. 53.

[110] Duchesne, *Liber*, i. 444–8. There is some confusion as to the exact length of the pope's sojourn at Saint-Denis, but it seems that he remained at least until the end of July 754.

[111] 'But since winter-time was near, [Pepin] asked the most holy pope to go with his entire retinue to the venerable monastery of Blessed Dionysius for the winter' ('Sed quia tempus inminebat hyemalis [Pippinus] eundem sanctissimum papam cum omnibus suis in Parisio apud venerabliem monasterium beati Dionisii ad exhibernandum pergere rogavit'); ibid. 448.

[112] 'Et [Stephanus] adsumens ex huius sanctae Dei ecclesiae sacerdotibus et clero, id est Georgium episcopum Hostense, Wilcharium episcopum Numentano, Leonem, Philippum, Georgium et Stephanum presbiteros, Theophylactum archidiaconum, Pardum et Gemmulum diaconos, Ambrosium primicerium, Bonifacium secundicerium, Leonem et Christoforum regionarios, seu et ceteros, XV die novembris mensis praedicte VII indictionis, a civitate Papia movens suum Franciam profectus est iter'; ibid. 446–7. *Numentano* and *Hostense* probably refer to 2 Roman suburbs, Nomentum (present-day Mentana) and Ostia (see Graesse *et al.*, *Orbis*, iii. 34, s.v. 'Nomentum'; ii. 255, s.v. 'Hostia'). Gams places Bishops Wilcharius in Nomentum and Georgius in Ostia for the year 753; Gams, *Series*, xii, p. iv.

Such an unprecedented arrival of so many liturgical experts from Rome certainly occasioned demonstrations of the Roman rite in the abbey, perhaps on the high feasts of Easter and Pentecost, which fell during the extended visit of the pope.[113] This is all the more likely because the chief musical instructors of the Roman *Schola Cantorum*, the *Primicerius* and *Secundicerius*, were present.[114] And since not all the clerics who accompanied the pope were drawn from the Lateran or from Saint-Peter's, it is probable that the ceremonies of the various stational and regional churches of the area around Rome were represented as well.[115] Both pope and king had reason to honour Saint-Denis by having it serve as a kind of centre for the diffusion of the new liturgy: Stephen declared that he had undergone a miraculous recovery from a serious illness while at Saint-Denis,[116] and Pepin held Fulrad in high esteem for his exemplary work as abbot, ambassador, and *capellanus*. Netzer suggests that the coronation ceremony itself, in uniting these three persons at Saint-Denis to effect the launching of a new dynasty, may also have served by analogy as point of departure for the new liturgical regime whose instruction would have continued to emanate thence.[117]

The ubiquitous Abbot Fulrad had also placed Saint-Denis in the limelight by proving his worth to Pepin as *capellanus* of the royal chapel and as *archipresbiter* of the realm, as mentioned earlier. The hospitality he extended to Stephen at Saint-Denis and his willingness to accompany the pope on his return voyage to Italy in 754 no doubt won him favour with the pontiff as well.[118] And Fulrad clearly showed an interest in the ongoing liturgical reform when he attended Chrodegang's Council of Attigny of 762.[119] At least one famous liturgical book of Roman ancestry, a Gelasian sacramentary (I:Rvat, Reg. lat. 316), was copied in the area of Paris in the middle of the eighth century, probably at the nunnery of Chelles and possibly for Saint-Denis. Certainly this region and especially the abbey of Saint-Denis under Abbot Fulrad were in political and ecclesiastical favour at this time. Taken in sum, the facts suggest that Saint-Denis in fact stood at the centre of a political and liturgical reform of great consequence.

113 J. Boe has recently advanced the theory that the Old-Roman Gloria for the Easter Vigil (melody No. 39 in Bosse, *Gloria*), 'Gloria A', might have been 'brought north from Rome with the Roman rite by individual Romanizing Frankish bishops and later spread by the ecclesiastical policies of Pippin and Charlemagne'; Boe, 'Gloria', 36–7. If this is the case, then one of the first performances of the melody in Gaul might have occurred at Saint-Denis, perhaps even at the pontifical Mass at Saint-Denis on Easter Eve 754.

114 See the recent review of the composition of the *Schola*, with extensive bibliography, in Tomasello, 'Ritual', 447–9.

115 The liturgy of the presbyteral churches of Rome played a significant role in the formation of the Gelasian sacramentary of the type I:Rvat, Reg. lat. 316, treated in Ch. 7.

116 Duchesne, *Liber*, i. 448.

117 Netzer, *Introduction*, 31–2.

118 See Félibien, *Histoire*, 48–9.

119 His name is in the list of signatories; see Werminghoff, *Attiniacense*, i. 73, conc. 13.

ABBOT FULRAD AND THE CULT OF RELICS

Besides ingratiating himself with King Pepin as court *capellanus*, Fulrad set out to secure the privileges that Bishop Landericus had only begun to grant a century earlier. Whereas Saint-Denis had been freed from administrative interference from the church of Paris in the seventh century, under Fulrad it still remained under the spiritual direction of its bishop. To remove the monastery from Parisian domination once and for all, the abbot invoked the presence of an *episcopus* in the monastery. This office, he claimed, had existed at Saint-Denis 'from ancient times and up to the present'. He argued, moreover, that because the duty of this bishop was already the 'pastoral care' of Saint-Denis, the dependency of the abbey upon the Bishop of Paris was an unnecessary duplication. As a result, by 772 the abbey was at last liberated from the Parisian episcopate. But the price was high, for Saint-Denis was now linked to a monastic bishop.[120] The presence of this bishop, who had no place under the Rule of Saint Benedict, again underlines the mixed nature of the community at Saint-Denis which persisted almost 200 years after monastic rule—also a hybrid—had been instituted.

Besides engineering the spiritual independence of Saint-Denis, Fulrad wielded his extraordinary power to satisfy yet another obsession which eventually bore directly on the liturgy of the abbey: the acquisition of the relics of Saints Hipploytus, Cucuphas, and others for the monasteries and priories which he had founded in Alsace.[121] He may have obtained Hippolytus' relics in Rome,[122] profiting no doubt from his intimacy with Pope Stephen II during his embassy there in 754 and 755.[123] The remains of Saint Cucuphas were sent to Alsace from Spain some time during Fulrad's abbacy. Both relics later found their way to Saint-Denis, probably under Abbot Hilduin (814–41).[124] A mid-ninth-

[120] Fulrad's wishes are known to us, not through his original letter to Pope Stephen III (reg. 768–72), but in the confirmation bull of Pope Hadrian I, addressed to Fulrad's successor, Abbot Maginaire (784–93), on 1 July 786; see Félibien, *Histoire*, *PJ*, pt. i, p. xli, No. lx, and Jaffe, *Regesta*, i. 300–1, No. 2454. Levillain discusses the monastic bishops at Saint-Denis in 'Études' (1926), 315–17, 330–9. By ignoring the passage cited above on p. 11, Levillain found no examples of a monastic bishop at Saint-Denis before Fulrad's time; 'Études' (1926), 334.

[121] Dubruel, *Moines*, 135–8.

[122] Félibien and others believed that Fulrad made a special trip to Rome *c.*763 for the relics, since it had been rumoured that Pope Paul I had just unearthed many saints' bodies; *Histoire*, 53. While Sigebert de Gemblous (11th c.) recorded that Chrodegang made such a journey at this time, he gives no indication that Fulrad went as well; *Chronicon*, 88.

[123] Dubruel, *Moines*, 137.

[124] Although earlier authors have disagreed about the time of arrival of these relics (see Cucuphas: *AASS*, July vi, 155; Hippolytus: ibid. Aug. iii, 10–11), the consensus of the Bollandists of the *AASS* is that the translations happened during Hilduin's abbacy, not Fulrad's.

century manuscript of readings for the day Hours from Saint-Denis (I:VEcap LXXXVIII) contains the text of the proper Office for Cucuphas, and the late ninth-century calendars of the sacramentaries F:Pn, lat. 2290 and F:Psg 111 likewise verify the cult of the two martyrs at Saint-Denis, although only Saint Hippolytus had a place in the actual formularies contained in these books for the Mass.[125] The Office for Cucuphas in I:VEcap LXXXVIII is a full monastic Office, and may well have been composed by Abbot Hilduin in the ninth century. By the eleventh century the extant sources show that the feasts for both saints had been supplied with music as well.

CAROLINGIAN REFORMS OF THE LATE EIGHTH CENTURY: CHANT AND RULE

Near the end of the eighth century, Charlemagne received several Gregorian liturgical books from Rome and cantors highly trained in the art of Roman *cantilena*.[126] Nothing less than the 'correction' of Gallican chants was their heavy charge, for Charlemagne had been convinced of the corruption of his native melodies by comparison with the purer versions that he had heard in Rome. Together with Pepin the Short's previous endeavours, Charlemagne's renewed efforts resulted initially in a disappearance of Gallican chants from the earliest manuscripts written after the Carolingian reform, to judge from the extant sources.[127] This music was by no means forgotten, however. The somewhat bolder character of Gallican melodies had an appeal that was wanting in Roman counterparts, and, as always, deeply rooted local traditions

Other arguments to support this assessment can be mentioned. First, while the placement of relics in some of the churches of Rome began as early as the 4th c., churches both in the Holy City and especially in areas far removed from it were commonly erected without relics well into the 9th c. Second, no historical sources, royal charters, or letters prior to the 9th c. mention any relics in the church of Saint-Denis other than those of the saint and his 2 companions. Third, the crypt of the new church, the reconstruction of which was completed by 775, was modelled on the Roman annular type. Its shape was semicircular around a single, central recess in which only the relics of Saint Denis and friends were contained (Crosby, *Abbey*, 59–61). On the other hand, Hilduin's chapel, added to the east end of the church in 832, housed 3 altars which were dedicated to the Virgin, John the Baptist, and all the saints (see the charters of Louis the Pious and Hilduin; Félibien, *Histoire*, *PJ*, vol. i, pp. lvi–lvii, Nos. lxxv–lxxvi; and on Hilduin's chapel, Crosby, *Abbey*, 87–94). This final altar could easily have provided a resting-place for the relics of Saints Hippolytus and Cucuphas. As we will see, moreover, the Rule of Saint Benedict, whch assumes the presence of relics in a monastery (see Fry, *Rule*, 268–9, ch. 58), was reaffirmed at Saint-Denis in 832, just prior to the construction of Hilduin's chapel.

[125] See Appendix A, 25 July (Cucuphas) and 13 Aug. (Hippolytus).

[126] The anecdotal accounts of Charlemagne's acquisition of books and singers from Rome are all after the fact and vary greatly in detail, but there is no reason to dismiss them in substance; see Van Dijk, 'Schola', which evaluates the reports by John the Deacon and by Notker Balbulus.

[127] Huglo, 'Gallican', 114.

could not easily be removed. Consequently, the forbidden repertoire, preserved mainly through oral practice, began to resurface gradually in the eleventh century, long after the initial era of prohibition, at such centres as Saint-Denis.[128]

Just as Charlemagne sought out masters from Rome to refine ecclesiastical singing in Gaul, so also he turned to Monte Cassino for the instrument by which he intended to reclaim order and discipline in the monasteries of his kingdom. At the beginning of the ninth century, an authentic text of the Rule of Saint Benedict made its way into Gaul.[129] As we have seen, the administrative and spiritual aspects of the Rule, practised in conjunction with parts of the Columbanan and other formulas, had been known in Gaul since the beginning of the seventh century, but there is little evidence that the Benedictine *cursus* was actually followed. In a letter accompanying the Rule, the author recommends, though without enjoinder, the Benedictine weekly arrangement of the Psalter:

> If the division of the psalm-singing over the individual weekdays which the Blessed Father [Benedict] established seems better to a house, then he gives them permission to sing in this way that they have deemed better. But, if it please you [Charlemagne], those monks who now sing the psalms in the Roman manner should not be coerced to divide them according to the arrangement of this holy *regula*. Rather, they may, with your permission, undertake the *regula* of a more structured life, while continuing to sing in their accustomed [Roman] manner.[130]

The final sentence again emphasizes the distinction that was still made between the *regula* of Saint Benedict and its *cursus*. The *cursus* was clearly an option considered to be only coequal with the Roman arrangement of the Psalter, which Pepin had introduced in Gaul a few decades earlier.[131]

In fact, because the Benedictine *cursus* was adapted largely from the traditions of the Roman urban monasteries and, to a lesser degree, of

[128] Huglo, 'Gallican', 114. The earliest notated MSS from Saint-Denis transmit a number of Gallican chants (see Ch. 4).

[129] A letter to Charlemagne arrived along with the rule. Many sources attribute the epistle to Theodomar, abbot of Monte Cassino, although modern scholars have proposed other authors. The contents of the letter suggest it dates from the early 9th c.; see Hallinger, *Initia*, 152–4.

[130] 'Nam et de psalmorum canendorum per singulos septimane dies divisione, si cui melius visum fuerit quam ipse beatus pater instituit, ab ipso habet licentiam, ut melius aestimaverit, canere. Nec debent cogi monachi, si tamen vestro sapientissimo cordi ita placet, qui nunc Romano more psallunt, iuxta institutionem sacre huius regule psalmos dividere; sed possunt, si vobis ita videtur, solito more canentes, artioris vitae normam suscipere'; ibid. 161–2.

[131] For further discussion of the close association of the Benedictine rule and the Roman *Ordo officii*, see Semmler, 'Beschlüsse', 23–9. The exposition on various types of *cursus* in the *Ratio de cursus qui fuerunt eius auctores* from around 767 likewise emphasizes the similarities between these two uses; see Hallinger, *Initia*, 91.

the Roman cathedrals, the two systems shared many features.[132] Both *cursus* specified Pss. 4, 90, and 133 for Compline.[133] The multisectional Ps. 118 was a prominent feature of both Roman and Benedictine Prime and Little Hours (Terce, Sext, None) alike. Both series of psalms for Matins (called *Vigiliae*) ended on Saturday with Ps. 108, and the Vespers psalms recommenced on Sunday with Ps. 109. In the Benedictine *cursus*, however, the psalms of Lauds (called *Matutini*), Prime, and the Little Hours varied daily. This diversity was possible because Benedict limited the number of psalms at Matins to twelve. Furthermore, the Benedictine Rule, like that of Saint Columbanus, was composed for a rural rather than an urban monastery, and had to allow for periods of outdoor labour. For this reason, Prime and the Little Hours were shortened from the Roman model to contain three psalms each.[134] There were four instead of five psalms for Vespers, and Benedict halved a greater number of the lengthy psalms. These abridgements provided more variety and less repetition of psalms during the course of the week.

To determine where the abbey of Saint-Denis stood on the question of the *cursus* at the end of the eighth century requires a certain amount of deduction to augment the scant evidence that the texts provide. Theodomar's letter confirms that the customary order of psalm-singing in Gaul was the Roman one. Probably Saint-Denis would have undertaken this method under the influence both of Pepin and of Pope Stephen II's clerics during the winter of 754. The earliest manuscripts provide no corroboration of this arrangement, but historical evidence strongly indicates that the Benedictine *cursus* had not yet been adopted at Saint-Denis.

ABBOT HILDUIN (814–41) AND THE BENEDICTINE LITURGY

In 817 certain inhabitants of the abbey precipitated a great crisis when they attempted to secularize the community.[135] This event came as no surprise, for the previous century was fraught with signs that the *Ordo regularis* had but tenuous hold on the abbey. Not least of these was the fact that abbots such as Fulrad and Fardulph (793–806) were all too

[132] The text of the Benedictine plan is found in Fry, *Rule*, 202–15, chs. 8–18; see also his discussion of the sources of the liturgical code in ibid. 379–400; and Vogüé and Neufville's treatment of the weekly psalter in *Benoît*, i. 102–3; v. 434, 545–54.

[133] Numbering of psalms follows the Vulgate version of the Psalter; see Leroquais, *Psautiers*, i. xxv.

[134] Actually, the Benedictine *cursus* specified the first 4 sections of Ps. 118 for Prime on Sunday, but throughout the rest of the week this Hour included only 3 psalms.

[135] See Levillain, 'Études' (1925), 35–43; Oexle, *Forschungen*, 112–19.

often preoccupied with their political manoeuvres.[136] Like Fulrad, Abbot Hilduin (814–41) held the title *archicapellanus* of the chapel of Emperor Louis the Pious (814–40) early in his career, and he was no less ambitious and influential than his predecessor. In addition to these posts, Hilduin also served as abbot of the Parisian abbey of Saint-Germain-des-Prés, the first of many Sandionysian abbots to do so.[137] The closeness that he and his followers forged between these two establishments may well be reflected in the contents of three manuscripts from Saint-Denis (F:LA 118, F:Pn, lat. 2290, and F:Psg 1186), and in two sources which were once ascribed to the abbey (I:Rvat, Ott. lat. 313; and F:Pn, lat. 2291).[138]

Under Hilduin's reign, a schism over the internal organization of the monastery divided the monks of Saint-Denis into two camps. Those, on the one hand, who wished to remain faithful to their monastic vows were banished from the abbey. The rest simply divested themselves of monastic dress, if they had ever worn it, and began living in the abbey as canons, perhaps according to Chrodegang's Rule.[139] The liturgical prescriptions of this Rule were similar to those of the Roman *cursus*, as described by the ninth-century liturgical commentator Amalarius of Metz.[140] This general state of organizational uncertainty prevailed at Saint-Denis from 817 until 832. To the confusion was added the year-long exile of Hilduin to Corvey (830–1) for his participation in plots against Emperor Louis the Pious.[141] During these years, several councils and synods attempted reforms of the abbey, but it was only in 832 that Louis was able finally to confirm that the Sandionysians had once again donned their monastic garments and were living in accordance with the Rule of Saint Benedict: '[the monks of Saint-Denis] have drawn up three documents . . . in which they have declared openly that they are

[136] Levillain, 'Études' (1925), 36. The Lombard Abbot Fardulph seems never to have embraced monastic life, choosing instead to remain a secular priest throughout his term of Office; Ayzac, *Histoire*, i. xxv. His appointment to the abbacy, far from a promotion for his piety, was a reward from Charlemagne for his revelation of an intrigue against the life of the King; Félibien, *Histoire*, 62–3.

[137] The 2 houses were supervised off and on by the same abbot until 987. Carolingian kings regularly granted multiple abbacies to their loyal supporters; see James, *Origins*, 112.

[138] See Chs. 6 and 7. The rapport between Saint-Denis and Saint-Germain is also evident in the passage of other non-liturgical books between the 2 monasteries; see Nebbiai-Dalla Guarda, *Bibliothèque*, 56–8.

[139] Ibid. 68, and Levillain, 'Études', (1925), 36–7. It should be recalled that even after the imposition of monastic rule at Saint-Denis a secular element had remained in the community.

[140] See the discussion of Chrodegang's liturgical code in Carpe, 'Chrodegang', 157–80.

[141] Although Hilduin was almost immediately restored to favour with Louis the Pious in 831, he never recovered his position as *archicapellanus*. Compare, for example, Louis's charter of 10 Nov. 827, in which he addresses Hilduin as 'monasterii Sancti Dyonisii abba, sacrique palatii nostri archicapellanus' (Tardif, *Monuments*, 83, No. 119; original = F:Pan, K 9, No. 4), with a letter of 26 Aug. 832, in which he calls Hilduin simply *abbas* (Tardif, *Monuments*, 87, No. 124; original = F:Pan, K 9, No. 6).

willing to observe the *regula* established by the Blessed Father Benedict.'[142]

It would be imprudent to assume simply on the basis of this charter that the reimposition of the Rule at Saint-Denis included also the *cursus* of Saint Benedict, especially in view of Theodomar's letter to Charlemagne only 40 years earlier which still distinguished clearly between the administrative and liturgical portions. Nevertheless, the widespread diversity of the Divine Office had been the focus of considerable attention throughout this period. The prime mover in all aspects of the Frankish monastic reform was Benedict of Aniane, already mentioned as adviser both to Charlemagne and to Louis the Pious.[143] Under Benedict's direction, several councils at Aix-la-Chapelle had attempted to impose the Benedictine ritual universally between 816 and 818 or 819.[144] As early as 802, the acts of a synod recorded in the *Chronicon* of Moissac state: 'It is commanded that each bishop in the entire kingdom and in his own jurisdiction, along with his presbyters, should perform the *officium* just as the Roman church sings it . . . Likewise in the monasteries which follow the Rule of Saint Benedict they should perform its *officium* just as the Rule teaches.'[145]

Throughout the land, however, monks found it difficult to carry this out for various reasons, and a number of meetings in Paris several years after the death of Benedict of Aniane addressed this problem along with others.[146] Among the excuses for their innattention to the *Opus dei*, the monks claimed that they were not receiving the sustenance necessary to perform it. As a result, the report of the Paris Council of 829 admonishes 'that [abbots] should not neglect . . . to govern with fatherly affection and to administer the necessary stipends to the [monks], lest perchance on account of some deprivation even the Divine Offices should be neglected'.[147] At Saint-Denis, Abbot Hilduin tried to remedy this

[142] '[monachi Sancti Dionysii] tres cartulas conscripserunt . . . in quibus se a beato patre Benedicto . . . descriptam regulam sunt servare velle professi'; Tardif, *Monuments*, 89.

[143] See the translation of Benedict's biography by the monk Ardo in Cabaniss, *Monk*; and the more recent discussion of Benedict's activities in Grégoire, 'Benedetto'.

[144] The pertinent passages from these councils are edited in Hallinger, *Initia*, 435, 442, 458, 517.

[145] 'Mandavit autem, ut unusquisque episcopus in omni regno vel imperio suo, ipsi cum presbyteris suis, officium sicut psallit ecclesia Romana, facerent . . . Similiter et in monasteriis sancti Benedicti servantibus regulam ut officium ipsium facerent, sicut regula docet'; ed. Pertz, *Chronicon*, 306–7; and the discussion of this document in Semmler, 'Reichsidee', *passim*, esp. 63–5.

[146] Benedict died in 821 and so did not live to see the Benedictine Rule finally established at Saint-Denis. He was evidently involved in the early attempts at reform of the abbey, however, for Louis the Pious recalls in 832 that he had sent Benedict, along with Arnoul, abbot of Noirmoutier, to inspect the situation there somewhat earlier (for Louis's letter, see Werminghoff, *Monasterio*, 685).

[147] 'ut [abbates] . . . paterno affectu gubernare eisque [monachis] necessaria stipendia adminis-

situation in 832 by dividing the goods of the abbey so that a portion of the revenues might go to the nourishment and care of his monks.[148] Yet neither Hilduin nor the Council of Paris nor the synods held at Saint-Denis speak directly of the Office that had suffered such neglect.[149] It appears that the chief mission of Emperor Louis and Abbot Hilduin was first and foremost to re-establish monastic rule at Saint-Denis. This is understandable, for those 15 years of internal strife had threatened the very existence of the now richly endowed royal abbey. If Louis and Hilduin were at all concerned at this time with designating the type of *cursus*, Roman or Benedictine, which was to be sung, they did not express that concern. What mattered was that monks—and not canons—should do the singing.

Indeed, if the Benedictine or monastic Office, a hallmark of which is the presence at Matins on feast-days of twelve lessons and twelve responsories (four of each in each of three Nocturns), had begun to take hold, one might expect to find it superseding the Roman, secular Office, which had only three lessons and responsories in each of three Nocturns at Matins (nine in all). But this is not the case in the first monastic antiphoners. The earliest complete extant antiphoner of the Western European group[150] is the late-ninth-century manuscript F:Pn, lat. 17436.[151] On the basis of its content, Jacques Froger has suggested that the book was originally destined for the monastery of Saint-Médard of Soissons, and that it had close connections with Saint-Denis.[152] In spite of its possible monastic beginnings, the manuscript contains only one example of a twelve-responsory, monastic office, the Translation of Saint Benedict (11 July).[153] Authors earlier were reluctant to attribute it to a monastery because of the preponderance of secular Offices.[154] However, Froger justified his assessment by recalling that it was in fact the secular office of the cathedrals that the

trare non neglegant, ne forte propter aliquam inopiam et divina officia neglegantur'; Werminghoff, *Parisiense*, 676, ch. 18.

[148] Tardif, *Monuments*, 84–6, No. 123 (original = F:Pan, K 9, No. 5); Werminghoff, *Monasterio*, 688–94; Félibien, *Histoire*, 71; *PJ*, vol. i. pp. xlix–li, No. lxxii.

[149] See, in addition to the documents listed in the 2 preceding notes, the acts of the synods at Saint-Denis; Werminghoff, *Monasterio*, 683–94.

[150] For the geographical division of the earliest antiphoners, see Huglo, 'Antiphoner', 483–9; idem, *Livres*, 84.

[151] This source is also known as the 'Compiègne antiphoner' because it later came into the library of Saint-Corneille of Compiègne.

[152] Froger, 'Lieu', 349–53. The author explains that the MS contains material proper to the liturgies of 3 monasteries: Saint-Médard, Saint-Denis and Saint-Germain-des-Prés. The connection between these 3 places was established during the time of Hilduin, who after about 820 was abbot of all 3 houses simultaneously.

[153] F:Pn, lat. 17436, fos. 70ᵛ–71ᵛ; see also Hesbert, *CAO*, i, No. 1024.

[154] Froger, 'Lieu', 338–45.

monasteries initially celebrated. They adopted the Benedictine liturgy only gradually, and at a later date.[155]

Froger's argument for the monastic destination of F:Pn, lat. 17436 complements the witness of the texts dealing with the early history of Saint-Denis. The office in the abbey clearly did not assume a Benedictine, monastic form for several centuries. From the days of its foundation as a *domus basilicae* under the control of the Parisian bishop, Saint-Denis practised a liturgy like that of the cathedral of Paris. In terms of the office, this was probably the *Ordo officii* handed down by the Council of Tours in 567, except for two brief periods when it was replaced by perpetual psalmody. The basilica submitted to the administrative and spiritual guidance of two monastic rules, those of Saints Columbanus and Benedict, in the middle of the seventh century without entirely adopting the liturgy of either one. Furthermore, a secular contingent remained in the abbey. At the outset of the Carolingian period, Fulrad, who was simultaneously abbot of Saint-Denis and *capellanus* of the secular, royal chapel, rid the abbey of Parisian episcopal domination while at the same time acknowledging the presence of a monastic bishop. Meanwhile, King Pepin introduced the Roman *cursus* in Gaul and no doubt personally urged its adoption at Saint-Denis. Not until the eleventh century do we find confirmation in the manuscripts from Saint-Denis that a monastic Matins service was being celebrated in the abbey. In most other places the transition from secular to monastic liturgy was comsummated around the same time.[156] But the councils at Aix and the mixture of nine- and twelve-responsory offices in F:Pn, lat. 17436 demonstrate that in the ninth century the process was under way. And what office could more appropriately inaugurate this event than one for the feast of Saint Benedict?

Abbot Hilduin should in fact be credited with taking the first step toward the establishment of the Benedictine liturgy at Saint-Denis. It was probably he who, around 835, altered the Office of Saint Denis from its old Gallican version, which no doubt came under Roman influence in the eighth century, to what we now call the monastic form. The aforementioned Compiègne antiphoner (F:Pn, lat. 17436) contains the earliest extant testimony of an *officium* for the saint, but this manuscript transmits the secular, nine-responsory office.[157] One must

[155] Ibid. 346. Further confirmation of this view can be seen in the late 8th-c. *Ordines XVI* (chs. 15, 16) and *XVII* (ch. 81) of the *Ordines romani*, which incorporate elements of the Benedictine Matins service without increasing the number of lessons and responsories to 12; Andrieu, *Ordines*, iii. 148–9, 186.

[156] The slow adoption of the Benedictine liturgy is clearly demonstrated by the mixture of monastic and Roman Offices that persists in the late 10th- or early 11th-c. Hartker antiphoner from Saint-Gall, CH:SGs 390–1 (facsimile edn. in *PM*, 2nd ser., i). See also Hesbert, *CAO*, vol. ii, pp. vii–viii.

[157] F:Pn, lat. 17436, fos. 79^{v}–80^{v}; Hesbert, *CAO*, i, No. 114b. Cf. ibid. ii, No. 114.

look elsewhere, namely, in the contemporaneous texts, for evidence that the twelve-lesson Office for the feast of Saint Denis did exist in the first half of the ninth century.[158]

For several tranquil years after the abbey had reaffirmed its obedience to the *regula* of Saint Benedict, literary and artistic industry flourished at Saint-Denis. Hilduin's construction of a chapel in the crypt around 832 and the composition of the *Miracula sancti Dionysii* and of the *Gesta Dagoberti* bear witness to the monks' zeal. In gratitude for his recent restoration to the throne, Louis the Pious asked Hilduin in 834 to compose a history of the life of Saint Denis.[159] The abbot willingly complied with this request, but he did so in a way that went well beyond the bounds of scholarly enquiry, adding fuel to what was to become one of the fiercest debates of the Middle Ages.

ABBOT HILDUIN AND THE 'NEW' SAINT DENIS

The argument centred on the identity of Saint Denis. In constructing his *vita* of the patron saint, Hilduin ignored Gregory of Tours's authoritative work on Dionysius, third-century bishop of Paris. Instead, he used two other passions,[160] along with the works of a fifth- or sixth-century philosopher, Pseudo-Dionysius the Areopagite. Pseudo-Dionysius was the shadowy author of four influential, neo-Platonic treatises on metaphysics, works which have earned him the epithet 'father of Christian mysticism'.[161] Despite the immense popularity of his writings, we know little about Pseudo-Dionysius. Possibly a native of Syria, the mystic evidently tried to enhance the popularity of his

[158] The earliest MS evidence for the complete monastic Office that I have seen is the MS of Mont-Renaud (*PM*, xvi, fos. 105^v–6^v), and the first extant source from Saint-Denis that contains this service is F:Pm 384, fo. 190^v (textual incipits only, no musical notation).

[159] *Epistolae*, MGH, *Karolini Aevi*, iii. 325–7, No. 19. For further information on the high regard which Louis had for Saint Denis, see Spiegel, *Chronicle*, 23–4.

[160] See Luscombe, 'Denis', 137–40.

[161] See Rorem, *Symbols*, 7. A new summary of Dionysian philosophy is found in Louth, *Denys*; and a new English translation of the 4 treatises of Pseudo-Dionysius (*The Divine Names*, *The Mystical Theology*, *The Celestial Hierarchy*, *The Ecclesiastical Hierarchy*) has recently appeared in Luibheid and Rorem, *Pseudo-Dionysius*. The Byzantine emperor, Michael the Stammerer, had sent a Greek MS (F:Pn, grec. 437) of the works of Pseudo-Dionysius to Louis the Pious in 827. Hilduin's translation of the treatises, made with the help of monks who were only somewhat familiar with Greek (see Théry, *Études*; Huglo, 'Acathiste', 56–7), was less than satisfactory, and Louis's son Charles the Bald commissioned a new translation from John Scottus Eriugena between 860 and 862 (see Moran, *Philosophy*, 48–51). Eriugena's commentary on *The Celestial Hierarchy*, which strongly influenced 12th-c. perceptions of Pseudo-Dionysius, is edited in Barbet, *Johannis* (for further information on Eriugena's life and works, see the new studies in O'Meara, *Eriugena*, and Moran, *Philosophy*; also Cappuyns, *Jean*, 150–1; Haren, *Thought*, 72–82, [with bibliog. on 239, 243–4, 251, 255–6]; Dronke, *History*, 29 and *passim*; Roques, *Jean*; Allard, *Jean*; bibliography in Zinn, 'Suger', 38, n. 13).

works by adopting the name of Dionysius the Areopagite, a first-century Greek philosopher and disciple of Saint Paul.[162] This deception seems to have worked, for Pseudo-Dionysius became one of the most revered authors of the Middle Ages. Abbot Hilduin, well aware of his reputation, seized the opportunity to promote the association of this jumbled Pseudo-Dionysius/Dionysius the Areopagite figure with the true, third-century patron of the abbey, Saint Denis.

Naturally, Hilduin's work substantially advanced the monastery not only in the eyes of Louis the Pious but also in those of subsequent monarchs for centuries to come. In the process, he conflated the three men who shared the name Dionysius into a personage who was to become the subject of long-lasting controversy.[163] In the hands of Hilduin, Saint Denis, no longer simply the third-century Roman bishop and apostle to Gaul, had now become an Athenian convert of Saint Paul, a bishop of Athens, a visitor to Rome, a papal emissary and proselytizer in Gaul, a philosopher, and a martyr in Paris—all rolled into one.[164] It is altogether understandable that the abbey would have wanted to perpetuate this expedient confusion of identities. After several centuries of doing just this, the monks of the late Middle Ages naturally believed or at least clung with fervour to their tripartite Saint Denis.[165]

To Hilduin's embellished history of Saint Denis, Louis commanded that the abbot append some hymns and an Office for the saint.[166] In this way the liturgy of the abbey served as propaganda for the association of Saint Denis with the Areopagite figures. Indeed, the ritual was the first

[162] The story of Dionysius' conversion by Paul is found in Acts 17: 22–34.

[163] The fundamental studies of the various aspects of the profoundly important theory of Areopagitism at Saint-Denis include Théry, 'Contribution'; idem, *Études*; Loenertz, 'Légende'. For summaries of the history of the Areopagite controversy at Saint-Denis, see Panofsky, *Suger*, 18; Spiegel, *Chronicle*, 23–4, n. 43; Beaune, *Naissance*, 84–96; Gerson, 'Iconographer', 183, 186; Crosby, *Abbey*, 4–5; Luibheid and Rorem, *Pseudo-Dionysius*, 33–4; and Luscombe, 'Denis'. In the latter article Luscombe demonstrates that, whereas Abbot Hilduin was the catalyst in promoting the identification of the 3 Denis figures, he did not invent the whole story. For bibliographies of the vast literature on Pseudo-Dionysius, see Rorem, *Symbols*, 151.

[164] See Luscombe, 'Denis', 133.

[165] Their belief was no doubt enhanced by the number of translations and commentaries on Pseudo-Dionysius throughout the Middle Ages. Apart from the work of John Scottus Eriugena, mentioned above, Jean Sarrazin translated the Dionysian corpus around 1167, and Robert Grosseteste retranslated it in 1235. Important commentaries include those of Hugh of Saint-Victor (1125–37), Albertus Magnus in 1248, and Thomas Aquinas in 1256–9. (For a bibliography of all the translations of Pseudo-Dionysius to 1954, see Roques, *Univers*, 8–9; and for a recent summary of Pseudo-Dionysius' influence on the Western Middle Ages, see the introd. to the translation of Pseudo-Dionysius' works by Jean Leclercq in Luibheid and Rorem, *Pseudo-Dionysius*, 25–32; Louth, *Denys*, 120–7.) The belief in the tripartite personage of Saint Denis, although contested from time to time, went well beyond the Middle Ages (see Luscombe, 'Denis', 149–52), for the first of the 3 modern historians of Saint-Denis, Doublet, was still identifying Saint Denis as the Areopagite as late as the 17th c. (see Doublet, *Histoire*).

[166] 'una cum ymnis [*sic*], quos de hoc gloriosissimo martire atque pontifice habes, et officium nocturnale subiungas'; *Epistolae*, MGH, *Karolini Aevi*, iii. 327, No. 19.

aspect of the church to assume this function, for only in the twelfth century would the Areopagite connection be visible in artistic, architectural, philosophical, and historiographical areas as well.[167]

References to Pseudo-Dionysius in the liturgical texts of Saint-Denis fall into two categories, biographical and philosophical, both of which are treated in Chapter 4. The former often portray Saint Denis as a Greek who was sent to Rome and thence Paris by Pope Clement I, the successor to Saint Peter. This is a compound error, of course, since the true patron of the abbey was a Roman missionary of the third—not first—century.[168] The neo-Platonic philosophy of Pseudo-Dionysius as well as themes more particular to him crop up in the liturgy: the hierarchical ordering of the heavenly beings, and the concept of light, leading from the material to the immaterial world, as the principal source of faith.[169] In addition to Hilduin's Office for Saint Denis and one of the hymns just mentioned, an eleventh-century rhymed Office, and a number of twelfth-century tropes and thirteenth-century sequences contain these and other tell-tale associations. From the late twelfth century on, the monks even sang a Mass for the Octave of Saint Denis (16 October) in Greek, recalling the supposed native tongue of the Pseudo-Areopagite.

Hilduin's conflation of the life of the saint, the *Historia sancti Dionysii* or *Post Beatam ac Salutiferam*, has come down to us,[170] but the Office, which he probably wrote into a *libellus*, is harder to trace.[171] It is only in antiphoners from the late ninth century on that we find secular and then monastic Offices for Saint Denis. How then can we say that the monastic Office, the first extant manuscript evidence of which is from the eleventh century, probably dates from Hilduin's abbacy? Part of the answer may rest in texts from the ninth century.

[167] See Leclercq's introd. to Luibheid and Rorem, *Pseudo-Dionysius*, 26–7. Recent works on the Pseudo-Dionysian influences in Abbot Suger's 12th-c. church, which review much of the earlier literature on this subject, include Lillich, 'Glass', on the meaning of the deep blue colour in Suger's stained glass; Gerson, 'Iconographer', on the west façade of the church; Spiegel, 'History', on Suger's historiographical writings; Zinn, 'Suger'; Schueller, *Idea* (344, 348), on the philosophical thought of Suger; see also the numerous passing references in Crosby, *Abbey*, and in Panofsky, *Suger*.

[168] The incorrect association of Saint Denis with Pope Clement was actually a separate mistake which began to circulate in versions of an early vita of Saint Denis before 520 and thus pre-dated Hilduin's tripartite Saint Denis by at least 2 centuries; see Crosby, *Abbey*, 454, n. 11; Luscombe, 'Denis', 135.

[169] See e.g. the opening lines of *The Celestial Hierarchy* of Pseudo-Dionysius: '"Every good endowment and every perfect gift is from above, coming down from the Father of lights." But there is something more. Inspired by the Father, each procession of the Light spreads itself generously toward us, and, in its power to unify, it stirs us by lifting us up. It returns us back to the oneness and deifying simplicity of the Father who gathers us in'; Luibheid and Rorem, *Pseudo-Dionysius*, 145.

[170] Hilduin, *Areopagitica*, *PL*, cvi. 13–50.

[171] The only contemporaneous allusion to his actual composition of the Office is found in Hilduin's response to the emperor's request; *Epistolae*, MGH, *Karolini Aevi*, iii, chs. 5–7, 330–1.

Around 836, the monk Adrevaldus from Saint-Benoît-sur-Loire reported the translation of some relics of Saint Denis, Rusticus, and Eleutherius to Fleury.[172] In granting permission for their transferral, Hilduin exacted a promise from Abbot Boson of Saint-Benoît: that the feast of Saint Denis be celebrated at Fleury 'in the monastic fashion' (*more monastico*).[173] Since Saint-Benoît-sur-Loire was already a monastery, such a stipulation has little meaning unless it refers to the twelve-lesson Office which Hilduin was eager to promote, having recently recast it at the bidding of Emperor Louis.[174] During his tenure, Hilduin had proved his skill in liturgical matters when he composed an Office for the feast of Saints Corneille and Cyprian (14 September)[175] and possibly the monastic Office for Saint Cucuphas found in the collection of readings for the day Hours I:VEcap LXXXVIII. He was likewise meticulous in distinguishing between various types of practice, having specified, for instance, that the 'Roman Office' be sung in the chapel he built in 832.[176] In addition, an expression with the opposite meaning, *more canonico*, was current in the ninth century. This term appears in many sources, including the capitular acts from Aix-la-Chapelle, where it indicates a shortened form of the Office of Matins which was used by canons and some monks on Maundy Thursday, Good Friday, Holy Saturday, Easter, and during Easter Week.[177] Since both expressions were known, there is every reason to suppose that Hilduin meant something quite specific in referring to the celebration of the feast of Saint Denis in *more monastico*.

Hilduin would naturally have enjoined the monks of Saint-Denis to sing his newly created Office. When he could find sufficient excuse to

[172] Mabillon, *AASS Ordinis Sancti Benedicti*, Saec. ii, 383–4. The life of King Robert II (996–1031) by Helgaud of Fleury records that there was an altar dedicated to Saints Denis, Rusticus, and Eleutherius in the church at Fleury; see Bautier and Labory, *Helgaud*, 116–19. On Adrevaldus, see *PL*, cxxiv. 899; Chevalier, *Bio-Bibliographie*, i, col. 53.

[173] 'ut quotannis adveniente natalitio eorumdem Martyrum [sanctorum Dionysii, et al.] celeberrima apud nos [monachos Floriacenses] ipsorum festivitas *more Monastico* haberetur'; Mabillon, *AASS Ordinis Sancti Benedicti*, Saec. ii, 384.

[174] The 2 extant breviaries from Saint-Benoît-sur-Loire, F:O 776 (fos. 375^{v}–76^{v}) and F:O 125 (fos. 245^{v}–47), contain precisely the same antiphons and responsories in the Office for Saint Denis as the sources from the abbey (cf. F:Pn, lat. 17296, fos. 227–32; Hesbert, *CAO*, ii, No. 114).

[175] The 12th-c. hagiographical codex F:R(m) 1391 (U. 39) states (fo. 95): 'In veneration of Saints [Corneille and Cyprian] a night Office with antiphons and responsories was written by the aforementioned archchancellor Hilduin to be sung with most pleasing melody' ('In quorum [Cornelii et Cypriani] veneratione . . . officium nocturnale cum antiphonis et responsoriis a supradicto archicancellario [Hilduino] compositum est cum commodissima modulatione canendum'); see 'Catalogus', 184. The text and music of the Office are contained as an addition in the 12th-c. antiphoner from Saint-Denis, F:Pn, lat. 17296, fos. 352–34, as well as in several later sources. I am indebted to M. Huglo for drawing my attention to Hilduin's Office for Corneille and Cyprian.

[176] See Ch. 4.

[177] See Hallinger, *Initia*, 535; and for later appearances of the phrase, see Symons *et al.*, *Regularis*, 108, n. 2.

promulgate the service outside the claustral walls, as on the occasion of the translation of relics from Saint-Denis to Fleury, he probably did so. More than two centuries must have been required for this and other twelve-responsory offices like the one for Saint Cucuphas to find permanent places in monastic antiphoners. The sole monastic Office for Saint Benedict in F:Pn, lat. 17436 and the hybrid nature of the liturgy of the early eleventh-century Hartker antiphoner (CH:SGs 390–1) attest to the slow pace at which the monastic *cursus* entered the written tradition. Nevertheless, the beginning of the progressive adoption of the Benedictine liturgy at Saint-Denis seems to have occurred in the first part of the ninth century in the literary output of the prolific Hilduin.

NORMAN INVASIONS

The activities of the 830s were temporarily suspended in 841 when Hilduin was forced to flee the first of several Norman invasions that shook much of Western Europe. Taking with him the saints' relics and what treasures he could carry, the dispossessed abbot sought refuge at Ferrières.[178] On three later occasions, the monks did likewise,[179] and by 890 they had twice lodged in the area around Reims.[180] During the last of these sojourns, the relics of Saint Denis actually remained in the Abbey of Saint-Denis of Reims for approximately three years.[181] The mingling of local liturgical and musical practices that such visits must have caused is probably reflected in the contents of F:LA 118, a combined gradual, sacramentary, and lectionary. The gradual portion of this book shows a mixture of the usages of Saint-Denis with those of Laon, located near Reims. There is good reason to suppose that the individual sections of F:LA 118 came into the area of Reims/Laon at the end of the ninth century, when the monks of Saint-Denis, chased from their abbey, would have needed such books to celebrate Mass in exile.

Nor was the monastery itself spared the rapacity of the Normans. On 20 October 865 the intruders occupied Saint-Denis, and over the next

[178] Félibien, *Histoire*, 80.

[179] Crosby, *Abbey*, 94–5.

[180] In 876, the monks hid their precious cargo in the church of Saint-Martin of Consevreux (between Laon and Reims), a territory which Princess Berthe, daughter of Charlemagne, had conceded to Saint-Denis; see Mabillon, *AASS Ordinis Sancti Benedicti*, Saec. ii/2, 361, ch. 1.

[181] The chronicler Flodoard confirms the presence of the monks and relics of Saint-Denis in Reims; Heller and Waitz, *Flodoardi*, 573, lib. iv, ch. 8. Later authors supply the precise location and the duration of their stay (*c*.887–90); see Félibien, *Histoire*, 99; *GC*, ix. 288.

three weeks carted away the riches they found within its walls.[182] This catastrophe no doubt wrought the destruction or theft of numerous products of the scriptorium of Saint-Denis, whose monk-copyists were active in spite of the unwelcome interruptions. Of those manuscripts which have survived, the sacramentary and lectionary of F:LA 118 and the gradual F:Psg 111 probably issued from the scriptorium during these troubled times. Similarly, the annalistic chronicle I:Rvat, Reg. lat. 309, which contains important information about the thirteenth-century cantor William, was also begun there in the second half of the ninth century.[183] Another sacramentary, F:Pn, lat. 2290, was probably copied for Saint-Denis in the northern Abbey of Saint-Amand during the abbacy of Gozlin (877–87), who governed Saint-Denis, Saint-Amand, and Saint-Germain-des-Prés simultaneously.

LAY ABBOTS AND CLUNIAC REFORM

The misfortunes that the monastery suffered from the foreign invaders only added to the woes they had experienced earlier at the hands of local seigniorial predators. To cope more effectively with their predicament, the monks entrusted their internal government to members of the royal house in the mid-ninth century.[184] Emperor Charles the Bald, lay abbot after about 870,[185] showed his predilection for Saint-Denis in several ways, often spending Easter and other high feast-days in the abbey.[186] His frequent presence there accounts in part for the connections of the sacramentary F:Pn, lat. 2290 with the monastery, and it inspired scholars in the past to attribute four other sumptuous liturgical codices (D:Mbs, Clm. 14000; F:Pn, lat. 1141; F:Pn, lat. 1152; F:Pn, lat. 2292) to the scriptorium of Saint-Denis. The library of the abbey was certainly enriched through Charles's patronage, for he bequeathed many manuscripts from his personal collection to the monks.[187] While Saint-Denis profited in this way from the generosity of Charles and his successors, over the course of the next century the monks also lost some

[182] 'quia Nortmanni tertia decima Kalend. Novembris monasterium Sancti Dyonisii intraverunt; ubi viginti circiter diebus immorantes et cotidie praedam exinde ad suas naves ducentes'; Waitz, *Bertiniani*, 80.

[183] The first layer of entries in this chronicle notes the arrival of the Normans in Paris in 845: 'Nortmanni Parisius primitus veniunt'; Berger, '*Chronicon*', 274 (a. 845). Coincidentally, the record for the year 865, during which they ransacked the abbey's treasury, is itself all but obliterated; ibid. 273, n. 1.

[184] Félibien, *Histoire*, 81; see also Spiegel, *Chronicle*, 25; Crosby, *Abbey*, 94–6.

[185] Charles calls himself 'monasterii magni Dionysii abba' in a charter which dates from this year (see Tardif, *Monuments*, 132, No. 205). On the Office of lay abbot, see James, *Origins*, 112–13; McKitterick, *Kingdoms*, 122, and *passim*.

[186] Félibien, *Histoire*, 93–5.

[187] See McKitterick, 'Library', 28 ff.

of their autonomy as a result of the constant royal intervention.[188] In spite of this, lay abbots continued in the monastery until 968, when the incumbent abbot and later king, Hugh Capet, abolished the custom and reinstated the practice of electing the prelate from among the members of the convent.[189]

Contrary to the early history of Saint-Denis, musical and liturgical activity at the abbey in the tenth century is not well depicted by the extant sources. Probably the main development was the progressive adoption of the Benedictine form of the Office of Matins. Evidence of this can be seen in the tenth-century gradual and antiphoner of Mont-Renaud. Chapter 7 suggests that this manuscript did not originate at Saint-Denis, as has been previously proposed. Nevertheless, the combination of nine- and twelve-responsory Offices in the antiphoner portion of the book represents in a general way the progressive differentiation between the two types of service, secular and monastic, that took place during this era. If the liturgy of the monastery was moving toward the Benedictine ideal during the tenth century, the transition was accomplished by around 1000. As in the mid-eighth century, influences from outside the convent helped consummate the change. These external forces were not solely regal, they stemmed also from a new spirit of monastic fervour which swept the West.

During his brief nine-year reign, the first Capetian monarch Hugh Capet (987–96) evidently continued the liturgical restructuring that had been under way at Saint-Denis for more than 150 years. In abdicating his lay abbacy in 968, the king restored much of the monastery's former independence. He followed this act some 25 years later with a full-scale reform through which he hoped to place Saint-Denis under the influence of the newly established house of Cluny. To accomplish this task, Hugh sent Abbot Majolus (later Saint Majolus) to Saint-Denis. Majolus died on the way to the abbey, but Adémar of Chabannes records that his successor Odilo (later Saint Odilo), acting as abbot of Saint-Denis from 994 to 998, introduced the Benedictine model there, as interpreted by Cluny.[190] But the reform was far from all-pervasive in terms of the Divine Service, and it deserves to be scrutinized in some detail.

The music and liturgy of Saint-Denis stood apart from that of Cluny in several important ways. The calendar of feasts in the abbey incorpor-

[188] See Spiegel, *Chronicle*, 26.

[189] Félibien, *Histoire*, 111.

[190] Waitz, *Ademari*, 129; see also the summaries of this event in Félibien, *Histoire*, 115; *GC*, vii, col. 362; Sackur, *Cluniacenser*, ii. 32–3; Spiegel, *Chronicle*, 26–7; Rosenwein, *Rhinoceros*, 55; Crosby, *Abbey*, 96–7. See Fry's discussion of Cluniac adherence to the Rule after the reform; *Rule*, 125–7. For examples of Cluniac customaries which depict the liturgy in detail, see the editions and descriptions in *CCM*, vols. vii/2; vii/4; x.

ated only one Cluniac saint, Majolus, and the level of his cult was never particularly high, and the Cluny-inspired celebrations of All Souls (2 November) and Transfiguration (6 August) were adopted only reluctantly at Saint-Denis. Similarly, the abbey continued to use the Roman version of the service of Matins at Easter (three psalms, antiphons, lessons, and responsories), even after the Cluniac houses called for a return to the longer monastic form.[191] As Chapter 3 will show, the Gregorian music for the Mass at Saint-Denis was not altered to conform to books from Cluny, nor did the liturgy of the Offices bend much to Cluniac influence. In short, the monks of Saint-Denis clung to their own time-honoured usages in many instances.

Nevertheless, the liturgical practice of the abbey was in other ways affected by the reform. Every extant Sandionysian antiphoner and breviary, beginning with the early eleventh-century F:Pm 384, reflects the imposition of the monastic Office with regard to the performance of twelve lessons and responsories at Matins. The Cluniacs no doubt insisted on the strict observance of the Benedictine liturgy as part of their call for a return to adherence to the basic tenets of the rule. After five centuries, the Office at Saint-Denis was finally structured in accordance with the Rule of Saint Benedict. The use of processions to the lesser altars of the church played an important role in the Divine Service at Saint-Denis beginning in the twelfth century. The same practice can be documented at Cluny just after the mid-eleventh century, and Abbot Suger may have followed this Cluniac custom when he rebuilt the church of Saint-Denis in the 1140s. The monks might also have modelled some aspects of their performance practice on Cluniac customaries.

Many of the administrative aspects of Cluny seem likewise to have been adopted, and King Robert II (996–1031) was as zealous in enforcing them in the abbey as his father Hugh Capet had been.[192] Under the two subsequent monarchs, Henry I (1031–60) and Philip I (1060–1108), the abbey became involved in international dealings which had an impact on the shape of the Divine Office. Around 1053, the monastery of Saint-Emmeram near Ratisbon instigated a quarrel with Saint-Denis over the relics of the patron saint. Both houses insisted they possessed the authentic remains, and in the ceremony of identification which ensued, the monks of Saint-Denis openly displayed the bodies of the patron saint and his two companions to justify their own claim. The establishment of the feast of the Detection of Saint Denis (9 June) in the eleventh or twelfth century resulted from this event. But, perhaps more significantly, the fact that this controversy

[191] See Huglo, 'Office', 203.

[192] Félibien, *Histoire*, 116; Spiegel, *Chronicle*, 27.

even arose demonstrates that Saint Denis had by now achieved substantial fame both at home and abroad.

To be sure, the favoured royal protector was highly renowned in England. King Edward the Confessor in 1059 granted lands in Oxfordshire to the abbey,[193] and a decade later the priory of Deerhurst near Gloucester.[194] Edward's gift of Deerhurst was in part a thank-offering to Baldwin, a monk of Saint-Denis who had become Edward's personal physician.[195] Baldwin's faithful service likewise earned him the abbacy of Bury St Edmunds from William the Conqueror in 1069. This event may well have left an imprint on the liturgy of Saint-Denis, for the monks added an Office for Saint Edmund (20 November) around this time.

ABBOT SUGER (1122–51) AND THE GOTHIC CHURCH

Whereas the twelfth century began inauspiciously at Saint-Denis, it was to culminate in the attainment of the glorious destiny that the monks had long envisaged for their abbey. Once again, the personalities of those in command had much to do with the course of events. Under the abbacy of Adam (1099–1122), discipline at Saint-Denis declined to the point that the famous Peter Abelard, recently installed as a monk of the abbey, criticized the monks for their laxness.[196] He likewise committed the unpardonable sin of questioning the truth of the Saint Denis/Dionysius the Areopagite/Pseudo-Dionysius identification, a connection in which the monks now steadfastly believed. Ironically, his diatribe did not uncover the true Saint Denis of the third century; instead, he insisted that the patron of the monastery was yet another Dionysius, a more obscure second-century bishop of Corinth.[197]

Quite apart from this new affront to the patron saint, Adam had encountered problems with the royal house somewhat earlier. The abbey slipped noticeably from its favoured position when Philip I declined to be buried at Saint-Denis in 1108.[198] This was of no small concern to Adam, and to prevent the repetition of such a slight by future monarchs he founded an anniversary to commemorate the death

193 Tardif, *Monuments*, 171–2, No. 277 (original = F:Pan, K 19, No. 6).

194 See Knowles and Hadcock, *Houses*, 231.

195 Félibien, *Histoire*, 126–27; and Atsma and Vezin, 'Dossier', 233–4.

196 On Abelard's controversial sojourn at Saint-Denis, see Félibien, *Histoire*, 146–8; Panofsky, *Suger*, 17–18; Spiegel, *Chronicle*, 29; Crosby, *Abbey*, 112–13.

197 See Jeauneau, 'Abélard'; Luscombe, 'Denis', 147–8; Beaune, *Naissance*, 88–90.

198 From the death of Hugh Capet in 987 to the French Revolution, all but 3 kings—Philip I, Louis VII (d. 1180), and Louis XI (d. 1483)—were interred in the abbey. For more on the importance of Philip's insult to the abbey, see Spiegel, *Chronicle*, 28.

of Philip's most illustrious forebear, the Merovingian King Dagobert (d. 639). This ceremony, or another of slightly less pomp, was intended to be sung on the yearly remembrance of every king who was interred in the abbey. In its high level of splendour, the service for Dagobert stood as a reminder to subsequent rulers that their salvation was best assured when they entrusted their bodies to Saint-Denis.

If abbey and monarchy were thus estranged during Adam's time, their intimacy reached a zenith under Abbot Suger (1122–51). Educated for a time with the future Louis VI, Suger consolidated his influence with the young ruler early on.[199] The economic and political privileges that Louis conferred on Saint-Denis during this period were immense. In return, Suger's monks began to chronicle the lives of the French kings, retaining this important duty for almost four centuries.[200]

In the 1130s the abbot turned his efforts to beautifying the church. Since the ninth century, probably the only construction that had taken place at Saint-Denis had been the addition of a tower with funds from William the Conqueror in the late eleventh century.[201] Between about 1135 and 1144, Suger had the western and eastern parts of the church rebuilt.[202] Leaving the nave of the Carolingian structure largely untouched, he extended the church westward, constructing a new facade, and building a new chevet with radiating chapels on the east end (Pl. 2). In this way, Sugar inaugurated many aspects of the emerging Gothic style. He likewise made a number of changes to the ritual which complemented his expansive architectural and artistic ideas, unwittingly setting a precedent for a similar liturgical enhancement which would take place 100 years later. A host of magnificent stained-glass windows[203] and liturgical objects also date from Suger's tenure.[204] These, like other aspects of the new church, illustrate his acquaintance with the philosophy of Pseudo-Dionysius, as he understood it through the translations

[199] On the reigns of Louis VI and Abbot Suger, see ibid. *Chronicle*, 29–36, Constable, 'Administration'; Crosby, *Abbey*, 105–20; and on Suger's life and surroundings, see Benton, 'Life'; Crosby, *Abbey*, 105–20; Panofsky, *Suger*, 1–37.

[200] Although the composition of regnal histories actually began slightly before his time, it was undoubtedly Suger's influence that altered the style of these works to royal advantage in many ways; Spiegel, *Chronicle*, 39–40. In her study of Suger's life of Louis VI, Spiegel has pointed to the abbot's unusual way of writing, suggesting that he may have been 'more concerned with providing a cultural image of kingship and its role within a cosmologically defined hierarchy of being than with reporting the operations or administrative achievements of the monarchy in the political universe of twelfth-century France'; idem, 'History', 156. Suger's *Vita Ludovici grossi* is edited in Lecoy de la Marche, *Suger*, 5–149, and in Waquet, *Louis*.

[201] Crosby, *Abbey*, 96–101.

[202] See Crosby's study of Suger's church in ibid. 105–289.

[203] The principal work on Suger's windows is Grodecki, *Vitraux*. More recent studies include his 'Style'; Crosby, *et al.*, *Abbey*, 60–99; Gage, 'Glass'; Lillich, 'Glass'; Brown and Cothren, 'Window'; Caviness, 'Glass'; Cothren, 'Infancy'; Kidson, 'Panofsky', 10.

[204] See the descriptions of individual items in Crosby, *et al.*, *Abbey*.

and commentaries of John Scottus Eriugena and through the exegetical works of contemporaneous thinkers, especially Hugh of Saint-Victor (d. 1140/1).[205]

In similar fashion, some of the texts and music for the Office found in the antiphoner which was probably copied under Suger (F:Pn, lat. 17296) may reflect Pseudo-Dionysian doctrines on the Trinity and on the efficacy of light and clarity. Chapter 4 shows that the numerous ornate responsories and Benedicamus Domino and Ite Missa Est melismas, the tones for the Gloria Patri, and a few of the responsory prosulas are especially open to this interpretation. On the other hand, Suger may also have embodied a negative statement in the elaborate melismas and tropes in F:Pn, lat. 17296, for he largely ignored the Cistercian reform of excesses in plainchant of the 1130s,[206] even after Bernard of Clairvaux had commended him around 1127 for having eliminated some of the pomp and external splendour in the abbey.[207] But if ornate music was Suger's goal, his successors missed an opportunity to cultivate it when they seem to have disregarded the new polyphonic music which Canon Leoninus (*c.*1135–after 1201) of Notre Dame[208] and others created in and around Paris. With the possible exception of one French motet and one Latin *conductus*, described in Chapter 5, there is no evidence that polyphony was composed or sung at Saint-Denis. Some reasons for this apparent conservatism will be suggested in Chapter 4.

The influence of the ubiquitous Suger extended to the ritual of another house, Saint-Corneille of Compiègne.[209] In 1150, Pope Eugene III instructed him to reform the canons of this institution, and to this end Suger installed monks of Saint-Denis there. He must also have supplied Saint-Corneille with Sandionysian liturgical books, for the extant sources for the next two centuries are based in many striking ways on those of Saint-Denis.

While significant information on the history of the liturgy at Saint-Denis during Suger's abbacy has survived, the history of the second

[205] See the recent summary of the philosophies which Suger expressed in the new church, with relevant bibliography, in Rorem, *Symbols*, 144–6; and the subsequently published studies in Zinn, 'Suger'; Crosby, *Abbey*, 108–11, 117–18; Radding and Clark, 'Abélard', and Schueller, *Idea*, 344, 348. On Eriugena's influence on Suger, see Moran, *Philosophy*, 274; and on the philosophical underpinnings of the 1st half of the 12th c. in general, see Dronke, *History*; Haren, *Thought*, 104–16; Schueller, *Idea*, 344–72.

[206] The musical aspects of the Cistercian reform are treated in Marosszéki, *Origines* (see esp. 70–3, which deal with the amputation of long melismas); and in Waddell, 'Origin'; idem, *Hymnal*, i. 76–87, 105. On the philosophy behind this reform, see Schueller, *Idea*, 357–9.

[207] See Félibien, *Histoire*, 157–61; Panofsky, *Suger*, 10–15. The text of Bernard's letter to Suger is given in *PL*, clxxxii. 191–9 (for a list of Bernard's other missives to Suger, see Crosby, *Abbey*, 477, n. 16).

[208] See the new biography of Leoninus in Wright, 'Leoninus'.

[209] See Robertson, 'Transmission'.

half of the twelfth century is largely a void, owing to the lack of extant sources. The translations of several saints' relics, among them three virgins of Cologne in 1168, occurred during this period, although the feast commemorating their martyrdom was not celebrated at Saint-Denis until the thirteenth century. The only abbot of note, William of Gap (1173–?1186), was probably responsible for the compilation of the Greek Mass which was sung on the Octave of Saint Denis (16 October).

LATE MIDDLE AGES

In contrast to the late twelfth century, the numerous liturgical and historical documents which have survived from the thirteenth century make it possible to chart closely the growth of the Divine Office and of musical activities in general at Saint-Denis. The late medieval expansion of the ritual was due primarily to two factors: the continued desire for relics and yet another reconstruction of the church (1231–81, Pl. 3).[210] The origins of many new feasts can be traced directly to the acquisition or recovery of sacred remains and objects. Similarly, the reconstruction of Saint-Denis under Abbots Eudes Clément (1228–45), William of Macouris (1246–54), Henry Mallet (1254–8), and Matthew of Vendôme (1258–86) caused the elevation in rank of numerous ceremonies and an increase in the number of processions in the chevet of the church. This newly heightened level of devotion no doubt prompted Abbot Eudes to found a confraternity in honour of Saint Denis. A new ordinary (F:Pn, lat. 976) and a notated missal (F:Pn, lat. 1107) were copied to incorporate these changes, and these books replaced, among other sources, an earlier ordinary (F:Pm 526) which depicts the liturgy of Saint-Denis as it stood in the early 1200s and perhaps in the time of Suger as well.[211] Musicians of some renown flourished in the abbey during the thirteenth century. An anonymous monk-trouvère, styling himself simply *Li Moines de saint denis*, was actively composing around 1230, while a cantor named William gained fame through his stunning performance in Notre Dame Cathedral during the ceremony of the Reception of the Crown of Thorns in 1239. Two monks from the early fourteenth century, Guido and Petrus, bear witness to the study of music theory by persons connected with the abbey.

These centuries also mark the final stage of development of the liturgy of Saint-Denis until the advent of the Congregation of Saint

[210] On the 13th-c. reconstruction of Saint-Denis see Bruzelius, *St-Denis*.

[211] For a discussion of many aspects of the daily *cursus*, as represented in F:Pm 526, see Foley, 'Ordinary', ii. 77–183.

Maur in 1633.[212] The services that were sung as late as the mid-sixteenth century are anticipated in the fourteenth-century missal GB:Lva 1346–1891 and in the breviary GB:Ob, Can. Lit. 192. That the liturgy at Saint-Denis apparently ceased to grow is understandable, for the end of the quest for relics did away with the primary reason for the creation of new feasts.[213] But the later sources are far from silent about other types of ceremony that took place at Saint-Denis. Endowments poured in for the various altars of the church, especially for the chapels that were added on the north side of the nave, at the start of the fourteenth century (Pl. 4).[214] In addition, a daily Mass for the Virgin was established at the end of the fourteenth century. And three liturgical accessories, resulting once again from the close ties between abbey and royal palace, were instituted in celebration of three of the most momentous times in the lives of the king and queen.

The first and most solemn of these occasions was the burial or anniversary of a king. The notion of Saint-Denis as the royal necropolis was not new, of course, since royalty from as early as the sixth century lay buried there. But only in the twelfth century did the monks create the extraordinary service for Dagobert to commemorate their monarchs, as mentioned earlier. So elaborate were some of these sombre Offices that many important saints' feasts paled in comparison. Quite a different kind of Mass was sung to request the safe conduct of the king and the protection of the realm during periods of war. Saint-Denis housed many regal emblems, including the elaborate regalia, the symbols of authority which were used at kingly consecrations in the cathedral of Reims.[215] One special insignia, the banner of Saint-Denis, was identified in the days of Louis VI (1108–37) as the *Oriflamme*, a standard carried at the head of the French armies until the early fifteenth century.[216] The

[212] Levillain, 'Office', 54; and on the introduction of the Maurist reform at Saint-Denis, see Félibien, *Histoire*, 449–64.

[213] The interest in new relics was temporarily renewed in the late Middle Ages during the heated controversy which arose between the canons of Notre Dame and the monks of Saint Denis over who possessed the true head of the patron saint. The affair culminated in a widely publicized trial which took place in 1410 (see Delaborde, 'Procès', 297 ff.).

[214] On the 14th-c. additions to the church see Bruzelius, *St-Denis*, 15–17.

[215] See Spiegel, *Chronicle*, 31–3; Crosby *et al.*, *Abbey*, 114–15; Beaune, *Naissance*, 112–20; Crosby, *Abbey*, 10–11. The ordinaries of Reims from the 13th and 14th cs. name the objects which constituted the regalia and describe their use in the coronation. They make it clear, in addition, that the abbot of Saint-Denis was always present to watch over these treasures: 'the abbot of Saint-Denis-en-France has to bring all of these [regalia] to Reims from his monastery, and he stands at the altar [during the ceremony] to guard them' ('que omnia abbas beati dyonisii in Francia de monasterio suo debet Remis adportare, et stans ad altare custodire'); F:Rsc 330 (14th c.), fos. 105–5v. Approximately the same passage is likewise found in F:Rsc 328 (13th c.) and in F:Rsc 329 (14th c.). On these coronation *ordines* from Reims, see Vogel, *Liturgy*, 186; Jackson, *Vive*, 222; idem, 'Manuscrits', 74.

[216] Louis VI describes his reception of the standard in 1124; Tardif, *Monuments*, 217, No. 391 (original: F:Pan, K 22, No. 4); also Félibien, *Histoire*, 154.

Oriflamme likewise lay in the safekeeping of the monks. The king customarily received the standard during the Mass celebrated just before he departed for battle. Yet a third type of Mass marked the crowning of queens in the abbey, a custom which officially began in the late fifteenth century. The special music performed for these coronations did not emanate from the monks, however, but from members of the king's own chapel.

COMMENDATORY ABBOTS AND DISPERSION OF THE LIBRARY

Indeed, royal influence grew so strong in the sixteenth century that the king himself began choosing the abbot in 1529 to assure that a person sympathetic to his own interests would occupy the office. The new commendatory abbots seemed to have little interest in the ritual at Saint-Denis, though, for the execution of the Divine Service remained about as it had been since 1350, as just noted.[217] The latest book surveyed in this study, the first printed breviary of Saint-Denis of 1550 (F:Pn, Rés. B. 5209), shows that services were performed approximately as in the fourteenth-century breviary GB:Ob, Can. Lit. 192. And so, after the striking transformations of earlier times—the pre-monastic Martinian code and the brief interludes of perpetual psalmody, the reforms of the ninth and tenth centuries which slowly established the Benedictine Office, the ceremonial additions from the eleventh to the thirteenth century—the late fourteenth-century liturgy of Saint-Denis was complete. Apart from the new endowments which were made after this time, little change came about until the monastery was reformed once again in 1633 by the Congregation of Saint-Maur.[218]

Unsettling as the seventeenth-century reforms must have been, they did not compare with the earlier catastrophic events which all but destroyed the library of Saint-Denis, a facility which by 1465 had numbered some 1,600 volumes.[219] In October 1567, a band of Huguenots began a ruinous occupation of Saint-Denis.[220] The full force of their destruction was only in part averted by their leader Louis of Bourbon, Prince of Condé, who had been raised from boyhood in the

[217] Louis, Cardinal of Bourbon, was the 1st of these abbots; ibid. 382–3. See the list of commendatory abbots in Ayzac, *Histoire*, vol. i, p. cxxix.

[218] The Maurists reworked many proper services in the breviary and missal of Saint-Denis as well as the Greek Mass to make them conform to their standardized versions.

[219] Carolus-Barré, 'Pillage', 97; Nebbiai-Dalla Guarda, *Bibliothèque*, 101.

[220] Accounts of the event are edited in Carolus-Barré, 'Pillage', 98–9, and in Nebbiai-Dalla Guarda, *Bibliothèque*, 125–8.

monastery.[221] Unfortunately, Louis could not prevent the pillage and dispersion of the library, but the monks must have hidden or spirited away a few musical and liturgical manuscripts, for the sacramentary F:Pn, lat. 9436 and missal F:Pm 414 appear in inventories of books from Saint-Denis up to the French Revolution. Other sources found their way to the Bibliothèque Nationale and to other libraries in France, England, and Italy by way of private collectors who profited from the losses of the abbey. The library of Saint-Denis was never fully reconstituted after this sixteenth-century dispersal; the fury in Protestant guise had effectively scattered the great legacy of the medieval scriptorium and library of Saint-Denis throughout western Europe. The service-books of the monks are the subject of the chapters that follow.

[221] Félibien, *Histoire*, 398. This prince was the nephew of the 1st commendatory abbot of Saint-Denis Louis of Bourbon.

2

Calendar of Feasts, Anniversaries, and Royal Observances

For Abbot Hilduin (814–41) of Saint-Denis the name of King Dagobert (died *c*.639) proved an entrée to the Carolingian throne in the ninth century. By invoking that name in 1108, Abbot Adam (1099–1122) intended to establish Saint-Denis permanently as the royal necropolis. And Adam very nearly succeeded, for the earthly remains of almost every French ruler from 1137 until the Revolution lay in homage alongside the relics of the patron saint of the monarchy. To aid in the fusion of the royal and the saintly, the names of kings were inscribed next to those of martyrs and confessors in the liturgical calendar of the abbey, which served as an official register of this covenant.[1] Unlike the purely necrological references that many manuscripts with regal connections contain,[2] such obits did more than lend the calendar of Saint-Denis its distinctive appearance.[3] They marked the days on which the special anniversary services for members of the royal household and others were to be celebrated.

This enhancement of the Divine Ritual of the abbey boded something further. Of all aspects of monastic life, the established liturgy was the most resistant to change. To infuse it with commemorations for deceased rulers was to introduce ceremonies that often rivalled the most ancient festivals in splendour. And just as the principal observances of the *sanctorale* were inviolable, so too would be the alliance between the monastery and the crown, once the royal necrology was systematically incorporated into the calendar of Saint-Denis. Or so Abbot Adam and his successors sought to make this royal–monastic relationship.

[1] The 1st extant calendar that contains royal obituary notices is the early 13th-c. Chapel Hill psalter (e.g. Appendix A, MS CH, 6 Oct.). Although no calendar from the era of Abbots Adam and Suger survives, it is likely that similar indications would have been included in them. Other MSS from the 12th c. do incorporate traces of royal ceremonies, e.g. the contemporaneous antiphoner F:Pn, lat. 17296, with the service *In natali Dagoberti regis* (fo. 327–30; Hesbert, *CAO*, ii, No. 146). Likewise, around 1144 Suger describes a storm that arose during the celebration for Dagobert; Panofsky, *Suger*, 108.

[2] E.g. the 13th-c. psalter of Queen Ingeburge (see Leroquais, *Psautiers*, i. 138–43).

[3] The presence of these mentions is in fact a hallmark of calendars from Saint-Denis from the 13th to the 16th cs., one that is noted as a distinguishing feature in catalogues which describe these sources from the abbey.

CALENDAR AND MARTYROLOGY

The calendar of Saint-Denis is a useful introduction to the history of feasts in the abbey. A calendar is a list of festivals and saints' days, ordered according to the course of the year, which are meant to be observed in the ritual.[4] Seventeen manuscripts connected with Saint-Denis include calendars, although the calendars in F:Pn, lat. 9436, F:Pn, lat. 103, and Vendôme, Bibl. Mun. 17C also contain influences from outside the abbey.[5] Aside from the foreign elements in these sources, the calendars and the texts they introduce depict the liturgical usage of Saint-Denis from the end of the ninth to the middle of the sixteenth century.

During this time, a number of older festivals passed from the earliest to the latest documents with few changes. Many were ancient Roman observances which had come into France by way of the Gregorian sacramentary, while others were present in the Frankish Gelasian books when the new sources from Rome arrived.[6] The mixture of these feasts into one series resulted in the basic calendar of the Carolingian era, which served as the point of departure for most French churches beginning in the ninth century. Subsequently each house began to accept new festivals into its calendar and liturgy. The monks of Saint-Denis, for example, established the observance of the Detection of Saint Denis (9 June) in the eleventh or twelfth century to commemorate an event particular to their community. In the 1290s they responded to the universal decree which instituted the widely honoured feast of Saint Louis (25 August). In this way, calendars were everywhere the products both of inheritance and of addition. An institution guarded its liturgical legacy with respect, at the same time admitting new celebrations in response to parochial and ecumenical exigencies alike.

In copying the names of feasts into a calendar, a scribe probably consulted two documents. First he would have used an old calendar, and along with this he would have had to hand a martyrology, a more general source which presented the complete conspectus of saints honoured on a certain day regardless of whether or not liturgical

[4] See Frere, *Kalendar*, 7–10; 'Calendar', 161; Eisenhöfer and Lechner, *Liturgy*, 228–9; Fiala, 'Versuch', 131–4; Dubois, *Martyrologes*, 16–17.

[5] Throughout this chapter, references to feasts will be made by name and date, e. g. Saint Denis (9 Oct.). The reader should consult App. A to locate the observances in the calendar. See also the introduction to the calendar of Saint-Denis in App. A for the abbreviations used in the calendars.

[6] See the convenient list of Gregorian and Gelasian feasts in Leroquais, *Bréviaires*, vol. i, pp. cxxx–cxxxii; and the discussion of the early sacramentaries in Ch. 6.

[7] See Frere, *Kalendar*, 7; see also Eisenhöfer and Lechner, *Liturgy*, 39–40; Dubois, *Martyrologes*, 16–17.

celebration was planned for all of them.[7] The prototype of the early martyrologies was a document attributed to Saint Jerome, but which was actually composed between the fifth and seventh centuries.[8] Over the next 200 years, the so-called historical martyrology, with its fewer but more detailed entries, won favour.[9] A celebrated martyrology of this type, composed by the monk Usuard of Saint-Germain-des-Prés between 850 and 865,[10] was one of the principal sources of the official Roman martyrology of 1584. References to martyrologies at Saint-Denis pre-date the earliest extant calendars, and it is likely that they were regularly employed in the production of new calendars.[11]

RANKS OF FEASTS

While many aspects of the calendar of Saint-Denis remained fixed over the centuries, its physical appearance changed noticeably. The ninth-century calendars F:Psg 111 and F:Pn, lat. 2290, for instance, provide geographical as well as liturgical information.[12] For the feast of Saint Felix (14 January) they write 'in Campania, in the city of Nola, Felix, presbyter and confessor',[13] while the later manuscripts write simply 'Felix, presbyter and confessor'.[14] In addition, the calendar of F:Psg 111 contains certain abbreviations which apparently describe how services were celebrated: *Pl. mis.*, *mis. in gl.*, and *pl. of. Pl. mis.* seems to stand for *plena missa* ('full Mass'),[15] *mis. in gl.* for *missa in Gelasii* ('Gelasian Mass'),[16] and these designations are added to feasts for which Masses

[8] Ed. in *AASS*, Nov. ii/2. On the history of the martyrology of Saint Jerome, see Dubois, *Martyrologes*, 29–37; *DACL* x/2, col. 2530; and Frere, *Kalendar*, 8–10.

[9] Dubois, *Martyrologes*, 37–45; *DACL*, x/2, col. 2599.

[10] Ed. with extensive commentary in Dubois, *Usuard*. See also idem, *Martyrologes*, 45–56; earlier studies in *DACL*, x/2, col. 2500; Quentin, *Martyrologes*, 1–4.

[11] In a letter to King Louis the Pious (*c*.835), Abbot Hilduin refers to a Greek martyrology ('Habemus tamen Graecae auctoritatis Martyrologion') which he claims offers evidence to support his promotion of the identification of Saint Denis with the 2 Areopagite figures; *Epistolae Variorum*, MGH, *Karolini Aevi*, iii. 332.

[12] These 2 calendars, which appear to have been derived from the martyrology of Saint Jerome, transmit certain precisions of Roman topography that are preserved in no other source; *DACL*, x/2, cols. 1560–1. They are published in App. A (MSS G and N1) and in Delisle, *Sacramentaires*, 313–25.

[13] *In Campania, Nola civitate, Felicis, presbiteri et confessoris*, ibid. 314. For a discussion of topographical details in martyrologies, see Dubois, *Martyrologes*, 71–9.

[14] *Felicis presbiteri et confessoris* (calendar of the 13th-c. missal F:Pn, lat. 1107).

[15] Delisle suggests these resolutions for the abbreviations in the calendar of F:Psg 111; Delisle, *Sacramentaires*, 313. See the introduction to the calendars for the manner of notating these signs in App. A.

[16] Spelling of *Gelasii* [*sic*] is probably ellipsis for *missa in [sacramentario] Gelasii* (see calendar of F:Psg 111, 28 Oct., feast of Simon and Jude; also Delisle, *Sacramentaires*, 322). Since, with only 2 exceptions (20, 24 Jan.), the days indicated by this abbreviation are all Gelasian feasts, Delisle's translation seems correct. Similar designations *ordo secundum Gelasium* and *secundum*

usually appear in the contemporaneous sacramentaries and graduals. Likewise, the term *plenum officium* (*pl. of.*) is assigned to most of the observances which carry the rank of twelve lessons in the later calendars of the abbey.[17] The subsequent antiphoners and breviaries of Saint-Denis demonstrate that this indication *pl. of.* denotes the majority of services, both proper and common,[18] that composed the Office of the royal monastery. While the abbreviation *pl. of.* in F:Psg 111 does not differentiate between proper and common services, it does designate the feasts on which full, nine- or twelve-lesson Offices were sung in the ninth century at Saint-Denis. This information thus provides a list of observances which foreshadows the contents of the later antiphoner of the abbey.

Beginning in the thirteenth century, the calendar of Saint-Denis incorporated a new element: the rank of feasts.[19] The earliest extant calendar with rankings is found in the missal F:Pm 414 (*c.*1216–35). This document, along with the calendars in the other thirteenth-century missals F:Pn, lat. 1107 and I:Rc 603, uses the markings 'xii' and 'iii' to indicate feasts with twelve and three lessons at Matins, respectively. The calendars of the ordinaries F:Pm 526 and F:Pn, lat. 976 from roughly the same time contain similar information, and the texts of these two manuscripts provide more details. They distinguish four levels of ceremonies with twelve lessons and responsories in the three Nocturns at Matins, given here in descending order of solemnity:

Gregorium appear in the augmented sacramentary of Saint-Denis F:Pn, lat. 9436, fos. 58ᵛ (Pl. 11) and 63ᵛ, respectively, and these directions refer to services drawn from 2 types of sacramentary: the so-called 'Gelasian of the 8th c.' and the *Hadrianum* (discussed in Ch. 6).

[17] In the 9th c. the word *plenum* probably implied only 9 lessons and responsories, as found in secular and monastic institutions alike. In only 2 instances does an entry designated 'full Office' (*pl. of.*) in the calendar of F:Psg 111 fail to become a 12-lesson service at Saint-Denis: Saints Vitus, Modestus and Crescentia (15 June), and the Translation of Saints Hilary, Innocent, and Peregrinus (22 Aug.). The reasons for this are clear. The relics of Saint Vitus were present at Saint-Denis only until their translation to Corbie-en-Saxe in 836 (*AASS*, June iii, 522; also Félibien, *Histoire*, 78), and it is therefore understandable that vestiges of the special cult reserved for saints whose relics the abbey possessed would have died out by the end of the 9th c., with the service being replaced with a less elaborate Office of 3 lessons. The Translation of 22 Aug. was ousted by the Octave of the Assumption, but Saints Hilary and Peregrinus have 'full Offices' elsewhere in F:Psg 111 (25 Oct. and 16 May, respectively).

[18] Proper Offices were those which derived the texts of some or all of their chants and lessons from a literary selection particular to the occasion, such as a saint's *vita*. Common Offices, on the other hand, drew the sung portions of the Hours from sections of antiphoners and breviaries which contained a collection of material for various classes of saint, the 'common of saints' or *commune sanctorum*. A few festivals mixed proper with common chants. On rare occasions, the abbreviation for *commune* (*com.*) is used in F:Psg 111 to specify use of material from the *commune sanctorum* (see the entry for Saint Firminus, 25 Sept. in App. A).

[19] Ranks are symbols which denote the form and level of ceremony that an observance was to have. See the discussion of grades of feasts in 'Calendar', 165; Tolhurst, *Breviary*, vi. 146–8; and Eisenhöfer and Lechner, *Liturgy*, 240.

(1) principal (*principale*) feasts,[20] (2) duplex feasts,[21] (3) duplex feasts in which the fourth responsory is duplex,[22] and (4) simplex feasts of twelve lessons, which often lacked a full Office of First Vespers, replacing it with a Commemoration.[23] The differences in these services involve, among other things, the numbers of performers on various chants; their placement in the church; the use of incense, of special chants and of processions; the order of the procession at Mass; and the vestments worn.[24] In addition, ceremonial variations exist even within feasts of the same rank. Aside from the twelve-lesson feasts, the ordinaries recognize two lower levels of celebration: feasts of three lessons, which contain only two Nocturns at Matins; and, finally, the simple commemorations, which usually consist of a proper antiphon and oration at the end of Vespers and Lauds, and sometimes of a morning Mass (*missa matutinalis*) in honour of the saint.

In the fourteenth century, the calendar designated the degrees of feasts even more meticulously, and this new level of precision remains virtually unchanged through the sixteenth century. The five festivals marked *principale* in the thirteenth century were now called *annuale*,

[20] Christmas, Easter, Pentecost, Assumption (15 Aug.), Saint Denis (9 Oct.); F:Pm 526, fo. 16.

[21] See the ranks and descriptions of feasts in App. A for the method of denoting these grades of 12-lesson ceremonies in App. A. The term *duplex* is puzzling, and there is no general concensus about its precise meaning in the Middle Ages; see Cross, *Dictionary*, s.v. 'Double feasts'. Some have suggested that the word originally referred to the presence of a double Vespers service, one for the weekday, the other for the feast; e.g. Eisenhöfer and Lechner, *Liturgy*, 240; see other possible meanings discussed in Foley, 'Ordinary', ii. 221–2. The Saint-Denis ordinaries use the term *duplex* in different ways, all of which call for special attention to one or more aspects of the ceremony in question. The ordinaries sometimes place the word at the beginning of a feast, e.g. 'fiat dupplex festum' on the feast of Hilary of Poitiers (13 Jan.; F:Pm 526, fo. 98^{v}; F:Pn, lat. 976, fo. 70). This instruction seems to refer to the entire festival, although how it is to be carried out is unclear. In some services the term is connected specifically with the service of Matins, e.g. 'Ad matutinas omnia duppliciter fiant', on the feast of John the Baptist (24 June; F:Pm 526, fo. 137; F:Pn, lat. 976, fo. 99). In this instance the word might call for the performance of the repeated portion (*repetendum*) of some of the 12 responsories after the verse and after the Gloria Patri (see also n. 184 below). Occasionally the term seems to imply the double ringing of the bells at First Vespers, e.g. on King Dagobert's anniversary (19 Jan.): 'De domne [*sic*] dagoberto rege fiat dupplex festum hoc modo: campane *duppliciter* sonent'; F:Pn, lat. 976, fo. 71; see also F:Pm 526, fo. 99^{v}. Similar wording is found in a description of the enhancement of Saint Osmanna's feast in F:Pn, n.a.l. 1509, p. 407 [409] (see n. 152 below). The designation *duplex* is occasionally limited to 1, 2, or 3 responsories, as on the feast of Peter's Chair (22 Feb.): 'Fiant xii lectiones, quartum responsorium sit dupplex'; F:Pm 526, fo. 111; F:Pn, lat. 976, fo. 79. Here the implication may be that only the 4th responsory is to be performed with its *repetendum*. And finally, the designation *duplex* may refer to the fact that both the Magnificat at Vespers and the Benedictus at Lauds are performed twice on duplex feasts, whereas they are chanted 3 times on *semiannuale* and *annuale* festivals and once on feasts lower than duplex (see Ch. 5).

[22] Chair of Peter (22 Feb.), Detection of Saint Denis (9 June), Commemoration of Paul (30 June), Lawrence (10 Aug.), Bernard of Clairvaux (23 Aug.), Demetrius (17 Oct.), Martin (11 Nov.). On the Octave of Epiphany, the 4th, 8th, and 12th responsories are duplex.

[23] Described in F:Pm 526, fo. 85.

[24] See the discussion of many of these items in Ch. 5.

and the feast of the Dedication of the Church (24 February) in the calendars of GB:Lva 1346–1891 and GB:Ob, Can. Lit. 192 was likewise accorded this highest rank.[25] Duplex rank was split into two categories in the fourteenth century: the higher *semiannuale* and the lower duplex. Eleven feasts were *semiannuale* by 1350: Saint John (27 December), Epiphany (6 January), Purification (2 February), Annunciation (25 March), Invention of Saint Denis (22 April), Ascension, Peter and Paul (29 June), Nativity of Mary (8 September), Octave of Saint Denis (16 October), All Saints (1 November), and Conception of Mary (8 December). These festivals were slightly less elaborate than the *annuale* observances, but they still shared some of the special signs of festivity with the principal feasts. Duplex designation was given to feasts of saints whose relics were kept in the abbey, as well as apostles, doctors of the church, and others. Semiduplex observances include two feasts that had been celebrated with the fourth responsory duplex in the the thirteenth century (Octave of Epiphany, Chair of Peter), as well as other twelve-lesson services which were somewhat more ornate than those labelled simply *xii*. The later calendars, like the ones from the thirteenth century, also include simplex feasts of twelve lessons, feasts of three lessons, and commemorations (*memoriae*).[26]

PARISIAN AND FRENCH FEASTS

While the Gregorian and Gelasian saints formed the 'common denominator'[27] of individual liturgies in the ninth century, another handful of names that differed from place to place distinguished the earliest calendars along regional lines. At Saint-Denis, as elsewhere, these local saints fell into two categories. Particular to the abbey were the ones whose relics came into the Carolingian church in increasing numbers in the ninth century and thereafter. A second group comprised those who were specially regarded in the area of Paris and throughout much of France and Europe. Veneration of these latter saints was by no means limited to Saint-Denis,[28] although many of them had some direct

[25] Even though the Dedication became an *annuale* feast, the 14th-c. ordinary F:Pan, L 863, No. 10 continues to name only 5 'principal' feasts: 'Quando vero ante quinque festa principalia, scilicet, Natale domini, Pascha, Pentecosten, Assumptionem B[eate marie] etc. et festum Beati Dionisii'; F:Pan, L 863, No. 10, fo. 135.

[26] See Levillain, 'Office', 58–60.

[27] Expression coined by Leroquais (*Bréviaires*, vol. i, p. cxxx). For the most part, the Gregorian and Gelasian feasts do not need to be treated here since they were common to most other places. But they cannot be ignored altogether, for in some instances the Sandionysians changed the ranks of these services, as shown below.

[28] In fact, when these Parisian and French festivals, along with the Gregorian and Gelasian feasts, are removed from consideration, the only differences between the 13th-c. calendar of Saint-

historical connection with the monastery and were honoured with full offices (*pl. of.*)—probably first with nine lessons and responsories and later with twelve-lesson services.

One cherished Parisian saint was Geneviève, patron of Paris and founder of the earliest church of Saint-Denis. The date of her martyrdom, or *natale*, on 3 January was celebrated with twelve lessons, and the feast was later moved to 5 January, giving way to the anniversary for Philip V (d. 1322). The popularity of Lucian of Beauvais (8 January) at Saint-Denis may have been due to his assumed association with Dionysius the Areopagite.[29] Saint Germanus (28 May), who as bishop of Paris would also have presided over the basilica of Saint-Denis in the sixth century, probably compelled the monks of the abbey to sing the psalms according to the fiat of the Council of Tours (567).[30] The feasts of Saints Medard of Soissons (8 June) and of Germanus of Auxerre (31 July) recall the time prior to the mid-seventh century when Saint-Denis shared its status of *basilica senior* with the houses dedicated to these saints. The abbey of Saint-Médard, moreover, was one of three that Abbot Hilduin of Saint-Denis governed simultaneously in the first half of the ninth century.[31] Repeated Norman invasions shortly thereafter drove the monks and relics of the abbey more than once to asylum in the area of Reims.[32] The observance of the Translation of the titular Saint

Denis and that of a neighbouring church such as the cathedral of Paris (see the calendar in F:Pn, lat. 5185cc), are: (1) the varying observances for saints with relics in the 2 churches, (2) the anniversaries in the Saint-Denis calendars, and (3) a handful of 3-lesson celebrations. The 2 former elements are clearly the ones which distinguish the liturgies of these houses from one another. Thus the feasts described in this section—some of which are Parisian, some French, and some even more widely observed—are by and large common both to Saint-Denis and to other churches in Paris, and they came into the ritual of Saint-Denis as part of 'local heritage', perhaps stemming in part from the time when Saint-Denis was under the control of the cathedral of Paris. They consequently define the ceremony of Saint-Denis only as 'Parisian' or as 'French', rather than as 'proper' to the abbey (cf. Foley, who combines these festivals with the anniversaries and feasts of saints whose remains were in the abbey, claiming that they are all 'distinctive or "proper" to St.-Denis'; 'Ordinary' ii. 188–249).

[29] *AASS*, Jan. i, 459 ff. While Saint Lucian was honoured by a feast of 12 lessons at Saint-Denis, his rank at the Paris cathedral was a simple commemoration (see F:Pn, lat. 5185cc, calendar).

[30] A Translation for Germanus on 25 July (date according to the martyrology of Usuard; see *AASS*, July vi, 2) is added to the calendar of F:Pn, lat. 2290. This feast was never permanently incorporated into the liturgy of the abbey, no doubt due to the conflict with the services for Cucuphas and James.

[31] By the 11th c., the calendars link Saint Gildard, archbishop of Rouen, to Saint Medard, and the day is subsequently shared between them (see *AASS*, June ii, 67–9). Saint Bathildis, who imposed monastic rule on all 3 basilicas, was commemorated in the abbey on 30 Jan. by a feast of 3 lessons. Her name does not appear in the 9th-c. calendars, however, even though her cult can be traced prior to 822 (see Brouette, 'Bathildis', *NCE*, ii. 164). It is possible that the impetus for the veneration of Bathildis came from her beatification by Pope Nicholas II (reg. 1059–1061), for she is not present in any calendar from Saint-Denis before to this time (*VSB*, i. 619). For discussion of her veneration in other monasteries, see Folz, 'Tradition'.

[32] On the movement of relics in general during the 9th-c. Norman incursions, see Boussel, *Reliques*, 39–43.

Remigius (1 October) at Saint-Denis bespeaks not only the political alliance that was thereby forged but also the liturgical affinity that is evident in the near identity of their alleluia-lists.[33] Saint Eligius (1 December) was known in the abbey for his role in the adornment of the church in the seventh century, and for the miracle that he once performed there on the Vigil of Saint Denis.

For almost all of these saints, the calendar of F:Psg 111 indicates that the Offices were already 'full' services in the ninth century.[34] The later antiphoners and breviaries from the abbey show that the feast of Saint Germanus of Auxerrre included proper chants for the fourth, eighth and twelfth responsories as well as for the antiphons to the Magnificat and Benedictus.[35] The other observances, following the more usual custom, derived the material for their twelve-lesson Offices from the *commune sanctorum*. The twelve-lesson services for other parochial saints, notably Clodoaldus (7 September),[36] Leodegarius (2 October), and Maximinus (15 December), were handed down in like fashion in the Saint-Denis manuscripts.

Proper Offices for Benedict and Maurice, two saints of particular historical interest at Saint-Denis, appear in the antiphoner of Saint-Denis. Benedict, founder of the order to which the majority of monasteries in Gaul belonged by the middle of the ninth century, was commemorated by the thirteenth century in four separate feasts each year at Saint-Denis: his *natale* (21 March), his Translation (11 July) with its Octave (18 July), and his Illation (4 December). The proper Offices for the *natale* and the Translation, which share many of the same pieces, are conflated in idiosyncratic fashion in the antiphoners F:Pm 384 and F:Pn, lat. 17296.[37] The twelve antiphons for the psalms

[33] On the alleluia lists, see Ch. 3. The Translation of Remigius is the principal feast for this saint. By the 11th c. the Translations of Saints Vedast and Germanus of Auxerre had been joined to the celebration for Remigius (see *AASS*, Oct. i, 2, 4) in the calendar and liturgy of Saint-Denis (e.g. F:Pn, lat. 1107, fo. 270). These services were separated in the 14th c. so that Remigius retained the rank of 12 lessons, while the observance of Germanus and Vedast was converted to a simple Commemoration. The association between the abbeys of Saint-Denis and Saint-Vaast of Arras was particularly strong in the 11th c., as witnessed in the origin and provenance of F:Pn, lat. 9436. Hence it is not surprising that the feast of Saint Vedast (6 Feb.), which was celebrated with only 3 lessons at Paris cathedral (see F:Pn, lat. 5185cc, calendar), was a simplex feast of 12 lessons at Saint-Denis.

[34] The abbreviation *pl. of.* is given for all except Germanus of Auxerre and Eligius, for whom the term *com.* (*commune*) is used.

[35] The office books from Saint-Denis transmit these pieces just as they are found in F:Pn, lat. 17296, fos. 199–200 (Hesbert, *CAO*, ii, No. 102[10]). For discussion of the melismas which some antiphoners provide for the responsories of this Office, see Steiner, 'Melismas', 115–20.

[36] Clodoaldus' name is joined with that of Saint Evortius in the later Saint-Denis calendars, probably because their feasts happen to fall on the same day (see, e.g. F:Pn, lat. 976, fo. 123; F:Pn, lat. 1107, fo. 262). The Parisian calendar F:Pn, lat. 5185cc, however, assigns a feast of 9 lessons to the titular saint of Saint-Cloud, while relegating Evortius to a simple Commemoration.

[37] F:Pm 384, fos. 171^{v}–172; F:Pn, lat. 17296, fos. 77–83^{v} (also Hesbert, *CAO*, ii, No. 505a–c, and pp. xi–xii.).

and the first eight responsories appear under the rubric *In natale sancti benedicti abbatis*. These pieces are common to both services, as confirmed in the later breviaries.[38] The final Nocturn with its four responsories, however, and the ensuing antiphons for Lauds were sung only on the day of the Translation.[39] For the *natale*, the ordinaries and breviaries specify instead the corresponding pieces listed by the antiphoners under the rubric *In transitu sancti benedicti*.[40] The Octave of the Translation and the Illation of Benedict, like the observance for his sister Saint Scholastica (10 February),[41] were simplex feasts of twelve lessons in the later Saint-Denis sources. While the former service draws its Office from the Translation, the Illation retains only the fourth, eighth, and twelfth responsories, substituting pieces from the common of one confessor (not a bishop) in place of the others.[42]

The early liturgy of Saint-Denis owed more than two brief interludes of continuous psalm-singing to the practice of Saint-Maurice-en-Valais. The names of Maurice and his friends of the Theban Legion were replaced by those of Saint Denis and companions in the Ant. *Insignes preconiis*, which survives in several sources from the abbey as an example of Gallican chant. Louis IX further nurtured the cult of Saint Maurice in the thirteenth century by presenting the abbey with relics of one of the Valais saints in 1262,[43] and this gift may account for the brief period during which an Octave was celebrated for Maurice.[44] The earliest Office for Maurice in F:Pm 384 (*In natali sancti Mauricii*[45]) lists proper pieces for only four of the Matins responsories, for the antiphons of Lauds, and for the Magnificat, while a second service in this manuscript (*Item in festivitate Sancti Mauricii*[46]) adds the proper

[38] GB:Ob, Can. Lit. 192, fos. 335–337ᵛ (*natale*), 380–381ᵛ (Translation); F:Pn, Rés. B. 5209.

[39] Hesbert speculates on the basis of the texts of these pieces that they may have been intended for the Translation (*CAO*, vol. ii, pp. xi–xii), but it is the Saint-Denis ordinaries that actually confirm this arrangement and destination of the repertoire (F:Pm 526, fo. 145; F:Pn, lat. 976, fo. 105ᵛ).

[40] The ordinaries state that the 4 final lessons of the *In transitu* service are to be grafted onto the *natale*: 'Quatuor extreme lectiones de transitu eius. Resp. *Eodem vero anno*', etc. (F:Pm 526, fo. 114ᵛ; F:Pn, lat. 976, fo. 82).

[41] F:Pn, lat. 2290, places her feast on 11 Feb., either through error or possibly because this is the date that is given in a small number of martyrologies; *AASS*, Feb. ii, 506.

[42] Octave of Translation: F:Pm 526, fo. 147; F:Pn, lat. 976, fo. 108. Illation: F:Pn, lat. 976, fo. 152ᵛ.

[43] *AASS*, Sept. vi, 389; Félibien, *Histoire*, 532. Grodecki suggests the year 1245, which Félibien records for the dedication of the altar of Saint Maurice in the chevet (Pl. 3 and Table 4.1), as another possible date for Louis's gift of the relics of Maurice to the abbey; *Vitraux*, 31. The presence of relics of Saint Maurice is also attested in F:Pn, n.a.f. 1098, fo. 65; see Delisle, 'Peintures', 447.

[44] Both F:Pm 414 and F:Pm 526 anticipate the Octave of Saint Maurice by 1 day in their calendars (28 instead of 29 Sept.), and the text of F:Pn, lat. 976, also includes a feast of 12 lessons (fo. 175), which was later removed from the liturgy.

[45] F:Pm 384, fos. 189ʳ⁻ᵛ.

[46] Ibid. fos. 189ᵛ–90.

antiphons for Matins and the remaining responsories. The twelfth-century antiphoner F:Pn, lat. 17296 seems to conflate the two, while making various substitutions of proper chants not given in F:Pm 384.[47] As the ceremonies at Saint-Denis were standardized in the fourteenth century, all but the final responsory of each Nocturn were replaced with chants from the common of many martyrs.[48]

EARLY FEASTS OF SAINTS WITH RELICS IN THE CHURCH

The saints just mentioned were commemorated at Saint-Denis as a result of the Parisian ancestry of the abbey rather than by design of the monks. On another level, the translations of sacred relics into the abbey inspired the creation of observances that were distinctively Sandionysian. An eleventh-century mass in honour of the saints 'whose bodies lie in this church' names the 15 relics that the abbey possessed at this time.[49]

[47] F:Pn, lat. 17296, fos. 216ᵛ–22 (Hesbert, *CAO*, ii, No. 111).

[48] GB:Ob, Can. Lit. 192, fos. 447–9; F:Pn, Rés. B. 5209. The same tendency away from individuality in services is evident in the 14th-c. Offices of Saints Cucuphas and Hilary of Mende, discussed below.

[49] All relics known to have been kept at Saint-Denis can be listed with the help of this and other documents. F:Pn, lat. 2185 (fo. 88) names 15 saints 'quorum corpora in presenti requiescunt ecclesia': Denis, Rusticus, Eleutherius, Eugene, Peregrinus, Hippolytus, Cucuphas, Innocent (one of the Holy Innocents), Eustace, Patroclus, Firminus, Hilary (of Poitiers), Hilary (of Mende), Romanus, Osmanna. By the 12th and 13th cs., chapels in the chevet of the church were dedicated to these saints (see Table 4.1), and these were no doubt the major relics that the abbey possessed at the time F:Pn, lat. 2185 was copied. But other sacred remains and objects, often consisting of only portions of relics, were apparently present. A propagandistic document which the monks composed in the late 11th c., the *Descriptio qualiter Karolus Magnus clavum et coronam Domini a Constantinopli Aquisgrani detulerit qualiterque Karolus Calvus haec ad Sanctum Dionysium retulerit* (ed. in Castets, '*Iter*'), reports that Charlemagne had obtained a nail of the Passion, the Crown of Thorns (which the cathedral of Notre Dame also claimed to have in the 13th c.; see Perdrizet, *Calendrier*, 199–200), and an arm of Saint Simeon Senex in the late 8th c., all of which Charles the Bald supposedly later brought to Saint-Denis. Levillain has shown that these relics probably arrived in the abbey only in the mid-11th c. ('Essai', 275 and *passim*), and many documents subsequently refer to them, including the *Pèlerinage de Charlemagne* (ed. in Burgess and Cobby, *Pilgrimage*, 70–1); the writings of Abbot Suger (Lecoy de la Marche, *Suger*, 330, 358; Panofsky, *Suger*, 86–9) and of the chronicler Rigord (Delaborde, *Œuvres*, i. 134); the historical compilation from 1317 (F:Pn, lat. 5286, fo. 187ᵛ); see also Perdrizet, *Calendrier*, 98–9. In the 12th c. Abbot Suger recalls that Charles the Bald had likewise presented the following to Saint-Denis: an arm bone of Saint James, an arm of Saint Stephen (to whom a chapel in the crypt of the 12th-c. church was dedicated; see Table 4.1), and an arm of Saint Vincent; Lecoy de la Marche, *Suger*, 354; Panofsky, *Suger*, 66–71, 128–9. 13th-c. documents witness the presence of yet more relics, although the circumstances of their arrival in the abbey are not always clear: part of the head of Saint Peter (F:Pn, n.a.l. 1509, p. 402 [403]), an arm-bone of John the Baptist (ibid. 389 [390]), a portion of the Holy Cross, some hair and parts of the purple robe and burial linen of Jesus, another thorn from the Crown of Thorns, a rib and tooth of Saint Philip (these 6 presented by Philip Augustus in 1205; see Delaborde, *Œuvres* i, 162–3; Félibien, *Histoire*, 215; Baldwin, *Philip*, 377), and some unspecified relics of Saint Clement, to whom a separate chapel was dedicated (Walters [Robertson], 'Reconstruction', 202). 6 other relics were present: of Saint Maurice (discussed above), and Dionysius of Corinth, Sanctinus and Antoninus, the Eleven Thousand Virgins, and Benedict (all treated below).

No contemporaneous evidence suggests that any transfers took place before the ninth century, and indeed the veneration of multiple relics in Frankish churches was not common before this period.[50] It is likely, therefore, that the early feasts of saints with relics at Saint-Denis came into the liturgy between the ninth and eleventh centuries.

Abbot Hilduin probably installed several saints' remains at Saint-Denis during his reign, including those of Saint Hippolytus.[51] Hippolytus' *natale* on 13 August appears in the first calendars, with the indication in F:Psg 111 that a full Office was sung in the ninth century. A second service on 12 May, the *Commemoratio sancti Ypoliti*, seems to have been almost unique to the abbey.[52] Drawing its content from the proper Office of the *natale* and from the *commune*, this feast is absent from the earliest calendars of Saint-Denis and appears first in the eleventh-century antiphonary list F:Pm 384.[53]

The relics of Saints Cucuphas (25 July) and Hilary of Mende (25 October) were likewise specially venerated at Saint-Denis from the days of Hilduin.[54] The proper, monastic Office for Cucuphas existed in the ninth century, and the services for both saints were sung at Saint-Denis until the thirteenth century,[55] at which time a gradual reduction in the number of proper chants began with the suppression of most of the antiphons for Matins and Lauds.[56] In the fourteenth century and

[50] See Boussel, *Reliques*, 33–8; Kraus, *Translatio*, 3; Heinzelmann, *Translationsberichte*, 99.

[51] Hesbert summarizes the literature that deals with the possible events of the translation of Hippolytus; *CAO*, vol. ii, p. xii, n. 2.

[52] Of the liturgical MSS described in Leroquais's catalogues, only the 12th-c. missal of Saint-Père de Chartres (F:T 894; Leroquais, *Sacramentaires*, i. 235) contains this feast. Until 1236, the relics of Saint Hippolytus had a special place in the abbey in an altar in the middle of the nave, and thereafter in the 1st chapel west of the north transept arm (see Pl. 4; Walters [Robertson], 'Reconstruction', 192–3; Bruzelius, *St-Denis*, 127).

[53] Fo. 182. 2 martyrologies describe this feast as the Commemoration of the Translation of Saint Hipolytus from Rome to Saint-Médard of Soissons and thence to Saint-Denis (*AASS*, May iii, 3–4), but other accounts of the Translation do exist.

[54] See the discussion of these 2 saints in Ch. 1. Hesbert recapitulates the events of their Translations; *CAO*, vol. ii, pp. xii–xiii. Here he mentions that the relics of Hilary of Mende (to be distinguished from Hilary of Poitiers) were present at Saint-Denis in 636, a date which is also admitted by the Bollandists (*AASS*, Oct. xi, 619–20). However, none of the documents that they cite to substantiate this claim is contemporaneous with the supposed Translation. These accounts of the arrival of the remains of Saints Hilary, Patroclus, and Romanus of Blaye come instead from the 9th-c. narrative of the adventures of King Dagobert, a highly embellished source. In the light of this, it is probably the later sources from the 8th c., referring to the placement of the relics of Saint Hilary in one of the dependencies of Saint-Denis (*AASS*, Oct. xi, 620–1) and their subsequent Translation into the abbey, which are the most accurate.

[55] Cucuphas: I:VEcap LXXXVIII, fos. 76–9; F:Pm 384, fo. 185ᵛ; F:Pn, lat. 17296, fos. 193ᵛ–198ᵛ (Hesbert, *CAO*, ii, No. 102⁸). Hilary: F:Pm 384, fos. 191ʳ⁻ᵛ; F:Pn, lat. 17296, fos. 234–237ᵛ (Hesbert, *CAO*, ii, No. 114⁸). See the discussion of the Office for Saint Hilary in which the antiphons and responsories for Matins are ordered in ascending numerical order by mode (a numerical Office); Crocker, 'Matins', 449–53, 469, 475.

[56] Cucuphas: F:Pm 526, fo. 150; F:Pn, lat. 976, fo. 110ᵛ. Hilary: F:Pm 526, fo. 186ᵛ; F:Pn, lat. 976, fo. 139ᵛ. The changes are first apparent in F:Pn, lat. 976, written *c*.1258.

thereafter, the first three responsories of each Nocturn were replaced with chants from the common of one martyr for Cucuphas and from the common of one confessor for Hilary—further evidence of a progressive loss of specificity in the celebration of many saints' festivals in the later Middle Ages.[57]

The relics of Saint Eugene (15 November) also came into the abbey during the ninth century. Several mysteries shroud both his identity and the particulars of his martyrdom at Deuil and subsequent Translations, yet the various components of his legend closely parallel the Areopagitist texts that emanated from the abbey under the direction of Abbot Hilduin at this time.[58] The Office for Eugene is not labelled *plenum officium* in F:Psg 111; moreover, it is unevenly transmitted in the later manuscripts in terms of number and choice of proper responsories.[59]

Of the feasts for Saint Denis himself, Abbot Hilduin would have called for the celebration of the Vigil (8 October) and the *natale* (9 October). Both observances date from the Merovingian period, and it was probably Hilduin himself who reworked the latter into a twelve-lesson, monastic Office in the ninth century. The earliest calendars likewise incorporate the Dedication of the Church, which had been observed on 24 February since the consecration of the Carolingian building under Charlemagne in 775. The antiphonary list in F:Pm 384 includes 28 different responsories for Matins of the Dedication,[60] and the later Office-books select the usual number of twelve.[61] As if to personalize the service, the final responsory from each Nocturn is one of the chants for the patron saint, while the others are taken from the Office for the Dedication of a church. The Office of the Invention of Saint Denis (22 April), which consists of borrowings from his *natale* and from the *commune*, was likely celebrated even before Hilduin's reign.[62] And just as Hilduin tampered with the narration of events that

[57] Cucuphas: GB:Ob, Can. Lit. 192, fos. 390–2; F:Pn, Rés. B. 5209. Hilary: GB:Ob, Can. Lit. 192, fos. 478^{v}–480; F:Pn, Rés. B. 5209.

[58] See Gaiffier, 'Légende', 329–49; also Hesbert, *CAO*, vol. ii, pp. xiii–xiv.

[59] Ibid. xiv, n. 4; F:Pm 384, fo. 193; F:Pn, lat. 17296, fos. 252–3 (Hesbert, *CAO*, ii, No. 117^{3}); GB:Ob, Can. Lit. 192, fos. 499–500^{v} (mistakenly rubricated 'De sancto Eligio'); F:Pn, Rés. B. 5209. Beginning in the 13th c., the calendars of Saint-Denis describe Eugene as bishop and martyr (*episcopus et martyr*). This title differs from his epithet in Parisian calendars, wherein he is called simply *martyr* (see Félibien, *Histoire*, 196–7; the 13th-c. calendar of Notre Dame contained in F:Pn, lat. 5185cc; and App. A, Notes to the Calendar, 15 Nov.).

[60] F:Pm 384, fos. 196^{v}–197.

[61] The Saint-Denis sources after F:Pm 384 follow the order given in F:Pn, lat. 17296, fos. 288–289^{v} (Hesbert, *CAO*, ii, No. 127).

[62] On Hilduin's attempt to conflate the theme of this service, the 'finding' of Saint Denis, with that of a 'Translation' of the saints' relics, see Ch. 1. The books of the Office from Saint-Denis transmit this service approximately as it is found in F:Pn, lat. 17296, fos. 152^{r-v} (Hesbert, *CAO* ii, No. 90^{4}).

gave rise to this feast, so also he apparently altered the account of Pope Stephen's visit to Saint-Denis in 754 to suggest that the pontiff consecrated an altar to Saints Peter and Paul.[63] The commemoration of this supposed occurrence, the feast of the Consecration of the Altar (28 July), is first documented in the calendars of F:Psg 111 and F:Pn, lat. 2290,[64] and the Office, found in later sources, synthesizes material from the feasts of the Dedication, Saint Peter, and the Commemoration of Saint Paul.[65]

Other translations cannot readily be linked to Hilduin's abbacy, and yet it is clear that holy relics continued to find their way to Saint-Denis. Among these were the remains of Saint Eustace, whose reliquary was sometimes carried in the processions of the abbey.[66] The popularity of his feast-day (2 November) had blocked the celebration of All Souls' Day until Abbot Eudes Clément called attention to this omission in 1241.[67] Even then Saint Eustace took precedence over the service for the faithful departed, which was sung instead on 3 November.[68] The antiphonary list F:Pm 384 is the first surviving witness from Saint-Denis of the proper Office for Eustace,[69] and this service probably replaced an earlier one from the *commune*, which is suggested in the

[63] Buchner, 'Vizepapsttum', 75–85.

[64] 'V. Kal. (Aug.) In Galliis, Parisiacense, consecratio altaris Petri et Pauli apostolorum in ecclesia sanctorum martyrum Dionysii, Rustici et Eleutherii, quod Stephanus papa de ipsorum reliquiis consecravit' (also published in Delisle, *Sacramentaires*, 318).

[65] GB:Ob, Can. Lit. 192, fos. 393^{v}–395^{v}; F:Pn, Rés. B. 5209.

[66] F:Pan, L 863, No. 10, p. 59. Cf. Hesbert, who ignores the 11th-c. list in F:Pn, lat. 2185 (see n. 49 above), stating that the relics of Saint Eustace were not present in the abbey prior to the 12th c.; *CAO*, vol. ii, p. xiii.

[67] Eudes writes: 'The Commemoration of the faithful departed [All Souls' Day] occurs throughout the whole Church on the day after All Saints [1 Nov.], but we have neglected [to observe] it on that day [2 Nov.] on account of the feast of Saint Eustace. We, therefore, wishing to follow the approved usage of the Church, ordain and establish that in the future the chapter reading which is customarily read on the feast of All Saints be done on the Vigil of All Saints, so that after Vespers [which is sung at the altar of] Saint Eustace the community might return into the choir. Then let *Placebo* [the first antiphon of Vespers for the dead] be intoned in a loud voice, just as it is done on the anniversaries of Kings Charles [the Bald] and Philip [Augustus], and then let Vespers and Matins for the faithful [departed] be sung successively' ('Praeterea cum in crastino omnium sanctorum fiet per totam Ecclesiam Dei memoria fidelium defunctorum, et eadem die propter festum sancti Eustachii omittebatur apud nos. Volentes sequi approbatum usum Ecclesiae, sic ordinamus et statuimus ut de cetero in Vigilia omnium Sanctorum fiat sermo in capitulo qui solet fieri in die festo omnium Sanctorum, ita vero quae fit post vesperas ad sanctum Eustachium, redeat Conventus in chorum et alta voce incipiatur *Placebo*, sicut fit in anniversariis Caroli et Philippi Regum, et ibi vesperae et Vigiliae pro fidelibus continuae decantentur'); F:Pan, LL 1159, pp. 1–2 (also published in Félibien, *Histoire*, *PJ*, i, No. clxx). The Bollandists treat Saint Eustace on 20 Sept., but they note that many martyrologies record his *natale* on 2 Nov.; *AASS*, Sept. vi, 117.

[68] The 16th-c. calendar of Saint-Denis, as represented by F:Pn, Rés. B. 5209, finally records All Souls' Day on 2 Nov. (see App. A). On the feast of All Souls, see Mershman, 'Souls', *CE*, i. 315–16.

[69] F:Pm 384, fo. 192; also see Hesbert, *CAO*, vol. ii, p. xiii. Actually, only the antiphons and the final 8 responsories are proper, and the 1st four responsories are drawn from the common of many martyrs.

calendar of F:Psg 111 (see Appendix A). The addition of an Octave to his feast underlines the Sandionysians' high regard for Eustace, for no such distinction was permanently accorded any other saint with relics in the abbey, with the exception of Denis himself.[70]

The remains of Saint Patroclus (31 January)[71] and of Saint Romanus of Blaye (24 November) were reputedly present in the abbey from the seventh century. Not only does the lack of contemporaneous evidence for a Translation under Dagobert cast doubt upon the alleged event, the earliest calendars of the abbey do not even include these saints. Their relics had come to Saint-Denis by the eleventh century, however, and their Offices, taken from the *commune*, were celebrated at duplex rank by the last third of the thirteenth century.

The ninth-century calendars of F:Psg 111 and F:Pn, lat. 2290 record the Translation of Saints Hilary, Innocent and Peregrinus to Saint-Denis (22 August),[72] but subsequent calendars replace this notice with the Octave of Assumption. It appears that the Hilary named in this triple Translation is the bishop of Mende who was mentioned earlier,[73] although the relics of Hilary of Poitiers also resided in the abbey by the eleventh century. Tradition had it that remains of Hilary of Poitiers came to Saint-Denis as spoil of one of King Dagobert's seventh-century campaigns, and a similar legend existed for Hilary of Mende.[74] The tale about the bishop of Poitiers probably has little basis in fact,[75] but the earliest calendars attest the veneration of him on 13 January and on 14 January by the fourteenth century.[76] His feast of twelve lessons was drawn largely from the *commune*. The Saint Innocent named here appears to be one of the Holy Innocents. Charlemagne was said to have brought back a relic of this saint from the Holy Land, and documents from the ninth to the thirteenth century witness its presence at Saint-Denis.[77] The third saint named in the Translation of 22 August is

[70] An Octave for the feast of Saint Maurice (28 Sept.) existed only briefly in the 13th c., whereas the Octaves for John the Baptist (1 July) and Peter and Paul (6 July) were widely celebrated and were not particular to Saint-Denis.

[71] This saint is not the *martyr* Patroclus of Troyes, honoured on 21 Jan. (see *AASS*, Jan. ii, 342–9); rather, he is the *bishop and martyr* (location uncertain) whose feast is celebrated on 31 Jan.; *AASS*, Jan. ii, 1110. Benedictine Monks, *Saints* (4th edn.), gives the Patroclus of Troyes of 21 Jan., and none on 31.

[72] 'Et translatio corporum sanctorum in cenobio sancti Dionysii, id est Hilarii, episcopi et confessoris, et sancti Innocentii martyris, atque sancti Peregrini, episcopi et martyris' (published in Delisle, *Sacramentaires*, 320).

[73] *AASS*, Oct. xi, 620, 624.

[74] F:Pn, lat. 5286, fos. 154ᵛ–155; also published in Delisle, 'Peintures', 450, 466–7.

[75] The Bollandists review the theories for and against this translation; *AASS*, Jan. i, 801–2.

[76] A rearrangement of feasts caused this change of day, see App. A.

[77] See the 9th-c. calendars in App. A (22 Aug.); the 11th-c. MS F:Pn, lat. 2185 (fo. 88; see above, n. 49); and F:Pn, n.a.l. 1509, p. 393 [394]: 'De parvulo innocente qui passus est cum aliis sub herode.' Abbot Suger had one of the altars in the chevet dedicated to Saint Innocent in 1144 (see Table 4.1), and a reliquary and stained-glass window for this martyr existed in the 13th-c. church (see Gauthier, 'Reliques').

Peregrinus, the first bishop of Auxerre. No date is given for the arrival of his bones at Saint-Denis,[78] but the designation of a full Office for his feast (16 May) in the calendar of F:Psg 111 suggests that they were in the abbey in the ninth century. By the eleventh century at the latest, Peregrinus was incorporated in the liturgy,[79] and his twelve-lesson service, likewise taken from the *commune*, was probably raised to duplex rank shortly after 1234.[80]

Like the relics of Saint Eustace, those of Saints Firminus and Simeon Senex were also conveyed in procession.[81] As in other instances already mentioned, the monks probably invented the account of a seventh-century Translation of Firminus under Dagobert,[82] but the calendars demonstrate that he was venerated, and probably therefore present at Saint-Denis, by the ninth century. The calendar of F:Psg 111 indicates that his Office consisted of material from the *commune sanctorum*, and his feast (25 September) was celebrated at duplex rank sometime after 1234. The cult of Saint Simeon Senex was limited to the prominent display of his arm in processions. His feast-day, which would have conflicted with the Vigil of Saint Denis (8 October), was not kept in the abbey.

Saint Osmanna was the only virgin apart from Mary for whom there was a chapel in the choir-level of the chevet of Saint-Denis (Pl. 3). It is not clear whether this seventh- or eighth-century figure was the Irish maiden who settled in Brittany or a nun of Jouarre near Paris.[83] Equally obscure are the circumstances of her Translation, but the list of saints in F:Pn, lat. 2185 shows that her remains lay in the abbey by the eleventh century. Osmanna's feast-day, with its Office drawn from the *commune*, was later moved from 16 August to the more widely accepted 9 September.[84]

[78] F:Pn, lat. 5286, fos. 156^{r-v}; also published in Delisle, 'Peintures', 474–5.

[79] F:Pm 384, fo. 183.

[80] The alteration in degree is noted by a later hand in F:Pm 526, fo. 127^{v}; and the changes in ceremony that normally signify duplex celebration are found in F:Pn, lat. 976, although this MS never actually calls the feast duplex (see below).

[81] There are many references to the relics of these 2 saints in the 3 ordinaries of Saint-Denis and in the writings of Abbot Suger. They include, for Firminus: F:Pm 526, fos. 48, 66^{v}, 121; F:Pn, lat. 976, fos. 22^{v}, 38; F:Pan, L 863, No. 10, p. 37; and for Simeon: F:Pm 526, fos. 16, 48, 60, 112, 140^{v}; F:Pn, lat. 976, fos. 22^{v}, 80^{v}, 102; F:Pan, L 863, No. 10, pp. 37, 41; and Panofsky, *Suger*, 101, 109, 133.

[82] F:Pn, lat. 5286, fos. 155^{r-v}, 187^{v}; published in Delisle, 'Peintures', 449.

[83] *VSB*, ix. 186–7. Osmanna does not appear in the Roman martyrology; she represents instead the category of saint who is venerated according to 'approved cult' (see Benedictine Monks, *Saints*, 4th edn., p. xiii).

[84] While the Bollandists discuss Osmanna on 9 Sept. (*AASS* Sept. iii, 417–25), the calendars of F:Pn, lat. 9436 (by addition) and F:Pm 414 place her on 16 Aug., the text of F:Pn, lat. 16820 has the festival after Assumption (fo. 122), and the copyist of F:Pm 526 inscribes her feast after the Octave of Assumption (fo. 161^{v}). A later hand adds a service for Osmanna on 9 Sept. (F:Pm 526,

FEASTS OF THE TWELFTH CENTURY

Thus the early liturgy of Saint-Denis was an amalgamation of the ancient ceremonies of the Western Church and of saints' days having regional, historical, and intramural significance. By the early thirteenth century, the calendar had been enriched with other feasts of twelve lessons, the establishment of which was often connected with coeval events. Only rarely did the monks compose new Offices for these services; most of the time they simply borrowed material from the *commune sanctorum*.

This procedure is evident in the creation of a service for Saint Clarus (4 November). It was only natural that the Crown should grant landholdings to the favoured royal abbey, and the record of dependencies of Saint-Denis both in France and abroad extends back to Carolingian times.[85] Louis VII's gift of the château and priory of Saint-Clair-sur-Epte in 1153 probably instigated the observance of its titular saint at Saint-Denis.[86] His *natale* (4 November) is not recorded in the original hand of any extant calendar prior to the thirteenth century,[87] nor is his Translation (17 July) noted until the fourteenth.[88] Similarly, the short-lived calendar entry of Saint Walaburga (1 May), in whose honour an altar in the crypt was consecrated in 1144,[89] may well recall the abbey's ownership of the priory of Sainte-Gauberge by the mid-twelfth century.[90] The commemoration of her Translation on 1 May is completely overshadowed by the feast of Philip and James on the same day,

fo. 167), which is the date given in all subsequent MSS. It appears, then, that the change in date had occurred by the time F:Pn, lat. 976 was copied (*c*.1258), probably around the time Saint Bernard was incorporated into the calendar on 23 Aug.

[85] On the 8th-c. possessions of Saint-Denis, see Félibien, *Histoire*, 60–61. Edward the Confessor granted the abbey the priory of Deerhurst in Gloucestershire around 1059; Knowles and Hadcock, *Houses*, 64. Félibien lists the churches in which the abbot had the *jus patronatus* as well as the priories belonging to Saint-Denis; *Histoire*, *PJ*, ii, No. ix.

[86] F:Pan, K 23, No. 20 (Tardif, *Monuments*, 275–6, No. 525). In the following year, Louis conceded to the abbey an annual fair near this priory (F:Pan, K 23, No. 21; Tardif, *Monuments*, 276–7, No. 529). See also Félibien, *Histoire*, 195. The 13th-c. cartulary F:Pan, LL 1158 reproduces these and other documents dealing with Saint-Clair (fos. 389–96). On Saint Clarus, see *AASS*, Nov. i/1, 444–5; *VSB*, xi. 125.

[87] Clarus first appears in the 11th-c. calendar of F:Pn, lat. 103 as an addition, presumably made in the 12th c. There are no twelfth-century calendars from Saint-Denis and only a few liturgical sources from this period. Hence, unless documents yet to be found prove the contrary, it is reasonable to associate Louis's charter with the beginning of the veneration of Saint Clarus at Saint-Denis.

[88] The Bollandists place the Translation on 18 July (*AASS*, July iv, 349), a date which would have conflicted with the celebration of the Octave of Saint Benedict at Saint-Denis.

[89] Panofsky, *Suger*, 119 (see also Table 4.1).

[90] Félibien, *Histoire*, 195–6; Cottineau, *Répertoire*, ii, col. 2691.

and by the fourteenth century no trace of Walaburga is left in the ritual.[91]

Two new feasts for Saint Denis were incorporated into the liturgy of the abbey before the end of the twelfth century. The Detection of Saint Denis (9 June) commemorated the opening of the reliquary of the saint around 1053. This ceremony was planned as a public rebuttal to the community of Saint-Emmeram, who made the startling claim that they possessed the body of the first bishop of Paris.[92] A shadowy monk of Saint-Denis with the ubiquitous name Haimon reported the event, but his original epistle (*Detectio corporum macharii Areopagitae Dionysii sociorumque ejus*) no longer exists.[93] Haimon's account includes references to the newly established feast, and scholars for some time debated whether it was contemporaneous or whether it dated from the late twelfth century. Levillain adopts the latter view, and he suggests that the festival was celebrated at Saint-Denis beginning in 1192.[94] His dating of the feast is supported by its absence from the twelfth-century portion of the gradual F:Pm 384 (fo. 159ᵛ). On the other hand, the Detection is a relatively early addition to the calendar of the mid eleventh-century psalter F:Pn, lat. 103, and it is written in the original hand of the mid-twelfth-century lectionary F:Pn, lat. 16820, suggesting that it may in fact have been celebrated in the eleventh and twelfth centuries. Like the Invention of Saint Denis (22 April), the service for the Detection drew on chants from the *commune* by the thirteenth century, while interjecting some proper responsories from the *natale* into the Nocturns of Matins.[95] It is possible that the short-lived rhymed Office for Saint Denis in F:Pm 384, described in Chapter 4, was intended for this service.

Until the end of the twelfth century, the Mass for the Octave (16 October) of Saint Denis consisted of material from the *commune sanctorum*.[96] Shortly thereafter, and probably under Abbot William of Gap (1173–?1186), the monks substituted a series of Greek translations of the ordinary and proper texts of the Mass for their Latin counterparts. This unique compilation, through which they intended to promote the identity of Saint Denis and the two Areopagite figures, was sung in the abbey in one of two versions until the French Revolution.

91 The Roman martyrology gives the observance of Saint Walaburga on 25 Feb., but it is her Translation to Eichstätt on 1 May that is the principal observance in many places; *AASS*, May i, 2.

92 The 2 accounts of the supposed Translation of Saint Denis from Paris to Saint-Emmeram (ed. in Hofmeister, *Translationis*, and in Köpke, *Translatio*) are examined in Kraus, *Translatio*; idem, 'Saint-Denis'.

93 Félibien is the only source for Haimon's letter, which he claims to have copied from an 'ancien ms. de Saint-Denys'; *Histoire*, *PJ*, ii, No. ii.

94 I.e. 9 June 1192; Levillain, 'Essai', 267–70.

95 F:Pm 526, fo. 132; F:Pn, lat. 976, fo. 95ᵛ.

96 The Octave first appears in F:Pm 384, fo. 135 (Hesbert, *Graduel*, 235).

While the feasts named above provided the liturgy of Saint-Denis with its distinctive character, so too, in a negative way, did the festivals that were not adopted there. One searches the calendar of Saint-Denis largely in vain for traces of Cluniac influence. The abbot-saints Odo (d. 942), Odilo (d. 1049), and Hugh (d. 1109) are absent, and the commemoration of All Souls' Day (2 November, 3 November at Saint-Denis) was slow to take hold.[97] The feast of the Transfiguration (6 August) was celebrated in the abbey, but without the Office composed by the abbot of Cluny Peter the Venerable (1092–1156).[98] A service for the Cluniac Saint Majolus (d. 994; feast 11 May) had, however, entered the Saint-Denis liturgy by the thirteenth century.[99] And Cluny may in fact have inspired the adoption of the Octave of Saint Martin (18 November) at Saint-Denis,[100] although the order of his proper antiphons in sources from the abbey does not agree with that given in the antiphoner from Saint-Maur-des-Fossès (F:Pn, lat. 12584), which may represent Cluniac tradition.[101]

The cults of certain local saints were recognized relatively late in France, and for this reason their names do not appear in the earliest calendars from Saint-Denis. The translations which first encouraged devotion to Saints Maurus (15 January) and Julian (27 January) did not take place until the ninth century, and the earliest mention of them in a Saint-Denis calendar comes in the eleventh-century augmented sacramentary F:Pn, lat. 9436.[102] Saint Blaise (3 February), who was popular in Armenia, came to be venerated only later in the West.[103] Whereas

[97] Saint Odilo is thought to have instituted this feast in the 11th c.; see Leroquais, *Bréviaires*, vol. i, pp. civ–cv; and Hourlier, 'Odilon'. The calendar of F:Pn, lat. 976 is the earliest to include the service, giving it the rank of 3 lessons. By the 14th c., the level of observance was duplex. For the Cluniac calendar of the 11th c., see Elvert, *Clavis*, 21–32.

[98] The Cluniac Office is published in Leclercq, *Pierre*, 379–90. At Saint-Denis the feast of the Transfiguration consisted largely of material borrowed from the Office of Trinity. The antiphons for the Magnificat at First Vespers (Ant. *Assumpsit jesus*), at Second Vespers (Ant. *Descendentibus illis de monte*) and the antiphon for the Benedictus at Lauds (Ant. *Visionem quam vidistis*) were the only proper pieces used; see GB:Ob, Can. Lit. 192, fo. 402; and F:Pn, Rés. 5209.

[99] The calendars combine Majolus with Saint Mamertus, no doubt because the 2 observances happened to fall on the same day. While their feast of 12 lessons was never duplex in the abbey, it was celebrated at this rank by the 1st half of the 14th c. in monasteries more closely allied to Cluny. Apparently the statute of 1310 that called for duplex feasts for all of the abbot-saints of Cluny was revoked in 1343, on account of its non-observance by the majority of houses of the order; Valous, *Monachisme*, i. 422.

[100] Cluny established this feast between 926 and 942; ibid. 421.

[101] The MSS for the Office from Saint-Denis transmit the antiphons for this service just as they are found in F:Pn, lat. 17296, fos. 251–2 (Hesbert, *CAO*, ii, No. 117[2]). Cf. F:Pn, lat. 12584 (ibid.) and Hesbert's discussion of the Offices for the day and Octave of Martin; ibid., p. xiii.

[102] In 868 Saint Maurus was translated to the abbey near Paris that later took his name (Saint-Maur-des-Fossés); *AASS*, Jan. i, 1053. 30 years earlier the elevation and translation of the relics of Saint Julian to Le Mans had occurred (*VSB*, i. 537), and his name is added to the calendar of F:Pn, lat. 9436.

[103] *VSB*, ii. 65. Saint-Denis possessed the priory of Saint-Blaise de Grandpuits before the end of the 12th c.; Cottineau, *Répertoire*, i, col. 1330.

some of the earliest martyrologies, including Usuard's, record his feast on 15 February, the more common day 3 February was later established.[104] Saint Landericus should have been remembered as architect of the abbey's freedom from the church of Paris in the seventh century; nevertheless, he does not figure in the original hand of any Saint-Denis calendar prior to the thirteenth century. The celebration of his feast (10 June) in the abbey was perhaps linked to the placement of his relics at Saint-Germain-l'Auxerrois in 1171 by Bishop Maurice of Sully,[105] for previous evidence of his cult is limited to his inclusion in eleventh-century litanies.[106] The earliest calendar to record the name of Saint Maglorius (24 October) in the original hand is that of the eleventh-century psalter F:Pn, lat. 103. This is not surprising, since the Translation of his relics to Paris occurred only in the tenth century.[107] As was true of the majority of twelve-lesson feasts that were added to the liturgy of Saint-Denis, all these observances drew on the *commune sanctorum* for the substance of their Masses and Offices.

Services for two illustrious English martyrs at Saint-Denis were compiled in the same way. King Edmund of East Anglia (d. 870; feast 20 November) was widely venerated on the Continent by the thirteenth century,[108] and the people of Toulouse claimed to possess his relics after 1219.[109] His cult was no doubt enhanced, if not instigated, in the abbey by the accession of Baldwin, a monk of Saint-Denis, to the abbacy of Bury St Edmunds in 1069. Baldwin's term of tenure precedes the earliest record of Edmund's cult at Saint-Denis as an addition to the calendar of F:Pn, lat. 103. Abbot Suger furthered the devotion to this saint when he dedicated one of the altars in the crypt to him in 1144.[110]

The sojourns of Thomas of Canterbury in France during his lifetime likewise popularized his martyrdom (1170) all the more on the Continent. Saint-Denis incorporated his feast-day (29 December) into the liturgy somewhat belatedly, in the mid-thirteenth century.[111] The abbey did not, however, adopt one of the popular rhymed, proper Offices for the saint,[112] using instead chants from the *commune*. The

[104] *VSB*, ii. 65; Dubois, *Usuard*, 180. F:Pn, lat. 9436, which was copied at or influenced by Saint-Vaast of Arras, transmits both days.

[105] *AASS*, June ii, 292–4.

[106] F:Pm 384, fo. 94 (Hesbert, *Graduel*, 153).

[107] *AASS*, Oct. x, 779.

[108] The indexes of Leroquais's catalogues provide ample witness of the extent of the cult of Saint Edmund in France.

[109] Bordier, *Reliques*, 16–18.

[110] Panofsky, *Suger*, 119 (see also Table 4.1).

[111] The Cistercians, for example, had accorded him the dignity of celebration by two Masses in 1191, and the church of Paris commemorated the Translation of his relics (7 July) in 1220; Leroquais, *Bréviaires*, vol. i, pp. xcviii, cxiii. Thomas is omitted from the early 13th-c. calendar of F:Pm 414 and appears first in that of F:Pm 526 (see App. A). On the spread of his cult in the 12th c., see Foreville, 'Diffusion'.

[112] A. Hughes has catalogued at least 300 examples of this Office, each of them 'different in some substantial way from the others'; Hughes, 'Offices', 34.

feast-day was important enough in the monastery to warrant an Octave for Thomas (4 January), although this service seems to have been dropped by the fourteenth century.

If the compilation of new services from material provided in the *commune* was the norm at Saint-Denis between the tenth and thirteenth centuries, the monks set aside this procedure in three exceptional circumstances to add proper Offices to the liturgy. The antiphons for the Octave of Saint Martin have already been mentioned. In addition, the more recently composed Offices for Saint Mary Magdalene (22 July) and Saint Nicholas (6 December) were adopted at Saint-Denis. Saint Nicholas is not found in F:Pm 384, and his proper Office first appears in the twelfth-century antiphoner F:Pn, lat. 17296.[113] The service for Mary Magdalene may not have been sung at all in the abbey until the twelfth century, for it appears as a slightly later addition to F:Pn, lat. 17296.[114] The entry of this proper feast into the liturgy may have happened under Abbot of Suger, who ordered it to be celebrated at duplex rank around 1130, as will be shown in Chapter 4.

FEASTS OF THE THIRTEENTH AND FOURTEENTH CENTURIES

In comparison with the earlier era, the thirteenth and fourteenth centuries have left us with abundant evidence about the state of the liturgy at Saint-Denis. More than half the extant calendars and almost a quarter of the surviving manuscripts from the abbey date from this period. This wealth of sources at once confirms the presence of feasts that were established earlier and identifies the additions of new services with some precision. The two subsequent calendars (F:Pn, lat. 1072; F:Pn, Rés. B. 5209) effectively duplicate the schedule of feasts that had been fixed 200 years earlier.[115] By their agreement, these later sources verify that the fires under the liturgical crucible at Saint-Denis had all

[113] Fos. 261–264^{v}; Hesbert, *CAO*, ii, No. 120^{2}. Hesbert notes that the Office for Saint Nicholas falls at the end of the *temporale/sanctorale* cycle of F:Pn, lat. 17296, whereas other antiphoners place the service within Advent; ibid. xiv. This may be due to the fact that F:Pm 384, which places Nicholas similarly, seems to have served as a model for F:Pn, lat. 17296, as discussed in Ch. 6. The copyists of F:Pn, lat. 17296 respected the arrangement of feasts in F:Pm 384 (or in some list derived from it) by failing to place Saint Nicholas squarely within the period of Advent within which his feast invariably falls.

[114] Fos. 348–51. Hesbert points out that the novelty of this Office is attested by the variety and codicological placement of the formulas through which it is transmitted; *CAO*, vol. ii, p. xix, and Nos. 146^{4}, 105^{2}. For a study of the appearance of the Office in breviaries and some antiphoners, see Saxer, *Culte*.

[115] The only additions in F:Pn, lat. 1072 and F:Pn, Rés. B. 5209 are obits.

but died by around 1350—to be rekindled only after 1633 in the sweeping changes that accompanied the advent of the Maurist regime.

And yet in the thirteenth and fourteenth centuries festivals were added to the calendar in no small number. A Vigil (23 February) was attached to the service of the Dedication of the church when the rank of this feast was elevated to *annuale* in the fourteenth century.[116] Aside from this modification, the number of ceremonies for the titular saint of the abbey remained the same. But the lack of new services for their patron in no way implied that the monks' ardour for him had flagged. The mid-thirteenth-century composition of a *vita* of Saint Denis in the vernacular publicized his deeds to an ever-wider audience.[117] In so doing, this work and others like it again stressed the identity of Saint Denis with the Areopagite figures, a point which was still unresolved in the abbey. Pope Innocent III had tried to settle the issue as early as 1216 when he sent the abbey relics of yet another Dionysius, the second-century bishop of Corinth.[118] His feast-day (8 April) was thereafter celebrated at Saint-Denis with material for the Mass and Office taken from the common of one confessor.

In 1233 a miracle was said to have occurred at Saint-Denis. The abbey claimed to possess a nail of the Holy Passion since the ninth century, and on the feast of the Dedication of the Church (24 February) in 1233 the monks announced that the relic had been lost. Miraculously, the nail was recovered and returned to the monastery on Good Friday of the same year.[119] This grandiloquent story is full of fanciful passages, and it is possible that the community exaggerated it at least in part to compete with the cathedral of Notre Dame, which likewise boasted relics of the Cross.[120]

Fabricated or not, the event was the object of a short-lived commemoration in the abbey which was celebrated on Friday of Easter week. F:Pm 526 is the only extant manuscript that includes the festival, entitled *In invencione sacri clavi*.[121] According to the usual practice for Easter week, the feast had only three lessons at Matins, and it drew

[116] In making this addition, the monks transferred the feast of Saint Matthias to the following day.

[117] F:Pn, lat. n.a.f. 1098, fos. 1–28 (see n. 134 below; and Delisle, 'Peintures', 445–6, 452–3).

[118] See F:Pn, lat. 5286, fos. 201^{v}–202. Félibien describes the reception of these relics in the church of Saint-Denis-de-l'Estrée and their subsequent solemn Translation to the abbey on 22 Feb. 1216; *Histoire*, 219–20. Apparently Pope Innocent intended to fill the abbey with all available Dionysian relics so that the authentic ones would perforce be present (see also Spiegel, *Chronicle*, 24, n. 43).

[119] The account of the nail is contained in F:Pn, n.a.l. 1509, pp. 419–95, edited in Aubry, 'Clou'. See also Félibien, *Histoire*, 228–32.

[120] Perdrizet, *Calendrier*, 199–200.

[121] Fos. 60^{r-v}. While the service for the *Inventio* appears in full in the text of F:Pm 526, it is contained in no calendar (including that of F:Pm 526) nor in any other MS from the abbey.

largely on the *officium* of the Exaltation of the Holy Cross (14 September) for material for the Mass and Office. The community performed the Hours and Mass of the *Inventio* with the splendour reserved for celebrations during Easter week, which mirrored the solemnity of the *annuale* feasts. The monks even created a new chant for the procession after Terce. Carrying the nail and other relics, they proceeded first to the altar of the Virgin in the chevet and thence, if time permitted, into the nave. Here three singers chanted the solo portions of the Resp. *Clavus refulgens* and its Ver. *Dicant nunc*. *Dicant nunc* is the familiar verse from the Easter Resp. *Christus resurgens*, but the text *Clavus refulgens* resists identification and must have been designed especially for the occasion. F:Pm 526 gives only this brief incipit, but the accentuation, syllable count and vowels of these two words hint strongly that they were meant to imitate the text of *Christus resurgens*, which was sung during the procession in the nave on Easter.[122] On a different level, the recovery of the nail inspired another liturgical change: the addition of the Ant. *Salve regina* to the end of Compline.[123]

The monks focused again on the relics of the abbey in the thirteenth century by establishing a festival in their honour.[124] Celebrated at duplex rank on the first Sunday after Ascension, the feast of the Relics seems to have been instigated by the community's desire to have a common observance for all saints whose bones rested in the abbey, as well as for such sacred objects as the Holy Nail:

> We have in our church innumerable relics both of saints' bodies and of their various ornaments . . . But because [the celebration of these relics one at a time] could not be accomplished easily—or at all—we decree wisely and rationally, with the unanimous resolve of the elders of this church, that a general celebration for all the relics be made publicly each year, so that none of the saints of whom these are the very remains should be defrauded of the service due to them. Let there be a duplex feast on the first Sunday after the Ascension of the Lord, just as it was established for almost the same reason for those for whom the Feast of All Saints is customarily celebrated on 1 November.[125]

[122] 'In navi, *Christus resurgens*, Ver. *Dicant nunc* a tribus'; F:Pm 526, fo. 57; F:Pn, lat. 976, fo. 30.

[123] F:Pn, lat. n.a.l. 1509, pp. 435–6 (published in Aubry, 'Clou', 300).

[124] F:Pm 526, fos. 69^{v}–70; F:Pn, lat. 976, fos.41^{r-v}; F:Pm 414, fos. 36^{v}–37; F:Pn, lat. 1107, fos. 163^{v}–163^{a} (recto); I:Rc 603, fos. 134^{v}–135; GB:Lva 1346–1891, fo. 175^{v}.

[125] 'Apud nos in presenti continentur ecclesia innumerabiles reliquie sive ex sanctorum corporibus sive ex diversis eorundem ornamentis . . . Sed quia id non de facili aut omnino non poterat fieri, unanimi consilio antiquorum patrum huius ecclesie sano quidem et discreto decretum est: ut communiter de omnibus reliquis generalis fiat per singulos annos celebritas ut nemo sanctorum quorum sunt ipse reliquie a debito sibi servitio defraudetur. Et fit festum duplex in instanti dominica post ascensionem domini, pariter ut dictum est de omnibus eodem fere in quo in kalendis novembris festivitas omnium sanctorum celebrari consuevit'; F:Pn, n.a.l. 1509, pp. 416–17.

The feast of the Relics naturally encompassed the major relics of the abbey. But inasmuch as many of these saints (e.g. Hilary of Mende) already had duplex feasts of their own, chapels dedicated to them, and other signs of a special cult, the motive for instituting the service was apparently different. Most likely the celebration was meant to recognize the remains of saints such as Simeon Senex, who did not have the intense observances that the more important relics enjoyed, even though his arm was a regular sight in the processions at Saint-Denis. The feast of the Relics consisted of selections from the common of many martyrs and of material from Ascension.

In the twelfth and thirteenth centuries, the abbey of Saint-Denis was affected by one of the most significant events in medieval monastic history: the reaction against the centralizing tendencies of Cluny. This rebellion resulted in the creation of new orders and ideals of monasticism as early as the eleventh century. And whereas the monks of Saint-Denis had declined to acknowledge most of the abbot–saints of Cluny in their liturgy, they were not so remiss in regard to the chief organizers of two of the younger institutions. The founder of the Franciscans was canonized in 1228, and the abbey of Saint-Denis first celebrated the feast-day of Francis of Assisi (4 October) between 1234 and 1241 (Table 6.2). Likewise, the commemoration of Saint Bernard of Clairvaux (23 August) was belatedly established by Abbot Eudes Clément in 1241.[126] According to the customary method of compiling new feasts of twelve lessons, the material for the Mass and Hours of Saint Francis came from the common of one confessor. The ceremony for Saint Bernard was slightly more elaborate, with its fourth Resp. *Sancte Bernarde* sung *duplex et festivum*, as Abbot Eudes had specified. The entire feast was raised to duplex level in the fourteenth century.

New services at Saint-Denis were normally adopted, as mentioned earlier, when relics arrived. In the case of the feast of Saint Ursula and the Eleven Thousand Virgins (21 October), however, there was apparently a hiatus between these two occurrences. The cult of this

[126] Though canonized in 1174, the abbot of Clairvaux was not incorporated into the liturgy of Saint-Denis until Abbot Eudes Clément called for his veneration in 1241: 'We ordain and establish that the feast of that holy confessor and distinguished teacher [Bernard of Clairvaux] be celebrated solemnly by us every year on the day following [the feast of] Saint Ouen. The fourth responsory should be performed duplex and festively, and all the other things pertaining to the observance of this feast should be done, both in terms of the lighting and whatever else we customarily do on those feasts in which the fourth responsory is made duplex and festive' ('ordinamus et statuimus ut festum ipsius pii confessoris et doctoris egregii in crastino sancti Audoeni singulis annis a nobis sollempniter celebretur, ita quod quartum R. fiat duplex et festivum, et omnia alia circa servitium ejusdem festi fiant tam de luminari quam de aliis quae facere consuevimus in festis illis, in quibus quartum R. fit duplex et festivum'); F:Pan, LL 1159, pp. 1–2; Félibien, *Histoire*, *PJ*, i, No. clxx; Walters [Robertson], 'Reconstruction', 193. Eudes called for the feast to be celebrated on 25 Aug. (i.e. the day following Saint Ouen, 24 Aug.), but calendars from the abbey record 23 Aug.

saint and her holy companions grew rapidly in the twelfth century as a result of the alleged discovery of many of their bones at Cologne.[127] This event inspired the religious orders to try to secure portions of the relics, and much attention focused on the celebration of the feast in the thirteenth and fourteenth centuries.[128] While the Saint-Denis *Chronicon ad Cyclos Paschales* records that the bodies of three of the Virgins were brought to the abbey in 1167 or 1168,[129] the extant calendars and manuscripts indicate that the feast was not celebrated there before about 1234.[130] By 1259 this service, which drew its Office from the common of one virgin and from other parts of the *commune*, was celebrated at duplex rank.[131] The commemoration of another virgin, Saint Catherine (25 November), also entered the liturgy of Saint-Denis and elsewhere in the thirteenth century.[132] Her feast of twelve lessons, taken entirely from the *commune*, reached only semiduplex rank in the fourteenth century.

By the mid-fourteenth century, the calendar was enriched with new feasts in honour of five supposed companions of Dionysius the Areopagite.[133] The relics of Saints Sanctinus and Antoninus, reputedly witnesses to the martyrdom of Dionysius, were given to the abbey by the chapter of Meaux in 1259.[134] Since the feast-day which commemor-

[127] *VSB*, x. 683–6.

[128] The Cistercians, for example, assigned the rank '12 lessons, 1 Mass' in 1260; see Leroquais, *Bréviaires*, vol. i, xcix, c–ci.

[129] The entry appears between the years 1167 and 1168: 'Hoc anno allata sunt tria corpora virginum de Colonia in ecclesiam Beati Dyonisii'; Berger, 'Chronicon', 278, 288. See also the account in F:Pn, lat. 5286, fos. 199ᵛ–200.

[130] This service is an addition to the calendar of the Chapel Hill psalter and to the texts of F:Pm 414 and F:Pm 526. It is absent altogether from the calendar of F:Pm 414, but does appear in the original hand of the calendar of F:Pm 526, an indication that this calendar was copied slightly after the rest of the MS. Since both calendar and text of F:Pm 526 were copied between 1234 and 1241, we may assume that the feast of the Virgins was added during this period.

[131] See F:Pn, lat. 976 (copied *c*.1258), fo. 138ᵛ.

[132] The cult of Saint Catherine did not begin in the West until the 11th c., and it spread through the religious orders in the 13th c. (see *VSB*, xi. 862–3). Saint-Denis may have followed the example of Cîteaux, which adopted this feast in 1207 (see Leroquais, *Bréviaires*, vol. i, p. xcviii).

[133] It is noteworthy that observances for saints associated with Dionysius the Areopagite were among the small number of celebrations incorporated into the liturgy after the middle of the 13th c. Whether the monks made such additions deliberately to support the Areopagite theory is not known. We have evidence, none the less that they actually solicited the bones of Saints Sanctinus and Antoninus, and that they continued to invoke the names of these and other colleagues of Dionysius well into the 17th c.; see Doublet, *Histoire*, 52–60.

[134] The Dean of Meaux states that the request for these relics had come from the abbey: 'Notum facimus quod nos [totum capitulum Meldense] . . . petitioni ipsorum [conventus beati Dionysii] qua de sanctorum qui in nostra Meldensi ecclesia requiescunt, reliquiis videlicet beatorum Sanctini et Antonini confessorum Christi sibi a nobis dari cum humilitate maxima petierunt . . . costam unam de corpore sancti Santini praefati, et unum de ossibus brachii sancti Antonini praedicti eisdem Abbati [Matthew of Vendôme] et Conventui in perpetuum liberaliter duximus conferendum'; Félibien, *Histoire*, *PJ*, i, No. clxxvi ('copiées sur l'original'). There is also evidence that the monks had become interested in these 2 saints just prior to this Translation. Only 9 years

ated them at Meaux (11 October) would have fallen within the octave of Saint Denis (9–16 October), the monks placed this twelve-lesson service instead on the first available day (19 October) after the conclusion of the festivities.[135] Likewise, in the fourteenth century they added observances with three lessons for Saint Taurinus (20 October), whose *vita* incorrectly associates this bishop of Evreux with the Areopagite,[136] and for another presumed comrade of Dionysius, Saint Eutropius (30 April). King Philip IV (1285–1314) and his wife Jeanne of Navarre instituted the cult of Eutropius at Notre Dame in 1296, and his adoption at Saint-Denis is possibly further evidence of royal influence in the abbey.[137] And although Saint Jonas (12 August) may have been a contemporary of the true Saint Denis (third-century bishop of Paris),[138] the monks likewise connected him with the Athenian Dionysius, giving him a feast of three lessons in the fourteenth century.[139]

The newly composed services for Corpus Christi and Saint Louis (25 August, Octave on 31 August) were universally adopted in the late thirteenth and fourteenth centuries, and Saint-Denis was no exception in embracing these celebrations.[140] The hearings which preceded the canonization of Saint Louis were held at Saint-Denis in 1282,[141] and the

earlier (1250), the scriptorium of the abbey produced an illustrated account of the life of Saint Denis in French (F:Pn, lat. n.a.f. 1098), to which was added a legend of Saints Sanctinus and Antoninus; see Delisle, 'Peintures', 453, 460.

[135] On the various days on which this feast was celebrated, see *AASS*, Sept. vi, 292. The 2nd ordinary (F:Pn, lat. 976) and the notated missal F:Pn, lat. 1107 aptly demonstrate the incorporation of this feast into the liturgy. The service first appears as an addition to the calendar and text of F:Pn, lat. 976, but it is written in the original hand of all subsequently copied MSS, beginning with F:Pn, lat. 1107.

[136] In spite of the fact that scholars now reject the connection of these 2 saints (see *AASS*, Aug. ii, 638), monks of Saint-Denis as late as the 17th c. accepted it (see Doublet, *Histoire*, 58). In any case, the date on which they chose to commemorate him (20 Oct.) is given in no other tradition that I have seen. The Bollandists assign 11 Aug., and Leroquais lists a variety of dates, including 5 Aug. and 11 Sept. With reference to the point made in n. 133, it would be interesting to know if the placement of the celebrations of Saints Sanctinus, Antoninus, and Taurinus in the calendar was intended to fill the 2 vacant days (19 and 20 Oct.) nearest those of the feast and Octave of Saint Denis with commemorations for his missionary cohorts.

[137] See Guérard, *Cartulaire*, iv. 182. It is also plausible that the king and queen actually endowed the same feast at Saint-Denis, though no record of such an action survives.

[138] *VSB*, ix. 444.

[139] Doublet, *Histoire*, 57–8. The Bollandists place Saint Jonas on 5 Aug. (*AASS*, Aug. ii, 13–15), the day which is likewise given in the Parisian calendar F:Pn, lat. 5185cc. There is evidence that relics of Jonas, and perhaps his feast, may have been present at Saint-Denis as early as 1284. The *Comptes de la Commanderie* of Saint-Denis (F:Pan, LL 1240–56) record an entry 'for the payment of Saint Jonas' ('de censu sancti yonis') in this year; F:Pan, LL 1240, fo. 27.

[140] Both services are additions to the 13th-c. missals F:Pn, lat. 1107 (fos. 283^v–285) and I:Rc 603 (fos. 178^v–179^v), while figuring in the original hand of the 14th-c. MSS F:Pn, lat. 10505 (Corpus Christi only: fo. 89^v) and GB:Lva 1346–1891 (Corpus Christi: fos. 191–192^v; Saint Louis, fos. 286^v–287). On the possible authorship of the Office and Mass of Corpus Christi by Saint Thomas Aquinas, see Gy, 'Office'; and for arguments against this view, see Mathiesen, 'Office'.

[141] Vauchez, *Sainteté*, 659.

Comptes de la Commanderie of the monastery show that the monks recognized Louis IX as Saint Louis between 1296 and 1297,[142] at which time they probably adopted his feast-day.[143] But while other observances were established or gained currency before the end of the fifteenth century,[144] almost none of them came into the liturgy of the abbey. Missing altogether are the feasts for Saint Thomas Aquinas (7 March) and Saint Anne (26 July), both of which were widely celebrated in France in the fourteenth and fifteenth centuries.[145] Such omissions may well have been necessitated by the rigorous and ever-expanding schedule of anniversary services that were solemnized throughout the year in the royal abbey. The feast of the Conception of the Virgin (8 December), on the other hand, was firmly established at Saint-Denis during this period. The service first appears in the calendars of the two thirteenth-century ordinaries (F:Pm 526; F:Pn, lat. 976), although there is no trace of it in the texts of these manuscripts. In the fourteenth century, this observance surfaced again between around 1304 and 1321,[146] and, like the Nativity of Mary (8 September) whence its Mass and Office come, the feast attained *semiannuale* rank. The arrival of the feast of the Conception completed the cycle of major Marian celebrations in the abbey, which included, in addition to the services just mentioned, the feasts of Purification (2 February), Annunciation (25 March), and Assumption (15 August). Unlike many other late medieval houses, however, Saint-Denis remained untouched by the almost hysterical spread of Mariology in the West, eschewing such immensely popular feasts as the Visitation (2 July) and Presentation of the Virgin (21 November).[147]

LITURGICAL CHANGES

Just as the concentration of extant calendars in the mid-thirteenth to mid-fourteenth centuries aids the study of the development of feasts at

[142] For the years 1296–7, F:Pan, LL 1240 records payments 'pro pitancia ludovici regis', fo. 172. By 1297–8, the wording had been changed: 'pro pitancia sancti ludovici' (fo. 187v), and this designation continues in all subsequent references.

[143] R. Folz suggests that the feast of Saint Louis was first celebrated on 25 Aug. 1298; Folz, 'Sainteté', 31.

[144] See e.g. the lists of feasts given in Leroquais, *Bréviaires*, vol. i, pp. xcvii–cxvii.

[145] Ibid. Other late medieval feasts, such as the Name of Jesus, the Five Wounds, and the Crown of Thorns (see Pfaff, *Feasts*, 62–97), were likewise ignored at Saint-Denis.

[146] From 1321 on, the *Comptes de la Commanderie* show payments for a 'pitancia conceptionis beate marie'; F:Pan, LL 1241, fo. 9v; F:Pan, LL 1230A, fo. 6, etc. The documents up to 1303–4 (F:Pan, LL 1240) make no mention of this feast, and there is a lacuna between these accounts and the ones of 1321.

[147] On these festivals, see Eisenhöfer and Lechner, *Liturgy*, 233; Holweck, *Calendarium*.

Saint-Denis, so the greater specificity of these documents indicates that a wholesale inflation of liturgical rank took place at this time. The degrees of feasts, noted in every calendar beginning with F:Pm 526, show various types of change. The Holy See ordered duplex observance for the festivals for the twelve apostles, the four evangelists, and the four doctors of the church in 1295.[148] In other instances, the call for such enhancement apparently originated within the monastery itself. The monks elevated to full duplex rank a number of simple twelve-lesson services and celebrations in which only the fourth responsory was duplex: Matthias (24–5 February), the Invention of the Holy Cross (3 May), the Detection of Saint Denis (9 June), Barnabas (11 June),[149] the Commemoration of Saint Paul (30 June), Lawrence (10 August), the Octave of Assumption (22 August), Bernard (23 August), the Exaltation of the Holy Cross (14 September), Demetrius (17 October), and Martin (11 November). The feasts of the apostles James (25 July) and Bartholomew (24 August) had likewise been declared duplex by 1259.[150] The services for almost all the saints whose relics lay in the abbey, many of which had twelve lessons but no further indication of rank in F:Pm 526, were also elevated to duplex between 1234 and 1259: Patroclus (31 January), Dionysius of Corinth (8 April), Firminus (25 September), Hilary of Mende (25 October), and Romanus of Blaye (24 November).[151] Only the feasts of Peregrinus (16 May) and Osmanna (16 August, 9 September) were not labelled duplex by the time the later ordinary F:Pn, lat. 976 was written (*c*.1258), although most of the customary features of this solemnity are given in the text of the manuscript.[152]

[148] Duchesne, *Liber*, ii. 169; Leroquais, *Bréviaires*, vol. i, cxvi.

[149] A chapel in the crypt was dedicated to Barnabas under Abbot Suger in 1144; Panofsky, *Suger*, 119 (see also Table 4.1).

[150] While there are no ceremonial changes in the services for James, the text of F:Pn, lat. 976 calls his feast duplex (fo. 111), whereas F:Pm 526 writes 'fiat xii lectiones de ipso' (fo. 150ᵛ). The 14th-c. calendars move his festival to 26 July, no doubt to avoid conflict with the duplex celebration of Saint Cucuphas. Bartholomew appears in F:Pm 526 with twelve lessons (fos. 162ʳ⁻ᵛ), and in the original hand of F:Pn, lat. 976 with 12 lessons and the 4th responsory duplex (fos. 120ʳ⁻ᵛ). Another scribe altered this rank to 'duplex' and erased some of the performance indications, but without inserting the new rubrics which would have reflected the usual numbers of soloists for duplex ceremonies.

[151] It is difficult to know whether the feast of Saint Clement (23 Nov.), which was duplex in F:Pn, lat. 976, was likewise duplex in F:Pm 526, since the text of this earlier ordinary has a lacuna at the beginning of the feast (fos. 194ᵛ–195). Since, however, both F:Pm 526 and F:Pn, lat. 976 stipulate 2 cantors for the introit at Mass with 4 others in the procession, it is likely that Clement's feast was duplex in both sources.

[152] Fos. 92ᵛ (Peregrinus), 124 (Osmanna). The fact that the rank of Peregrinus' feast is raised to duplex by a later hand in the text of the 1st ordinary shows that this was the intended level; F:Pm 526, fo. 127ᵛ. A call for the enhancement of Osmanna's feast is found in F:Pn, n.a.l. 1509, p. 407 [409]: 'It is remarkable that the observance for each of the saints whose bodies rest in this church is performed in albs and in silk copes with the bells doubly rung. But the feast of this virgin

Apart from the festivals of saints whose relics were in the church, the feast of Saint Benedict (21 March) was also raised to duplex during the same period, as was his Translation (11 July) in F:Pn, lat. 976.[153] Changes in the numbers of persons assigned to the important chants and actions on the Octaves of Christmas and Pentecost, and on Annunciation (25 March), when it fell on Monday after Palm Sunday, similarly enhanced these festivals to a level that closely resembles duplex.[154] Finally, the ranks of four feasts were elevated from three to twelve lessons: John at the Latin Gate (6 May), the Ten Thousand Martyrs (22 June), John and Paul (26 June), and Cosmas and Damian (27 September). In conjunction with the increase in ceremony, ferial processions to the relics in the chevet were added to these and other celebrations. This mid-thirteenth-century embellishment of the rite was brought about not only for liturgical reasons but partly for architectural ones, for the changes went hand in hand with the completion of portions of the reconstruction of the church, which was executed between 1231 and 1281.[155]

When two feasts of twelve lessons fell on the same day, the more important, usually ranked at least duplex, kept its place, while the other moved to the nearest available slot. This type of displacement was fairly common at Saint-Denis by the late Middle Ages owing to the number of anniversary services. In other cases, conflict arose between two feasts of the regular liturgy. The *natale* of Saint Martial (30 June), which was originally celebrated with the Commemoration of Saint Paul, began to be observed on the Octave of his feast (7 July) in the thirteenth century.[156] The feast of Saint Demetrius (17 October at Saint-Denis)

[Osmanna] is being celebrated in an exceedingly inferior manner. This is believed to have happened undoubtedly through the negligence and lack of foresight of our forebears. For since holiness and virginity are a double good, then holy virginity and virgin-like holiness in this virgin are worthy to be doubly honoured [i.e. honoured with a duplex feast].' ('Unde mirandum est quod de singulis sanctis quorum corpora in presenti requiescunt ecclesia in albis et capis sericis pulsatis duppliciter campanis sollempnitas agitur. Huius autem virginis inferiori valde modo festivitas celebratur. Quod utique per neglegentiam antiquorum et minorem providentiam creditur accidisse. Cum enim duplex bonum sit sanctitas et virginitas, in virgine ista sancta virginitas et virginalis sanctitas debuit non immerito duppliciter honorari.')

153 F:Pm 526 calls for 12 lessons for the Translation (fos. 145^r–v), but the rubrics for numbers of participants are like those for duplex ceremonies. In 1401, portions of the head and arms of Saint Benedict were given to the abbey by the Duke of Berry, and as a result the feast of Saint Benedict (21 Mar.) was said to have been celebrated with even greater solemnity at Saint-Denis; see Juvénal, *Charles VI*, 145; Bellaguet, *Chronique*, ii. 780–3; Félibien, *Histoire*, 317–18. The 15th- and 16th-c. calendars (F:Pn, lat. 1072; F:Pn, Rés. B. 5209), however, give no indication that the rank of the feast was raised beyond duplex. Félibien's 18th-c. drawing of the interior of the church (Pl. 4) shows that a chapel for Benedict existed in the south transept at this time; *Histoire*, 529.

154 The services, however, were not actually designated as duplex.

155 See Ch. 4; Walters [Robertson], 'Reconstruction', 192–9.

156 Saint Martial was one of the 7 bishops who, along with Saint Denis, was supposedly sent to Gaul to preach in the area around Limoges; see Doublet, *Histoire*, 40.

was first commemorated in the abbey between 1234 and 1259, probably as a result of an endowment, as will be shown in Chapter 4.[157] His festival, like that for Saint Simeon Senex, was never celebrated on the customary day (8 October), probably because it too would have conflicted with the Vigil of Saint Denis. Similarly, the feast of All Saints displaced the commemoration of the fifth-century bishop of Paris, Saint Marcellus (1 November). Instigated at Saint-Denis perhaps by the translation of Marcellus to Paris in 1200,[158] this celebration was assigned to 5 November instead of the more customary 3 November.[159] Several feasts of three lessons were likewise moved to the next day when they were overshadowed by duplex or twelve-lesson services: Crispin and Crispinian, which conflicted with Hilary of Mende on 25 October; Faro, which yielded to Simon and Jude on 28 October; and Theodore, ousted by the Octave of Eustace on 9 November.[160]

In like fashion, many three-lesson feasts were demoted to commemorations in the fourteenth century, giving way to services of higher rank. Such was the fate of the feast of Saint Simeon Stylites (5 January), which made a place for the twelve-lesson observance of Saint Geneviève, transferred to this day from 3 January to avoid conflict with the Anniversary of Philip V. Saints Felix and Remigius (14 January) were also converted to commemorations when the feast of Hilary of Poitiers was moved to 14 January from the previous day, which it shared with the Octave of Epiphany. The feast of Saint Leo (28 June) yielded to the more important Vigil of Peter and Paul; the feast of Christopher (25 July) gave way to Cucuphas; Paulinus (31 August) to the Octave of Saint Louis; and Priscus (1 September) to Giles and Lupus. Most of the remaining festivals that were reduced from three lessons to *memoriae* in the fourteenth century were ancient observances from the Gregorian and Gelasian ranks, which never merited solemn observance at Saint-Denis.[161]

In the fourteenth century, the monks likewise modified the celebration of days within the octaves of several major feasts. Normally, these

[157] See Table 6.2. The calendar of F:Pm 526, copied between 1234 and 1241, contains Demetrius as an addition, and he is inserted in the text of the MS. His feast is contained in the original hands of both text and calendar of F:Pn, lat. 976 (copied *c.*1258).

[158] Leroquais, *Bréviaires*, vol. i, cxiii.

[159] The Parisian calendar F:Pn, lat. 5185cc places Marcellus on 3 Nov., as do the vast majority of MSS cited in Leroquais's indexes. As mentioned earlier, the feast of Saint Eustace (2 Nov.) at Saint-Denis caused the Commemoration of All Souls to occupy 3 Nov., thus leaving 5 Nov. as the first available day for Marcellus. He is listed in the calendars of F:Pm 526 and I:Rc 603 on 1 Nov., the day on which he was perhaps originally commemorated at Saint-Denis.

[160] In these 3 instances, the calendars of the 13th-c. ordinaries (F:Pm 526 and F:Pn, lat. 976) list the 3-lesson observances on their original days, but the texts of these MSS transfer them to the following day.

[161] See App. A: Processus and Martinian (2 July); Felix and Adauctus (30 Aug.); Protus and Hyacinth (11 Sept.); Euphemia, Lucy, and Geminian (16 Sept.); and Damasus (11 Dec.).

days consisted of feasts of three lessons in honour of the principal feast, drawing their material entirely from the main observance. But the calendar often contradicts the text of a manuscript by including a number of three-lesson services within these octaves which have nothing to do with the chief celebration. Most of these observances date from the ninth to the twelfth centuries, and they were no doubt preserved in the calendar simply as a matter of record, even after the more important octaves were added. To make the calendar conform to the way in which the octaves were actually observed (with three-lesson feasts in honour of the primary festival), the community abolished all three-lesson celebrations immediately following the feast of Assumption (15–22 August). Likewise, the octave of Saint Denis (9–16 October) was cleared of its one encumbrance, Saint Callistus (14 October). The later calendars also removed the feast of Paul the Hermit (10 January) from within the octave of Epiphany, Saint Leonard (6 November) from the octave of All Saints, and Saint Anianus (17 November) from the octave of Martin (11–18 November), reassigning this festival to the day after the Octave (19 November). Similarly, the feast of Saint Barbara (4 December) disappeared from the week folowing Saint Andrew's feast.

The creative energy that informed the liturgical calendar of Saint-Denis over the centuries had spent itself by 1350. While the monks of earlier eras strove to enrich the liturgy with new feasts, the late thirteenth and early fourteenth centuries saw the standardization of the Divine Service along two important lines. Economy of means was the guiding principle in the compilation of new observances. The chants for the Masses and Offices of these celebrations were almost invariably drawn from the appropriate portions of the *commune sanctorum*.[162] Even the proper antiphons and responsories from the Offices of Saints Cucuphas (25 July) and Hilary of Mende (25 October), whose cults were more particular to Saint-Denis, were largely replaced by pieces from the *commune*. Similarly, the monks achieved uniformity with regard to degrees of festal solemnity. The rebuilding of the church between 1231 and 1281 had facilitated the celebration of the Divine Office in terms of movement and acoustics. As if to restructure and regularize their performance of the *opus dei* accordingly, the liturgists assigned a specific level of elaboration to each ceremony. Furthermore, they ensured consistency in this matter by imposing the same rank on feasts of equal stature. The heightening of certain celebrations occasionally required that those of lesser consequence yield place, and, with this final reshuffling, the liturgical year at Saint-Denis was complete.

[162] The widely distributed proper services for Corpus Christi and for Saint Louis (25 Aug.) which the abbey adopted are the only exceptions.

The establishment of new observances at Rome, in Paris, and elsewhere, such as those for Saints Valery, Joseph, and Lazarus, found no imitator in the abbey. Indeed, by 1350 the calendar of Saint-Denis already had a surfeit of entries requiring annual observance. The monks' reluctance to incorporate yet more festivals at the end of the Middle Ages was undoubtedly due in part to the large number of royal commemorations required of them. Such memorials, unique both in level of splendour and in longevity at Saint-Denis, precluded the addition of many apocryphal or legendary saints who were added so freely to the rituals of other churches.

ANNIVERSARIES

It is, to be sure, the regalian rites that give the liturgy of Saint-Denis its special character. The anniversary that Abbot Adam instituted for King Dagobert was not the first celebration of its kind at Saint-Denis. Charles the Bald, among others, had made foundations in the abbey for himself and for members of his family, but they did not survive the vicissitudes that the abbey endured in the tumultuous ninth century.[163] As if mindful of the transience of Charles's earlier attempt, Abbot Adam devised a commemoration of greater solemnity in 1108 to honour the legendary founder of the abbey.[164] In doing this, he created a prototype to which the monks had recourse for centuries to come. Even after the addition of new obits to the calendar had ceased, twelve anniversaries for kings and more than twice that number for queens, nobles, prelates, and abbots continued to be sung until the middle of the sixteenth century.

King Dagobert (d. 639) was the first monarch to be laid to rest in the monastery.[165] By the end of the tenth century the tradition of burying kings in the abbey was established, and, with only three exceptions, the custom continued in force until the French Revolution. The favour that the abbey won as a result was its crowning glory. Given the significance of these interments, one might expect to find them carried out with elaborate pageantry. Certainly this was the case in the Renaissance and thereafter, to judge from the *pompes funèbres* which have survived.[166]

[163] See Erlande-Brandenburg, *Roi*, 73, 98; and the acts of Charles the Bald that mention these anniversaries in Giry *et al.*, *Recueil*, ii, Nos. 246, 247; also Tardif, *Monuments*, Nos. 186, 187, 205.

[164] R. Barroux suggests the year 1108 for Adam's charter; 'Anniversaire', 146.

[165] The only royalty known to have preceded Dagobert are the 6th-c. Queen Arnegonde and Prince Dagobert (son of King Chilperic I); Erlande-Brandenburg, *Roi*, 69.

[166] Royal funerals in Renaissance France are treated in Giesey, *Funeral*. During this period, the services at Saint-Denis were only the final stage of the ceremony which often stretched over several days and included a service at Notre Dame Cathedral.

But even these detailed documents make little or no mention of the manner of performance of the Office and Mass for the Dead, describing instead the order of persons in the funeral cortège, the solemn décor of the church, and the like.[167] In the Middle Ages, references to the way in which services were executed are even fewer. Some documents note summarily that the burial was carried out *cum magno honore*.[168] Abbot Suger, for example, summarizes the funeral of Louis VI (d. 1137) with these few words: '[the King] was laid to rest in the royal manner with a number of prayers and hymns, and with the most distinguished and devout funeral office.'[169] In like manner, the successor to the chronicler Guillaume le Breton only hints at the special attention that was given to the performance of the Requiem for Philip Augustus (d. 1223):

> The bishop of Porto and the archbishop of Reims celebrated the funeral Mass at the same time in unison at two neighbouring altars. The rest of the bishops, along with the clerics and monks, of whom there was a large multitude, stood by and responded to them as though to one person.[170]

Descriptions with even these modest details about the manner of performance are rare in medieval sources, and one almost never finds the names of specific pieces, other than the Ps. *De profundis* or the Intr. *Requiem eternam*.

But the brevity of these mentions by no means implies that royal medieval burials at Saint-Denis, at least from the twelfth century on, were not elaborate. When Abbot Suger speaks of the 'most distinguished and devout funeral office', he refers to the formula *In natali Dagoberti regis*, which his predecessor Adam had recently compiled for the anniversaries of kings. Subsequently composed services for royalty all drew to some extent on the musical, liturgical, and ceremonial stipulations that Adam—possibly with the assistance of his successor Suger—

[167] The record of the funeral of Henry II (d. 1559) is exceptional in its account of the celebration of 4 Masses at Saint-Denis on the day of the burial, and then a fifth Mass, which was a Requiem. The Cardinal of Lorraine, who was abbot at this time, officiated, and the choir was composed of singers from the royal chapel (see Godefroy, *Cérémonial de France*, 445–6).

[168] Taken from the description of the services for Pepin the Short (d. 768) in these terms; Krusch, *Fredegarii*, 193; Pertz, *Mettenses*, 335.

[169] 'Ubi cum orationum et hymnorum frequentia, et celeberrimo devotoque exequiarum officio, more regio depositus'; Lecoy de la Marche, *Suger*, 148–9.

[170] 'Missam autem exequialem celebrarunt simul Portuensis episcopus et Remensis archiepiscopus, una voce ad duo altaria propinqua, ceteris episcopis cum clericis et monachis, quorum aderat innumera multitudo, assistentibus et eis respondentibus sicut uni'; Delaborde, *Œuvres*, i. 325. There is also a rhymed version by Philippe Mouskes: 'Tout à lor cos à St-Denis/ En liu qui fu biaus et ounis/ Plorant, criant et batant paumes/ Et li clergiés en disant saumes/ Et, se parmi le voir envois/ Doi arcevesque à une vois/ Cantérent la messe à seniestre/ Fu li uns et li autre à diestre/ Et li clergiés ki s'atendoit/ Les arcevesques respondoit'; Reiffenberg, *Chronique*, ii, ll. 23869–84. For further discussion of the burial of Philip, see Baldwin, *Philip*, 389–91.

set forth in the early twelfth century.[171] The differences between them lay largely in the realm of performance practice, and it is this aspect that now claims our attention.

King Dagobert (d. 639)

Abbot Adam's original charter of 1108 is lost, but fortunately a seventeenth-century copy has survived.[172] The document is written in the style of a ceremonial rather than an ordinary, so that the text elaborates on clerical garb and on the decoration of the church, while it skims or omits altogether the incipits of chants, readings, and prayers. Other manuscripts from the abbey fill in these lacunae to provide a vivid picture of the Mass and Hours for Dagobert's anniversary. In a service entitled *In natali Dagoberti regis*, the twelfth-century antiphoner F:Pn, lat. 17296 includes the antiphons and psalms for Vespers, the special series of responsories for Matins, and the antiphon for the Benedictus at Lauds.[173] The thirteenth- and fourteenth-century ordinaries likewise provide the textual incipits of the chants for Prime, the Little Hours, and Mass, as well as the date of the anniversary (19 January), and other information about the performance of the ritual.[174] The presence of the lesser hours in the anniversary for Dagobert is significant, for the Office for the Dead did not, as a rule, contain these services.[175] The music for the *Requiem* Mass, for the Seq. *De profundis* and for the Gallican Ant. *Salvator omnium deus*, which was sung before the gospel, are preserved in the notated missal F:Pn, lat. 1107.[176] The three later books for the Office add no new items, but they do confirm that this service was still current from the fourteenth to the sixteenth century.[177]

[171] R. Barroux has noted several features of Adam's charter which suggest the collaboration or at least the influence of Suger; 'Anniversaire', 146–7.

[172] *Archives municipales de Saint-Denis*, GG 14, fos. I–II; ed. in R. Barroux, 'Anniversaire', 148–51.

[173] F:Pn, lat. 17296, fos. 327–30 (Hesbert, *CAO*, ii, No. 146). It is interesting to note that the Benedictus Ant. *Salvator omnium deus*, a remnant of Gallican chant, was replaced in the later sources (e.g. F:Pn, lat. 976, fo. 71^{v}) by the Ant. *Cognoscimus domine*. *Salvator omnium* did not disappear from the service altogether, however, for it was sung before the gospel at Mass. The beginning of Matins is missing from F:Pn, lat. 17296 due to the loss of a folio. Hesbert has reconstructed the list of missing pieces using the 15th-c. Book of Hours of Saint-Denis F:Pn, lat. 1072 (fos. 224^{v}–226^{v}); Hesbert, *CAO*, vol. ii, p. xv.

[174] F:Pm 526, fos. 99^{v}–101; F:Pn, lat. 976, fos. 71–2; F:Pan, L 863, No. 10, fos. 137–138^{v}. Since the ensuing discussion of the Hours and Mass for Dagobert's anniversary is taken entirely from these folios and from the source named in n. 176 below, the citations are only repeated when specific texts are analysed in the notes. The extract from F:Pm 526 and F:Pn, lat. 976 is published in Martène, *De ritibus* (1690), 505–7; see also Martimort, *Documentation*, 545.

[175] See Tolhurst, *Breviary*, vi, 107; Foley, 'Ordinary', ii. 113–18.

[176] F:Pn, lat. 1107, fos. 329–330^{v}, 347^{v}–348.

[177] GB:Ob, Can. Lit. 192, fos. 539^{v}–540; F:Pn, lat. 1072, fos. 224–227^{v}; F:Pn, Rés. B.

Like other feast-days at Saint-Denis, this anniversary service had three ceremonial highpoints: First Vespers, Matins, and High Mass. Even before Vespers, however, the monks in the fourteenth century prepared for this grand occasion by reading a text (*sententia*) in honour of Dagobert, probably a selection from the *Gesta Dagoberti*, during the chapter Office on the day prior to the festival (18 January).[178] Later, at Vespers, the church was decorated in a manner appropriate to Christmas, Pentecost, and the feast of Saint Denis, all of which were principal (*annuale*) celebrations.[179] There were in fact two Vespers services, the first for Saint Lomer (also 19 January) and the second for Dagobert. The bells rang during Lomer's Vespers to signal the forthcoming solemnity for the king. At Vespers for Dagobert, four senior monks (*antiquiores*) in copes positioned themselves in the choir. The *primus*, perhaps the most senior of these monks, intoned the first antiphon to the psalms, *Placebo domino*, in a loud voice, while the others began the individual psalms. The *priores* initiated the remaining antiphons. Adam states that *cantores* in copes chanted the solo parts of the Resp. *Congregati sunt* after the chapter reading, and F:Pan, L 863, No. 10 adds that they were the four *antiquiores* who had executed the first antiphon and the psalms. Two boys sang the versicle after the hymn, after which the Antiphon to the Magnificat *Ego sum resurrectio* was performed three times. Two priests in copes carried the two thuribles, and the final versicle *Requiescant in pace* was chanted on the melisma *Clementiam* by four soloists in copes.

The hour of Matins follows the model of the secular Office for the Dead, which contains only nine lessons and responsories, three in each of three Nocturns. Matins commenced with the Inv. Ant. *Regem cui omnia* and its Ps. *Venite exultemus* (Ps. 94), which was executed by four soloists wearing copes. Adam stipulates that two of these singers should remain in the choir to chant the responsories, as was the custom on duplex feasts at Saint-Denis in the thirteenth century.[180] The

5209. For a study of the liturgy of the dead in the early centuries, see Sicard, *Liturgie*; also the works he cites on pp. xxviii–xxix.

[178] F:Pan, L 863, No. 10, fos. 137–138ᵛ. A priest chanted the lesson. This reading and those for other anniversaries may have been transferred to the day before the celebration because there was no time for them on the actual feast-day, as is perhaps implied in the rubrics for Dagobert's service in the two 13th-c. ordinaries F:Pm 526 and F:Pn, lat. 976: 'non dicatur in capitulo sententia, sed evangelium Omne quod'. On the structure of the chapter Office, see Foley, 'Ordinary', ii. 131–6.

[179] 'Ecclesia tota ut in Natali Domini vel Pentecoste pallietur'; Barroux, 'Anniversaire', 148–9. Adam's stipulations for this anniversary are taken from these pages. For further information on performance practice at Saint-Denis, see Ch. 5.

[180] Within the directions for the feast of Saint Stephen (26 Dec.), F:Pm 526 states (fo. 17): 'in all feasts which are executed as duplex, four [soloists] in copes will sing the invitatory and two will remain in the choir' ('in omnibus festis que duppliciter fient quatuor invitatorium in cappis cantabunt et duo in choro remanebunt').

ordinaries, however, augment this number to four, and call for the soloists who sang the invitatory to stand between the principal altar and the matutinal altar in the lower choir (*inter duo altaria*).[181] This change is significant, for it indicates that by the thirteenth century Dagobert's service surpassed the level duplex and ranked among such feasts as Christmas and the handful of other *annuale* ceremonies wherein such decorum was observed.[182] Indeed, Abbot Adam probably intended the same degree of splendour even though the number of soloists was smaller, for he specifies that the church should be draped as if for Christmas or Pentecost.[183]

The similarities between Dagobert's anniversary and the *annuale* celebrations are even more obvious in the comparison of the performance of the responsories for Matins on these occasions. Adam seems to imply that each of these chants was sung by only two soloists,[184] and he may well have been citing the usual number of singers for the highest-ranking feasts in the twelfth century. The later ordinaries are again more detailed in their directions for these two occasions (see Table 2.1). The third, sixth, and ninth responsories from the service for Dagobert correspond to the fourth, eighth, and twelfth for Matins on Christmas. These chants, being the final ones in each Nocturn, are executed more elaborately than the others. The numbers of performers for the solo portions of each of these responsories are: four monk-priests in the

[181] 'Invitatorium inter duo altaria a quatuor in cappis. Quatuor qui cantaverunt Venite remanebunt in choro usque ad tertium responsorium'; F:Pan, L 863, No. 10, fo. 137ᵛ. See also F:Pm 526, fo. 100; F:Pn, lat. 976, fo. 71. Yet in spite of the numbers of soloists cited in the preceding note, both ordinaries refer to the anniversary as a duplex feast: 'De domno dagoberto rege fiat duplex festum hoc modo'; F:Pm 526, fo. 99ᵛ; F:Pn, lat. 976, fo. 71; and Martène, *De ritibus* (1690), 505. On the location of the spot *inter duo altaria*, see Walters [Robertson], 'Music', 167–8; Foley, 'Ordinary' ii. 272–5.

[182] F:Pm 526 (fos. 14ᵛ–15) specifies the following performance practice for the beginning of Matins on Christmas: 'Invitatorium *Christus natus est* quod cantetur a quatuor in cappis inter duo altaria. Et remanebunt quatuor cantores in choro et dicant singulas antiphonas.'

[183] On the one hand, Adam evokes the image of a ceremony whose proportions match those of Christmas, and yet much of his scanty description resembles that of a duplex feast. We should bear in mind, however, that there are no other extant descriptions of duplex feasts at Saint-Denis under Adam's abbacy, nor in fact during any part of the 12th c. The first detailed evidence of duplex festivals comes in the 13th-c. ordinaries (F:Pm 526; F:Pn, lat. 976). It is reasonable then to conjecture that a ritual which would have been classed only as duplex around 1250 might actually have been the ceremonial equivalent of the principal feasts of the early 12th c. A substantial heightening of celebration did occur within the short span of 50 years during which parts of Saint-Denis were rebuilt in the 13th c. Perhaps a similar enhancement took place after the completion of Suger's church in 1144, and this would account for the generally lower level of cult in 1108, the presumed date of Adam's charter.

[184] 'Responsoria singula duo decantent'; Barroux, 'Anniversaire', 149. Another interpretation of these words might be that some of the responsories were not duplex, that is, were not performed with the repetition of their second halves (*repetenda*) after the verse. If this is the case, then Adam's directions are incomplete, for they would certainly not pertain to the final responsory, which included the *repetendum* ('novenum responsorium post versum repetatur'); F:Pn, lat. 976, fo. 71.

Table 2.1. *Comparison of Dagobert's Anniversary with Christmas*

Dagobert's anniversary[a]	Christmas[b]
Primum responsorium *Absolve domine* a quatuor in cappis, secundum *Manus tue* a duobus pueris, tertium *Quomodo confitebor* a quatuor sacerdotibus in cappis qui remanebunt in choro ad peragendum officium, quartum responsorium *Cognoscimus domine* a duobus juvenibus de Raya, quintum *Ne tradas domine* a tribus antiquis, sextum *Libera me domine* a quinque prioribus in cappis, septimum *Rogamus te* a duobus juvenibus de stallo, octavum *Deus eterne* a tribus antiquis, novenum *Congregati sunt* a septem in cappis.	Primum responsorium *Hodie nobis celorum* a quatuor in cappis, pro secundo responsorio *Hodie nobis de celo* duo pueri, pro tertio *Quem vidistis* duo juvenes de Raya, pro quarto responsorio *O magnum mysterium* quatuor sacerdotes qui remanebunt in choro ad officium peragendum, pro quinto *Beata dei genetrix* duo juvenes de Raya, pro sexto *Beata viscera* duo sacerdotes, pro septimo *Beata et venerabilis* tres antiqui, pro octavo *Sancta et immaculata* abbas cum quatuor prioribus, pro noveno *O regem celi* duo juvenes de stallo, pro decimo *In principio* duo antiqui, pro undecimo *Verbum caro* tres de antiquioribus, pro duodecimo *Descendit de celis* cantor cum aliis sex.

[a] F:Pan, L 863, No. 10, fo. 137^{v}. The names of the responsories, which are not listed in this MS, have been supplied from the contemporaneous breviary GB:Ob, Can. Lit. 192, fos. 539^{v}–40.

[b] F:Pan, L 863, No. 10, p. 2, under the general rules for Christmas, Assumption, and the feast of Saint Denis. Responsory incipits also taken from GB:Ob, Can. Lit. 192, fos. 73–5.

choir, five singers, and seven singers,[185] respectively. This gradual increase in vocal force reflects the mounting importance of the Nocturns themselves. Likewise, the personnel are assigned in ascending order of dignity within each Nocturn. Apart from the first responsory, which is executed by four unspecified soloists in copes, the remaining chants are sung as indicated in Table 2.2.

By comparison with this royal anniversary, even the major duplex feasts at Saint-Denis seem pallid. The ceremony for a saint as highly esteemed as Hilary of Mende, whose relics the abbey possessed, did not approach this level of sumptuousness. The final responsories in each Nocturn of his *natale* (25 October) were sung by three, four, and five singers, respectively, and the remaining chants were assigned only two soloists apiece.[186] A final outstanding ceremonial feature of this service was the censing of the altars, the tomb of Dagobert, and the whole community, which took place at the end of each Nocturn.

The celebration of the Requiem Mass also mirrored the solemnity of the festivities of Christmas Day. Here Adam's charter seems to agree with the specifications in the later sources.[187] The psalm verse of the introit was sung by three *cantores* standing in the choir, through the midst of which the abbot, seven deacons, and seven subdeacons passed.[188] The directives for Christmas are almost identical,[189] while those for Hilary of Mende and other duplex feasts usually call for only five deacons and subdeacons in the procession to the main altar.[190] Four persons chanted the Kyrie *Clemens rector*,[191] the Grad. *Si ambulem*,[192] and the Seq. *De profundis* during Dagobert's Mass, and while these

[185] The directions for Christmas, which are more detailed than those for Dagobert, name the soloists for the 8th (abbot and 4 priors) and 12th (abbot and 6 others) responsories.

[186] F:Pn, lat. 976, fo. 140.

[187] Another 12th-c. document, Abbot Suger's *De Consecratione* (written between 1144 and 1147), includes a report of the celebration of Mass on Dagobert's anniversary. The occasion was considered important enough to warrant the presence of Geoffroy, Bishop of Chartres, as officiant, and the service was performed festively at the main altar; Panofsky, *Suger*, 108–9.

[188] 'Ad missam, omnes in cappis, tres Cantores, sex procedentes cum diacono, et sex cum subdiacono et dominus abbas ingrediantur per medium chori, ut dictum est in die natalis domini'; F:Pan, L 863, No. 10, fo. 138 (cf. F:Pm 526 and F:Pn, lat. 976, which give fewer details about the procession). Adam's charter states: 'Missa solenniter celebretur, tres cantores in choro assistant, procedentes sex sacri Evangelii lectorem comitentur et totidem subdiaconum contextibus'; Barroux, 'Anniversaire', 149.

[189] 'Ingrediatur domnus abbas ad altare cum septem diaconibus et totidem subdiaconibus et aliis senioribus cui obviam precedant monachi a capicio'; F:Pm 526, fo. 16v.

[190] Ad magnam missam tres cantores et sint omnes in cappis, quatuor procedentes'; F:Pn, lat. 976, fo. 140 (feast of Hilary, 25 Oct.). 'Quatuor procedentes' is probably an abbreviated rubric for 'quatuor procedentes cum diacono et quatuor cum subdiacono'.

[191] In F:Pm 526 and F:Pn, lat. 976, the number of singers for the Kyrie is given only on the anniversaries of Dagobert, Robert, and Charles the Bald; for Charles the soloists are further instructed to 'sing well'.

[192] F:Pan, L 863, No. 10 reduces this number to 3 not only for Dagobert but also for Christmas and other *annuale* ceremonies (e.g. p. 24).

TABLE 2.2. *Comparison of Matins of Christmas with Matins of Dagobert's Anniversary*

Christmas			Dagobert		
First Nocturn					
Resp.	1	4 in copes	Resp.	1	4 in copes
	2	2 boys		2	2 boys
	3	2 youths on choir floor			
	4	4 monk-priests in copes in choir		3	4 monk-priests in copes in choir[a]
Second Nocturn					
Resp.	5	2 youths on choir floor	Resp.	4	2 youths on choir floor
	6	2 monk-priests			
	7	3 senior monks		5	3 senior monks
	8	abbot and 4 *priores* (= 5)		6	5 *priores* in copes
Third Nocturn					
Resp.	9	2 youths in choir stalls	Resp.	7	2 youths in choir stalls
	10	2 senior monks			
	11	3 more senior monks		8	3 senior monks
	12	cantor and 6 others (= 7)		9	7 in copes

[a] F:PM 526 calls for 3 soloists, probably through error.

were being performed, the bells behind the choir and in the tower rang. As at Christmas and on other *annuale* and *semiannuale* feasts, the monks sang an antiphon prior to the reading of the gospel. In this case, the antiphon was *Salvator omnium deus*, a chant drawn from the ancient Gallican liturgy and also from its store of plainchant. Given the pedigree of this piece, it is possible that the monks chose it deliberately to reaffirm the longevity of the association between Saint-Denis and the monarchy.[193] From the beginning of the gospel to the end of the offertory, two monk-priests again censed Dagobert's sepulchre.

The other Hours were less elaborate. Adam gives no information on the performance of Lauds, but the three ordinaries show that the distribution of personnel virtually duplicates that of First Vespers. The *cantor* for the week (*hebdomadarius*) began the first psalmodic antiphon, and the rest were intoned by the *priores*. Four soloists in copes chanted the Resp. *Tuam deus* after the reading,[194] and two boys sang the versicle following the hymn. The antiphon to the Benedictus, *Beati qui elegisti*,[195] was peformed three times, and two thurifers were on hand. Four soloists in copes, perhaps the same ones who executed the responsory, likewise sang *Requiescant in pace* on the melisma *Quorum vallatus* to end the service. Prime, along with each of the Little Hours (Terce, Sext, None) featured two *hebomadarii* on the responsory, a chant which did not normally appear in these Offices.[196] Two boys sang the versicles, and two *hebomadarii*, probably the same ones who were assigned to the responsory, concluded the hour with *Requiescant in pace*. Second Vespers for Dagobert mirrors First Vespers in its use of four soloists in copes on the great responsory, and in the threefold singing of the antiphon to the Magnificat.

Foundation of King Charles V (d. 1380)

In establishing an anniversary for King Dagobert, Abbot Adam probably had more on his mind than the mere prestige of the abbey. He must have foreseen the enrichment that such services could bring to the church, for other kings who would be commemorated in anniversaries would pay for the honour. Services for kings, as for others, were set up through foundation, often in the will of the person to be remembered. A foundation generally took effect at the time of its creation, that is, the

[193] See Walters [Robertson], 'Reconstruction', 203–31; and the discussion in Ch. 4.

[194] F:Pm 526 assigns 2 to this responsory (fo. 100ᵛ), and a later hand notes in the margin that F:Pn, lat. 976 calls for 4.

[195] In the 12th c. a different chant was sung, the aforementioned Gallican Ant. *Salvator omnium* (F:Pn, lat. 17296, fo. 330).

[196] Numbers of soloists given in F:Pan, L 863, No. 10; evidence of the responsory in all 3 ordinaries.

donor usually provided for a Mass to be sung on a certain day (or days) each year up until his death. Upon his death, this service was to be converted to an anniversary.

The endowment of Charles V in 1373 provides an interesting example of how foundations were made.[197] Charles ordered two Masses to be celebrated daily in the chapel of John the Baptist (Pl. 4), the place which he likewise designated for his burial. In addition, he called for special prayers for his soul in the votive Masses for the Holy Spirit on Mondays, for John the Baptist on Fridays, and for the Virgin on Saturdays. He provided for eight monks to carry out these celebrations, and also for candles and other appurtenances in the chapel. After his death, the Masses would become four solemn anniversaries. The one on the day of his death should be celebrated like that of Philip IV, described below. Three other anniversaries were to be executed in the weeks following the feasts of Pentecost, Assumption, and Saint Denis, respectively, and two Masses should be recited daily for the Virgin, John the Baptist, and Saints Denis and Agnes.

These details of Charles's foundation are among the most extensive recorded at Saint-Denis; other foundations tend to be less specific. No polyphony or other specially composed music is mentioned here or in any other endowment at Saint-Denis. The ordinaries of Saint-Denis, and especially F:Pan, L 863, No. 10, provide more information on how the anniversaries were actually carried out. The instructions in these sources are similar to those for the liturgical festivals of the church, so much so that it is possible to compare the different levels of anniversaries with the various ranks of feasts that have already been discussed, as will be evident from the anniversaries described in F:Pan, L 863, No. 10.

King Philip Augustus (d. 1223) and King Philip IV (d. 1314)

The solemn anniversary described earlier for Dagobert was employed twice annually in the thirteenth century: on 19 January for Dagobert and, with a few changes, for King Philip Augustus (d. 1223) on 14 July.[198] By the mid-fourteenth century, however, only Dagobert was

[197] Records of Charles V's foundation in the Saint-Denis archives are found in several documents, among them F:Pan, LL 1177, pp. 147–57; and F:Pan, LL 1323, fos. 38^{r-v}.

[198] The service for Philip appears in F:Pm 526, fos. 146^{r-v}; and in F:Pn, lat. 976, fos. 107^{r-v}. While the descriptions of First Vespers, Matins, and Mass given above for Dagobert pertain to the commemoration of Philip as well, the other hours of Philip's anniversary belonged to Saint Phocas, with whom he shared the day (14 July). Other marks of slightly lessened ceremony for Philip include the performance of the reading about Philip in the chapter office by a youth from the choir stalls (*juvenis de stallo*) instead of by a priest, and the singing of the invitatory psalm by 4 soloists in the choir rather than *inter duo altaria*.

honoured in this fashion, and the elaborateness of Philip's service had diminished. The performance of his Vespers and Matins henceforth was like that of Hilary's duplex feast described above,[199] and the number of participants in the Mass was similarly reduced.[200] F:Pan, L 863, No. 10 shows that Philip IV (29 November) and other monarchs with strong ties to the abbey were honoured in like fashion:[201] Charles IV (1 February), Louis X (5 June), Philip III (5 October), and Louis VIII (6, 7, or 8 November). Robert II (20 July) and Louis VI (2 August) had approximately the same type of observance, except that a youth from the choir-stalls (*juvenis de stallo*) read a lesson in their honour in the chapter Office on the day before their respective anniversaries.[202] Earlier in the thirteenth century, the Requiem Mass for Robert was more ornate. Celebrated much like the service for Dagobert, it included the censing of his tomb from the beginning of the gospel to the end of the offertory.[203]

The anniversary of Charles the Bald (6 October) was likewise ushered in by a youth from the stalls, who read a lesson in the chapter office on the previous day.[204] Matins for Charles was evidently less sumptuous early in the thirteenth century, with only two, three, and four soloists on the third, sixth, and ninth responsories.[205] These numbers were increased to three, four, and five by the time F:Pn, lat. 976 was copied (*c.*1258), and the responsories themselves were changed

199 Specifically, the first psalmodic antiphon at First Vespers was intoned by the *hebdomadarius* and the others by those in the choir. The responsory was sung by 4 in copes, the versicle by 2 boys, and the Magnificat antiphon was chanted twice. 2 thurifers were present. At Matins, the 9 responsories were performed by: (1) 2 soloists in the choir, (2) 2 boys, (3) 3 monk-priests, (4) 2 youths on the floor of the choir, (5) 2 senior monks, (6) 4 *priores*, (7) 2 youths in the choir stalls, (8) 2 senior monks, and (9) the cantor with 4 others (5 in all); F:Pan, L 863, No. 10, fo. 140.

200 The rubrics for Mass state 'et celebretur magna missa festive'; ibid. It is likely that 'festive' refers to the anniversary for Philip IV (d. 29 Nov. 1314) which, because it falls earliest in the liturgical year, is written out in full at the beginning of the section of anniversaries in F:Pan, L 863, No. 10, fos. 135ᵛ–136 (Table 6.5). In this service, 2 *cantores* in copes were stationed in the choir for the introit at Mass, and 5 deacons and 5 subdeacons took part in the procession. The 2 singers in the choir performed the soloistic parts of the gradual, and 4 monk-priests in copes chanted the sequence, while the bells were rung as in the Mass for Dagobert. There is no mention of incense during this service; F:Pan, L 863, No. 10, fo. 136. The only other slight variation was at Lauds, where the antiphon to the Benedictus was chanted twice instead of 3 times. Many of the succeeding services in this MS hark back to Philip IV.

201 Ibid. For the death-dates of these kings, see the notes to the calendar in App. A. Their anniversaries are found in F:Pan, L 863, No. 10, fos. 135ᵛ–141ᵛ (Table 6.5). The only differences between the anniversaries for these kings and that for Philip Augustus were at Matins, where the 8th responsory was executed by 2 instead of 3 senior monks; and at Lauds, where the antiphon to the Benedictus was chanted once instead of twice.

202 F:Pan, L 863, No. 10, fo. 140ᵛ. Louis is also mentioned in F:Pm 526 (fo. 153ᵛ), where the rubrics hark back to the anniversary for Robert.

203 Fos. 108ᵛ–109. F:Pm 526 gives almost the same instructions, except that the procession to the altar consists of 5 instead of 7 deacons and subdeacons (fo. 148).

204 F:Pn, lat. 976, fo. 132ᵛ; F:Pan, L 863, No. 10, fo. 141.

205 F:Pm 526, fos. 178ʳ⁻ᵛ.

to the special series which was reserved for the most highly esteemed royalty.[206] Paradoxically, his Mass was more festive in the first ordinary F:Pm 526, which calls for a ceremony like Dagobert's, whereas F:Pn, lat. 976 and F:Pan, L 863, No. 10 reduce the Mass to the level of Philip Augustus and Philip IV.[207]

Queen Margaret of Provence (d. 1295)

The ordinary F:Pan, L 863, No. 10 provides a simpler format for Margaret of Provence (23 December), wife of Louis IX, and for other nobility. This service differs in several respects from the solemnity shown the kings named above, and it most closely resembles the twelve-lesson feasts in the regular liturgy of the abbey. The antiphon to the Magnificat at First Vespers was chanted only once. At Matins the important third, sixth, and ninth responsories were sung by two, three, and four soloists, respectively. The two singers on the floor who ruled the choir performed the first responsory, and the remaining pieces were executed by one boy on the second responsory, one youth from the floor of the choir (*juvenis de raya*) on the fourth, one senior monk on the fifth, one youth from the choir-stalls on the seventh, and one senior monk on the eighth. The celebrations of Lauds and of Mass were like those for the kings just named, except that no thurifers are mentioned at Lauds.[208] In addition to Margaret, the royalty commemorated in this slightly less solemn fashion included: King Philip V (3 January), Count Philip of Boulogne (18 January),[209] Queen Isabel of Aragon (28 January), Count Alphonse of Poitou and Toulouse (26, 27 August), and Queen Blanche of Castille (27 November).[210]

Abbot Giles (d. 1325)

The anniversaries of five abbots of Saint-Denis and one cardinal, described in F:Pan, L 863, No. 10, combine elements of the obsequies

[206] F:Pn, lat. 976 states that Charles's anniversary (fo. 132^{v}) is to be conducted like that of King Robert, which called for these same responsories (see Ch. 3).

[207] Ibid.; and F:Pan, L 863, No. 10, fo. 141.

[208] Ibid. fos. 136^{r-v}.

[209] F:Pan, L 863, No. 10, fo. 137. F:Pm 526 contains only a title rubric for this feast (fo. 99^{v}), and F:Pn, lat. 976 (fo. 161^{v}) states simply that his anniversary is to be celebrated like that of Abbot Suger, described below. The anniversary for Philip of Boulogne is the last one contained in F:Pn, lat. 976, and it appears in a the section at the end of the MS marked *Incipiunt anniversaria*, following the observance for Suger. It seems clear that there were once other anniversaries in the subsequent folios, which are now lost. The calendar of F:Pn, lat. 976 records many additional obits (see App. A), and the services for Suger and Count Philip, which are the first and second, respectively, of the calendar year (12/14 and 18 Jan.), were naturally entered at the head of this truncated section of the MS. The anniversaries in F:Pan, L 863, No. 10 are ordered similarly, except that they occur in the order of the liturgical year, beginning with Philip IV on 29 Nov.

[210] See the notes to the Calendar in App. A for more information on these persons.

already mentioned. The service for Abbot Giles (30 December), standing as the prototype for the others, calls for a youth from the choir floor to read the lesson in the chapter Office on the preceding day. First Vespers and Mass were celebrated as on the anniversaries of Philip IV and Philip Augustus, while Matins and Lauds were patterned after the equivalent hours in Margaret's anniversary.[211] Giles's observance is slightly higher in rank than Margaret's, on account of the reading in the chapter Office and because the antiphon to the Magnificat was sung twice at First Vespers. His service probably corresponds to the semi-duplex observances at Saint-Denis. Besides Giles, the persons commemorated in this way were Abbots Guido of Châtres (21 February), Renaud Giffart (11 March),[212] Eudes Clément (5 May), Matthew of Vendôme (26 September), and Cardinal William of Braye.[213] The anniversary for the ever-popular Abbot Suger (12, 14 January) was solemnized in this manner in the fourteenth century,[214] but in the thirteenth century, his Mass apparently was even more splendid. F:Pn, lat. 976 calls for a Requiem like Dagobert's, except that five, instead of seven, deacons and subdeacons took part in the procession to the altar.[215]

Abbot Peter of Auteuil (d. 1229)

The anniversaries of two other abbots, along with a princess and three prelates, were somewhat less ornate in the fourteenth century. The observance for Abbot Peter of Auteuil (7 February) calls for only one *cantor* as soloist on the ninth responsory at Matins, which was changed from the usual *Congregati sunt* to *Libera me de morte*.[216] The remaining hours and Mass were conducted in the same manner as the services for Queen Margaret. Anniversaries celebrated in this way, in addition to Peter's, were those for Abbot William of Macouris (4 March),[217] Pope

[211] F:Pan, L 863, No. 10, fo. 136^{v}.

[212] The anniversary for Renaud is exceptional in the omission of the chapter reading; F:Pan, L 863, No. 10, fo. 139^{v}.

[213] For information on all except William of Braye, see the notes to the calendar in App. A. William's name does not appear in any extant calendar. He served variously as dean of the cathedral of Laon, archdeacon of Reims, and cardinal at Saint Mark's, and he died at Orvieto on 19 or 29 Apr. 1282; Chevalier, *Bio-Bibliographie*, i. 1934. It is not clear what his connection with Saint-Denis might have been.

[214] F:Pan, L 863, No. 10, fo. 137.

[215] F:Pn, lat. 976, fos. 161^{r-v}. The rubrics for the service for Count Philip of Boulogne (18 Jan.) refer back to Suger; ibid. fo. 161^{v} (see n. 209 above).

[216] F:Pan, L 863, No. 10, fos. 138^{v}–139.

[217] William's anniversary is also described in a 13th-c. necrology: 'In Vigilia dicti anniversarii primos versus puer incipiat a *Placebo* et *Dirige*, priores cantabunt vi responsa in frocis, in crastino per tres fiat commendatio. Deinde celebretur missa ad majus altare. Ebdomadarius et ministri altaris habeant vestimenta pulcriora que fecit R. [responsorium] a iii in capis, et tractus a iiii in cappis'; Molinier, *Obituaires* i/1, 311.

Martin IV (29 March), Archbishop Peter of Cosenza (1 April), Princess Blanche,[218] and Cardinal John Cholet (30 July).[219]

Abbot Yves (d. 1173?)

Certain others were not accorded a full day of services, but only a morning Mass (*missa matutinalis*) celebrated in copes. In the morning Mass, there was no commendation after Terce and no procession to the altar. The choir was ruled by two youths on the floor, who also chanted the solo sections of the introit and gradual. Four monk-priests sang the tract. The anniversaries observed in this way were for Abbot Yves (14 February),[220] Queen Mary of Brabant (?),[221] Abbot Adam (19 February), Abbot Hugh of Milan (18 April), Pope Innocent III (16 July), Abbot William of Gap (29 July), Kings Louis III and Henry I (commemorated together on 4 August), Queen Constance (7 October),[222] Abbot Hugh Foucault (26 October), and the triple anniversary of the three Abbots Hilduin, Eudes of Deuil, and Eudes Taverny (30 October).

Other Descriptions of Anniversaries

The record of anniversaries found in F:Pan, L 863, No. 10, is the most complete source of its kind from Saint-Denis. Similar information continues down to the seventeenth and eighteenth centuries, but with fewer specifics. A fourteenth-century necrology, for instance, includes this type of entry: 'Ob. Suggerii abbatis. Semiduplum'.[223] Other documents, given such titles as 'Syllabus Anniversariorum'[224] or 'Extrait du partage du sujet des obits Anniversaires et fondations',[225] list anniversaries by rank. There are slight differences from one list to the next concerning who is placed at what level; but Dagobert's service is always the most splendid, other kings are next, followed by queens, abbots of Saint-Denis, and others, arranged among the various degrees of ceremony, just as we have seen in F:Pan, L 863, No. 10.

The monks were faithful to their charge to keep these services alive, and indeed their seriousness of purpose is evident both in the perdur-

[218] Blanche (d. 17 June 1320), daughter of Louis IX, does not figure in any calendar of Saint-Denis; see Molinier, *Obituaires*, i/1. 340.

[219] See the notes to the calendar in App. A for information on these persons.

[220] Yves is the model for this service; F:Pan, L 863, No. 10, fo. 139.

[221] Not found in the calendar of Saint-Denis. By her placement in F:Pan, L 863, No. 10, she is probably Queen Mary of Brabant, the 2nd wife of Philip III. She died on 10 Jan. 1321; Saillot, *Reines*, 206; cf. Molinier, *Obituaires*, i/1. 338, who reports the year 1322.

[222] Constance's anniversary also appears in F:Pm 526, fos. 178ᵛ–179. The only difference in this description is the assignment of 3 to the tract instead of 4.

[223] Molinier, *Obituaires*, i/1. 338 (from F:Pan, LL 1320).

[224] F:Pan, L 836, No. 1.

[225] Ibid. No. 3.

ability of the anniversaries in the liturgy and in the high level of solemnity that was assigned to many. Sometimes the very inscription of an anniversary into the calendar graphically depicts the respect that the Sandionysians nurtured for their benefactors. The precise death-day of Louis VIII (8 November) was guarded in the thirteenth-century calendar, even at the expense of unseating the Octave of All Saints by one day. Although the situation was corrected by reversing the two observances in the fourteenth century, their initial placement suggests that the monks preferred historical accuracy over liturgical uniformity.[226] In a similar decision, mentioned earlier, the anniversary of the recently deceased King Philip V (d. 3 January 1322) ousted the feast of Saint Geneviève, transferring it to 5 January, a remarkable occurrence given that she was the patron saint of Paris and that her feast had been celebrated at Saint-Denis on 3 January since time immemorial. Anniversaries for royal figures sometimes caused other observances that fell on the same day to be reduced to commemorations: King Philip Augustus (d. 1223) overshadowed the feast of Phocas on 14 July, and Count Alphonse of Poitou (d. 1271) similarly eclipsed the feast of Saint Rufus (27 August).

RECEPTION OF THE *ORIFLAMME* AND CORONATIONS OF QUEENS

Dagobert's anniversary, the oldest and most solemn of all these services, stood unchanged from the twelfth to at least the mid-sixteenth century. Two other royally motivated observances likewise were heard in the abbey, but neither lasted as long as this. Beginning in the twelfth century, the king traditionally received the battle standard of France, the *Oriflamme*,[227] from the abbot of Saint-Denis. The ceremony took place during a solemn Mass celebrated in the presence of the king, who came to the abbey to pray for the success of his campaign and to take up the emblem.[228] Preliminary ceremonies were held in the Chapel of Saint Clement in the cloister, after which the monarch made his way processionally into the church. He prayed at the main altar on which the relics of Saints Denis, Rusticus, and Eleutherius were customarily displayed for the duration of the strife. The *Oriflamme* was blessed by touching it to the holy relics, while the choir, on the occasion of Charles VI's reception of the standard before his campaign against the Duke of

[226] No doubt the pressure to maintain the correct day for Louis's anniversary diminished as time separated the abbey from the year of his death (1226). In addition, the commemoration of the Octave of All Saints on the wrong day must have become awkward.

[227] On the history of the *Oriflamme*, see the discussion above in Ch. 1; Contamine, 'Oriflamme'; Crosby, *Abbey*, 11–12; Spiegel, *Chronicle*, 30–1, all of which give further bibliography.

[228] On the liturgy of the *Oriflamme*, see Contamine, 'Oriflamme', 203–13.

Burgundy in 1414, chanted the Ant. *O beate Dyonisi.*[229] The abbot then sang Mass and, having blessed the banner, presented it to the king.[230] The chroniclers of Charles VI mention the precise moment of the delivery of the standard, reporting that the king received the *Oriflamme* 'toward the end of Mass, namely, at the Agnus Dei'.[231] No specially created music is known to have been written for these events, and the ritual died in the fifteenth century, when Charles VII (1422–61) adopted the *cornette blanche* as the principal banner of France.[232]

While the consecration of kings usually took place in the cathedral of Reims,[233] the coronation of Anne of Brittany at Saint-Denis in 1491 set a precedent for the location of subsequent coronations of French queens in the abbey.[234] Because of the importance and grandeur of these services, the elaborate accounts which have survived tell who was present, what they wore, how the church was decorated, and the like. Most often, however, the information on the coronation Mass itself is disappointing, revealing simply that the ceremony was extremely solemn.[235] Only on rare occasions are there precious details describing some of the music that was heard in the church. The account of the coronation of Claude of France (1517), wife of Francis I, is exception-

[229] On the liturgy of the *Oriflamme*, see Contamine, 'Oriflamme', 207.

[230] The continuator of the chronicle of Guillaume de Nangis describes the reception of the *Oriflamme* by Philip VI in 1328 in these terms; Géraud, *Chronique*, ii. 92–3; see also Félibien, *Histoire*, 270.

[231] Juvénal, *Charles VI*, 275; Bellaguet, *Chronique*, v. 284–5; Félibien, *Histoire*, 333.

[232] Ibid. 335. On the decline of the use of the *Oriflamme*, see Contamine, 'Oriflamme', 234–44.

[233] On the crowning of French kings, see the recent work of Jackson, *Vive*; idem, 'Manuscrits'; and the classic study of Schramm, *König*, all of which deal with the history of the coronation in France and cite relevant bibliography. The 1st king to be anointed, Pepin the Short (751) was anointed a 2nd time at Saint-Denis in 754 along with his sons Charlemagne and Carloman, as mentioned in Ch. 1. In the 12th c., the monks' claim of Saint Denis as royal protector grew (with the help of a forged charter attributed to Charlemagne) to the point that they challenged the primacy of Reims in the matter of coronations; Schramm, *König*, i. 131–42, 204–5; Folz, *Coronation*, 217–21; Schramm, *König*, i. 131–42. In fact, certain kings put on their crowns a second time at Saint-Denis (Louis VII in 1131, Philip Augustus in 1180, Louis XII in 1498, and Francis I in 1515), after having earlier been consecrated at Reims. The partisan accounts of these 'crownings' at Saint-Denis, usually written by persons connected with the abbey, overemphasize the role of the monastery in this ceremony (Félibien, *Histoire*, 203–4, 371, 377; also Folz, *Coronation*, 219–20; Baldwin, *Philip*, 375), for any act of receiving the crown, whether at Saint-Denis or at Reims, was secondary to the more important ceremony of anointment (see Jackson, *Vive*, 3), which the monks of the abbey were never able to appropriate for themselves. In any case, no musical details of the kingly coronations at Saint-Denis have survived; see e.g. Félibien's terse statement that Francis I was crowned 'with great solemnity' (*Histoire*, 377).

[234] On the coronation of Anne, wife of Charles VIII and later of Louis XII, see Schramm, *König*, i. 141–2; Godefroy, *Cérémonial françois*, i. 469; Félibien, *Histoire*, 368. The biographers of Philip Augustus, Rigord and Guillaume le Breton report that Philip's wife, Isabel of Hainaut, had been consecrated at Saint-Denis in 1180 (Delaborde, *Œuvres*, i. 20–1, 180; Félibien, *Histoire*, 203–4), but this seems not to have been a regular occurrence until the late 15th c.

[235] See e.g. the descriptions of the coronations of Marie of England in 1514 (Godefroy, *Cérémonial françois*, i. 471; Félibien, *Histoire*, 376), and of Catherine of Medici in 1549 (Godefroy, *Cérémonial françois*, i. 510; Félibien, *Histoire*, 391–2).

ally rich in particulars.[236] The new queen customarily arrived at Saint-Denis on the eve of her coronation, and Claude was greeted at the door of the abbey with hymns and orations. The following day, she entered the church as the *Te Deum* was sung. After a prayer, she was anointed and crowned in front of the high altar and then was conducted to her throne. The celebration of Mass ensued, with the cardinal legate of Luxembourg officiating. Singers from the royal chapel formed the choir, and several instruments accompanied them.[237] Claude, who had remained seated since the beginning of the Mass, rose at the reading of the gospel to signify her intention to defend the faith.[238] At the end of the service, the new queen returned to her lodgings to the strains of joyful music.

Clearly, the abbot and monks of Saint-Denis were not solely responsible for these festivities for the queen—they effectively handed over the execution of the Mass to musicians and prelates from outside the abbey. At most they may have assumed a subservient role as singers for certain parts of the Mass, but their musical training probably did not include the special motets and other compositions which were no doubt used. When polyphonic music and instruments were heard in the abbey during these majestic ceremonies, it was apparently not a sound they were particularly accustomed to, nor was it of their making.

Apart from the obituary notices, the calendar of Saint-Denis contains few striking or inexplicable features. The abbey, like every religious house in Western Christendom, recognized the ancient feasts of the Gregorian and Gelasian traditions. Similarly, the saints whose deeds often accounted for numerous pages in the early history of the region of Paris were commemorated by all churches in the area. The dispersal of relics throughout France distinguished one community from another, and each house was liturgically solicitous of the handful of saints whose

[236] Godefroy, *Cérémonial de France*, 168–80; idem, *Cérémonial françois*, i. 477–8; Félibien, *Histoire*, 378–9.

[237] Reports of this Mass clearly state that instruments were played: 'Le Cardinal de Luxembourg commença la messe qui fut chantée par les chantres de la chapelle du Roy au son de plusieurs instrumens'; ibid. 378; Godefroy, *Cérémonial françois*, i. 477–8; idem, *Cérémonial de France*, 167. While the a cappella Mass was the norm in the 15th c., instruments came to be used increasingly in the church in the 16th c., and their presence on such important occasions as a queen's coronation was certainly possible; McKinnon, 'Representations', 44–52. On the composition of the royal chapel in the early sixteenth century, see Brenet, *Musiciens*, 45–71. The instrumentalists may well have come from Francis's *musique de chambre*, described in Prunières, 'Musique', 219–36. Singers from the royal chapel were likewise present for the coronation of Eleanor of Austria at Saint-Denis in 1531, although no instruments are mentioned; Godefroy, *Cérémonial françois*, i. 487 ff.; and Félibien, *Histoire*, 384–6.

[238] An antiphon was sung just before the gospel on the highest feasts and on the most important anniversaries (see Ch. 4 and 5). Descriptions of the coronation Mass, however, do not mention the chant.

remains it possessed. Especially after the tenth century, monastic calendars were influenced by such central forces as Cluny and Rome, but Saint-Denis often resisted these authorities, just as it later refused to adopt several of the new Marian feasts greatly favoured by the lay populace. While the liturgies of other churches continued to take shape almost until the Council of Trent,[239] the Saint-Denis calendar was a *fait accompli* by the mid-fourteenth century.

The force that probably caused the cessation of growth in the abbatial calendar, while those at other churches continued to expand, were the anniversaries. These constituted the truly distinctive element of the liturgy of Saint-Denis and were in place in large number by the fourteenth century.[240] With the consent of no pontiff, the monks effectively canonized their ancient champion King Dagobert when they reckoned him among the number of saints worthy of highest esteem.[241] The services that commemorated this Merovingian monarch and several of his royal successors served only to enhance his cult. In matters of ceremony, these anniversaries were comparable to the *annuale* of Christmas at the highest level, and to the major duplex celebrations of saints with relics in the abbey at the lowest.[242] What is more, their introduction into the calendar and the liturgy in the twelfth century coincided precisely with the inception of the chronicle tradition at Saint-Denis.[243] Just as the *Gesta Gentis Francorum* first betrays the royalist viewpoint that was to become characteristic of the chronicles, so the Saint-Denis calendar took on a regal aspect at this time. The steady stream of obituary services that transfused the liturgy in fact parallels the era of composition of royal histories in the abbey, and these celebrations endured even after the completion of the *Grandes Chroniques* in the fifteenth century. Recent scholarship has determined that the historical works that emanated from Saint-Denis in the Middle

[239] By the end of the Middle Ages, divergence among calendars was so great that the official Roman calendar, contained in the new breviary (1568) and missal (1570), was imposed on all churches who were unable to prove a heritage of at least 2 cs. of distinctive usage; 'Calendar', 165.

[240] Foley, basing his observations on the liturgy of Saint-Denis on the content of a single ordinary (F:Pm 526), considers the anniversaries to be relatively unimportant because they were fewer in number in the brief time during which F:Pm 526 was in effect (1234 to *c.*1258 at the latest, and probably only until about 1241); 'Ordinary', ii. 222–3, 234–8, 241–4, and *passim*. His limited analysis does not account for the numerous anniversaries that had been added to the ritual of Saint-Denis by 1364.

[241] Hesbert points out that the use of the word *natale* (In *natale dagoberti regis*) in the rubric that introduces the anniversary service in F:Pn, lat. 17296 (fo. 327; *CAO*, ii, No. 146) reveals the monks' would-be portrayal of Dagobert as saint; ibid. p. xiv.

[242] The choice of colour for the names listed in the calendar of the mid-14th-c. missal GB:Lva 1346–1891 aptly illustrates the monks' regard for Dagobert's feast in the mid-14th c. His entry (19 Jan.) is written in gold letters which, apart from the obit for the recently deceased Abbot Guido of Châtres (d. 1350, obit 21 Feb.), are reserved for the *annuale* feasts: Christmas, Saint Denis, etc.

[243] Spiegel, *Chronicle*, 11, 40–1, 125.

Ages made the monks worthy of the title 'official custodians of the royal myth'.[244] Their activities as keeper of the regalia were not limited to writing royalist chronicles—indeed, they sanctified their alliance with the Crown by interpolating anniversaries of kings into their sacred calendar and liturgy.

[244] Ibid. 11.

3

Introduction to Liturgy and Music at Saint-Denis

The special feasts and rites described in Chapter 2 shaped the calendar of Saint-Denis over several centuries and distinguished the abbey from other houses. Within these celebrations, certain ceremonial and musical features likewise stand apart from those of pre-eminent institutions in Paris and throughout the West. Chapters 3 and 4 survey the most telling of these traits. The history of the chant tradition at Saint-Denis is treated first, followed by a discussion of the series of alleluias for the Sundays after Pentecost and the lists of responsories for Matins of the Office of the Dead. The hymns for the Office, the tones for the invitatory, the Gloria Patri, and the neumas of the Sandionysian liturgy are sketched to the extent that they are available for study in the extant sources. The repertories of tropes and sequences at Saint-Denis are then described in some depth, along with the collections for the Benedicamus Domino and Ite Missa Est, melodies of particular importance at Saint-Denis. These significant aspects of the liturgy naturally are not the only ones represented in the extant manuscripts, but they are the most prominent.

Chapter 4 continues the discussion of a different aspect of Sandionysian ritual and music. There, the focus is on the special ways in which the liturgy was connected to the architectural, artistic, and political fabric of the Church. In both chapters the contemporaneous uses of other establishments serve in some cases as points of comparison, so that the ritual and music at Saint-Denis can be evaluated not only in the light of the overall liturgical history of the abbey, but also alongside customs that existed side by side with them.

CHANT TRADITION

In the volumes of *Le Graduel romain* currently available, the monks of Solesmes have set out to establish a critical edition of the Roman gradual, trying to recreate as closely as possible the 'authentic' state of the book that was disseminated in the Carolingian empire at the end of the eighth century.[1] In a comparison of portions of the Gregorian

[1] To date vols. ii, iv/1, and iv/2 have appeared. See the summary of the process employed by Solesmes in *GR*, iv/2. 91–2; and in Froger, 'Edition'.

repertory in some 400 manuscripts, the first phases of the project uncovered nine principal lines of the chant tradition, each represented by a different source. So far it has proved impossible to extract from these branches one or more lines which are closer to the 'archetype', and it seems that these nine versions are more or less independent and equal in their level of descent from the presumed original source. The remaining manuscripts fall into groups which revolve around one of the nine main branches. Sources within the same group tend to favour one another in terms of their place of origin, their musical notation, the history of the houses in which they were written, and the languages spoken in the areas from which they come.

One of the nine fundamental traditions, representing the region of the Île-de-France and its environs, is headed by the earliest extant gradual from Saint-Denis, the eleventh-century F:Pm 384. Along with the slightly later augmented sacramentary F:Pn, lat. 9436, F:Pm 384 depicts the chant of Saint-Denis in its oldest recoverable state.[2] F:Pm 384, moreover, seems to preserve features characteristic of a period prior to the eleventh century, among which are the alleluia list and the trope to the Comm. *Video celos*, discussed further on. In the light of the dependency of Saint-Denis on the cathedral of Paris in the Merovingian period, one might assume that the readings in F:Pm 384 and F:Pn, lat. 9436 would resemble those in Parisian books. Such might well have been the case in the ninth century, but the surviving sources from the cathedral date from the late Middle Ages, a time at which a more recent chant tradition took hold, and these books have little in common with F:Pm 384. For this reason, the music in F:Pm 384 is singularly important, not only for the history of the ancient French tradition in general, but also because it is apparently the most faithful representative of the Gregorian tradition among extant Parisian sources. The monks of Saint-Denis must have taken fierce pride in their venerable practice, for Solesmes comparisons likewise show that sources for the Mass from the abbey kept their autonomy even after the Cluniac reform of the late tenth century.[3]

Other manuscripts, though not from Saint-Denis, also portray the state of Gregorian chant found in the old Saint-Denis tradition, for example the tenth-century Mont-Renaud manuscript,[4] and a number of English books.[5] The presence of insular sources seems surprising, but these manuscripts evidently transmit many of the musical readings

[2] *GR*, iv/1. 261–2. [3] Ibid., and 258–60.

[4] See the discussion of this source in Ch. 6.

[5] These include the 12th-c. Irish gradual GB:Ob, Rawl. c. 892, and the 13th-c. antiphoner and gradual from Worcester, GB:WO, F 160 (edited in *PM*, xii); see *GR*, iv/1. 261–2. For others, see Hiley, 'Traditions', 30.

which may have come to England during the monastic reforms of the second half of the tenth century.[6] The precise reasons for the connection between these sources and the early Saint-Denis books (F:Pm 384 and F:Pn, lat. 9436) are difficult to pin-point, since the extent of the participation of Saint-Denis in these reforms is unclear. The similarities between the Mont-Renaud manuscript and the early Saint-Denis sources, on the other hand, parallel the liturgical and musical relationships discussed in Chapter 7. But Solesmes shows that there are differences due to the geographical separation of the Saint-Denis and Mont-Renaud books,[7] and other discrepancies likewise suggest that the Mont-Renaud source more closely reflects the practices either of Corbie or of Saint-Éloi of Noyon.

The newer Sandionysian sources for the Mass studied by Solesmes are the thirteenth- and fourteenth-century missals F:Pn, lat. 1107 and F:Pn, lat. 10505. These books depict the music of Saint-Denis in a more recent state, one which departed from the older tradition probably when the shift from neumatic to square notation occurred,[8] and one which is closer to other Parisian sources, especially in the repertories of sequences and tropes.[9] In this later form the music of Saint-Denis was transmitted from Saint-Denis to Saint-Corneille of Compiègne in the twelfth and thirteenth centuries, as witnessed in the agreement of musical readings from these houses.[10]

Adopting a similar methodology, Dom Hesbert searched diligently for the 'archetype' Roman antiphoner, analysing the content and arrangement of the responsory series for the Office of Matins for Advent and for the rogation days in Advent, and scrutinizing the choice of verses for the Advent responsories.[11] In this quest, Hesbert employed some 900 antiphoners and breviaries, including F:Pm 384, F:Pn, lat. 17296, and GB:Ob, Can. lit. 192 from Saint-Denis. While his methodology is currently under review,[12] his findings generally seem to corroborate the studies of Solesmes, showing a tendency toward antiquity in the liturgy of the abbey. The manuscripts from Saint-Denis form a remarkably homogeneous group, one which lies at the heart of a collection of sources which Hesbert calls the 'French monastic group', centred in the area of the Île-de-France.[13] He likewise suggests that this group was elaborated from the older 'French Roman group' by the

[6] These include the 12th-c. Irish gradual GB:Ob, Rawl. c. 892, and the 13th-c. antiphoner and gradual from Worcester, GB:WO, F 160 (edited in *PM*, xii); see *GR*, iv/1. 261–2. For others, see Hiley, 'Traditions', 9.

[7] *GR*, iv/2. 39.

[8] Ibid. 261–2, 282.

[9] See Hiley, 'Traditions', 26, 28.

[10] See Robertson, 'Transmission'.

[11] Hesbert, *CAO*, vols. v, vi. Another explanation of the author's comparative techniques can be found in Hesbert, 'Sarum'.

[12] See e.g. the recent discussion in Möller, 'Research', which summarizes the criticisms of other authors.

[13] Hesbert, *CAO*, v. 372, 440, 477–80.

addition of three responsories to the nine of the Roman series. This particular 'French Roman group', Hesbert concludes, represents the type used in the area of Tournai–Reims–Chartres, and is a branch of the French Roman series which broke away no later than the eleventh century from the Germanic version that lies closest to the original source.[14] In this indirect way, Hesbert proposes a relationship of the Saint-Denis manuscripts to the 'archetype' in terms of the liturgical ordering of the items he studied.

Hesbert demonstrates that one late Parisian source, the fifteenth-century breviary from Saint-Magloire F:Pm 346, preserves the ancient Île-de-France tradition along with the three Saint-Denis manuscripts just mentioned.[15] Not surprisingly, the nearest neighbours to the Saint-Denis sources at Hesbert's next 'level of distance' are those from Mont-Renaud and Saint-Corneille of Compiègne, which likewise show affinities for the books for the Mass from Saint-Denis.[16] The subsequent level includes several manuscripts from north-eastern France (Amiens, Corbie) and England (Ely, Hyde Abbey, Worcester).[17] Like the gradual of Saint-Denis, the Office-books from the abbey owe little to the influence of Cluny. On the contrary, it is clear from the close agreement of all the Sandionysian sources and their attachments to books of similarly ancient traditions that the monks of Saint-Denis resisted the musical and liturgical standardizations of the Cluniac reform.

ALLELUIAS FOR SUNDAYS AFTER PENTECOST

The alleluias for Mass on the Sundays between Pentecost and Advent provide an important clue to the place of use of a manuscript.[18] The order of chants for these 23 or more weeks became fixed late in the evolution of the gradual, and consequently the alleluias often do not appear within individual services in manuscripts of the ninth and tenth centuries.[19] Instead, they are grouped into a list at the end of the Pentecost cycle, while a rubric such as *quale volueris* ('whichever one you wish') in each Mass formulary indicates that an alleluia should be selected freely from this collection. The choices that each church made were highly individual, and, after a time, a series of alleluias was

[14] Ibid. 372; vi. 147–9, 237.

[15] Ibid. v. 427. [16] Ibid. 430. [17] Ibid. 432.

[18] See the study of a number of post-Pentecost alleluia lists from England and northern France in Hiley, 'Traditions', 2–3. The author points out that, although Walter Frere discovered this method of connecting a source with a particular establishment, Dom Gabriel Beyssac was the first scholar who systematically applied it, mostly in unpublished work; ibid. 11, n. 3; also Beyssac, 'Mont-Renaud', 133; Huglo, 'Listes', 219; idem, 'Remarques'.

[19] Examples of this peculiarity are given in Hesbert, *AMS*, pp. cxix–cxx.

formalized in each institution and remained invariable in the later sources from that place. Because the arrangement differs from one house to another, it serves as a test of origin for a gradual or missal. By the twelfth century, either the alleluias were written within each Mass after Pentecost, or their incipits directed the cantor to the collection at the end of the *temporale*.[20]

The verses of alleluias were drawn from the texts of psalms, and most establishments arrange the post-Pentecost series in ascending numerical order according to the Book of Psalms.[21] In contrast, the alleluia lists of several churches—among them, Saint-Corneille of Compiègne, Reims, Saint-Denis of Reims, Meaux, Angers, Verdun, Saint-Médard of Soissons, Saint-Martin of Tours, Senlis, Corbie, Metz, and Winchester in England—all begin with the Ver. *In te domine speravi*, based on Ps. 30 (Vulgate numbering).[22] They subsequently differ from one another to varying degrees, taking the psalms in random numerical order. The series that is particular to Saint-Denis joins those that begin with the Alle. Ver. *In te domine speravi* (Table 3.1).

This list from Saint-Denis is distinct not only from those in which *In te domine speravi* comes at the head, but also from the numerically ordered lists established for the standardized Cistercian, Dominican, and Franciscan orders.[23] The cathedral of Metz begins its series of alleluias with *In te domine speravi*, and it is possible that this church, so intimately involved in the Carolingian reforms of the late eighth century, may have initially promulgated the lists that start with this verse. A master series issuing from Metz could have been rearranged in the various locations mentioned above, as well as in churches like Notre Dame, whose earliest alleluia series also begins with *In te domine speravi*.

The sequence of alleluias for Pentecost Sundays was firmly implanted at Saint-Denis by the mid-eleventh century (F:Pn, lat. 9436) and remained in use there at least through the time of the last extant missal, the mid-fourteenth century GB:Lva 1346–1891. Only one earlier manuscript varies slightly from the usual order. The eleventh-century gradual F:Pm 384 has two alleluias on the nineteenth Sunday, *Adorabo ad templum* and *Eripe me* (Table 3.1), while *Eripe* appears alone on this Sunday in all later sources from the monastery. *Adorabo* also occurs on Sunday XIX in the closely related lists of Corbie, Meaux, Tours,

[20] In some sources, the alleluias for the Easter season were also notated separately from their Masses; see Hughes, *Manuscripts*, 140–2.

[21] See e.g. the list that is characteristic of Laon in Table 6.4.

[22] Listed in Huglo, 'Remarques', Table I; idem, 'Listes', 226; idem, *Livres*, 104.

[23] D. Delalande gives a comparative table of alleluia lists which includes the Saint-Denis gradual F:Pm 384, along with MSS of German, Italian, Aquitanian, French, English (Sarum), Cistercian, Dominican, and Franciscan provenance; *Prêcheurs*, 15–18.

TABLE 3.1. *Alleluias at Saint-Denis for Sundays after Pentecost compared with the Early Series from Notre Dame*

Sunday	Psalm	Saint-Denis alleluias[c]			Notre Dame alleluias[d]
I	30	*In te domine speravi*			–[a]
II	17	*Diligam te*			–
III	94	*Venite exultemus*			–
	94	*Preoccupemus faciem*			n.g.[b]
IV	104	*Confitemini domino*			–
V	113	*Qui timent dominum*			–
VI	89	*Domine refugium*			–
VII	46	*Omnes gentes*			–
VIII	94	*Quoniam deus magnus*			–
IX	146	*Qui sanat*			–
X	121	*Letatus sum*			–
			XI	80	*Exultate deo*
XI	107	*Paratum cor meum*	XI		–
XII	80	*Exultate deo*			n.g.
XIII	92	*Dominus regnavit*	XII		–
XIV	99	*Jubilate deo*	XIII		–
XV	87	*Domine deus*	XIV		–
XVI	116	*Laudate dominum*	XV		–
XVII	7	*Deus judex*	XVI		–
XVIII	147	*Qui posuit*	XVII		–
XIX	137	*Adorabo ad templum*[e]	XVIII		–
	58	*Eripe me*[f]			n.g.
			XIX	113	*Qui timent dominum*
			XIX	64	*Te decet hymnus*
XX	77	*Attendite popule*	XX	?	*Domine . . .*
XXI	64	*Te decet hymnus*	XXI	129	De profundis
	64	*Replebimur in bonis*			n.g.
XXII	129	*De profundis*	XXII	110	*Redemptionem*
XXIII	117	*Dextera dei*	XXIII		–

[a] –: same alleluia. [b] n.g.: alleluia not given.
[c] Based on F:Pm 384; F:Pn, lat. 9436; F:Pn, lat. 1107; F:Pn, lat. 10505; GB:Lva 1346–1891.
[d] Based on marginal additions in I:Rvat, Ott. lat. 313, ed. in Wilson, *Gregorian*, 168–76.
[e] Given only in F:Pm 384.
[f] Given in all MSS.

Winchester, Bury St Edmunds, Senlis, Reims, and Saint-Denis of Reims. Since F:Pm 384 is the first extant source from the abbey that incorporates an alleluia list, the presence of the Ver. *Adorabo* may suggest that there was originally greater liturgical affinity between Saint-Denis and some of the centres that sang *Adorabo ad templum*.

The correspondences would have diminished as these houses consolidated their own customs in the later Middle Ages.

Another instance of lessening similarity is found in the comparison of two series of post-Pentecost alleluias from Notre Dame with the list from Saint-Denis. The first known series from the cathedral, added to I:Rvat, Ott. lat. 313, strongly resembles the Saint-Denis list (Table 3.1). Only later did Notre Dame adopt an arrangement that begins with the Alle. *Deus judex* (Ps. 7) and continues with the psalm verses in numerical order.[24] The long affiliation of Saint-Denis with Notre Dame during the Merovingian era might explain the kinship of the series from the abbey with the earlier list from Notre Dame. The two houses were disjoined administratively and spiritually by the end of the eighth century, and their liturgies slowly diverged during the ninth and tenth centuries. For a while both churches evidently kept similar alleluia lists for the Sundays after Pentecost, both of which began with *In te domine speravi*. But in the gradual liturgical alienation that followed, Notre Dame eventually reorganized its sequence of alleluias, while Saint-Denis kept the older list.

RESPONSORIES FOR OFFICES OF THE DEAD

Like the order of alleluias for the Sundays after Pentecost, the sequence of responsories for Matins of the Office of the Dead can assist in the localization of manuscripts. The arrangement of these chants differs from one place to another, and may sometimes suggest a region or even a particular house as place of use of a manuscript. While the information thus gained about the history of a manuscript is not always conclusive, the ordering of responsories does vary enough, particularly in the high Middle Ages, to delineate broad geographical patterns of usage.[25] Many establishments had a single list of responsories for Matins, but Saint-Denis used three.[26] Two of these series are unique to the abbey, and hence serve to distinguish some of the Office manuscripts from Saint-Denis to an unusual degree.

In monastery and cathedral alike, the hour of Matins for the Office of the Dead was celebrated in the secular manner, with nine responsories instead of twelve. At Saint-Denis, the earliest example of the standard cycle of responsories for Matins *pro defunctis* survives in the early

[24] See Wright, *Notre Dame*, 65–6.

[25] Dr Knud Ottosen of the Univ. of Aarhus in Denmark has charted these affinities by means of a data base which traces Offices for the Dead from hundreds of medieval institutions. I am grateful to him for sharing his information with me in correspondence noted below.

[26] Only the 2nd and 3rd Offices discussed here are treated in Hesbert, *CAO*, vol. ii, pp. xiv–xv.

thirteenth-century Chapel Hill psalter, and this list also appears in Sandionysian books for the Office from the fourteenth to sixteenth centuries. The list was used for ordinary services of the Dead:[27]

Resp. 1. *Qui lazarum*
2. *Credo quod*
3. *Heu michi*
4. *Ne recorderis*
5. *Domine quando veneris*
6. *Peccantem me*
7. *Domine secundum actum*
8. *Quomodo confitebor* (in the Chapel Hill psalter and F:Pn, lat. 1072)
Memento mei deus quia ventus (in all manuscripts except Chapel Hill)
9. *Libera me domine de viis*

Concordances for the series with *Memento mei* as the eighth responsory are easy to find in other houses in the region of Paris, and even in a few places in England and Germany.[28] The arrangement became fairly standard in late medieval Paris.

A more 'proper' series of responsories for the Office of the Dead at Saint-Denis is found in F:Pm 526[29] and in F:Pn, lat. 976:[30]

Resp. 1. *Absolve domine*
2. *Credo quod*
3. *Manus tue domine*
4. *Ne recorderis*
5. *Domine quando veneris*
6. *Libera me domine de morte*
7. *Domine secundum actum* (used for ordinary Office of the Dead)
Peccantem me (used for certain anniversaries)
8. *Libera me domine de viis*
9. *Ne tradas domine*

The list with *Domine secundum actum* as the seventh responsory provided an option to the one just described for the normal Office for the Dead at Saint-Denis. By replacing *Domine secundum actum* with *Peccantem me* in the third nocturn, the same series was adapted for some of the anniversaries that the monks celebrated annually: Kings

[27] Chapel Hill, Univ. Lib., Rare Book Coll. 11, fos. 165ᵛ–170ᵛ; GB:Ob, Can. Lit. 192, fos. 538–9; F:Pn, lat. 1072, fos. 200–213ᵛ; F:Pn, Rés. B. 5209.

[28] Correspondence with Dr K. Ottosen.

[29] Fos. 70ᵛ, 148, 178.

[30] Fos. 41ᵛ, 161ᵛ.

Robert II (d. 1031) and Charles the Bald (d. 877),[31] Count Philip of Boulogne (d. 1234), Louis VI (d. 1137), and Abbot Suger (d. 1151). This list appears to have been particular to Saint-Denis.[32]

For the burials of the most beloved kings, the monks of Saint-Denis created another series of Matins responsories. These chants are found in the antiphoner, breviaries, and book of Hours under such rubrics as *In natali dagoberti regis*,[33] *In anniversario domni dagoberti*,[34] *In anniversario solemni*,[35] and in the descriptions of anniversaries in the ordinaries. They were used for the observances of Dagobert (d. 639), Philip Augustus (d. 1223), and for Robert II (d. 1031) and Charles the Bald (d. 877) in F:Pn, lat. 976:

Resp. 1. *Absolve domine*
2. *Manus tue*
3. *Quomodo confitebor*
4. *Cognoscimus domine*
5. *Ne tradas domine*
6. *Libera me domine de morte*
7. *Rogamus te*
8. *Deus eterne*
9. *Congregati sunt*[36]

This special list, found first in F:Pn, lat. 17296, was probably compiled by Abbot Adam, who composed the service for Dagobert around 1108. Like the second series given above, the selection and order of responsories in the distinctively 'royal' list appears to have been particular to Saint-Denis. By the late thirteenth or early fourteenth century the monastery of Saint-Corneille of Compiègne had adopted it with only minor reshuffling.[37]

The monks had a good reason for keeping the special *cursus* for Dagobert and other kings alongside the standard list. They buried, after all, not only their colleagues, but also the most august persons in the land, and they were obliged to re-enact the royal interments annually. Accordingly, the community needed distinct levels of ceremony and fine shades of variation within the Office of the Dead to differentiate between occasions of greater and lesser solemnity. In this instance, therefore, the abbey did not bow completely to the tendency

[31] Only F:Pm 526 assigns these responsories to Robert and Charles the Bald; F:Pn, lat. 976 uses the 2nd series below for these 2 kings.

[32] Correspondence with Dr K. Ottosen.

[33] F:Pn, lat. 17296, fos. 328–30.

[34] GB:Ob, Can. Lit. 192, fo. 540.

[35] F:Pn, lat. 1072, fos. 224v–226v; F:Pn, Rés. B. 5209.

[36] The history and dissemination of this final Resp. *Congregati sunt* has been treated in some detail in Hesbert, 'Office', 404–15, and in Sainte-Beuve, 'Répons'.

[37] See Robertson, 'Transmission', 507.

toward standardization of services, as it did on so many other occasions. And this stand-offishness is one of the unique features of the liturgy of Saint-Denis.

OFFICE HYMNS

The Office hymn has formed part of the canonical Hours since the sixth-century Rule of Saint Benedict.[38] Most late medieval hymnals were composed mainly of chants drawn from two sources, now called the Old and New Hymnals.[39] Used until around 800, the Old Hymnal consisted of two types of hymn: a collation attributed to Saint Ambrose, Caesarius, Aurelianus, Bede, and others; and a somewhat more elaborate version that provides hymns for most of the Offices.[40] In the ninth and tenth centuries a New Hymnal, which seems to have originated in France, gradually added chants to the Old Hymnal. This collection, which was again revised beginning at the end of the eleventh century, forms the basic repertory of hymnals in most medieval establishments.[41]

We can glean the content and ordering of the hymnal of Saint-Denis, but not the melodies, nor all of the texts, since no notated hymnal from the abbey survives. The titles of hymns and, in some cases, their texts are preserved in six manuscripts. The two earliest sources from the eleventh century are psalters (F:Psg 1186 and F:Pn, lat. 103),[42] books which regularly included hymnals at this time. The thirteenth-century ordinaries F:Pm 526 and F:Pn, lat. 976 contain the textual incipits of hymns, and the later breviaries GB:Ob, Can. Lit. 192 and F:Pn, Rés. B. 5209 incorporate the incipits and a few texts of hymns.

[38] See the liturgical chapters of the Rule, edited in Fry, *Rule*, 202–15; and Fry's commentary on the difference between the two terms that Benedict uses for hymn, *Ambrosianus* and *hymnus*; ibid. 401.

[39] On the Old and New Hymnals, see Gneuss, *Hymnar*, 1–75; Wieland, *Hymnal*, 1–7; Steiner, 'Hymn'; and for a general introduction to Latin hymnodists and hymn sources, see Szövérffy, *Hymnody*.

[40] On the early hymns in particular, see Walpole, *Hymns*.

[41] Recent studies have shown that there was tremendous variety in local hymnals. The first revision of the Cistercian hymnal of the 12th c. reestablished the use of only the ancient Ambrosian hymns. Some time before 1147, the hymnal was again reworked and expanded according to the dictates of the liturgical reform that took place during this period; see Waddell, *Hymnal*, i. 76–87, 105.

[42] Gastoué treats the hymnal of F:Psg 1186 in 'Origines' (1903/4), 13–15. Neumes were added to 1 hymn in F:Pn, lat. 103: *Veni creator spiritus* for Pentecost (fo. 154^v; see Pl. 10). A 9th-c. patristic MS that probably comes from Saint-Denis, F:Pn, lat. 528, contains hymns in a separate gathering on fos. 84–90. These pages are written in a different hand from the rest of the MS, and the book soon passed from Saint-Denis to Saint-Martial of Limoges. It is thus difficult to determine whether or not the hymnal represents the usage of Saint-Denis, since it is quite possible that this section of the MS did not originate in the abbey. In any case, the hymnal is incomplete and was not long in use; see Gneuss, *Hymnar*, 20; Nebbiai-Dalla Guarda, *Bibliothèque*, 298.

The two early collections in F:Psg 1186 and F:Pn, lat. 103 show that the eleventh-century hymnal of Saint-Denis consisted of the usual round of chants for the *temporale* and common of saints, as found in the Old and New Hymnals. Besides these, there were a handful of proper hymns for saints. Those for Mary,[43] Benedict,[44] John the Baptist,[45] Peter,[46] Michael,[47] Martin,[48] and Nicholas[49] might have been heard in almost any house whose liturgy likewise included selections from the New Hymnal. The chants which distinguish F:Psg 1186 and F:Pn, lat. 103, on the other hand, are a few hymns for saints who had stronger connections with Saint-Denis and with the city of Paris: *Ecclesie speculum patrie* for Saint Germanus (28 May),[50] *Celi cives adplaudite* and *Fortem fidelem militem* for Saint Denis (9 October),[51] *Barcinon lete Cucuphas* for Saint Cucuphas (25 July),[52] and *Adsunt o populi* for Saint Hippolytus (13 August).[53] The presence of proper hymns for the two latter saints is not surprising, since their relics were kept in the abbey, and the hymn for Saint Germanus may recall the period in the ninth and tenth centuries when Saint-Denis and Saint-Germain-des-Prés were governed by the same abbot. In the later books from the monastery, only the two hymns for Saint Denis are still listed, and these pieces served to differing degrees as propaganda for the identification of Saint Denis with Dionysius the Areopagite and Pseudo-Dionysius, as discussed in Chapter 4. Like many proper items in the Sandionysian liturgy, however, the hymns for Saints Germanus, Cucuphas, and Hippolytus disappeared in the late Middle Ages, replaced by the normal series of common hymns for martyrs and confessors. Other proper hymns in the sources from the abbey include the incipits of the hymns for the later-added feasts of Corpus Christi and Saint Louis (25 August), which appear in GB:Ob, Can. Lit. 192[54] and in F:Pn, Rés. B. 5209.

[43] *O quam glorifica luce*, *Quem terra pontus*, *Ave maria stella dei*, *Fit porta christi*, *Quod chorus vatum*, *Virgo dei genetrix*; F:Psg 1186, fos. 212–13; F:Pn, lat. 103, fos. 154ᵛ–155, 159.

[44] *Christe sanctorum decus atque virtus*; F:Psg 1186, fo. 213; F:Pn, lat. 103, fo. 158.

[45] *Ut queant laxis*; F:Psg 1186, fos. 213ᵛ–214; F:Pn, lat. 103, fo. 155ᵛ.

[46] *Aurea luce et decore roseo*; F:Psg 1186, fo. 214ᵛ; F:Pn, lat. 103, fo. 156.

[47] *Tibi christe splendour*, *Christe sanctorum decus angelorum rector*; F:Psg 1186, fos. 215ᵛ–216; F:Pn, lat. 103, fos. 155ʳ⁻ᵛ.

[48] *Rex christe martini decus*; F:Pn, lat. 103, fo. 161.

[49] *Exultet aula celica*; F:Psg 1186, fo. 221ᵛ.

[50] F:Psg 1186, fo. 215. This hymn is also found in the 14th-c. breviary of Saint-Germain-des-Prés F:Pn, lat. 13239, fos. 304ᵛ–305. The text is published in Dreves, *Hymni*, *AH*, xi. 146; see also Gastoué, 'Origines' (1903/4), 15; Mearns, *Hymnaries*, 31.

[51] The hymns for Saint Denis are discussed in Ch. 4.

[52] F:Pn, lat. 103, fo. 159ᵛ; text ed. in Blume, *Hymnodia*, *AH*, xxvii. 150–2. See also Chevalier, *Repertorium*, No. 2317; Szövérffy, *Hymnendichtung*, 150; Mearns, *Hymnaries*, 14.

[53] F:Pn, lat. 103, fo. 160; text ed. in Blume, *Hymnodia*, *AH*, xxvii. 183–4. See also Chevalier, *Repertorium*, no. 552; Szövérffy, *Hymnendichtung*, 150, 154; Mearns, *Hymnaries*, 3.

[54] Corpus Christi: at Vespers, *Pange lingua* (fo. 142; a 6th-c. hymn by Fortunatus); at Matins,

INVITATORY

The invitatory is the opening chant of Matins, also known as the Venite, the first word of the text of Ps. 94 (Vulgate numbering) *Venite exultemus domino*.[55] In performance, the eleven verses of the Venite are grouped into five sections, and an antiphon is usually sung before the first and following each odd-numbered section. The second half of the antiphon is chanted after the even numbered sections and after the Lesser Doxology (Gloria Patri) which is sung as the sixth section at the end of the psalm. The melodies both for this chant and for its antiphons were established at a rather late date, and the Middle Ages has handed down many tones for the Venite. Hence repertories of invitatories vary widely from house to house, and for this reason they may prove to be liturgical and musical features that can help establish the proper features of a particular ritual.[56] Steiner shows, for example, that some houses had only a few tones for the Venite, while others used more than twenty.[57] Likewise, earlier manuscripts which contain Venites often assign antiphons of different modes to one and the same Venite, while later books tend to organize the Venite and its antiphons in a tonary fashion without mixing modes.[58]

Several fragmentary sources for the Venite and its antiphons, both unnotated and notated, survive from Saint-Denis. The unnotated books include the early eleventh-century antiphonary list in F:Pm 384; the three ordinaries F:Pm 526; F:Pn, lat. 976 and F:Pan, L 863, No. 10; and the two breviaries, GB:Ob, Can. Lit. 192 and F:Pn, Rés. B. 5209. The music for some Venites and their antiphons is given in two manuscripts. The twelfth-century antiphoner F:Pn, lat. 17296 records more than 50 invitatory antiphons and a number of Venite incipits within the Offices for saints and feast-days, and a separate collection of five tones for the Venite appears near the end of the book.[59] In addition, the tonary of the theorist Guido of Saint-Denis, discussed in Chapter 5,

Sacris solemnis (fo. 142^v; see Chevalier, *Repertorium*, No. 17713); at Lauds, *Verbum supernum* (fo. 144^v; ed. in Dreves, *Hymni*, *AH*, xii. 32). Saint Louis: Vespers, *Pulset celum laus* (fo. 422); Matins, *Nocturni cursus tempore* (fo. 422^v); Lauds, *Laus matutina suscitet* (fo. 424^v). The texts of the hymns for Louis are ed. in Dreves, *Hymni*, *AH*, xi. 178–9.

55 For studies of the invitatory in other houses, see Frere, *Introduction*, 62–4, 95 (Sarum use); Steiner, 'Invitatory'; idem, 'Tones', 142–4; idem, 'Repertory' (Cluny), wherein further bibliography on the invitatory is given in nn. 2 and 4. Steiner has recently announced her forthcoming comparative study of the invitatory in 'Traditions', 131.

56 Ibid. 137.

57 Ibid. 134–5.

58 See discussion of the various ways of ordering the melodies in Steiner, 'Repertory'.

59 The first 2 Venites, corresponding respectively to Guido's tones for Modes IV2 and IV3 (Ex. 3.4), are written out on fos. 346–347^v. The 3rd tone (fo. 347), which matches Guido's melody for Mode 3 (Ex. 3.3), is interrupted. The last part of a 4th melody and the beginning of a

gives incipits for the Venite, along with sample invitatory antiphons (see Table 3.2; Exs. 3.1–3.8).

In his treatise Guido presents fourteen tones for the Venite: one in Modes 1, 2, 3, 5, 7, and 8, five in Mode 4, and three in Mode 6. His distribution of the melodies is unusual, since tones for the Venite are generally thought to exist only in Modes 2–7. Guido explains his curious arrangement in an extensive commentary to the musical examples, printed here for the first time, where he tries to justify the inclusion of the first and eighth modes. He also mentions in passing the use of the invitatory in the cathedrals at Paris and Amiens. It is clear that his tone for the first mode is actually the same as his fifth tone in Mode 4 (IV^5), whereas his melody for the eighth mode is the equivalent of his third tone in Mode 6 (VI^3). Thus in total he gives only twelve different melodies for the Venite, a standard number in many practices, including the Sarum Use.[60]

Ex. 3.1. *Guido of Saint-Denis's Antiphon and Tone for the Invitatory, Mode 1*
GB:Lbm, Harl. 281, fo. 78ᵛ [82ᵛ]

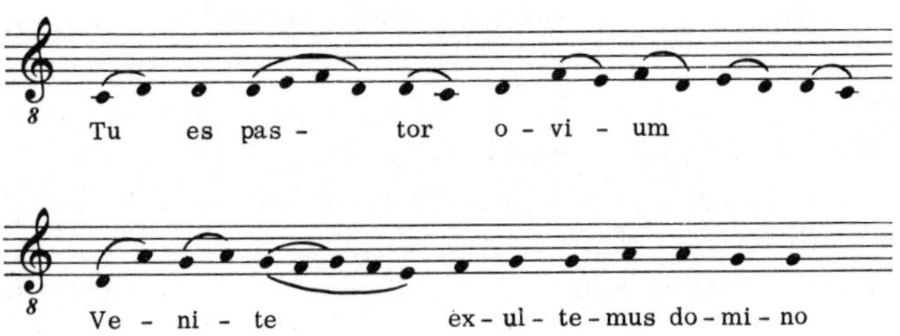

Guido's fictitious tone for the Venite in the first mode is shown in Ex. 3.1. He precedes this Venite with the Ant. *Tu es pastor*, which the Sarum and other traditions assign to Mode 2.[61] The melodies of a number of other antiphons at Saint-Denis are identical to or based on *Tu es pastor*: *Eternum trinumque*, *Regem regum dominum . . . adoremus quia ipse*, and *Sancte paule apostole*. Almost all these antiphons are reserved in the abbey for feasts of saints whose relics were in the church. This token of the monks' solicitude for their most beloved saints is but

5th tone, corresponding to Guido's example for Mode 1 (Ex. 3.1), are given on fo. 348. Since the series of Venites in F:Pn, lat. 17296 is incomplete, it is not possible to know whether all the melodies that Guido gives were also in use at the time F:Pn, lat. 17296 was copied in the mid-12th c.

60 For Sarum, see Frere, *Introduction*, 62–4; idem, *Use*, ii, app., x–liii.

61 Frere, *Introduction*, 62.

TABLE 3.2. *Invitatory Antiphons at Saint-Denis*

Invitatory antiphon	Fo. in N1	Fo. in G	Mode	Liturgical placement of antiphon
Adoremus christum regem	234		II	*Hilary of Poitiers, *Dionysius of Corinth, *Hilary of Mende (M1, N1), Octave of Martin (M1, N1)
Adoremus deum quia ipse redemit	213^{v}		IV	Exaltation of Cross
Adoremus dominum qui fecit nos	Given only in unnotated sources			Thursdays after Epiphany and during Lent
Adoremus regem apostolorum	32		IV^{1}	John
Adoremus regem magnum dominum qui	200		IV	Invention of *Stephen
Adoremus regem seculorum	261		IV	Nicholas
Alleluia alleluia alleluia	142^{v}		VI^{3}	Monday after Octave of Easter
Alleluia ascendit christus	156		V	Ascension, Octave of Ascension
Alleluia spiritus domini	160^{v}		V	Pentecost
Alleluia surrexit dominus vere	136		V	Easter
Alleluia jubilemus deo	142		IV^{5}	Octave of Easter, Sundays I–IV after Octave of Easter, Feast of Relics, Sunday after Ascension, saints' feasts during Eastertide
Alleluia regem regum dominum . . . adoremus quia ipse	Given only in unnotated sources (cf. *Regem regum dominum* below)			Invention of Holy Nail, Invention and Detection of *Denis during Easter and Pentecost seasons
Ave maria	206^{v}	90 [93]	VII	Saturdays for Mary, Annunciation, Vigil of Assumption, week-days during octaves and Octaves of Assumption and of Nativity of Mary

Invitatory antiphon	Fo. in N1	Fo. in G	Mode	Liturgical placement of antiphon
Christum natum	27		IV	*Stephen
Christum regem regum	175^{v}		IV	*Peter and Paul, Andrew
Christus apparuit nobis	44^{v}		IV^{3}	Epiphany and week after
Christus natus est	19^{v}	84 [88]	IV^{3}	Christmas and days after, Sunday after Octave of Christmas, Saturdays for Mary between Christmas and Purification
Christus natus est Alleluia . . .	85			Septuagesima (M1, N1)
Confessorum regem adoremus	77^{v}		II	Benedict
Deum verum unum	165	84 [88]	IV^{1}	Octave of Pentecost, Transfiguration
Dominum deum nostrum	Given only in unnotated sources			Saturdays after Epiphany and during Lent
Dominum qui fecit nos	106, 313	85^{v} [89^{v}]	V	Sundays, Fridays after Epiphany, Fridays in Lent, Third Sunday in Lent, Sundays XVIII–XXVI after Octave of Pentecost
Ecce venit ad templum	65^{v}		IV^{5}	Purification
Ecce venit plenitudo	9		IV^{5}	Advent III and IV
Ecce venit rex	1^{v}	84 [88]	IV^{5}	Advent I and II
Eternum trinumque	194		I	*Patroclus, *Cucuphas, *Firminus, *Eugene, *Clement, Lawrence (M1)
Exultemus domino	287		II	Dedication of Church, Consecration of Altar
Hodie scietis	18		IV	Vigil of Christmas
Hodie si vocem	116		IV^{5}	Passion Sunday

In manu tua	93, 301^{v}		V	Wednesdays after Epiphany and during Lent, Quinquagesima, Sundays X–XVII after Octave of Pentecost
Ipsi vero	121		IV	Palm Sunday
Jubilemus deo	290^{v}		IV	Mondays, Tuesdays after Octave of Epiphany, Tuesdays in Lent, Sundays I–IX after Octave of Pentecost, Monday after Pentecost XXII, Mark, Philip and *James, Commemoration of Hippolytus
Justus florebit in domo	276		IV	One martyr
Laudemus deum nostrum	Given only in unnotated source			Conversion of Paul (M1)
Martinus ecce migrat	246^{v}		II	Martin
Nativitatem virginis	210		IV	Nativity of Mary
Non sit vobis	97		VII	Lent I
Pastorum summo jubilemus	180^{v}		I	Octave of *Peter and Paul
Populus domini et oves pasche	111		VII	Lent IV
Preoccupemus faciem	52		VII	Fabian and Sebastian
Psallamus domino	Given only in neumed source			Found only in M1 in the rhymed Office for Saint Denis (see discussion in Ch. 4)
Quoniam deus magnus	89		VII	Septuagesima (N2, M2, B, R), Sexagesima
Regem apostolorum	265		IV	Matthias, Barnabas, during Octave of *Peter and Paul, Octave of *Peter and Paul, James, Bartholomew, Matthew, Simon and Jude
Regem celorum	222^{v}	80 [84]	II	Michael

Invitatory antiphon	Fo. in N1	Fo. in G	Mode	Liturgical placement of antiphon
Regem confessorum dominum	279^{v}		IV	Confessors, Octave of Martin (B, R), *Hilary of Mende (B, R)
Regem cui omnia [= cuncta] vivunt		87 [91], 92^{v} [95^{v}]	VI^{3}, VIII	Office of the Dead, anniversaries
Regem evangelistarum	268^{v}		III	Evangelists
Regem martyrum dominum	208^{v}, 272^{v}		Only incipit is given	Martyrs, Decollation of *John Baptist (M1, N1)
Regem precursoris		81^{v} [85^{v}]	III	Days within octave and Octave of *John Baptist, Decollation of *John Baptist (M2, N2, B, R)
Regem regum dominum . . . adoremus quia ipse	227, 239		I	Invention of *Denis (M1, N1), *Hippolytus (M2, N2, B, R), *Maurice, *Denis, All Saints
Regem sanctarum	Given only in unnotated sources			Bathildis
Regem sanctorum	Given only in unnotated sources			All Souls, days within octave of All Saints
Regem sempiternum	188^{v}	80 [84]	II	Lawrence
Regem venturum	Given only in unnotated sources			Mondays and Wednesdays in Advent
Regem virginum dominum	284		IV	Virgins
Repleti sunt	Given only in unnotated sources			Monday, Thursday after Pentecost
Sancte paule apostole	181		I	Conversion, Commemoration of Paul
Surrexit dominus vere	138	87 [91]	VI^{1}	Monday–Thursday, Saturday after Easter

Tu es pastor	180^{v}	78^{v} [82^{v}]	I	Chair of *Peter, Octave of *Peter and Paul, *Peter's Chains
Unanimes regem laudemus	348^{v} (damaged folio)		Cannot be determined	Mary Magdalene
Venite adoremus dominum qui in sanctis	38^{v}, 202^{v}	87 [91]	VI^{2}	*Innocents, *Eustace, *Hippolytus (M1, N1), *Maurice (M1)
Venite adoremus et procidamus	101^{v} (damaged folio)		Cannot be determined	Lent II
Venite adoremus regem precursoris	169		IV	*John Baptist
Venite adoremus regem regum cuius	206^{v}	84 [88]	IV	Assumption
Venite exultemus		84 [88]	IV^{4}	Mondays in Lent
Vincentem mundum adoremus	60		I	*Vincent

Abbreviations: N1 = F:Pn, lat. 17296. G = Treatise of Guido of Saint-Denis (GB:Lbm, Harl. 281). M1 = F:Pm 384. M2 = F:Pm 526. N2 = F:Pn, lat. 976. B = GB:Ob, Can. Lit. 192. R = F:Pn, Rés. B. 5209. * = relics of saint at Saint-Denis.

one way in which they tailored the liturgy to highlight the relics with appropriate music.

The second mode likewise has only one melody for the Venite, as in the Sarum practice.[62] Guido quickly explains, however, that this Venite was not even used at Saint-Denis. The twelfth-century antiphoner F:Pn, lat. 17296 confirms this omission, for no second-mode Venite appears there. Guido says that the chant was sung at Notre Dame (see Ex. 3.2):

Note that we do not use this Venite nor any in this tone. But in order to give an example when I did not have one, I prefered to put in this example rather than not have one at all. This Venite is used not only in the church at Paris but also in many others, in fact, in just about all others.[63]

Ex. 3.2. *Guido of Saint-Denis's Antiphons and Tone for the Invitatory, Mode 2*
GB:Lbm, Harl. 281, fo. 80 [84]

The antiphons for this tone, like those mentioned earlier, are assigned to feasts of saints, many of whose remains the monks possessed.

Like the previous modes, Guido's third mode has only one tone for the Venite, and the same is true in Sarum usage[64] (see Ex. 3.3). The model antiphon for this mode, *Regem precursoris* for John the Baptist,

[62] Frere, *Introduction*, 62; idem, *Use*, ii, app., xvii.

[63] Ibid. 62; idem, *Use*, ii, app., xvii.

[63] 'Nota tamen quod istud Venite non habemus in usu nec aliquod huius toni. Gratia vero exempli quod hic mihi deficiebat malui ponere exemplum de illo quam deficere in exemplo. Istud enim Venite habet in usu non solum parisiensis ecclesia immo etiam plures alie et quasi omnes'; GB:Lbm, Harl. 281, fo. 80 [84]. Guido probably draws his information on the usage of Notre Dame of Paris from a portion of Johannes de Garlandia's treatise on plainchant which is evidently no longer extant; see Baltzer, 'Johannes'.

[64] Frere, *Introduction*, 63; idem, *Use*, ii, app., xxi.

Ex. 3.3. *Guido of Saint-Denis's Antiphon and Tone for the Invitatory, Mode 3*
GB:Lbm, Harl. 281, fo. 81v [85v]

has the same melody as the other antiphon from this tone, *Regem evangelistarum* from the common of evangelists.

The fourth mode is the most popular, as in the Sarum Rite and in all other uses.[65] Guido provides five melodies for the Venite,[66] pointing out that the fifth looks like the tone for Mode 1, and that the same Venite can occur in the first, fourth, or even the second mode, depending on the mode of the antiphon which accompanies it. To bolster his argument, he cites the authority of Johannes de Garlandia (see Ex. 3.4):

> You should not be surprised that in one place I said that this last Venite was in the fourth mode, while earlier in another place I said that this same Venite was in the first mode. For according to Master Johannes de Garlandia, who was a musician of great fame, it is possible in some cases for the same Venite to be [used] in different modes with respect to a number of Invitatory antiphons, in the same way that the same *Seculorum amen* can be [used] in different modes with respect to different antiphons, just as I noted earlier in the third *differentia* of this mode after the Ant. *Tuam crucem*. I must say something else about these two [Venites]: [1] that [the mode] of any Venite ought to be determined according to the invitatory [antiphon] or antiphons with which it is connected, as the aforementioned Master [Johannes de Garlandia] states, so that in this way the same Venite may at any time be [used] in different modes; and [2] that it is not necessary to attach in front of the Venite [only] an invitatory [antiphon] of the same mode, [since an antiphon] of another mode may [be used] at any time. And quite often in our monastery I notice that not only the aforementioned Venite [no. IV⁵] but also the first Venite of this mode [IV¹] are combined with the Inv. Ant. *Christum regem* and with many others of the fourth mode, as well as with the Inv. Ant. *Regem regum dominum* and with certain others of the first mode, and even occasionally with some [invitatory antiphons] of the second mode, for example, the Inv. of the angels

[65] Frere, *Introduction*, 63; idem, *Use*, ii, app., xxx–xxxi.

[66] In Table 3.2 the different tones for the 4th and 6th modes are designated with superscript nos.: IV1 (= IV5 in Sarum; cf. Frere, *Introduction*, 95), IV2, IV3 (= IV3 in Sarum), IV4 (= IV4 in Sarum), IV5.

Ex. 3.4. *Guido of Saint-Denis's Antiphons and Tones for the Invitatory, Mode 4*
GB:Lbm, Harl. 281, fo. 84 [88]

Mode IV¹

Mode IV²

Mode IV³

Mode IV⁴

Mode IV[5]

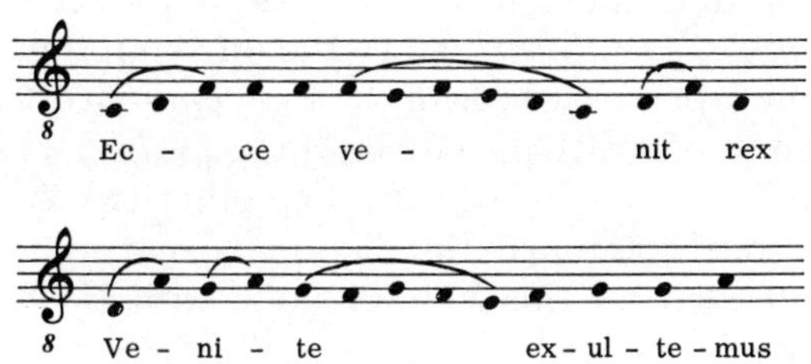

Regem celorum. And I believe that this is done mainly on account of the joyousness of the chant itself and on account of its gentleness and beauty.[67]

The Ant. *Vincentem mundum adoremus* and its Venite show how a fourth-mode Venite can be combined with a first-mode antiphon. *Vincentem mundum* ends on *d* and lies in the range of the first mode, while the Venite to which it is assigned is Guido's first melody for Mode 4 (IV[1]). Since many invitatory antiphons in F:Pn, lat. 17296 are not followed by incipits for the Venite, it is often impossible to know which fourth-mode Venite was assigned to the large number of antiphons ending on *e*. Several antiphons share the same melody, namely those for the commons of apostles, confessors, and virgins (*Regem apostolorum*, *Regem confessorum dominum*, *Regem virginum dominum*), and a number of them were probably intended for the second melody for the Venite. The antiphons for the third tone in Mode 4 have identical tunes: *Christus natus est* for Christmas and for the Saturdays for Mary during Christmas season, and *Christus apparuit nobis* for Epiphany. In the earlier sources, *Christus natus est alleluia* is used on Septuagesima

[67] 'Nec mireris si modo dictum sit istud ultimum Venite esse quarti toni cum supra dictum sit istud idem esse primi toni. Secundum enim magistrum Johannem de Garlandia qui fuit magne reputationis musicus non est inconveniens idem Venite esse diversorum tonorum diversis respectibus, scilicet per respectum ad diversa invitatoria sicut idem seculorum amen per respectum ad diversas antiphonas potest esse diversorum tonorum prout notavi supra in tertia differencia huius toni post illam Antiphonam *Tuam crucem*. Alterum enim istorum duorum necesse est dicere videlicet vel quod de quolibet Venite secundum suum invitatorium seu invitatoria ad que applicatur debeat judicari, sicut dicit magister predictus, et sic quandoque idem Venite sit diversorum tonorum vel quod non supra oportet invitatorio Venite eiusdem toni applicari sed quandoque alterius toni. Et hoc maxime et frequenter secundum usum presentis monasterii video evenire non solum in predicto Venite immo etiam in primo Venite huius toni quod scilicet aliquando Invitatorio *Christum regem* et multis aliis sui toni scilicet quarti alioquin vero Invitatorio *Regem regum dominum* et quibusdam aliis eiusdem toni cum ipso scilicet primi nec non etiam interdum aliquibus secundi sicut Invitatorio de angelis, scilicet *Regem celorum* applicatur alioquin et hoc sicut credo maxime fit propter festivitatem cantus ipsius et comitatem vel etiam venustatem'; GB:Lbm, Harl. 281, fo. 84 [88].

Sunday,[68] while the later books call for *Quoniam deus magnus*. The fourth Venite in Mode 4 begins with the text of the second verse of the Venite, *Jubilemus deo salutari*, since the one antiphon to which it is assigned uses the opening words of the Ps. *Venite exultemus*. Guido's model antiphon for the fifth melody in Mode 4 is *Ecce venit rex* for the first and second Sundays in Advent. The other two *Ecce* antiphons, assigned to the third and fourth Sundays in Advent and to Purification, are likewise intended for this Venite, along with *Hodie si vocem* for Passion Sunday.

Guido's fifth mode has a single melody for the Venite, as in the Sarum rite[69] (see Ex. 3.5). His sample antiphon *Dominum qui fecit nos*, used on various days during the weeks after Epiphany, during Lent, and after Pentecost, is melodically similar to the antiphons for Ascension, Pentecost, and Easter: *Alleluia ascendit christus, Alleluia spiritus domino, Alleluia surrexit dominus vere*. The fifth-mode Ant. *In manu tua* serves other days during the Epiphany, Lenten, and post-Pentecost seasons.

Ex. 3.5. *Guido of Saint-Denis's Antiphon and Tone for the Invitatory, Mode 5*
GB:Lbm, Harl. 281, fos. 85ᵛ–86 [89ᵛ–90]

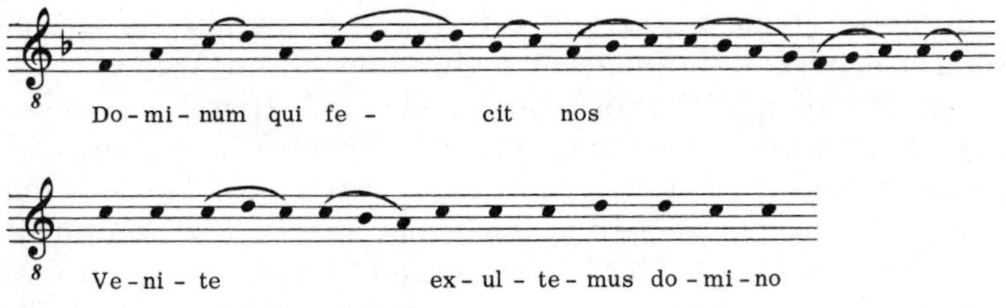

Although the sixth mode at Saint-Denis has three tones for the Venite, as in Sarum usage, the two practices differ both melodically and in the ordering of the tunes[70] (see Ex. 3.6). Guido's first and second melodies have only one antiphon apiece: *Surrexit dominus vere* for Eastertide, and *Venite adoremus dominum qui in sanctis* for Holy Innocents and Eustace and for Saints Hippolytus and Maurice in the earlier manuscripts. The representative antiphon for the third Venite, *Regem cui omnia vivunt*, was sung in the Office of the Dead and on anniversaries. Ironically, the only other antiphon which derives its

[68] See Steiner, 'Traditions', 133–4.

[69] Frere, *Introduction*, 63; idem, *Use*, ii, app., xxxv–xxxvi.

[70] Frere, *Introduction*, 64; idem, *Use*, ii, app., xlii–xliii. Guido's VI1 = Sarum VI2; Guido's VI2 = Sarum VI1; Guido's VI3 = Sarum VI3.

Ex. 3.6. *Guido of Saint-Denis's Antiphons and Tones for the Invitatory, Mode 6*
GB:Lbm, Harl. 281, fo. 87 [91]

Mode VI[1]

Mode VI[2]

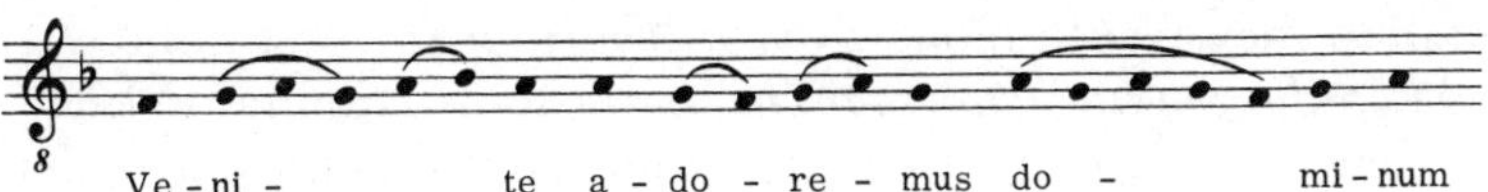

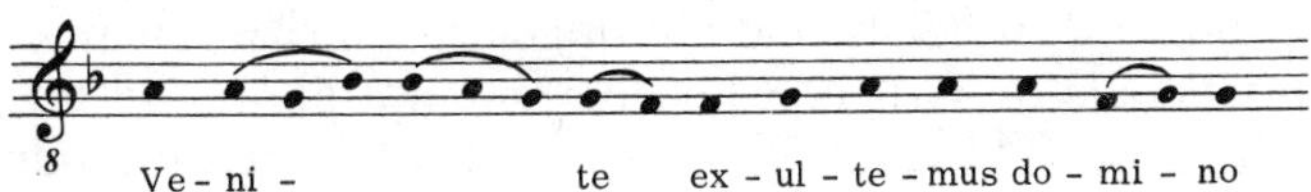

Mode VI[3]

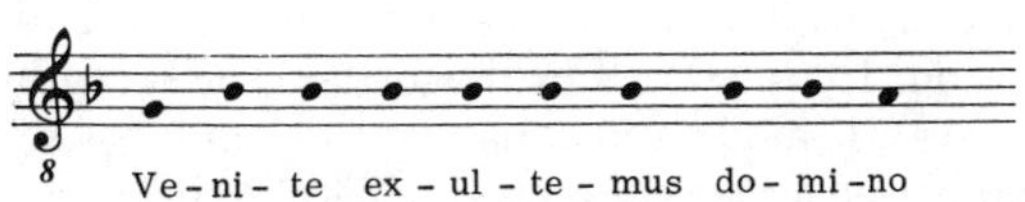

music from the tone for this sombre text is the joyful Ant. *Alleluia alleluia alleluia* for Easter.

Whereas the Venite of the seventh mode in Sarum usage has three different endings,[71] Guido's Venite has only one melody (see Ex. 3.7): 'Note that if this Venite is said to be in the eighth mode, it should not be notated as it is notated here, but as will be seen further down [in the

[71] Frere, *Introduction*, 64; idem, *Use*, ii, app., li–liii.

Ex. 3.7. *Guido of Saint-Denis's Antiphon and Tone for the Invitatory, Mode 7*
GB:Lbm, Harl. 281, fo. 90 [93]

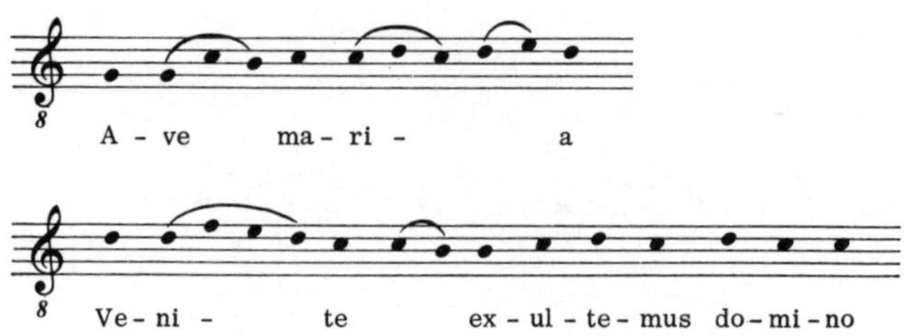

discussion of] the eighth mode.'[72] The model antiphon for this Venite, the Marian Ant. *Ave maria*, shares the beginning of its melody with the Ant. *Preoccupemus faciem* for Fabian and Sebastian and *Quoniam deum magnus* for Septuagesima and Sexagesima. Two other antiphons likewise fall in the seventh mode: *Non sit vobis* for the first Sunday in Lent, and *Populus domini et oves pasche* for the fourth Sunday in Lent.

In his discussion of the eighth mode, Guido admits at the outset that this tone usually does not have a Venite.[73] He then explains at length why he includes an eighth-mode melody, citing as authority Johannes de Garlandia and Petrus de Cruce, who give one antiphon and one Venite apiece in this mode.[74] In reality, however, Guido's eighth-mode melody is the same as the third example from Mode 6, except that the latter uses *b*-flat and ends on *f*, while the former closes on *g* and does not contain *b*-flat.

I should note that some say that there is no Venite in the eighth mode. They claim that, just as there are seven days in the week and seven gifts of the Holy Spirit, so also the spiritual fathers of the Church, who established the singing of invitatories in ancient times by 'inviting' us to ask for the sevenfold grace of the Holy Spirit, began on the first day with the invitatory of the first mode and then [sang the others] in succession. In this way they finished on the seventh day with the invitatory of the seventh mode and thus fixed the number of invitatories according to the number of the seven days which are in the week. Whatever you might think about this, I can say that, according to the aforementioned Master Johannes [de Garlandia], who speaks for the use of Paris, and [according] to Master Petrus de Cruce, who is a great singer and has closely observed the customs of the church at Amiens, there are at least two invitatory antiphons in this mode: one for which the above named Master

[72] 'Nota tamen quod si istud Venite dicatur esse octavi toni non notaretur ut hic notatum est sed sicut infra in octavo tono videbitur'; GB:Lbm, Harl. 281, fo. 87 [91].

[73] Sarum and other usages do not recognize an 8th-mode Venite.

[74] See Petrus de Cruce's tonary, ed. in Harbinson, *Petrus* (Venite in the 8th mode on p. xxiv). Because the use of the 8th-mode Venite is rare, Guido's description, given here in full, is especially relevant.

Petrus gives an example which, along with its Venite, we do not use, but which seems to be accepted use in the church at Amiens, namely *Preoccupemus* [see Mode 7 above]; and another for which the aforementioned Master Johannes de Garlandia gives examples [*see Ex. 3.8*].

Ex. 3.8. *Guido of Saint-Denis's Antiphon and Tone for the Invitatory, Mode 8*
GB:Lbm, Harl. 281, fo. 92ᵛ [95ᵛ]

This example does not contradict what I said earlier in the treatise and [showed] in the examples of invitatory antiphons and Venites of the sixth mode. There I put the invitatory [Ant. *Regem cui omnia*] with its Venite in the sixth mode so that you could see that they can be notated two ways: [1] there with round or soft *b* and thus end on *f grave*, that is, on the first *f fa ut*, which as I said in the first part of this work is the final letter of the sixth mode; and [2] here they are written without soft or round *b* and thus they end on *g grave*, that is, on the first *g sol re ut*, which is the final letter of the eighth mode. And thus in different cases they can be in different modes, just as I mentioned earlier concerning the same *Seculorum amen* with regard to different antiphons, and concerning the same Venite with regard to different invitatory [antiphons]. In fact, if anyone wishes to investigate closely how the same antiphon notated in different ways can be in five different modes, certain people will tell you it is in one mode and others in another, as for example the Ant. *Me suscepit*.[75]

[75] 'Notandum est quod sicut aliqui dicunt nullum est Venite octavi toni dicunt enim quod sicut sunt septem solum dies in ebdomada et septem dona spiritus sancti, ita etiam spirituales ecclesie doctores qui nos invitando ad postulandam septiformem spiritus sancti gratiam invitatoria statuerunt cantari antiquitus incipiebant prima die ab invitatorio primi toni et sic deinceps ita videlicet quod septimo die in invitatorio septimi toni finiebant et sic numerum invitatoriorum juxta numerum septem dierum qui sunt in ebdomada statuerunt. Quicquid tamen sit de hoc potest dici secundum magistrum Johannem predictum qui allegat usum parisiensis ecclesie et magistrum Petrum de Cruce qui fuit optimus cantor et ambianensis ecclesie consuetudinem specialiter observavit aliqua invitatoria sunt istius toni saltem duo. Unum videlicet de quo ponit exemplum ille magister Petrus qui apud nos non est in usu nec eius Venite sed videntur esse de usu ambianensis ecclesie sumpta scilicet *Preoccupemus*. Aliud vero de quo ponit exempla prefatus magister Johannes de Garlandia videlicet istud quod sequitur: [*Ex.* 3.8]. Nec istud est contrarium illi quod supra dixi tractando et exempla ponendo de invitatoriis et Venite sexti toni vel istud invitatorium cum suo Venite positum fuit tamquam sexti toni sicut enim ibi potest videri ambo notantur cum *b rotundo* vel *molli* et sic in *f gravi* idest in primo *f fa ut* terminantur que ut dictum est in prima parte operis huius est finalis littera sexti toni, hic vero sine *b molli* vel *rotundo* notantur et sic in *g gravi* id est in primo *g sol re ut* que est octavi toni finalis littera terminantur. Et

Regem cui omnia vivunt, the only antiphon assigned to this mode, is the same antiphon that accompanies the third Venite of the sixth mode, as Guido explains.

Table 3.2 shows that a number of changes in the repertory of invitatory antiphons at Saint-Denis occurred from the time of the earliest eleventh-century source (F:Pm 384) to the mid-thirteenth century, after which all subsequent sources seem to agee. The number of antiphons apparently grew, as shown in the unnotated sources which contain chants not found in the books with music: *Adoremus dominum qui fecit nos*, *Alleluia regem regum dominum . . . adoremus quia ipse*, *Dominum deum nostrum*, *Laudemus deum nostrum*, *Regem sanctarum*, *Regem sanctorum*, *Regem venturum*, and *Repleti sunt*. Perhaps some of these antiphons were newer compositions. The earliest sources, F:Pn, lat. 17296 and F:Pm 384, sometimes offer two choices of antiphons, whereas the later manuscripts give only one. In addition, the common antiphon for confessors, *Regem confessorum dominum*, is preferred in the later manuscripts, while the usual antiphon for saints with relics at Saint-Denis, *Adoremus christum regem*, occurs more often in F:Pn, lat. 17296 and in F:Pm 384. This type of standardization in the later sources removes some of the colour from the celebrations of even the most honoured saints of the abbey, and it stands in direct contrast to the strongly individual emphasis that the early liturgical books place on the services of the treasured relics. Chapter 2 has shown a similar de-emphasis on other aspects of the proper Offices for Maurice, Cucuphas and Hilary of Mende in the thirteenth- and fourteenth-century manuscripts, and we will see the same tendency in the monks' steadily decreasing use of proper chants for the Benedicamus Domino and Ite Missa Est in the late Middle Ages.

GLORIA PATRI OF GREAT RESPONSORIES

The Gloria Patri, or lesser doxology, is a praise to the Trinity, performed at the end of almost all psalms and canticles: *Gloria patri et filio et spiritui sancto. Sicut erat in principio et nunc et semper et in secula seculorum Amen*. When it appears in Western responsories, only the first half of the versicle is sung: *Gloria patri et filio et spiritui*

sic diversis respectibus possunt esse diversorum tonorum sicut etiam supra dictum est de eodem *seculorum amen* respectu diversarum antiphonarum et de eodem Venite respectu diversorum invitatoriorum. Immo etiam si quis diligenter velit inspicere quando eadem antiphona secundum diversum modum notandi eam posset esse et est quinque diversorum tonorum itaque a quibusdam dicitur esse unius toni ab aliis alterius sicut est de Antiphona *Me suscepit*'; GB:Lbm, Harl. 281, fos. 92^{r-v} [95^{r-v}].

sancto.[76] The music for the text, which is normally fairly simple, comes from the psalm tone or responsory verse with which it appears. The twelfth-century antiphoner F:Pn, lat. 17296 includes several examples of Gloria Patri within responsories. Similarly the tonary of Guido of Saint-Denis gives a Gloria Patri for each of the eight modes, and he elaborates on the Gloria Patri of the first mode, mentioning other houses that follow the use of Saint-Denis (see Ex. 3.9):

Ex. 3.9. *Guido of Saint-Denis's Tone for the Gloria Patri, Mode 1*
GB:Lbm, Harl. 281, fo. 78ᵛ [82ᵛ]

Note that this way of singing not only the aforementioned Gloria of this tone with the responsory but also those of the other tones, which are given below each in their turn, is commonly observed by monks [i.e. in monasteries], although other churchmen [i.e. non-monastic institutions] follow a different usage. But at the church of Amiens [non-monastic], according to the [Gloria] tones of Master Petrus de Cruce and the examples which he writes there [i.e. in his tonary] conform rather to our usage and [to that] of other monks [i.e. monastic houses] in this respect.[77]

In addition to the Gloria Patri in Guido's tonary, a collection of 25 special tones for the Gloria Patri is given in F:Pn, lat. 17296 (Table 3.3).

Like the tunes for the Benedicamus Domino and Ite Missa Est, discussed below, these Gloria Patri are identified by cues which point to the sources of the melodies. The music for each Gloria Patri is written on the first two-thirds of a line in F:Pn, lat. 17296, and then a musical incipit showing the beginning of the responsory verse appears at the end of the line. In Ex. 3.10, the cue refers to the Ver. *Replebitur majestate* from the responsory for Trinity *Benedictus dominus deus*. The sources of the remaining Gloria Patri in F:Pn, lat. 17296 are invariably responsory verses, but they do not always copy the parent tunes exactly. Rather, they embellish their models in some places, usually by placing

[76] See discussions of the Gloria Patri in Chew, 'Doxology', 600; Hughes, *Manuscripts*, No. 204.

[77] 'Et nota quod iste modus cantandi in responsorio non solum predictam gloriam huius toni immo etiam ceterorum tonorum sicut infra in suo ordine notantur communiter a monachis observatur, licet ab aliis ecclesiasticis viris aliter habeantur in usu. Ambianensi tamen ecclesia secundum tonos magistri Petri de Cruce et exempla que ponit ibidem nostro potius et ceterorum monachorum usui quo ad hoc conformari videtur'; GB:Lbm, Harl. 281, fo. 78ᵛ [82ᵛ]. The remaining tones for the Gloria Patri are found on fos. 79ᵛ (Mode 2), 81ᵛ (Mode 3), 84 (Mode 4), 85ᵛ (Mode 5), 87 (Mode 6), 90 (Mode 7), 92 (Mode 8) [= fos. 83ᵛ, 85ᵛ, 88, 89ᵛ, 91, 93, 95]. See Petrus de Cruce's tones for the Gloria Patri, ed. in Harbinson, *Petrus*.

TABLE 3.3. *Collection of Tones for the Gloria Patri in F:Pn, lat. 17296*

Cue from Resp. verse	Resp. source of melody	Feast and No. of responsory	Fo. No. of responsory
Fo. 170			
1. *Deus [misereatur]*	*Benedicat nos deus*	Trinity, No. 1 at Matins	165v
2. *Replebitur [majestate]*	*Benedictus dominus deus*	Trinity, No. 2 at Matins	165v
3. *Notam [fecisti]*	*Quis deus magnus*	Trinity, No. 3 at Matins	166
4. *Magnus [dominus]*	*Magnus dominus*	Trinity, No. 4 at Matins	166
5. *Da gaudiorum [premia]*	*Gloria patri genite*	Trinity, No. 5 at Matins	166v
6. *Trinitati [lux perhennis]*	*Honor virtus et potestas*	Trinity, No. 6 at Matins	167
7. *Timentibus [deum]*	*Deum time et mandata*	Trinity, No. 7 at Matins	167
8. *Prestet [nobis graciam]*	*Summe trinitatis*	Trinity, No. 8 at Matins	167
Fo. 170v			
9. *Benedictus [es domine]*	*Benedicamus patrem*	Trinity, No. 9 at Matins	167v
10. *Quoniam [magnus es tu]*	*Te deum patrem*	Trinity, No. 10 at Matins	167v
11. *Et benedictum [nomen]*	*Tibi laus tibi gloria*	Trinity, No. 11 at Matins	168

12. *Tibi laus* [*tibi gloria*]	*O beata trinitas*	Trinity, No. 12 at Matins	168
13. *Tanto namque*	*Valerius igitur*	Vincent, No. 7 at Matins	63
14. *Gabrielem* [*archangelum*]	*Gaude maria virgo*	Purification, No. 12 at Matins	68^{v}
15. *Incessanter* [*pro nobis*]	*Pater insignis*	Benedict, resp. at First Vespers	77
16. *Cum orasset*	*Cornelius centurio*	Peter and Paul, resp. at First Vespers	175
17. *Cui sacerdos*	*Igitur dissimulata*	Invention of Stephen, No. 2 at Matins	185
18. *Karitati*[*s gracia*]	*Ecce jam coram te*	Invention of Stephen, No. 4 at Matins	185^{v}
19. *Ut tuo* [*propitiatus*]	*Sancte dei preciose*	Invention of Stephen, No. 8 at Matins	186^{v}
20. *Qui pro tuis*	*O martirum gemma*	Feast of Stephen, No. 4 at Matins	29
21. *Cherubin* [*quoque*]	*Te sanctum dominum*	All Saints, No. 3 at Matins	240
Fo. 171[a]			
22. *Pro eo* [*ut me*]	*Vir iste in populo*	Andrew, No. 12 at Matins	160^{v}
23. *Jam quodam modo*	*Dum vero adhuc*	Nicholas, No. 2 at Matins	262^{v}
24. *Erat autem*	*Quatuor animalia*	Common of Evangelists, No. 6 at Matins	270^{v}
25. *Constantes* [*esto*]	*O juda et jerusalem*	Christmas, resp. at First Vespers	19^{v}

[a] See the facsimile of fo. 171 in Robertson, '*Benedicamus*', fig. 2.

Ex. 3.10. *Gloria Patri* Replebitur

F:Pn, lat. 17296, fos. 170 (Gloria Patri) and 165ᵛ (Ver. *Replebitur majestate*, from Resp. *Benedictus dominus deus*)

two-note neumes on words that are set syllabically in the original responsory verses. In other instances, they simplify the sources. The Gloria Patri in Ex. 3.10 follows its model faithfully up to the final cadence, at which point it deviates from the source by avoiding the repeated *e* and *d*.

The organization of the Gloria Patri collection in F:Pn, lat. 17296 is also deliberate. The author of this grouping evidently wanted to provide a complete set of Gloria Patri tones for the responsories for Matins of the feast of Trinity, for twelve melodies appear in the order of the responsories as they are given a few folios earlier in the feast itself (F:Pn, lat. 17296, fos. 165ᵛ–168). The emphasis on the Trinity festival is explained partly by the fact that the text of the versicle deals with the Trinity. But the concept of the Trinity was also central to the iconography of Abbot Suger's church, with which F:Pn, lat. 17296 was closely connected. These dozen tones for the Trinity add musical and liturgical evidence to the artistic witness of Trinitarian symbolism that is evident in the decoration of the new church.[78]

[78] See the discussion in Ch. 4. The emphasis on Gloria Patri tones for the Office of Trinity seems to be rare. Only Saint-Corneille of Compiègne, a house which derived its liturgy directly from Saint-Denis, preserves all 12 tones for Trinity, among others, in the gradual F:Pn, lat. 17329

The remaining 13 chants for the Gloria Patri occur in almost perfect calendar order, probably for easy reference, beginning with the feast of Saint Vincent (22 January) and ending with Christmas (25 December). Only the Gloria Patri *Qui pro tuis* (No. 20) for the Stephen Resp. *O martirum gemma* seems to break this arrangement, since Stephen's feast falls on 26 December. The reason for this placement is understandable, however, for the tone is grouped with three other melodies for the feast of the Invention of Stephen (3 August).

NEUMAS

The neuma was a melisma added to the ends of important antiphons, and it served as the standard ornament of the plainsong of the Divine Office.[79] Each of the eight modes had its own neuma, which could be attached to chants of the same mode. Drawing evidently on Guillaume of Auxerre, Guido's tonary describes the use of neumas at Saint-Denis in some detail, explaining how they were added to antiphons, responsories, sequences, and other chants.[80] He presents the melismas in the standard way, writing a neuma at the beginning of every chapter, alongside the model antiphon that introduces each mode (Ex. 3.11).

The ordinaries of Saint-Denis likewise mention some of the uses of the neumas of antiphons. F:Pan, L 863, No. 10 calls for their addition to the antiphons of *annuale* and *semiannuale* feasts at Vespers, Matins, and Lauds, unless it was prohibited in the directions of individual feasts. This regulation covered some 17 festivals, excluding Easter because of the already jubilant nature of the services on this day. On Pentecost, on the other hand, neumas were sung both at Vespers and at Matins.[81] The sources do not specify precisely which antiphons had neumas at these services, and it was possible to ornament either the psalmodic antiphons or the antiphons to the canticles. Outside Saint-

(fos. 240^{v}–246^{v}). More typical is the collection in the antiphoner from Saint Peter's in Gloucester (Oxford, Jesus College, MS 10), which has a small collection of 8 Gloria Patri without cues (fo. 189^{v}), added in the early 14th c. (see Van Dijk, *Handlist*, ii. 136–6b). Only the 4th melody in this group, *Magnus dominus*, is taken from the verse of the Trinity Resp. *Magnus dominus et magna* (= Table 3.3 No. 4).

[79] On the neuma, see Hiley, 'Neuma', Huglo, *Tonaires*, 388–90; idem, *Livres*, 24–5; Hughes, *Manuscripts*, No. 621.

[80] GB:Lbm, Harl. 281, fos. 72^{v}–75^{v} [76^{v}–79^{v}]. See Huglo's discussion of the source of Guido's section on the neuma; Huglo, 'Guy'.

[81] The regulation for *annuale* and *semiannuale* feasts reads: 'In festis annualibus et semiannualibus ad antiphonas dicentur neumata tam ad matutinas videlicet quam ad laudes et utrasque vesperas nisi contrarium inveniatur notatum'; F:Pan, L 863, No. 10, p. 2; see also pp. 51–3; F:Pm 526, fo. 56. The use of neumas on Pentecost is found in F:Pan, L 863, No. 10, pp. 63–4.

Ex. 3.11. *Guido of Saint-Denis's Neumas*

GB:Lbm, Harl. 281, fo. 76 [80]—Mode 1

GB:Lbm, Harl. 281, fo. 79ᵛ [83ᵛ]—Mode 2

GB:Lbm, Harl. 281, fo. 80ᵛ [84ᵛ]—Mode 3

GB:Lbm, Harl. 281, fo. 82ᵛ [86ᵛ]—Mode 4

GB:Lbm, Harl. 281, fo. 85 [89]—Mode 5

GB:Lbm, Harl. 281, fo. 86ᵛ [90ᵛ]—Mode 6

GB:Lbm, Harl. 281, fo. 88 [92]—Mode 7

GB:Lbm, Harl. 281, fo. 90ᵛ [93ᵛ]—Mode 8

Denis, the neumas of antiphons sometimes served as tenors of motets in houses which cultivated polyphony.[82]

During the Middle Ages neuma also signified 'melisma' in general, and hence the melismatic tropes that were inserted in responsories at Saint-Denis are sometimes termed neumas. In addition, the melismas taken out of responsories and those drawn from other forms of chant to create melodies for the Benedicamus Domino and Ite Missa Est were also called neumas. Neuma likewise designated the vocalize of a sequence as described by Guido of Saint-Denis and others. Saint-Denis made extensive use of the neuma in all these forms, generating new music and embellishing its plainsong in much the same way that polyphony did in other Parisian centres.

TROPES

The word 'trope' includes introductions and insertions in the chants of the Mass and Office. It encompasses additions of melody, of text, and of both melody and text to the music of the high feasts of the year.[83] Such pieces, scattered here and there, are found in a wide range of manuscripts from Saint-Denis. But no troper, properly speaking, is extant from the monastery, nor are large sections of any of the surviving books devoted to this type of composition. For this reason it is difficult to know just how extensively the monks employed these pieces in their heyday in the tenth to twelfth centuries. To judge solely from the examples in the extant manuscripts, the abbey did not rival the major centres such as Winchester (Saint-Swithin), Saint-Martial, Saint-Gall, or Benevento in production of tropes. And yet the tropes that remain in the sources from Saint-Denis represent most of the kinds of composition that come under the general heading of the term, and a few of these compositions are unique to the monastery. Clearly the abbey shared the Western fascination with tropes—indeed, for at least 500 years, some form of troping was practised at Saint-Denis.

Melismatic Tropes and Responsory Melismas

Probably the earliest kinds of trope were untexted melismas, inserted in chants of special importance.[84] The ninth-century Frankish liturgist

[82] See the list of sources in Hiley, 'Neuma', 123.

[83] For recent definitions of the word 'trope', see Jonsson, *CT*, i, 11, n. 3; Marcusson, *CT*, ii, 7; Steiner, 'Trope', 172. For the Kyrie trope, D. Bjork distinguishes between the words trope, prosula, and Latin-texted Kyrie; 'Kyrie', 2–3.

[84] Handschin, 'Trope', 128.

Amalarius of Metz describes a melismatic trope that was famous in the Middle Ages: the so-called neuma triplex.[85] As its name implies, the melisma actually consists of three different melodies, each designed to ornament a statement of the final portion, or *repetendum*, of a great responsory. Amalarius says that the neuma triplex was originally added to the Resp. *In medio ecclesie* for the feast of John (27 December), but that singers in his day had transferred it to the Christmas Resp. *Descendit de celis*.[86] Evidently the melisma gained even greater renown after Amalarius, for it passed from one responsory to another.

The twelfth-century antiphoner F:Pn, lat. 17296 from Saint-Denis preserves this melody on three different feasts (Tables 3.4 and 3.5): Christmas, John (27 December), and Saint Denis (9 October). The neuma triplex is easy to recognize as an added trope, not only because of its length, but also because it appears in F:Pn, lat. 17296 after the fully written-out responsory and verse. On Christmas, the syllable which the neuma embellishes in the *repetendum* is *fa-*, from the final words *fabrice mundi* of the Resp. *Descendit de celis*, and this is the same syllable which is set much more simply in the original statement of the responsory. The monks of Saint-Denis sang this fabulously elaborated responsory on Christmas Day, whereas on the Octave of Christmas the community evidently performed *Descendit* without the melismas.[87] Because there is no indication that the melismas were executed in a special way, it is likely that these and other purely melismatic tropes in F:Pn, lat. 17296 were chanted by the choir.[88] The first melisma of the neuma triplex likewise appears in the final responsory for John, *In medio ecclesie*, on the closing words *et intellectus*, and a texted version of the neuma, the prosula *Et intellectus johannem*, is given on the same folio.[89] The entire neuma triplex occurs in the first responsory for the feast of Saint Denis, *Post passionem*, on the last syllable of its antepenultimate word *ecclesi-a*.

Two different versions of the Ver. *Quicum imminere* accompany *Post passionem*, and the first of these was performed by two soloists on the

[85] Hanssens (ed.), *Amalarii*, iii. 54. For transcriptions of and commentary on the neuma triplex, see Apel, *Chant*, 240, 343, 441; Stäblein, 'Tropus', ex. 9 following col. 816; Handschin, 'Trope', 143–4; Holman, 'Tropes', 37; Hofmann-Brandt, 'Die Topen', i. 12–15; Hoppin, *Medieval Music*, 147; Steiner, 'Responsories', 171–7; idem, 'Chant'; Hofmann-Brandt, 'Die Tropen', i. 56–72; Kelly, 'Melisma', 163–4; idem, 'Neuma'. Further discussion of the word 'neuma' is given below.

[86] Steiner questions Amalarius' assertion that the neuma triplex originated in the Resp. *In medio ecclesie*; 'Chant', 250–1.

[87] 'Et non cantetur festive'; F:Pn, lat. 976, fo. 2^{v}.

[88] On the performance of responsory tropes, see Kelly, 'Melisma'. The author shows that the use of the choir is suggested in MSS in which the responsories were embellished only with melismas which 'contain no division marks [and which] are found sometimes as alternative endings, but sometimes also as part of the Responsory itself'; ibid. 178.

[89] See below, pp. 147–8.

TABLE 3.4. *Untexted Responsory Melismas in the Saint-Denis Antiphoner F:Pn, lat. 17296*

Responsory	Fo.	Feast	Location of Melisma	Bibliography on Melisma
Accinxit beata maria[a]	349v	Mary Magdalene	Mat. 8: *sem*-piternam	
Beatissumus cucuphas[b,c]	195v	Cucuphas	Mat. 1: *po*-pulis[g]	
Beatus Nicholaus[a,d]	263v	Nicholas	Mat. 8: o-*por*-tet	H, 42; HB, 453
Benedicamus patrem[a,c]	167v	Trinity	Mat. 9: *se*-cula	R2, 25 ff.
Benedicat nos deus[a,c]	239v	All Saints	Mat. 1: fi-*nes*	R2, 19 ff.
Centum quadraginta[b,c]	41v	Innocents	Mat. 12: *de*-i	S5, 120–3
Christi miles[a,d,e]	63v	Vincent	Mat. 9: verna-*ba*-ntur	HB, 115, 712–13; R2, 24 ff.
Confessor dei nicholas[a]	262v	Nicholas	Mat. 1: *pro*-vehi	H, 42
Cornelius centurio[a,d,e]	175	Peter, Paul	Vesp.: quid *te* oporteat facer-*e*	HB, 204, 216, 549; K2, 385, 387; R2, 19 ff.
Descendit de celis[b,c,d]	21	Christmas	Mat. 4: *fa*-brice mundi[h]	See n. 85
De supernis[a,c]	245v	Eustace	Mat. 6: *fi*-liis[i]	
Diluculo valde surgens[a,c]	350	Mary Magdalene	Mat. 9: *pre*-ciosis	R2, 26 ff.
Ecce jam coram te[a,c,d,e]	185	Invention of Stephen	Mat. 4: *Ec*-ce	HB, 157, 172; S5, 120–2
Ecce vir prudens[a,d]	237	Hilary of Mende Confessor	Mat. 11: *Ec*-ce	HB, 570
Ver. *Erat autem*[a,c] (Resp. *Quatuor animalia*)	270v	Common of Evangelists	Mat. 6: ani-*ma*-lia	R2, 23 ff.
Ver. *Et respicientes*[a,c,e] (Resp. *Et valde mane*)	137v	Easter	Mat. 3: respici-*en*-tes[j]	R1, 839
Et valde mane[a,f]	137	Easter	Mat. 3: *Et*	HB, 116; R1, 839
Ex ejus tumba[a,d]	264	Nicholas	Mat. 11: *sos*-pes	

Responsory	fo.	Feast	Location of Melisma	Bibliography on Melisma
Expoliavit veste[a,c]	204^{v}	Hippolytus	Mat. 8: frue-*re* militi-*e*[g]	
Famulo christi[a,c]	197^{v}	Cucuphas	Mat. 10: *fi*-dem[i]	
Gaudeat exultans[a,e]	252^{v}–253	Eugene	Mat. 12: desti-*na*-vit	R2, 20 ff.
Gaude maria[a,d,f]	68^{v}–69	Purification	Mat. 12: invio-*la*-ta	HB, 341–6, 348, 351, 355; K2, 379; R1, 847
Gloriosi domine[a,d,e]	61^{v}	Vincent	Mat. 3: *oc*-cumbere	HB, 447; R2, 24–ff.
Gloriosus dei amicus[a,d]	64	Vincent	Mat. 12: *ce*-los	HB, 86
Ver. *Hi empti sunt*[a,c,d] (Resp. *Centum quadraginta*)	41^{v}	Innocents	Mat. 12: Hi *emp*-ti[j]	
Hodie martyrum flores innocentes[a,c]	40^{v}	Innocents	Mat. 8: *se*-cula[k]	
Hodie martyrum flores thebeorum[a,c]	220	Maurice	Mat. 4: *se*-cula[k]	R2, 23 ff.
Honor virtus et potestas[a]	167	Trinity	Mat. 6: per-*hen*-ni	H, 42
Illuminare illuminare jerusalem[a,d]	45^{v}	Epiphany	Mat. 3: super *te*	HB, 652, 673
Inito consilio[a]	78^{v}	Benedict	Mat. 3: sig-*no*	H, 42
In medio ecclesie[b]	36	John	Mat. 12: *et* intellectus[h]	
In tempesta noctis[a]	81	Benedict	Mat. 11: *om*-nem	
Jussit decius[a]	204^{v}	Hippolytus	Mat. 9: reve-*re*-or	
Lapides torrentes[b,c,d]	30	Stephen	Mat. 8: ani-*me*	S5, 112–13
Magne pater nicholae[a]	264	Nicholas	Mat. 12: *sus*-tine	H, 43
Magnus sanctus paulus[a,d]	184^{v}	Commemoration of Paul	Mat. 11: *pos*-sidere	H, 42; HB, 505

Miles christi[a,d,f]	252^{v}	Eugene	Mat. 7: *a*-blue	A, 166; D, 74, 88–9, H, 43; HB, 142; K2, 382; R1, 526 (No. 7); S1, 176–7, 246, 259
Ver. *Misit dominus*[a,c,d] (Resp. *In medio ecclesie*)	35^{v}	John	Mat. 12: *Mi*-sit[j]	
O beata trinitias[a,d]	168	Trinity	Mat. 12: *O* beata (at beginning), *o* beata (at end)	HB, 454; K2, 380
O beati viri[a,c,d]	80^{v}	Benedict	Mat. 8: *con*-junctus	HB, 133, 464; K2, 79; S5, 113
O constancia martyrum[a,d]	205	Hippolytus	Mat. 12: *tem*-pore	HB, 334, 335, 479
O felix felicis[a,d,e]	350^{v}	Mary Magdalene	Mat. 12: *com*-menda	HB, 469; R2, 20 ff.
Operibus sanctis[a]	262^{v}	Nicholas	Mat. 4: sacer-*do*-tii	H, 43
Patefacte sunt[b,c,d]	31^{v}	Stephen	Mat. 12: *co*-ronatus	S5, 110–11
Post passionem[b,c]	229^{v}	Denis	Mat. 1: ecclesi-*a*[h]	See n. 91; W, 219–21
Preciosus confessor[a,e]	83	*Transitus* of Benedict	Mat. 12: *as*-cendit	R2, 25 ff.
Preciosus domini[a,e,f]	231^{v}	Denis	Mat. 11: Preci-*o*-sus	See n. 200; R1, 619 (No. 30), 629 (No. 73); R2, 23 ff.
Quicum audissent[a,d,e,f]	263	Nicholas	Mat. 7: cle-*men*-ciam	See n. 200; A, 167; HB, 123, 592–4; R1, 734 (No. 619); R2, 14 ff.; S2, 405–7; S3, 88–90, 350
Ver. *Quicum imminere*[b,c] (Resp. *Post passionem*)	229^{v}	Denis	Mat. 1: Qui-*cum*[j]	See n. 91; W, 219–21
Qui vicerit faciam[b,c]	34	John	Mat. 4: jerusa-*lem*	S4, 129

Responsory	fo.	Feast	Location of Melisma	Bibliography on Melisma
Quis deus magnus[a]	166	Trinity	Mat. 3: mi-*ra*-bilia	H, 42
Sancta et immaculata[b,d]	22	Christmas	Mat. 8: contu-*lis*-ti	
Sancte dei preciose[a,d]	186^{v}	Invention of Stephen	Mat. 8: *col*-legio	S4, 169
Sancte paule apostole[a,f]	184^{v}	Commemoration of Paul	Mat. 10: qui *te* elegit	A, 167; H, 42; L, i/1, 95; ii, 78–9; R1, 735 (No. 621); S2, 405–7; S3, 88, 350
Servus dei nicholaus[a]	263^{v}	Nicholas	Mat. 10: fu-*ga*-vit	H, 42
Solem justicie[a]	212	Nativity of Mary	Mat. 12: pro-*ces*-sit	H, 43; HB, 288, and vol. i, 95
Stephanus autem[b,c]	28^{v}	Stephen	Mat. 1: *po*-pulo[g]	
Styrps jesse[a,d]	211	Nativity of Mary	Mat. 8: *al*-mus	H, 43; HB, 65, 563
Summe dei confessor[a,d]	263^{v}	Nicholas	Mat. 9: *pos*-se	H, 42; HB, 332
Summe trinitati[a]	167	Trinity	Mat. 8: *or*-bem	
Valde honorandus est[b,c]	33^{v}	John	Mat. 1: commen-*da*-vit	S4, 124
Valerius igitur[a,d,e]	63	Vincent	Mat. 7: a-*la*-criter	HB, 586; R2, 20 ff.
Videns ergo flentem[a,d]	349	Mary Magdalene	Mat. 4: *re*-suscitavit	HB, 158; K1, 469
Vir inclitus dionysius[a,e]	231, 241^{v}	Denis, All Saints	Mat. 8: ange-*lo*-rum	R2, 7 ff.
Ver. *Virgo dei*[a,d,e,f] (Resp. *Styrps jesse*)	211^{v}	Nativity of Mary	Mat. 8: *e*-jus	See n. 200; HB, 613, 702; R1, 837; R2, 11 ff.; S2, 406

Abbreviations: Mat.: Matins, No. Vesp.: Vespers, No. A.: Anderson, 'Chants'. B: Bukofzer, 'Aspects'. D: Dittmer, *Worcester*. H: Holman, 'Tropes'. HB: Hofmann-Brandt, 'Die Tropen', ii, No. K1: Kelly, 'Elaboration'. K2: Kelly, 'Music'. L: Ludwig, *Repertorium*. R1: Reaney, *Manuscripts*. R2: Robertson, '*Benedicamus*'. S1: Sanders, *Music*. S2: Smith, 'Florence'. S3; Smith, 'Notre Dame', i. S4; Steiner, 'Responsories'. S5: Steiner, 'Melismas'. W: Walters [Robertson], 'Reconstruction'.

[a] Melisma integrated into responsory (or verse).
[b] Melisma written separately after responsory and verse.
[c] Melisma found in different responsory or other chant at Saint-Denis or elsewhere.
[d] Melisma found with prosula text in other houses.
[e] Melisma also used as Benedicamus Domino or Ite Missa Est at Saint-Denis.
[f] Melisma found as tenor in polyphony in other houses.
[g] Melismas designated with [g] have the same melody.
[h] Melismas designated with [h] use one or more of the neuma triplex melismas.
[i] Melismas designated with [i] have the same melody.
[j] Melismas designated with [j] have the same melody.
[k] Melismas designated with [k] have the same melody.

less important Octave of Saint Denis.[90] The more elaborate second version, which was sung on the feast-day and which may be a remnant of the old Gallican verse,[91] contains a melisma which appears in four other places in F:Pn, lat. 17296 (Table 3.4): in the Gloria Patri following the first neuma triplex in *Descendit de celis*, in the Ver. *Et respicientes* from the third Easter Resp. *Et valde mane*, in the Ver. *Misit dominus* from the twelfth responsory for John *In medio ecclesie*, and in the Ver. *Hi empti sunt* from the final responsory for Innocents *Centum quadraginta*.[92]

Besides the neuma triplex, the Saint-Denis antiphoner contains other melismatic tropes which are likewise well known in numerous medieval sources. The melisma on *Inviolata* (Table 3.4) from the responsory for Purification *Gaude maria* was widely disseminated both with and without a text. The melody alone appears in F:Pn, lat. 17296, but the thirteenth-century ordinaries show that a prosula *Inviolata maria* was also used at the close of the third nocturn of Matins:[93] 'the Resp. *Gaude maria*. After the verse [the responsory] is repeated and the Prosa *Inviolata maria* is sung well by two.'[94] Evidently the responsory and its verse were sung through once, and as the responsory was repeated, the choir stopped singing just before the final words *inviolata permansisti*. Two soloists then interpolated the prosula, and when they finished, the choir probably joined in to finish the text of the responsory.[95] In later sources the melisma was underlaid with another text, *Inviolata intacta et casta es Maria*. This prosa is found among the Marian sequences in the thirteenth- and fourteenth-century missals of Saint-Denis F:Pn, lat. 1107 and GB:Lva 1346–1891 (see Table 3.9). The fourteenth- and sixteenth-century breviaries call for the perform-

[90] 'Resp. *Post passionem*, Ver. *Quicum imminere* in cantu privato a duobus'; F:Pm 526, fos. 183[r–v]; F:Pn, lat. 976, fo. 137.

[91] For a transcription of the entire responsory and verse, see Handschin, 'Wende', 46–9. The 2 versions of the Ver. *Quicum imminere* are given in Walters [Robertson], 'Reconstruction', 220; see also the discussion in ibid. 219–21.

[92] Even though the melisma is incorporated into the original statement of the Ver. *Hi empti*, it is clearly a trope, for the verse later appears without the melisma in this same MS on the feast of All Saints (1 Nov.) on fo. 241[v].

[93] The word 'prosa' is often used interchangeably with 'prosula', but Steiner suggests that the former be reserved 'for independent works in syllabic style intended for specific liturgical functions', while the latter should be used 'where a text is written for a melisma that originated in a piece of Gregorian chant'; 'Melismas', 111, n. 8; see also Kelly, 'Melisma', 163; Huglo, *Livres*, 30–2.

[94] 'Resp. *Gaude maria*. Post Ver. repetatur et cantetur Prosa *Inviolata maria* a duobus bene cantantibus'; F:Pm 526, fo. 106[v]; F:Pn, lat. 976, fo. 76. At least 2 prosulas begin with these same 2 words: *Inviolata maria dei* and *Inviolata maria intacta permanens* (see Hofmann-Brandt, 'Die Tropen', ii, Nos. 351, 352). The one sung at Saint-Denis is probably the latter, which is the more widely disseminated.

[95] The text just cited suggests this manner of performance, and Kelly documents similar instructions in 'Melisma', 169–70.

ance of *Inviolata intacta* in place of the hymn at Second Vespers on Purification.[96]

Like *Inviolata*, the melisma 'Contulisti' for the eighth responsory for Christmas *Sancta et immaculata* is untexted in F:Pn, lat. 17296 (see Table 3.4).[97] The common Prosa for this responsory, *Beata es virgo*, subsequently appears in the thirteenth-century sequentiary (see Table 3.9) with music that is not related to that of the responsory melisma. In its final verse, *Beata es virgo* likewise contains a trope of the Gloria Patri *Doxa patri semper ingenito*.[98]

If the neuma triplex and the melismas on *Inviolata* and *Contulisti* were derived ultimately from other sources, the latter have not been uncovered, and it may be that these melodies were in fact popular, original compositions which circulated throughout the West. Certain melismas in the antiphoner F:Pn, lat. 17296, on the other hand, come from another class of chant, the offertory of the Mass. The melismas on 'anime' from the Resp. *Lapides torrentes* and on 'dei' from the Resp. *Centum quadraginta* (Table 3.4) are borrowed from the Offer. *Gressos meos* and *Benedicite gentes*, respectively.[99] The ordinaries show that by the thirteenth century *Lapides torrentes* had moved from its original position at Matins to Second Vespers.

Since the melismas discussed thus far vary in form, one might ask whether the term 'trope' actually encompasses them all. It is in fact likely that these and other melismas in Table 3.4 that wander freely from one chant to another are tropes, despite their different origins. Some of the melodies, as just noted, do not even confine themselves to a single genre of chant, for example the melismas 'anime' and 'dei', which move from offertory to responsory. These 'wandering melismas', along with the melismas on 'coronatus' (Resp. *Patefacte sunt*), 'jerusalem' (Resp. *Qui vicerit faciam*), and 'commendavit' (Resp. *Valde honorandus est*) appear after their responsories as alternate versions for simpler settings in F:Pn, lat. 17296, while in other books they are not given at all. Since none of these melismas seems to have originated in the chant with which it appears, they fit the definition of trope as a later melodic insertion.[100] In contrast, a few melismas in Table 3.4 that are

[96] 'Prosa loco hymno, *Inviolata intacta es*'; GB:Ob, Can. lit. 192, fo. 322^{v}; also F:Pn, Rés. B. 5209. Kelly discusses uses of the prosula *Inviolata* both as a processional piece and as a sequence; Kelly, 'Music', 388. See also Steiner, 'Melismas', 113, n. 17.

[97] Evidently the Resp. *Sancta et immaculata* had been transferred from Matins to Second Vespers by the 13th c., for the ordinaries record it in this place; see F:Pm 526, fo. 17.

[98] See Hofmann-Brandt, 'Die Tropen', ii, No. 166, for concordances for this Gloria trope in other sources.

[99] Steiner identifies the offertories and gives other concordances for the melodies; Steiner, 'Melismas', 112–13, 120–3. The movement of melismas to and from offertories has been treated in ibid.; in idem, 'Prosulae'; and in Levy, 'Origin'.

[100] It is particularly difficult to determine whether a responsorial melisma is an added trope or

integrated into their responsories and which have not yet been discovered in other contexts or sources,[101] or which have not been found independent of their host chants,[102] may on the one hand be added tropes, or may have been written with their responsories from the outset.

The Offices at Saint-Denis were not the only services that included melismatic tropes, for the Mass contained at least one trope of this type: the melisma found in the early eleventh-century gradual F:Pm 384 in the Communion for Saint Stephen *Video celos*. The first syllable of the final word 'faciunt' contains a lengthy, sequential melisma which is notated in neumes.[103] This interpolation seems to be peculiar to Saint-Denis, since it has not surfaced in any other source for the ubiquitous *Video celos*. Because of the uniqueness of the trope for Saint Stephen, Michel Huglo suggests that the melody may have been composed at Notre Dame during the era of its dedication to Stephen prior to the ninth century. Saint-Denis, a dependency of the cathedral in the Merovingian era, may have adopted the trope and then preserved it in later manuscripts such as F:Pm 384.[104] If it is true, as Handschin stated, that troping with melismas was both first to appear and first to die out, then the preservation of this and other melismatic tropes at Saint-Denis well into the twelfth century—long after other forms were cultivated elsewhere—points to the monks' tendency to hold to ancient tradition in matters of liturgical practice.

A glance at the antiphoner F:Pn, lat. 17296 reveals many other melismas embedded in responsories and in some antiphons. Unlike the melismatic tropes for the Office mentioned above, these embellish-

not, since the earliest sources from the 9th and 10th cs. most often preserve only the words of the responsory, which indicate neither the presence nor the absence of a trope. Scholars differ over their criteria for what constitutes a melisma that tropes a responsory. Holman considers that most responsorial melismas are musical tropes for four reasons: '(1) In most instances they appear in one fixed place in the responds (immediately before the end); (2) a large number of melismas have a melodic repeat structure (AA, AAB, ABA, ABAC, etc.) that is foreign to the style of the neumatic and syllabic parts of the responsories; (3) they are often stylistically different from the rest of the respond in which they are found even when the melismas do not have a repeat structure; and (4) long melismas are much more common in recent responsories, originating in the 10th to the 13th centuries when troping was common, than in the reponsories that originated in the 9th century or earlier'; 'Tropes', 39–40. Steiner takes a more cautious approach: 'In some cases, the melisma is incorporated in the Responsory and can be identified as added material only if the Responsory (or its melody, with different words) is found elsewhere without the melisma, or if the melisma can be shown to be borrowed from another chant'; 'Melismas', 109–10. Kelly has repeated this opinion: 'Lengthy melismas by themselves are no sure sign of a lurking trope'; 'Elaboration', 461.

[101] i.e. those with no entries in the 'Bibliography' column.

[102] i.e. those with symbols relating them to other melismas but without entries in the 'Bibliography' column.

[103] F:Pm 384, fo. 9. See facsimiles of this fo. in Hesbert, *Graduel*, 9; in Huglo, 'Débuts', 106; and the transcription in idem, 'Aux Origines', 48.

[104] Idem, 'Débuts', 105.

ments are not notated separately after the responsory; instead, they are written within the responsory, usually on a final syllable or sometimes in the accompanying verse (Table 3.4). In this case, it is more difficult to know whether the melodies are tropes or whether they were composed along with the responsory from the start. Those which wander through other genres of chant (e.g. *Ecce* from Resp. *Ecce jam coram te*) may be tropes, as noted earlier. Others, however, are found in newer Offices, such as the services for Mary Magdalene and Nicholas, in which the more important responsories often contained melismas as integral parts of the chants. While these melismas may not have begun as tropes, many houses turned them into textual tropes through the addition of prosula texts.[105] Saint-Denis likewise cultivated some prosulas, but the monks evidently preferred to make a different use of many melismas listed in Table 3.4. They separated them altogether from their responsories and retexted them as independent chants for the Benedicamus Domino and Ite Missa Est, as described below.[106]

Prosulas in F:Pn, lat. 17296

The few examples of texts, or prosulas, which are added to responsories in the Saint-Denis antiphoner are significant because of their rarity. These pieces embellish eleven responsories for Matins and Lauds and one Gloria Patri (Table 3.5). All but one were sung on the three feast-days after Christmas (Stephen, John, Innocents), while the remaining prosula is assigned to the Nativity of Mary (8 September).

Ten of the prosulas in Table 3.5 seem to be unique to F:Pn, lat. 17296 (*Christo nato*, *Et intellectus johannem*, *Gloria deo patri magno*, *Hebreorum gens*, *Hodie processit regina*, *Inter hec frendet* [Pl. 13], *Judicabunt innocentes*, *Justus johannes*, *Justus virginitate* [Pl. 14] and *Non vos quos elegi*),[107] and it is entirely possible that the texts and

[105] See Table 3.5. The prosulas that were sung on these melismas in other institutions are catalogued in Hofmann-Brandt, 'Die Tropen', ii. On the texting of responsory melismas, see ibid. i. 2–4; Kelly, 'Elaboration', 468–72. Kelly concludes that it is usually the internal melismas that determine the structure of the prosulas, and not the other way around.

[106] In practices outside Saint-Denis, several melismas from Table 3.4 served either as integral tenor voices or as parts of longer tenors in polyphonic compositions. (See the bibliog. in Table 3.4 for responsories designated with the number 6; see also Robertson, '*Benedicamus*', 48–51; Kelly, 'Melisma', 175–6). The Notre Dame sources, for example, include 2- and some 3-voice settings of the Ver. *Et respicientes* and *Virgo dei*, the Resp. *Et valde mane*, *Quicum audissent*, and *Preciosus domini*, and clausulas also exist for many of these works. The clausula *Te*, based on the Resp. *Sancte paule apostole*, likewise hails from the Notre Dame repertory. Similarly, the English source GB:Lwa 33327 uses the melisma *Ablue* from the Resp. *Miles christi* in the motet *Ave miles de cuius/Ave miles*, *O Edlkude/Quartus cantus/Ablue*. Because of their multi-functional nature in polyphonic as well as monophonic guises, these peripatetic melismas remain some of the most intriguing of all chant-segments.

[107] See Hofmann-Brandt, 'Die Tropen', i. 11. These tropes do not appear in any other extant source from the abbey, and were probably not in use after the 12 c. Similarly, they are not found in

TABLE 3.5 *Prosulas for Responsories and Gloria Patri in the Saint-Denis Antiphoner F:Pn, lat. 17296*

Prosula	Fo.	Chant to which prosula is attached	Text troped	No. of trope in		Feast	Service
				Hofmann-Brandt	*CAO*, iv		
Christo nato de virgine[b]	39v–40	Resp. *Sub altare dei*		114	7713	Innocents	Mat. 8
Et intellectus johannem[b]	36	Resp. *In medio ecclesie*	. . . *et intellectus* (end of responsory)	182	6913	John	Mat. 12
Gloria deo patro magno[b]	30v	Gloria patri Resp. *Impetum fecerunt*	Gloria patri (lesser doxology)	257	6885	Stephen	Mat. 9
Hebraeorum gens[b]	30v–31	Resp. *Impii super justum*		282	6887	Stephen	Mat. 10
Hodie processit regina[a,b]	212	Resp. *Solem justitie*		288	7677	Nativity of Mary	Mat. 12
Inter hec frendet[b]	29v–30 Pl. 13	Resp. *Lapidabant stephanum*		339	7072	Stephen	Mat. 6
Judicabunt innocentes[b]	42–42v	Resp. *Cantabant sancti*	Alle. *Judicabunt sancti*	369	6266	Innocents	Lauds
Justus johannes[b]	37v–38 Pl. 14	Resp. *Iste est johannes*	Alle. *Justus germinabit* (*LU*, 1192)	372	7001	John	Mat. 8
Justus virginitate[b]	37v Pl. 14	Resp. *Iste est johannes*	Alle. *Justus ut palma* (*LU*, 1207)	374	7001	John	Mat. 8
Non vos quos eligi[a,b]	36v–37	Resp. *Qui sunt isti*		426	7484	John	Lauds
Qui scis infirma[c]	29–29v Pl. 13	Resp. *O martyrum gemma*		558	7276	Stephen	Mat. 4
Stephanus dei gratia plenus[c]	30v	Resp. *Impetum fecerunt*		661	6885	Stephen	Mat. 9

[a] Text only, no music.
[b] Prosula unique to Saint-Denis.
[c] Prosula found in other sources.

music of some if not all of these were composed in the abbey. Neither *Hodie processit regina* nor *Non vos quos elegi* are notated in F:Pn, lat. 17296, and thus we cannot compare them musically to the responsories which they accompany. In *Non vos quos elegi*, the added prosula phrases strongly emphasize the concept of light which (as we will see in Chapter 4) is found in neo-Platonic philosophy. Hofmann-Brandt points out that the syllable count (left column below) of *Hodie processit* fits the final melisma on 'proces-sit' from the Resp. *Solem justitie*:[108]

13 *Hodie processit* regina angelorum	[Today appears the queen of angels
13 et liberatrix animarum perditarum	and liberator of lost souls,
12 salus medicinaque christicolarum	the health and medicine of Christians.
12 fugatrix omnium clara tenebrarum	That bright (lady) who puts to flight
cessit ad ortum.	all darkness is born.]

This prosula uses rhyme and two pairs of lines of thirteen and twelve syllables each. In its regularity, it resembles the early examples of the rhymed, metrical liturgical poetry that are the hallmark of the later Middle Ages, and it may therefore have been written near the time of copying of F:Pn, lat. 17296, possibly in the late eleventh or early twelfth century. The prosula was probably performed as an interpolation in the reprise of the responsory, as described above for *Inviolata maria*.

The music for the prosula *Et intellectus johannem* is not original: it comes from the first melisma of the neuma triplex.[109] The text, on the other hand, is evidently particular to the Saint-Denis antiphoner F:Pn, lat. 17296:[110]

Et intellectus johannem quem elegerat virginem ex omni populo quemcumque plasmavit christus redemptor et moriturus, pendens in cruce Mariam preciosam parentem discipulo castitatis prerogativa prae cunctis ornato commisit et claro sapientia *intellectus*.

(Christ the redeemer fashioned John as the purest out of all the people he had chosen. When he was about to die, hanging on the cross, he entrusted his precious mother Mary to this disciple [John], distinguished above all through his preference for purity, and bright in wisdom.)

The words are set syllabically to the melody in straightforward manner, often following the ligatures of the neuma. The prosula text frequently employs the vowel *e* in assonance with the final words of the responsory (*et intellectus*). These features are characteristic of the earliest stage of

the large number of MSS that Hofmann-Brandt inventories. Hesbert has edited the texts in *CAO*, iv.

[108] 'Die Tropen', i. 95; ii, No. 288.

[109] The trope is published in Stäblein, 'Tropus', *MGG*, xiii, ex. 9.

[110] Hofmann-Brandt, 'Die Tropen', i. 57; ii, No. 182.

prosula composition.[111] The metre and rhyme-scheme are not regular, although two almost iambic, eight-syllable lines do appear at the beginning: 'Et intellectus johannem/quem elegerat virginem'. Thus the prosula may have been composed in the early eleventh century and then preserved in subsequent manuscripts like F:Pn, lat. 17296. The execution of the piece was probably the same as mentioned earlier for *Inviolata maria* and *Hodie processit*.

By contrast, the texts of three other prosulas, *Christo nato*, *Hebreorum gens*, and *Inter hec frendet*, are perfectly metrical and rhyming. These compositions represent the final stage of evolution of the prosula, in which the music of the trope is independent of its parent responsory (Ex. 3.12),[112] and they probably date from the twelfth century, perhaps just before the time F:Pn, lat. 17296 was copied (1140–50).

Hebreorum gens and *Inter hec frendet* contain six lines of poetry each, while *Christo nato* adds a seventh line to make a smooth textual transition back to the *repetendum* of the responsory. All three prosulas have eight-syllable lines throughout. In *Christo nato*, the ends of line-pairs rhyme (aa bb cc d); in *Hebreorum gens* the first four lines rhyme, while the last two form a couplet (aaaa bb); and in *Inter hec frendet*, all lines rhyme on *-us*. The melodies of these prosulas are more ornate than usual, employing two-note neumes on some words and short melismas at the ends of phrases. The exceptionally high *tessitura* of *Christo nato* may indicate that boys chanted the piece, an appropriate choice since it was sung on the feast of Holy Innocents. In performance, these prosulas seem to have been interpolated after the repetition of the responsory and just before the *repetendum*, which is indicated by a textual cue after the prosula: responsory—verse—responsory—PROSULA—*repetendum*.

In contrast, *Justus virginitate*, *Justus johannes*, and *Judicabunt innocentes* have the hallmarks of older compositions. These prosulas serve as tropes for three alleluias (*Justus ut palma*, *Justus germinabit*, and *Judicabunt sancti*, respectively), a kind of troping that reached its height in the tenth and eleventh centuries, although some twelfth-century sources preserve the pieces.[113] The prosulas may well have been composed to be sung with alleluias at Mass at Saint-Denis in the tenth or early eleventh century, and then, when they were no longer 'in style' for the Mass, they were recycled as pseudo-responsory tropes in the antiphoner F:Pn, lat. 17296 in Offices for Saint John and Holy Innocents (Ex. 3.13). No trace of them remains in any extant books of

[111] For a discussion of the methods of prosula composition, see Kelly, 'Music', 367–74.

[112] See ibid. 387–8.

[113] Steiner, 'Prosula', 310. The sources of prosulas for the alleluia, catalogued in Marcusson, *CT*, ii. 10–13, date mostly from the 10th and 11th cs.

Ex.3.12. *Sandionysian Prosulas* Christo nato, Hebreorum gens, *and* Inter hec frendet

F:Pn, lat. 17296, fos. 39v–40

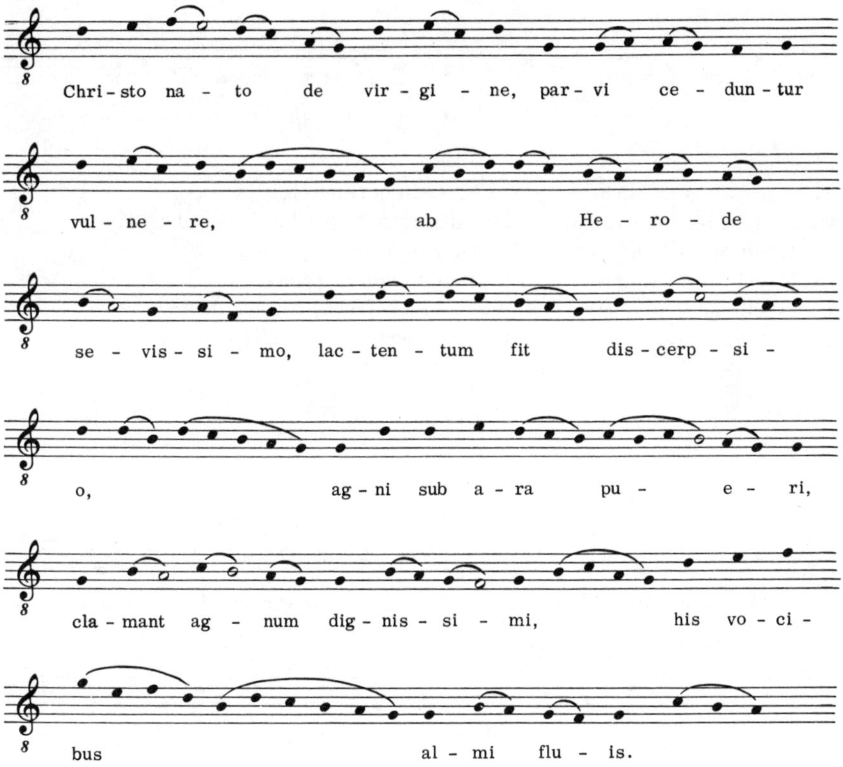

Chri - sto na - to de vir - gi - ne, par - vi ce - dun - tur

vul - ne - re, ab He - ro - de

se - vis - si - mo, lac - ten - tum fit dis - cerp - si -

o, ag - ni sub a - ra pu - e - ri,

cla - mant ag - num dig - nis - si - mi, his vo - ci -

bus al - mi flu - is.

Christo nato de virgine,
parvi ceduntur vulnere,
ab Herode sevissimo,
lactentum fit discerpsio,
agni sub ara pueri,
clamant agnum dignissimi,
his vocibus almifluis.

[When Christ was born of the Virgin,
the little boys were submitted to a calamity:
the tearing apart of the suckling children,
carried out by the most horrible Herod.
The most worthy boys
cry from the altar of the lamb
with these flowing words.]

F:Pn, lat. 17296, fo. 31

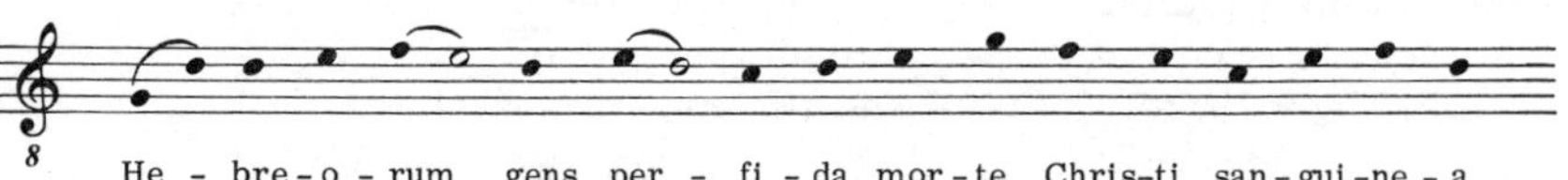

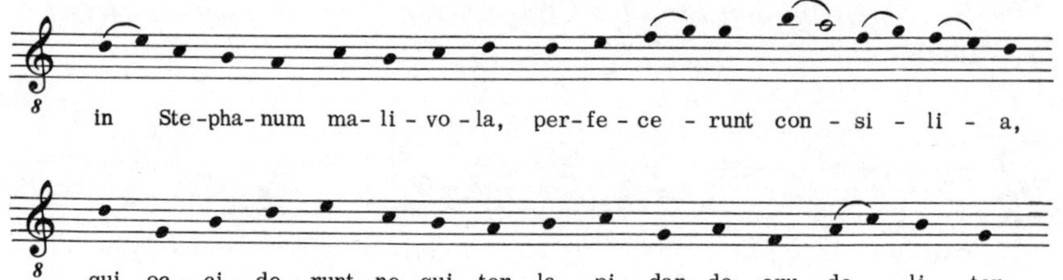

Hebreorum gens perfida,
morte Christi sanguinea,
in Stephanum malivola,
perfecerunt consilia,
qui occiderunt nequiter
lapidando crudeliter.

[The treacherous Hebrew people,
bloodthirsty from the death of Christ,
carried out on Stephen
their malevolent plans.
They killed (him) miserably
by stoning (him) cruelly.]

F:Pn, lat. 17296, fos. 29v–30

Inter hec frendet populus,
in Stephanum judaicus,
eius membra lapidibus,
perurgens totis viribus,
et levita dignissimus,
orat Christum his vocibus.

[In the midst of these things,
the Jewish people crush Stephen,
forcing stones on his limbs
with all their might.
And this most worthy Levite
beseeches Christ with these words.]

the Mass from the abbey. Despite the fact that a text similar to the one given for *Justus johannes* in F:Pn, lat. 17296 appears in some Aquitanian sources, it is evident that none of these three prosulas was widely disseminated.[114] Indeed, it is possible that *Justus virginitate*, which hints at Pseudo-Dionysian and Eriugenian philosophy, as described in Chapter 4, was composed at Saint-Denis.

All three prosulas are written in F:Pn, lat. 17296 after their 'adoptive' responsories: *Justus virginitate* and *Justus johannes* both follow the Resp. *Iste est johannes* for John, and *Judicabunt innocentes* appears after the Ver. *Sub throno dei* of the Resp. *Cantabant sancti* for the Innocents. The Resp. *Iste est johannes* is actually given twice in F:Pn, lat. 17296: first with the two Ver. *Iste est johannes cui christus* and *Johannes hic theologus* as the eighth responsory at Matins for John (fos. 34^{v}–35), and then following Lauds it is repeated out of order (fos. 37^{v}–38), this time without its verses, and with the two *Justus* prosulas, evidently as a way of providing an alternative version for the eighth responsory. Only the first prosula, *Justus virginitate*, is followed by a cue to the *repetendum* of the Resp. *Iste est johannes*, and this piece serves as a substitute for the missing responsory verse.[115] The second prosula *Justus johannes* was probably performed after the *repetendum* of the responsory, though it is not clear whether the *repetendum* was then repeated at the very end. Likewise, there is no indication in F:Pn, lat. 17296 of a return to the *repetendum* of the Resp. *Cantabant sancti* after the execution of its prosula *Judicabunt innocentes*.

The texts of these three prosulas are interjected between the words of the three parent alleluias, so that the verses are transformed from melismatic to mostly syllabic settings.[116] Typically, prosulas for the alleluia use vowel imitation, and these three in F:Pn, lat. 17296 are no exception. The ends and sometimes middles of many words of the prosula texts echo either the final vowel of the verse words they follow, or the vowel on which the original melismas were sung. In *Judicabunt innocentes*, for example, the prosula words 'gent*es*' and 'omn*es*' imitate the verse word 'nation*es*'. 'Super*a*', 'p*a*lm*a*', 'be*a*t*a* Glori*a* nov*a*',

[114] None is contained in Marcusson, *CT*, ii. The prosula *Justus johannes* is discussed briefly in Pothier, '*Alleluia*', 169–70.

[115] Hofmann-Brandt, 'Die Tropen', ii. 75, No. 374. Although not tropes properly speaking, two other chants in F:Pn, lat. 17296 are rubricated as verses and serve like *Justus virginitate* as additional or substitute responsory verses. These are the Ver. *Felix inquam virgineum* and *Eia nunc clarissimo*, respectively the 2nd and 3rd verses of the 1st responsory for John *Valde honorandus est*. Of the 12 sources edited by Hesbert, *Felix inquam virgineum* and *Eia nunc clarissimo* appear only in F:Pn, lat. 17296 (see *CAO*, iv. 446, No. 7817). Although this suggests that the 2 verses may be unique to Saint-Denis, it would be necessary to search many more antiphoners before claiming that the chants originated in the abbey.

[116] Steiner gives examples of other alleluia prosulas, found in F:Pn, lat. 1118, and their relationship to the parent alleluias and verses, in 'Prosulae', 375–92.

Ex. 3.13. *Sandionysian Prosulas* Justus virginitate, Justus Johannes, *and* Judicabunt Innocentes

F:Pn, lat. 17296, fo. 37^v

Jus- tus vir-gi-ni-ta-te cla- rus *ut pal- ma* Jo-han-nes

or-na-tus pu-di-ci-ti-a *flo-ru*-it et i-de-o *si-cut ce-drus*

pa-ra-di-si nec-ta-re ir-ri-ga-tus un-di-que mun-do ple-ne

e-ruc-ta-vit ar-ca-na the-o-ri-e que an-ge-li vix va-lent

per-ci-pe-re qua-prop-ter ei-us ho-no-re gau-det pro-les ec-cle-si-e

que doc-tri-na ei- us *mul-ti- pli-ca- bi- tur.*

[Righteous John has blossomed bright in virginity, adorned with chastity like the palm, and like the cedar tree he is watered with the nectar of paradise. He has preached openly in all parts of the world the secrets of philosophy which the angels are scarcely able to understand. For this reason the progeny of the Church, which will multiply through his teaching, rejoice in his honour.]

F:Pn, lat. 17296, fos. 37^v–38
[not notated]

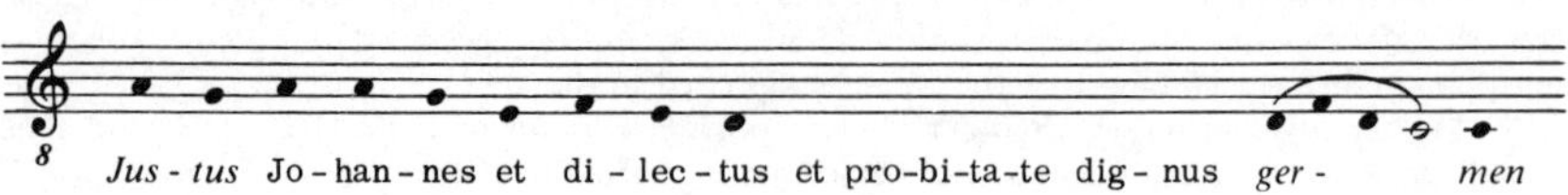

[John, righteous and beloved and worthy in goodness, will always hold the sweetly scented branch, the palm tree of propriety, like the lily, whitened with brightness. He who was chosen by the Lord as the pure one and who has remained worthily pure for ever before the Lord shone in the flower of virginity and of the fully evangelizing law.]

F:Pn, lat. 17296, fos. 42r–v

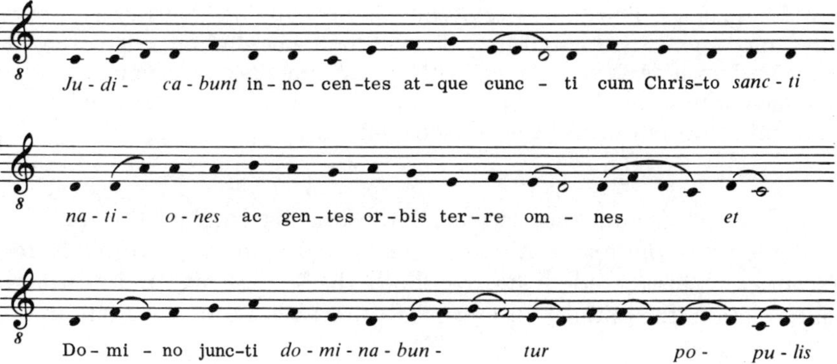

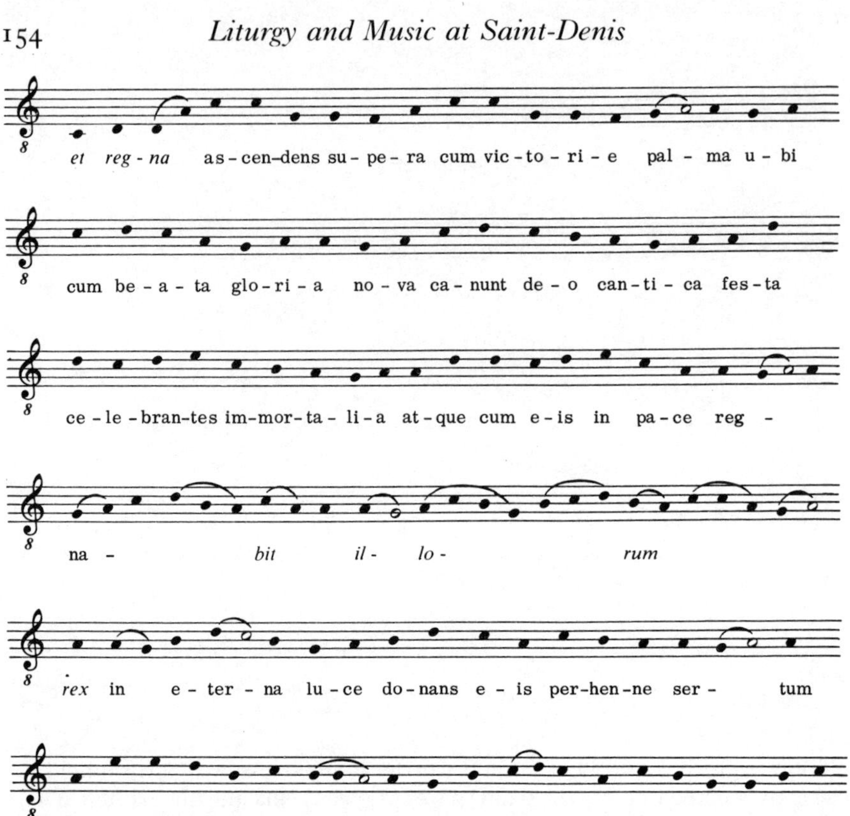

[The innocents and all the holy ones with Christ will judge the nations and all the peoples of the earth, and those united with the Lord will have dominion over the peoples. Their king ascends into the heavenly kingdoms with the palm of victory where with blessed glory they sing new songs to God, celebrating the immortal feasts. And he will reign with them in peace in eternal light, speaking eternally with them. We ask that our portion be holy so that we can climb to the heavenly kingdom with them to rejoice for ever.]

'c*a*ntic*a* fest*a*', and 'inmort*a*li*a*' of the prosula emulate the melisma syllable -*na*- of 'regnabit'; and 'luc*e*', 'p*e*rh*e*nn*e*', 'parc*e*m', '*esse*', 'scand*ere*', and 'gaud*ere*' mirror both the -*e*- in 'rex' and, through anticipation, the initial *e*- in 'eternum', on which the melisma falls in the alleluia verse.

While *Justus virginitate*, *Justus johannes*, and *Judicabunt innocentes* were possibly unique to Saint-Denis, three other prosulas in the repertory of the monastery were popular throughout Europe. *Qui scis infirma* from the responsory for Stephen *O martyum gemma* was sung at Saint-Denis at least until the sixteenth century, as witnessed by its appearance with text and music in F:Pn, lat. 17296 (Table 3.5, Pl. 13), and with text alone in the fourteenth- and sixteenth-century breviaries GB:Ob, Can. lit. 192 and F:Pn, Rés. B. 5209.[117] In contrast to the aforementioned prosulas in the late style, *Qui scis infirma* was created by the easiest means possible: a poetic text added to the melisma on *-pla-* of 'contemplatione', with one syllable assigned to each note. The text of the prosula imitates the melisma-vowel *-a-* and the final vowel *-e-* of 'contemplatione' through assonance. *Qui scis infirma* also appears in neumatic notation in the notated breviary Vendôme, Bibl. Mun. 17C (fos. 34ᵛ–35), which may come from a house dependent on Saint-Denis. The musical reading in this breviary varies slightly from that in the Saint-Denis antiphoner on the words 'vitiorum' and 'fragilissime'.

Another prosula for Stephen, *Stephanus dei gratia plenus*, appears in F:Pn, lat. 17296 and in other manuscripts as well.[118] This text is set syllabically to a simple melody which is not related to the parent Resp. *Impetum fecerunt*.[119] The music comes instead from the tone of the lesser doxology (Gloria Patri), which is likewise troped with the text *Gloria deo patri magno* (Ex. 3.14):

Ex. 3.14. *Gloria Patri Trope* Gloria deo patri magno
F:Pn, lat. 17296, fo. 30ᵛ

[117] GB:Ob, Can. lit. 192, fo. 291ᵛ. For concordances outside Saint-Denis, see Hofmann-Brandt, 'Die Tropen', ii, No. 558.

[118] See ibid. No. 661.

[119] On this responsory, see Steiner, 'Responsories', 167–8.

9	Gloria deo patri magno	[Glory to God the great Father
12	eiusque filio sibi digne nato	and to His Son, born worthy of him,
9	ac utriusque flammi sacro	and to the Holy Flame of them both,
13	per omnia secula seculorum amen.	world without end, Amen.]

(Syllable count of each line given in left column.)

This brief Gloria trope alternates between lines of nine and twelve/thirteen syllables and uses end-rhymes and internal emphasis on the vowel *-o*. In F:Pn, lat. 17296, *Gloria deo patri magno* occurs after the Prosula *Stephanus dei gratia plenus*, and just before a second Ver. *Positis autem*. The order of the items suggests the following performance of the elaborate Resp. *Impetum fecerunt*: Resp. *Impetum*—prosula *Stephanus dei—repetendum* of responsory—Gloria trope *Gloria deo—repetendum* of responsory—Ver. *Positis autem—repetendum* of responsory.

One other *prosula*, the widely disseminated *Sospitati dedit egros* from the responsory for Saint Nicholas *Ex ejus tumba*, is perhaps the only prosula that came into the liturgy of the abbey after the twelfth century, for it is not found in F:Pn, lat. 17296. The Office of Saint Nicholas was something of a novelty in the twelfth century, but it does occur in one of the original hands of F:Pn, lat. 17296, which was copied around 1140–1350.[120] While later sources from Saint-Denis naturally include the service, they alter the sequence of responsories for Matins. According to the newer arrangement, the Resp. *Ex ejus tumba* is conspicuously placed last in the series. The new ordering allows for the prominent display of the prosula *Sospitati dedit egros* (Table 3.6).[121] The ordinary F:Pn, lat. 976 states that *Sospitati* was performed by two monks,[122] and it is possible that these soloists chanted the phrases of this rhymed, metrical trope antiphonally.

Tropes for the Mass Proper

The proper of the Mass at Saint-Denis included at least four tropes of the text-and-music variety, and traces of these are preserved in the thirteenth-century sources. The Christmas and Easter tropes *Hodie cantandus est* and *Quem queritis* are named in the unnotated ordinaries F:Pm 526 and F:Pn, lat. 976, but none of the musical manuscripts

[120] Fos. 261–264^{v}; Hesbert, *CAO*, ii, No. 120^{2}.

[121] Like the prosulas just discussed, *Sospitati* is also late in style. It is not surprising then to find this piece missing from such 12th-c. MSS as F:Pn, lat. 17296 and added to other books for the Office of approximately the same age.

[122] '[Et dui monachi cantent prosam] *Sospitati*'; F:Pn, lat. 976, fo. 153^{v}. Bracketed words are partially erased in the MS.

TABLE 3.6. *Transmission of the Responsory* Ex ejus tumba *in the Saint-Denis Sources*

Twelfth century[a]	Thirteenth to sixteenth centuries[b]
Matins responsories	*Matins responsories (differences only)*
1. *Confessor dei nicholaus*	
2. *Dum vero adhuc*	
3. *Quantam denique*	
4. *Operibus sanctis*	4. *Servus dei*
5. *Quadam die tempestate*	5. *Operibus sanctis*
6. *Audiens christi confessor*	6. *quadam die*
7. *Quicum audissent sancti*	7. *Audiens christi*
8. *Beatus nicholaus*	8. *Quicum audissent*
9. *Summe dei confessor*	
10. *Servus dei nicholaus*	10. *Beatus nicholaus*
11. *Ex ejus tumba*	11. *Magne pater*
12. *Magne pater nicholae*	12. *Ex ejus tumba* (with prosula *Sospitati dedit*)

[a] F:Pn, lat. 17296, fos. 262–4; Hesbert, *CAO*, ii, No. 120[2].
[b] The Office of Saint Nicholas, along with the prosula *Sospitati*, is found in F:Pn, lat. 976, fos. 153–153[v]; GB:Ob, Can. lit. 192, fos. 281–4; and in F:Pn, lat. Rés. B. 5209.

records them. Performance indications for these pieces, however, are expressly stated in the ordinaries:

Following the procession [after terce], certain ones who sing well should go up next to the altar of the holy martyrs [the altar of Saint Denis] and stand some on the right side, others on the left side. They should sing correctly and respectfully the trope *Quem queritis*, answering back and forth antiphonally. And when they intone [the part] 'quia surrexi dicens patri', then the *archicantor* and two of his colleagues standing in the choir and holding staves in their hands should begin the Introit for Mass *Resurrexi*.[123]

The stationing of singers around the most sacred altar in the church, the altar of Saint Denis and his companions, emphasizes the solemnity of the tropes, for this position was used only for the highest moments in the Divine Service.[124]

Although the music for *Hodie cantandus est* and *Quem queritis* has not survived in sources from Saint-Denis, the thirteenth-century missal

[123] 'Post processionem ascendant juxta sancta sanctorum quidam bene cantantes, alii in dextro latere, alii in sinistro latere assistantes bene et honorifice tropas, scilicet *Quem queritis* conjubilantes et sibi invicem respondentes. Et cum intonuerint "quia surrexi dicens patri", mox archicantor et duo socii ejus assistentes in choro regias virgas in manibus tenentes incipiant officium ad missam *Resurrexi*'; F:Pm 526, fo. 57; F:Pn, lat. 976, fo. 30[v]. The execution of the Christmas trope *Hodie cantandus est* is described with similar rubrics in F:Pm 526, fo. 16[v].

[124] See Walters [Robertson], 'Reconstruction', 231; Foley, 'Ordinary', ii. 268–70.

F:Pn, lat. 1107 records melodies for the Easter tropes *Ab increpatione* and *Laus, honor, virtus* for the Offer. *Terra tremuit* and Comm. *Pascha nostrum*, respectively (Ex. 3.15, Pl. 17).[125]

Ex. 3.15. *Easter Tropes* Ab increpatione *and* Laus, honor, virtus
F:Pn, lat. 1107, fos. 145^{r-v} (Pl. 17)

[125] F:Pn, lat. 1107, fos. 145–6. The text of the trope *Ab increpatione* agrees with that which is contained in the majority of earlier MSS cited in Björkvall *et al.*, *CT*, iii. 53, 139, 68, 69, and in Planchart, *Tropes*, ii. 215–19, except the final stanza *Ipso resurgente*, which appears in no other MS inventoried in these studies. Similarly, F:Pn, lat. 1107 preserves the text of *Laus, honor, virtus* roughly as it is found in the majority of earlier tropers (see Björkvall *et al.*, *CT*, iii. 133, 158, 134; Planchart, *Tropes*, ii. 228–30).

F:Pn, lat. 1107, fos. 145v–146

Along with the chants, the missal specifies the method of their performance. The phrases of the trope, assigned to *cantores*,[126] alternated with lines of the offertory or communion, which were executed by the choir. When this exchange had been completed, the entire chant was repeated

[126] F:Pn, lat. 1107 does not specify the number of *cantores*, but the ordinaries F:Pm 526 (fo. 57) and F:Pn, lat. 976 (fo. 30v) state that the archicantor and two of his colleagues are present in the choir.

without the trope. The earlier ordinaries give a few additional details. The two soloists appointed to sing the trope stood in front of the eagle lectern, located in the middle of the choir.[127] When they had chanted a verse of the trope, the cantor then intoned a line of the offertory or communion.[128] The choir would undoubtedly have joined in on the rest of the verse. Once again, the ordinaries make it clear that these expansions to the offertory and communion were sung in a special place in the church, that is, before the eagle lectern.

Although texted tropes for the proper of the Mass at Saint-Denis were evidently popular in the thirteenth century and perhaps earlier, their use seems to have died out in the fourteenth century. The missals F:Pn, lat. 10505 or GB:Lva 1346–1891 and the ordinary F:Pan, L 863, No. 10 contain no tropes at all, and they aptly depict the waning in production and use of tropes in the late Middle Ages. It is more difficult to determine precisely when tropes disappeared from Office chants in the abbey, since no notated Office manuscript later than F:Pn, lat. 17296 has survived. Probably the purely melismatic tropes were the first to go.[129] All prosulas in Table 3.5 except *Qui scis infirma* also seem to have vanished after the twelfth century; at least they are not mentioned in any subsequent manuscript. The melismas *Inviolata* and *Contulisti* were probably dropped from the Office, although the prosas that were created from them survived in the sequentiary. Other responsory melismas that can be traced are those which were transformed into Benedicamus Domino and Ite Missa Est, discussed below. Only the prosulas *Qui scis infirma* and *Sospitati dedit egros*, which remained standard throughout the Middle Ages and Renaissance, appear consistently in the later sources from Saint-Denis.

Tropes for the Mass Ordinary: The Kyriale

The ordinary of the Mass at Saint-Denis, like the proper chants, contained more tropes in the thirteenth century (and no doubt earlier) than at the end of the Middle Ages. The *Kyriale* is found in the

[127] On the location of the eagle, see Foley, 'Ordinary', i. 297–9.

[128] Trope to the offertory: 'Interim offertorium cantetur ita. Duo cantent *Ab increpatione ira*. Dicto versu incipiat cantor *Terra tremuit*'; F:Pm 526, fo. 57^{v}; F:Pn, lat. 976, fo. 31. For the communion: 'Ante communionem duo cantent prosam ante aquilam *Laus, honor, virtus*, et cantor respondeat *Pascha nostrum*'; ibid.

[129] Some support for this idea can be drawn from the transmission of the Office for Saint Denis. The 1st responsory for Matins, *Post passionem*, has both a simple and an elaborate setting for its Ver. *Quicum imminere* in F:Pn, lat. 17296 (fo. 229^{v}), as described above. The subsequent, unnotated breviaries from the 14th and 16th c. (GB:Ob, Can. lit. 192; F:Pn, Rés. B. 5209) preserve only 1 verse in this place and make no mention of an alternate version. It may, then, be fairly assumed that these later books imply the simpler version without the melismas.

thirteenth- and fourteenth-century missals F:Pn, lat. 1107[130] and GB:Lva 1346–1891.[131] A few troped ordinary pieces appear in F:Pn, lat. 1107, and a larger number of florid melodies whose texts had long since disappeared are given in both missals. These tunes are also named in the three ordinaries of Saint-Denis, which describe the liturgical placement of the melodies for the Kyrie throughout their rubrics.

As Table 3.7 shows, the contents and arrangement of the *Kyriales* in F:Pn, lat. 1107 and GB:Lva 1346–1891 differ somewhat. F:Pn, lat. 1107 (N in Table 3.7) groups the items of the ordinary separately, while GB:Lva 1346–1891 (V) pairs Kyrie with Gloria in three instances, as if to form the beginnings of a complete cycle. This is not surprising in the light of the trend toward the unification of the Mass ordinary which had its roots in the fourteenth century. Four troped pieces are notated in F:Pn, lat. 1107: the Gloria *Spiritus et alme*, the Sanctus *Principium sine principio*,[132] and the two Agnus *Quem Johannes*,[133] and *Gloriosa spes reorum*.[134] GB:Lva 1346–1891 includes none of these texts, although it does have the melodies for the Sanctus and Agnus *Gloriosa*, again demonstrating the gradual abandonment of texted interpolations in the later sources. The rubrics in GB:Lva 1346–1891 stress this point by labelling chants, not by the names of their tropes, but by their liturgical destinations. The earlier F:Pn, lat. 1107, on the other hand, uses text incipits to introduce three Kyries, *Pater creator*, *O christi pietas*, and *Orbis factor*, even though the words had already ceased to be sung in the abbey. *O christi pietas* is not the name of a trope at all, but rather of an antiphon for the feast of Saint Nicholas (6 December) which lends its melody to this Kyrie.

The earlier ordinaries F:Pm 526 and F:Pn, lat. 976 show that certain Kyrie melodies had disappeared by the time F:Pn, lat. 1107 and

[130] Fos. 392ᵛ–395. One Kyrie and 1 Gloria are given in the Easter Vigil service on fo. 143; the Kyrie (Melnicki No. 50) is designated for vigils in the *Kyriale*, and the Gloria (Bosse No. 51) also reappears at the end of the MS without rubric.

[131] Fos. 364–9. The Easter Vigil in this MS (fo. 153) includes a Kyrie (Melnicki, *Kyrie*, No. 58) and Gloria (Bosse, *Gloria*, No. 51). The mid-11th-c. augmented sacramentary F:Pn, lat. 9436 likewise contains a small *Kyriale*, notated in neumes, at the beginning of the MS (fos. 1ᵛ–2ᵛ). It contains 3 Kyries, 4 Glorias, 1 Credo, 3 Sanctus, and 1 Agnus Dei. The 4 Gloria melodies, which can be identified, also appear in the later *Kyriale* of the abbey (see Table 3.7): the 1st Gloria is written both in Greek and Latin (see the discussion of the Greek Mass), the 2nd is Bosse, *Gloria*, No. 56, the 3rd is Bosse, *Gloria*, No. 51, and the Agnus is Schildbach, *Agnus*, No. 226 (cf. Schildbach, *Agnus*, 126–7).

[132] The text is ed. in Blume and Bannister, *Tropi*, *AH*, xlvii, No. 270.

[133] The order of phrases of this trope differs from source to source. The version in F:Pn, lat. 1107, in which the order is *Quem johannes*, *Lux indeficiens*, *Qui sede*, and *Rex regum*, most resembles the arrangement found in 2 Beneventan MSS: I:BV VI. 34 (*Quem*, *Rex*, *Lux*, *Qui*), and I:BV VI. 40 (*Quem*, *Rex*, *Qui*, *Lux*); see Iversen, *CT*, iv. 82. The assignment of this trope to the feast of Epiphany is the most common one; ibid. 247; Planchart, *Tropes*, ii. 327–8.

[134] See Blume and Bannister, *Tropi*, *AH*, xlvii, No. 470. and the Gloria *Spiritus et alme*.

TABLE 3.7. *The* Kyriale *of Saint-Denis in the Thirteenth and Fourteenth Centuries, according to F:Pn, lat. 1107 and GB:Lva 1346–1891*[a]

Chant	MS and rubric		Name of trope	No. of trope melody in				
	N	V		MEL	BOS	THAN	SCHILD	*LU*
Kyrie	*In vigiliis*	n.g.		50				
Kyrie	*xii lectionibus*	n.g.		151–var.				
Kyrie	Item [*xii lec.*]	n.g.	217					
Kyrie	*In privatis diebus*	See below		144				
Kyrie	*Pater creator*	See below	[*Pater creator*]	68				XIV
Kyrie	*O christi pietas*	See below	[Ant. *O christi pietas*]	96				
Kyrie	*Orbis factor*	See below	[*Orbis factor*]	16				XI
Kyrie	*Dominicis diebus*	n.g.		155				
Kyrie	*In precipuis festivitatibus*	*In festis annualibus et semiannualibus*	[*Fons bonitatis*]	48				II
Gloria	See below	–			56			IV
Kyrie	–	*In festis sanctorum quorum corpora requiescunt in ecclesia*	[*Cunctipotens genitor*]	18				IV
Kyrie	See above	*In festis duplicibus quando conventus est in cappis*	[Ant. *O christi pietas*]	96				
Kyrie	See above	*In festis duplicibus et semiduplicibus et in xii lectionibus*	[*Orbis factor*]	16				XI

Kyrie	See above	*Dominicis diebus*	[*Pater creator*]	68			XIV
Kyrie	n.g.	*Quando fit de beata maria et vigiliis annualium*	[*Cunctipotens orbis factor*]	58			XII
Gloria	See below	–			51		XI
Kyrie	n.g.	*In festis xii lectionum et feria V quando fit de beato dyonisio*		214– var.			
Gloria	See below	–			11		XIV
Kyrie	See above	*In festis iii lectionum de aliquando sancto*		144			
Gloria	n.g.	*Ad missam matutinalem quando cantatur simpliciter*			43		XV
Kyrie	n.g.	*Quando fit de tempore*		7			
Kyrie	n.g.	*Pro defunctis*		60			
Gloria	–	see above			56		IV
Gloria	–	see above			11		XIV
Gloria	–	see above			51		XI
Credo	n.g.	–					
Sanctus	–	see below	*Principium sine principio*			49	IV
Sanctus	See above	*In festis annualibus et et semiannualibus*	[Trope not given]			49	IV
Sanctus	*In dominicis diebus*	*Dominicis diebus et festis duplicibus et sabbato de beata maria ad magnam missam*				32– var.	XVII
Sanctus	*In xii lectionibus*	*In xii lectionibus et die jov. de beato dyonisio*				223– var.	XV
Sanctus	*In privatis diebus*	*In iii lectionibus de uno sancto vel pluribus et quando fit de magna missa pro defunctis*				41– var.	

Chant	MS and rubric		Name of trope	No. of trope melody in				
	N	V		MEL	BOS	THAN	SCHILD	*LU*
Sanctus	–	n.g.				41–var.		
Agnus	*In epyphania domini*	n.g.	*Quem johannes in jordane*				226	II
Agnus	See below	*In festis annualibus et semiannualibus*					136	IV
Agnus	n.g.	*In festis duplicibus et semiduplicibus et diebus dominicis*					209	XV
Agnus	*In dominicis diebus et in xii lection-ibus*	*In xii lectionibus de sancto dyonisio*					164	XVI
Agnus	*Privatis diebus*	n.g.					86	
Agnus	*In diebus festis*	See above					136	IV
Agnus	n.g.	*In iii lectionibus de uno vel de pluribus sanctis et quando fit de feria magna missa pro defunctis*					101–var.	
Gloria	–	n.g.	*Spiritus et alme*		23			IX
Agnus	–	See below	*Gloriosa spes reorum*				114	IX
Agnus	See above	*Sabbato de beata maria*	[Trope not given]				114	IX

Abbreviations: N: F:Pn, lat. 1107. V: GB:Lva 1346–1891. var.: Varies from reading in MEL, BOS, THAN, or SCHILD. n.g.: Melody not given in MS. –: Melody present but rubric absent. [name of trope in brackets]: trope text absent. MEL: Melnicki, *Kyrie*. BOS: Bosse, *Gloria*. THAN: Thannabaur, *Sanctus*. SCHILD: Schildbach, *Agnus*. *LU*: *Liber Usualis*.

[a] The arrangement of material in this table is a conflation of the order found in MSS N and V so that the peculiarities of each MS will be evident.

GB:Lva 1346–1891 were written. The ordinaries name a total of eight Kyries in their rubrics: *Orbis factor, Clemens rector, Fons bonitatis, Cunctipotens genitor, Rex genitor, Pater creator, O christe precamur,*[135] and *O christi pietas* (Table 3.7). The *Kyriale* of F:Pn, lat. 1107, which slightly post-dates the ordinaries, omits *Clemens rector,*[136] *Rex genitor*, and *O christe precamur*, while the fourteenth-century missal GB:Lva 1346–1891 and ordinary F:Pan, L 863, No. 10 record the five melodies found in F:Pn, lat. 1107, along with *Cunctipotens orbis factor*.

Although the rubrics in Table 3.7 give some indication of the liturgical placement of the trope melodies within the ceremony of Saint-Denis, the ordinaries offer even more precise witness for the assignment of these tunes (Table 3.8). As might be expected, the arrangement of melodies for the ordinary of the Mass was closely connected to the ranks of feasts.[137] Clearly, *Fons bonitatis* was the most solemn, being reserved for the handful of festivals called *principale* or *festum precipuum* in the thirteenth century, or *annuale* and *semiannuale* by the mid-fourteenth century. Along with these ornate services, four solemn anniversaries merited this most important Kyrie: Dagobert (19 January),[138] Philip Augustus (14 July), Saint Louis (25 August), and Charles the Bald (6 October). Second in importance were the twelve-lesson, duplex ceremonies for saints with relics in the church, and these usually had their own Kyrie, *Cunctipotens genitor*.[139] Services for saints whose relics were not present, but who were celebrated in other respects, like those whose bones lay in the abbey, used the Kyrie *O christi pietas*. Other duplex and semiduplex festivals employed the Kyrie *Rex genitor* or, especially in the fourteenth century, *Orbis factor*. *Orbis factor* also appeared on a number of feasts *in albis* of the *temporale*, and *Rex genitor* served the octaves of *annuale* feasts and on Mondays within these octaves.[140] The Kyrie *Pater creator* was reserved for simplex

[135] Presumably, *O christe precamur* refers to the melody of a trope, for both ordinaries name the melody (Table 3.8; F:Pm 526, fos. 59^{v}, 145, 182; F:Pn, lat. 976, fos. 32^{v}, 106, 135^{v}). It is not given, however, in Melnicki, *Kyrie*, nor in *AH*.

[136] Although F:Pn, lat. 1107 does not contain the Kyrie *Clemens rector*, the series of Benedicamus Domino melodies does include the chant (fo. 396).

[137] The same is true of the ordering of chants for the Benedicamus Domino and the Ite Missa Est.

[138] Actually, the earliest of the 3 ordinaries, F:Pm 526, records the Kyrie *Clemens rector* for Dagobert, but the 2nd ordinary F:Pn, lat. 976 gives *Fons*. The change was probably made to bring this service into alignment with the highest *annuale* feasts of the year, as it is in other respects. The choice of *Clemens* is not illogical, however, for it is specified for other funereal occasions: the anniversary of King Robert (20 July) and the Commemoration of the Dead. In addition, *Clemens* was sung on the feast of Saint Stephen (26 Dec.). For other instances of the melody *Clemens rector* on this day, see Planchart, *Tropes*, ii. 244–5.

[139] For other uses of this melody, see ibid. 247–9.

[140] See also ibid. 250–1.

TABLE 3.8. *Liturgical Placement of Melodies of the* Kyriale *at Saint-Denis, based on the Ordinaries*[a]

Date	Feast	Melody and/or rubric	Rank of feast	No. of fo. in		
				M	N	A
TEMPORALE						
December						
	Advent I	Orbis factor		7ᵛ		
24	Vigil of Christmas	*festive*		14ᵛ		
25	Christmas:					
	Mass I	Orbis factor		15ᵛ		
	Mass II	*festive sicut in xii lec.*		16		
	Mass III	*festive*	12, 12 a	16ᵛ		
26	Stephen	Clemens, *a quatuor bene cantantibus*	12, 12 d	17ᵛ		
27	John	Fons bonitatis, *a quatuor bene cantantibus*	12, 12 sa	18ᵛ		
28	Innocents*	Cunctipotens	12, 12 d	19ᵛ		
January						
1	Octave of Christmas	*festive*		23	2ᵛ	
5	Vigil of Epiphany	*ut in xii lec.*		24	3ᵛ	
6	Epiphany	Fons bonitatis	12, 12 sa	25	4	
12	Octave of Epiphany	Rex genitor		26ᵛ	5ᵛ	
	Septuagesima	Orbis factor		33ᵛ		
	Lent I	Orbis factor		37	13ᵛ	
	Lent IV	Orbis factor		45	20	
	Palm Sunday	Orbis factor		48ᵛ	23	
	Maundy Thursday	Orbis factor		51ᵛ	25ᵛ	

Easter:	Fons bonitatis	3, [3] a	57^{v}	30^{v}	
Monday	Rex genitor		58^{v}	31^{v}	
Tuesday	Pater creator		59	32	
Wednesday	O christe precamur		59^{v}	32^{v}	
Octave of Easter	Rex genitor		61^{v}	33^{v}	
Rogation days:					
Monday	*ut in xii lec.*		66^{v}	37^{v}	
Wednesday	*ut in xii lec.*		68	39	p. 58
Ascension	Fons bonitatis	12, [12] sa	69	40^{v}	
Commemoration of the Dead	Clemens rector		70^{v}	41^{v}	
Pentecost:	Fons bonitatis	3, [3] a	74	44	
Monday	Rex genitor		74^{v}	44^{v}	
Tuesday	Pater creator		75	45	
Wednesday	O christi pietas		75^{v}	45	
Missa de jejunio	*ut in privatis diebus*		75^{v}	45	
Thursday	*ut in xii lec.*		76	45^{v}	
Saturday	*ut in xii lec.*		76^{v}	45^{v}	
Octave of Pentecost	Kyrie = Rex genitor		77^{v}		
	Gloria = *sicut in xii lec.*		77^{v}		
	Kyrie, Gloria = *festive*			47	
	Sanctus, Agnus = *festive*		77^{v}		
Monday, Tuesday, Wednesday,	*feriale*		79^{v}	50	
Friday	Sanctus, Agnus = *ferialis et omnibus diebus privatis similiter*		80		
Thursday, Saturday	*sicut in xii lec.*			82	50^{v}
	Sanctus, Agnes = *ut in xii lec.*		83		
1st Sunday after Octave	Kyrie, Gloria = *privatim*			52	
Corpus Christi	O christi pietas				p. 71

Date	Feast	Melody and/or rubric	Rank of feast	No. of fo. in		
				M	N	A
SANCTORALE						
13	Hilary of Poitiers*	Cunctipotens	12, 12 d	99	70	
14	Suger (A)	*festive*			161^v	
19	Dagobert (A)	Clemens rector	9 d	100^v		
		Fons bonitatis			71^v	
22	Vincent	Orbis factor	12 d			p. 88
25	Conversion of Paul	Orbis factor	12, 12 d	103	74	p. 89
February						
1	Vigil of Purification	*ut in xii lec.*		106	75^v	
2	Purification	Fons bonitatis	12, 12 sa	107	76^v	
22	Chair of Peter	Orbis factor	12, 12 sd			p. 95
24	Dedication of Church	Fons bonitatis	12 d, 12 a	112^v	80^v	
March						
12	Gregory	Orbis factor	12, 12 d	114	82	
21	Benedict	Orbis factor	12, 12 d	115		
25	Annunciation	Orbis factor	12, 12 sa	115^v		
		Fons bonitatis			83^v	
June						
24	John Baptist*	Cunctipotens	12 d	137^v	100	106
		Ante agnus dei dicatur Quem johannes in jordane		138		
29	Peter, Paul	Fons bonitatis	12 d, 12 sa	140^v	102	
30	Commemoration of Paul	Orbis factor	12, 12 d	141	102^v	

July						
11	Translation of Benedict	O christe precamur	12, 12 d	145	106	
14	Philip Augustus (A)	Fons bonitatis			107v	
20	Robert (A)	Clemens rector		148		
		festive			109	
22	Mary Magdalene	O christi pietas	12 d	149	109v	
25	Cucuphas*	Cunctipotens	12 d	150v	111	
26	James	O christi pietas	12, 12 d	151	111	
28	Consecration of Altar	Orbis factor	12, 12 sd	152	112	
August						
1	Peter's Chains	*festive*	12, 12 sd		113v	
		Orbis factor				112
10	Lawrence	*festive*	12, 12 d		115v	
		Orbis factor				113
13	Hippolytus*	Cunctipotens	12 d	157v	116v	
14	Vigil of Assumption	*festive ut in vigilia natalis domini*		158v	117	114
15	Assumption	Fons bonitatis	12, 12 a	159	117v	
	First day after	Rex genitor		159v	118v	
		Orbis factor				115v
	Second day after	Orbis factor				115v
22	Octave of Assumption	Rex genitor	12, 12 d	161	119v	
		O christi pietas				116
23	Bernard of Clairvaux	O christi pietas	12, 12 d		120	
		Orbis factor				116v
24	Bartholomew	Pater creator	12, 12 d	162	120v	
25	Saint Louis	Fons bonitatis	12, 12 d			117
28	Augustine	Orbis factor	12, 12 d			117v
29	Decol. of John Baptist	Rex genitor	12, 12 sd	164	121v	
		Orbis factor				117v

Date	Feast	Melody and/or rubric	Rank of feast	No. of fo. in		
				M	N	A
September						
8	Nativity of Mary	Fons bonitatis	12 d, 12 sa	166v	123v	119
	Tuesday after	*ut in xii lec.*		168		
		Sanctus, Agnus = *ut in xii lec.*		168	125	
9	Osmanna*	Cunctipotens	12, 12 d		124	119v
14	Exaltation of Cross	Rex genitor	12, 12 d	170	126v	
		O christi pietas				120v
21	Matthew	Pater creator	12, 12 d	172v		
		festive			128	
22	Maurice*	Cunctipotens	12 d	173v	128v	122
25	Firminus*	Cunctipotens	12, 12 d	174v	129	122v
29	Michael	Cunctipotens	12 d	176	130	123
October						
6	Charles the Bald (A)	Fons bonitatis, *a quatuor bene cantantibus*	9 d	178v		
7	Constance	Orbis factor		179	132v	
8	Vigil of Denis	*festive de precipuis vigiliis*		180	133v	
		ut in sabbato quando fit de beata maria virgine				124
9	Denis*	Fons bonitatis	12, 12 a	181	134v	124v
	First day after	Rex genitor		181v		
		festive			135	
		Orbis factor				125
	Second day after	Pater creator		181v		
		festive			135	
		Orbis factor				125

	Third day after	O christe precamur		182	135^{v}	
		Orbis factor				125^{v}
16	Octave of Denis	Fons bonitatis	12, 12 sa	184	137	
	Gloria = *Doxa en ipsistis*		184	137		
		Credo = *Pisteuo*				
		Sanctus = *Agyos*				
		Agnus dei = *O amnos tou theu*[b]				
17	Demetrius	Orbis factor	12, 12 d			126
25	Hilary of Mende*	pater creator	12, 12 d	187	140	
28	Simon, Jude	Rex genitor	12, 12 d	188	141	
November						
1	All Saints	Fons bonitatis	12 d, 12 sa	189^{v}	142	128
2	Eustace*	Cunctipotens	12 d	190	143	128^{v}
3	All Souls	Orbis factor	3, 12	191		
9	Octave of Eustace	Orbis factor	12		145^{v}	130^{v}
11	Martin	O christi pietas	12, 12 d		146^{v}	131
15	Eugene*	Cunctipotens	12 d	194	148	131^{v}
23	Clement*	Cunctipotens	12, 12 d	195	150^{v}	
		Orbis factor				132^{v}
24	Romanus of Blaye*	Deus [= Pater] creator	12, 12 d	195^{v}		
		Cunctipotens			151	132^{v}
30	Andrew	O christi pietas	12, 12 d		152	
December						
6	Nicholas	O christi pietas	12, 12 d		153^{v}	

Abbreviations: M: F:Pm 526. N: F:Pn, lat. 976. A: F:Pan L 863, No. 10. (A): Royal anniversary. * Relics of saint at Saint-Denis.
sd: *semiduplex*. d: *duplex*. sa: *semiannuale*. a: *annuale*.

[a] All melodies listed here are for the Kyrie unless otherwise stated.
[b] See the discussion of the Greek Mass in Ch. 4.

feasts of twelve lessons and for Tuesdays during important octaves.[141] The elusive Kyrie *O christe precamur* was sung on Wednesdays during the octaves of Easter and Saint Denis, and on the feast of the Translation of Saint Benedict (11 July). By the mid-fourteenth century, the monks freely substituted the melody *Orbis factor* for almost any tune that was used in the thirteenth century.[142] *Cunctipotens orbis factor*, notated only in GB:Lva 1346–1891, is evidently not mentioned in the ordinaries, which record only the first word *Cunctipotens*, probably designating *Cunctipotens genitor*.[143] The directions in GB:Lva 1346–1891 and in F:Pan, L 863, No. 10 (Table 3.8), however, show that *Cunctipotens orbis factor* was performed on the Vigils of *annuale* feasts and during the Saturday Masses for Mary in the fourteenth century.

The precise instructions that the ordinaries provide for the ceremonial use of the chants of the *Kyriale* of Saint-Denis might lead us to consider the *ordinarium* of the abbey as unique. Actually, the content of the *Kyriale* is similar to the repertories of neighbouring institutions, for example, the *Kyriale* of Notre Dame of Paris, which provides a convenient point of reference.[144] The number of chants for the Kyrie at Saint-Denis and at Notre Dame is identical: fourteen in both churches. Of this number, the two houses share eleven Kyries.[145] For the other chants of the ordinary, the concordances between Saint-Denis and Paris are also striking. The six melodies for the Gloria in the Parisian *Kyriale* include the five that were sung in the abbey.[146] Three of the four chants for the Sanctus in the Saint-Denis repertory were also in use at the cathedral.[147] Likewise, five of the seven melodies for the Agnus Dei at Saint-Denis were sung at Paris.[148]

[141] Planchart, *Tropes*, ii. 257–8. It is interesting to note that, even though the relics of Hilary of Mende had been present in the abbey since the 9th c., the saint did not receive duplex treatment of his *natale* until the middle of the 13th c. It is probably for this reason that the Mass for Hilary employed the Kyrie *Pater creator*, rather than *Cunctipotens genitor* as would have been expected.

[142] This reduction in specificity in the assignment of melodies for the Kyrie reflects once again the shift from proper to common items in the Mass and Office at Saint-Denis in the 14th c.

[143] Since *Cunctipotens orbis factor* is not given in the missal F:Pn, lat. 1107, which falls chronologically between the 13th-c. ordinaries and GB:Lva 1346–1891, it probably was not used at all in the 13th c.

[144] On the Parisian Kyriale, see Wright, *Notre Dame*, 81–96. Wright's study is based on the notated missal of Paris use F:Pn, lat. 861 (*c.*1318).

[145] Saint-Denis alone employs Melnicki's Kyrie Nos. 50, 96, and 151 (Table 3.7), and lacks melody Nos. 102, 171, and 210, all of which were sung at the cathedral. Both establishments sang the Kyrie *Clemens rector*. Of the 3 Sandionysian Kyries just mentioned (Melnicki's Nos. 50, 96, 151), all can be found in other Parisian MSS: No. 50 appears in the Parisian missal F:Psg 1259 (see Melnicki, *Kyrie*), No. 96 in I:Ac 695 from Reims and Paris (Hiley, 'Ordinary', 13), No. 151 in F:Pn, lat. 14452 from Saint-Victor (ibid. 48).

[146] In addition to the Gloria tunes given in Table 3.7, Notre Dame employed Bosse, *Gloria*, No. 12.

[147] Parisian sources lack Thannabaur, *Sanctus*, No. 32, but they add No. 154, which was not performed at Saint-Denis.

[148] MSS from Notre Dame do not include Schildbach Nos. 86 and 114, although they do incorporate No. 236, which was not used at Saint-Denis.

Paris, in contrast, uses fifteen distinct cycles, each containing a melody, or at least a rubric, for a Kyrie, Gloria, Sanctus, and Agnus. The cycles are arranged according to the days of the octave in an involved way which is explained in the rubrics.[149] Saint-Denis, on the other hand, only begins to group compositions into Kyrie–Gloria pairs in the fourteenth century. The directions in the sources from the abbey are more concise, referring simply to the name of a trope or to the rank of a feast (Table 3.7).

Despite the differences in arrangement of these two repertories, the number of coincidences in choice of melody is telling. Almost all the prominent melodies for the Kyrie at Saint-Denis (*Pater creator*, *Orbis factor*, *Fons bonitatis*, *Clemens rector*, *Cunctipotens genitor*, and *Cunctipotens orbis factor*) were also in use in the Paris cathedral. If the Parisian collection is by and large representative of the 'city tradition',[150] the monks of Saint-Denis apparently borrowed from this usage rather than attempting to establish a truly distinctive set of melodies, as they did for their Benedicamus Domino and Ite Missa Est.

The general agreement between the *Kyriales* of Saint-Denis and of Notre Dame is naturally due both to the geographical proximity of the two houses and to the fact that their liturgies were at one time intertwined. The role that geographical separation plays in distinguishing repertories can be seen in a brief comparison of the *Kyriale* of Saint-Denis with that of another roughly coeval, though distant, establishment. The Scottish source of Notre Dame polyphony W_{I}[151] shows that differences in choice of melody increase with geographical separation. The third, eighth, ninth, and eleventh fascicles of W_{I} contain polyphonic settings of selections from the ordinary of the Mass.[152] The *Kyriale* of Saint-Denis shares only two *cantus firmi* for Kyries with the seven that are found in the eleventh fascicle of W_{I}, and no Glorias are common to the two manuscripts. In slight contrast, four of the seven Sanctus and three of the five Agnus Dei chants in W_{I} were also used at Saint-Denis, although the abbey includes none of the trope texts for these concordances.

These observations about the heritage of the *Kyriale* of Saint-Denis lead to the question of the overall nature of the trope repertory of Saint-Denis. On the one hand, the majority of tropes of Saint-Denis seem not particularly innovatory, for those for the proper and ordinary of the Mass were also heard in other houses in Paris. And yet the surviving

[149] See Wright, *Notre Dame*, 81–96.

[150] See Hiley, 'Observations', 67–8. Hiley finds slightly less concordance (75–84%) between Notre Dame and Saint-Denis in his comparisons between I:Ac 695 from the cathedral and F:Pn, lat. 1107 from the abbey; idem, 'Traditions', 5–6, 26 (diagram 3).

[151] D:W 677 [Helmstedt 628], published in Baxter, *St. Andrews*.

[152] See the discussion and tables of this material in Hiley, 'Observations'.

manuscripts preserve a handful of prosulas for the Office that have little or no concordance in other repertories. Here the monks may have exercised true creativity, even to the point of saturating certain texts with what they thought was Pseudo-Dionysian philosophy. The number of festivals for which tropes are provided encompasses Christmas, Easter, the *natale* and Invention of Stephen, John, the Innocents, the Purification and Nativity of Mary, and the feasts of Saint Denis, Cucuphas, and possibly others. Moreover, the tropes of the proper of the Mass played a conspicuous role in the Divine Service at Saint-Denis: they received special consideration in terms of performance practice on high feasts, their phrases being alternated between soloists who stood in special parts of the church, as performers of polyphony did in other houses. The rubrics for these pieces often admonish soloists to 'sing well'. The tropes for Matins usually come in prominent places in the fourth, eighth, or twelfth responsories, or in the great responsories for Vespers or Lauds. When a trope appeared with any other Matins responsory, the monks sometimes tampered with the order of the responsories, shuffling the chants to place the troped one in a more important position and thereby to exhibit it to greater advantage. The community's willingness thus to rearrange a long-established list of responsories, one which would have been copied from one manuscript to another, shows that its eagerness to display a new or unique composition dominated over the feeling of obligation to adhere slavishly to tradition. In this way the monks made their liturgy more proper to Saint-Denis.

What is more, the extant sources from Saint-Denis also provide a glimpse into what may have been a more extensive tradition of troping in an earlier era. The three alleluia tropes *Judicabunt innocentes*, *Justus johannes*, and *Justus virginitate*, the responsory trope *Non vos quos elegi*, and the trope to the Comm. *Video celos* for Stephen allude to the presence of more tropes in the Mass in the tenth and eleventh centuries. At given times, the community evidently preferred certain types of trope over others. Wordless, melismatic forms predominate in the sources through the twelfth century, while prosulas increase in numbers in the thirteenth century and thereafter. The *Kyriale*, although not rich in textual tropes, contains a substantial number of ornate melodies that once included texts, and the community assigned them rigorously to feasts according to the rank of the service. In sum, the repertory of original and borrowed tropes at Saint-Denis greatly enhanced the highest celebrations, contributing substantially to the splendour appropriate to the festivals of the royal abbey.

SEQUENCES

Sequences, with their highly colourful poetry and straightforward music, lauded the deeds of saints and enriched the important feasts of the *temporale* throughout the West up to the Council of Trent. These chants were sung at Mass between the alleluia and the gospel, or, on the highest festivals at Saint-Denis, between the alleluia and the antiphon before the gospel. The monks performed sequences on observances of duplex rank and higher, and on some twelve-lesson celebrations as well. The abbey created a significant number of new sequences in the thirteenth century, having earlier adopted selections from the repertory that circulated in Paris in the twelfth and thirteenth centuries.

The first evidence of sequences at Saint-Denis comes from the thirteenth century, although the monks undoubtedly cultivated them much earlier. Two fully notated sequentiaries have survived in the thirteenth-century missal F:Pn, lat. 1107[153] and in the mid-fourteenth-century missal GB:Lva 1346–1891.[154] F:Pn, lat. 10505 includes only a few textual incipits for proses, and the three ordinaries F:Pm 526; F:Pn, lat. 976 and F:Pan, L 863, No. 10 contain verbal cues for the sequences in their rubrics. The late thirteenth-century theorist Guido of Saint-Denis uses a number of sequences in his tonary. Table 3.9 names the sequences that were sung in the abbey and signals the editions of their texts in *Analecta Hymnica*.[155] The table shows that the monks' choice of sequence sometimes changed between the thirteenth and fourteenth centuries. When two different sequences are listed for a feast, the thirteenth-century sources often assign the same sequence, while the fourteenth-century books record another.[156] Evidently, however, the thirteenth-century cantor was free to select the sequence for the day, for the two ordinaries (M, N1) occasionally offer two or more sequences for the same Mass,[157] or they differ completely in their choices.[158] The fourteenth-century sources, on the other hand, witness a more fixed repertoire, agreeing in all but one instance.[159]

153 Fos. 340–92.

154 Fos. 370–430^{v}. The texts of the sequences in this MS are edited in Misset *et al.*, *Analecta*, 530–41.

155 The Saint-Denis sequences are contained in vols. vii–x, xxxvii, xl, xlii, xliv, liii–lv (see Bibliog., under Blume, Bannister, Dreves).

156 Table 3.9: Advent I, Christmas Masses 2 and 3, etc.

157 See the Saturday Masses for the Virgin between Pentecost and Advent, Saints Vincent (22 Jan.), Peregrinus (16 May), John the Baptist (24 June), Cucuphas (25 July), Octave of Assumption (22 Aug.), Maurice (22 Sept.), Saint Denis (9 Oct.), Hilary of Mende (25 Oct.), and Clement (23 Nov.).

158 See the Octave of Pentecost, Saint Patroclus (31 Jan.), Invention of Saint Denis (22 Apr.), feast, ferial days and Octave of Saint Denis (9 Oct.), and the feast of Romanus of Blaye (24 Nov.).

159 On the feast of Purification (2 Feb.), GB:Lva 1346–1891 calls for *Letabundus exultet*, while F:Pan, L 863, No. 10 assigns the prosa *Inviolata, intacta*.

TABLE 3.9. *Sequences in the Saint-Denis Sources*

Feast	Sequence	Century: 13th			13/14th	14th			
		M	N1	N2	G	N3	V	A	*AH*
TEMPORALE									
Advent I	*Gaudia mundo*	x		x					37:44
	Salus eterna					x	x	x	7:28, 53:3
Advent II	*Regnantem sempiterna*	x		x		x	x	x	7:30, 53:5
Advent III	*Qui regis*	x		x	x	x	x	x	7:31, 53:8
Advent IV	*Jubilemus omnes*	x		x	x		x	x	7:33, 53:9
Christmas									
Mass 1	*Nato canunt*	x		x			x	x	7:49, 53:41
Mass 2	*Letabundus exultet*	x		x	x				54:5
	Nato nobis					x	x	x	54:155
Mass 3	*Christi hodierna*	x		x					7:42, 53:25
	Letabundus exultet					x	x	x	54:5
Stephen	*Magnus deus*	x		x					7:221, 53:353
	Heri mundus						x		55:341
John	*Alma cohors*	x							7:238, 55:392
	Gratulemur ad festivum			x		x	x		55:215
Innocents*	*Celsa pueri*	x		x		x	x	x	53:264
Octave of Christmas	*Letabundus exultet*	x	x			x		x	54:5
Saturday Mass for Mary between Christmas and Purification	*Letabundus exultet*		x						54:5
Octave of Stephen	*Hic sanctus*						x		n.g.
Octave of John	*Clare sanctorum*						x		53:367
Octave of Innocents	*O dulces innocentum*						x	x	53:265 (st. 20)

Epiphany	*Epiphaniam domino*	x		x	x	x	x	x	7:53, 53:47
Octave of Epiphany	*Letabundus exultet*	x	x						54:5
	Magi stella					x	x	x	7:53, 53:47 (st. 13)
Easter	*Fulgens preclara*	x	x	x					7:57, 53:62
	Zima vetus				x		x	x	54:227
Vespers 2	*Victime paschali*	x	x						54:12
Monday	*Mane prima*	x	x	x					54:214
	Victime paschali						x		54:12
Tuesday	*Zima vetus*		x						54:227
	Victime paschali						x		54:12
Wednesday	*In maxilla mille*		x						54:227 (st. 12)
	Victime paschali						x		54: 12
Invention of the Holy Nail	*Victime paschali*	x							54:12
Thurs.–Sat.	*Victime paschali*						x		54:12
Octave of Easter	*Victime paschali*	x	x	x					54:12
	Lux illuxit						x	x	54:220
Sundays 1–4 after Easter	*Victime paschali*	x	x				x		54:12
Ascension	*Rex omnipotens*	x	x	x			x	x	7:83, 53:111
Commemoration of Relics	*Superne matris*	x		x					55:45
	Christo inclita	x	x		x				7:132, 53:201
Pentecost	*Sancti spiritus*	x	x	x			x		53:119
Octave of Ascension	*O deus maris*						x		53:112 (st. 20)
(Pentecost)									
Monday	*Alma cohors*	x	x	x					7:238, 53:392
	Veni sancte spiritus						x	x	54:234
Tuesday	*Laudes deo devotas*	x	x	x					54:21
	Veni sancte					x			54:234
Wednesday	*Almiphona*	x							7:93, 53:132
	Veni sancte		x	x			x		54:234

Feast	Sequence	Century: 13th			13/14th	14th			
		M	N1	N2	G	N3	V	A	*AH*
Thurs.–Sat.	*Veni sancte*			x			x		54:234
Octave of Pentecost	*Laudes deo devotas*	x							54:21
	Profitentes unitatem		x				x		54:249
Saturday Mass for Mary between Pentecost and Advent	*Ave maria*	x	x						54:337
	Letabundus exultet	x	e						54:5
	Salve sancta	x	x						9:60
Corpus Christi	*Lauda syon*			a			x		50:584
Octave of Corpus Christi	*Ecce panis angelorum*			a					50:584 (st. 10)
SANCTORALE									
January									
8 Lucian of Beauvais	*Mirabilis deus*						x		7:231, 53:372
13 Hilary of Poitiers*	*Superne matris*	x	x	x					55:45
	Christo regi glorie						x	x	42:219
19 Dagobert (A)	*De profundis*	x	x	x					40:69
20 Fabian, Sebastian	*Mirabilis deus*						x	x	7:231, 53:372
21 Agnes	*Virgines egregie*						x		55:28
22 Vincent	*Ave stella*[a]	x	e						See n. *a*.
	Superne matris	x	x	x					55:45
	Ecce dies preoptata						x	x	55:377
25 Conversion of Paul	*Clare sanctorum*	x	x						53:367
	Jubilemus salvatori						x	x	10:286
31 Patroclus*	*Ave stella*	x							See n. *a*.
	Superne matris		x	x			x		55:45

February								
2 Purification	*Letabundus exultet*	x	x			x		54:5
	Inviolata intacta						x	H-B, No. 346; *RH*, 9093
5 Agatha	*Virgines egregie*					x		55:28
22 Chair of Peter	*Clare sanctorum*					x		53:367
24 Dedication of Church	*Christo inclita*	x	x		x	x		7:132, 53:201
24 Matthias	*Clare sanctorum*					x		53:367
March								
21 Benedict, *natale*	*Laudum carmina*		x	x	x	x	x	7:145, 53: 223
25 Annunciation	*Ave maria*	a	x	x		x		54:337
April								
4 Ambrose	*Superne matris*					x		55:45
8 Dionysius of Corinth*	*Superne matris*		x			x		55:45
22 Invention of Denis	*Superne armonie*	x						9:141
	Gaude turma triumphalis		x					9:140
	Superne matris			x				55:45
	Salve pater dyonisi					x	x	44:104
Denis, Thursday Mass between Easter and Pentecost	*Gaude prole grecia*	x	x					55:130
25 Mark	*Psallat chorus corde*					x		55:130
May								
1 Philip, James	*Clare sanctorum*	x	x			x		53:367
3 Invention of Cross	*Laudes crucis*	x	x					54:188
	Salve crux arbor					x		54:192
6 John at Latin Gate	*Clare sanctorum*					x		53:367
16 Peregrinus*	*Ave stella*	x						See n. *a*.
	Superne matris	x						55:45
	Gaude plebs		x	x		x		44:239

Feast	Sequence	Century: 13th			13/14th	14th			
		M	N1	N2	G	N3	V	A	*AH*
June									
9 Detection of Denis	*Superne matris*	x	x						55:45
	Salve pater						x		44:104
11 Barnabas	*Clare sanctorum*						x		53:367
24 John Baptist*	*Christo inclita*	x			x				7:132, 53:201
	Superne matris	x							55:45
	Ad honorem tuum		x	x			x	x	55:200
29 Peter, Paul	*Laude jocunda*	x	x	x					7:201, 53:339
	Roma petro glorietur						x		55:321
30 Commemoration of Paul	*Clare sanctorum*	x	x						53:367
	Paule doctor gentium						x	x	40:263
July									
11 Benedict, Translation	*Laudum carmina*	x	x	x	x		x		7:145, 53:223
14 Philip Augustus (A)	*De profundis*		x						40:69
20 Robert II (A)	*De profundis*		x						40:69
22 Mary Magdalene	*Mane prima*	x	x	x			x		54:214
24 Christina	*Virgines egregie*						x		55:28
25 Cucuphas*	*Ave stella*	x							See n. *a*.
	Superna matris	x							55:45
	Letabundus exultet		x				x		42:189
25 James	*Clare sanctorum*	x	x				x		53:367
28 Consecration of Altar	*Christo inclita*	x	x		x		x		7:132, 53:223
August									
1 Peter's Chains	*Clare sanctorum*	x	x				x		53:367
3 Invention of Stephen	*Magnus deus*	x	x				x	x	7:221, 53:353

6 Transfiguration	*Veni sancte spiritus*					x	x	54:234
10 Lawrence	*Stola jocunditatis*	x	x	x				54:86
	Prunis datum					x	x	55:245
13 Hippolytus*	*Christo inclita*	x	x		x			7:132, 53:223
	Laudemus omnes					x		42:220
14 Vigil of Assumption	*Hac clara*					x		7:115, 53:168
15 Assumption	*Aurea virga*	x	x	x		x		7:122, 53:186
Day 1 after	*Hac clara*			x				7:115, 53:168
	Ave virgo virginum				x	x		54:432
Day 2 after	*Salve sancta*			x				9:60
	Marie preconio					x		54:391
Day 3 after	*Regine nunc*	x						7:124
	Verbum bonum			x	x	x		54:343
Days 4–6	*Hodierne lux diei*			x				54:346
	Ave maria			x				54:337
	Inviolata intacta					x		H-B, No. 346; RH, 9093
22 Octave of Assumption	*Regine nunc*	x						7:124
	Salve sancta	x	x					9:60
	Hodierne lux					x		54:346
23 Bernard of Clairvaux	*Superne matris*		x			x		55:45
24 Bartholomew	*Clare sanctorum*	x	x			x		53:367
25 Saint Louis	*Gaude prole francia*			a		x		43:212
28 Augustine	*Augustino presuli*					x		10:137
29 Decollation of John Baptist	*Superne matris*	x	x					55:45
	Precursorem summi regis					x	x	55:202
September								
8 Nativity of Mary	*Alle celeste*	x	x	x		x		7:111, 53:166
Saturday	*Marie preconio*					x		54:391

Feast	Sequence	Century: 13th			13/14th	14th			
		M	N1	N2	G	N3	V	A	*AH*
9 Osmanna*	*Plebs fidelis*	a	xc	x			x		8:196
14 Exaltation of Cross	*Laudes crucis*	x	x	x			x	x	54:188
21 Matthew	*Clare sanctorum*	x	x				x		53:367
22 Maurice*	*Alludat letus*	x	x						7:193, 53:305
	Superne matris	x		x					55:45
	Mirabilis deus						x		7:231, 53:372
25 Firminus*	*Vocis cum camena*	a	x	x			x		8:129
29 Michael	*Ad celebres*	x	x	x					7:195, 53:306
	Laus erumpat ex affectu						x		55:288
30 Jerome	*Superne matris*						x		55:45
October									
9 Denis*									
Morning Mass	*Mirabilis deus*	x							7:231, 53:372
	Salve pater dyonisi	x					x		44:104
Main Mass	*Superne armonie*	x							9:141
	Gaude prole	x	x	x	x		x		55:130
Day 1 after	*Ecce pulcra*	x							7:130, 53:200
	Alludat vox ecclesie		x	x					8:118
	Ave pater gallie				x		x		42:193
Day 2 after	*Mirabilis deus*	x							7:231, 53:372
	Gaude turma		x	x					9:140
	Doctorem egregium						x		42:193
Day 3 after	*O alma trinitas*	x							7:110
	Salve pater		x	x			x		44:104

Days 4–6	*Mirabilis deus*						x		7:231, 53:372
16 Octave of Denis	*Superne armonie*	x							9:141
	Gaude prole		x				x		55:130
17 Demetrius	*Superne matris*		x				x		55:45
18 Luke	*Superne matris*		a						55:45
	Psallat chorus						x		55:11
21 Eleven Thousand Virgins*	*Ave lux insignis*		x	x			x		9:261
25 Hilary of Mende*	*Superne matris*	x	x	x			x		55:45
	Laudis odas	x							9:283
28 Simon, Jude	*Clare sanctorum*	x	x				x		53:367
November									
1 All Saints	*Christo inclita*	x	x	x	x		x		7:132, 53:223
2 Eustace*	*Corde puro*	x	x	x			x		9:152
11 Martin	*Superne matris*		x	x					55:45
	Gaude sion que						x		55:278
15 Eugene*	*Psallat cum tripudio*		x	x			x		9:151
22 Cecelia	*Virgines egregie*						x		55:28
23 Clement*	*Ave stella*	x	x						See n. *a*.
	Superne matris	x	x	x					55:45
	Glorietur gallia						x		10:156
24 Romanus of Blaye*	*Laudis odas*	x							9:283
	Superne matris		x				x		55:45
25 Catherine	*Adest triumphalis*						x		8:165
30 Andrew	*Sacrosancta hodierne*		x	x		x	x		54:42
December									
6 Nicholas	*Congaudentes exultemus*		x	x	x	x	x	x	54:95
7 Octave of Andrew	*Clare sanctorum*						x		53:367
13 Lucy	*Virgines egregie*						x		55:28
21 Thomas	*Clare sanctorum*		x			x	x		53:367

Feast	Sequence	Century: 13th			13/14th	14th			
		M	N1	N2	G	N3	V	A	*AH*
Unassigned Marian sequences									
	Salve stella mundi lumen			x					9:70
	Inviolata intacta			x			x		H-B, No. 346; *RH*, 9093
	Mellis stilla maris			x					9:71
	Beata es virgo			x					H-B, No. 77, *RH*, 2330
	Mundamini mundamini			x					9:70
	Ave maris stella			x					9:72
	Stella maris o maria			x					H-B, No. 660, *RH*, 19456
	Veni virgo virginum			x					54:393
	Veneremur virginem			x					54:328
	Marie preconio			x			x		54:391
	Ave virgo virginum			x	x		x		54:432
	Virginis marie laudes			x			x		54:31
	Tibi cordis in altari						x		54:422
	Benedicta es celorum						x		54:396

Abbreviations: x: Sequence present in MS. * Relics of saint in church. e: Sequence erased. a: Sequence added later. st: Stanza. (A) Royal anniversary. H-B: Hofmann-Brandt, 'Die Tropen', ii. *AH*: *Annalecta Hymnica*, vol.:p. *RH*: Chevalier, *Repertorium*. M: F:Pm 526. N1: F:Pn, lat. 976. N2: F:Pn, lat. 1107. G: Treatise of Guido of Saint-Denis in GB:Lbm, Harl. 281. N3: F;Pn, lat. 10505. V: GB:Lva 1346–1891. A: F:Pan, L 863, No. 10.

[a] This incipit appears only in the unnotated ordinary F:Pm 526, and the amount of text is not sufficient to determine which *Ave stella* sequence this is. Since almost all the sequences beginning with this incipit are for Mary, it is likely that the one intended here is *Ave stella gloriosa/Gemma martyrum preciosa/Georgi martyr spes unica* (*AH*, ix. 165; *RH*, No. 23878) which serves for George and a number of other saints.

These later books, moreover, show that the level of cult at Saint-Denis was inflated in the late thirteenth and fourteenth centuries. Whereas the thirteenth-century missal F:Pn, lat. 1107 places sequences only at the end of the book, both F:Pn, lat. 10505 and GB:Lva 1346–1891 notate them with textual and sometimes musical incipits both in the individual formularies for Masses and in a fully notated sequentiary at the end of GB:Lva 1346–1891. Furthermore, the celebrations for three of the four doctors of the Church (Ambrose, Augustine, Jerome), raised to duplex in the late thirteenth and fourteenth centuries (Appendix A), also acquired sequences at this time. Similar elevations of the feasts of Saints Matthias (24 February), Mark (25 April), and Barnabas (11 June) included the addition of sequences to their liturgies. By the mid-fourteenth century, in fact, the common sequence *Hic sanctus*, with its variant forms for a virgin (*Hac sancta*) and for many martyrs (*Hii sancti*), could be heard on every simplex observance of twelve lessons, and even in a few three-lesson services in the monastery.[160]

Special attention was given to the manner of performance of sequences at Saint-Denis on at least four high feasts. Guido of Saint-Denis discusses the use of textless melismas, or neumas, in the sequences for Assumption, Michael, Christmas, and Epiphany:

> [A neuma] appears in that Seq. *A[u]rea virga* [for Assumption], where the text *sanctum neuma descendet in te casta* is sung, and also . . . in that Seq. *Ad celebres* [for Michael], where the words *Novies distincta neumatum sunt agmina per te facta* are sung. . . . [A neuma] is heard in the sequence for Christmas *Nato canunt omnia*, where it is sung in the second verse *Sillabatim neumata perstringendo organica*, and in the Seq. *Epiphaniam domino*, in its verse *Omnes nunc caterva tinnulum jungat organi laudibus neuma*.[161]

Presumably the stanzas that Guido mentions were chanted first with text, and then the melody was repeated on a single vowel. Other

[160] *Hic sanctus*, *Hac sancta*, and *Hii sancti*, omitted from Table 3.9 because they occur so regularly, are given throughout the notated missal GB:Lva 1346–1891 on the following feasts: Octave of Stephen (2 Jan.), Geneviève (5 Jan.), Maurus (15 Jan.), Julian (27 Jan.), Blaise (3 Feb.), Vedast and Amandus (6 Feb.), Scholastica (10 Feb.), Mamertus and Majolus (11 May), Hippolytus *et al.* (12 May), Medard and Gildard (8 June), Primus and Felician (9 June), Gervase and Protase (19 June), Ten Thousand Martyrs (22 June), Translation of Martin (4 July), Octave of Martial (7 July), Apollinaris (23 July), Christopher (27 July), Germanus of Auxerre (31 July), Ouen (26 Aug.), Leodegarius (2 Oct.), Francis (4 Oct.), Clarus (4 Nov.), Marcellus (5 Nov.), Octave of All Saints (8 Nov.), Brice (13 Nov.), Edmund (20 Nov.), Eligius (1 Dec.), Maximinus (15 Dec.), Thomas of Canterbury (29 Dec.), Silvester (31 Dec.).

[161] '[Neuma] apparet in sequencia illa *Area virga* ubi dicitur *sanctum neuma descendet in te casta* sive etiam . . . in sequencia illa *Ad celebres* ubi dicitur *Novies distincta neumatum sunt agmina per te facta*. . . [Neuma] accipitur in illa sequencia de natali *Nato canunt omnia*, ubi dicitur in secundo versu *Sillabatim neumata perstringendo organica*, et in sequencia *Epiphaniam domino* in illo versu *Omnes nunc caterva tinnulum jungat organi laudibus neuma*'; GB:Lbm, Harl. 281, fos. 72^{v}–73 [76^{v}–77].

medieval sources allude to this practice, and in some cases the text and melisma were executed in *alternatim* style between the two sides of the choir.[162] Another performance convention at Saint-Denis was the abbreviation of sequences on certain Octaves and on ferial days within important Octaves. This method of designating the sequences in the ordinaries and missals shows that the singers began, not from the start, but from the middle of the chant (Table 3.9): *O dulces innocentum* (stanza 20 of *Celsa pueri*) for the Octave of Holy Innocents, *Magi stella* (from *Epiphaniam domino*) for the Octave of Epiphany, *In maxilla mille* (from *Zima vetus*) on Wednesday of Easter week, *O deus maris* (from *Rex omnipotens*) for the Octave of Ascension, and *Ecce panis angelorum* (from *Lauda sion*) for the Octave of Corpus Christi.

The repertory of sequences at Saint-Denis, like that of the major Parisian centres of sequence composition,[163] includes selections both from the first era of composers such as Notker of Saint-Gall (d. 912)[164] and from the more recent period, in which Adam Precentor (*olim* of Saint-Victor, d. late 1140s) and others cultivated rhymed, metrical poetry.[165] A number of sequences in the later style are named in the earliest witness of sequences from Saint-Denis, the ordinary F:Pm 526 (M) from the 1230s.[166] In all likelihood, though, these late sequences were in use at Saint-Denis in the twelfth century as well, for even in Paris the first surviving sources of this twelfth-century music come from the early and mid-thirteenth century.[167]

Eleven sequences for saints whose relics were present in the abbey were evidently composed at Saint-Denis in the thirteenth century (Table 4.5). This unusually large number of new sequences for a single establishment demonstrates that Saint-Denis was rather prolific in the realm of sequence composition at this time.[168] With respect to the music for these poems, only one melody (*Salve pater*) seems to have originated in the abbey, as we will see in Chapter 4. Apart from these pieces, the remaining repertory is not merely compiled fom Parisian melodies; in most instances, it follows the specific melodic tradition of the majority of houses in the area of Paris, rather than the distinctive one

[162] See Hiley, 'Neuma', 125.

[163] The 1st extant Victorine repertory is discussed in Fassler, 'Adam' (esp. table 2, pp. 245–7), and in her forthcoming book on the Victorine sequences. On the sequences from Notre Dame, in addition to the works just cited, see Hesbert, *Prosaire*; Husmann, 'Notre-Dame'.

[164] Texts for these sequences are ed. in Dreves, *Prosarium*, *AH*, vii; and in Blume and Bannister, *Prosarium*, *AH*, liii.

[165] See Blume, *Prosarium*, *AH*, lv; Blume and Bannister, *Prosarium*, *AH*, liv.

[166] See Table 3.9. Sequences in the later style are those whose texts are ed. in *AH*, liv.

[167] See the discussion of the earliest Parisian MSS in Fassler, 'Adam', 240–51.

[168] I am grateful to Margot Fassler for her opinion of the significance of these 11 sequences from Saint-Denis.

created at Saint-Victor in the late twelfth century.[169] The local melodic variants that do occur at Saint-Denis were passed to the abbey of Saint-Corneille of Compiègne,[170] which drew virtually its entire liturgical practice from Saint-Denis.

CLOSING VERSICLES FOR OFFICE AND MASS

Benedicamus Domino ('Let us bless the Lord') served as the final sentence for the Offices, for Mass during penitential seasons, and on a few other occasions. An older chant, Ite Missa Est ('Go, the Mass is ended'), was the normal closing versicle of Mass. Jungmann believes that there was probably a concluding formula at Mass in the earliest liturgies, and he speculates that the Ite Missa Est probably dates back to the beginnings of the Roman rite.[171] The first *Ordo Romanus* of the mid-eighth century uses the Ite,[172] but it does not mention the Benedicamus as an alternative formula in more sombre Masses. Evidently Ite Missa Est simply was or was not chanted, according to the directions of the specific *ordo*.[173] Only in the eleventh century was the characteristic distinction between Ite as a jubilant sentence and Benedicamus as the solemn expression firmly established.[174]

It is not clear when the Benedicamus entered the liturgy of the Offices. The Benedictine Rule from the early sixth century makes no

[169] Fassler treats several salient melodic variants and the wholesale recomposition of sequences; 'Adam', 252–63.

[170] See Hiley, 'Traditions', 26 (diagram 3), based on F:Pn, lat. 1107 (Saint-Denis) and F:Pn, lat. 16823 (Saint-Corneille).

[171] Jungmann, *Mass*, ii. 432–7. Drawing from Jungmann's work, Barclay also gives a brief summary of the early history of the Ite and of the Benedicamus; 'Repertory', i. 5–10. See also Eisenhöfer and Lechner, *Liturgy*, 330.

[172] *Ordo I* states: 'When the oration is finished, one of the deacons whom the archdeacon will have chosen looks at the pontiff in order to nod to him, and he says to the people: *Ite missa est*. [They] respond *Deo gratias*' ('Qua [oratione] finita, cui praeceperit archidiaconus de diaconibus aspicit ad pontificem, ut ei annuat, et dicit ad populum: *Ite missa est*. Resp. *Deo gratias*'); Andrieu, *Ordines*, ii. 38–9, 107. See also the similar references to the Ite in the 8th and 9th c. in *Ordo IV* (ibid. 167), *Ordo V* (ibid. 226), *Ordo VI* (ibid. 250), etc. For a brief overview of the contents and dates of the *Ordines Romani*, see Andrieu's preliminary comments on each *ordo*; and Vogel, *Liturgy*, 135–224.

[173] It seems clear, however, that the notion of the Ite as a jubilant text was at least beginning to take hold at the end of the 8th c. *Ordo XXXA*, which originated in Flanders or Lotharingia in the 2nd half of the 8th c., forbids the singing of the Ite at the close of Mass on Maundy Thursday, stating instead that the participants should bow without speaking and then leave the church; Andrieu, *Ordines*, iii. 455. On the other hand, the northern French *Ordo XXXB* from about the same time specifies that the Ite be sung at the end of this same Mass and at the close of the Mass on Holy Saturday; ibid. 470, 474. *Ordo XXII* from late 8th-c. Gaul likewise allowed the singing of the Ite during Lent, although it placed some restrictions on the performance of the Kyrie, Gloria, and alleluia; ibid. 260–2.

[174] Jungmann, *Mass*, ii. 435.

mention of it,[175] and other ancient descriptions of the *opus dei*, which are generally quite sketchy, are vague about the final versicle.[176] Not until the late eighth and ninth centuries, in fact, does the Benedicamus begin to appear in descriptions of the *cursus*. Jungmann surmises that this addition to the divine service probably happened in Gaul, for there is no trace of the Benedicamus in Roman sources until some time later.[177] It clearly formed part of the Offices by the time of the early ninth-century Frankish liturgist Amalarius of Metz. In his treatise on the Rule of Saint Benedict, Amalarius tries to reconcile his use of the formula Benedicamus Domino with the fact that Saint Benedict omits it.[178] Besides the witness of Amalarius and his contemporaries,[179] other evidence suggests that the Benedicamus may have been employed somewhat earlier. The Benedictine customary, *Memoriale Qualiter*, written at the end of the eighth century, or at least prior to the reforms of Benedict of Aniane in the early ninth century, hints at the existence of the versicle. At the end of the noonday meal a certain *ordo* states: 'Then the prior should say "Benedicamus Domino," and they should respond "Deo gratias"'.[180] Since the Benedicamus is not connected here with a particular Office, it is possible that the versicle originated in this way as a traditional closing for services outside the eight standard Hours, and was then absorbed into the daily *cursus* and Mass at the beginning of the ninth century. A third phrase, *Requiescant in pace*,

175 At the end of First Vespers, Saint Benedict provides for the recitation of the Lord's Prayer 'immediately before the dismissal' ('oratione dominica fiant missae'); Fry, *Rule*, 212–13. The closing formula for the Little Hours as well as for Compline is also termed 'the dismissal' ['missae']; ibid. (See Fry's commentary on the liturgical chapters of the rule; ibid. 379–417; and esp. his discussion of the vocabulary of the rule, pp. 400–8. The term 'missa' is treated separately on pp. 410–12.) In the description of Lauds, the rule records simply that the Office 'is finished' ('et completum est'); ibid. 206–9. (Fry translates these words slightly more freely: 'and the conclusion'; ibid. 207.) One or more closing sentences may have been sung at these Offices, but they were not named.

176 The *Regula Magistri*, on which the Benedictine Rule was based, speaks of the 'concluding verse' of Compline ('versum clusoriae'); Latin text in Vogüé, *Maître*, ii. 194; trans. in Eberle, *Rule*, 200. The lexicons of early rules in Kasch, *Vokabular*, and in Clément, *Lexique*, do not contain the expression 'Benedicamus Domino', suggesting that it was not in use in the early cs.

177 Jungmann, *Mass*, ii. 435.

178 In a redundantly worded passage, he demonstrates its aptness at the end of the hours: 'The priest bids farewell to those dismissed, and after that he is greeted by those who are blessing the Lord most fittingly at the end and saying "*Deo gratias*". The priest says most appropriately "*Benedicamus domino*", and they all respond most suitably "*Deo gratias*"' ('Quos disiungendos communiter salutans, resalutatur postquam a cunctis, congruentissime Dominum in fine benedicentes et "*Deo gratias*" dicentes, aptissime dicit sacerdos: "*Benedicamus Domino*", aptissime cuncti respondent: "*Deo gratias*"'); Hanssens, *Amalarii*, iii. 294. See also the mentions of the Benedicamus in Amalarius' *Liber Officialis* (ibid. ii. 541); and the commentary to his *Liber de ordine antiphonarii* (ibid. iii. 139–42).

179 Jungmann, *Mass*, ii. 435.

180 'Tunc item dicat prior *Benedicamus domino*, respondeant *Deo gratias*'; Hallinger, *Initia*, 276. On the date of the *Memoriale*, see ibid. 224–5.

was chanted in place of Benedicamus or Ite at the ends of the Mass and Offices of the services for the dead.

Music for the Benedicamus and Ite first appears in eleventh-century manuscripts or as eleventh-century additions to earlier sources.[181] The variety of the music that was written for the versicles—troped and polyphonic settings as well as monophonic ones—witness the importance of these chants in the medieval liturgy. The monophonic repertory grew when melismatic passages were borrowed from other forms of chant and underlaid with the text Benedicamus Domino or Ite Missa Est. Peter the Venerable, abbot of Cluny, explained this procedure around 1146,[182] and the Sarum Rite witnesses its use a century later.[183] In these descriptions, Benedicamus are created from responsory melismas, while tunes for the Ite, on the other hand, seem to be based on Kyries as frequently as on responsories, at least in the later Middle Ages. Both versicles were also formed from other types of chant: alleluia verses, antiphons, and sequences. Frank Harrison discovered a series of Benedicamus in a thirteenth-century Sarum missal from Exeter, GB:Mr, lat. 24, which draws on all these genres except the alleluia verse.[184] The thirteenth-century missal from Saint-Denis, F:Pn, lat. 1107,[185] contains similar collections of Benedicamus and Ite, and this important repertory contributes significantly to the history of the development of these chants.

[181] For a summary of the early MSS in which Benedicamus occur, see Huglo, 'Débuts', 135–49; Barclay, 'Repertory', i. 50–91; Robertson, '*Benedicamus*', 10–11. Serious study of the melodies for the Ite Missa Est has only recently been undertaken, and Eifrig has begun a catalogue of tunes for this chant in his paper, 'Ite'.

[182] 'And I add that at Vespers and Lauds on those same solemn feasts [Easter, Pentecost, Peter and Paul, Assumption], as well as on whichever other major feasts you might wish, the Benedicamus Domino should be sung according to the melody of that very new, yet good, and already popular verse which many sing on the nativity of the blessed mother of the Lord: *Virgo dei genitrix est, flos filius ejus*. The melody is not taken from the whole verse, however, but from the end of the verse, that is *Flos filius ejus*. The purpose for this ordinance was that on more festive days a more solemn chant is preferable, and so that this greater variation of melodies might increase the devotion of those singing' ('Additum est et hoc, ut in eisdem solemnitatibus et in quibuslibet, prout libuerit, maioribus ad Vesperos vel ad Laudes cantetur *Benedicamus domino* iuxta cantum novi quidem sed boni et iam publici versus illius, qui in Nativitate beatae Matris Domini a multis canitur, *Virgo dei genitrix virga est, flos filius eius*. Sumptus est autem cantus non de toto versu, sed de fine versus, hoc est *Flos filius eius*. Causa instituti huius fuit, ut et solemnioribus diebus magis congrueret solemnior cantus et ut ipsa cantuum variatio maior esset cantantium devotio'); Hallinger, *Benedictinae*, 103.

[183] 'On duplex feasts and on feasts when the invitatory is sung by three, some appropriate *Benedicamus* from the historia [*i.e.* the Matins responsories] of the feast with which it deals or some other which is appropriate to the feast is sung' ('In festis vero duplicibus et in festis quando Invitatorium a tribus canitur, dicitur aliquod proprium *Benedicamus* de historia festi de quo agitur vel aliquid aliud quod festo conveniat'); Frere, *Use*, i. 254. Harrison cites this passage in his discussion of the Benedicamus; *Britain*, 74–5; and in his 'Benedicamus', 37.

[184] Harrison, 'Benedicamus'.

[185] Fos. 395^{v}–397 (Pl. 18).

In fact, the Benedicamus Domino and Ite Missa Est at Saint-Denis are the most striking and individual musical features in the liturgy of the monastery. The chants are characterized first and foremost by the length and range of many of the melismas.[186] This ornateness immediately suggests that the melodies were sung on special occasions, and the three ordinaries (F:Pm 526; F:Pn, lat. 976; and F:Pan, L 863, No. 10) confirm that the Benedicamus and Ite were performed on the higher feast-days.[187] The tradition of their use at Saint-Denis was an important one, to judge from its longevity. Traces of the melodies appear in the extant manuscripts of the abbey for more than 600 years—from the mid-twelfth century (F:Pn, lat. 17296) to the late eighteenth century (F:Pn, n.a.l. 1420). The monks even bequeathed this usage to the abbey of Saint-Corneille of Compiègne, which preserves many of the Benedicamus and a few Ites from Saint-Denis in the thirteenth-century missal F:Pn, lat. 17329.[188]

Benedicamus Domino[189]

The repertories of Benedicamus Domino in F:Pn, lat. 1107 from Saint-Denis and F:Pn, lat. 17329 from Saint-Corneille are remarkably similar in format and content (Table 3.10). The manuscripts introduce almost every melody with a rubric that reveals the source of the Benedicamus melisma, and the two series share some 20 melodies. Cues to the sources appear in the ordinaries of the two abbeys, where rubrics such as 'Benedicamus ut *Quorum vallatus*' at the end of Lauds on the feast of Saint Vincent (22 January) are given.[190] This hint refers both to the melody and to the liturgical use of the Benedicamus. In the example just given, the rubric points to the Office of Saint Vincent, in which the words *Quorum vallatus* form part of the text of the Resp. *Beatus dei athleta*. The sources of many of the other Benedicamus, which include Kyries, alleluias, sequences, and antiphons in addition to responsories, likewise come to light with the aid of the ordinaries.

[186] See Ex. 3.16; Robertson, '*Benedicamus*', Ex. 2.

[187] At Prime, the earlier ordinaries state that the Benedicamus was not sung on feasts of fewer than 12 lessons: 'Ad finem orationum dicatur *Per dominum nostrum* et Benedicamus Domino si duodecim lectiones fuerint. Si vero non fuerint dicatur tantummodo *Per christum dominum nostrum*'; F:Pm 526, fo. 79; F:Pn, lat. 976, fo. 48.

[188] See Robertson, 'Transmission'; idem, '*Benedicamus*', ex. 2; and Table 3.10 of the present study. See also the facsimiles of the Benedicamus collections from Saint-Denis and Saint-Corneille in Robertson, '*Benedicamus*', fig. 1; and in idem, 'Transmission', fig. 1.

[189] For further details on the Benedicamus at Saint-Denis and discussion of the chant in other repertories, see idem, '*Benedicamus*'.

[190] Saint-Denis ordinaries: F:Pm 526, fo. 102; F:Pn, lat. 976, fo. 73; Saint-Corneille ordinaries: F:Pn, lat. 18044, fo. 67; F:Pn, lat. 18045, fo. 65.

The Benedicamus in F:Pn, lat. 1107 are not the earliest examples of these melodies at Saint-Denis. What appears to be an unfinished collection of six Benedicamus is found in the mid-twelfth-century antiphoner F:Pn, lat. 17296,[191] inserted in the proper Office for John the Baptist. None of the Benedicamus in F:Pn, lat. 17296 provides a cue to the origins of the melodies, but all of them reappear in the missal F:Pn, lat. 1107. The presence of these chants in a book for the Office results naturally from the customary association of the Benedicamus with the canonical Hours. By the mid-thirteenth century, the Benedicamus collection at Saint-Denis had expanded to the point where the chants were placed side by side with other items having multiple liturgical assignments—Kyrie, Gloria, Sanctus, Agnus, and Ite Missa Est—in the troper–proser section of such Mass books as F:Pn, lat. 1107.[192]

The ordinaries of Saint-Denis explain the ceremonial use of the Benedicamus.[193] These books prescribe one or more Benedicamus for feasts whose rank is duplex or higher, and they specify Benedicamus most of the time for First and Second Vespers. Two famous melismas which were sung as Benedicamus Domino served *annuale* and *semi-annuale* celebrations: *Flos filius* at First Vespers and *Clementiam* at Second Vespers. Other Benedicamus for First and Second Vespers were selected from the music of the feast in question.[194] *Secundum ordinem* and *Posuisti*, based on common alleluia verses for confessors and martyrs, respectively, served as the *commune sanctorum* of Benedicamus for feasts of saints in these two categories.

Whereas the majority of Benedicamus are assigned to the two Vespers services, the monks performed the Benedicamus *Amborum sacrum* at Lauds on the high feast-days of Christmas, Pentecost, and Assumption. The same melody was chanted at Lauds on the feast of Saint Vincent (22 January), and on the anniversaries for Robert II (d. 1031) and Abbot Suger (d. 1151), where the text *Requiescant in pace* replaced Benedicamus Domino. The use of these melodies at Matins is rare. *Quorum vallatus* is the only tune specified in the ordinaries at this Hour on the anniversaries of Philip Augustus (d. 1223) and Charles the Bald (d. 877), where it was sung as *Requiescant in pace*. Although they are hardly ever used at Matins in any case, the restricted employment of

[191] Fo. 171; see Robertson, '*Benedicamus*', 27, and fig. 2.

[192] There is ample precedent for the appearance of Benedicamus in missals, for in earlier sources they are regularly found in the tropers whose contents later passed into graduals and missals. Benedicamus based on pre-existing material apparently were not sung at Mass in place of the Ite during penitential seasons. A simple tone for the Benedicamus would have been used instead.

[193] See Robertson, '*Benedicamus*', 33–9, and table 2.

[194] Table 3.10, Nos. 3–8, 12, 15–17, 19, 22.

TABLE 3.10. *The Benedicamus Domino at Saint-Denis and Saint-Corneille, based on F:Pn, lat. 1107*

Cue	Source of melody[a]	Solo or choral part of responsorial source	Feast and location of source	No. of melody in F:Pn, lat. 17329
1. *Secundum ordinem*	Alle. *Juravit dominus*	Solo	Common of one confessor N2, fo. 309^{v}	2
2. *Angelorum*	Resp. *Vir inclitus dionysius*	Choral	Saint Denis N1, fo. 231	3
3. *Pax*	Ant. *Pax eterna*		Dedication of Church N1, fo. 346	n. g.
4. *Quid te*[b]	Resp. *Cornelius centurio*	Choral	Saints Peter and Paul N1, fo. 175	6
5. *Fines terre*	Resp. *Benedicat nos deus*	Choral	All Saints N1, fo. 239^{v}	7
6. *Commenda*	Resp. *O felix felicis*	Choral	Saint Mary Magdalene N1, fo. 350^{v}	8
7. *Destinavit*[c]	Resp. *Gaudeat exultans*	Choral	Saint Eugene N1, fos. 252^{v}–253	9
8. *Alacriter*[d]	Resp. *Valerius igitur*	Choral	Saint Vincent N1, fos. 62^{v}–63	10
9. *Clementiam*[e]	Resp. *Qui cum audissent*	Choral	Saint Nicholas N1, fo. 263	11
10. *Flos*	Verse Virgo dei, Resp. *Styrps jesse*	Solo	Nativity of Mary N1, fos. 211^{r-v}	12
11. n. g.	Ant. *O christi pietas*		Saint Nicholas N1, fo. 264^{v}	20
12. *Balaam*	Sequence *Epiphaniam domino*		Epiphany N2, fo. 346^{v}	15
13. *Clemens*	Kyrie *Clemens rector*		(Melnicki, No. 102)	n. g.
14. *Posuisti*	Alle. *Posuisti domine*	Solo (= *jubilus*)	Common of one martyr N2, fo. 292^{v}	16
15. *Preciosus*	Resp. *Preciosus domini*	Solo	Saint Denis	13

16. *Erat autem*	Verse *Erat autem* Resp. *Quatuor animalia*	Solo	Common of evangelists N1, fo. 270	1
17. *Per omnia secula*	Resp. *Hodie martyrum*	Choral	Saint Maurice N1, fo. 220	n. g.
18. *Occumbere*	Resp. *Gloriosi domine*	Choral	Saint Vincent N1, fos. 61r–v	n. g.
19. *Vernabantur*	Resp. *Christi miles*	Choral	Saint Vincent N1, fo. 63v	14
20. *Quorum vallatus*	Resp. *Beatus dei athleta*	Choral	Saint Vincent N1, fo. 64	21
21. *Surrexit dominus*	Alle. *Surrexit dominus*	Solo	Easter N2, fo. 149v	n. g.
22. *Benedictus ascendit*	Resp. *Preciosus confessor*	Choral	Translation of Benedict N1, fo. 83	17
23. *In secula*[f]	Resp. *Benedicamus patrem*	Choral	Trinity N1, fo. 167v	4
24. *Aromatibus*	Resp. *Diluculo valde surgens*	Choral	Saint Mary Magdalene N1, fo. 350	n. g.
25. *Amborum sacrum*	Kyrie *Cunctipotens genitor*		(Melnicki, No. 18)	18
26. n. g.			N2, fo. 393v (Huglo, No. 411)	19
Unnotated Benedicamus named in Paris, Archives Nationales, L 863, No. 10:				
O quam suavis	Ant. *O quam suavis* (same melody as Ant. *O christi pietas*)		Corpus Christi (14th c.): text in GB:Ob, Can. Lit. 192, fo. 142v, and in F:Pn, Rés. 5209.	

Abbreviations: N1: F:Pn, lat. 17296. N2: F:Pn, lat. 1107. Melnicki: Melnicki, *Kyrie*. Huglo: Huglo, 'Débuts', 150–4.

[a] For the melodies of the Benedicamus in F:Pn, lat. 1107, see Robertson, '*Benedicamus*', ex. 2.

[b] Also given in the 12th-c. antiphoner N1, fo. 171, Benedicamus No. 2.

[c] Ibid. No. 4.

[d] Ibid. Nos. 1 and 6.

[e] Ibid. No. 5.

[f] Ibid. No. 3.

melismatic Benedicamus at Matins and Lauds is probably related in part to the method of execution of the chants. When the ordinaries specify who should sing the Benedicamus, they call for boys,[195] and these youngest members of the convent probably did not participate constantly in the night and early-morning services of Matins and Lauds.

The sheer size of the collections of Benedicamus and Ite in F:Pn, lat. 1107; F:Pn, lat. 17329; and GB:Mr, lat. 24 is unusual, but other houses did have smaller repertories, consisting usually of the most famous tunes. Notre Dame cathedral, for example, used only a few simple tones for the Benedicamus, along with *Flos filius*, *Clementiam*, and a Benedicamus built on *Quem queritis* from the Easter dialogue.[196] Many Benedicamus that might be considered particular to Saint-Denis were known elsewhere, too, and they have gone unrecognized only because the sources of their melodies were not known. These widely disseminated Benedicamus include *O christi pietas*, *Balaam*, *Amborum sacrum*, *Clemens*, *Preciosus*, *Vernabantur*, *Quorum vallatus*, *Pax*, and the unidentified Benedicamus in Table 3.10 (No. 26), in addition to *Flos filius* and *Clementiam*.[197] But whereas many of the tunes were quite popular, the existence of fully notated and rubricated collections like those from Saint-Denis, Saint-Corneille, and Exeter is rare. These highly organized series probably represent 'reference copy' versions of the Benedicamus Domino and Ite Missa Est. The chants hardly needed to be written down because they were created from previously memorized material, and could be performed *extempore* and without the aid of notated sources. The soloist had only to keep the original melody roughly in mind while adding the new text Benedicamus Domino or Ite Missa Est so that it matched the parent source in terms of pitches, vowel sounds, and phrasing.[198] The choir could likewise join in this type of oral composition in singing the response Deo Gratias ('Thanks be to God'), since the majority of melismas come from the choral parts of responsories and alleluias (Table 3.10).

[195] There are many examples of the use of boys in the Saint-Denis ordinaries: on the Vigil of Pentecost, 'Benedicamus a duobus pueris' (F:Pm 526, fo. 72^{v}); and on Monday after Assumption, 'Benedicamus solempniter a duobus pueris et similiter duobus sequentibus diebus' (F:Pan, L 863, No. 10, fo. 115^{v}). In other instances, only the rubric 'a duobus' is given. Other houses employ 1–6 soloists for the Benedicamus, and they specify priests, clerics, rulers, cantors, and *hebdomadarii* as well as boys as performers. For an overview of the execution of the Benedicamus in other establishments, see Robertson, '*Benedicamus*', 5–10.

[196] On the Benedicamus Domino at Notre Dame, see Barclay, 'Repertory', i. 353–470; and her table on pp. 354–7.

[197] Robertson, '*Benedicamus*', 39–45, and table 3.

[198] Ibid. 30–1, 52–4, and ex. 2. See also Ex. 3.16 in the present study, where the text Benedicamus Domino is written beneath the 10 Ites which are built on the same melismas.

The Benedicamus melismas from Saint-Denis likewise existed in two other musical forms: responsory tropes and tenors in polyphony. The melodies *Quid te*, *Commenda*, *Alacriter*, *Clementiam*, *Flos filius*, *Occumbere*, and *Vernabantur* were sung with texts, or prosulas, in a number of establishments outside Saint-Denis.[199] Whereas none of these prosulas was performed in the abbey, their presence in other houses with the same melodies as the Benedicamus at Saint-Denis further emphasizes the popularity and transferability of the melismas. In the same way, the monophonic Benedicamus *Flos filius*, *Clementiam*, *Balaam*, *Preciosus*, and *Surrexit dominus* served as tenor voices of polyphonic compositions in other rituals.[200]

Ite Missa Est

Ten of the 26 melodies for the Benedicamus in F:Pn, lat. 1107 were also sung as Ite Missa Est at Saint-Denis (Ex. 3.16, Pl. 18). Unlike the Benedicamus collection, however, the Ite series begins with three melodies whose sources are not named. These are simple tones, designated for use on twelve-lesson feasts and on ordinary Sundays. Thirteen more elaborate Ites follow, each introduced by a textual and musical incipit. Besides F:Pn, lat. 1107, three other manuscripts from the abbey witness to melodies for the Ite. The two thirteenth-century ordinaries F:Pm 526 and F:Pn, lat. 976 give textual incipits for two Ites that are otherwise undocumented at Saint-Denis: *O christe precamur* and *Judicabunt sancti*. *O christe precamur* is especially intriguing, since an unknown Kyrie tune with the same name is also mentioned in the ordinaries.[201] The evangeliary F:Pn, n.a.l. 1420 shows that the practice of singing melismatic Ites even continued to the eighteenth century, at which time the two Ite melodies *Omni prosequenda* and *Alma* were added to this manuscript.

The liturgical destinations of the Ites at Saint-Denis are not documented as extensively as those for the Benedicamus (Table 3.11).[202]

[199] Table 3.4; Robertson, '*Benedicamus*', 45–8, and table 4.

[200] Table 3.4. *Clementiam* and *Flos* appear as tenors of 2- and 3-voice Benedicamus at Notre Dame; see Barclay, 'Repertory', i. 354–7. Examples of *Balaam* and *Flos* in other types of polyphony can be found in the index to Reaney, *Manuscripts*, 829, 841. A polyphonic responsory built on *Preciosus* exists in several forms in the Notre Dame polyphonic MS I:Fl, Pluteo 29.1 (= F; published in Dittmer, *Florence*); and the Alleluia *Surrexit dominus* (*et occurrens mulieribus*) is preserved in F and in W1 (D:W 677 [Helmstedt 628]; published in Baxter, *St. Andrews*) The tenor of the 2-voice organum and clausula on *Preciosus* in F is the source for the French motet *He! mounier porrai je moudre*, preserved in W2 (D:W 1206 [Helmstedt 1099]; ed. in Dittmer, *Wolfenbüttel*); and in the Montpellier MS (F:MO, H 196; ed. in Rokseth, *Polyphonies*; and in Tischler *et al.*, *Montpellier*). For more information on *Preciosus* and *Surrexit dominus*, see Robertson, '*Benedicamus*', 48–51.

[201] See Table 3.11. As noted earlier, I have been unable to locate the source of the tune.

[202] See Robertson, '*Benedicamus*', 33–9, and table 2.

Ex. 3.16. *Melodies for the Ite Missa Est at Saint-Denis, based on F:Pn, lat. 1107*[1]

Abbreviations:

N1: F:Pn, lat. 17296. Melnicki: Melnicki, *Kyrie*.
N2: F:Pn, lat. 1107. BD: Benedicamus Domino.

	Cue	*Source of melody*	*Solo or choral part of responsorial source*	*Feast and location of source*	*Mode*
1	*In xii lectionibus*				7
2	*Item in xii lect.*	Kyrie		Melnicki No. 205	7
3	*In dominicis diebus*				1

1: I - te mis - sa est

2: I - te mis - sa est

3: I - te mis - sa est

[1] Fos. 396^{v}–97 (Pl. 18). The text underlay of the Benedicamus Domino melodies in F:Pn, lat. 1107 is also included in this example for comparison with that of the Ite Missa Est. The musical readings, however, sometimes differ, and the ones given here are those for the Ite. For the music of the Benedicamus at Saint-Denis, see Robertson, '*Benedicamus*', ex. 2.

4 *Quorum vallatus* (BD 20)	Resp. *Beatus dei athleta*	Choral	Saint Vincent N1, fo. 64	1

q^o^ vallat'   I – te mis – sa est

(Be – ne-di – ca – mus do – mi – no)

. . . quo-rum val – la – tus ca – ter – va

5 *O christi pietas* (BD 11)	*Ant. O christi pietas*		Saint Nicholas N1, fo. 264v	6

O xp̃i pietas   I – te mis – sa est

(Be – ne – di – ca – mus do – mi – no)

O chri – sti pi – e – tas

Cue	Source of melody	Solo or choral part of responsorial source	Feast and location of source	Mode
6 *Joseph*	Alle. *Missus est angelus gabriel*	Solo	Annunciation N2, fo. 232	2
7 *Omni prosequenda*	Ant. *O christi pietas*		Saint Nicholas N1, fo. 264v; F:Pn, n.a.l. 1420, fo. 127	5

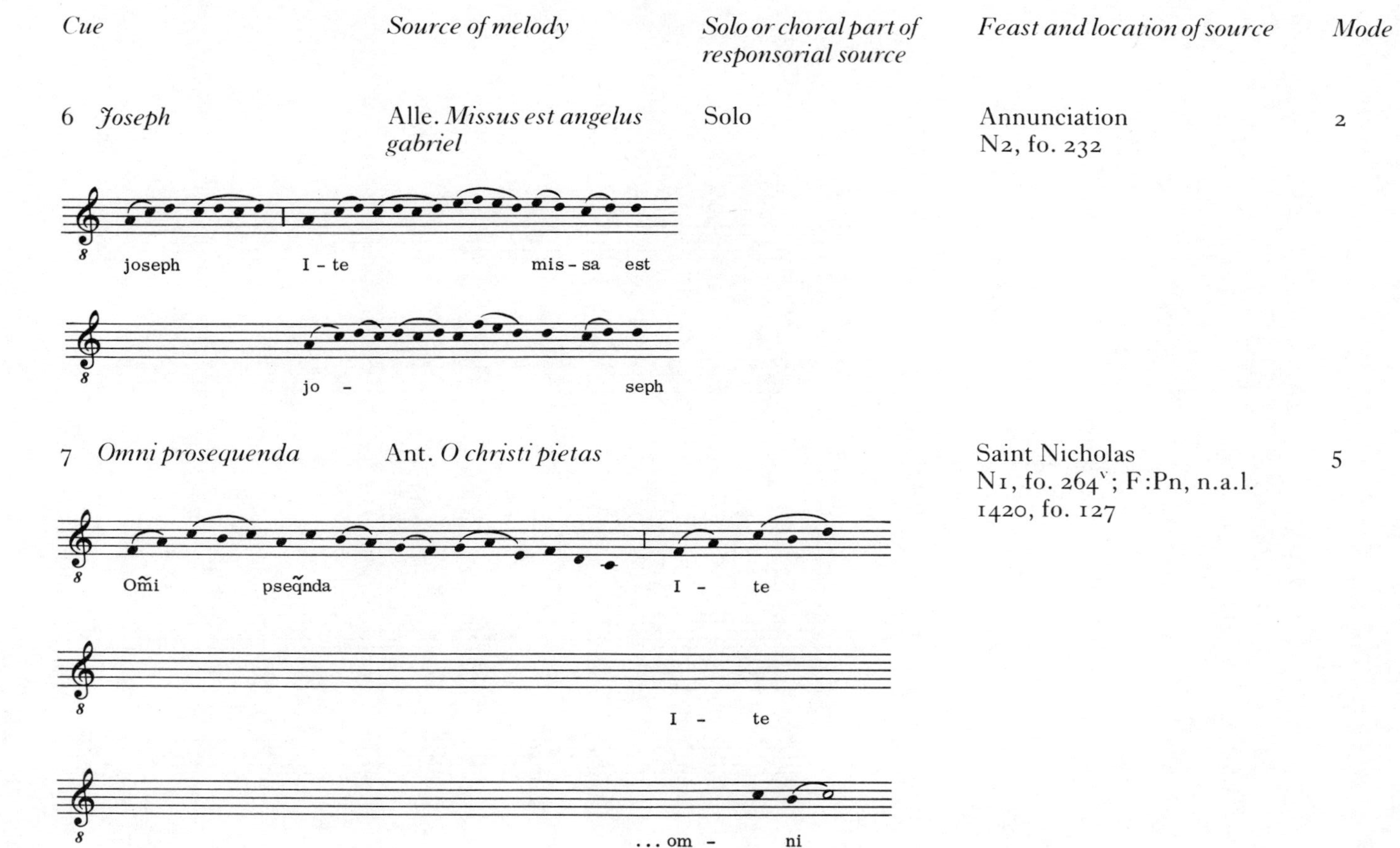

8 *Vernabantur* (BD 19) | Resp. *Christi miles* | Choral | Saint Vincent N1, fo. 63^v | I

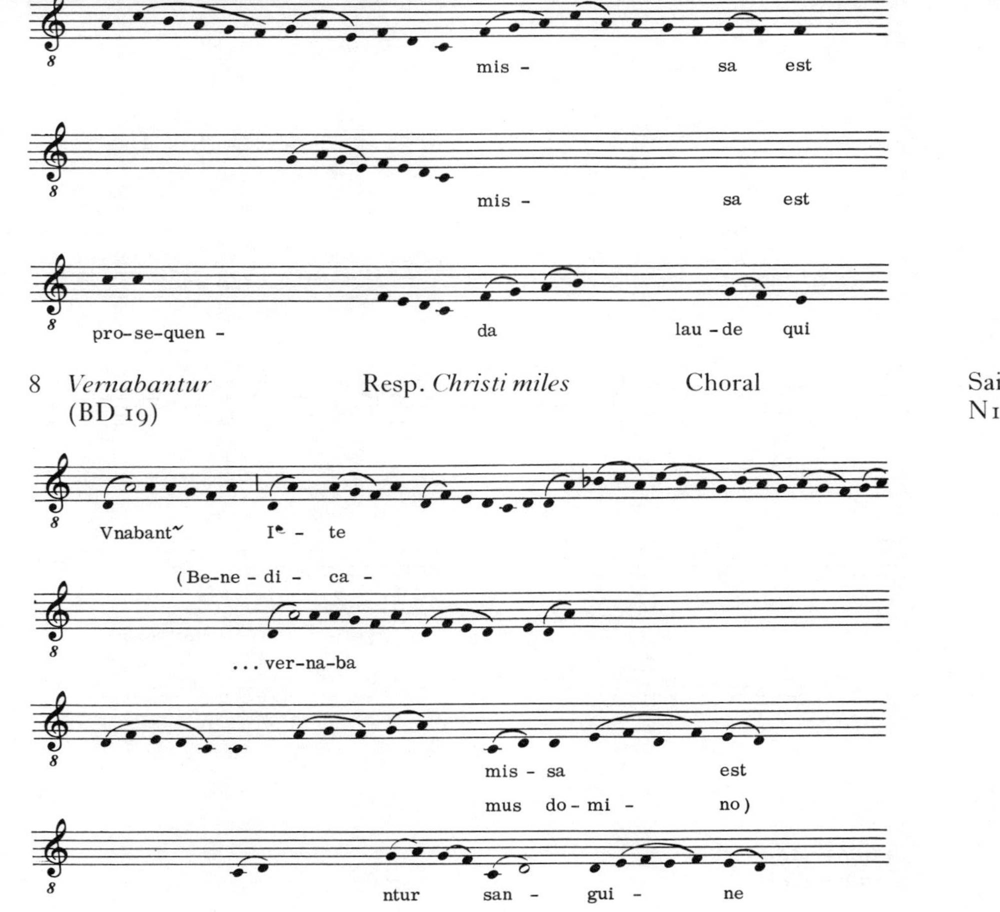

	Cue	*Source of melody*	*Solo or choral part of responsorial source*	*Feast and location of source*	*Mode*
9	*Ecce jam coram te*	Resp. *Ecce jam coram te*	Solo	Invention of Stephen N1, fo. 185	I

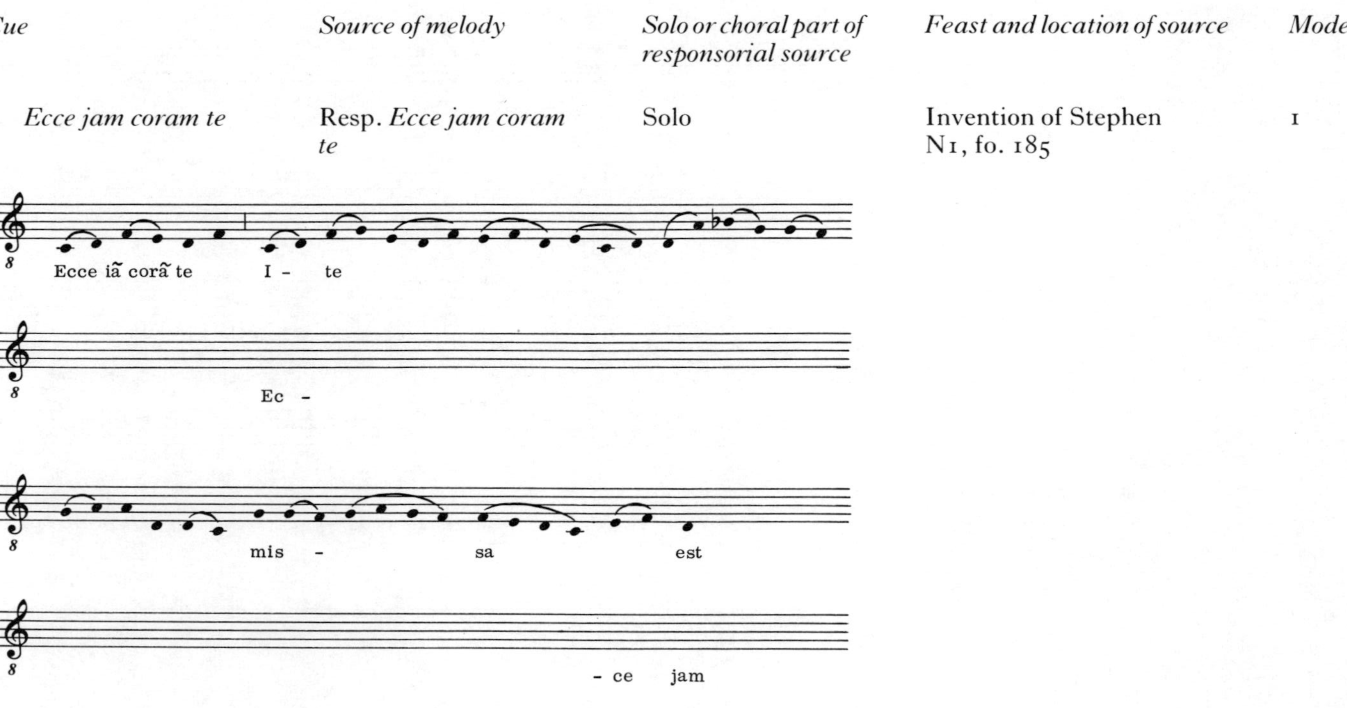

10	*Surrexit dominus* (BD 21)	Alle. *Surrexit dominus*	Solo	Easter N2, fo. 149^{v}	I
11	*Posuisti* (BD 14)	Alle. *Posuisti domine*	Solo (= *jubilus*)	Common of one martyr N2, fo. 292^{v}	I

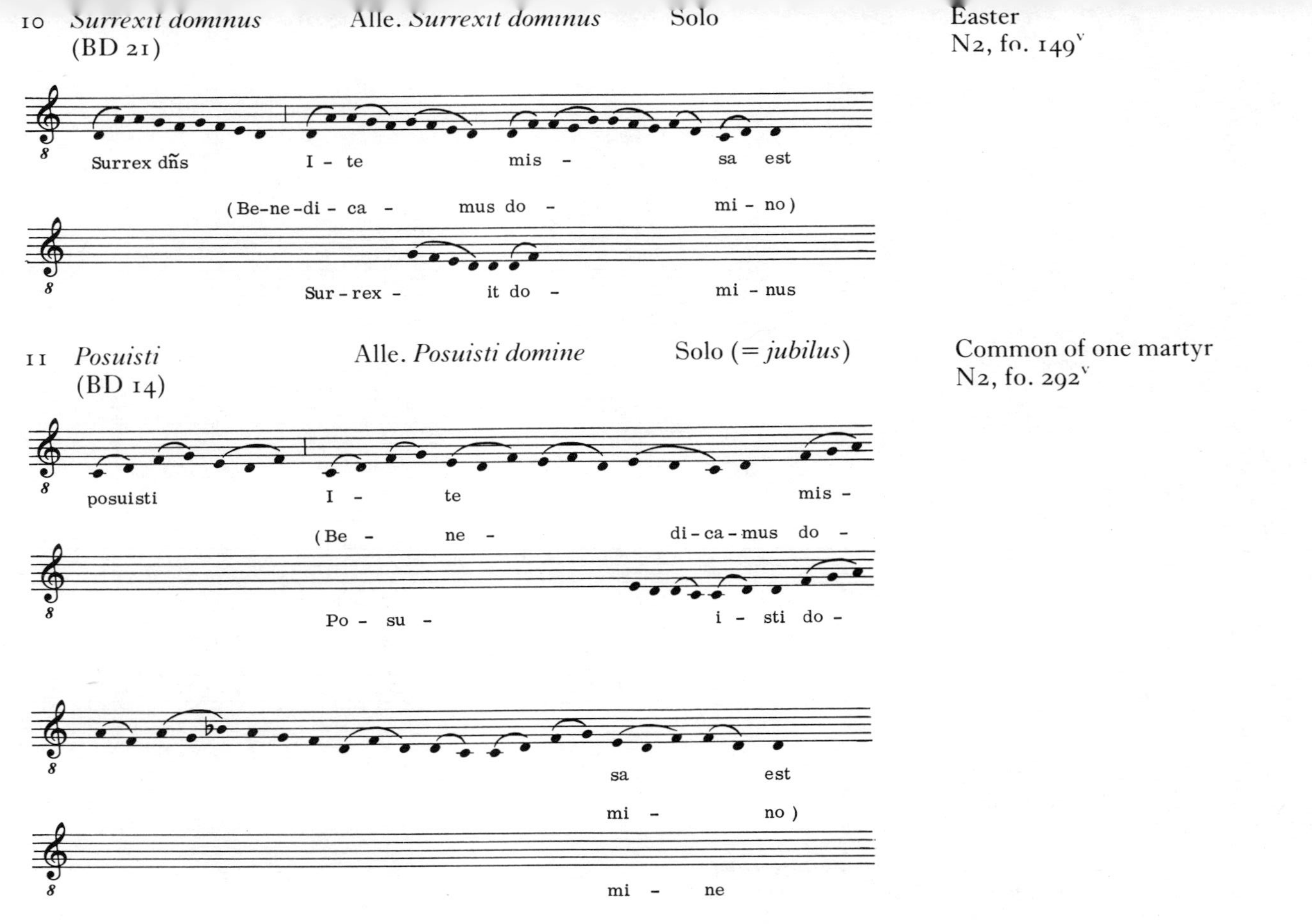

Cue	*Source of melody*	*Solo or choral part of responsorial source*	*Feast and location of source*	*Mode*
12 *Angelorum* (BD 2)	Resp. *Vir inclitus dionysius*	Choral	Saint Denis N1, fo. 231	I

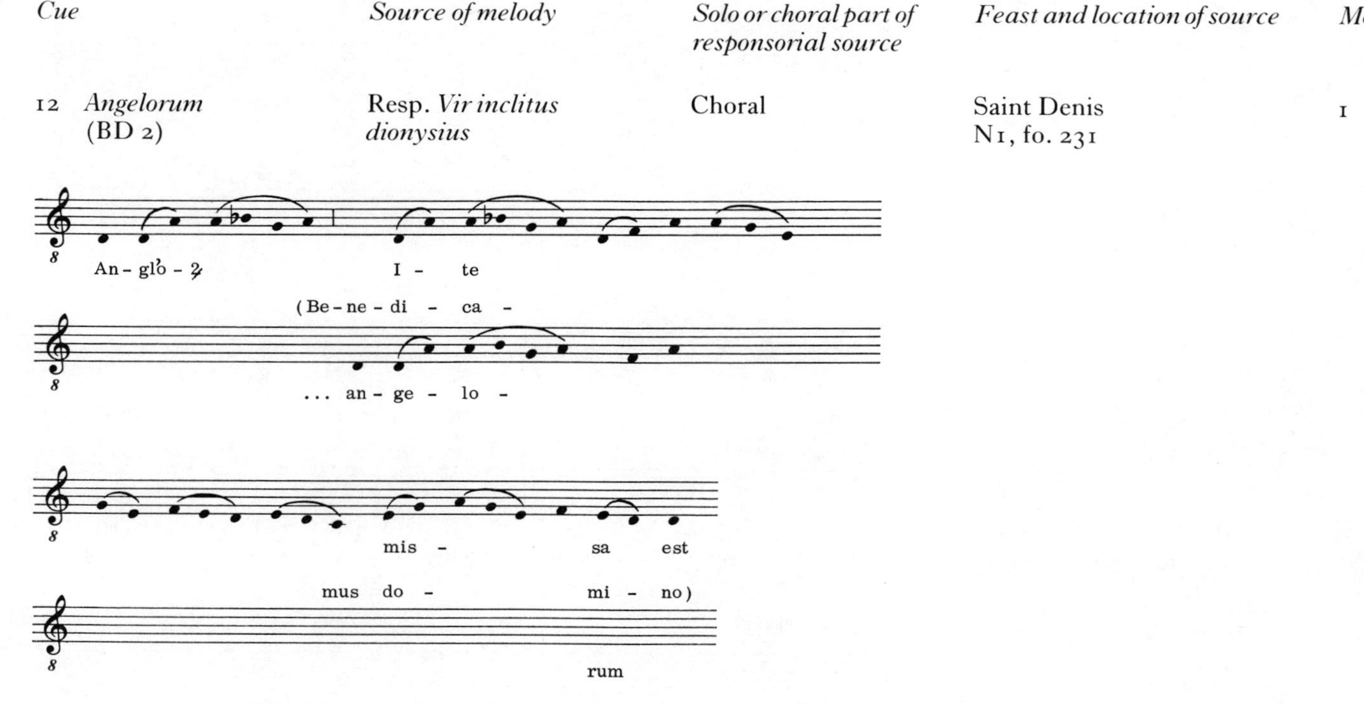

13 *Preciosus* (BD 15) | Resp. *Preciosus domini* | Solo | Saint Denis N1, fo. 231v | 1

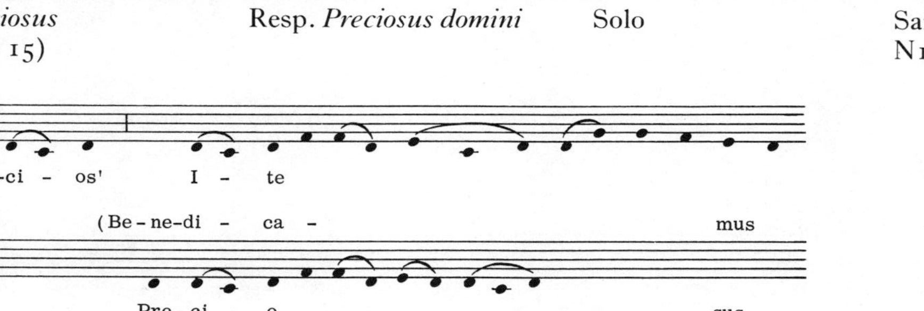

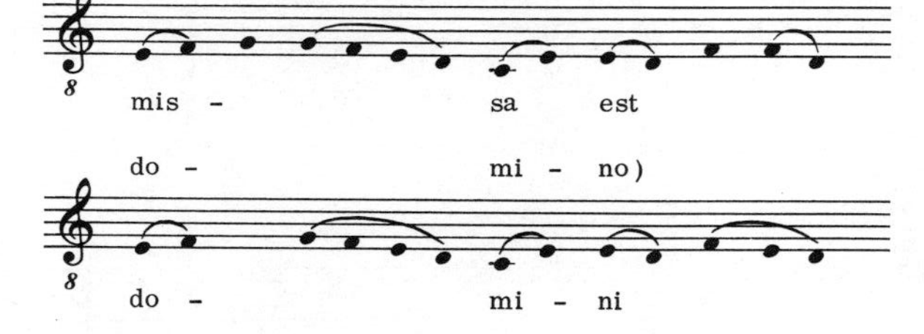

14 *Clementiam* (BD 9) | Resp. *Qui cum audissent* | Choral | Saint Nicholas N1, fo. 263 | 5

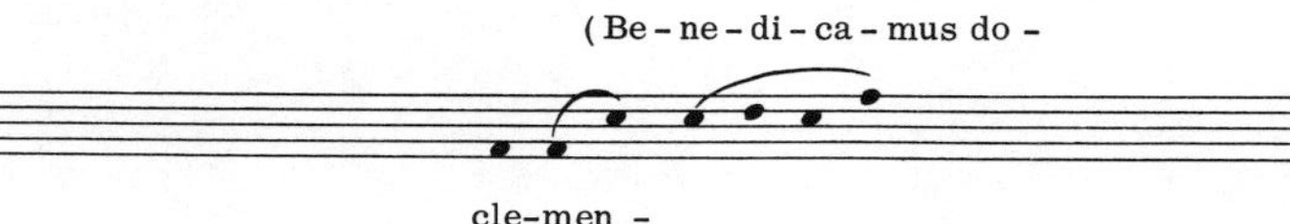

Cue	Source of melody	Solo or choral part of responsorial source	Feast and location of source	Mode
14 *Clementiam* (*cont.*): (BD 9)				
15 *Commenda* (BD 6)	Resp. *O felix felicis*	Choral	Saint Mary Magdalene N1, fo. 350ᵛ	7

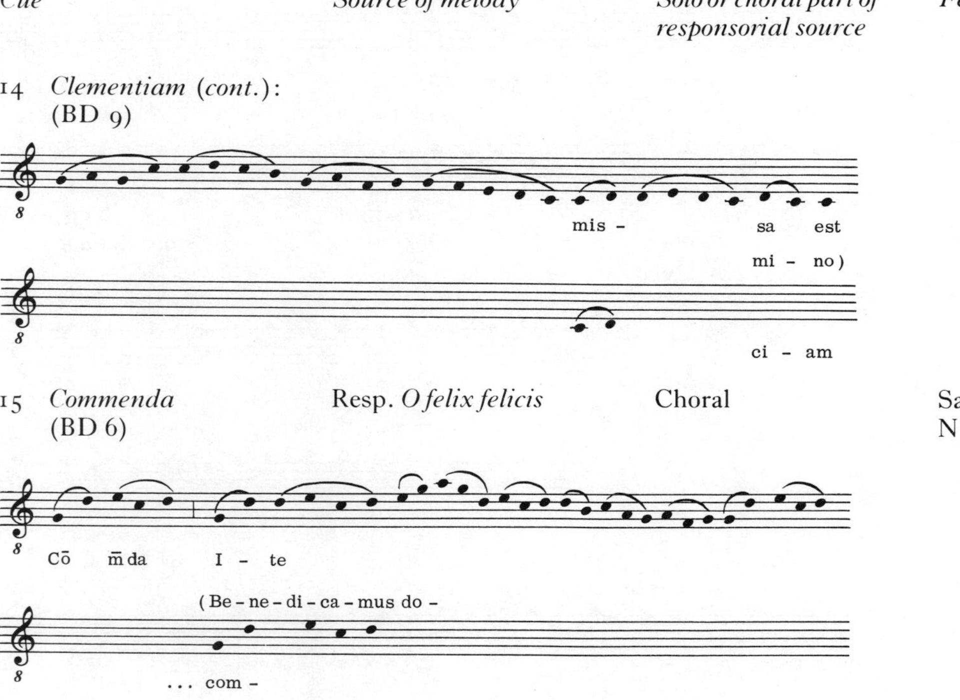

16 *Quid te* (BD 4) | Resp. *Cornelius centurio* | Choral | Saints Peter and Paul N1, fo. 175 | 1

Cue	Source of melody	Solo or choral part of responsorial source	Feast and location of source	Mode
Notated Ites given in F:Pn, n.a.l. 1420, fo. 127:				
1 *Omni prosequenda* (Ite 7)	Ant. *O christi pietas*		Saint Nicholas N1, fo. 264^{v}	1
2 *Alma*	Ant. *Alma redemptoris mater*		Marian antiphon	5

I - te mis - sa est

Cue	Source of melody	Solo or choral part of responsorial source	Feast and location of source	Mode
Unnotated Ites named in F:Pm 526 and F:Pn, lat. 976:				
O christe precamur			Unknown, probably same as source of Kyrie *O christe precamur* (Table 3.5)	
Judicabunt sancti	Alle. *Judicabunt sancti*	Solo	Common of many martyrs N2, fo. 300^{v}	5

TABLE 3.11. *Liturgical Placement of Melodies for the Ite Missa Est at Saint-Denis*[a]

Ite melody	Feast to which assigned	Date	Rank
1.	12 lessons		
2.	12 lessons		
3.	Sundays		
4. *Quorum vallatus*			
5. *O christi pietas*	Ascension		12 sa
	Eustace (14th c.)	2 Nov.	12 d
	Clement (14th c.)	23 Nov.	12 d
	Romanus of Blaye	24 Nov.	12 d
	Nicholas (14th c.)	6 Dec.	12 d
Requiescant in pace	Commemoration of Dead		
6. *Joseph*			
7. *Omni presequenda*	Christmas (14th c.)	25 Dec.	12 a
	Easter (14th c.)		3 a
	Ascension		12 sa
	Pentecost		3 a
	Dedication of Church (14th c.)	24 Feb.	12 a
	Assumption	15 Aug.	12 a
	Saint Louis (14th c.)	25 Aug.	12 d
	Nativity of Mary (14th c.)	8 Sept.	12 sa
	Denis	9 Oct.	12 a
	All Saints	1 Nov.	12 sa
8. *Vernabantur*			
9. *Ecce jam coram te*			
10. *Surrexit dominus*	Easter		3 a
	Ascension		12 sa
	Vigil of Pentecost (14th c.)		3
	Mary Magdalene	29 July	12 d
	Exaltation of Cross (14th c.)	14 Sept.	12 d
11. *Posuisti*	Eugene	15 Nov.	12 d
	Clement	23 Nov.	12 d
12. *Angelorum*	Michael	29 Sept.	12 d
	Octave of Denis	16 Oct.	12 sa
13. *Preciosus*	Detection of Denis	9 June	12 d
14. *Clementiam*	Nicholas	6 Dec.	12 d
Requiescant in pace	Philip Augustus (d. 1223)	14 July	
15. *Commenda*	Mary Magdalene	22 July	12 d
16. *Quid te*	Peter and Paul	29 June	12 sa
17. *Omni prosequenda* (F:Pn, n.a.l. 1420)	*In festis annualibus et semiannualibus*		
18. *Alma* (F:Pn, n.a.l. 1420)	*In festis beate Mariae sicut in annualibus, vel sicut Alma*		

Ite melody	Feast to which assigned	Date	Rank
19. *O christe precamur* (F:Pn, lat. 976)	Abbot Suger (d. 1151)	14 Jan.	
20. *Judicabunt sancti* (F:Pm 526; F:Pn, lat. 976)	Eustace	2 Nov.	12 d

[a] The order of this table is based on the order of the Ite melodies in F:Pn, lat. 1107 (see Ex. 3.16). Information on liturgical placement comes from the ordinaries F:Pm 526; F:Pn, lat. 976; F:Pan, L 863, No. 10; and from the evangeliary F:Pn, n.a.l. 1420. Feasts designated '14th c.' occur only in F:Pan, L 863, No. 10. Numerals under *Rank* refer to nos. of lessons in feasts; letters signify *semiduplex* (sd), *duplex* (d), *semiannuale* (sa), *annuale* (a). Entries in this table are conflated from all 3 ordinaries.

Four of the 16 melodies have no assignments at all in the ordinaries, and many important feasts do not name an Ite for Mass.[203] In some cases, however, it is possible to guess which one might have been chosen by observing how other melodies are assigned. *Omni prosequenda* was clearly reserved for the most festive occasions. This melody appears to have become increasingly popular in the fourteenth century,[204] and it was chanted on the most important occasions at Saint-Denis right up to the eighteenth century.[205] The chant served as a kind of common Ite for *annuale* and *semiannuale* feasts in the fourteenth century, whereas the more proper Ite *Surrexit dominus* was sung on the *annuale* celebration of Easter in the thirteenth century.[206]

In other houses, however, *Omni prosequenda* seems not to have enjoyed this premier status. Of the 16 melodies for the Ite Missa Est in F:Pn, lat. 1107, only *O christi pietas* and *Joseph* were widely known, and these melodies were undoubtedly two of the most popular in the Ite repertory.[207] A preliminary search for concordances for the Ites in F:Pn, lat. 1107 uncovers *O christi pietas* and *Joseph* consistently in manuscripts of many different locations and uses (Table 3.12). *Joseph* seems to be the older Ite, appearing in at least one source from the twelfth century. The Ite *O christi pietas*, on the other hand, is found

[203] The earliest ordinary, for instance, does not assign a specific melody for Christmas, indicating only that the Ite Missa Est should be sung 'festively'; F:Pm 526, fo. 17. Similarly, Ites are not named for many of the saints who were specially venerated in the monastery, as we will see further on.

[204] It is listed more often in F:Pan, L 863, No. 10 than in the 13th-c. MSS.

[205] Witness its addition to F:Pn, n.a.l. 1420 (Table 3.11).

[206] This shift in liturgical assignments in the 14th c. is another example of the gradual loss of proper items from the ritual of the abbey in the 14th c.

[207] Eifrig first pointed out the popularity of these melodies in his paper, 'Ite'.

more often in thirteenth- and fourteenth-century manuscripts.[208] Because the number of concordances for the remaining chants in F:Pn, lat. 1107 is much smaller, the ubiquity of *O christi pietas* and *Joseph* is even clearer. The Ite *Preciosus* appears in the *cantatorium* and lectionary from Saint-Denis of Reims F:RSc 265.[209] *Angelorum* and *Omni prosequenda* are found in the gradual from Saint-Corneille F:Pn, lat. 17329, which likewise drew many Benedicamus and much of the rest of its rite from Saint-Denis.[210] The simple tones without rubrics also appear in other sources.

The ceremonial placement of the Ite *O christi pietas* is clear from the ordinaries (Table 3.11). Like the Kyrie *O christi pietas* (Tables 3.7 and 3.8), this Ite was chanted most often on duplex feasts, and it also served as *Requiescant in pace* for the Mass of the Commemoration of the Dead. Other houses likewise employ *O christi pietas* in duplex ceremonies[211] and later on feasts of the Virgin,[212] while the Sarum tradition assigns the chant to festivals of only three lessons, which can encompass the Saturday Mass for Mary.[213] The feast of Saint Nicholas (6 December) at Saint-Denis clearly demonstrates the uses of *O christi pietas*. In the fourteenth-century liturgy, the melody was heard no fewer than four times on this day: at the beginning and end of Mass as the Kyrie and Ite, before the Magnificat at Second Vespers in the Ant. *O christi pietas*, and finally—as if to conclude the festival with the melody that had served as the 'musical theme' for the day—as the Benedicamus Domino at Second Vespers. The practice of singing the Kyrie and the Ite on the same tune was common in the Sarum tradition,[214] and the fourfold appearance of *O Christi pietas* on Nicholas's feast is perhaps analogous to the use of a cycling theme as the tenor voice in polyphonic settings of the ordinary of the Mass in the Renaissance. In this connection it is noteworthy that the monks of Saint-Denis actually increased the

[208] Eifrig has also noted the greater antiquity of *Joseph*, which he found in the 11th-c. troper F:Pn, lat. 887. His concordances for *O christi pietas* include only MSS of the 13th c. and later; ibid.

[209] Separated from 7 other Ites which are notated at the top of the fo., the chant is situated instead in the midst of 7 melodies for the Benedicamus Domino (see Robertson, '*Benedicamus*', 41, 43).

[210] See idem, 'Transmission'.

[211] See Table 3.12: F:Pa 595; GB:Cjc, D.27; F:Pn, lat. 1108; F:Pn, lat. 829; F:Pa 201, fo. 8ᵛ; F:RSc 233.

[212] F:Pa 201, fo. 9ᵛ.

[213] Oxford, Corpus Christi College, MS 394; Oxford, Pembroke College, MS 1; Sandon, *Salisbury*, 82.

[214] Many MSS of the Sarum rite witness this usage: 'When Mass includes one of *Kyries* I–IX, Ite missa est is sung to the melody of the first "Christe" of the same chant' (ibid. 81); and 'let it be known that whichever of these following chants is sung at Mass for the Kyrie, the same follows for the Ite missa est' ('Et notandum est quod quiscumque cantus istorum subsequencium dicitur ad missam supra Kyrie, idem etiam sequitur supra Ite Missa est'); Oxford, Corpus Christi College, MS 394, fo. 110).

TABLE 3.12. *Short List of Concordances for the Ite Missa Est at Saint-Denis*

Ite melody[a]	MS	Date	Provenance
1.	F:RSc 265, fo. 49^v, No. 5	12th	Saint-Denis, Reims
	F:Pn, lat. 1112, fo. 308^v, No. 7	*c*.1225	Notre-Dame, Paris
	F:AM 184,[b] fo. 66	1291	Amiens, France
2.	F:Pn, lat. 1112, fo. 308^v, No. 6	*c*.1225	Notre-Dame, Paris
	F:Pn, lat. 15615, fo. 353^v; 354^v, No. 1	13th	Sorbonne, Paris
3.			
4. *Quorum vallatus*			
5. *O christi pietas*	F:AM 184,[c] fo. 270	1291	Amiens, France
	F:Pn, lat. 17329, fo. 249, No. 1	13th	Saint-Corneille, Compiègne, France
	Oxford, Jesus College, MS 10, fo. 190, No. 5, Ites added in 14th c.	14th	Saint-Peter, Gloucester, England
	GB:Cjc, D.27, fo. 13^v, No. 3	14th	Saint-Mary, York, England
	F:Pn, lat. 842, fo. 126^v, No. 1	14th	Châlons-sur-Marne, France
	F:Pn, lat. 1108, fo. 49, No. 1	14th	Saint-Denis-de-Carcere, Paris
	F:Pn, lat. 829, fo. 123, No. 1	14th	Capua, Italy
	F:Pa 110, fo. 271, No. 1	14th	Notre-Dame, Paris
	Oxford, Corpus Christi College, MS 394, fo. 110, No. 3	1398	Sarum
	F:Pa 595, fo. 246, No. 5	13–14	Saint-Étienne, Châlons-sur-Marne, France
	Oxford, Pembroke College, MS 1, fo. 127, No. 3	15th	Sarum
	F:Pa 201, fos. 8^v, 9^v	15th	Roman
	F:Pn, Rés. 1750, p. 13, No. 1	15th	Franciscan, Paris
	F:RSc 233, fo. 351^v, No. 1	15th	Paris
	Sandon, *Salisbury*, p. 82, No. XII	14th–16th	Sarum

6. *Joseph*	F:RSc 265, fo. 49^{v}, No. 2	12th	Saint-Denis, Reims
	F:AM 184,[d] fo. 53^{v}	1291	Amiens, France
	F:Pn, lat. 17329, fo. 249, No. 25[c]	13th	Saint-Corneille, Compiègne, France
	F:Pa 595, fo. 246, No. 3	13th–14th	Saint-Étienne, Châlons-sur-Marne, France
	Oxford, Jesus College, MS 10, fo. 190, No. 7, Ites added in 14th c.	14th	Saint-Peter, Gloucester, England
	GB:Cjc, D.27, fo. 13^{v}, No. 2	14th	Saint-Mary, York, England
	F:Pa 110, fo. 271, No. 4	14th	Paris
	F:Pn, lat. 1108, fos. 49^{r-v}, No. 2	14th	Saint-Denis-de-Carcere, Paris
	F:Pn, lat. 829, fo. 126, No. 1	14th	Capua, Italy
	Oxford, Corpus Christi College, MS 394, fo. 110, No. 4	14th	Sarum
	F:Pa 201, fo. 9, No. 2	15th	Roman
	Oxford, Pembroke College, MS 1, fo. 127, No. 4	15th	Sarum
	F:RSc 233, fo. 351^{v}, No. 2	15th	Paris
	Sandon, *Salisbury*, p. 82, No. XIII	14th–16th	Sarum
7. *Omni prosequenda*	F:Pn, lat. 17329, fo. 249	13th	Saint-Corneille, Compiègne, France
8. *Vernabantur*			
9. *Ecce jam coram te*			
10. *Surrexit dominus*			
11. *Posuisti*			
12. *Angelorum*	F:Pn, lat. 17329, fo. 249	13th	Saint-Corneille, Compiègne, France
13. *Preciosus*	F:RSc 265, fo. 49^{v}, Ite No. 8	12th	Saint-Denis, Reims
14. *Clementiam*			
15. *Commenda*			
16. *Quid te*			

[a] Numbering of melodies follows the order found in F:Pn, lat. 1107 (Ex. 3.16).
[b] Edited in Durand, *Ordinaire* (see pl. 11).
[c] See n. *b* above.
[d] See n. *b* above.
[e] In this MS, the Ite *Joseph* is rubricated as *Missus*, recalling the 1st word of the parent source, the Alle. *Missus est angelus gabriel*.

number of times they sang *O christi pietas* from three to four after the thirteenth-century ordinaries were written, for these earlier books call for the performance of the Ite *Clementiam*, and not *O christi pietas*, at the end of Mass. When the community replaced *Clementiam* with *O christi pietas*, they unified the Mass and feast for Nicholas to a greater degree.

In other instances, too, a single melody was used both for the Benedicamus at First Vespers and for the Ite at Mass: the melisma *Posuisti* on the feasts of Eugene (15 November) and Clement (23 November),[215] *Angelorum* on the feast of Michael (29 September), *Preciosus* on the Detection of Saint Denis (9 June), *Commenda* on the feast of Mary Magdalene (22 July), and *Quid te* for Peter and Paul (29 June). As in Nicholas's feast, these melismas were sometimes heard yet a third time as part of the responsories or alleluias from which they were derived.

Given the widespread use of *O christi pietas* and *Joseph*, it is curious that the ordinaries of Saint-Denis contain no liturgical assignation for *Joseph*. Fortunately the source of the melody, until now unrecognized, explains both how the chant was used and why it was so popular. The melisma comes from the music for the word *Joseph* in the Alle. for Annunciation *Missus est angelus Gabriel*.[216] This Marian connection no doubt made the Ite *Joseph* appropriate for feasts of the Virgin in the numerous houses that sang the chant, and it probably served on Annunciation and on other festivals of Mary as well at Saint-Denis. A number of manuscripts in Table 3.12 give other uses for *Joseph*, providing such rubrics as *in omnibus festis duplicibus* (GB:Cjc, D.27), *in festis annualibus* (F:Pn, lat. 1108), *in festis novem lectionum* (F:RSc 233), *in terciis dupplicibus* (F:Pa 595), and *in semiduplicibus* (F:Pn, lat. 829),[217] which imply that the melody was sung on festivals of anywhere from semiduplex to *annuale* level. Churches following Sarum use prescribe the Ite *Joseph* only for three-lesson celebrations, but the rubrics for other melodies of the ordinary of the Mass at this level include the Saturday commemorations for Mary. *Joseph* even appears in extant polyphonic settings of the Ite and Deo Gratias, including the Marian motet *Ave regina/Mater innocencie/(tenor)* by Marchettus of Padua and the Ite motet which ends the Mass of

215 Compare Table 3.11 with Robertson, '*Benedicamus*', table 2.

216 The identification of *Joseph* in F:Pn, lat. 1107 with the melisma from *Missus est Gabriel* is also established from the appearance of *Joseph* in the gradual from Saint-Corneille F:Pn, lat. 17329 (fo. 249; see Table 3.12), where it is rubricated as *Missus*; see Robertson, 'Transmission' 508, 512, 514.

217 F:Pa 201 writes *in majoribus semiduplicibus*.

218 Eifrig discovered *Joseph* in these 2 motets; Eifrig, 'Ite'. Two English polyphonic settings of Deo Gratias from the 14th c. likewise use *Joseph* as tenor: 1) GB:Cu, Kk.i.6, fo. 246 (edited in

Tournai.[218] In these two pieces at least it is clear that *Joseph* was used as the tenor voice because the compositions were intended for the Virgin.

The remaining liturgical assignments for the Ite at Saint-Denis are usually determined by the appropriateness of a melody for a particular feast. The Ite *Posuisti*, taken from an alleluia for the common of one martyr, served the Masses for two martys, Eugene (15 November) and Clement (23 November).[219] Similarly, *Judicabunt sancti* from the common of many martyrs was sung for the feast of Eustace and his companions (2 November).[220] *Commenda* and *Quid te* are assigned to the feasts of Mary Magdalene (22 July) and Peter and Paul (29 June), respectively, from which their sources come.[221] Likewise, the melodies *Angelorum* and *Preciosus* enhanced two festivals for Saint Denis, and *Angelorum* does double service for the Archangel Michael. *Clementiam* was used not only for Saint Nicholas (6 December), but also for the *Requiescant in pace* at the Requiem Mass and at First Vespers on the anniversary of King Philip Augustus (d. 1223).

Apart from *Joseph*, most of the other Ites without liturgical assignments were probably heard on the feasts from which their melodies were borrowed. *Ecce jam coram te* might have concluded Mass either for the feast of Saint Stephen (26 December) or for his Invention (3 August), and *Vernabantur* was likely used for Saint Vincent (22 January). Since *Quorum vallatus* also comes from a responsory for Saint Vincent, it would seem that one of the two Ites is superfluous. The liturgical assignment of *Quorum vallatus* as a Benedicamus Domino, however, suggests a possible use for this tune as an Ite. The Benedicamus *Quorum vallatus* was chanted not only at the end of Lauds for Vincent, but also as the *Requiescant in pace* for Matins and Lauds on the anniversaries of Philip Augustus (14 July), Robert II (20 July), Charles the Bald (6 October), and Abbot Suger (14 January). Only two of these anniversaries are assigned specific Ites in the ordinaries: Philip Augustus (*Clementiam*) and Suger (*O christe precamur*). Perhaps one or both of the other services for Robert or Charles

Harrison *et al.*, PMFC, xvi. 68; facsimile in Summers, *Polyphony*, pl. 28, No. 2); and 2) London, Lincoln's Inn, MS Hale 146 (Misc. 26), fo. A^{r}, second item (facsimile in Lefferts and Bent, 'Sources', 331). I am grateful to Peter Lefferts for bringing these pieces to my attention. The Ite Missa Est on *O christi pietas* was also composed in polyphony, and Elizabeth Keitel identified the tenor of the Ite in the Mass of Guillaume de Machaut with *O christi pietas*; 'Mass', 314, n. 26.

[219] By the 14th c., century, the Ite for Clement was *O christi pietas*, probably because the ordinary F:Pan, L 863, No. 10 reduces the specificity of services and tends to assign this Ite to a greater number of duplex ceremonies.

[220] Whereas this Ite is not notated in F:Pn, lat. 1107, the melody is preserved in F:Pn, lat. 17329 from Saint-Corneille; see Robertson, 'Transmission'.

[221] The 13th-c. ordinaries likewise offer *Surrexit dominus (et occurrens mulieribus)* as an alternative Ite for Mary Magdalene, no doubt because of her presence at the tomb and encounter with Jesus on Easter morning.

employed *Quorum vallatus* as the *Requiescant in pace*. F:Pn, n.a.l. 1420 reserves the Ite *Alma*, sung at Saint-Denis in the eighteenth century, for Marian feasts.

A notable omission from the ordinaries is information on the Ite Missa Est for many of the feasts of saints whose relics were kept in the church. Only Eustace, Clement, Romanus of Blaye, and Eugene are named in Table 3.11, and no Ites are prescribed for a number of important duplex feasts for other saints, including Firminus, Osmanna, Maurice, Peregrinus, Cucuphas, and Hilary of Mende, to name only those to whom chapels in the chevet were dedicated (Pl. 3). Possibly the common Ites *Posuisti* or *Judicabunt* were intended for those who were martyrs, or the Benedicamus specified at First Vespers was meant to be repeated as the Ite Missa Est at Mass. But there may also be another solution. For most of these saints, one Kyrie, *Cunctipotens genitor*, was heard at Mass. If the Sarum ordinance cited above was also in use at Saint-Denis, then the melody for this Kyrie would have been chanted as Ite Missa Est. Similarly, the tunes *Pater creator*, *Rex genitor*, and *Orbis factor*, sung both as Kyrie and as Ite in the Sarum rite,[222] might have served the same two chants in the ritual of Saint-Denis. This theory then accounts for the Ites of the remaining feasts, and it provides other examples of the unification of the Mass ordinary by means of a recurring tune.

The actual performance of the Ite Missa Est is discussed only once in the ordinaries. In the description of the second Mass for Christmas Day, F:Pm 526 states that a deacon chanted it,[223] and the choir would then have responded with the Deo Gratias on the same melody. How the deacon or choir would have adapted the text Ite Missa Est or Deo Gratias to the parent melismas no doubt mirrors the process that was used in the creation of the Benedicamus. The musical and textual incipit preceding each Ite reminded the soloist or chorus how the melody should begin. The singer(s) then composed the versicle orally, using assonance and phrasing as primary guides for setting words to melody. When one or more of the vowels of the Ite text corresponded to those of the original source, then assonance largely determined how the Ite should go. In *Joseph* (Ex. 3.16, No. 6), the syllable *-te* of Ite rhymes with *-cen-* and *-tes* of *dicentes*. Similarly, the vocalist matched the *-e* of *I-te* with like sounds in *Omni prose-quen-da* (No. 7), *Ec-ce jam coram te* (No. 9), *Sur-rex-it dominus* (No. 10), *Cle-men-tiam* (No. 14), and *Quid te* (No. 16). Although the longest part of the melisma usually occurs on *-te* of Ite, the *-i* of 'missa' has a short melisma that mirrors the one on *-i* of *pi-etas* in *O christi pietas* (No. 5).

222 See e.g. Sandon, *Salisbury*, 81; Oxford, Corpus Christi College, MS 394, fos. 110^{r-v}.
223 Fo. 16.

In many instances, the phrasing of the melisma also provided the performer with landmarks. *O christi pietas*, *Omni prosequenda*, and *Clementiam* have medial cadences on *c*, and it is here that the word 'missa' of Ite Missa Est begins. The same text placement occurs in *Surrexit* and in *Quid te*, where 'missa' starts after the internal cadences on *d*. Where little or no similarity of vowel-sounds exists, the points of articulation in the melisma are all the more important in the underlay of the Ite text. In *Vernabantur* (No. 8), the 38-note melisma on *-te* of Ite corresponds to the one on *-ba* of *Vernabantur*, and the change to 'missa' comes when the melody plunges a sixth from *a* down to *c*. The movement from the word 'Ite' to 'missa' in the Ite *Posuisti* (No. 11) happens when the melody shifts register from the lower half of the first mode, which circles around *d*, to the upper half on *f*.

Like the Benedicamus, some of the melismas for Ites are found in other repertories with prosula texts (Table 3.13). The use of these melismas both as prosulas and as melodies for the Benedicamus Domino and Ite Missa Est attests not only to the renown of these tunes, but also to their capacity to move from one type of chant to another. As Benedicamus and Ite, moreover, the melismas achieve a new stature, for they stand entirely separate from their parent sources as independent chants. The manuscripts from Saint-Denis which preserve these repertories are thus singularly important in providing detailed information about the musical and ceremonial aspects of this important tradition. How these melismas may have accommodated the philosophical and political designs of the monks as well is treated in the next chapter.

Table 3.13. *Correspondences between Melismas for Ite Missa Est and Responsory Prosulas*

Ite melisma from Saint-Denis (Ex. 3.16)	Responsory prosula (from Hofmann-Brandt catalogue)	Sources for prosulas (from Hofmann-Brandt)	Parent responsory
8. *Vernabantur*	115. *Christo regi nostro laus*	F:AUT, S. 178, fos. 128^{r-v}	*Christi miles*
	712. *Vernabant nunc supernorum*	F:TO 149, fos. 466^{v}–467	
	713. *Vernabas roseo Vincenti*	F:B 66, fos. 344^{r-v}	
		CH:Fcu, L. 61, fo. 227^{v}	
		CH:Fcu, L. 322, fo. 255	
9. *Ecce jam coram te*	157. *Digne caritatis*	F:Pa 153, fos. 41^{v}–42	*Ecce jam coram te*
		F:Pn, lat. 1266, fos. 72^{r-v}	
		F:Pn, lat. 12035, fos. 28^{r-v}	
	172. *Ecce quem manus*	Barcelona, Bibl. Central, M 662	
		Barcelona, Bibl. Central, M 706	
		Montblanch, Archivo de la Iglesia de Santa Maria (no number—15th-c. antiphoner), fos. 149^{v}–150	
14. *Clementiam*	123. *Clementem te praebe rex*	Barcelona, Bibl. Central, M 662	*Qui cum audissent*
		E:Gm 19	

		Montblanch, Archivo de la Iglesia de Santa Maria (no number—13th–14t-c. antiphoner)	
		Montblanch, Archivo de la Iglesia de Santa Maria (no number—15th-c. antiphoner), fos. 149^{v}–150	
		F:Pn, n.a.l. 1535, fos. 5^{r-v}	
	592. *Sancte Nicolae reatus*	A:KN 1010, fo. 1	
		D:Mbs, Clm 12201c, fos. 68^{v}–69	
	593. *Sancte Nicolae tu nos*	I:CFm XLVII, fos. 147^{v}–148, 151^{v}	
	594. *Sancte Nicolae tu vota*	D:W 522, fo. 130	
15. *Commenda*	469. *O rerum summo mulier*	F:AN 112 (104),m fos. 72^{v}–73	*O felix felicis*
		F:Pa 279, fos. 426^{v}–427	
		F:R(m) 245, fos. 252^{r-v}	
		F:R(m) 251, fo. 136^{v}	
		Vendôme, Bibl. mun., 17E, 431^{v}–432	
16. *Quid te*	204. *Facere quo duce*	F:Pn, lat. 12044, fos. 60^{r-v}, 61	*Cornelius centurio*
	216. *Factus sospes*	F:Pm 386, fos. 96–7	
		F:TO 158, fos. 180^{v}–181^{v}	
	549. *Quid te maerore affligis aegre*	Montblanch, Archivo de la Iglesia de Santa Maria (no number—13th–14th-c. antiphoner)	

4

Interaction of Ritual and Music with Art, Architecture, and Politics

The Divine Ritual at Saint-Denis was performed in a church that had enviably close ties with the Crown, a sumptuously decorated building which was reconstructed no fewer than three times. This unique setting cannot be overlooked in the study of the liturgy of Saint-Denis, for it deeply affected the ceremony of the monastery. Even before the first extant liturgical books from Saint-Denis were copied, Merovingian documents attest to the recognition the abbey was beginning to win from French monarchs. As time passed, the burials of kings in the church gradually established the notion that Saint-Denis should be the royal necropolis, and the patronage bestowed on the abbey by living monarchs only enhanced its position. The strength of this association grew immensely in the ninth century, when Abbot Hilduin of Saint-Denis consciously furthered the fusion of the identity of the patron of the church, Saint Denis, with those of the more famous Dionysius the Areopagite and Pseudo-Dionysius, the neo-Platonic philosopher. From this time onwards, aspects of the ritual were interlaced with traces of the tripartite Saint Denis, and these politico-liturgical 'slogans' helped further the monks' belief.

Like the political history of Saint-Denis, the changes in the architecture of the church inspired ceremonial and musical modifications as well.[1] The earliest church was a basilica, built over the relics of Saint Denis by Saint Geneviève around 475. King Dagobert had this edifice enlarged and refurbished between 629 and about 639, but not until the abbacy of Fulrad (750–84) was a new Carolingian church actually erected around the old basilica at Saint-Denis between 755 and 775.[2] Under Abbot Hilduin (814–41) a chapel was built at the eastern end of Fulrad's church around 832, and this enlarged Carolingian structure remained in use for some 300 years. In the mean time, a poorly fashioned tower was placed adjacent to the church with the help of funds from William the Conqueror at the end of the eleventh century, but it fell shortly after it was finished. Between *c.*1135 and 1144, Abbot Suger (1122–51) began the second reconstruction of Saint-Denis.

[1] Details on the structures mentioned in this paragraph are taken from Crosby, *Abbey*, and Bruzelius, *St-Denis*.

[2] Dates according to Crosby, *Abbey*, 56.

Many of the remarkable features he used in the eastern and western extremities of the church inaugurated a new period in the history of architecture, now termed the Gothic. Suger died before the other parts of the church were finished, leaving the completion of his work to four abbots who presided over the campaigns which took place between 1231 and 1281. This Saint-Denis of the thirteenth century is essentially the church that now stands on the northern outskirts of Paris. Later changes included several minor alterations in the fourteenth and sixteenth centuries and one final restoration in the nineteenth century.

In many ways, of course, the development of the Sandionysian ritual during these reconstructions mirrored that of other churches in the West, as described in Chapter 2: it followed current local trends, and it yielded to the dictates of higher authorities. But at the same time this liturgy contained liturgical and musical items that had special significance in the abbey, ones that inspired or were inspired by the different buildings in which the Divine Office was performed. The sources allow glimpses of these features, and a discussion of the ritual of the abbey from the vantage-point of the art, architecture, and politics will bring them to light.

THE MEROVINGIAN PERIOD

There is little specific information on the performance of the Divine Office at Saint-Denis in the Merovingian era. What can be inferred is that the community that grew up around the basilica constructed by Saint Geneviève held services there at least by the last quarter of the fifth century. The Mass and Hours followed some brand of the old Gallican ritual, and around 567 the church of Paris probably imposed the liturgical dictates of the Council of Tours on Saint-Denis, as outlined in Chapter 1. The Merovingian building could certainly have accommodated these practices. Although simple and rectangular in shape, the size of Geneviève's chapel was sufficiently large to distinguish it from other Merovingian churches in Gaul.[3] The presence of an altar, which stood at the eastern end of the church,[4] likewise suggests that a ritual was regularly celebrated there.

[3] Crosby believes that this chapel measured about 20.6 m. (= *c*.67½ ft.) long by 9.5 m. (= *c*.31 ft.) wide within the church walls; ibid. 22.

[4] Crosby demonstrates that the altar was probably situated directly above the actual tomb of Saint Denis; ibid. 26.

Perpetual Psalmody

In the seventh century, the monks were twice required to adopt the practice of perpetual psalmody, first under Dagobert and then under his son Clovis II. The church in which they carried out this onerous practice differed significantly from the original basilica. Crosby has shown that between 629 and *c.*639 Dagobert added a semicircular apse to the east of the rectangular shrine, moved the main altar into this new part of the church, lengthened the nave westward, and provided it with side aisles.[5] Such was his devotion to Saint Denis that he also sent Eligius (later Saint Eligius) to redecorate the church. Although the descriptions of this splendid refurbishment post-date Dagobert, enough evidence survives to show that no expense was spared.

In the light of his attachment to Saint-Denis, the importance of Dagobert's establishment of *laus perennis* must not be underestimated. In calling for perpetual psalmody, Dagobert accomplished several things. First, he paved the way for his son Clovis to institute the monastic order that would be necessary to perform the endless chanting, as noted in Chapter 1. Second, both Dagobert and Clovis no doubt had a personal reason for promoting the establishment of a rule at Saint-Denis. Since the late sixth century, the basilica had been the site of burials of members of the royal house. In such a place Dagobert and Clovis would naturally want the practice of *laus perennis* to continue in perpetuity. Not only was this usage a fitting ritual for a place as lofty as Saint-Denis, but in executing it, the monks were making constant atonement for the souls of the members of the royal line who were interred there.[6]

THE EIGHTH CENTURY

More than a century after Dagobert, Abbot Fulrad of Saint-Denis built a new church. While no documents relative to the edifice have survived, the physical remnants of parts of the structure, excavated by Crosby, permit a reconstruction of the entire plan.[7] Crosby shows that the

[5] On Dagobert's church, see ibid. 29–50.

[6] The medieval penitential system was responsible in part for the important relationship that existed between royalty and its favoured monasteries during the Middle Ages. A king founded or lavished gifts upon an institution, and in return the inhabitants of that house prayed continually for his soul (see Lawrence, *Monasticism*, 61–3; and on the penitential process in general, see Vogel, *Liturgy*, 188–90, esp. n. 207).

[7] Crosby, *Abbey*, 51–83. Since Crosby's work was completed, a text from *c.*799 describing the Carolingian church in some detail, the *Descriptio Basilicae Sancti Dyonisii*, has been published in Stoclet, '*Descriptio*'; and in Bischoff, 'Beschreibung'. In her editorial comments to Crosby's book, P. Blum says that 'further study is needed to analyse and evaluate the information provided by the

church, erected between 755 and 775, was built 'in the Roman fashion' (*Romano more*) like the Roman basilica-type churches. The plan probably included a rectangular enclosure at the eastern end of the nave, a *solea-schola*, through which liturgical processions made their way to the easternmost part of the church. In Roman churches, boys and monks stood here in double lines to form the processional route for the celebrant. At Saint-Denis, this space would have been the forerunner of the liturgical choir of the ninth- and twelfth-century buildings.[8]

Ordo Romanus XLI

Crosby suggests that the lengthy stay of Pope Stephen II at Saint-Denis in 753/4 may have provided a reason for the reconstruction.[9] The pope's visit placed Saint-Denis at the centre of things in terms of the emerging Carolingian dynasty, and it also made the abbey a natural place—at least in the area of Paris—for the diffusion of the new liturgy from Rome. Of the many services that were celebrated during the pontiff's sojourn, some would doubtless have involved expositions of the Roman papal and suburban rituals. For such sumptuous and unfamiliar Roman rites, the monks of Saint-Denis probably viewed their old Merovingian basilica as an inadequate show-case and undertook a reconstruction.

One of these Roman practices was probably related to an *ordo* which Charlemagne witnessed at Saint-Denis on 24 February 775. Honouring the basilica with his presence at the dedication of the reconstructed church on this day, Charlemagne later described the event with these words: 'For the salvation of our soul, we endow the church of Saint-Denis, where the relics of the precious Saint and his companions rest, where the venerable Abbot Fulrad presides, and where we with Christ's favour have built a new church and ordered that it be dedicated *in a manner of great distinction*.'[10] Unfortunately, Charlemagne leaves all too few details about the actual dedication ceremony. But it is perhaps

Descriptio in terms of the archaeological information presented in this [Crosby's] chapter and of the author's [Crosby's] reconstruction of the Carolingian basilica'; Crosby, *Abbey*, 471, n. 52. The *Descriptio*, while rich in architectural details, sheds little direct light on the performance of the Divine Office, stating only that the 1,250 lamps in the church were filled 3 times on each feast-day ('Habet ipsa ecclesia luminaria mille CCL et mittunt in illa luminaria de oleo modios VIII et ad unamquemque festam in anno semper per tres vices'); Stoclet, '*Descriptio*', 104.

[8] Crosby, *Abbey*, 79–80.

[9] Ibid. 54, 56.

[10] All spellings *sic*: 'donamus pro anime nostrae remedio ad ecclesiam sancti Diunisii ubi ipse praeciosus domnus cum sociis suis corpore quiescunt et venerabilis vir Fulradus, abba, praeesse videtur, et nos, Christo propitio, a novo aedificavimus opere et modo cum magno honore jussimus dedicare'; Tardif, *Monuments*, 58–9, No. 72 (original = F:Pan, K 6, No. 4; facsimile in Bruckner and Marichal, *ChLA*, xv. 90–3 [No. 615]).

no accident that *Ordo XLI* of the *Ordines romani*, a document which deals with the placement of relics in a church, began to circulate in France at exactly this time.[11] This ritual involves a processional entry into the new church, including three knocks at the door by the presiding pontiff. The Ant. *Tollite portas* was sung, and a great litany, a prostration, and the Agnus Dei ensued. Orations were chanted, followed by a ceremony in which the alphabet was traced on the floor. A number of other actions, chants, and prayers concluded the service.

In addition to the date of *Ordo XLI,* the ancestry of this ritual offers good reasons to connect it directly to Saint-Denis. First, *Ordo XLI* was a direct outgrowth of the liturgical reform undertaken by Pepin and Charlemagne, coming from a 'Gallicanized' collection of Roman *ordines*.[12] It drew heavily on the old Gelasian sacramentary from Rome—the best representative of which was written in close proximity to Saint-Denis (I:Rvat, Reg. lat. 316)—and to a small extent on the eighth-century Gelasian sacramentary. The author evidently compiled this *ordo* around 775.[13] Second, it is unlikely that a formula for the dedication of a church would have been composed without reference to a specific event. We may therefore suggest that *Ordo XLI* was compiled for the dedication of Saint-Denis. The need for such a service at the abbey in precisely this year, along with the fact that Charlemagne himself ordered that an elaborate ceremony take place, are wholly compatible with the date, provenance, and author of the *ordo*. Charlemagne, in stipulating that the church be consecrated 'in a manner of great distinction', would have meant precisely the ritual of *Ordo XLI*, which he himself had called into being.

THE NINTH CENTURY

Hilduin's Chapel

Hilduin, the next great abbot of Saint-Denis, constructed a building on the east end of the crypt of Fulrad's church around 832. Crosby shows that this structure completely enveloped Fulrad's apse, and that it contained three parallel chapels, after the manner of the Byzantine *ecclesia triplex*.[14] Hilduin dedicated the chapel to Mary and to all the saints, and he placed many relics in the new edifice.[15] Two of the

[11] *Denuntiatio cum reliquiae sanctorum martyrum ponendae sunt. Ordo quomodo ecclesia debeat dedicari*; see Andrieu, *Ordines*, iv. 336, 339–47; Vogel, *Liturgy*, 180.

[12] Andrieu, *Ordines*, iv. 336.

[13] Vogel, *Liturgy*, 180.

[14] Crosby, *Abbey*, 87–94.

[15] 'Idcirco ego . . . criptam ante pedes sanctissimorum martyrum nostrorum ad laudem et gloriam nominis Domini, in honore sanctae et intemeratae semperque virginis genetricis Dei

remains that he doubtless brought to Saint-Denis around this time were those of Saints Hippolytus and Cucuphas, which Fulrad had deposited in churches belonging to the abbey some time earlier. Hilduin was probably also responsible for the transfers of the relics of Saints Hilary of Mende, Innocent, and Peregrinus, whose translations to Saint-Denis are recorded in the calendars of F:Pn, lat. 2290 and F:Psg 111 on 22 August.[16] Of these five saints, the liturgical manuscripts confirm that Hippolytus was commemorated at Saint-Denis with a separate Mass in his honour by the end of the ninth centuy, and that Cucuphas had a proper Office, the latter possibly composed by Hilduin himself. In addition, both F:Pn, lat. 2290 and the sacramentary portion of F:LA 118 contain a 'Mass for special saints' (*Missa specialium sanctorum*), which names saints whose relics were present in the abbey, including Dionysius, Rusticus, Eleutherius, Hippolytus, Cucuphas, Innocent, Hilary of Poitiers, and Hilary of Mende.[17] This votive Mass was celebrated weekly on Thursdays in the late ninth and tenth centuries,[18] and it was probably the forerunner of the Thursday Mass for Saint Denis which Abbot Suger established in the twelfth century. During the actual Translation, some or all of the processional antiphons *ad reliquias* [*deducendas*], listed at the end of F:Psg 111, were probably sung.[19] This collective Mass seems little more than an afterthought. And yet, taken in conjunction with the historical texts and with the evidence of a structural addition to the abbey in the early ninth century, they demonstrate that the monks venerated a group of particularly chosen saints along with Denis, Rusticus, and Eleutherius at Saint-Denis in the ninth century. By the eleventh century, and probably earlier, observances for these saints were incorporated into the *sanctorale* of the gradual and antiphoner of the abbey, with the proper

Mariae omniumque sanctorum aedificavi, in qua multa pretiosissima sanctorum pignora auxiliente Domino collocavi'; Félibien, *Histoire*, *PJ*, pt. i, p. lvi, No. lxxv.

[16] 'Et translatio corpora [*sic*] sanctorum in cenobio sancti Dionisii, id est Hilarii, episcopi et confessoris, et sancti Innocentii martyris, atque sancti Peregrini, episcopi et martyris' (also published in Delisle, *Sacramentaires*, 320).

[17] F:Pn, lat. 2290, fo. 129v; F:LA 118, fo. 35 (the latter MS omits Hilary of Mende). See the discussions of these sources in Ch. 6; also Leroquais, *Sacramentaires*, i. 20, 67.

[18] Ibid. On the category of *missa votiva per hebdomadem* into which this Mass falls, see 'Votive Mass'.

[19] See Hesbert, *AMS*, No. 212a. (I have supplied the word *deducendas*, which completes the rubric for these antiphons, by comparison with the rubrics of the antiphoners from Compiègne [F:Pn, lat. 17436] and Corbie [F:Pn, lat. 12050]; Hesbert, *AMS*, No. 219). Given the fact that the placement of relics in Frankish churches was not widespread before the 9th c., it is possible that some of these processional antiphons are not much older than the late 9th-c. MSS, such as F:Psg 111, which transmit them. Their absence from late 8th-c. sources corroborates this view (see Hesbert, *AMS*, p. cxxi). Perhaps the old-Roman melodies for the antiphons *Ecce populus*, *Cum jucunditate*, and *Ambulate* were used at Saint-Denis as a result of the papal presence there in the mid-8th c. On the history of the old-Roman melodies for these antiphons, see Huglo, 'Antiennes', 136–9.

Offices for Hippolytus, Cucuphas, and Hilary of Mende that are described in Chapter 2. And by the thirteenth century their relics had been moved to separate chapels within Abbot Suger's church.

Hilduin's new chapel was dedicated, appropriately enough, on the feast of All Saints (1 November), at which time the abbot called for the performance of services in the *oratorium*:

> And by common assent, we have established that eight monks of this holy community, following one another by turns, should execute all the time in this [chapel] the day and night Office in the Roman manner, and that they [. . . *lacuna* . . .] should celebrate together the established Offices and antiphons . . . with daily diligence.[20]

Because of the lacuna in this passage, it is not clear which ceremony 'for Mary and all the saints' Hilduin established. The use of the words 'day and night Office' seems to imply a full *cursus* of Hours and probably Mass as well. If the precise nature of the service is obscure, the manner of its execution is clearer. The assignment of shifts of eight monks to the small chapel was entirely feasible, since there were on average 150 monks at Saint-Denis in the ninth century. Presumably Hilduin meant that at the appropriate Hour the monks would enter the chapel, sing the Office or Mass, and then leave. Later, when it was time for the next Hour, another group of eight would perform the task.[21] Since the choral singing of the psalms was by now common, the psalmody mentioned in the passage may have been performed by eight monks divided into two groups of four to chant in *alternatim* fashion. In terms of the physical placement of Hilduin's chapel, the performance of a service in the oratory at the same time as or just following the regular Office in the choir was possible. The new chapel was situated far enough from the choir to allow the same Hour to be recited simultaneously in both places without mutual interference.

If Mass was one of the services performed in Hilduin's chapel, then the sacramentary F:R(m), A. 566 may well have served in the celebrations in this location. The ninth-century portion of this manuscript was a small book (*libellus*), just the size that would have been appropriate. The seven Masses in this part of the MS are for Mary and All Saints, just as the new oratory was likewise dedicated to these persons. It is possible that this *libellus* was written for use in Hilduin's chapel in the

[20] 'Communi etiam voto statuimus ut octo ex monachis hujus sanctae congregationis succedentes sibi per vices; omni tempore in ea tam diurnum quam nocturnum *more Romano* officium faciant et constituta officia vel antiph . . . [*lacuna*] . . . cotidiana assiduitate concelebrent'; Félibien, *Histoire*, *PJ*, pt. i, p. lvi, No. lxxv.

[21] At first glance, Hilduin's description of an *officium omni tempore* recalls the earlier practice of perpetual psalmody at Saint-Denis. However, it is clearly something quite different, since *laus perennis* involved not only the Office Hours but also all the time between them.

ninth century and later was combined with the other two parts of F:R(m), A. 566. If so, these seven masses may represent services which, like the fourteenth-century Lady Mass at Saint-Denis, were specifically intended to be performed in a chapel outside the choir.

Indeed, the Office in Hilduin's chapel is the first service known to have been celebrated outside the choir at Saint-Denis,[22] and for this reason alone Hilduin's endowment in the new oratory is significant.[23] Yet this foundation was by no means an isolated occurrence in the history of the Divine Service at Saint-Denis. Both the recitation of Offices in the various chapels of the abbey and the simultaneous performance of two services in different parts of the church figure prominently in the ceremonies of the abbey beginning in the twelfth century.

The Hymn for Saint Denis

A proper hymn for Saint Denis, *Celi cives*, probably emanated from Saint-Denis in the ninth century. Portions of the text of this piece aptly demonstrate the connection that Abbot Hilduin sought to enhance between Saint Denis, Dionysius the Areopagite, and Pseudo-Dionysius in the early ninth century.

1	
Celi cives adplaudite mundi jocundo lumine quo inlustratur celitus huius diei gratia . . .	[Rejoice heavenly citizens in the wonderful light of the world by which the beauty of this day is illustrated in the heavens . . .
3	
Areopago Athene regis sumpsit diadema celestis gemmam fulgidam Dionisium sophistam.	In Areopagus of Athens the royal diadem provided itself with the shining gem of the heaven, Dionysius the philosopher.
4	
Paulo docente speculum habet fides fidelium	The faith of the faithful has a mirror of Paul's teaching,

[22] No doubt the chapter Office (*officium capituli*) was done at Saint-Denis at this time, since it had been in existence in France since the 8th c. Foley documents its presence in the daily prayer of the abbey in the 13th c., but he mentions that the chapter room which is described by modern sources dates back only to the 12th c.; 'Ordinary', ii. 131–6, 331–4.

[23] Félibien says that the use of services such as the one established in Hilduin's chapel was common elsewhere; *Histoire*, 72. Apart from the *officium capituli*, references to Offices celebrated in different locations within a church are not readily available in texts from the 8th and 9th cs. One exception is Angilbert of Centula, who calls for daily Masses *per diversa altaria* under certain conditions; Hallinger, *Initia*, 293.

et spiculum gentilitas	and the heathen a thorn [in their side]
quem ante murum noverat.	whom they had known in front of their wall.
5	
Miro clarescens dogmate	Shining with wondrous teaching
inluminavit Greciam	he enlightened Greece,
et inclitus hinc pontifex	whence the renowned pontiff
urbem romanam adiit.	came to the city of Rome.
6	
Clemente rome presule	At the bidding of the Roman Pope Clement,
jubente venit Galliam	Dionysius came to Gaul,
cui jubar solis splendidi	which the splendour of the shining sun
inluxit signis, famine.[24]	brightens in signs and in speech.]

Not only is Saint Denis identified as the Areopagite (stanza 3), he is also placed in the first century through the references to Saint Paul and to Pope Clement (stanzas 4, 6), and stanza 5 portrays him preaching both in Greece and in Rome. The references to light throughout this text are of course central to neo-Platonic and hence to Pseudo-Dionysian philosophy. Hilduin attributed this hymn to Saint Eugene,[25] no doubt to lend it an air of authority, since the piece formed part of the newly composed Office for Saint Denis that he was commissioned to write for Emperor Louis the Pious. But it seems clear that the abbot himself, or one of his circle, penned the poem in order to assist in the conflation of the personages of Saint Denis and Dionysius the Areopagite.[26]

Another proper hymn for Saint Denis, *Fortem fidelem*, is less convincing as a propagandistic poem:

1	
Fortem fidelem militem	[The people cry out with heart and voice:
celi secutum principem	'Brave, faithful soldier,
Dionysium martyrem	follower of the prince of heaven,
plebs corde, voce personet.	the martyr Dionysius'.
2	
Clemente Roma presule	While Clement was Pope in Rome
ab urbe missus adfuit	he was sent out from the city

[24] F:Psg 1186, fos. 216r–v; GB:Ob, Can. Lit. 192, fo. 466; entire text ed. in Dreves, *Hymni*, *AH*, xix. 119. See also Chevalier, *Repertorium*, No. 3473; Mearns, *Hymnaries*, 16.

[25] 'Who can wonder why we should have the hymn about Saint Denis by Saint Eugene of Toledo?' ('Nec mirari quis poterit, cur ymnum sancti Eugenii Toletani de beato Dionysio habeamus?'); *Epistolae*, MGH, *Karolini Aevi*, iii. 331, ch. 7.

[26] See the discussion of this attribution in Dreves, *Hymni*, *AH*, xix. 120; Levillain, 'Études' (1921), 33–5; Théry, 'Aréopagitisme', 119–23; Dubois, 'Eugène', 89–90; Szövérffy, *Hymnendichtung*, 154–5; idem, *Hymnody*, 34–5; Gaiffier, 'Légende', 333–8.

verbi superni seminis	to be the fruit of the seed
ut fructus esset Gallie.[27]	of the celestial word in Gaul.]

Like *Celi cives*, the first two stanzas of *Fortem fidelem* bolster the erroneous connection of Saint Denis with the first-century Dionysius by associating him with the reign of Pope Clement (stanza 2), and several authors have ascribed the poem likewise to Hilduin.[28] Hilduin, however, claimed that the famous and ancient hymn-writer Fortunatus wrote this hymn about Saint Denis,[29] and Levillain accepts Fortunatus' authorship of *Fortem fidelem*, for while the poem does place Dionysius in the first century, it does not specifically identify him with the Pseudo-Areopagite.[30]

The Office for Saint Denis

These two hymns formed part of Hilduin's new Office for Saint Denis, which he offered to Louis the Pious around 835. The Office likewise conveyed the Areopagite theme, although not prominently. Drawn largely from the *vita* that Hilduin composed to establish the Areopagite connection (*Post beatam ac salutiferam*),[31] the Office avoids the parts of this text which overtly ascribe the Pseudo-Areopagite's teaching to Saint Denis. It does, however, place him in the first century (instead of the third) by connecting him with Pope Clement, and calls Dionysius 'teacher of the Athenians':

Matins Ant. 1. Sanctus Dionysius qui, tradente beato Clemente Petri apostoli successore, verbi divini semina gentibus parturienda susceperat. Ver. Quae Atheniensium magister Paulo docente didicerat Galliis ministravit.

[With Blessed (Pope) Clement the successor of Peter the Apostle confiding (in him), Dionysius, who had taken up the seeds of the Divine Word that had to be brought forth to the Gentiles, ministered to the Gallic (people) those things which this teacher of the Athenians had learned from Paul's teaching.][32]

[27] F:Pn, lat. 103, fo. 161; GB:Ob, Can. Lit. 192, fos. 463–6; entire text ed. in Blume, *Hymnarium*, *AH*, li. 176. On the dissemination of these 2 hymns for Saint Denis, Gastoué points out that *Celi cives* was more or less restricted to Saint-Denis, while *Fortem fidelem* circulated in many other churches at least through to the 18th c.; 'Origines' (1903/4), 15; see also the list of concordances in Dreves, *Hymni*, *AH*, xix. 119; and in Blume, *loc. cit.*

[28] See ibid.; Chevalier, *Repertorium*, No. 6468; Gaiffier, 'Légende', 334.

[29] 'Vir prudens et scolasticissimus Fortunatus qui plura et frequenter ad eundem [Dionysium] scripserat, ymnum rithmice compositionis pulcherrimum de isto gloriosissimo martyre composuerit'; *Epistolae*, MGH, *Karolini Aevi*, iii. 333.

[30] Levillain, 'Études' (1921), 12–13.

[31] The *vita* is found in *PL*, cvi. 23–50. The MSS from Saint-Denis that give the texts of the Office are: F:Pn, lat. 17296, fos. 227^{v}–32 (Hesbert, *CAO* ii. 114a, b, full texts in vols. iii and iv); F:Pm 384, fo. 190^{v}; GB:Ob, Can. Lit. 192, fos. 468–70; F:Pn, Rés. 5209 (no fo. nos.).

[32] F:Pn, lat. 17296, fos. 227^{r-v} (text ed. in Hesbert, *CAO*, iii. 462, No. 4775).

The other parts of this Office concentrate largely on the later years of Dionysius' mission to Paris, especially his imprisonment, vision of Christ, and martyrdom. It is curious that this Office is quite restrained in its expression of Hilduin's objective of promoting the Areopagite message. Perhaps the abbot feared that too much emphasis on this new-fangled theme would arouse suspicion and prompt a closer examination of such correct, historical texts on Saint Denis as the account of Gregory of Tours, mentioned in Chapter 1.[33] Whatever his reason, the Office only hints at the full story that Hilduin was eager to tell.

THE TENTH AND ELEVENTH CENTURIES

Prosulas

The use of the Areopagite theme in the liturgy certainly did not die with Hilduin. In at least two Sandionysian prosulas from the tenth or early eleventh century, the monks were careful to inject traces of this philosophy. The prosula for Saint John *Non vos quos elegi* (see Table 3.5), preserved although not notated in F:Pn, lat. 17296, is based on a verse from John 15: 16 (biblical text in italics):

Non vos quos elegi de hoc mundo me patris summi dei verbum *elegistis sed ego* iudices seculi *vos et* fratres meos amicos electos vocavi et lucernas *posui vos ut* supra iubaris radios fulgentes et splendoure virtutum nitentes in tenebris residentes scelerum orbis terre splendescatis et dignum *fructum* germinaque *feratis* gentibus atque populis *et fructus* omnibus fidelibus superne fidei jugiter *vester maneat*.[34]

[You whom I have elected from this world have not chosen me and the word of the highest God the Father, but I have called you judges of the world and my brothers, my chosen friends. I have fashioned you as lamps so that, glistening above the rays of brightness and glittering with the splendour of virtue, you might shine while yet residing in the shadows of wickedness of the earthly sphere, and bear worthy fruit and seed to the nations and peoples, and your fruit might remain continually for all the faithful of the highest faith.]

The characteristic neo-Platonic emphasis on light as the means to salvation is clearly expressed here. The juxtaposition of the opposing concepts of 'shining' and the 'shadows of wickedness' recalls Pseudo-Dionysius' use of dissimilarities in language in his interpretation of the neo-Platonic doctrine of the 'procession and return.'[35] This notion

[33] Hilduin purposely plays down Gregory's account; see *Epistolae*, MGH, *Karolini Aevi*, iii. 331, chs. 8, 12; Levillain 'Études' (1921), 35.

[34] F:Pn, lat. 17296, fos. 36v–37; ed. in Hesbert, *CAO*, iv. 369, No. 7484.

[35] See the discussion of this concept in Rorem, *Symbols*, 58–131.

presumes that the Divine first manifests himself, and then that man is uplifted to Him through the interpretation of the Scriptures and the liturgy. The former action is characterized as a procession downward, the latter as an upward return. Words with opposing meanings, such as 'shining' and 'the shadows of wickedness', are used at the very lowest point of the 'procession' to promote the 'return' movement.[36]

The text of *Non vos* is unnotated in F:Pn, lat. 17296, a fact that supports the idea that the piece was composed prior to the twelfth century, copied from an earlier source into the antiphoner, and left without music because it was no longer sung. Another factor which seems to corroborate this dating is the proximity of three other alleluia prosulas (*Judicabunt innocentes*, *Justus johannes*, *Justus virginitate*), which likewise probably come from the tenth or eleventh century, on nearby folios of F:Pn, lat. 17296. The structure of the text of *Non vos* is like that of the alleluia prosulas, especially in the use of vowel imitation. The *-o-* sounds in 'Non' and 'vos' in the original biblical text no doubt influenced the choice and placement of the words 'qu*o*s', 'h*o*c', 'mund*o*', 'me*o*s', 'amic*o*s', 'elect*o*s', and radi*o*s in the prosula, while the *-u-* in 'ut' and 'fructus' of the Biblical text is also emulated in the trope.

One of the alleluia tropes just mentioned, the prosula for Saint John *Justus virginitate* (Ex. 3.13) likewise conveys an aspect of Areopagitist thought. In this chant, the Evangelist preaches 'in all parts of the world the secrets of philosophy which the angels are scarcely able to understand', a topic treated at length in Chapter 4 of *The Celestial Hierarchy* of Pseudo-Dionysius.[37] In addition, the ninth-century translator and commentator John Scottus Eriugena uses remarkably similar language to characterize these obscure mysteries, relating them to John's visions in the Apocalypse.[38] Influenced by Saint Augustine, Eriugena saw John as a mystic who, transcending the human mind, could glimpse 'the nature of the divine plan itself.'[39] If in fact John Scottus' interpretation that is embodied in this tenth- or eleventh-century text of *Justus virginitate* alongside that of Pseudo-Dionysius, it is one of the few witnesses we have of his impact on the tenth or eleventh century, for the main revival of Eriugenian philosophy came in the twelfth century.[40] His work was certainly known prior to this time, however, and we

[36] See ibid. 84–96; Louth, *Denys*, 45–7.

[37] See Luibheid and Rorem, *Pseudo-Dionysius*, 156–9. A letter to John, supposedly from Pseudo-Dionysius, is included in the works of Pseudo-Dionysius, but its authenticity has been questioned; ibid. 288–9.

[38] Barbet, *Johannis*, p. 74, esp. ll. 372–5. For information on the MSS of Eriugena's translations of Pseudo-Dionysius that were housed in the library of Saint-Denis, see Nebbiai-Dalla Guarda, *Bibliothèque*, 245–6.

[39] Moran, *Philosophy*, 79. Moran is commenting here on Eriugena's *Homily on the Prologue to St. John's Gospel*, found in O'Meara, *Eriugena*, 158–76.

[40] On John Scottus' influence up to the 12th c., see ibid. 269–73.

would expect that the composer of *Justus virginitate*, presumably a monk of Saint-Denis, would have been versed in the writings of this famous translator of Pseudo-Dionysius.

The Rhymed Office for Saint Denis

Whereas Hilduin's ninth-century Office for Saint Denis, described above, was somewhat tentative in its assertion of the Areopagite theme, a rhymed Office for Saint Denis from the mid-eleventh century makes a bolder statement. This Office appears in one manuscript only, the early eleventh-century gradual F:Pm 384, in a section added near the end (fos. 160–161^{v}; see Pl. 9). It is written in a different and probably slightly later hand from the main part of the book. The Office is incomplete: it includes only the responsory for First Vespers and the Invitatory and eleven responsories for Matins, with no trace of antiphons for Vespers, Matins, and Lauds.[41] The notation, discussed in Chapter 6, is neumatic and contains a few significative letters denoting aspects of pitch or rhythm.

ELEVENTH-CENTURY RHYMED OFFICE FOR SAINT DENIS IN F:PM 384

Vespers Resp. [*fo. 160; leftmost column indicates numbers of syllables*]

5	Cum sol nocturnas	[When the bright sun
9	preclarus ab orbe tenebras	drives out of the world the shadows of night,
7	excuteret patriae	from our noble fatherland
8	fulsit lux altera nostrae	another light lightened
10	nobilis heliacas superas	the sun's higher rays
6	qua gallia flammas.	as far away as Gaul.
Verse		
7	Membra dyonisii	The limbs of the very blessed Dionysius,
10	reteguntur namque macharii	who illuminated you
5	qui te divinae	with the light of divine wisdom,
8	lustravit luce sophiae.	are laid bare.
Matins Inv.		
6	Psallamus domino	Let us sing
8	concordi mente supremo	with the highest unity of mind

[41] On the contents of rhymed Offices, see Hughes, 'Offices', 33, 45. I am especially grateful to Prof. Hughes for his advice on this Office for Saint-Denis.

6 qui dyonisio	to the Lord who has given
9 tribuit caelestia sancto.	heavenly gifts to Dionysius.
Resp. 1	
5 Errorum captas	When Paul strives
9 laqueis dum paulus athenas	with many words to call Athens,
6 perstudet ad vitae	imprisoned in the snares of sin,
8 callem verbose[42] vocare	to the pathway of life,
7 vana dyonisius	the joyful Dionysius soon afterward
9 mox respuit ydola letus	cast aside the empty idols,
Verse	
7 ut meruit proprium	as he became worthy to know
8 factorem noscere christum.	Christ his own Maker.
[Vana]	
Resp. 2	
5 Despectis vanae	Dionysius, having rejected
8 decretis phylosophiae	the principles of the empty philosophy,
5 sec-[*fo. 160*^{v}]-tator christi	chooses to be considered
10 dyonisius optat haberi	a follower of Christ,
Verse	
5 Pauli doctrinis	once he has been shown the way of light
8 monstrato tramite lucis.	through Paul's teaching.
[Sectator]	
Resp. 3	
7 Gentibus helladicis	His own mind having been changed,
8 mutata mente relictis	the celebrated Dionysius
7 visitat ausonias	left the Greek people
10 dyonisius inclitus horas	and visits the regions of Rome
6 suadeat ut christum	and urges that Christ
9 gentilibus esse colendum.	should be worshipped by the Gentiles.
Verse	
6 Semina doctrinae	He scatters everywhere the seeds
8 vitalis spargit ubique.	of the life-giving teaching.
[Suadeat]	
Resp. 4	
6 Sancte dyonisi	Saint Dionysius,
8 martyr clarissime christi	brightest martyr of Christ,
6 caelestis patriae	offer us the joys
8 tu nobis gaudia posce	of the celestial fatherland,

42 Text gives *verbore*.

Verse		
7	quo sine fine frui	so that we may be worthy to enjoy
9	mereamur luce perhenni.	light eternal without end.
[Caelestis]		
Resp. 5		
6	Clementis citius	Quickly following
8	ierarchae iussa sequutus	the orders of Pope Clement,
6	christi signa ferens	he journeys to see the borders of the Gauls,
8	gallorum visere fines	bearing the sign of Christ
7	tendit ut ad dominum	in order to turn the hearts
8	convertat corda reorum.	of the condemned to the Lord.
Verse		
6	Parisius tandem	Dionysius finally arrived
10	dyonisius advenit urbem.	in the city of Paris.
[Ut]		
Resp. 6 [fo. 161]		
8	Non virgae non aequuleus	Neither rods nor rack
9	non ignea fornax	nor fiery furnace
?	ferreus haud lectus [la-	nor even the bier
?	cuna?] ieiunave belva	nor even the hungry beast
7	terret adhletam [*sic*] christi	frightens the struggling warrior of Christ,
8	certantem pectore forti.	strong in spirit.
Verse		
7	Hostica barbaries	Seeing this,
8	desaevit talia cernens.	the hostile barbarian rages.
[Athletam]		
Resp. 7		
7	Sacra dyonisius	Dionysius, thrown in prison,
9	caelebrans in carcere trusus	duly celebrates the sacred mysteries
8	misteria angelicis	with the angelic companies
9	comitatum rite catervis	of the hosts
7	mirifica specie	and is worthy to see you
9	meruit te christe videre	in a wonderful vision, O Christ,
Verse		
7	premia pro meritis	who gives eternal rewards
8	qui das aeterna beatis.	to the deserving blessed.
[Mirifica]		
Resp. 8		
6	Dans dyonisio	Jesus, giving to Saint Dionysius
9	hiesus sacra mistica sancto	the sacred mysteries,
7	inquit laetare meum[43]	says: 'Gladden my saint,
8	sanctum nunc accipe munus	and now accept the gift

[43] Text gives *meus* to accommodate the rhyme.

6 quod tibi complebo	which I will soon give you
7 mox una patre summo.	in the company of the Highest Father'.
Verse	
6 Est etenim merces	Truly Your greatest mercy
7 mecum tua maxima semper	is with me always,
6 atque salus cunctis	and there is salvation for all those
9 tibi consentire paratis.	who are prepared to believe in You.
[Quod tibi]	
Resp. 9	
5 Armatos hostes	The truth-telling witness of Christ,
9 furiato corde [*fo. 161v*] ruentes	his heart enraged,
6 veridicus testis	trusts in the powerful virtue of God
8 christi devincit inermis	and conquers the armed enemies
6 pneumatis excelsi	going to their ruin
8 fretus virtute potenti.	with their defenceless spirits.
Verse	
6 Cedere tormentis	The holy man cannot yield
8 vir sanctus nescit acerbis.	to the harsh torments.
[Pneumatis]	
Resp. 10	
6 Carnificis duram	The saint submits
9 sancto subeunte dolabram	to the hard axe of the executioner,
7 protinus acephalum	and immediately his beheaded body,
8 corpus vita vidua tum	deprived of life,
6 fert caput abscisum	then carries his truncated head,
9 caeli comitante caterva.	attended by the heavenly throng.
Verse	
6 Principe devicto	The prince of darkness
9 tenebrarum sanguine fuso.	is overcome by his spilled blood.
[Fert]	
Resp. 11	
6 Affectus variis	Dionysius, martyred by diverse punishments
9 pro christi nomine poenis	for the name of Christ
5 gallorum genti	when he disclosed the secrets of the Truth
9 dum detegit abdita veri	to the people of the Gauls,
6 sideream tandem	finally ascends
9 scandit dyonisius arcem.	to the heavenly fortress.
Verse	
6 Nactus perpetuam	He obtains the everlasting crown
8 praeclara morte coronam.	through his noble death.]
[Sideream]	

Resp. 12

I [*Office ends here; only this initial 'I' is given.*]

Like Hilduin's Office described above, this rhymed Office seems to be taken from the abbot's ninth-century *vita* for Saint Denis, and it succeeds in confusing the adventures of Saint Denis with those of Dionysius the Areopagite. The first five responsories for Matins tell the story of the conversion of Dionysius the Areopagite (the Greek disciple of Paul), his supposed journey to Rome, and his commission from Pope Clement to preach to the people of Gaul. Here the legend of the true Saint Denis takes over: his mission to Gaul and his martyrdom by decapitation are recounted in Resp. 5–11. Neo-Platonic teachings, although not exclusive to Pseudo-Dionysius, are embedded in this Office in the references to light and to its opposition to the 'shadows of night' in the responsory for Vespers, the invitatory, and the second and fourth responsories for Matins.

Although the rhymed Office goes beyond Hilduin's ninth-century Office in displaying the biographical aspect of the Areopagitist motif directly, its content echoes the abbot's earlier version in at least one place. The eighth responsory of the rhymed Office (see above), which deals with Saint Denis's vision of Christ and his receipt of Holy Communion while in prison, seems to be adapted directly from the fourth responsory from Hilduin's Office:

Resp. Dum sacrum misterium sanctus dyonisius celebraret in carcere, apparuit ei Dominus Hiesus Christus cum multitudine angelorum. Dansque illi sancta, dixit: Accipe hoc, care meus, quod mox complebo tibi una cum patre meo. Ver. Mecum enim est maxima merces tua, et his qui audierint te salus in regno meo. [Dansque][44]

The musical notation of the rhymed Office cannot be transcribed accurately, since it is preserved only in the neumatic source F:Pm 384. It is clear, however, that the responsories are ornate, with several melismas appearing on final or penultimate words. The Vespers responsory contains a lengthy melisma on the final word 'flam-*mas*'. Sequentially structured melismas appear on the fourth-to-last word 'mox' of the first Matins responsory, and on the penultimate word '*gau*-dia' of the fourth responsory. Other melismas occur in the second responsory ('hab-*e*-ri'), the seventh responsory ('chris-*te*'), and the ninth responsory ('pot-*en*-ti'). This rather generous use of responsory melismas is not surprising: as we have seen, they are a feature of many responsories in the twelfth-century antiphoner from Saint-Denis F:Pn, lat. 17296 (see Table 3.4).

The poetry of this Office is in leonine hexameters, lines of six feet having rhyme between the syllable before the caesura and the final

[44] F:Pn, lat. 17296, fos. 230^{r-v}; ed. in Hesbert, *CAO*, iv. 143, No. 6559. Both versions are drawn from Hilduin's *vita*, *PL*, cvi. 45.

syllable of each line.[45] Leonine rhyme, used both in the Classical period and in the Middle Ages, was especially popular in the eleventh century.[46] Assonance replaces actual rhyme in a few places, for example, in Resp. 5 ('ferens', 'fines'), Resp. 6 ('fornax', 'belva'; 'barbaries', 'cernens'), Resp. 8 ('merces', 'semper'; 'meum', 'munus'), although in the latter instance the scribe evidently tried to force a rhyme by writing 'meus'. Resp. 6 appears to be defective in ll. 3–4 ('ferreus haud lectus [lacuna?] ieiunave belva'), and the rhyme scheme of its first four lines is abab, instead of the expected aabb. Otherwise the Office is quite straightforward.

What prompted the community to compose this Office, probably in the mid-eleventh century, is not known, but we can hazard a guess. The debate over the relics of Saint Denis, stirred up by the monks of Saint-Emmeram, happened in 1053, causing the eventual establishment of the feast of the Detection of Saint Denis (9 June). In the aftermath of this event, the community might well have wanted to publicize anew its possession of the remains of the saint. The text of this rhymed Office does not seem to serve this end, however, since it is more appropriate for the feast of Saint Denis (9 October) than for the Detection. But there is no reason to expect that the service for the Detection would specifically mention the acrimonious controversy with Saint-Emmeram, and later sources in fact show that the Detection borrowed chants from the *natale* of Saint Denis. On the basis of this, we can surmise that the eleventh-century rhymed Office, if it dates from as late as the middle of the century, may have been composed for the feast of the Detection. The service was clearly valuable as another piece of Areopagitist liturgical dogma. Oddly enough, however, it appears not to have lasted at Saint-Denis—at least it does not recur in any later extant service book fom the monastery.[47] Fleeting as it may have been, the Office shows that the connection of Saint Denis with the two Areopagite figures, first introduced into the Sandionysian liturgy in the ninth century, was destined to span the centuries.

THE TWELFTH CENTURY

The rhymed Office for Saint Denis is the last example of the Pseudo-Dionysian connection in the liturgy of the abbey before the time of

[45] I have split the lines at the caesuras to show the rhymes.

[46] Raby, *History*, 227.

[47] The Office in F:Pm 384 may well be unique; I have found it in no other source, and it is not edited in *AH* (for a discussion of the volumes devoted to rhymed Offices, see Hughes, 'Offices', 33–4).

Abbot Suger. The reconstruction of Saint-Denis that he instigated began at the western end of the church around 1135.[48] Suger extended the nave westward and built a new façade which embodied many themes related to the history of the abbey.[49] Between 1140 and 1144, he created a new chevet around the old crypts at the eastern end of the church. This revolutionary structure contained nine radiating chapels at the choir-level and nine directly underneath in the crypt. The walls of the chevet served as borders for the luminous stained-glass windows which not only brightened the church as a whole but at the same time illustrated the Pseudo-Dionysian contrast of light and darkness which Suger so thoroughly admired. The liturgical choir, or monks' choir, remained in the eastern part of the nave, exactly where it had been in the Carolingian church,[50] but Suger replaced the cold marble and copper seats with warmer wooden ones.

Suger wrote about the reconstruction and about other aspects of his administration of the abbey as well.[51] In these writings he refers to parts of the liturgy, and sometimes he seems to have more in mind than simply a record of what was sung. When the corner-stone for the new chevet was laid on 14 July 1140, for example, Suger mentions that the Ps. *Fundamenta ejus* (Ps. 86) and Ant. *Lapides preciosi* from the service of dedication were chanted.[52] Crosby points out that the psalm, which speaks of the holy city of Mount Sion, likens the chevet to Mount Sion, and that the antiphon was sung as the participants in the ceremony deposited precious gems (*lapides preciosi*).[53] When the church was finally consecrated on 11 June 1144, Suger recounts the dedication of the 21 altars by 21 different prelates both in the choir and in the crypt of the new church (Table 4.1). He then states that these persons performed Mass, each at his assigned altar:

> After the consecration of the altars all these [dignitaries] performed a solemn celebration of Masses, both in the upper choir and in the crypt, so festively, so solemnly, so different and yet so concordantly, so close [to one another] and so joyfully that their song, delightful by its consonance and unified harmony, was deemed a symphony angelic rather than human; and that all exclaimed with heart and mouth: 'Blessed be the glory of the Lord from His place.'[54]

[48] On Suger's church, see Crosby, *Abbey*, 105–277.

[49] On the west façade, see ibid. 167–213; Simson, *Cathedral*, 108–15; Blum and Crosby, 'Portail'; Gerson, 'Facade'; idem, 'Iconographer'.

[50] Bruzelius, *St-Denis*, 36, 38.

[51] See Suger's essays *De Administratione* and *De Consecratione*, published in Panofsky, *Suger*; and the various charters ed. in Lecoy de la Marche, *Suger*.

[52] Panofsky, *Suger*, 102–3. These chants appear in the Office for the Dedication in the 12th-c. antiphoner F:Pn, lat. 17296, fos. 287–289ᵛ (Hesbert, *CAO*, ii, No. 127).

[53] Crosby, *Abbey*, 216–17.

[54] Trans. in Panofsky, *Suger*, 118–21. The final text quoted here is the 12th and last antiphon for the feast of the Dedication; see F:Pn, lat. 17296, fo. 287ᵛ.

TABLE 4.1. *Records of the Dedications of the Altars in the Chevet of Saint-Denis*[a]

Suger, 11 June 1144[b]		F:Pn, lat. 976, fos. 157–8			Félibien, *Histoire*, 535–6		
Saint honoured	Dedicator	Saints honoured	Dedicator	Date	Saints honoured	Dedicator	Date
Choir level							
1. INNOCENT	Simon, b. of Noyon	FIRMINUS, angels, Matthew, Firminus, Urban, Alexander, Eventius and Theodore, Clarus, Thomas, Dionysius (of Corinth), Eligius, Lupus, Ouen, Anianus, Evortius, Columba, Faith, Thecla, Anastasia	Guy, b. of Carcassone (reg. 1210–33)	19 July 1218	n.g.		
2. OSMANNA	Peter, b. of Sens	OSMANNA, Holy Cross, Mary, Thomas, Lucian, Quintinus, Crispin, Crispinian, Silvester, Remigius, Vedast, Amandus, Eleven Thousand Virgins, Geneviève, Cecilia, Lucy, Agatha, all virgins	Guillaume, b. of Orléans (reg. 1237–58).	n.g.	All those listed in N, plus Ten Thousand Martyrs, Agnes[c]	Same as N	8 Oct. 1243

Suger, 11 June 1144[b]		F:Pn, lat. 976, fos. 157–8			Félibien, *Histoire*, 535–6		
Saint honoured	Dedicator	Saints honoured	Dedicator	Date	Saints honoured	Dedicator	Date
3. EUSTACE	Guy, b. of Châlons	MAURICE, Mary, Simon, Jude, Barnabas, Maurice, Innocent, Marcellinus, Peter, Apollinaris, Corneille, Cyprian, Franciscus, Martial, Germanus, Marcellus, Christina, Catherine, Margaret, Valerie, Barbara	Darius, b. of Saint-Pol of Léon (reg. 1234–1237[d])	19 July 1218	All those listed in N, plus Holy Innocents, Sulpicius, all the saints	Same as N	1245
4. PEREGRINUS	Hughes, archb. of Auxerre	PEREGRINUS, Holy Sepulchre, Andrew, Peregrinus, Cosmas, Damian, Gregory, Augustine, Jerome, Perpetua, Felicitas, Emerentiana, Bathildis	Yvonne, b. Saint-Pol of Léon (d. 1186)	n.g.	All those listed in N, plus Sebastian	Same as N	'During the reign of Louis IX and with Eudes [Clé-ment] abbot of this church.'

5. MARY	Hughes, archb. of Rouen	MARY, Holy Cross, Mary, James, Nicase, Patroclus, Hilary (of Poitiers), Ambrose, Athanasius, Dominic, Eulalia, Basilisca, Brigida, Radegunda	Peter, b. of Paneas (?) in Phoenicia[e]	n.g.	All those listed in N, plus Firminus	Same as N	1253
6. CUCUPHAS	Alvise, b. of Arras	CUCUPHAS, Bartholomew, Cucuphas, Stephen, Vincent, Lawrence, Felix, Corneille, Cyprian, Fabian, Sebastian, Germanus of Auxerre, Landericus, Austregisilius, Theobald, Appolonia, Juliana, Faith, Hope, Charity	Guillaume, b. of Madytus in Thrace.[f]	n.g.	All those listed in N: (1) except Felix; (2) plus Christina, Catherine, all the saints	Same as N	1244
7. EUGENE	Algare, b. of Coutances	EUGENE, Matthew, Luke, Eugene, John, Paul, Martin, Brice, Perpetua, Potentiana, Praxedes, Euphemia	Peter, b. of Carinola (reg. 1233–52).[g]	n.g.	n.g.		

Suger, 11 June 1144[b]		F:Pn, lat. 976, fos. 157–8		Félibien, *Histoire*, 535–6			
Saint honoured	Dedicator	Saints honoured	Dedicator	Date	Saints honoured	Dedicator	Date
8. HILARY OF MENDE	Rotrou, b. of Évreux	HILARY OF MENDE, Mark, Demetrius, Leodegarius, Apollinaris, Gorgonius, Gervase, Protase, Hilary (of Mende), Nicholas, Julian, Maglorius, Majolus, Mamertus, Bernard, Maximinus, Benedict, Maurus, Scholastic, Prisca, Juliana	Hemericus, b. of Tibertiade[h]	n.g.	All those listed in N, plus Mary, all the saints	Same as N	1 Jan. 1247
9. JOHN BAPTIST and JOHN EVANGELIST	Nicholas, b. of Cambrai	ROMANUS, John Baptist, John Evangelist, Linus, Cletus, Romanus, Hyreneus, Simeon (monk), Medard, Gildard, Mary Magdalene, Martha, Mary of Egypt	Nicholas, b. of Cambrai	n.g. (probably 1144)	n.g.		

Crypt

1. LUKE	Eudes, b. of Beauvais
2. GEORGE, WALABURGA	Manasseh, b. of Meaux
3. BARNABAS	Manasseh, b. of Meaux
4. SIXTUS, FELICISSIMUS, AGAPITUS	Milon, b. of Térouanne-
5. MARY	Jeffrey, archb. of Bordeaux
6. CHRISTOPHER	Elias, b. of Orléans
7. STEPHEN	Jeffrey, b. of Chartres
8. EDMUND	Guy, archb. of Sens
9. BENEDICT	Jocelin, b. of Soissons

Abbreviations: b.: Bishop. n.g.: Not given. N: F:Pn, lat. 976.

[a] The nos. to the left refer to the corresponding numerals in Pl. 3. For the altars in the crypt, which are situated directly beneath those in the choir, I have re-used the same numbers, respectively (e.g. altar No. 1 in the crypt lies under altar No. 1 in the choir). The name of the principal dedicatee of each altar appears in small capital letters.

[b] Taken from Suger's *De Consecratione* (ed. in Panofsky, *Suger*, 118).

[c] F:Pn, lat. 976 calls for processions to Osmanna's altar on the feasts of the Ten Thousand Martyrs (fo. 98v) and Agnes (fo. 72v), even though the MS does not list them as patrons.

[d] *GC*, xiv. 977.

[e] This bishop is found neither in Gams, *Series* nor in Eubel, *Hierarchia*.

[f] Likewise not found in Gams, *Series* nor in Eubel, *Hierarchia*.

[g] Gams, *Series*, 870; Eubel, *Hierarchia*, i. 157.

[h] The earliest-named 13th-c. bishop of Tiberiade is Eustorgius (*c*.1256–73), but Eubel cites a letter of Innocent IV (4 Aug. 1243) mentioning 'a bishop of Tiberiade'; ibid. 484.

Suger's emphasis on the angelic effects of this ceremony may reflect his Pseudo-Dionysian leanings. The service itself was clearly a pointed display of the new string of chapels, for while the side-altars of Saint-Denis were frequently visited, the simultaneous use of them in one service was not a common occurrence. The only other evidence of such employment of multiple altars comes in the burial service for Philip Augustus in 1223, described in Chapter 2.

Suger's Liturgical Enhancements

The new chevet was in fact Suger's crowning achievement. It is hardly surprising, then, that he would have prescribed a regular programme of processions to the radiating chapels, although no twelfth-century documents attest to them. The later ordinaries from the thirteenth and fourteenth centuries, on the other hand, give abundant information on the processions to the chapels of Saint-Denis. Since the earliest of these documents (F:Pm 526) was written between 1234 and 1236, at the beginning of the reconstruction of the twelfth-century church, we may assume that most of the processions contained in it were celebrated in Suger's church as well. The abbot certainly did not invent the custom of processing to the altars of saints venerated at various places in a church, for the Cluniac customaries from the previous century already call for this practice.[55] It was, however, Suger's revolutionary new chevet with its arc of chapels that provided a perfect opportunity for this custom to be enacted on a regular basis.

Perhaps Suger's interest in liturgical processions was in part an attempt to teach the community the doctrine of the 'procession and return', mentioned earlier.[56] The Bible and the liturgy, both vehicles in the procession and return, are central to Pseudo-Dionysian thought, and the emphasis Suger places on them in his new church are in keeping with what he understood of the philosopher. If processions to the chevet and elsewhere in the church symbolized this doctrine to Suger

[55] The *Liber Tramitis*, written at Cluny in the early 11th c., mentions processions to the altars of Saints Agatha and Benedict in the church; Dinter, *Liber*, 44, 63. The *Ordo Cluniacensis*, written by the monk Bernard in 1067, stipulates the visitation of the altars of the church as part of the dominical procession at Cluny; Herrgott, *Ordo*, 235, ch. xlv. Ulrich's customary, written at Cluny *c.*1080, calls for processions to the respective saints' altars on the Translation of Benedict, Assumption of Mary, and feast of Martin; *PL*, cxlix. 679. The Customs of Fruttuaria likewise specify processions to the altars of saints on the Octaves of their feasts, as well as on other important saints' days; Spätling and Dinter, *Consuetudines*, 252, 255, and *passim*. At Salisbury, on the other hand, daily processions to the altars of saints in the church did not form part of the liturgy of Salisbury Cathedral, for example, until the 13th c.; Bailey, *Processions*, 67.

[56] Suger mentions or describes processions in several places; see Panofsky, *Suger*, 45, 69, 97, 113, 115, 119.

by analogy, they would likewise have served a specific function in the twelfth-century church.

Suger's fascination with Pseudo-Dionysius and his reconstruction of the church clearly provided him with reasons to enhance the liturgy, but the abbot had actually begun to augment the ritual several years earlier. In spite of Bernard of Clairvaux's thunderings against the excesses that existed at Saint-Denis, Suger established a number of new services and raised the levels of older ones. He also founded an anniversary for Louis VI (2 August) around 1130,[57] and a decade later renewed a similar foundation for Charles the Bald (d. 877), which the monks had ceased to observe.[58] And in three documents the abbot made provisions for his own anniversary. Around 1130 he declared that the Ps. *Ad te levavi* (Ps. 24) from Matins of the Office of the Dead, which was sung daily at Saint-Denis,[59] be chanted for him during his lifetime on Thursdays and Saturdays and that after his death *De profundis* (Ps. 129) from the service of Lauds be sung in his memory on these same days. Both psalms come from the Office for the Dead. Suger's testament from around 1137 calls for the daily singing of a votive Mass for the Holy Spirit while he was alive, and for the continuation of this service and the addition of a daily Requiem Mass after he died.[60] On the yearly commemoration of his anniversary (12, 14 January), he commanded the monks to sing 50 psalms and ordered priests to chant the Mass and Office for the Dead.[61] Finally, Suger stipulated that his anniversary be celebrated at various churches in the area over which Saint-Denis had jurisdiction, and in addition that the Requiem Mass be sung weekly on Mondays and Tuesdays at Argenteuil, on Wednesdays at Saint-Denis-de-l'Estrée, on Thursdays at Corbeil, on Fridays at Metz, and on Saturdays at Lièpvre.[62] In 1138 he endowed an anniversary for himself at the nearby church of Saint-Paul's (see Pl. 1).[63]

Apart from the anniversaries, Suger made changes which bore on other portions of the Divine Office. Around 1130 he renewed the call for the weekly Office for the Virgin on Saturdays, a service which had evidently fallen into disuse at Saint-Denis:

[57] Lecoy de la Marche, *Suger*, 330 (original: F:Pan, K 22, No. 6). The lessons for this service are published in Martène, *Veterum*, vol. iv, pp. xxxvii–xl. The final 3 of the 9 readings come from Suger's biography of Louis; see Lecoy de la Marche, *Suger*, 140, 142, 145; F:Pm 543, fos. 232–66 (the 7th reading is also given in F:Pm 2013, fo. 264).

[58] Lecoy de la Marche, *Suger*, 355; also Erlande-Brandenburg, *Roi*, 102.

[59] On the daily Office of the Dead at Saint-Denis, see Foley, 'Ordinary', ii. 113–18.

[60] Lecoy de la Marche, *Suger*, 335. The Mass for the Holy Spirit to which Suger refers is probably the votive Mass contained in the missals from Saint-Denis: F:Pn, lat. 9436, fo. 128ᵛ; F:Pm 414, fo. 321ᵛ; F:Pn, lat. 1107, fo. 325ᵛ; I:Rc 603, fo. 264ᵛ; GB: Lva 1346–1891, fo. 355ᵛ.

[61] Lecoy de la Marche, *Suger*, 336; Félibien, *Histoire*, 191–2.

[62] Lecoy de la Marche, *Suger*, 338–40.

[63] Ibid. 346–7.

Wherefore . . . we order that those residing generally in our chapter should perpetuate, exalt, and honour the memory of the Holy Mother of God in this fashion: from henceforth in perpetuity [a feast for Mary] shall be celebrated every Saturday in the same way as on the last three days in the Octave of Pentecost, just as it is written in the ordinary [*in catalogo*] of this house, except that we forbid the omission of the seven [penitential] psalms with litany and the Vigil of the Dead.[64]

He also established a similar service for Saint Denis on Thursdays:

In addition, we further ordain [the feast] of our most glorious and sweetest patron Saint Denis and his companions . . . [to be celebrated] on Thursdays in the same way and with equal [ceremony] as the memorial of the holiest Mother of God.[65]

The thirteenth-century ordinaries of Saint-Denis provide directions for these weekly commemorations, pointing out the variations which occur within the various divisions of the liturgical cycle.[66] Suger himself allowed a deviation from the usual plan for these commemorations on the Vigil of a feast-day or during Lent.[67] The later ordinaries echo this, among other places, in the directions for Lent, where they limit these services basically to commemorations at Vespers and Matins and to the celebration of a morning Mass.[68] Whereas there is no evidence that polyphonic music was composed for or sung at these services for Mary and for Saint Denis, it is possible that a group of Marian sequences were intended for the former Office, as discussed below.

Evidence of Suger's other liturgical changes appears in the antiphoner F:Pn, lat. 17296, which Suger had copied during the reconstruction years in the 1140's. This book contains several feasts which the abbot raised to duplex rank in 1130: Epiphany (6 January), Ascension, John the Baptist (24 June), Mary Magdalene (22 July), the Nativity of Mary (6 September) and Saint Maurice (22 September).[69] All six festivals are

[64] 'Unde . . . in capitulo nostro generaliter residentes, ipsius sanctae Dei genetricis memoriam continuare, attollere, decorare constituimus: eo videlicet tenore, ut deinceps aeternaliter, secundum quod in catalogo hujus institutionis intitulatum est, omni die sabbati solemniter celebretur quemadmodum in octavis Pentecosten tribus extremis diebus; praeter quod septem Psalmos, cum Letania et Vigiliis mortuorum dimitti prohibemus'; Lecoy de la Marche, *Suger*, 327 (original = F:Pan, K 22, No. 6).

[65] 'Gloriosissimi praeterea et dulcissimi patroni nostri sanctissimi Dionysii sociorumque ejus, . . . hujus sanctissimae Dei Genetricis memoriam eo ordine et eadem paritate in quinta feria secundamus'; ibid.

[66] F:Pm 526, fos. 9, 10, 11^{v}, 36^{r-v}; 78^{v}–80^{v}, etc.; F:Pn, lat. 976, fos. 13, 47^{v}–48^{v}, etc.; F:Pan, L 863, No. 10, pp. 1, 13, etc.

[67] 'In ipsis celeberrimis memoriarum sanctarum diebus [i.e. the commemorations for the Virgin and Saint Denis], sive [fratres nostri] eas faciant, sive convenienter occasione alicujus praecipuae solemnitatis Vigiliarum aut Quadragesimae mutent'; Lecoy de la Marche, *Suger*, 328.

[68] 'Sciendum est quod a capite XL usque post octabas pasche nichil fiat de beato dyonisio neque in sabbato de beata maria nisi commemoratio tamen ad vesperas et ad matutinas et missa matutinalis, et ad missam, de beato dyonisio dicatur Tractus *Ave Maria*'; F:Pm 526, fos. 36^{r-v}; F:Pn, lat. 976, fo. 13; F:Pan, L 863, No. 10, p. 32.

[69] Lecoy de la Marche, *Suger*, 329.

labelled at least as duplex in the earliest calendars which contain rankings (Appendix A).

The Gloria Patri and Trinitarian Symbolism

F:Pn, lat. 17296 likewise includes twelve tones for the Gloria Patri for each of the twelve responsories for Matins of the feast of the Trinity. The presence of these special melodies is probably no accident, in view of Suger's emphasis on the concept of the Trinity in the central portal of the west façade.[70] A sculpture of the Trinity—God the Father holding the figure of Christ as a lamb, while the Holy Spirit hovers above in the form of a dove—appears on the highest point of this principal entrance to the church. Inspired by Pseudo-Dionysian philosophy by way of Saint Augustine,[71] Suger displayed prominently one of his favourite themes in this façade. Suger's emphasis on Gloria Patri tones for the feast of Trinity in F:Pn, lat. 17296 demonstrates that his predilection for symbolism extended to the music and liturgy of the abbey as well. Here too Suger was perhaps influenced by Pseudo-Dionysius' *Celestial Hierarchy*, where the mystic describes the songs of the seraphim, cherubim, and thrones—the first hierarchy—in these terms: 'And this first group passes on [in song] the word that the Godhead is a monad, that is one in three persons.'[72] These and other such sentiments[73] comprise the text of the Gloria Patri. Of the twenty-five melodies in the collection in F:Pn, lat. 17296, almost half (twelve) are for the feast of the Trinity, while only four of the remaining thirteen melodies are destined for any single festival (Invention of Stephen, 3 August), with other festivals represented by only one Gloria Patri apiece (see Table 3.3).

Melismas and Philosophy

Another aspect of current philosophy that Suger embraced was the theme of the transcendency of light, and evidence of this idea may even extend to the music in F:Pn, lat. 17296 and in the later missal F:Pn, lat. 1107. In the discussion of the tropes, Benedicamus Domino, and Ite Missa Est at Saint-Denis, we noted that the abbey was curiously old-fashioned, choosing melismatic, largely wordless forms of this music for feasts of duplex rank and higher. Apparently the Sandionysians

[70] For discussion of the Trinity iconography of the west portal, see Gerson, 'Iconographer', 192–4; Crosby, *Abbey*, 180, 191–2, 282–3.

[71] Gerson, 'Iconographer', 193.

[72] Luibheid and Rorem, *Pseudo-Dionysius*, 166; see the discussion of the Pseudo-Dionysian doctrine of the Trinity in Louth, *Denys*, 88–91.

[73] See also Luibheid and Rorem, *Pseudo-Dionysius*, 51–2, 53, 61–2, and *passim*.

enhanced their divine celebration little if at all with the new polyphonic forms that emerged in the twelfth and thirteenth centuries, in spite of the fact that they were unquestionably open to the newest trends in architecture. And if the surviving sources represent the true state of things, they likewise embraced relatively few texted tropes for the chants of the Mass and Office.

Instead, they used melismas as tropes, Benedicamus Domino, and Ite Missa Est—a practice hardly unique to Saint-Denis, of course. But the melismas may have had a meaning particular to the abbey, one which is both related to the architecture of the new church and which may help explain why the monks eschewed the avant-garde music of the twelfth century. In the context of architecture, Suger writes that the brightly gilded bronze doors of the central west portal 'should brighten the minds so that they may travel, through the true lights, to the True Light where Christ is the true door'. In similar fashion, the walls in Suger's chevet served as frames for the radiant windows which admitted the light that 'urg[es] us onward from the material to the immaterial'.[74] Even within the windows themselves, Suger's insistence on a dark blue colour emphasizes the typically Pseudo-Dionysian contrast between the light that partially penetrates the glass and the darkness that continually clouds our minds and inhibits our vision of God.[75]

The situation in music can be viewed as comparable. Like the gold and the light of Suger's doors and windows, a largely textless passage of vocal monophony exhibits a higher degree of 'clarity' than any other form of vocal music—even a passage of polyphony in the *organum purum* style of the Parisian composer Leoninus, whose period of activity began just after Suger's death. Nearly wordless, 'transparent' music is especially apt for an ineffable God who, according to Pseudo-Dionysius, reveals himself to us in the 'procession' and then uplifts us in the 'return' to this same ineffable Being.[76] But try as we may, we cannot do away with the words altogether, and hence our songs, like the windows which mix light with darkness, allow us only momentary glimpses of God in the melismatic (lighter) parts, only to pull us away from Him in the texted (darker) regions. The window is the static image of this light/dark contrast, the melismatic chant its fluid counterpart. By analogy, therefore, the numerous melismatic tropes (Table 3.4) and the melismatic Benedicamus and Ite Missa Est melodies in F:Pn, lat. 17296 (Table 3.10) and in F:Pn, lat. 1107 (Ex. 3.16) can be

[74] Panofsky, *Suger*, 46–9, 74–5. For von Simson, the 'decisive aspect' of the Gothic style is likewise its transparency and diaphanousness; *Cathedral*, 4.

[75] On the interpretation of the blue in Suger's windows, see Lillich, 'Glass', 222–5; and Gage, 'Glass', 39–42; and on the 'darkness' theme in Pseudo-Dionysius in general, see Louth, *Denys*, 100–1.

[76] Rorem, *Symbols*, 112.

interpreted as music which helps lead from the material to the immaterial world.[77] The bits of text that encase the melismas serve, like the walls of the church and the dark blue in the windows, to highlight the untexted, unencumbered music which temporarily uplifts both the singer and the listener to the True Voice. A distracting prosula, or indeed the presence of competitive voices in polyphony, would in Suger's mind impede this music, binding it to the realm of the material world.

There is certainly support for this explanation of the importance of monophonic, melismatic music at Saint-Denis. A prevalent theme in twelfth-century philosophy was the neo-Platonic/neo-Pythagorean doctrine that the association between God and matter is analogous to the relationship between *unity* and multiplicity.[78] This belief was echoed in part by Pseudo-Dionysian writings such as the following excerpt from *The Divine Names*:

> Everything owes to the *One* its individual existence and the process whereby it is perfected and preserved. Given this power of God's *unity*, we must be returned from the many to the *One* and our *unique* song of praise must be for the *single* complete deity which is the one cause of all things and which is there before every *oneness* amid multiplicity.[79]

Rorem likewise hints at the efficacy of monophonic singing in his discussion of Pseudo-Dionysian symbolism: 'The *unison* of the Psalmic melody, says Dionysius, suggests the worshippers' union with the divine, within themselves, and with each other.'[80] Suger himself, in the passage cited earlier which describes the celebration of Mass in the church in 1144 by 21 different officiants, is careful to point out that the music was both 'so different and yet so *concordant*', and 'delightful by its consonance and *unified* harmony' (emphasis mine).[81] As such, monophonic song becomes perhaps the more expedient form of vocal praise, in a sense the 'high road' for adherents of Pseudo-Dionysius. Interpreting monophonic, melismatic chants in this way, Suger might well have defended his use of them in the face of the Cistercian

[77] This theory of the usefulness of melismas is strengthened when one realizes that for Pseudo-Dionysius the liturgy is even closer to the immaterial world than the Scriptures because it is a fluid tradition, unlike the Scriptures, which are a fixed record (ibid. 117–26).

[78] Gregory, 'Inheritance', 70–80; Louth, *Denys*, 88–91.

[79] Luibheid and Rorem, *Pseudo-Dionysius*, 129.

[80] Rorem, *Symbols*, 122.

[81] In his description of the dedication of 1140, Suger says 'we chanted a multifaceted praise' ('multimodam laudem . . . decantabamus'), and Panofsky translates this passage as 'we chanted . . . a polyphonic praise'; *Suger*, 96–7. Panofsky's use of the word 'polyphonic' is not warranted by the context. This dedication ceremony, witnessed by prelates from different places, was for a number of locations in the new church and honoured numerous saints. The words 'multimodam laudem' are typical of Suger's colourful language, and insofar as they have a specific meaning, they probably refer to the different chants in honour of these various saints, and not to polyphony *per se*.

reformers, who made pointed attempts to remove all melismas from their liturgy and had unsuccessfully urged similar action at Saint-Denis. Those who followed Suger in the second half of the twelfth century seemed disinclined to modify the liturgy in any case, but they too would have had grounds to argue against the use of the new Parisian polyphony in the royal abbey.

If Suger and his successors in fact cultivated melismas for these reasons, they had still another aspect of Pseudo-Dionysian philosophy on their side. At the beginning of *The Divine Names*, the mystic warns that 'we must not dare to resort to words or conceptions concerning that hidden divinity which transcends being, apart from what the *sacred scriptures* [italics mine] have divinely revealed'.[82] Subsequent references to 'songs of praise' throughout his treatises always associate the song texts with biblical quotations.[83] The texts of prosulas, on the other hand, are generally non-biblical insertions, and they would undoubtedly have been shunned by Pseudo-Dionysius, had they existed in his day. Thus, when there was a choice between retaining an old melismatic trope and adding a prosula text at Saint-Denis, the melisma was preferable.

Clearly these monophonic, untroped forms of responsory melismas, Benedicamus Domino, and Ite Missa Est were a tradition in their own right, one which seems to have served as an alternative practice in some houses. Those who heard the performance of the *opus dei* at Saint-Denis must have been struck by the extensive use that the monks made of melismas. As noted earlier, the cultivation of melismas was not new—on the contrary, it was perhaps the oldest means of enriching the high celebrations of the liturgical year. That Saint-Denis should be perceived as guardian of the past was as important to the inhabitants of the monastery as that it should stand at the forefront of architectural developments. In their musical practice, and particularly in their preference for florid tropes, Benedicamus Domino, and Ite Missa Est, the monks pointed to the past. At the same time, they remained true to their philosophy, as they understood it, and they rivalled the more innovative musical centres with the beauty of their expansive melismas.

[82] Luibheid and Rorem, *Pseudo-Dionysius*, 49. Rorem underscores the importance of this passage: '*The Divine Names* does not consider names for God in general but only those found in the Bible. . . Besides providing the subject matter for most of his [Pseudo-Dionysius'] treatises, the Scriptures are his supreme authority for *all* speech and thought about God'; *Symbols*, 23.

[83] See e.g. Luibheid and Rorem, *Pseudo-Dionysius*, 165–6, 213–14.

THE THIRTEENTH CENTURY

Several decades after Suger, a third reconstruction of Saint-Denis began in 1231 under Abbots Eudes Clément (1228–45), William of Macouris (1246–54), Henry Mallet (1254–8), and Matthew of Vendôme (1258–86).[84] Beginning this time in the eastern part of the church, the builders left the chapels of Suger's chevet practically untouched. They constructed a new transept with protruding arms which replaced Suger's non-projecting transept. The upper stories of the church were rebuilt, and the old Carolingian nave was finally widened. The church was completed by 1281. The new liturgical choir occupied the same place as its Carolingian predecessor, and Bruzelius points out that there was evidently little need to interrupt worship at Saint-Denis during the long enterprise, since 'the Carolingian nave, which fits neatly within the thirteenth-century piers, probably continued to be used while the new church was being constructed as an envelope around it, and may have been demolished only at a fairly late date, when the new choir was complete'.[85]

New Feasts and Ranks of Services

The legacy of these four abbots extended to more than the architecture of the building, for, as in the previous century, the music and ceremony which adorned the new church were altered in several important ways. We have seen that Abbot Eudes established the feast of Saint Bernard of Clairvaux (23 August) and renewed the observance of All Souls' Day (3 November). Abbots William and Henry may possibly have instituted some of the new ceremonies as well, although no evidence positively connects them to any of the thirteenth-century foundations. Besides adding feasts, these men enhanced the ritual of older ones and in general raised the level of pomp and circumstance in the liturgy between 1233/4 and 1259. Abbot Matthew was responsible for the installation of the feast of Sanctinus and Antoninus (19 October), and he acknowledged the work of his predecessors by incorporating their changes into a new ordinary (F:Pn, lat. 976) and missal (F:Pn, lat. 1107) for the church. In all, six new feasts were adopted, as we have seen in the discussion of the calendar: the short-lived feast of the Invention of the Holy Nail, and the feasts of Saints Bernard of Clairvaux (23 August), Francis (4 October), Demetrius (17 October), Ursula and the Eleven Thousand Virgins (21 October), and Sanctinus

[84] On the architecture of the 13th c. church, see Bruzelius, *St-Denis*.
[85] Ibid. 38.

and Antoninus (19 October). Eudes likewise founded his own anniversary (5 May) and one for Abbot Henry Troon (22 October),[86] as well as a triple anniversary for Abbots Hilduin, Eudes of Deuil, and Eudes Taverny (30 October)[87] during this time. Several other minor anniversaries,[88] the festival of the Relics, as well as the feasts of Saints Dionysius of Corinth (8 April), Catherine (25 November), and Louis (25 August) were added to the ritual in the thirteenth century, although it is clear that most of these were first observed either before or after the reconstruction years. Around 18 other services were promoted from three to twelve lessons, or from simplex or partial duplex to full duplex in the thirteenth century.[89] Abbot Eudes' zeal toward the ritual even extended to Cistercian and Premonstratensian houses, where, at his bidding, the rank of the feast of Saint Denis was raised in 1232 and again in 1236.[90]

The Confraternity of Saint Denis

Religious devotion, which often inspired the composition of new music in many late medieval churches, was fostered in special societies affiliated with a church, called confraternities or guilds. During his tenure as abbot, Eudes Clément founded a confraternity of Saint Denis in honour of Christ and of his 'karissimus patronus' Saint Denis. A copy of the charter of the foundation has survived.[91] According to Eudes' wishes, four *prepositi* were to head the confraternity, of whom two were clerics and two lay persons. Regulations for the purchase of food and for the notification of the abbey in the event of the death of a member of the confraternity were also set forth. The monks were to pronounce absolution for a departed brother of the confraternity in the chapter Office, and to include a special oration for his soul at Mass. On the day following the Invention of Saint Denis (22 April), the monks of the abbey and the ordained members of the confraternity should celebrate the Office for the Dead in honour of deceased persons of the confraternity, and their names should be written into a special book called the *charterel*. Four priests should celebrate one *annuale* service each year for departed members. Eudes granted a yearly allowance of 10 *livres* to

[86] F:Pan, LL 1157, pp. 85–7 (original = F:Pan, L 836, No. 8), pp. 91–3; F:Pan, LL 1159, pp. 54–6, 56–8. Henry Troon was abbot from 1204 to 1221.

[87] Ibid. 1–2. On these 3 abbots see the introd. to App. A.

[88] F:Pan, LL 1159, pp. 108, 121 (anniversaries established by Abbot Henry Troon for Petronilla, sister of the prior of Saint-Denis, Haymon, in 1209, and for Hugh de Touri in 1213); p. 121 (anniversary for Abbot Hugh Foucault [26 Oct.], founded in 1223); pp. 123–4 (anniversary for Hugh of Aties, instituted in 1235).

[89] See above, pp. 00.

[90] Félibien, *Histoire*, 227–8.

[91] F:Pan, LL 1183, pp. 37–58, a 14th-c. copy of Eudes' charter, written in both Latin (pp. 37–46) and French (pp. 47–58).

the confraternity, but new affiliates were required to pay 10 *sous* annually during the first two years of their membership. The confraternity also received support from outsiders who wished to be commemorated.[92] By the early fourteenth century, the confraternity had its own chapel on the north side of the nave (see Pl. 4).

While Eudes' charter provides the details given above, it mentions no special music that the organization might have sung, unlike the documents from some fourteenth- and fifteenth-century confraternities and guilds in Brussels, Bruges, Antwerp, and elsewhere.[93] The foundation also contains a notated Office for the Dead, which follows the outline of the normal Office *pro defunctis* at Saint-Denis.[94]

Processions

Another important aspect of the liturgical enhancement of the thirteenth century was the increase in rubrics for processions in the chevet to the chapels of saints highly regarded at Saint-Denis. As Table 4.2 shows, these saints included not only the ones whose relics were actually present in the abbey, but also the majority of those who were accorded feasts of twelve lessons, a total of some seventy-two by the time the later of the two thirteenth-century ordinaries (F:Pn, lat. 976) was written.[95] Only nine of these saints were principal dedicatees of the altars in the chevet in the choir level at any one time, but almost all the remaining saints were subdedicatees of these nine altars.[96] Fewer than two-thirds

[92] Ibid. 159. This list of persons appears immediately after Eudes' charter: 'Premierem[en]t Madame Marguerite de Flandres, Messire Pierre de Craon, Messire Jaques de Langres, Estienne de Besancon, Edelot Quidente, Messire Lorenz Leburre, Suer Gille de Gallereu, Maistre Jehan Perdriel.'

[93] See Forney, 'Music'.

[94] F:Pan, LL 1183, pp. 61 ff. Later records of the confraternity, contemporaneous with those of the churches mentioned above, might have been more specific on the question of music, but to my knowledge no other documents for this institution exist. It is probably significant, however, with regard to the question of the possibility of polyphony at Saint-Denis that the French translation of Eudes' document, which probably comes from the 14th c., makes no changes in the original 13th-c. specifications, suggesting that the musical practice, if it was monophonic, had not been altered.

[95] In the general rules for the period after Pentecost, F:Pn, lat. 976 calls for a procession in the chevet for certain feasts of 12 lessons: 'If a twelve-lesson feast shall occur there will be a procession in the chevet for that feast, if an altar shall have been consecrated in honour of the saint' ('Si XII lectiones contingerint erit processio in capicio de festo contingente si altare consecratum fuerit in honore sancti'); F:Pn, lat. 976, fo. 48; almost the same text in F:Pm 526, fo. 78v.

[96] See Table 4.1, which compares the dedications of the altars in the chevet which took place in the 12th and 13th cs. While Suger's consecrations all took place on 11 June 1144, the dates of the 13th-c. dedications, recorded partly in the contemporaneous ordinary F:Pn, lat. 976 and partly in the much later, 17th-c. testimony of Michel Félibien, are problematical. In general, F:Pn, lat. 976 is the more reliable since it comes from the 13th c., but it is likely that neither source is completely accurate in recording the dates, names of honourees, or names of dedicators of an altar. Because these elements represent layers of copying in any case, there is no way to determine which one is accurate when there is a conflict between the 2 sources; see Walters [Robertson], 'Reconstruction', 197–9; Delisle, 'Peintures', 448.

of these processions formed part of the liturgy of Saint-Denis when the earlier manuscript F:Pm 526 was written (Tables 4.2 and 4.3).

No complete processioner from Saint-Denis has survived,[97] and yet processional chants are recorded in the earliest extant graduals and antiphoners from the abbey. These early sources contain the antiphons that were sung for the placement of relics on a new altar, for the processions on rogation days, in Advent, at Christmas, on Sundays before and during Lent, on Palm Sunday, Easter, Pentecost, and for Saints Peter and Paul, and Saint Denis.[98] Whereas these books provide the texts and often the music for these antiphons, it is not until the thirteenth century that the ordinaries show how these pieces were used in the church. At this time, and probably earlier, there were processions on all kinds of occasion.[99] The major processions before and after Terce on Christmas Day illustrate the use that the monks made of the church and cloister area.[100] If Christmas fell on Sunday, the ceremony began in the cloister,[101] where persons carrying three crosses led the procession. Next came the bearers of the holy water and the thurible, followed by seven deacons dressed in white, then all the subdeacons carrying books, and finally a priest carrying the relic of Saint Simeon.[102] The cantor intoned the Ant. *O beata infancia* and the Resp. *Styrps jesse*, as the procession re-entered the church from the cloister and went up into the chevet (Pl. 3). They then proceeded to the chapel of the Virgin, where two boys performed the V. *Post partum virgo*, and the priest recited an oration.[103] As the cantor began the Resp. *Verbum caro*, the company moved into the nave, and the procession came to a halt probably in the centre. Here the solo portions of the Resp. *Descendit de celis* and its Ver. *Tamquam sponsus* were performed by three singers. The abbot himself chanted both the V. *Viderunt omnes* and the oration that followed. Returning to the entrance of the choir, the procession ended with the singing of the Ant. *Verbum caro* and, if necessary, the Resp. *Sancta et immaculata*. The tropes to the introit of Mass followed immediately.

[97] F:Pn, n.a.l. 306, a pontifical from Rouen, contains some material for the major processions at Saint-Denis in the 14th c.

[98] See F:Psg 111 (Hesbert, *AMS*, Nos. 201–12); F:Pm 384 (idem, *Graduel*, 17–28); F:Pn, lat. 17296 (fos. 330–341ᵛ; Hesbert, *CAO*, ii, Nos. 147–8).

[99] The roster of processions at Saint-Denis did not differ from those of many other Western churches. For a brief discussion of some of the processions which occur in the 13th-c. ordinary F:Pm 526, see Foley, 'Ordinary', ii, 357–63; and for general treatment of the topic, see Bailey, *Processions*; Kurzeja, *Liber*, 251–349; Tolhurst, *Breviary*, vi. 168–70, and *passim*.

[100] F:Pm 526, fos. 16ʳ⁻ᵛ; F:Pan, L 863, No. 10, p. 23.

[101] F:Pm 526, fo. 16. The 14th-c. ordinary F:Pan, L 863, No. 10 indicates that the procession in the cloister took place whether it is Sunday or not (p. 23).

[102] F:Pm 526, fo. 16. F:Pan, L 863, No. 10 assigns this relic to the *diaconus missae* (p. 23).

[103] Although neither of the ordinaries actually states that the station in the chevet was made at Mary's altar, this location is indicated by the use of a Marian responsory.

TABLE 4.2. *Daily (Non-Dominical) Processions for Saints in the Chevet of Saint-Denis (Thirteenth and Fourteenth Centuries)*

Date	Procession on feast of saint	To altar of saint	MS				Remarks
			M	N	A	L	
January							
3	Geneviève	OSMANNA		x	x		
8	Lucian of Beauvais	OSMANNA	x	x	x		
15	Maurus	HILARY OF MENDE		x			
20	Fabian, Sebastian	PEREGRINUS		x	x		
21	Agnes	OSMANNA		x	x		
27	Julian	HILARY OF MENDE		x	x		
31	Patroclus*	(MARY)			x		The MS states (p. 89): 'processio ad ejus [Patrocli] oratorium.' Whereas no altar was dedicated specifically to Patroclus, he is named among the dedicatees of the altar of the Virgin in N, fo. 158 (see Table 4.1).
February							
1	Vigil of Purification	MARY (after Vespers)	x	x	x		
2	Purification†	Chevet (after Terce)	x	x	x	x	
5	Agatha	OSMANNA	a	x	x		In M, a procession after First Vespers is added, fo. 107v.
6	Vedast, Amandus	OSMANNA		x	x		
10	Scholastica	HILARY OF MENDE		x	x		
		BENEDICT, in crypt	x				This altar was consecrated on 11 June 1144 (Table 4.1).
24	Matthias	EUGENE	a	x	x		In M, a procession after Matins is added, fo. 113.
	Dedication of church	MARY	x	x	x	x	

Date	Procession on feast of saint	To altar of saint	MS				Remarks
			M	N	A	L	
March							
12	Gregory	PEREGRINUS	x	x	x		
21	Benedict	HILARY OF MENDE	x	x	x		
25	Annunciation	MARY	x	x	x		
April							
8	Dionysius of Corinth*	EUSTACE	x				Lacuna, A
25	Mark	Chevet	x				No altar is named in M.
		HILARY OF MENDE		x			Lacuna, A until 11 May
May							
6	John at Latin Gate	ROMANUS OF BLAYE		x			
1	Mamertus, Majolus	HILARY OF MENDE		x			
28	Germanus	MAURICE	a	x			In M, a procession after First Vespers is added, fo. 129^{v}. Lacuna, A until 8 June
June							
2	Marcellinus, Peter	MAURICE		x			
8	Medard, Gildard	ROMANUS OF BLAYE		x			
10	Landericus	CUCUPHAS		x	x		
11	Barnabas	MAURICE		x	x		In N, the procession is written in margin of fo. 97, but the hand is contemporaneous with, if not identical to, that of the rest of the MS. The procession is probably not a later addition, but a correction.
19	Gervase, Protase	HILARY OF MENDE	x	x	x		
22	Ten Thousand Martyrs	OSMANNA	a	x			In M, a procession after First Vespers is added, fo. 136^{v}.

24	John Baptist†*	JOHN BAPTIST	x	x			What appears to be 2 is actually 1 altar. On 11 June 1144 the altar was consecrated in honour of John the Evangelist. By the mid-13th c. it had been re-dedicated to Saint Romanus, retaining the 2 Johns as co-dedicatees (see Table 4.1).
		ROMANUS OF BLAYE			x	x	
26	John, Paul	EUGENE		x			Lacuna, A until 4 July
29	Peter, Paul†*	MARY	x	x			
		Chevet				x	
July							
4	Translation of Martin	EUGENE		x			
7	Octave of Martial	MARTIN	x				No altar was dedicated specifically to Martin, as M seems to imply on fos. 144^{r-v}. Martial, however, is named among the dedicatees of the altar of Saint Maurice in N (see Table 4.1).
		MAURICE		x			Lacuna, A until 11 July
11	Benedict, Translation	HILARY OF MENDE					
		Vespers, Lauds	x	x			
		BENEDICT, in crypt					
		Morning Mass	x				
22	Mary Magdalene	JOHN BAPTIST	x	x			See note for 24 June. Lacuna, A until 31 July
24	Christina	MAURICE	x	x			
25	James*	MARY	x	x			
31	Germanus of Auxerre	CUCUPHAS	x	x			
August							
10	Lawrence	CUCUPHAS	x	x	x		
15	Assumption†	MARY	x	x	x		
		Chevet				x	

Date	Procession on feast of saint	To altar of saint	MS				Remarks
			M	N	A	L	
23	Bernard	HILARY OF MENDE		x	x		
24	Bartholomew	CUCUPHAS	x	x	x		
	Ouen	EUSTACE	x				
		FIRMINUS		x	x		
25	Saint Louis	Chevet				x	
28	Augustine	PEREGRINUS	x	x	x		
29	Decollation of John Baptist*	JOHN BAPTIST	x	x			See note for 24 June.
		ROMANUS OF BLAYE			x		
September							
1	Giles, Lupus	EGIDIUS, in crypt	x	x			I have found no record of an altar dedicated to Egidius (= Giles). It is likely that one of the oratories within the crypt, for which Suger records the consecration (Table 4.1), was re-dedicated to Egidius in the 13th c. when the honourees of some of the crypt altars (e.g. Luke and Barnabas) were added to those of various *oratoria* in the upper level.
7	Clodoaldus, Evortius	EUSTACE	x				
		FIRMINUS		x	x		
8	Nativity of Mary†	MARY	x	x	x		
		Chevet				x	
9	Osmanna*	OSMANNA	x		x		
	Gorgonius	HILARY OF MENDE	(x)	x	x		M, fo. 167, calls for a procession without naming an altar.
21	Matthew	EUSTACE	x				
		FIRMINUS		x	x		

22	Maurice*	MAURICE				An altar was consecrated in honour of one of the Holy Innocents on 11 June 1144. By the mid-13th c., however, this relic had been moved to the altar of Saint Maurice and the altar re-dedicated to Saint Firminus (see Table 4.1).
		Vespers, Matins	x	x	x	
		High Mass		x	x	
		INNOCENT				
		High Mass	x			
25	Firminus*	FIRMINUS			x	M, fo. 174^{v}, calls for High Mass at the altar of the Holy Trinity in the choir, not in the chevet. This rubric was later changed to *ad altare ipsius* in M, and this is the location specified for High Mass in N, fo. 129.
27	Cosmas, Damian	PEREGRINUS	a	x	x	In M, a procession after First Vespers is added, fo. 175.
29	Michael	EUGENE	x	x		Michael is not listed among the dedicatees of the altar of Saint Eugene (see Table 4.1).
30	Jerome	PEREGRINUS	x	x	x	
October						
1	Translations of Remigius *et al.*	OSMANNA	x	x	x	
2	Leodegarius	HILARY OF MENDE	(x)	x	x	M, fo. 177, calls for a procession without naming an altar.
4	Francis	MAURICE		x	x	
17	Demetrius	HILARY OF MENDE		x	x	
18	Luke	EUGENE		x	x	
		Chevet	x			
21	Eleven Thousand Virgins*	OSMANNA			x	
24	Maglorius	HILARY OF MENDE		x	x	
25	Hilary of Mende*	HILARY OF MENDE			x	
28	Simon, Jude	MAURICE	x	x	x	

Date	Procession on feast of saint	To altar of saint	MS				Remarks
			M	N	A	L	
November							
1	All Saints	Chevet	x	x	x	x	
2	Eustace*	Chevet			x		
9	Octave of Eustace	EUSTACE		x	x		
11	Martin	EUGENE		x	x		
13	Brice	EUGENE	(x)	x	x		M, fo. 193, calls for a procession without naming an altar.
15	Eugene*	EUGENE			x		
22	Cecilia	OSMANNA		x	x		Lacuna, M
24	Romanus of Blaye*	ROMANUS OF BLAYE			x		
25	Catherine	MAURICE	x	x	x		
30	Andrew	PEREGRINUS		x			Lacuna, M, A
December							
1	Eligius	FIRMINUS		x	x		Lacuna, M until 28 Dec.
4	Benedict	HILARY OF MENDE		x	x		
6	Nicholas	HILARY OF MENDE		x	x		
13	Lucy	OSMANNA		x	x		
15	Maximinus	HILARY OF MENDE		x	x		
21	Thomas	OSMANNA		x	x		
28	Octave of Thomas	FIRMINUS			x		
31	Silvester	OSMANNA		x	x		

Abbreviations: * Saint's relics present in the abbey, hence procession normally replaced by Vespers service or High Mass at saint's altar in M and N. † Processions for these feasts more elaborate than shown here, involving itineraries in and out of church grounds. x: Procession given in MS. a: Procession added to MS. M: F:Pm 526. N: F:Pn, lat. 976. A: F:Pan, L 863, No. 10. L: F:Pn, n.a.l. 306.

Other processions for the great feasts of the year were conducted somewhat differently, and they frequently extended beyond the interior of the church and cloister. On Palm Sunday and Corpus Christi, for instance, the peregrinations after Terce led as far afield as the neighbouring churches of Saint-Martin and Saint-Denis-de-l'Estrée,[104] and on the rogation days during Easter season, the monks made a veritable tour of these and three other churches in the town: Saint-Paul, Saint-Leodegarius, and Saint-Remigius (Pl. 1).[105] The differing descriptions of the processions after Sext on Ash Wednesday in the three ordinaries even seem to bear on the history of one of the chapels of Saint-Denis. These documents suggest that the chapel of Saint Clement, located probably in the north-east corner of the cloister,[106] was built or perhaps rededicated from a pre-existing infirmary between 1234 and 1259.[107]

The processions of the *sanctorale* employed varying degrees of solemnity. For saints whose relics the abbey possessed, the monks sang High Mass and sometimes Terce on days other than Sunday in their chapels in the thirteenth century,[108] while in the fourteenth century they performed Vespers in addition to Terce and High Mass at these oratories.[109] Often the celebration of a complete Hour or Mass in one of the chapels replaced the procession altogether in the thirteenth century.[110] The majority of feasts of twelve lessons had at least one and sometimes two or more processions to one of the radiating chapels by the time F:Pn, lat. 976 was written around 1258.[111] Saints held in especially high regard were venerated in processions before Mass, just following the Hour of Terce. If the feast fell on Sunday, the procession began in the cloister, continued in the chevet, and ended in the choir.[112]

[104] Palm Sunday: F:Pm 526, fo. 48; F:Pn, lat. 976, fo. 22^{v}; F:Pan, L 863, No. 10, pp. 37–8; Corpus Christi: F:Pan, L 863, No. 10, pp. 70–1.

[105] F:Pm 526, fos. 66^{v}–68; 121–2; F:Pn, lat. 976, fo. 38; 88^{r-v}; F:Pan, L 863, No. 10, pp. 56–7.

[106] See Ayzac, *Histoire*, ii. 189.

[107] See Walters [Robertson], 'Reconstruction', 202.

[108] F:Pm 526, fos. 105^{v}, 193^{v}; F:Pn, lat. 976, fos. 75, 148.

[109] F:Pan, L 863, No. 10, p. 3.

[110] See the directions for Saint Hilary of Mende, Table 4.2, 25 Oct.

[111] It should be noted that Table 4.2 lists only the processions in the chevet of Saint-Denis. A few chapels were situated in other locations of the church, e.g. that of Saint Hippolytus in the north wall of the nave (after 1236), just to the west of the northern transept wing (on the various locations of this altar, see Walters [Robertson], 'Reconstruction', 192–3). For the Translation of Hippolytus on 12 May, the ordinaries call for processions after Vespers and Lauds and for the performance of morning Mass at this altar; for his *natale* on 13 Aug., they specify the execution of Vespers and main Mass at his oratory (F:Pm 526, fos. 127, 157, 157^{v}; F:Pn, lat. 976, fos. 92, 116; F:Pan, L 863, No. 10, fo. 113^{v}).

[112] See e.g. the procession for the Birth of John the Baptist (24 June); F:Pm 526, fo. 137^{v}; F:Pn, lat. 976, fos. 99^{v}–100; F:Pan, L 863, No. 10, fo. 106^{v}.

On days other than Sunday, the procession remained inside the church, using the chevet and choir only.[113]

The simplest processions for saints at Saint-Denis were those which were assigned to feasts that fell on days other than Sunday. Occurring at the end of First Vespers and sometimes after Matins or Lauds, the procession moved from the choir to one of the chapels in the chevet (see Table 4.2). During the ceremony three items were chanted: a responsory on the way to the chevet, which was usually taken from the Matins of the festival, a versicle, and an oration, which ended the service.[114]

The schedule of these simple processions for saints changed dramatically during the early years of the thirteenth-century reconstruction. The earliest ordinary F:Pm 526, written between 1234 and 1236, includes 47 such ceremonies, whereas in the second ordinary F:Pn, lat. 976 (between 1241 and 1259, probably *c.*1258) this number rises to 72. (See Table 4.3.) Clearly, this increase was related to the physical enlargement of the church: either the number of processions in F:Pm 526 reflected the current usage of the 1230s, which may have been in place since the last rebuilding of the church under Abbot Suger in the twelfth century, or it demonstrates that some of these services had to be dropped while the speedy reconstruction of the chevet and transept arms took place in the 1230s and 1240s.[115] The new processions followed precisely the model just described, drawing responsories from the Office of the common of saints—or, in the cases of Saints Maurus, Fabian and Sebastian, and Martin, from their proper services. In several cases no responsory is named, and the rubric simply states *responsorium de festo*. Undoubtedly these were also chosen from a portion of the *commune*. Not only were the processions after Vespers the most numerous,[116] those after Matins were increasingly replaced by one after Lauds. None of the chapels in the crypt was used for the new processions; instead, the westernmost chapels of the choir (Firminus, Osmanna, Hilary of Mende, Romanus of Blaye) were assigned most often for the new ceremonies (Pl. 3). This is understandable, since

113 F:Pm 526, fo. 137v; F:Pn, lat. 976, fos. 99v–100; F:Pan, L 863, No. 10, fo. 106.

114 Evidently these simple processions were somewhat less elaborate than the corresponding ones at Salisbury. Sarum usage included, in addition, the censing of the saint's altar and a return to the choir, where still another versicle and prayer were sung (Bailey, *Processions*, 17–18). It may be that these items were simply taken for granted in the Saint-Denis ordinaries. On the other hand, since the majority of the processions given in Table 4.2 are only for subdedicatees of the altars in the chevet, it is possible that they were as unadorned as they are portrayed in the ordinaries.

115 On the chronology of the early phases of the reconstruction of Eudes Clément, see Bruzelius, *St-Denis*, 124–30.

116 There were probably more processions after First Vespers in the middle of the 14th c. than F:Pan, L 863, No. 10 shows (Table 4.2), for the contents of this MS are highly condensed, and it often omits items which are taken for granted because of their regular occurrence.

both arms of the transept were finished when the second ordinary F:Pn, lat. 976 was written around 1258, thereby allowing the chapels which bordered on the areas of reconstruction, evidently avoided at the time F:Pm 526 was copied, to be used once again. These 72 processions in the chevet of Saint-Denis were firmly fixed in the liturgy. A century later, only those for the Octaves of certain feasts had been added (Table 4.2).

One processional omission in F:Pm 526 is particularly striking. This earlier ordinary never assigns processions to the north-westernmost chapel in the chevet, the *oratorium* of Saint Firminus (Pl. 3), which was dedicated to this saint in 1218 (Table 4.2), long before F:Pm 526 was copied.[117] Instead, the ordinary diverts all processions associated with this altar in the later ordinary F:Pn, lat. 976 to the third chapel on the north side of the chevet, which was consecrated to Saint Eustace and late to Saint Maurice.[118] Bruzelius' analysis of the sequence of the reconstruction suggests that the north transept arm was under construction in the 1230s,[119] and the avoidance of Saint Firminus' altar in F:Pm 526 lends contemporaneous support to her view. Written during the early phases of the reconstruction, F:Pm 526 was clearly outdated almost as quickly as the initial steps of the rebuilding were accomplished. The new ceremonies inspired by the reconstruction of the church were sufficiently numerous to cause a new ordinary (F:Pn, lat. 976) and missal (F:Pn, lat. 1107) to be copied in the late 1250s in response to the changes made during the two previous decades.

Gallican Vestiges

Even as new processions were added to the thirteenth-century ritual of Saint-Denis, a substantial number of ancient liturgical and musical remnants were still being preserved. These came from the Gallican rite, which held sway in Gaul until the mid-eighth century. Only two liturgical sources from Saint-Denis in the Merovingian era, F:Pn, lat. 256 and I:Rvat, Reg. lat. 257, now remain. But it is clear that other Gallican books were once present, for in the ninth century Abbot Hilduin (814–41) spoke of 'missals . . . which are very old and almost

[117] The date of consecration of this altar is given in another 13th-c. source, F:Pn, lat. 976, and it is corroborated by the fact that the Bishop Guy of Carcassone, who dedicated the chapel, reigned precisely during this period (1210/1–23); see Gams, *Series*, 528; Eubel, *Hierarchia*, i. 172. Félibien does not mention this altar (see Table 4.1).

[118] The date of the rededication of this chapel is unclear. The contemporaneous source F:Pn, lat. 976 records 19 July 1218 (Table 4.1), while Félibien, a much later secondary source, gives 1245. Since the texts of the earlier and later ordinaries F:Pm 526 and F:Pn, lat. 976 mention both the Eustace and Maurice altars, it is not possible to say which date—if either—is correct.

[119] Bruzelius, *St-Denis*, 82–105, 124–7.

TABLE 4.3. *Processions for Saints in the Chevet of Saint-Denis: Additions or Reinstatements after 1234*[a]

Date	Procession on feast of saint	Time			MS		To altar of saint
		Vespers	Matins	Lauds	N	A	
January							
3	Geneviève	x			x		OSMANNA
			x			x	
				x	x		
15	Maurus	x			x		HILARY OF MENDE
				x	x	x	
20	Fabian, Sebastian			x	x	x	PEREGRINUS
21	Agnes	x			x	x	OSMANNA
				x		x	
27	Julian	x			x	x	HILARY OF MENDE
			x		x		
February							
5	Agatha	x			x	x	OSMANNA
			x		x		
				x		x	
6	Vedast, Amandus		x			x	OSMANNA
				x	x		
24	Matthias		x			x	EUGENE
				x	x		
May							
6	John at Latin Gate	x			x		ROMANUS OF BLAYE
11	Mamertus, Majolus	x			x		HILARY OF MENDE
			x		x		
28	Germanus	x			x		MAURICE
			x		x		

June							
2	Marcellinus, Peter	x			x		MAURICE
			x		x		
8	Medard, Gildard	x			x		ROMANUS OF BLAYE
			x		x		
10	Landericus		x			x	CUCUPHAS
				x	x		
11	Barnabas	x			x	x	MAURICE
22	Ten Thousand Martyrs	x			x		OSMANNA
26	John, Paul	x			x		EUGENE
July							
4	Translation of Martin	x			x		EUGENE
August							
23	Bernard			x	x	x	HILARY OF MENDE
September							
27	Cosmas, Damian	x			x	x	PEREGRINUS
October							
4	Francis	x			x	x	MAURICE
				x	x		
17	Demetrius		x			x	HILARY OF MENDE
				x	x		
24	Maglorius	x			x	x	HILARY OF MENDE
November							
1	Martin	x			x	x	EUGENE
			x			x	
December							
31	Silvester	x			x		OSMANNA
				x	x	x	

Abbreviations: N: F:Pn, lat. 976. A: F:Pan, L 863, No. 10.

[a] This table is an elaboration of Table 4.2, extracting the feasts which do not (or did not originally) have processions in F:Pm 526, when this is not the result of a lacuna in the MS. In this way, the processions which were added to, or reinstated into, the liturgy of Saint-Denis between 1234 (the earliest possilble date or F:Pm 526) and 1259 (the latest date for F:Pn, lat. 976) are shown together.

entirely consumed with age',[120] and he claimed to have rewritten the Gallican Office for Saint Denis, as will be seen in Chapter 5. Indeed, the Gallican ritual never completely died out after the imposition of Roman *cantus*. Instead, parts of this ancient tradition simply went underground for a period of time, resurfacing sporadically in later sources, among which are manuscripts from Saint-Denis.

The identification of chants as Gallican survivors is a complicated task, and one which requires several steps.[121] Certain chants in the earliest Gregorian service-books that have concordances in Mozarabic, Ambrosian, or Celtic books may be suspected as Gallican remnants. Their texts must then be examined for a literary style which is typical of Gallican texts and which differs from Roman style: petitions to the Son or the Holy Spirit rather than (or in addition to) the Father, and the use of rhetorical figures, repetitions, and vivid language. The musical style of suspected Gallican survivors is often melismatic, with ornate melodies appearing in genres that in the Roman style are normally simpler. Using these and other criteria, scholars have suggested Gallican origins for a number of chants, some of which were sung at Saint-Denis in the late Middle Ages.

One Gloria in Excelsis from the fourteenth-century missal from Saint-Denis GB:Lva 1346–1891 is considered to have Gallican traits.[122] This melody appears in modern chant sources (*LU*) as Gloria XV, and the *Kyriale* of GB:Lva 1346–1891 assigns the chant to morning Masses (see Table 3.7). Traces of the Gallican Mass may likewise include most of the offertories recently proposed as possible Gallican survivors by Kenneth Levy, many of which are found in the Saint-Denis graduals and missals.[123] One of these chants, the Offer. *Benedictus sit deus* for Trinity, preserves the Ver. *Y ta Cherubim*, also known as the *Cheroubikon* (see Table 4.9). This chant, which served as the offertory for the Greek Mass at Saint-Denis by the thirteenth century, entered the handful of Western sources in which it appears by way of the Gallican rite.[124] The unique melisma in the Comm. *Video celos* for Saint Stephen, used as a trope in the eleventh-century gradual from the

[120] 'Missales . . . antiquissimi et nimia pene vetustate consumpti'; *Epistolae*, MGH, *Karolini Aevi*, iii. 330.

[121] For discussions of this process, see Stäblein, 'Gallikanische', *MGG*, iv, cols. 1299–1325; Huglo, 'Gallican', 114–7; Levy, 'Toledo'; Walters [Robertson], 'Reconstruction', 208–9.

[122] Huglo, 'Gallican', 121.

[123] Levy, 'Toledo'. The Gallican traits in the Offer. *Elegerunt apostoli* for Stephen are likewise discussed in Huglo, 'Gallican', 116, 117. The author states that the earliest known occurrence of *Elegerunt* is in F:Psg 111, a sacramentary written at Saint-Denis for the cathedral of Senlis (see Ch. 7), and *Elegerunt* also appears in F:Pn, lat. 9436, an augmented sacramentary copied probably in the abbey of Saint-Vaast of Arras for Saint-Denis. None of the sources written both in and for Saint-Denis, however, preserves this chant.

[124] Huglo, 'Gallican', 122.

abbey F:Pm 384, may also hail from the Gallican liturgy, although it seems to have been dropped from later manuscripts, as described in Chapter 3.

Gallican remnants from the ritual of the Hours are numerous. A number of hymns by Merovingian poets such as Fortunatus survive in later sources, and Saint-Denis was only one of many houses which sang the Gallican hymns that found their way into the New Hymnal,[125] including the hymns for Good Friday *Crux fidelis* and *Pange lingua*. Fortunatus probably also composed one of the aforementioned hymns for Saint Denis, *Fortem fidelem militem*. In addition, the Saint-Denis hymnals F:Psg 1186 and F:Pn, lat. 103 preserve three texts for popular French and Parisian saints: *Ecclesie speculum patrie* for Saint Germanus, *Barcinon lete Cucuphas* for Cucuphas, and *Adsunt o populi* for Hippolytus, all of which may be Gallican in origin.[126]

Many of the great processional antiphons seem to have originated in the Gallican rite,[127] and the probable Gallican candidates *Cum audisset*, *Ave rex noster*, and *Collegerunt pontifices* appear in the eleventh-century gradual F:Pm 384[128] and in the twelfth-century antiphoner F:Pn, lat. 17296 (fos. 332–3). More directly connected to Saint-Denis is another processional antiphon and likely Gallican survivor *Benedicat nos deus pater*,[129] an ornate chant which was sung during the procession after Terce on the feast of John the Baptist when it fell on Sunday, and after the morning Mass between Pentecost and Advent.[130] This piece is

[125] See the reconstruction of the Gallican Hymnal; ibid. 121–2.

[126] These hymns are discussed in Ch. 3.

[127] See the discussions of these and other supposed Gallican chants mentioned in this section in Huglo, 'Gallican', 113–25.

[128] Fos. 11–12 (Hesbert, *Graduel*, 22–3).

[129] On the style of the Ant. *Benedicat nos deus pater*, see Gastoué, 'Gallican' (1938), 147; Stäblein, *Schriftbild*, 156.

[130] 'After terce [on the feast of John Baptist] . . . if it shall be Sunday, the procession should be made in copes through the cloister. Let the cantor begin the Ant. *Benedicat nos deus* and the Resp. *Benedictus dominus deus* or any other one for the Trinity' ('Post terciam . . . si dominica fuerit fiat processio per claustrum in cappis, et incipiat cantor Ant. *Benedicat nos deus* et Resp. *Benedictus dominus deus* vel aliud quodlibet de trinitate'); F:Pm 526, fo. 137^{v}; F:Pn, lat. 976, fos. 99^{v}–100; F:Pan, L 863, No. 10, fos. 106^{r-v}. For the first Sunday after Pentecost, F:Pm 526 stipulates (fo. 84^{v}): 'After the morning Mass . . . a procession should be made, and the Ant. *Ego sum alpha* or *Benedicat nos deus pater* should be sung. These two antiphons are to be performed alternately at the beginning of the procession on all Sundays until Advent unless there occurs some feast on which it should be omitted' ('Post missam matutinalem . . . fiat processio et incipiatur Ant. *Ego sum* vel *Benedicat nos deus pater*. Hec due antiphone alternatim ad processionis principium in omnibus dominicis diebus dicantur usque ad adventum domini nisi aliqua festivitas contingat per qua dimittatur'). Whereas F:Pan, L 863, No. 10 often omits the textual incipits of chants, it does provide the rubrics, and these correspond regularly to the ones named in F:Pm 526 and F:Pn, lat. 976. It is, then, safe to assume that F:Pan, L 863, No. 10, which gives the directions 'post terciam fiat processio in cappis, primo per claustrum cantando Ant. et Resp. de trinitate', implies the Ant. *Benedicat nos deus pater* and the Resp. *Benedictus dominus deus*, as supplied by F:Pm 526 and F:Pn, lat. 976.

transmitted in the sections of F:Pm 384 and F:Pn, lat. 17296 which are devoted to processional pieces, and it also appears in the late eleventh-century antiphoner from Saint-Maur-des-Fossés F:Pn, lat. 12584, under a rubric for processional antiphons for Sundays (Ex. 4.1).[131]

Ex. 4.1. *Sandionysian Processional Antiphon* Benedicat nos deus pater
F:Pn, lat. 17296, fo. 340v

[131] F:Pm 384, fo. 14 (also Hesbert, *Graduel*, 27–8); F:Pn, lat. 17296, fo. 340v (Hesbert, *CAO*, ii, No. 148b); F:Pn, lat. 12584, fo. 383 (Hesbert, *CAO*, ii, Nos. 148b, 149b). At Saint-Maur the antiphon was sung for the feast of Saints Peter and Paul, as witnessed by the substitution of their names in the text.

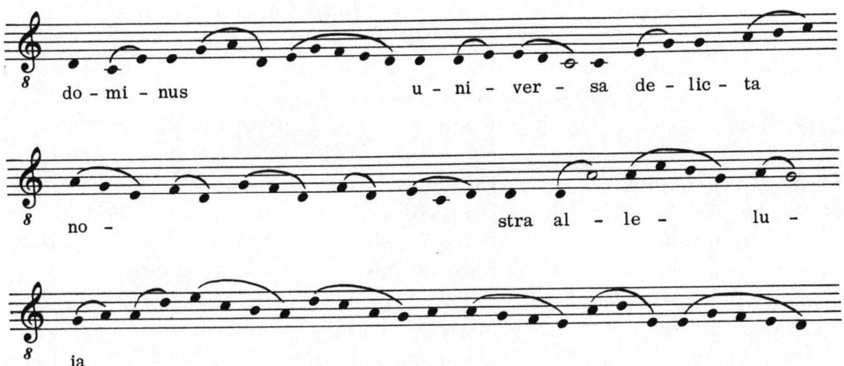

The Offices for Saint Denis and for the commemoration of Saint Paul in the antiphoner F:Pn, lat. 17296 include verses with the antiphons to the psalms at Matins,[132] and this is likewise assumed to be a Gallican trait.[133] The antiphon to the Magnificat at First Vespers on the feast of Saint Denis, *Insignes preconiis* (fo. 227), is considered Gallican because of an Ambrosian concordance in the feast of Saint Maurice. The Easter Ant. *Alleluia lapis revolutus est* (fo. 144^{v}) may likewise be Gallican because its initial *Alleluia* resembles the alleluiatic antiphons found in some Celtic fragments.[134] Likewise, the antiphon for the dedication of a church, *Pax eterna* (fo. 346), has a characteristically Gallican beginning. The Ant. *O crux benedicta quae* (fo. 155) for the Invention of the Cross similarly has a typical Gallican usage in its two final alleluias: a brief melisma on the syllable *-le-* instead of the first or last syllable *a-* or *-ia*.

Of all the Gallican antiphons in the late medieval liturgy of Saint-Denis, the most important are the antiphons which were chanted before the gospel at Mass (*antiphonae ante evangelium*). These pieces are preserved in F:Pn, lat. 17296 as antiphons to the Magnificat at Vespers, and they are named both in the individual Mass formularies of the ordinaries F:Pm 526; F:Pn, lat. 976; F:Pan, L 863, No. 10 and in the sequentiaries of the notated missals F:Pn, lat. 1107 and GB:Lva 1346–1891 (see Pl. 20).[135] These chants enhanced the 16 *annuale* and

[132] Fos. 227^{v}–232; Hesbert, *CAO*, ii, Nos. 114a, b.; fos. 181^{v}–182; Hesbert, *CAO*, ii, Nos. 102a, b.

[133] In addition to F:Pn, lat. 17296, all other Saint-Denis sources for the Office of the Saint contain this type of antiphon with verse for the psalms for Matins on the saint's feast-day: F:Pm 384, fo. 190^{v}; GB:Ob, Can. Lit. 192, fos. 468–70; F:Pn, Rés. 5209 (textual incipits in Hesbert, *CAO*, ii, No. 114, and full texts in vols. iii and iv). The Office of Saint Denis in the 10th-c. MS of Mont-Renaud (*PM*, xvi, fos. 105^{r-v}), a source previously thought to have issued from the abbey, does not include these verses.

[134] See Morin, 'Fragments', 344.

[135] See the discussion of the antiphons before the gospel at Saint-Denis, including a table showing the distribution of the chants in sources from the abbey and transcriptions of the music, in Walters [Robertson], 'Reconstruction', 205–38.

TABLE 4.4. *Antiphons before the Gospel at Saint-Denis*

Antiphon	Feast	Date
Crucem sanctam	Easter	
Ecce ego johannes	John	27 Dec.
Hodie celesti sponso	Epiphany	6 Jan.
Hodie completi sunt	Pentecost	
Hodie illuxit nobis	Peter and Paul	29 June
Hodie maria virgo	Assumption	15 Aug.
Homo erat in jerusalem	Purification	2 Feb.
Nativitas tua dei	Nativity of Mary	8 Sept.
O beate dyonisi	Dedication of Church	24 Feb.
	Invention of Denis	22 Apr.
	Natale of Denis	9 Oct.
	Octave of Denis	16 Oct.
O rex gloriae	Ascension	
O virgo virginum	Annunciation	25 Mar.
Salvator mundi salva nos	All Saints	1 Nov.
Salvator omnium deus	Anniversary of Dagobert	19 Jan.
	Anniversary of Philip Augustus	14 July
Verbum caro	Christmas	25 Dec.

semiannuale feasts and two important anniversaries in the monastery (Table 4.4). Among other features, the florid musical style of three of these antiphons makes them likely Gallican candidates: *Salvator omnium deus* for royal anniversaries, and its centonized relative *Hodie illuxit nobis*, a processional antiphon for Peter and Paul.[136] In addition to its elaborate melody, *Salvator omnium deus* ends with a typical choral response *Dicamus omnes miserere* from a Gallican *Preces*, the chant which followed the homily in the Gallican rite.[137] Like *Hodie illuxit*, *Salvator mundi salva nos* is both a processional piece and an antiphon for All Saints. Its litany-like text and its repetitious, triadic melody are rarely seen in Roman antiphons.[138] *O beate dyonisi* for feasts of Saint Denis and for the Dedication of the Church is probably revised from a Gallican version of the chant,[139] and the Easter Ant. *Crucem sanctam* is an apparent survivor of the Celtic repertory.[140] Other traces of antiphons before the gospel at Saint-Denis include *Deus omnipotens qui electis tuis*, an antiphon preserved in the Mass for Saint Denis in

[136] See the discussion of the antiphons before the gospel at Saint-Denis, including a table showing the distribution of the chants in sources from the abbey and transcriptions of the music, in Walters [Robertson], 'Reconstruction', 210–12.

[137] For examples of the *Dicamus omnes* in Gallican *Preces*, see De Clerck, *'Prière'*, 190–6.

[138] Walters [Robertson], 'Reconstruction', 213–15.

[139] Ibid. 217–22.

[140] Ibid. 215–17.

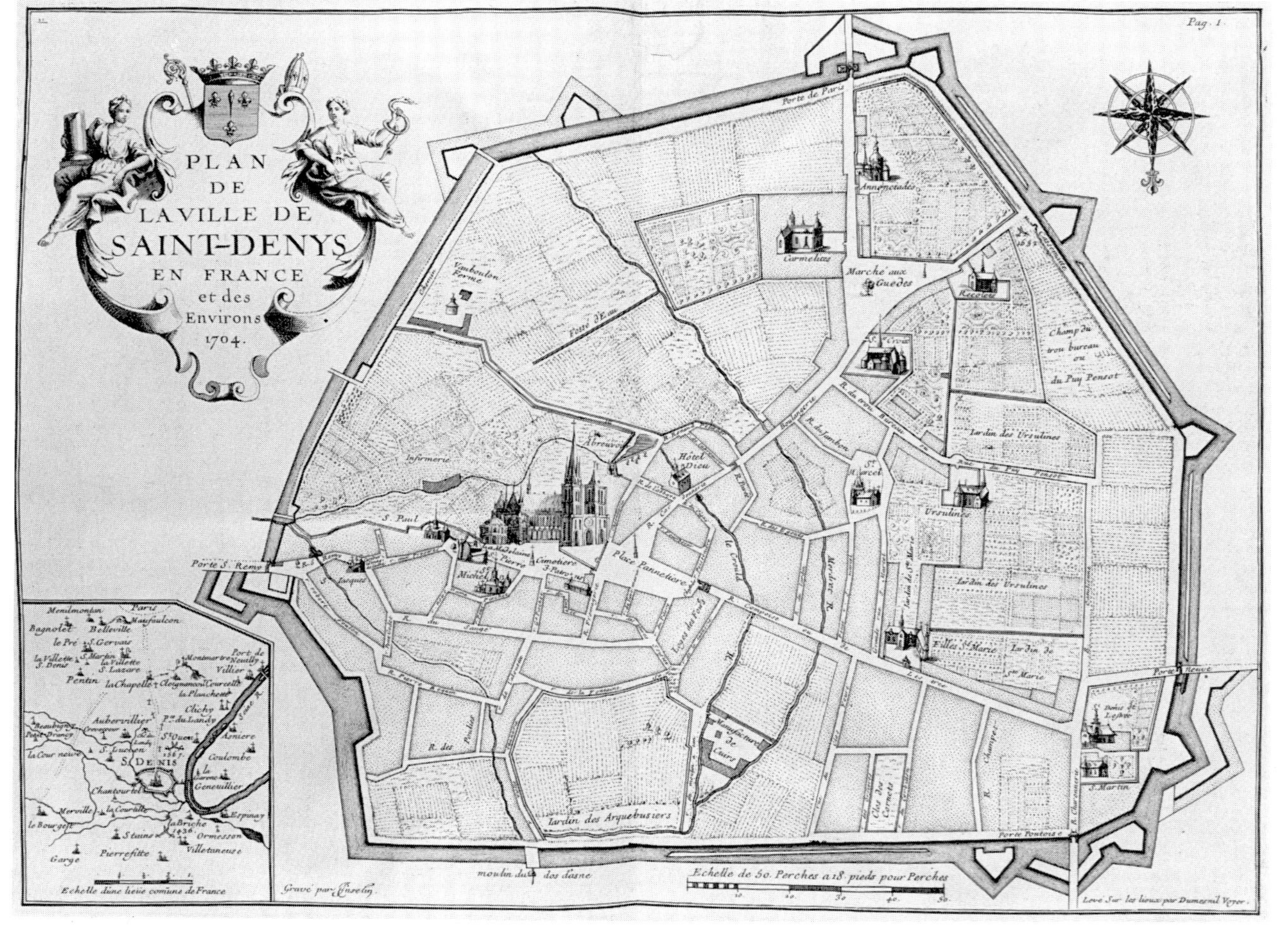

Plate 1. Plan of the City of St Denis in 1704 (from Félibien, *Histoire*).

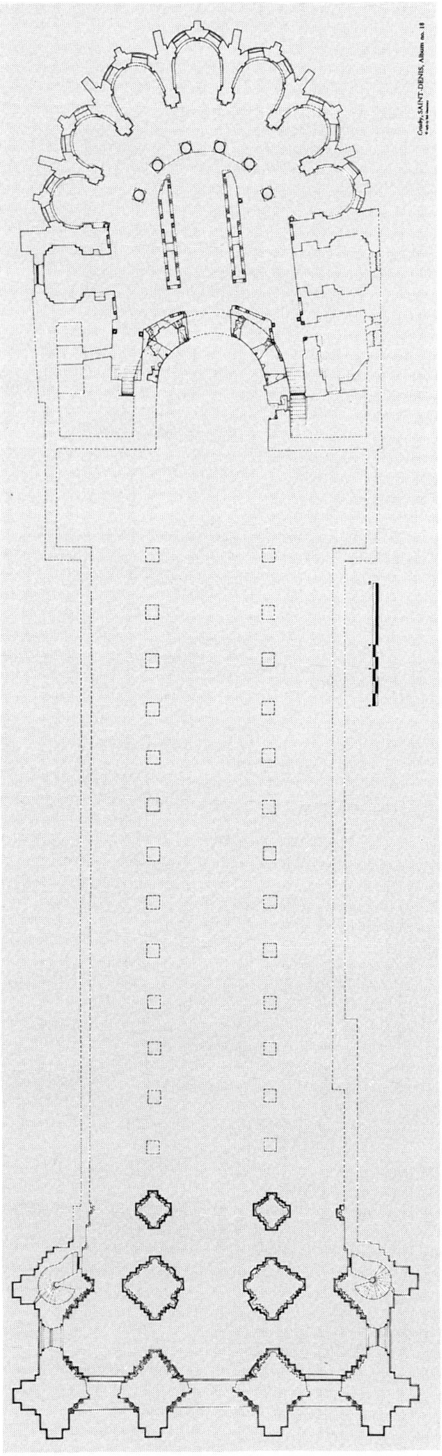

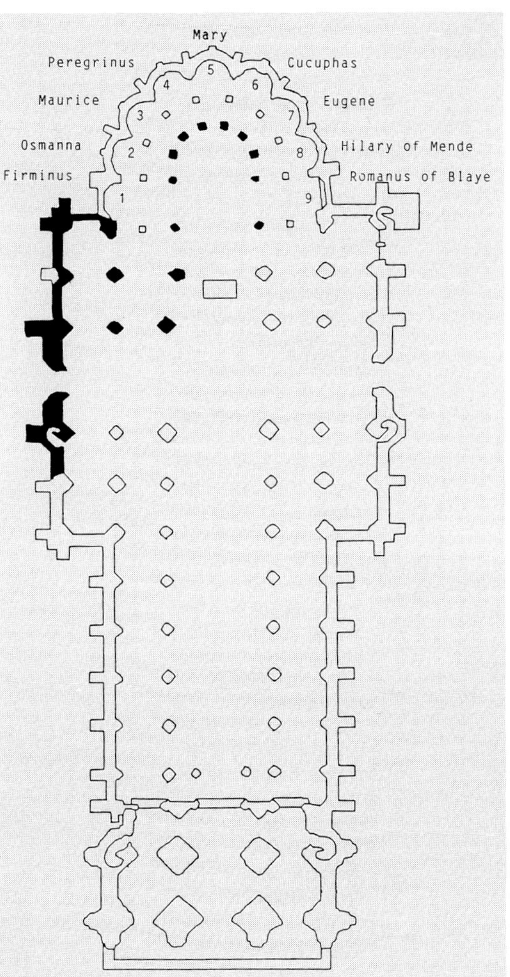

Plate 2 (*left*). Twelfth-Century Saint-Denis: reconstructed plan of the church showing Suger's campaign in the crypt, 1140–1144 (from Crosby, *Drawings*, No. 18; reproduced by permission of Yale University Press).

Plate 3 (*above*). Thirteenth-Century Saint-Denis: darkened areas showing the first phase of the reconstruction, begun in the 1230s (from Bruzelius, *St-Denis*, fig. 26; reproduced by permission of Yale University Press).

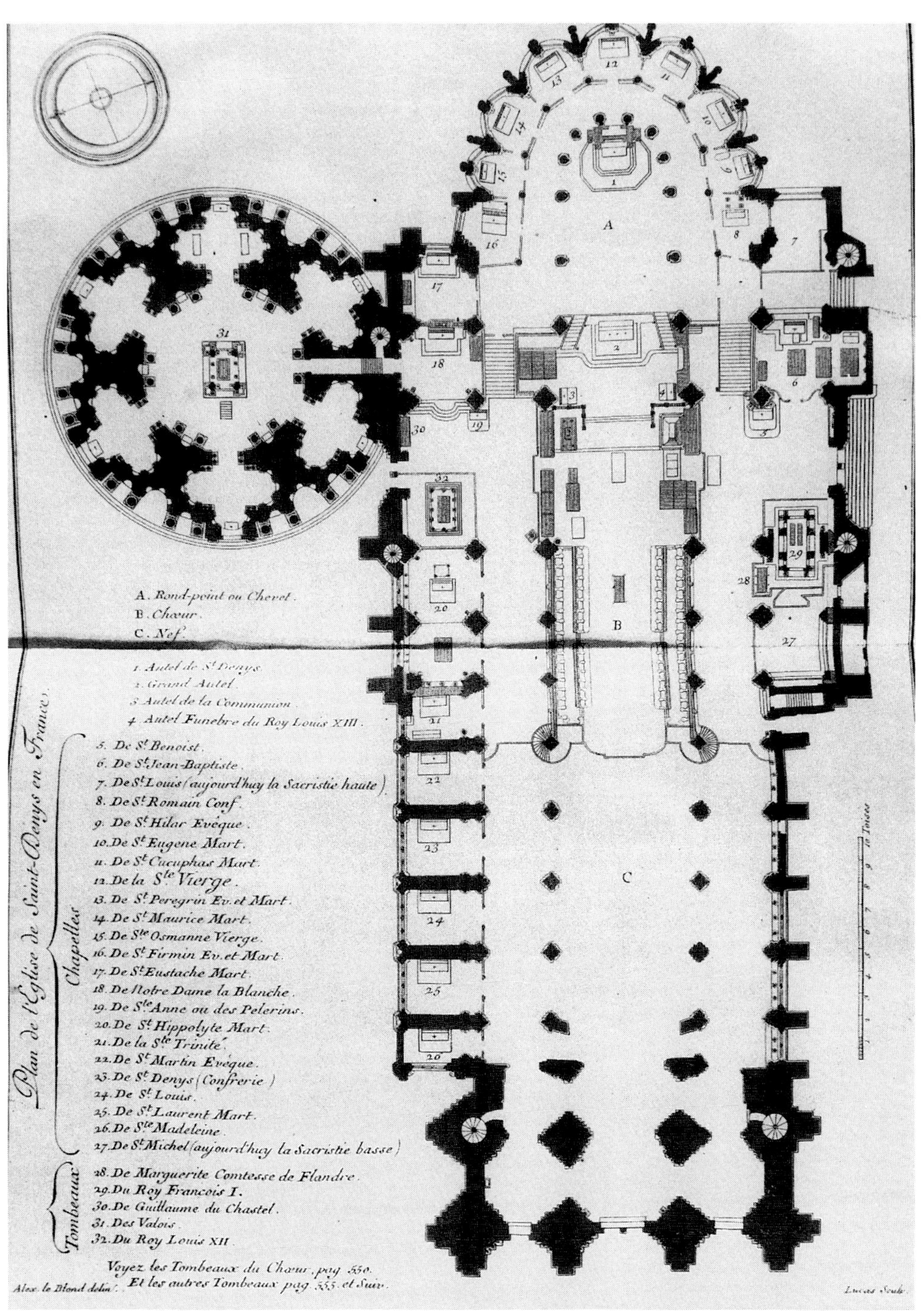

Plate 4. Early Eighteenth-Century Saint-Denis, showing the Fourteenth-Century Additions (from Félibien, *Histoire*, 529).

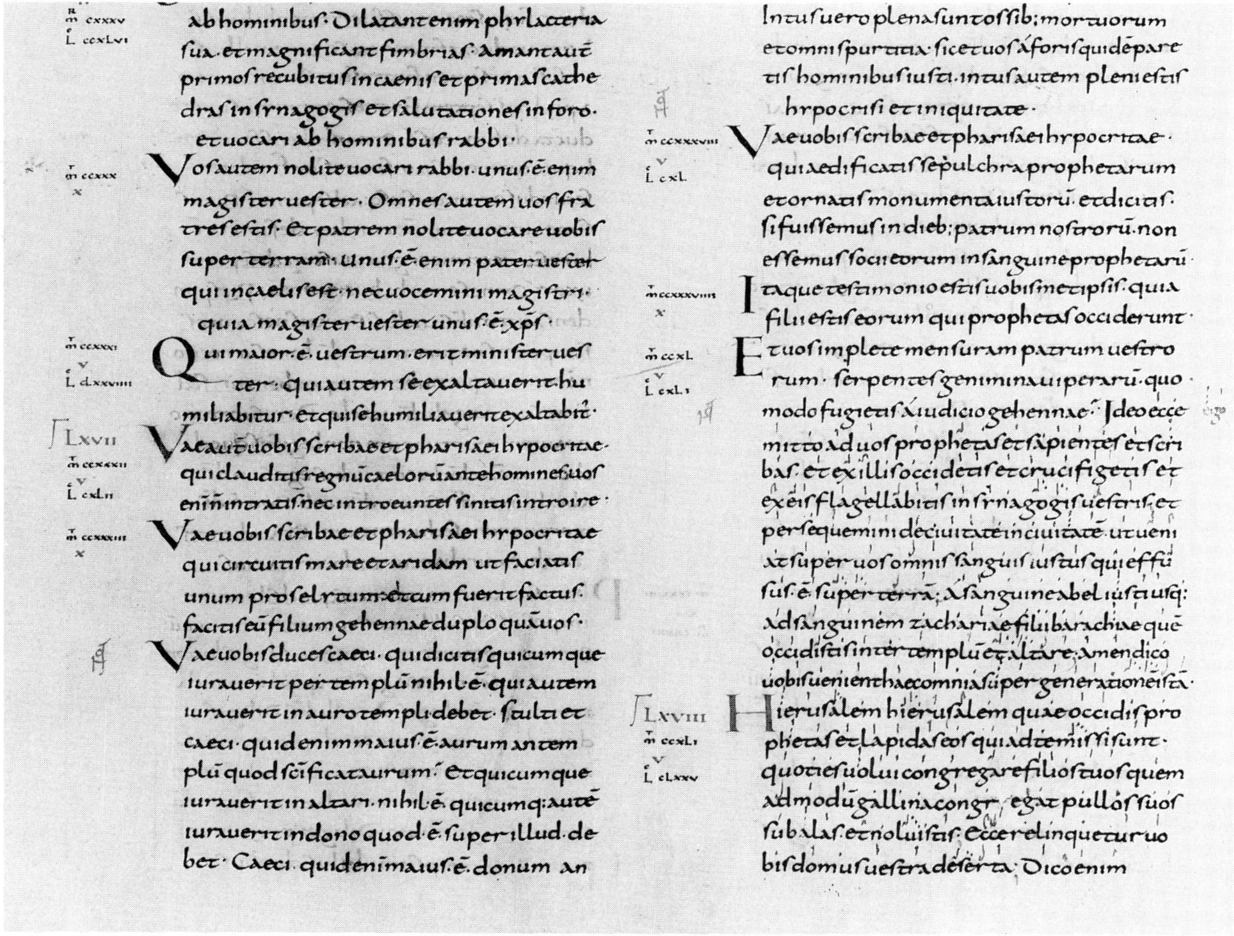

R m cxxxv e L ccxLvi

ab hominibus. Dilatant enim phylacteria
sua. et magnificant fimbrias. Amant aut
primos recubitus in caenis et primas cathe
dras in synagogis et salutationes in foro.
et uocari ab hominibus rabbi.

T m ccxxx x

Vos autem nolite uocari rabbi. unus e enim
magister uester. Omnes autem uos fra
tres estis. Et patrem nolite uocare uobis
super terram. unus e enim pater uester
qui in caelis est. nec uocemini magistri.
quia magister uester unus e xps.

T m ccxxxi e V L clxxviii

Qui maior e uestrum. erit minister ues
ter. Qui autem se exaltauerit hu
miliabitur. et qui se humiliauerit exaltabit.

Lxvii T m ccxxxii e V L cxLii

Vae autem uobis scribae et pharisaei hypocritae.
qui clauditis regnu caelorum ante homines uos
enim non intratis. nec introeuntes sinitis introire.

T m ccxxxiii x

Vae uobis scribae et pharisaei hypocritae
qui circuitis mare et aridam ut faciatis
unum proselytum. et cum fuerit factus.
facitis eu filium gehennae duplo quam uos.

Vae uobis duces caeci. qui dicitis quicumque
iurauerit per templu nihil e. qui autem
iurauerit in auro templi debet. Stulti et
caeci. quid enim maius e. aurum an tem
plu quod scificat aurum. Et quicumque
iurauerit in altari. nihil e. quicumq; autē
iurauerit in dono quod e super illud. de
bet. Caeci. quid enim maius e. donum an

Intus uero plena sunt ossib; mortuorum
et omni spurcitia. sic et uos a foris quidē pare
tis hominibus iusti. intus autem pleni estis
hypocrisi et iniquitate.

T m ccxxxviii e V L cxL

Vae uobis scribae et pharisaei hypocritae.
qui aedificatis sepulchra prophetarum
et ornatis monumenta iustoru. et dicitis.
si fuissemus in dieb; patrum nostroru. non
essemus socii eorum in sanguine propheta*ru*.

T m ccxxxviiii x

Itaque testimonio estis uobismet ipsis. quia
filii estis eorum qui prophetas occiderunt.

T m ccxL e V L cxLi

Et uos implete mensuram patrum uestro
rum. serpentes genimina uiperaru. quo
modo fugietis a iudicio gehennae. Ideo ecce
mitto ad uos prophetas et sapientes et scri
bas. et ex illis occidetis et crucifigetis et
ex eis flagellabitis in synagogis uestris. et
persequemini de ciuitate in ciuitate. ut ueni
at super uos omnis sanguis iustus qui effu
sus e super terra. a sanguine abel iusti usq;
ad sanguinem zachariae filii barachiae quē
occidistis inter templu et altare. Amen dico
uobis uenient haec omnia super generationem ista.

Lxviii T m ccxLi e V L clxxv

Hierusalem hierusalem quae occidis pro
phetas et lapidas eos qui ad te missi sunt.
quotiens uolui congregare filios tuos quem
admodu gallina congregat pullos suos
sub alas. et noluistis. Ecce relinquetur uo
bis domus uestra deserta. Dico enim

Plate 5. F:Pn, lat. 250, fo. 13^{v} (reproduced by permission of the Bibliothèque Nationale, Paris).

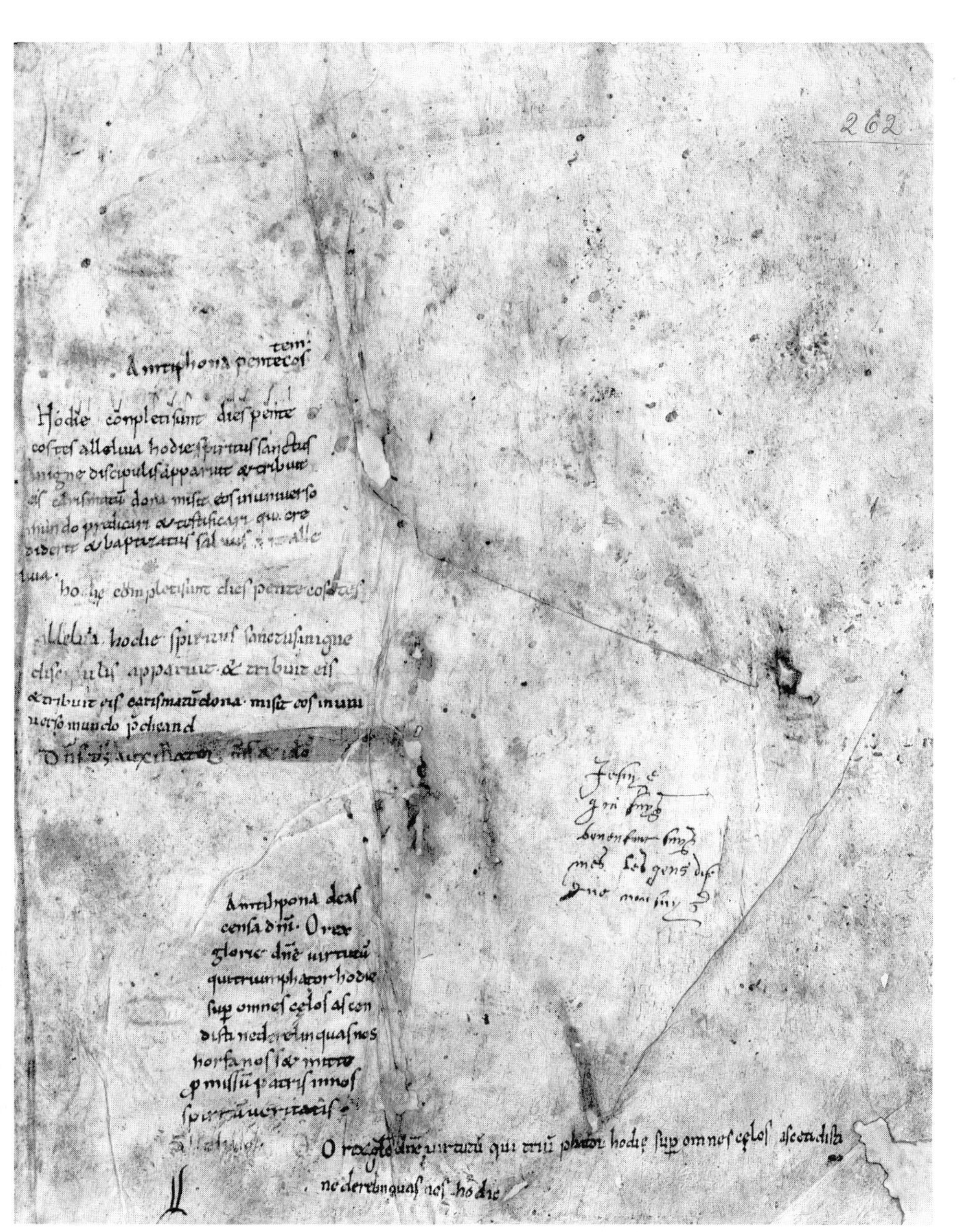

Plate 6. F:Pn, lat. 1647A, fo. 262 (reproduced by permission of the Bibliothèque Nationale, Paris).

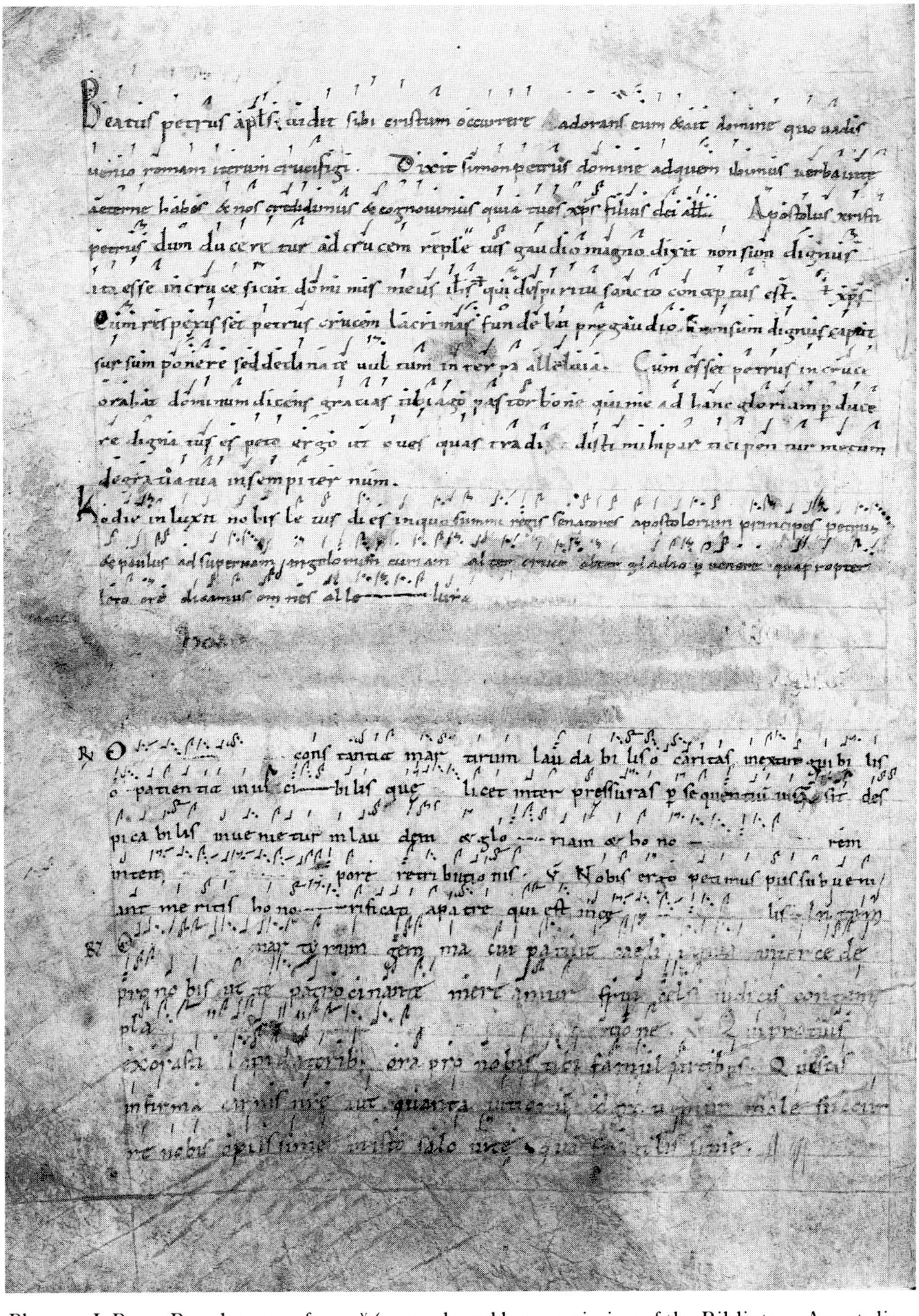

Plate 7. I:Rvat, Reg. lat. 255, fo. 79v (reproduced by permission of the Biblioteca Apostolica Vaticana, Rome).

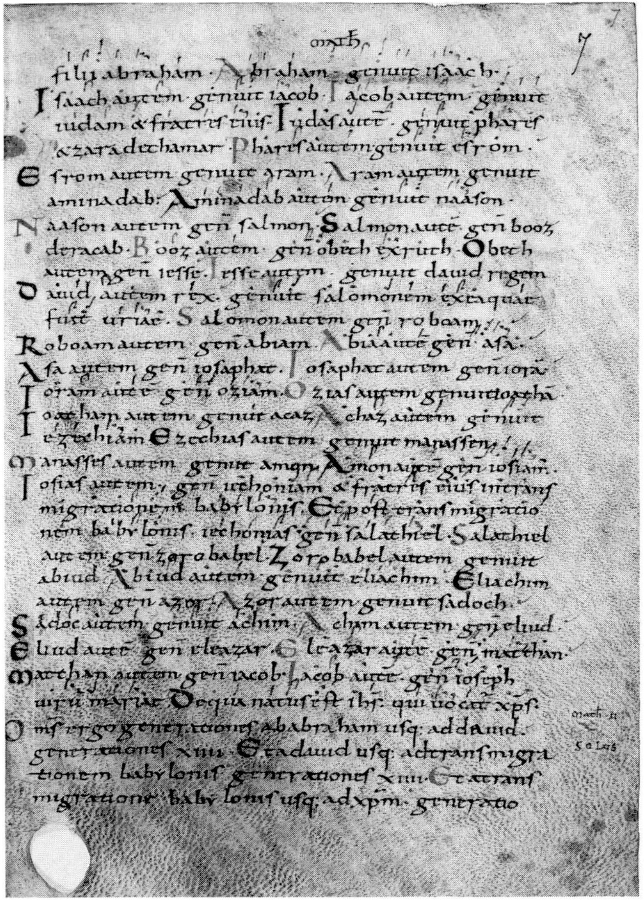

Plate 8. F:Pn, n.a.l. 305, fo. 7 (reproduced by permission of the Bibliothèque Nationale, Paris).

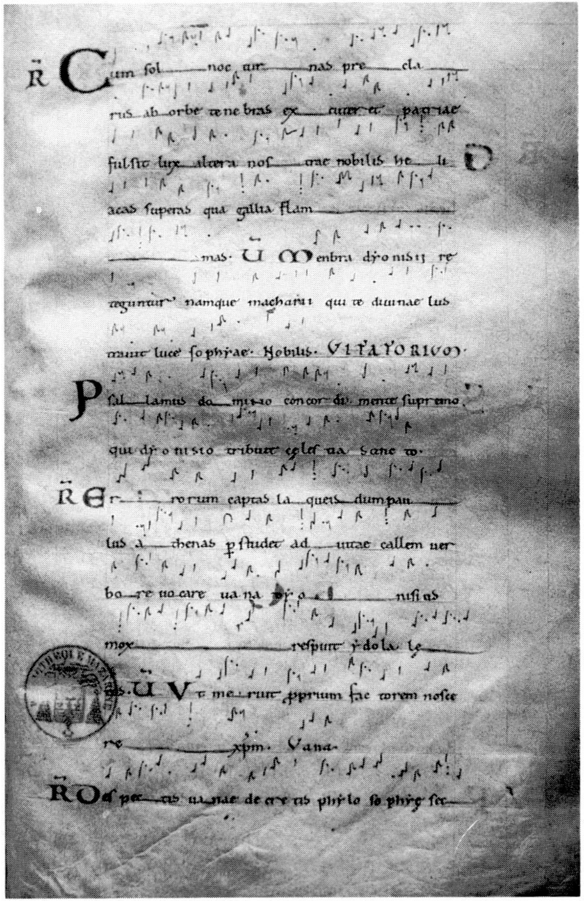

Plate 9. F:Pm 384, fo. 160 (reproduced by permission of the Bibliothèque Mazarine, Paris).

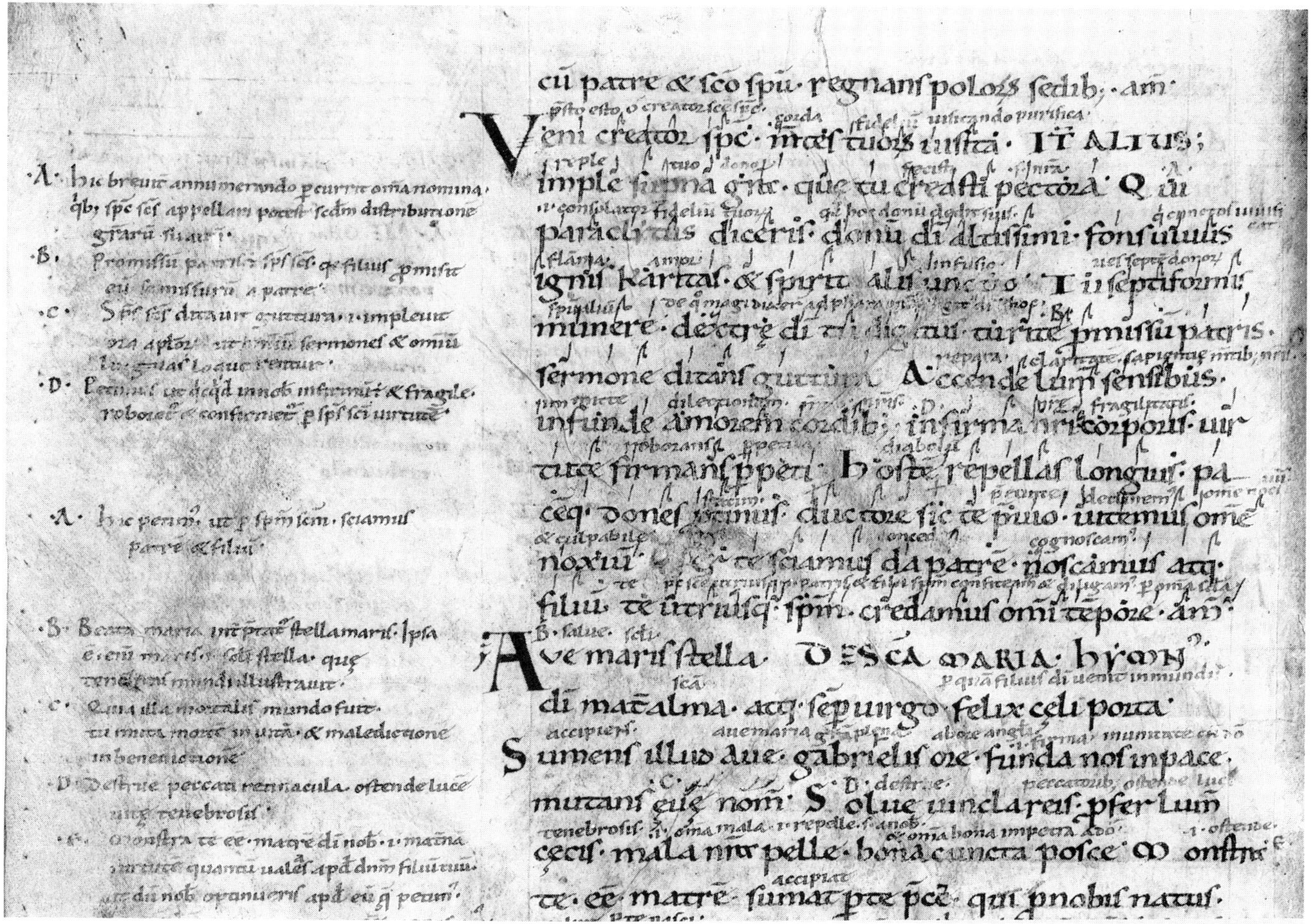

Plate 10. F:Pn, lat. 103, fo. 154v (reproduced by permission of the Bibliothèque Nationale, Paris).

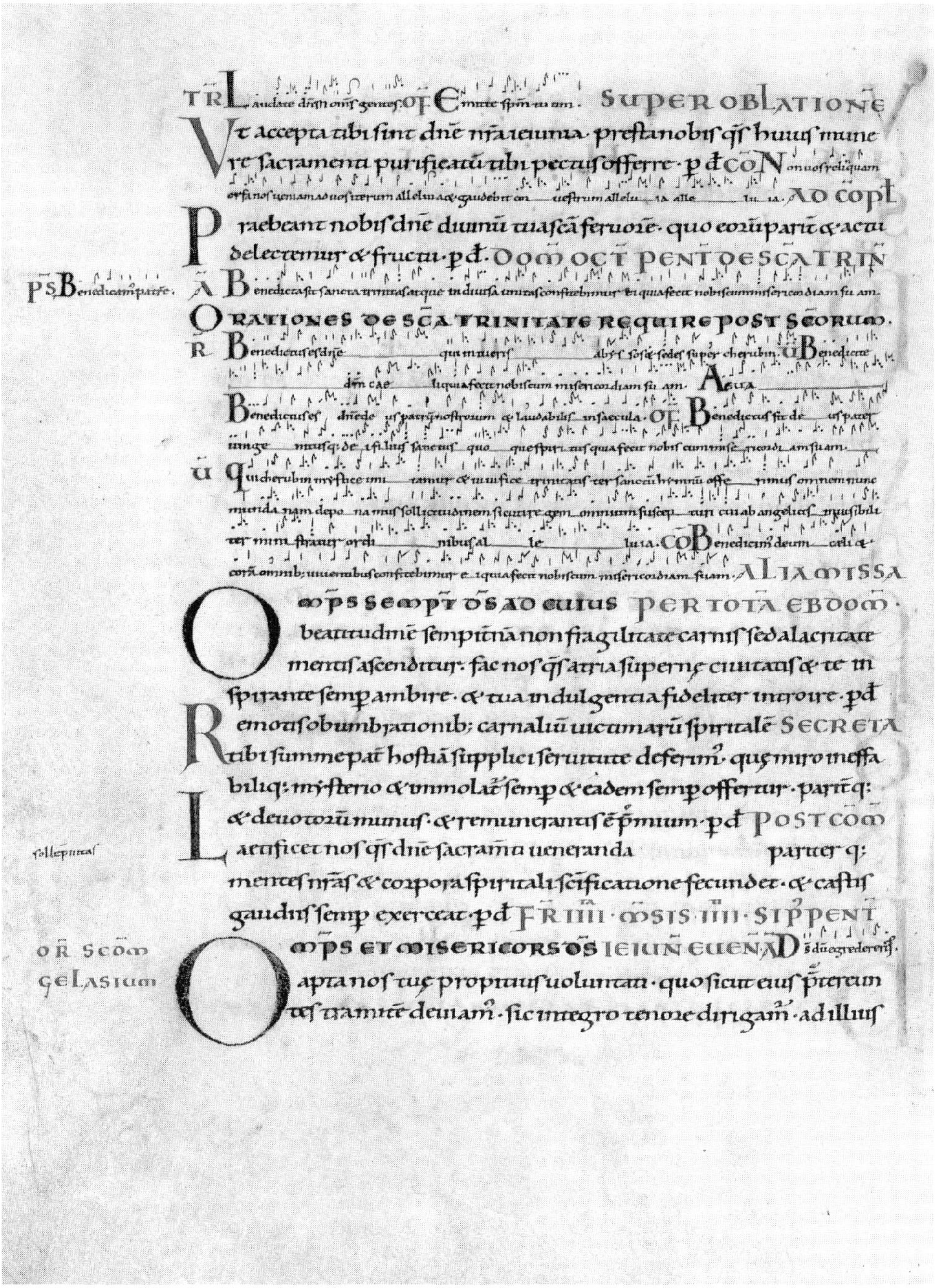

Plate 11. F: Pn, lat. 9436, fo. 58v (reproduced by permission of the Bibliothèque Nationale, Paris).

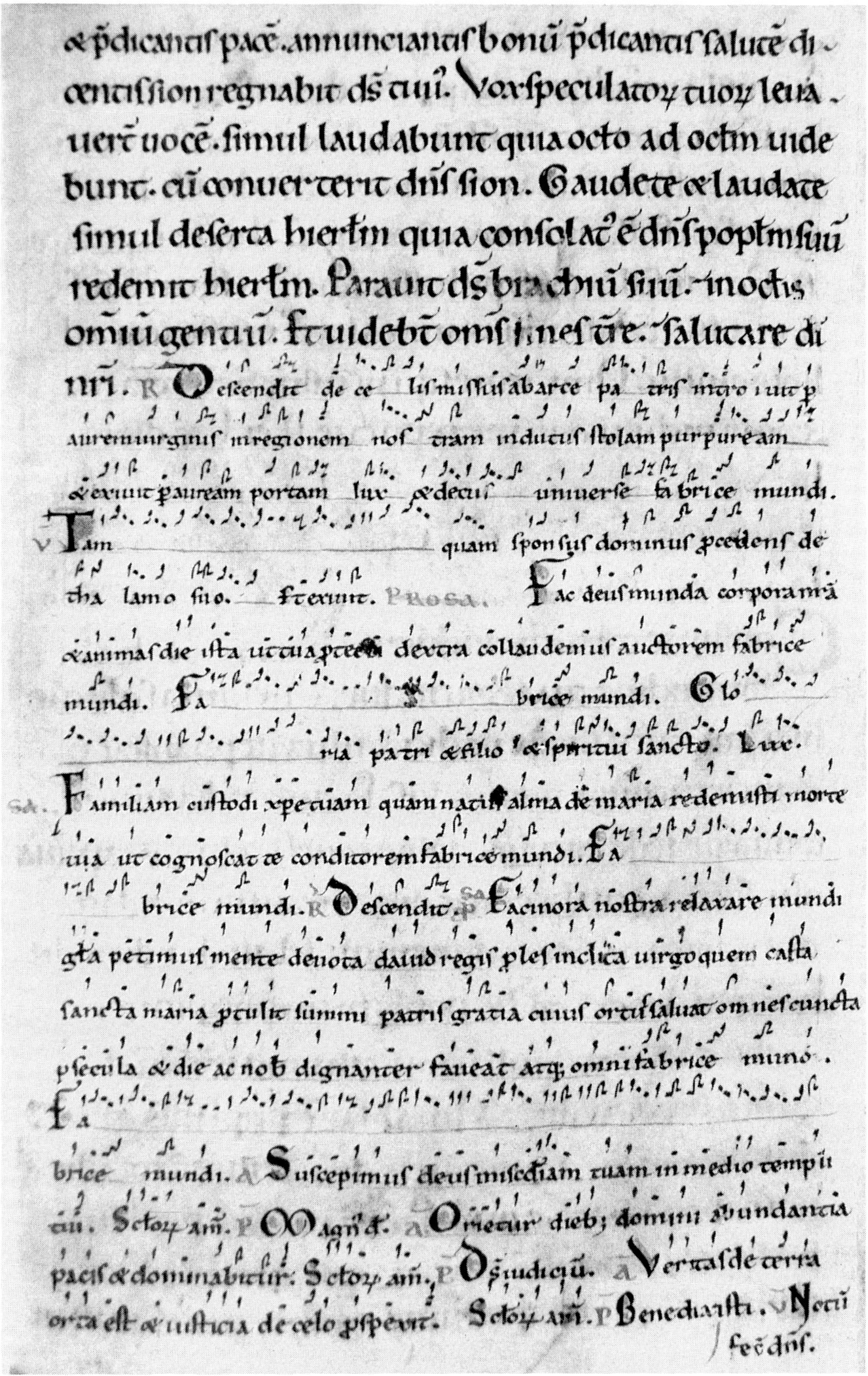

Plate 12. Vendôme, Bibliothèque Municipale, 17C, fo. 25v (reproduced by permission of the Bibliothèque Municipale, Vendôme).

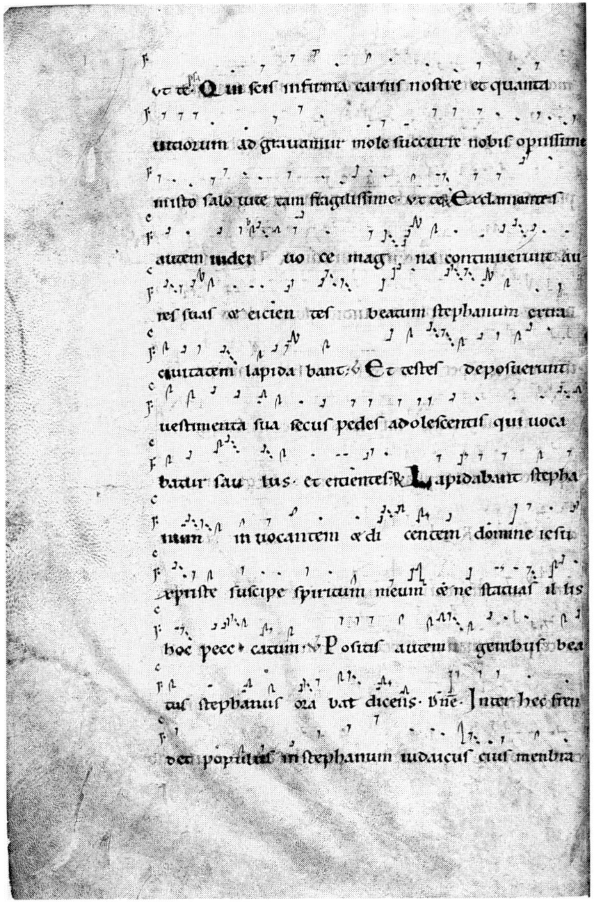

Plate 13. F:Pn, lat. 17296, fo. 29^{v} (reproduced by permission of the Bibliothèque Nationale, Paris).

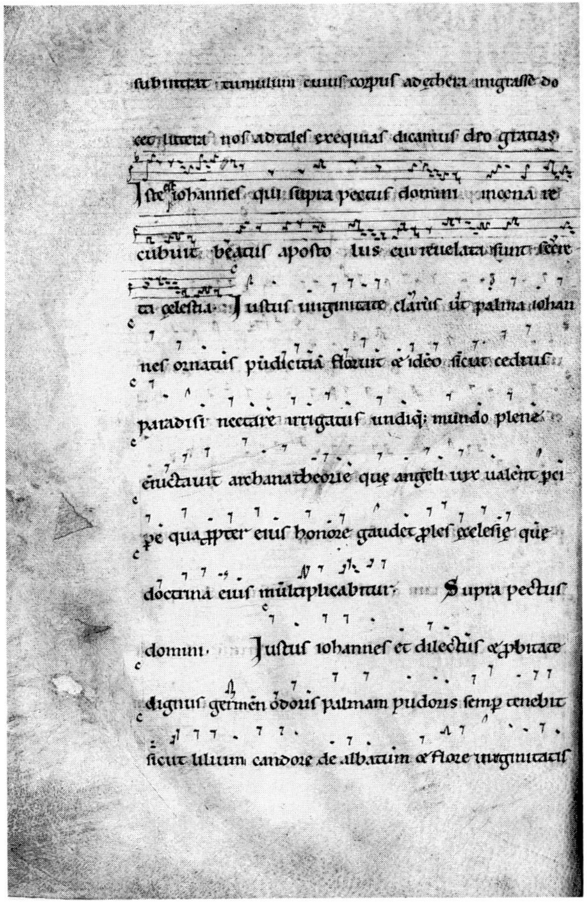

Plate 14. F:Pn, lat. 17296, fo. 37^{v} (reproduced by permission of the Bibliothèque Nationale, Paris).

Plate 15. F:Pm 414, fo. 245 (reproduced by permission of the Bibliothèque Mazarine, Paris).

Plate 16. F:Pm 414, fo. 245v (reproduced by permission of the Bibliothèque Mazarine, Paris).

Plate 17. F:Pn, lat. 1107, fo. 145v (reproduced by permission of the Bibliothèque Nationale, Paris).

Plate 18. F:Pn, lat. 1107, fo. 396ᵛ (reproduced by permission of the Bibliothèque Nationale, Paris).

Plate 19. F:Pn, lat. 10505, fo. 69v (reproduced by permission of the Bibliothèque Nationale, Paris).

Plate 20. GB:Lva 1346–1891, fo. 419 (reproduced by permission of the Victoria & Albert Museum Library, London).

F:Pm 384,[141] and *O rex glorie* for Ascension and *Hodie completi sunt* for Pentecost, two eleventh-century additions to the ninth-century manuscript from Saint-Denis F:Pn, lat. 1647A (Pl. 6).[142]

In addition to the *preces* response contained in *Salvator omnium deus*, a complete Gallican *Preces* survives in F:Pn, lat. 17296 in the Kyrie *Qui passurus* (Ex. 4.2).[143] This chant, performed after Lauds on the three days before Easter (*Triduum Sacrum*), looks like a troped Kyrie with its verses interpolated between phrases of the familiar Kyrie text.[144] The rubrics in Ex. 4.2 show that the Kyrie was performed in *alternatim* fashion between two soloists and the choir until the final phrase, which was sung by one soloist. The ordinaries add further: 'afterwards the Kyrie should be sung by two and the Ver. *Qui passurus* by another two, and the convent should respond *Domine miserere*.'[145]

Ex. 4.2. *Gallican Preces: Kyrie* Qui passurus
F:Pn, lat. 17296, fos. 129^{v}–130

[141] F:Pm 384, fos. 134^{v}–135 (Hesbert, *Graduel*, 234–5); see the discussion in Walters [Robertson], 'Reconstruction', 226–7.

[142] Ibid. 227–8.

[143] Huglo, 'Gallican', 122–3.

[144] For other sources of the Kyrie *Qui passurus*, see Symons *et al.*, *Regularis*, 108, n. 2.

[145] 'Post cantetur a duobus Kyrie, et ab *aliis duobus* Ver. *Qui passurus* et conventus respondeat *Domine miserere*'; F:Pm 526, fo. 53^{v} (also fos. 50^{v}, 55); F:Pn, lat. 976, fos. 24^{v}, 27^{v}.

Ky - ri - e - ley - son. V. Qui ex - pan - sis in
cru - ce ma - ni - bus trax - is - ti om - ni - a
ad te se - cu - la. V. Do - mi - ne mi - se - re - re.
Chri - ste - ley - son. V. Ag - no mi - ti ba - si - a cu - i
lu - pus de - dit ve - ne - no - sa. V. Do - mi - ne mi-se-re - re.
Chri - ste e - ley - son. V. Te qui vin - ci - ri vo - lu - i - sti
1.
nos qui a mor - tis vin - cu - lis e - ri - pui - sti.
V. Do - mi - ne chri - ste e - ley - son. V. Vi - ta in
lig - no mo - ri - tur in - fer - nus et mors lu - gens
Chorus
Duo cantores
spo - li - a - tur. Do - mi - ne mi - se - re - re. Ky - ri - e

[1] Syllable *vin-* not notated.

It is hardly surprising that liturgical and musical remnants of the Gallican rite persisted in the late medieval liturgy at Saint-Denis. The abbey, after all, was among the most ancient houses in France, with roots planted deep in Merovingian soil; it is understandable that ceremonial practices from the earlier period should have outlasted both the Carolingian and Cluniac reforms, the latter having little effect in any case. Some of these liturgical relics were not unique to Saint-Denis, of course, for many houses sang the old hymns, the Kyrie *Qui passurus*, and other chants mentioned above. But the number of probable Gallican vestiges at Saint-Denis is rather striking, and many of them stand in prominent places in the ritual. Moreover, the antiphons before the gospel with Gallican connections, the processional antiphons like *Benedicat nos deus pater* and *Deus omnipotens*, and the antiphons with verses certainly had special significance for the monks. In preserving these pieces, the community reminded themselves of a remote part of their past, a time which in fact coincided with the beginning of their alliance with the monarchy. Just as they 'resurrected' the memory of Dagobert (d. 639) in the twelfth century by instituting the anniversary service 'In natali Dagoberti regis', so the old Gallican elements in their liturgy—one of them a chant for Dagobert himself—symbolized the continuity of their associaton with the kings. Guarding their time-honoured traditions, as noted earlier, was as essential to the monks as appearing modern in some aspects of the architecture of the church.[146] Undoubtedly they hoped that the skilful combination of the old with the new in the ritual and architecture of the twelfth and thirteenth centuries would keep their venerability intact.

Music, Ceremony and Stained Glass

One of the most beautiful visual features of Saint-Denis is the medieval stained glass. Unfortunately, the entire work of the thirteenth century

[146] For further discussion, see Walters [Robertson], 'Reconstruction', 224–6, 231.

was dispersed or destroyed during the French Revolution, and only a portion of the original glass from the twelfth century was ever replaced in the church.[147] Of the magnificently stained windows that shone throughout the building at one time, perhaps the most arresting were those of the radiating chapels of the chevet. Witnesses from the seventeenth to the nineteenth centuries report that the chapel of Saint Firminus, dedicated in 1218 (see Table 4.1), once contained glass which depicted the history of his martyrdom, a scene that may well date from the thirteenth century.[148] The same is true of the chapel of Maurice, which included events from Maurice's life in one window and from the Martyrdom of the Holy Innocents, a subdedicatee of this chapel, in the other.[149] While this thirteenth-century glass is irrecoverable, some of Suger's twelfth-century windows have survived, and it is clear that many of these windows stood in the thirteenth-century church as well. Two panels from the time of Suger are particularly relevant to this section: a scene from the martyrdom of Saint Vincent, and portions of a window from the life of Saint Benedict.

Because of the vicissitudes suffered by the stained glass of Saint-Denis after the Middle Ages, the connection of certain fragmentary pieces with the abbey, among them the Vincent and Benedict panels, has been difficult to establish. A medallion from a window for Vincent, first documented at Saint-Denis only in the nineteenth century, was removed from the abbey and is now kept in the Dépôt des Monuments Historiques of the Château de Champs-sur-Marne.[150] Since no chapel was dedicated to Vincent during the Middle Ages, the appropriateness of such a scene in the church was difficult to establish, and authors earlier in this century suggested that the Vincent panel came from Saint-Germain-des-Prés, and not Saint-Denis.[151] Erwin Panofsky, however, argued convincingly for Sandionysian provenance by pointing out both that the abbey possessed a relic of Saint Vincent and that the figure of Saint Vincent in the panel closely resembles some of the stone sculpture of the west façade of the church.[152] To date, the medieval location of the window has never been established, although Panofsky and Grodecki conjecture that the medallion may have stood in one of the windows in the crypt.[153]

[147] See the bibliog on the 12th-c. stained glass at Saint-Denis in Ch. 1, n. 203.

[148] Grodecki, *Vitraux*, 30, 33, 36, 41, 115, 125.

[149] Ibid. 30–1, 103, 120, 146, 148.

[150] Ibid. 106–7, pl. xiii, and *passim*; Crosby *et al. Abbey*, 92–3.

[151] Lafond, 'Decoration', 154.

[152] Panofsky, *Suger*, 205–6.

[153] Ibid. 206; Grodecki, *Vitraux*, 107. Grodecki admits that his theory of the location of this window is little more than a guess, based on the fact that Abbot Suger records that there was stained glass in the crypt as well as in the upper level.

New liturgical evidence from the thirteenth century places the Vincent window at Saint-Denis with greater assurance, and also suggests a plausible location for the glass. First of all, the text of the proper Office for Saint Vincent in the twelfth-century antiphoner F:Pn, lat. 17296 describes in words the passion which the glass pictures.[154] This fact in itself is not conclusive, of course, for Vincent was widely honoured in the West as one of the standard saints of the Gregorian roster. His Office might have been found in any number of churches,[155] and consequently the stained glass would be suitable for many different places.

The unusual aspect of the cult of Vincent at Saint-Denis is the monks' predilection not only for the liturgy but also for the music from this service. The thirteenth-century missal F:Pn, lat. 1107 contains collections of melodies for the Benedicamus Domino and for the Ite Missa Est. Music for these ornate versicles comes from several classes of chant, but the majority of tunes are taken from Office responsories or their verses, as shown in Chapter 3. The Office of Saint Vincent contributes four of the 26 melodies, almost a sixth of the total repertory of Benedicamus at Saint-Denis: *Alacriter*, *Occumbere*, *Vernabantur*, and *Quorum vallatus*.[156] Music for Saint Vincent in fact accounts for twice as many melodies as any other Office in the liturgy of the abbey, including the Office for Saint Denis himself, from which only two Benedicamus melodies (*Angelorum* and *Preciosus*) were fashioned. The thirteenth-century ordinaries from Saint-Denis show that these Benedicamus tunes were sung throughout the feast-day of Saint Vincent (22 January). *Vernabantur* was chanted at the end of First Vespers, *Quorum vallatus* at the end of Lauds, and *Alacriter* at the end of Second Vespers.[157] The Ite Missa Est was likewise sung at Saint-Denis on the melismas *Quorum vallatus* and *Vernabantur*.[158] Clearly, the number of melodies in the Sandionysian liturgy from the music for Saint Vincent is too great to be dismissed as coincidence—the liturgists of the abbey must have placed special musical emphasis on Saint Vincent to pay homage to the precious relic they often carried in procession. The stained glass commemorating the martyrdom of this saint likewise complements the musico-liturgical glorification of his deeds.

[154] Fos. 60–5; Hesbert, *CAO*, ii, No. 46a.

[155] For an overview of the dissemination of this Office, see ibid.

[156] See Table 3.10, and Robertson, '*Benedicamus*', 43, and ex. 2, Nos. 8, 18, 19, 20.

[157] *Quorum vallatus* was likewise sung as the closing V. *Requiescant in pace* for Matins and Lauds of the Office for the Dead on the anniversaries of Charles the Bald, Robert II, Abbot Suger, and Philip Augustus; ibid. 43–4, and table 2.

[158] Although the ordinaries give no information about the liturgical placement of these Ites, they were certainly appropriate to Vincent's Mass and no doubt were used in this service.

One liturgical source from the thirteenth century even suggests where the Vincent panel may originally have been situated. When it was first documented in the nineteenth century, the Vincent medallion stood in the chapel which in the thirteenth century had been dedicated to Saint Maurice (See Pl. 3, chapel No. 3). Because there is no reason to associate Saint Vincent with Saint Maurice, a more convincing position for the glass in the thirteenth-century church must be found. The record of consecrations of chapels in the ordinary F:Pn, lat. 976 offers the most plausible answer (see Table 4.1). The first chapel to the south of the oratory for the Virgin, dedicated to Saint Cucuphas (Pl. 3, chapel No. 6), includes Saint Vincent as a secondary dedicatee. Since Vincent had a viable place in Cucuphas' chapel, it is entirely possible that one of the two windows in this oratory contained the Vincent panel, while the other held the scenes from Cucuphas' life.[159] By the fourteenth century, the monks who carried out both Vespers and High Mass at this very altar[160] would have chanted both the Benedicamus Domino and Ite Missa Est melodies from the music for Saint Vincent. If indeed the Vincent glass was located here, they had the added benefit of something relevant to gaze at while they sang.

The history of the Benedict panel is likewise unravelled in part through the study of liturgical sources from Saint-Denis. Unlike the Vincent medallion, the remnants of the Benedict window consist of more than a single fragment: the panel now kept in the Cluny Museum in Paris, and other pieces which are scattered in several collections.[161] No history of Saint-Denis mentions this window, and its presence in the abbey is confirmed only by the survival of drawings of parts of the panel made on location in the church by eighteenth- and nineteenth-century artists. Once again, certain peculiarities of the liturgy make this scene from the life of the founding father of all Benedictines particularly suitable for the abbey. We saw in Chapter 2 that the Office for the feast of Saint Benedict (21 March) has an unusual format in the Saint-Denis antiphoners F:Pm 384 and F:Pn, lat. 17296, and this disposition is also attested in the thirteenth-century ordinaries F:Pm 526 and F:Pn, lat. 976. The Office in F:Pn, lat. 17296 is introduced by the customary type of rubric, *In natale sancti Benedicti*, and the service contains the

[159] The medieval composition of the windows in this chapel is not known, although Grodecki suggests that a window illustrating the Passion of Christ may have stood there. He bases this estimation on the fact that the Passion glass should have stood in a chapel located in a place of central importance in the chevet, but he finds no evidence to support his hypothesis; see Grodecki, *Vitraux*, 105; also 121, 52, 53, 54, 64, 95, 103, 120, 129, 131, 146, 148.

[160] On the custom of performing Vespers and High Mass at the altar of saints whose relics were kept in the abbey, see p. 259 above.

[161] See Grodecki, *Vitraux*, 108–14, pl. xiv, and *passim*; Crosby *et al.*, *Abbey*, 88–9, and frontispiece.

normal number of chants for First Vespers, Matins, Lauds, and Second Vespers. Next should follow the feast of the Annunciation of Mary (25 March), but instead there is a second, brief Office for Benedict, entitled *In transitu sancti benedicti*. This service consists of four responsories for Matins and material for Lauds and Second Vespers. This second Office at first seems redundant, since the *transitus* or 'passing over' of the saint is really the same as the *natale* or 'birth into heaven', that is, the day of his death. But the thirteenth-century ordinaries F:Pm 526 and F:Pn, lat. 976 clear up the mystery of the adjacent Offices by showing that the four Matins responsories of the *transitus* service were actually used as the last four responsories of the *natale*, whereas the final four responsories of the *natale* service were used for the feast of the Translation of Saint Benedict (11 July).

The presence of the *transitus* rubric for Saint Benedict may well be peculiar to Saint-Denis.[162] The texts of this Office, compiled from other services for Benedict, deal with the events of his passage from this life, scenes which are likewise depicted in the Benedict panel. The last responsory is similar to the portrayal in the stained glass:

Preciosus dei confessor domini benedictus recto orientis tramite cum magno splendoris decore in celum ferebatur assistensque vir clarus ait duobus fratribus hac via dilectus domini celum benedictus ascendit.[163]

[Benedict, the precious confessor of the Lord God, was carried into heaven by the straight pathway with great glory of rising splendour, while a shining man stood by and said to the two monks:[164] 'By this road Benedict, beloved of the Lord, ascends to heaven.']

The final words are remarkably close to those in the glass, which Grodecki transcribes as: 'Hec est via qua dilectus domino beatus frater Benedictus celum ascendet' ('This is the way by which the blessed brother Benedict, beloved of the Lord, ascends into heaven').[165] Not only are these two texts similar, the music for the words 'benedictus ascendit' from the responsory provided the thirteenth-century monks of Saint-Denis with another florid melody for a Benedicamus Domino, which they chanted at the ends of First and Second Vespers on Benedict's feast-day.[166]

Another connection between the Benedict window and the thirteenth-century ceremony of the abbey is found in the itineraries of the simplest processions for saints at Saint-Denis. The three feasts for Benedict (see Table 4.2) have processions following First Vespers and Lauds, and in

162 See Hesbert, *CAO*, vol. ii, pp. xi–xii, and No. 505a.

163 F:Pn, lat. 17296, fo. 83.

164 These 2 monks are depicted in the panel looking upward to receive the words of the 'shining man'.

165 *Vitraux*, 109.

166 See Robertson, '*Benedicamus*', ex. 2, No. 22.

carrying them out, the monks proceeded from the choir to the chapel of Hilary of Mende in the chevet (Pl. 3, No. 8). In his study of the window, Grodecki has already shown that the sizes of the two apertures in Hilary's chapel were appropriate for the Benedict window.[167] By adding liturgical information to the results of Grodecki's measurements, we can speculate that the Benedict panel, along with the remaining glass, originally stood in a window of this *oratorium* where Benedict both served as a secondary dedicatee and was honoured with processions (see Table 4.2).[168]

Sequences for Saints with Relics in the Church

In addition to the stained-glass windows, the relics at the altars in the chevet also inspired the creation of special texts and music for sequences at Saint-Denis. By and large the monks of Saint-Denis drew their sequences from the repertory which circulated in Paris in the twelfth and thirteenth centuries, as noted in Chapter 3. By the thirteenth century, however, they had apparently succumbed to the urge to create new proses for a few of their special patrons. An extraordinary number of eleven sequences for nine saints whose relics Saint-Denis possessed were most likely written in the abbey sometime before the mid-fourteenth century (Table 4.5).[169] It is not surprising that such creativity should have occurred at a time when the reconstruction of the church between 1231 and 1281 prompted a general enhancement of the level of cult in the Divine Service. Indeed, most of these compositions are probably related to an important tradition at Saint-Denis in the thirteenth and fourteenth centuries: the singing of High Mass at the

[167] *Vitraux*, 112–14.

[168] Although Grodecki proposes the chapel of Hilary of Mende as a possible location for the Benedict window, he opts in the end for the location of the glass in the 2 windows of the Benedict chapel in the crypt (ibid. 114; see also Caviness, 'Glass', 259–60). The use of this chapel for processions and services on the feasts of Benedict, however, was limited to the celebration of morning Mass there probably only in the 1230s, i.e. at the time that the ordinary F:Pm 526 was copied (see Table 4.2). Since, on the other hand, the monks processed to the chapel of Hilary of Mende in the upper level no fewer than 6 times on Benedict's 3 feasts (Table 4.2), it is perhaps more likely that the glass stood in the Hilary window as an inspiration to those who took part in these ceremonies.

[169] The critical apparatus in *AH*, which provides concordances for each of the texts in Table 4.5, indicates that the poems for all these sequences were edited only from the Saint-Denis sequentiaries F:Pn, lat. 1107 or GB:Lva 1346–1891, except *Salve pater dyonisi*, which appears first in F:Pn, lat. 1107 and then in later, non-Dionysian sources from the 15th and 16th cs. The more extensive catalogue of sequences currently being completed by Nancy Van Deusen for the late Gordon Anderson will no doubt be useful in determining whether concordances exist for these compositions in books not used in *AH*. To date, Van Deusen informs me that she has not discovered these sequences in sources outside Saint-Denis. Another indication that the 11 sequences in Table 4.5 were composed in the 13th c. is that none of them is named in F:Pm 526, the earliest witness of the sequence repertory at Saint-Denis (Table 3.9).

altar of the saint whose day it was. Some of the oratories in the chevet and elsewhere in the church were dedicated to the saints whose proper sequences are named in Table 4.5, and the performance of sequences for the Masses that were sung in these locations must have been an attractive addition to these festivals. To be sure, the unassigned Marian sequences in F:Pn, lat. 1107 and GB:Lva 1346–1891 (Table 3.9) may be related in function to the proses just described, since two altars in the chevet, one on the choir-level and one in the crypt, were consecrated to the Virgin. These chants may have served during the Saturday Office for Mary, which might well have taken place in the chevet, although the ordinaries from Saint-Denis neither confirm nor deny the use of these chapels for this Office. In addition, the daily Lady Mass, performed from the late fourteenth century on in the chapel of Notre Dame *La Blanche* in the north transept (see Pl. 4), may have provided another opportunity for the use of the Marian sequences.

Although the poetry of the sequences in Table 4.5 was apparently written at Saint-Denis to honour these specially venerated martyrs and confessors, almost none of the melodies was original. Instead, the tunes were borrowed and adapted from pre-existing pieces, many of them for the Virgin. *Marie preconio* heads a family[170] of sequences which included *Christo regi glorie* for Hilary of Poitiers and *Doctorem egregium* for Saint Denis. Similarly, *Ave maris stella* lends its melody to three pieces: *Gaude plebs* for Pergrinus, *Vocis cum camena* for Firminus, and *Ave lux insignis* for the Eleven Thousand Virgins. *Ave virgo virginum/Ave lumen luminum/Ave stella previa* was imitated in *Plebs fidelis* for Osmanna and in *Ave pater gallie* (Pl. 17) for Saint Denis. This process of composing sequences through combining new texts with older music was a common means of creating fresh works for the myriad of local saints honoured with pieces in this genre in the late Middle Ages.[171]

In the three sequences for Saint Denis (*Salve pater dyonisi*, *Ave pater gallie*, and *Doctorem egregium*), moreover, the monks seized the opportunity to promulgate their Areopagitist tendencies. The wording of the three texts is similar, and they all contain references both to the Athenian Dionysius the Areopagite and, in *Salve pater*, to the philosophy of Pseudo-Dionysius.[172] The latter sequence describes Saint Denis as 'mirror and summit of the wise of Greece' (Ex. 4.3, st. 2). The text harks back frequently to the writings of the mystic in mentions of

[170] Fassler defines 'family' as a grouping that exists 'when two or more sequences are set to the same melody'; 'Adam', 251, n. 57.

[171] For discussions of this procedure, see the studies cited in n. 000 above; and Stevens, *Words*, 105–6.

[172] See the text and translation of *Salve pater* below. *Ave pater* and *Doctorem egregium* are edited in *AH*, xlii. 193.

TABLE 4.5. *Sequences Unique to the Saint-Denis Sources*

Sequence	Feast		N2	G	V	*AH*	*RH*	Source of melody
Ave lux insignis	21 Oct.	11,000 Virgins[a]	385		420v	9:261	1867	*Ave maris stella* *AH* 9:72
Ave pater gallie	10 Oct.	Denis[a,b] (day 2 after)		88 [92]	419	42:193	35651	*Ave virgo virginum* *AH* 54:432
Christo regi glorie	13 Jan.	Hilary of Poitiers[a]			389	42:219	36166	*Marie preconio* *AH* 54:391
Doctorem egregium	11 Oct.	Dens[a,b] (day 3 after)			419v	42:193	36788	*Marie preconio* *AH* 54:391
Gaude plebs Autrica	16 May	Peregrinus[a,b]	391v		396	44:239	6900	*Ave maris stella* *AH* 9:72
Laudemus omnes dominum in sanctis gloriosum	13 Aug.	Hippolytus[a,b]			403v	42:220	38604	*Epiphaniam domino* *AH* 7:53, 53:47
Letabundus exultet fidelis coetus	25 July	Cucuphas[a,b]			401	42:189	38532	*Letabundus exultet fidelis chorus* *AH* 54:5
Plebs fidelis jubila	9 Sept.	Osmanna[a,b]	377		414v	8:196	15086	*Ave virgo virginum* *AH* 54:432
Psallat cum tripudio	15 Nov.	Eugene[a,b]	388		424	9:151	15708	*Plebs devota* *AH* 9:146
Salve pater dyonisi	22 Apr. 9, 12 Oct.	Invention, Feast of Denis[a,b]	384		420v	44:104	18104	Original
Vocis cum camena	25 Sept.	Firminus[a,b]	379		416	8:129	22084	*Ave maris stella* *AH* 9:72

Abbreviations: [a] Relics of saint in church. [b] Altar in church dedicated to saint. G: Fo. no. in treatise of Guido of Saint-Denis in GB:Lbm, Harl. 281. N2: Fo. no. in F:Pn, lat. 1107. V: Fo. no. in GB:Lva 1346–1891. *AH*: *Analecta Hymnica*, vol.: p. *RH*: No. in Chevalier, *Repertorium Hymnologicum*.

Ex. 4.3. *Sandionysian Sequence* Salve pater dyonisi
F:Pn, lat. 1107, fos. 384–5

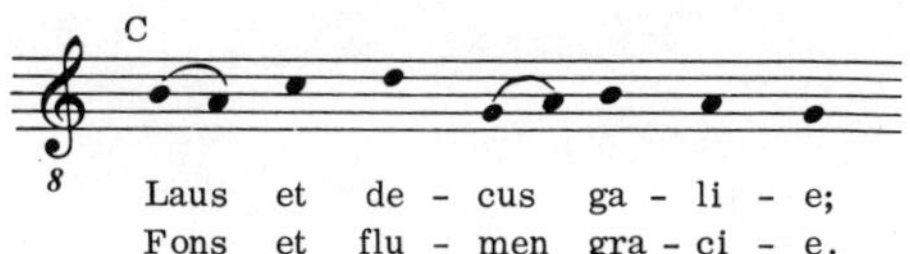

II

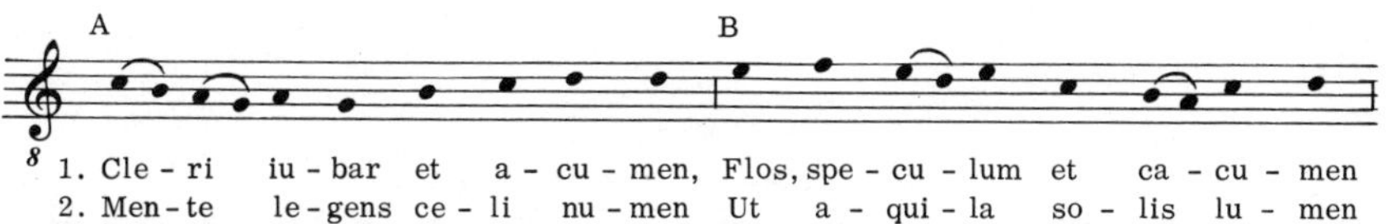

III

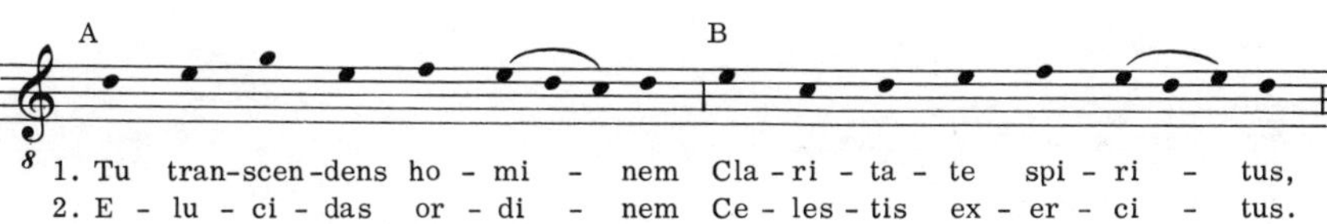

IV

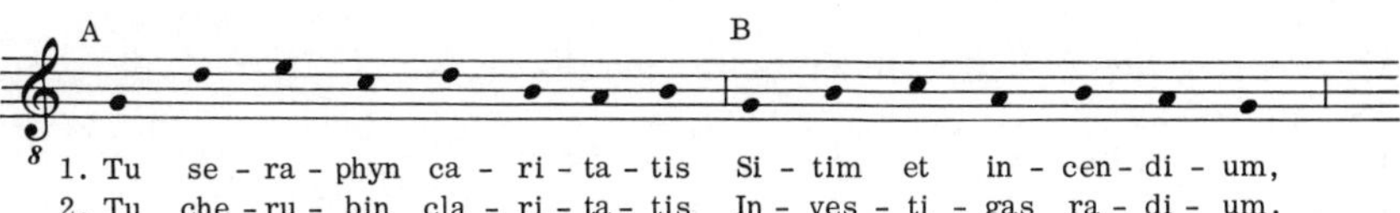

V

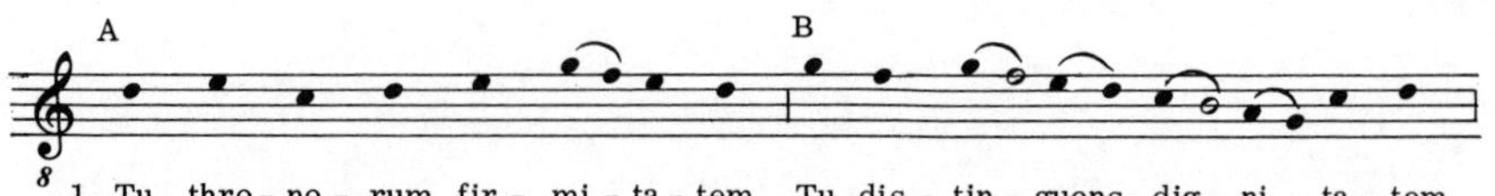

1. Tu thro - no - rum fir - mi - ta - tem, Tu dis - tin - guens dig - ni - ta - tem
2. Vim, na - tu - ram, pu - ri - ta - tem, O - pus, mo - tum, po - tes - ta - tem

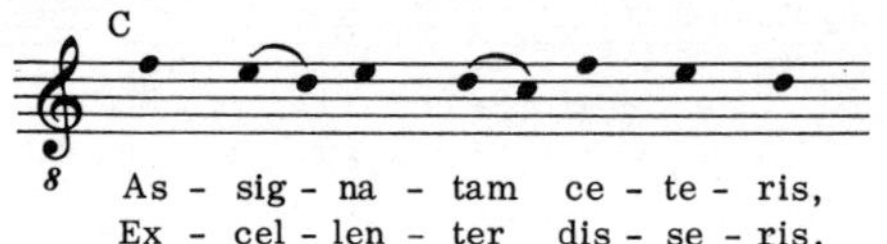

As - sig - na - tam ce - te - ris,
Ex - cel - len - ter dis - se - ris.

VI

1. Er - go, ro - sa glo - ri - o - sa, Bi - nis cum so - da - li - bus
2. Fer de - vo - ta no - stri vo - ta Cle - mens in ce - les - ti - bus,

VII

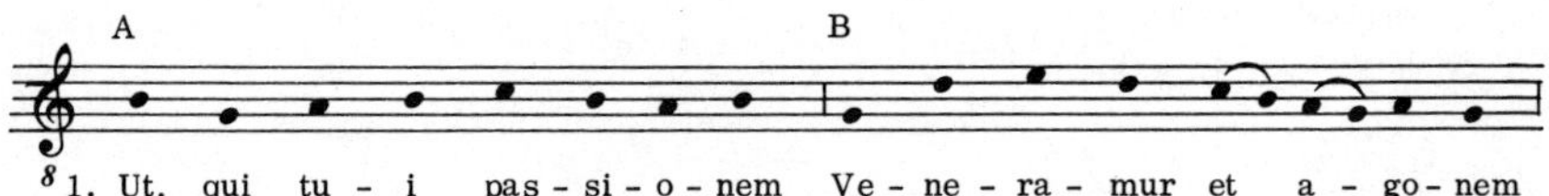

1. Ut, qui tu - i pas - si - o - nem Ve - ne - ra - mur et a - go - nem
2. Con - tem - ple - mur post la - bo - rem Fruc - tum ven - tris, ce - li flo - rem,

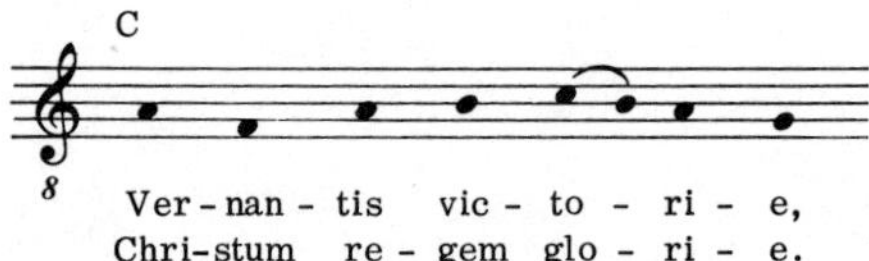

Ver - nan - tis vic - to - ri - e,
Chri - stum re - gem glo - ri - e.

A - men.

Variant readings in F:Pn, lat. 1107, fos. 384–85 (= N2), GB:Lva 1346–1891, fos. 393v–394 (= V):

I.1.B paradysi: V
I.1.C sapietum: V

II.2.B soli: V
IV.1.A seraphim: V
IV.2.A cherubim: V
V.1.B *c'* on *dig*-nitatem: V
V.2.B *c'* on *po*-testatem: N2, V
V.1.C assignatam: V
V.2.C dixeris: V
VI.1.A *e'd'-c'* on (glo)*ri-o*(sa): V
VI.2.A *e'd'* on (no)*stri*: V
VI.2.A *c'* on *vo*(ta): V
VII. *c'-b-a-a-b-c'-b-a-a-g* on *Amen*: V

Translation:

1

Hail, father Dionysius,
Light and beauty of paradise,
Glory and honour of Gaul,
Herald of life, trumpet of heaven,
Flame of love, furnace of zeal
Fountain and river of grace.

2

Splendour and keenness of the clergy,
Flower, mirror, and summit
Of the wise of Greece,
Elect in mind, godhead of heaven,
Light of the sun like the eagle
With his face not turned away.

3

You go beyond man
In clarity of spirit,
You illuminate the order
Of the heavenly army.

4

You, seraphim of love,
Search after desire and vehemence,
You, cherubim of clarity,
Seek the ray of light.

5

You determine the stability of thrones,
And the dignity
Assigned to the rest,
You sow strength, nature, purity,
Accomplishment, motion, and power
Excellently.

6

Therefore, glorious rose,
With both your companions[1]
Convey our devout offerings
Gently in the heavens.

7

So that we who worship your suffering
And the agony
Of your flowering victory
May behold after the labour
The fruit of the womb, the flower of heaven,
Christ the king of glory.

[1] Reference to the 2 co-martyrs of Denis, Rusticus and Eleutherius.

the 'order of the heavenly army', of the 'seraphim' and 'cherubim', and of their association with 'clarity' and 'light' (sts. 3 and 4). Indeed the very content of the first celestial hierarchy of Pseudo-Dionysius—seraphim, cherubim and thrones—is outlined in stanzas 4 and 5.[173] The 'eagle' (st. 2) is a Pseudo-Dionysian image for the angelic powers, and his ability to look directly into the sun is part of the legend of the bird.[174] *Salve pater* likewise seems to betray the influence of John Scottus Eriugena. The description of Saint Denis as 'trumpet of heaven' (*tuba celi*, st. 1) matches John's term 'brightest trumpet'.[175] Similarly, the association of the seraphim with *caritas*, and the further characterization of *caritas* as 'desire and vehemence' (*sitim et incendium*, st. 4) is a topic expounded not only in the Pseudo-Dionysian tracts, but also by John,[176] who explores the connection between 'clarity' and the 'ray' (st. 4) in some depth.[177]

Ave pater and *Doctorem egregium* have no overt references to Pseudo-Dionysian philosophy. *Ave pater* remarks on the 'order of angels' (st. 2) and cites the 'angelic hymns' (st. 4), which are reminiscent of the Hymn of the Cherubim (*Cheroubikon*) which was sung as the offertory in the

[173] See the pertinent chapter from *The Celestial Hierarchy*, trans. in Luibheid and Rorem, *Pseudo-Dionysius*, 161–6.

[174] Ibid. 189. The eagle is also a reference to Saint John, whose intellect is compared to the soaring eagle; see Moran, *Philosophy*, 79. John figures prominently in the philosophies both of Pseudo-Dionysius and of John Scottus Eriugena; see e.g. Eriugena's *Homily on the Prologue to St John's Gospel*, in O'Meara, *Eriugena*, 158–76.

[175] 'Quid ergo ad hanc magni theologi Dionysii preclarissimam tubam respondent', and further on: 'dum clarissime tuba prefata clamat'; Barbet, *Johannis*, p. 17, ll. 585, 587.

[176] Ibid. 86, l. 139; 95, ll. 139, 156, 166, 169; 96, l. 179; 210, l. 872.

[177] Ibid. 10, ll. 336–7. Hugh of Saint-Victor, who pondered John's discussion of Pseudo-Dionysius in the 12th c., likewise cites 'clarity' as one of the cognomens of the cherubim and elaborates on the 'dignity' of the 'thrones' (cf. st. 5) in his commentary on the *Celestial Hierarchy*; *PL*, clxxv. 1047.

Greek Mass on the Octave of Saint Denis. *Doctorem egregium* likewise mentions the 'heavenly army' (st. 3). On the other hand, both poems emphasize the apostolic connection of Saint Denis with Dionysius the Areopagite. *Ave pater* calls Saint Denis 'excellent and noble wonder of the wise teachers of Greece' (st. 1), and *Doctorem egregium* (st. 3) places the saint in the first century along with Saint Paul (*Paulo duce*) and Pope Clement (*legatus inclitus a Clemente*).

Whereas the melodies for *Ave pater* and *Doctorem egregium* were tailored from two Marian sequences (Table 4.5), the music and text for *Salve pater Dyonisi* was probably put together at Saint-Denis (Ex. 4.3). Not only do the words of the sequence include direct references to the Areopagite figures, but the structure of the text and music skilfully underlines the philosophy implanted in the work. The poem contains seven stanzas, each of which, in typical late-sequence fashion, consists of two halves chanted to the same music, producing the standard double-versicle form aa bb cc dd ee ff gg.

Within this form, however, the stanzas vary in numbers of lines and in numbers of syllables per line, and these differences create interest and diversion in the piece. The basic framework of the poem consists of four six-line stanzas (sts. 1, 2, 5, 7), each having a rhyme scheme (shown with letters) and syllable count (shown with numbers) that is common in the sequences of Adam Precentor (*olim* of Saint-Victor): A_8 A_8 B_7 A_8 A_8 B_7.[178] This neat structure is constantly interrupted, however, for the three remaining stanzas (3, 4, and 6) contain only four lines apiece. Stanzas 4 and 6 share a form that is also standard (A_8 B_7 A_8 B_7), while the third stanza has only seven syllables in each line (A_7 B_7 A_7 B_7). The use of stanzas with different numbers of lines is certainly not foreign to the Parisian sequence style,[179] but these irregularities in *Salve pater* are all the more glaring because of the brevity of the piece. The initial pattern is hardly established in the first two stanzas, when stanzas 3 and 4 disrupt what the ear has just come to expect. It is the ideas expressed in the text that seem to engender this structure, for the important Pseudo-Dionysian reference to 'the order of the heavenly army' appears prominently in the first irregular stanza (3). In addition, the use of ponderous masculine rhyme at the ends of every seven-

[178] On the use of this pattern, see Misset and Aubry, *Proses*, 38; and the general description of the 3 elements of Adam's poetry (ibid. 28–55): binary accent in trochees or iambs, the use of the same numbers of syllables in lines that rhyme, and the employment of masculine (strong) and feminine (weak) rhymes in specific ways. See also Fassler, 'Role', 358–61.

[179] Many unusual examples can be seen in the edition of sequences in Misset and Aubry, *Proses*. But when the 'classic' Parisian style is said to be represented in a single piece, the sequence chosen is usually one that has perfectly regular line lengths (see e.g. the analyses of *Exultantes collaudemus* in Hoppin, 'Sequence'; and of *O Maria stella maris* in Fassler, 'Role', 360–9). In comparison with these works, the structure of *Salve pater* is somewhat atypical of much of the Parisian repertory. See also the discussion of the regularity of this style in Stevens, *Words*, 100–2.

syllable phrase of stanza 3 break the mould of feminine–feminine–masculine (weak–weak–strong) rhymes found in each of the two previous stanzas.

Further emphasis on stanza 3 is achieved musically through the use of mode in the sequence. *Salve pater* is written in the seventh mode, and each stanza ends on g except the third and fifth, which close on d′. These two stanzas, moreover, explore the upper tetrachord of the authentic mode, hovering between d′ and g′, while the others remain for the most part in the lower part of the mode between g and d′, never reaching the high g′. Consequently, the 'heavenly army' not only comes in the first stanza that deviates from the poetic pattern established at the outset; its appearance is in effect proclaimed by use of a register that is noticeably higher than that of the the two preceding verses.

The cadence tones at the ends of the seven stanzas are symmetrical, with the final notes forming a double arch or palindrome around the fourth stanza (g g d′ g d′ g g). The internal cadences, however, override this structure slightly. The first stanza employs the higher note d′ only once at the end of the second phrase. The frequency of the d′ then increases to the point that it stands as final pitch to all three phrases in the fifth stanza, which serves as the climax of the sequence instead of the fourth. There was perhaps a design in this asymmetry. The text of the first half of stanza 5 is an obvious allusion to Pseudo-Dionysian doctrine of the ordering of the hierarchies of angels. In addition, the opening phrase, *Tu thronorum firmitatem . . . distinguens* ('You determine the stability of thrones'), has a possible double meaning: besides the Pseudo-Dionysian interpretation mentioned above, it may also be a reminder to temporal kings of their debt to Saint Denis, a dependence that the monks were only too happy to stress at every turn. The high pitches of the fifth stanza draw particular attention to these words, making the admonition more audible to angels, monarchs, and monks alike. At the same time, the lower *tessitura* of the surrounding fourth and sixth stanzas renders the fifth even more distinct by contrast.

If the community, consciously or subconsciously, had a musical model in mind when they created the initial phrase of *Salve pater*, they were perhaps inspired by the complex of sequences which are derived to greater or lesser extent from the the Seq. *Laudes crucis*, itself drawn from the Alle. *Dulce lignum*.[180] The characteristic descent of a fourth (c′-b-a-g) appears both in the alleluia and in the sequences that may be related to it, including the first phrase of *Salve pater* (on the word *Dyonisi*). The motive also serves at the start of the second stanza and as the final cadential figure in *Salve pater*. In like fashion, the opening

[180] See the discussion of these pieces in Stevens, *Words*, 400–3; Misset and Aubry, *Proses*, 130 (*timbre* 63).

four notes of the sequence (g-a-b-g) resemble the g-g-a-g at the beginning of a number of pieces that may have been influenced by *Laudes crucis/Dulce lignum*.[181]

The Greek Mass

The philosophy apparent in *Salve pater* and the other sequences for Saint Denis is also found in the *missa graeca* of Saint-Denis, one of the most intriguing rituals of the abbey. Here, the zeal of a community in pursuit of royal favour through insistence on its association with the Greek Areopagite permeates an entire ceremony. The monks' attachment to this service is clear from its longevity, for they chanted a Greek Mass from the Carolingian era until the French Revolution. But there were three distinct Greek celebrations that flourished at Saint-Denis during this millennium, and not all were particular to the monastery. The earliest Greek Mass in the West consisted in the performance of the chants of the ordinary in Greek.[182] Saint-Denis, like many other houses in the ninth to eleventh centuries, cultivated this usage, vestiges of which are found in the Latin transcriptions of Greek texts of the ordinary that occur in numerous early sources. These remnants of the Mass are Greek renditions of the last four pieces: Gloria (*Doxa en ipsistis* in the Greek translation), Credo (*Pisteuo ys ena theon*), Sanctus (*Agios, Agios, Agios*), and Agnus Dei (*O Amnos tu theu*).[183] Since the Kyrie Eleison was already in Greek, it was generally omitted from sources of the Greek Mass. This early *missa graeca* was intended for the highest feasts of the year, and the manuscript tradition indicates that it was most often associated with Pentecost.[184] Atkinson demonstrates that the various parts of the ritual probably came together between 827 and 835 to form the *missa graeca* of the West.[185] A host of sources from the late eighth to twelfth centuries, representing both east- and west-Frankish chant traditions, contain one or more portions of the ordinary in Greek. These manuscripts include books from several houses in the vicinity of Saint-Denis: Metz, Laon, Saint-Amand, Tours, Nevers, Fleury, and Chelles.[186] Three early sources

[181] Ibid. 401. Fassler points out further connections between *Salve pater* and the Parisian sequence repertory in her forthcoming book on the late medieval sequence.

[182] On this Greek Mass, see Atkinson, 'Entstehung'; Kaczynski, *Greek*, 101–4.

[183] Atkinson has shown that these texts were transmitted by oral dictation, and consequently that important regional variants in spelling frequently occur in MSS; 'Entstehung', 118–32; idem, '*O Amnos*', 19–21.

[184] Idem, 'Entstehung', 120–5, 132–3; Levy, 'Sanctus', 35.

[185] Atkinson, '*O Amnos*', 140–5. There is still some debate about the precise period of compilation of the Greek Mass in the West. Kenneth Levy believes this event took place during Charlemagne's reign, *c*.797–814; Levy, 'Sanctus', 35–42; idem, 'Archetype', 8.

[186] Atkinson, 'Entstehung', 120–5, 132–33; idem, '*O Amnos*', 9–14.

from Saint-Denis record chants and texts of the ordinary in Greek: the sacramentary F:Pn, lat. 2290, the sacramentary-portion of F:LA 118, and the augmented sacramentary F:Pn, lat. 9436 (Table 4.6).

Although Saint-Denis was not unique in celebrating this Greek Mass, its manuscripts do play an important role in preserving the service. F:Pn, lat. 2290 contains both the purest text of the Greek Gloria (*Doxa*)[187] and the oldest surviving example of the text of the Greek Agnus Dei (*O Amnos*), and it is the earliest extant source to include the Greek words of all four chants of the ordinary, besides the Kyrie.[188] Not until the eleventh century, however, do manuscripts from Saint-Denis preserve music in addition to text for two of these chants. The Gloria (*Doxa*) and Credo (*Pisteuo*) in F:Pn, lat. 9436 are notated in neumes that are written on top of the Greek words, which are transliterated in Latin characters. The Latin Gloria and Credo appear above the musical notation. While this melody for the *Doxa* has been 'translated' into square notation,[189] the *Pisteuo*, which is found in several other neumatic sources, can be deciphered with the help of a German source of the late fifteenth century.[190]

In the light of the activities of Abbot Hilduin (814–41), an interest in Greek liturgy at Saint-Denis comes as no surprise, and it is probably significant that his tenure as abbot encompasses the years in which Atkinson believes the Greek Mass in the West was compiled. Hilduin's work as translator of the writings of Pseudo-Dionysius and of other Greek texts certainly bears witness to his fascination with Byzantine culture. But there is no evidence that the early Greek Mass that Hilduin would have sung at Saint-Denis was specifically intended for the one celebration where it might have served these ends most readily: the feast of Saint Denis. Indeed, it is not until the thirteenth century that we find a Greek service in the abbey that is connected exclusively with the ritual for Saint Denis himself.[191] Henri Omont concludes that Abbot William of Gap (1172–86), a connoisseur of Greek manuscripts, was probably responsible for the compilation of this second *missa graeca*.[192] William was a learned man, a doctor turned monk, who brought several Greek sources to the abbey from Constantinople in

187 Idem, '*Doxa*', 93–4.

188 Idem, '*O Amnos*', 27–8; idem, 'Entstehung', 137.

189 See Huglo, 'Mélodie', 30–40.

190 D:BAa, Amtsbücherei 22788 (Inkunabel Hain 366a). K. Schlager has edited the text and melody of this *Pisteuo*, which was sung at Cologne, Würzburg, and Bamberg in the late 15th c.; see Schlager, 'Melodie'; Schlager and Wohnhaas, 'Choralgeschichte'. He compares the reading in this source to the one in F:Pn, lat. 9436 in 'Melodie', 228–30.

191 For earlier literature on the Greek Mass at Saint-Denis, see Huglo, 'Chants'; Vincent, 'Note'; Omont, 'Messe'; Leclercq, 'Grecque'.

192 Omont, 'Messe', 181–2. This opinion is repeated in Leclercq, 'Grecque', cols. 1583–4; and in Huglo, 'Chants', 74. A new overview of William's literary activities is given in Nebbiai-Dalla Guarda, *Bibliothèque*, 30–3.

TABLE 4.6. *Manuscripts Witnessing the Ordinary of the Mass in Greek at Saint-Denis (Ninth to Eleventh Centuries)*

MS	Portion of Mass	Fo.	Music	Text	Date
F:Pn, lat. 2290	*Doxa–Pisteuo–Agios–Amnos*	7v–8v		x	878–86
F:LA 118 (sacramentary)	*Doxa*	156v		x	Early 10th c.
F:Pn, lat. 9436	*Doxa–Pisteuo*	1v–2	x	x	Mid-11th c.

1167, before his elevation to abbot. Among these codices was the tenth-century manuscript of the works of Pseudo-Dionysius (F:Pn, grec. 933), which he translated into Latin.[193] His skill in the classical languages, along with a deep interest in the works of the Pseudo-Areopagite, make him, as Omont has proposed, the likeliest candidate for authorship of a Greek Mass for Saint-Denis in the twelfth century.[194]

New support for William as originator of the Mass comes in the twelfth-century lectionary from Saint-Denis F:Pn, n.a.l. 307 (see Table 4.6). This book shows that an important change in the epistle for the feast and Octave of Saint Denis took place around or shortly after the time of William. The proper lesson *Stans Paulus* is added to the beginning of the manuscript, as if to replace the Epistle *Hi sunt viri misericordie*, taken from the common of many martyrs.[195] *Stans Paulus* is the very text that was prescribed to be read both in Greek and Latin in the Greek Mass (Table 4.7), and it is the only part of the service that is taken from Paul's sermon in Areopagus, where he converted Dionysius the Areopagite (Acts 17: 22–34). As such, the epistle was tailor-made for a feast that promoted the identity of the true Saint Denis with the two Dionysius-figures. And what better sign of their devotion to the Areopagite could William and the monks have devised than a Mass which celebrated the supposed patron of the abbey not only with this proper reading but also in the language of the Greek disciple of Paul?[196]

[193] William's translations are preserved in 2 13th-c. MSS: F:Pn, lat. 2447 and F:Pn, n.a.l. 1509; see Nebbiai-Dalla Guarda, *Bibliothèque*, 32, n. 81.

[194] There is one other time, shortly after the abbacy of William, when this Greek Mass might possibly have originated. It is the period around 1216, when Pope Innocent III granted the relics of yet another Dionysius, bishop of Corinth, to the abbey. The gift of these bones was meant to settle the issue of whether or not the 'true Dionysius' (Saint Denis) was actually present in the monastery by ensuring that the reliquaries virtually overflowed with every known Dionysius. Whereas the addition of a Greek Mass to the liturgy could well have accompanied the arrival of the remains of Dionysius of Corinth, there seems no likely candidate at Saint-Denis at this time who might have composed the service. The reigning abbot, Henry Troon (1204–21), was certainly an important figure, but he is not known to have had a particular interest in Greek. The trafficking of several other relics from the East to Saint-Denis also occurred a few years earlier. In 1205 King Philip Augustus received from Emperor Baudoin of Constantinople a portion of the True Cross, some hair, linen, and part of the purple robe of Jesus, a thorn from the Crown of Thorns, and a rib and tooth of Saint Philip, all of which he entrusted to Henry Troon (see Delaborde, *Œuvres*, i. 162–3; Félibien, *Histoire*, 215–16).

[195] Although *Stans Paulus* appears at the beginning of the MS and thus is not assigned to a feast, the later sources from the abbey universally prescribe it for the *natale* and Octave of Saint Denis (F:Pm 414, fos. 242ᵛ, 245; F:Pn, lat. 1107, fos. 271ᵛ, 272ᵛ; GB:Lva 1346–1891, fos. 296, 297). The main body of F:Pn, n.a.l. 307, on the other hand, contains the Epistle *Hi sunt viri misericordie* for the feast of Saint Denis (fo. 109ᵛ). The addition of *Stans Paulus* to F:Pn, n.a.l. 307 is significant, then, for it suggests that a change from lesser to greater specificity in the liturgy for the feast-day and Octave of the saint happened in the 12th c. Indeed, this modification had apparently been accomplished by the end of the century, for the table of readings that was added to F:Pm 384 includes *Stans Paulus* (fo. 208).

[196] The use of Greek in this Mass was all the more important since the chants of the ordinary and proper, with the exception of the *Cheroubikon*, made no allusion to the Pseudo-Areopagite or to his

In short, the second Greek Mass at Saint-Denis was as political as it was religious. Moreover, unlike the earlier Greek Mass in the West, it belonged specially to the abbey, being assigned to one feast-day only: the Octave of Saint Denis (16 October). The surviving directions for the celebration, which post-date William of Gap by a half-century, are found in the two thirteenth-century ordinaries F:Pm 526 and F:Pn, lat. 976 (Table 4.7). Clearly, Greek was used in a larger portion of this

TABLE 4.7. *Description of the Thirteenth-Century Greek Mass in F:Pm 526 and F:Pn, lat. 976*[a]

De Octabis Beati Dionysii (1)

Ad missam tres cantores. Officium in greco *Zevete a gallya* (2). Sex (3) procedentes. V. *Zevete a gallia*. *Doxa Patri*. Kyrie *Fons bonitatis* (4). Post incipiat sacerdos *Doxa en (5) ipsistis*. Oratio *Protegat nos Domine* (6). Prima Epistola legatur (7) in greco, alia in latino: *Stans Paulus*. R. *Fobite (8) thon Kyrion* (9) V. *Yde ekzetontes* (10) a III. Alleluia (11) *Ekekraxan (12) dykei* (13) a IIII (14), Sequentia *Gaude prole* (15). Ante evangelium, Ant. *O beate Dyonisi*. Post legatur Evangelium in greco, aliud (16) in latino *Videns Jesus turbas* (17). Dicatur *Phisteuo* quod est Credo etiam si dominica non fuerit (18). Offertorium *Y ta Cherubyn* (19). Prefacio *Qui sanctorum*. *Sanctus, agyos, agyos* (20). Agnus, O amnos (21) tou (22) Theu et Agnus Dei III. Communio *Psallate (23) Ysu* (24). Postcommunio *Sumpsimus Domine pignus* (25). Ite Missa Est sicut *Angelorum*.

Variants:

1. *In Octabis Sanctorum Dyonisii, Rustici et Eleutherii*—M
2. *gallia*—M
3. Quatuor—M
4. *bonitatis*—n.g., M
5. *in*—M
6. *Domine*—n.g., M; *sepius*—added, N
7. legetur—M
8. *Phovicite*—M
9. *thon Kyrion*—n.g., M
10. *Yde ezecontes*—M
11. Alleluia a quatuor—M
12. *Ekekrassan*—M
13. *dikei*—M
14. a IIII—n.g., M
15. *Super[n]e armonie*—M
16. alia—M
17. *turbas*—n.g., N
18. Si dominica fuerit dicatur *Phisteno* quod est Credo et si dominica non fuerit non dicatur.—M
19. *Kerouvin*—M; Pref. *Qui sanctorum*—added, M
20. second *agyos*—n.g., M
21. *agnos*—M, N
22. *thon*—M
23. *Psallite*—M
24. *Yri*—M
25. *pignus*—n.g., M

Abbreviations: M: F:Pm 526, fo. 184. N: F:Pn, lat. 976, fos. 137^{r-v}.

[a] This table differs in several places from the one given in Huglo, 'Chants', 76.

philosophy. The Office of Saint Denis, on the other hand, contains more references to the presumed patron of the monastery.

thirteenth-century Mass than in the earlier Western setting of the ordinary alone. Some of the music likewise differs from that which was performed in the ninth to twelfth centuries. For the ordinary of the Mass, Huglo considered that the chants for the *Doxa* and *Pisteuo* which are preserved in the older Saint-Denis source F:Pn, lat. 9436 (see Table 4.6) were still used in the thirteenth century.[197] Manuscripts contemporaneous with the second Greek Mass (Table 4.8), however, point to different tunes for two reasons.

First, the melodies for the *Doxa* and *Pisteuo* in F:Pn, lat. 9436 are absent from the *Kyriale* that is written in the thirteenth- and fourteenth-century missals F:Pn, lat. 1107 and GB:Lva 1346–1891. Second, the unnotated missal F:Pm 414, hitherto unknown as a source of the Greek Mass, indicates melodies for the *Doxa* and the *Pisteuo* that vary markedly from those preserved in F:Pn, lat. 9436. The brief incipits for these two chants (Pls. 15 and 16) are the only music contained in F:Pm 414, aside fom some musical notation in the canon of the Mass. The *Doxa* and *Pisteuo* are included in the service for the Octave of Saint Denis on folios which were added in the fourteenth century. The tune for the *Doxa* appears to be the familiar Western Gloria IV.[198] Although the opening of the *Pisteuo* is not long enough to distinguish between Credo melodies I, II, and IV in the *Liber Usualis*, the incipit matches one of these usual tones, rather than the more elaborate opening that is recorded in F:Pn, lat. 9436. Moreover, the beginning of the *Pisteuo* in F:Pm 414 corresponds to the opening of the Credo in the *Kyriale* of GB:Lva 1346–1891.[199] F:Pm 414 is the only medieval witness for the music of the *Doxa* and *Pisteuo* that specifically assigns these chants to the Greek Mass on the Octave of Saint-Denis. The tunes transmitted in F:Pn, lat. 9436, on the other hand, are written at the beginning of the manuscript without reference to a feast. From the direct evidence of F:Pm 414, it is more likely that the *Doxa* and *Pisteuo* in this source were used on the Octave of the patron saint in the thirteenth and fourteenth centuries. The old melodies in F:Pn, lat. 9436 would by then have been forgotten or perhaps dropped from the liturgy of the abbey.

Apart from the incipits in F:Pm 414, other manuscripts support the notion that the second Greek Mass at Saint-Denis incorporated standard tones for the *Doxa* and the *Pisteuo*. The *Kyriale* of the thirteenth and fourteenth centuries in F:Pn, lat. 1107 and GB:Lva 1346–1891 contains these very melodies, albeit with Latin texts. Even more important, GB:Lva 1346–1891 pairs the melody of Gloria IV, alluded

[197] Huglo, 'Chants', 76–7.

[198] *LU*, xxvi; Bosse, *Gloria*, melody No. 56. This incipit is also found in the *Kyriale* of F:Pn, lat. 1107, fo. 393^{v}; and of GB:Lva 1346–1891, fo. 364.

[199] Fos. 367^{r-v}.

TABLE 4.8. *Manuscripts Witnessing the Greek Mass at Saint-Denis (Twelfth to Fourteenth Centuries)*

MS	Portion of Mass	Fo.	Music	Text	Date
F:Pn, n.a.l. 307[b]	Latin Epistle *Stans Paulus*	4		x	12th, added
F:Pn, grec. 375[a]	Greek Epistle *Stans Paulus*	56, 153, 194^{v}		x	12th–13th, added
	Greek Gospel *Videns jhesus*	154		x	12th–13th, added
F:Pn, n.a.l. 1420[b]	Latin Gospel *Videns jhesus*	97		x	Early 13th
F:Pm 526[a]	Complete description (incipits)	184		x	1234–6
F:Pn, lat. 976[a]	Complete description (incipits)	137^{r-v}		x	*c.*1258
F:Pn, lat. 1107[a]	Latin *Kyriale*	392^{v}–395	x	x	After 1259
F:Pm 414[b]	*Doxa-Pisteuo* (incipits)	245^{r-v}	x	x	14th, added
GB:Lva 1346–1891[b]	Latin *Kyriale*	364–9	x	x	1350
F:Pan, L 863, No. 10[b]	Gives only the rubric *Officium in graeco*	126		x	Copied in 18th, taken from 14th-c. MS (1350–64)
F:Pn, lat. 9387[a]	Greek epistles and gospels for				14th, added
	Christmas	153		x	
	Church Dedication	154^{v}		x	
	Easter	155^{v}		x	
	Pentecost	156		x	
	Saint Denis *natale*	157^{v}		x	

[a] MS identified in Huglo, 'Chants', or in Omont, 'Messe'.
[b] Newly identified source of the Greek Mass.

x: Text or music present in MS.

to in F:Pm 414, with the Kyrie *Fons bonitatis*. The accompanying rubric assigns this Kyrie to feasts of *annuale* and *semiannuale* rank, the latter of which had been prescribed for the Octave of Saint Denis—the day on which the Greek Mass was performed—by the fourteenth century. Since *Fons bonitatis* is named in the descriptions of the Greek Mass in F:Pm 526 and F:Pn, lat. 976 (Table 4.7), its appearance with Gloria IV in GB:Lva 1346–1891 probably indicates that the entire *ordinarium* for the Greek Mass was compiled from the chants which were designated for *annuale* and *semiannuale* feasts. Hence, the rubrics for the *Doxa* and the rest of the ordinary did not need to be written in F:Pm 526 and F:Pn, lat. 976.

If this is the case, then the intended melodies for the *Agios* and the *O Amnos* can also be inferred. Unlike the *Doxa* and *Pisteuo*, the *Agios* and *O Amnos* have left no musical traces in the early sources from Saint-Denis, although the texts are preserved in F:Pn, lat. 2290 (Table 4.6). But the later *Kyriale* of the abbey does provide tones for the Sanctus and the Agnus, and it was no doubt the festive melodies for *annuale* and *semiannuale* celebrations that were chanted as part of the later Greek Mass at Saint-Denis.[200]

In all probability, then, the monks had abandoned the old melodies for the *Doxa* and *Pisteuo* by the thirteenth century. In their place stood the current tunes for the most elaborate festivals, and these, along with the *annuale* and *semiannuale* melodies for the *Agios* and *O Amnos*, were performed in Greek on the Octave of Saint Denis. *O Amnos*, however, was somewhat exceptional in terms of its execution. This threefold supplication retained the Latin text in the first and third acclamations, alternating with Greek for the second statement: *Agnus, O amnos tou Theu et Agnus Dei III*.[201]

Another striking difference between the early Greek Mass and the thirteenth-century version for the Octave of Saint Denis is the inclusion of Greek propers in the later service.[202] The majority of these pieces come from the *commune sanctorum*. Omont identified the Latin chants

[200] The *Kyriale* of Saint-Denis gives Thannabaur's melody No. 49 (*LU*, IV) for the Sanctus, and Schildbach's melody No. 136 (*LU*, IV) for the Agnus on the highest feasts (Table 3.7).

[201] This alternation of Greek and Latin in the *O Amnos* has precedent in some Aquitanian sources; see Atkinson, '*O Amnos*', 25. Both the Credo and the Sanctus also appear to be designated both in Latin and in Greek (Table 4.7). The context of these rubrics, however, makes it clear that the Latin in each case serves simply as a reminder of which chant is intended. The Agnus Dei, on the other hand, seems a deliberate alternation of Latin, Greek, and Latin, and it does occur in both of the ordinaries represented in Table 4.7.

[202] Even this, however, was not a Sandionysian innovation. In the 11th c., the cathedral of Nevers employed Greek translations of some of the chants of the proper as well as the ordinary for the Mass on Pentecost; see Huglo, 'Chants', 75. The author also lists other MSS which include propers in Greek.

for two items: the Grad. *Timete dominum* and the Alle. *Clamaverunt*.[203] The texts of these pieces were borrowed from the Gregorian repertory and translated into Greek, using Latin characters. Latin correspondences for the Intr. *Zevete a gallia* and Comm. *Psallite Yri* (or *Ysu*), however, remain an unsolved mystery. The closest match for the Intr. *Zevete* would appear to be *Venite adoremus*, Ver. *Venite exultemus*, but Huglo points out that this introit is never assigned to a feast of the *sanctorale*.[204] The contemporaneous missals F:Pn, lat. 1107 and GB:Lva 1346–1891 give an equally unlikely solution: the Intr. *Intret in conspectu* (Table 4.8). The lesser doxology (*Doxa patri*), sung in Greek as part of the introit, either was translated from the Western version of the chant, or was the Byzantine doxology, which omits the text *sicut erat in principio*.[205] The identity of the Comm. *Psallite Yri (Ysu)*, which does not correspond to a known Gregorian Communion, is as elusive as that of the introit.[206] Again, the missals record a Communion which does not translate the Greek: *Posuerunt mortalia* (Table 4.10). No doubt the names of the introit and Communion are obscured by the strange spellings that are recorded—probably through oral dictation—in the two ordinaries.[207]

The Offer. *Y ta Cherubim* is the only portion of the Mass which actually originated in the Byzantine rite. This chant is the famous *Cheroubikon*, or Hymn of the Cherubim, sung for the procession of the Grand Entrance in the Eastern ritual.[208] In the West, the piece was handed down as a Gallican vestige in a Latin transliteration of the Greek, as the incipit *Y ta Cherubim* indicates. More often, however, the actual text is found as a Latin translation (*Qui cherubim mystice*) of the Greek words (Table 4.9).[209] Because the music for the *Cheroubikon* survives only in early, neumed sources, the references to the chant in the two thirteenth-century ordinaries of Saint-Denis are singularly important. Evidently the *Cheroubikon* was still known, at least at Saint-Denis, in the period of square notation. Unfortunately, however, it has not yet been found in manuscripts which might render the tune in a readable form.

[203] Omont, 'Messe', 180; see also Huglo, 'Chants', 78; Leclercq, 'Grecque', col. 1583.

[204] See Huglo's arguments against Omont's suggestions for the introit and communion; 'Chants', 77 (cf. Omont, 'Messe', 180).

[205] Huglo, 'Chants', 77–8.

[206] Ibid. 79–80.

[207] The numerous variant spellings of pieces in F:Pm 526 and F:Pn, lat. 976 (Table 4.7) suggest that the version in the latter MS was not copied directly from the former.

[208] On the *Cheroubikon* in the West, see Huglo, 'Chants', 78–9; Wellesz, *Elements*, 34; Jammers, *Neumenhandschriften*, pl. 9; Beyssac, 'Mont-Renaud', 139, 149; Handschin, 'Tropaires', 45–6. The Eastern version is treated in Wellesz, *History*, 165–6; and in Levy, 'Hymn', 162 ff.

[209] See the facsimile of the *Cheroubikon* in Pl. 11, from F:Pn, lat. 9436. Hesbert's facsimile edn. of F:Pm 384 also includes the *Cheroubikon* (Hesbert, *Graduel*, 271); see also the photograph in Huglo, 'Chants'.

TABLE 4.9. *Western Manuscripts Containing the* Cheroubikon

MS	Century	Fo.	Text	Music	Provenance
F:LA 118[b,c]	Late 9th	223^{v}	x		Saint-Denis/ Laon
Mont-Renaud[a,c]	10th	37^{v}	Incipit		Corbie/ Noyon
D:DÜl, D.2[a,d]	10th	203^{v}	x	x	Corvey
GB:Lbm, Har. 3095[a,c]	10/11th	111^{v}	x	x	German
F:Pm 384[a,c]	Early 11th	153	x	x	Saint-Denis
F:Pn, lat. 9436[b,c]	Mid-11th	58^{v}	x	x	Saint-Denis
I:Rvat, Reg. lat. 334[a,c]	11/12th	78^{v}–79	x	x	Sora

[a] MS identified in Huglo, 'Chants', 78–9.
[b] Newly identified source of the *Cheroubikon*.
[c] Latin translation from Greek.
[d] Latin transliteration from Greek.

x: Text or music present in MS.

The two new witnesses of the *Cheroubikon* in F:LA 118 and F:Pn, lat. 9436 (Pl. 7) illustrate the close association of this piece with Saint-Denis (Table 4.9). F:LA 118 is the oldest manuscript now known to include the text. Normally found as a verse of the Offer. *Benedictus sit deus pater* for the Mass for Trinity,[210] the *Cheroubikon* has a separate existence in F:LA 118 as the first of two offertories. In F:Pm 384, it also appears independently as the second offertory for the Mass. This rubrication of the chant as an offertory rather than a verse is significant, for it recalls the original role of the *Cheroubikon* as a separate piece in the Byzantine liturgy. The slightly later sacramentary F:Pn, lat. 9436, on the other hand, gives it a subordinate liturgical position as a verse of *Benedictus sit*. The version of the text found in these Saint-Denis sources is almost identical in all three manuscripts (Table 4.9):

Qui cherubim mystice imitamur et vivificae Trinitatis [F:LA 118—*trinitati*] ter sanctum hymnum offerimus, omnem nunc mundanam deponamus sollicitudinem sicuti regem omnium suscepturi cui ab angelicis invisibiliter ministratur ordinibus, alleluia.

[Let us who imitate the Cherubim mystically and offer thrice the holy hymn to the life-giving Trinity now put aside all worldly care as we are about to receive the King of all, who is attended invisibly by the angelic orders. Alleluia.][211]

[210] Huglo proposes that the *Cheroubikon*, in order to have matched the Offer. *Benedictus* modally, would have been sung in the 3rd mode; ibid. 79.

[211] Another translation, based on a slightly different reading of the text, is found in Neale, *History*, i. 430.

The one variant reading in F:LA 118 may be due to the dual heritage of the gradual portion of this manuscript (Saint-Denis and Laon), described in Chapter 6.

It may seem curious that the monks singled out the *Cheroubikon* for inclusion in the *missa graeca*, since the rest of the service uses more familiar Western chants. The reasons probably lie in the text of the offertory. References to the Trinity were a prominent theme both in the iconography of the central west portal and in the music for the Gloria Patri at Saint-Denis, as we have seen.[212] In addition, the mentions of cherubim are found, among other places, in Pseudo-Dionysian thought, as set forth in the *Celestial Hierarchy*.[213] According to the philosopher, the cherubim formed part of the 'first hierarchy' of beings. One of their duties was to emulate, 'as far as possible, the beauty of God's condition and activity'. While their comprehension of God is infinitely superior to ours, we can know something of Him and of the holiness of these celestial beings through the hymns that are provided for us to sing.[214] The *Cheroubikon* mirrors these sentiments from the human viewpoint. As the cherubim imitate God, so 'we . . . imitate the Cherubim mystically'. Perhaps the monks of Saint-Denis considered the song one that the cherubim might have revealed to mankind. For these reasons, the *Cheroubikon* would undoubtedly have been attractive to the community. The hymn gave them another means of linking their Greek service philosophically to what they believed about the Pseudo-Areopagite.

The two remaining chants of the proper, the Seq. *Superne armonie* (*Gaude prole* in F:Pn, lat. 976) and the gospel Ant. *O beate Dyonisi*, were performed in Latin probably because their texts, which were not drawn from the Bible, would have presented significant problems for a translator.[215] The Ite Missa Est, perhaps for similar reasons, was sung in Latin on the melisma *Angelorum* from the Resp. *Vir inclitus dionysius* from the feast of Saint Denis.[216] The epistle and gospel, chanted both in Greek and in Latin, could be found in any of the manuscripts of readings listed in Table 4.8. A summary of the parts of the second Greek Mass at Saint-Denis is given in Table 4.10.

Some time after the Middle Ages the contents of this Mass were altered. Huglo suggests that the Congregation of Saint-Maur, which introduced sweeping reforms at Saint-Denis in the seventeenth century,

212 And because of the reference to the Trinity, it is easy to see why the *Cheroubikon* was preserved within the Mass for Trinity in Western sources.

213 See esp. Luibheid and Rorem, *Pseudo-Dionysius*, 161–6.

214 Ibid. 165–6; see also the discussion of the angelic choirs in Louth, *Denys*, 33–51.

215 Huglo, 'Chants', 78.

216 Huglo mistakenly believed that the rubric *angelorum* signifies a melody from the votive *missa de angelis*; ibid. 77, n. 5. On the melodies for the Ite Missa Est at Saint-Denis, see Ch. 3.

TABLE 4.10. *Summary of the Greek Mass at Saint-Denis (Twelfth to Fourteenth Centuries)*[a]

Introit: ? (F:Pn, lat. 1107 and GB:Lva 1346–1891 give *Intret in conspectu*).
Gloria patri: *Doxa patri* (in Greek).
Kyrie: Kyrie *Fons bonitatis* (Melnicki No. 48; *LU* I).
Gloria in excelsis: *Doxa en ipsistis* (Bosse No. 56; *LU* IV).
Collect: *Protegat nos domine* (in Latin).
Epistle: *Stans Paulus* (in Greek and in Latin).
Gradual: *Timete Dominum* (in Greek).
Alleluia: *Clamaverunt* (in Greek).
Sequence: *Superne armonie* or *Gaude prole* (in Latin).
Antiphon before the Gospel: *O beate Dyonisi* (in Latin).
Gospel: *Videns Jesus turbas* (in Greek and in Latin).
Credo: *Pisteuo* (as in GB:Lva 1346–1891; in Greek).
Offertory: *Cheroubikon*.
Preface: *Qui sanctorum*.
Sanctus: *Agios* (Thannabaur No. 49; *LU* IV).
Pater Noster: in Latin.
Agnus Dei: *O amnos* (Schildbach No. 136; *LU* IV).
Communion: ? (F:Pn, lat. 1107 and GB:Lva 1346–1891 give *Posuerunt mortalia*).
Postcommunion: *Sumpsimus Domine* (in Latin).
Ite Missa Est: melisma *Angelorum* (in Latin).

[a] Based on the table in Huglo, 'Chants', 81, but with differences reflecting my own conclusions.

was responsible for the changes (Table 4.11).[217] The modifications were not as extensive as Huglo supposed, however, for the Greek Mass of the seventeenth century calls for the same melodies for the *Doxa*, *Agios*, and *O Amnos* (*LU* melody IV) that were indicated in the thirteenth- and fourteenth-century version (cf. Table 4.10). As in the earlier thirteenth-century Mass, the propers for the seventeenth-century service (Intr. *Sapientiam*, Grad. *Anima nostra*, Alle. *Justi epulentur*, Gospel *Attendite a fermento*, and Comm. *Dico autem vobis*) come from the common of many martyrs, although they are not the same chants that were sung in the late Middle Ages. The one Byzantine relative in the earlier celebration, the *Cheroubikon*, is replaced by the common Offer. *Exultabunt sancti* in the later Mass. Apart from the offertory, the differences between the two services consist largely in the choice of charts from the *commune sanctorum*.

[217] Huglo, 'Chants', 81–3.

TABLE 4.11. *The Greek Mass at Saint-Denis (Seventeenth to Eighteenth Centuries) according to Huglo*[a]

Introit: *Sapientiam* (in Greek).
Kyrie: *LU* IV.
Gloria in excelsis: *Doxa en ipsistis* (*LU* IV).
Collect: *Protegat nos domine* (in Greek).
Epistle: *Stans Paulus* (in Greek and in Latin).
Gradual: *Anima nostra* (in Greek).
Alleluia: *Justi epulentur* (in Greek).
Gospel: *Attendite a fermento* (in Greek and in Latin).
Credo: *Pisteuo* (*LU* V).
Offertory: *Exultabunt sancti* (in Greek).
Secret: *Hostias tibi domine* (in Latin).
Preface: 1. Common preface (in Greek).
2. Preface according to Paris usage (in Greek).
Sanctus: *Agios* (*LU* IV).
Pater noster: in Greek.
Agnus Dei: *O amnos* (*LU* IV).
Communion: *Dico autem vobis* (in Greek).
Postcommunion: *Sumpsimus domine* (in Greek).
Ite Missa Est: in Greek.
Episcopal benediction: in Greek.

[a] Huglo, 'Chants', 81. The table is drawn from edns. of the Greek Mass that appeared in 1658 and in 1777.

In sum, it was not until the twelfth and thirteenth centuries that the Sandionysians fashioned a Greek Mass that was their own, a service for the Octave of the patron saint which provided an apt conclusion to an intense week of celebration of the feast of Saint Denis. Prior to this time, the abbey, along with many other institutions, chanted the parts of the ordinary in Greek on one or more high feasts. As the monks grew more daring in the late twelfth century, emboldened perhaps by the memory of Abbot Suger, they added a Greek service to their ritual that was designed in the final analysis to illustrate their unique association with the Areopagite figures and thereby to win greater respect from the Crown. Certainly, the shadow of doubt that Peter Abelard had cast on the identity of Saint Denis several decades earlier, along with the centuries-long struggle of the monks to assert the oneness of Saint Denis and the Areopagite figures, was prodding the community to find a definitive form in which to state their position on this crucial matter. In choosing the liturgy, they only repeated an action taken a short time earlier to achieve a similarly political goal. This act was the establishment of an elaborate anniversary for King Dagobert, instigated by a challenge to the position of the abbey as royal necropolis, and created to demonstrate to future monarchs the high regard in which the monks held their presumed founder. If Dagobert merited such a commemoration, nothing less than an extraordinary service for Saint Denis would be fitting for their patron saint.

Just as the Merovingian Dagobert was singled out in part for the antiquity he could lend the abbey, so the chanting of this Mass in Greek also recalled the ties that Saint Denis had with a still more ancient patron, the church in Rome, for which Greek was the primordial tongue. When Latin supplanted the mother language in the middle of the third century, a handful of Greek vestiges retained prominent places in the Western Mass: the Kyrie Eleison, the Reproaches of the Good Friday service, the chanting of the epistle and gospel in Greek on the highest feasts, to name only a few. These items were well known at Saint-Denis, as elsewhere. But the conversion of virtually an entire Mass into Greek on a celebration other than an *annuale* feast was something special. More than mere homage to the Areopagite, the ceremony enhanced the venerability of the abbey by imitating the oldest speech of the Church of Rome itself in its rites for the Octave of Saint Denis.

Once adopted, the Greek Mass outlived even the realization that Saint Denis was not, after all, the Areopagite.[218] In fact, newly uncovered sources from Saint-Denis demonstrate that the Greek Mass, and probably the third version of it (Table 4.11), was sung in the abbey until the French Revolution. The eighteenth-century ordinary F:Pan, L 863, No. 10 (copied from a fourteenth-century exemplar) attests to the longevity of the Mass in a brief reference to its use on the Octave of the patron: 'Officium in graeco' (Table 4.8). But a more telling record is found in the notes of Ferdinand Albert Gautier, organist at Saint-Denis prior to and during the French Revolution: 'the Greek Mass that we customarily sang in this church on 16 October of each year took place for the last time on Sunday 16 October 1792.'[219] Only a few days earlier, the Benedictines themselves had been banished from their convent in the same frenzy that toppled the monarchy and, along with it, the *particularis patronus* of the kings of France.

[218] Huglo lists 4 18th-c. sources for the Greek Mass: the edns. of 1777 and 1779, and the MSS F:Pm 452 and F:Pm 4465; ibid. 81, n. 3. For further information on the MSS, see Nebbiai-Dalla Guarda, *Bibliothèque*.

[219] 'La messe grecque qu'on étoit dans l'usage de chanter en cette église le 16 octobre de chaque année, eut lieu pour la dernière fois le dimanche 16 octobre 1792'; F:Pn, franç. 11681, p. 99. Gautier also noted the last time the epistle and gospel were declaimed in Latin and Greek, as was the custom on festivals of *annuale* rank. This occurred several months earlier, on the feast of Pentecost; ibid. 97.

THE FOURTEENTH AND FIFTEENTH CENTURIES

The thirteenth-century reconstruction of Saint-Denis was the last major rebuilding of the church prior to the restoration of the nineteenth century. There were, nonetheless, smaller changes to the fabric of the church beginning in the fourteenth century (see Pl. 4).[220] Six new chapels were built on the north side of the nave, and a chapel to Saint Louis was added on the eastern side of the south transept arm in the early fourteenth century. The chapel of John the Baptist, located in the inside aisle of the east side of the south transept arm, was enlarged later in the fourteenth century. A chapel in honour of the Valois kings was attached outside the north transept arm in the sixteenth century and was subsequently destroyed in the early eighteenth century.

The roster of feasts of Saint-Denis seems to have been little affected by these architectural changes, for the greatest number of liturgical alterations had taken place in the wake of the thirteenth-century reconstruction between 1231 and 1281, as described earlier. The few additional festivals that entered the liturgy in the late thirteenth and early fourteenth centuries, moreover, pre-date the fourteenth-century architectural changes. These feasts include the Vigil of the Dedication of the Church (23 February), the Conception of Mary (8 December), Corpus Christi, Saints Taurinus (20 October), Eutropius (30 April), Jonas (12 August), Louis (25 August) and his Octave (31 August). Only the feast of Saint Louis, probably adopted *c*.1296–7, was directly connected with the chapel later built for him. On the other hand, at least one new votive Mass for Mary and numerous private endowments that can be traced to the later Middle Ages were related to the fourteenth-century side altars in the church. These services once again demonstrate the close interaction of the liturgy with the architecture of Saint-Denis.

Commemorations of the Virgin

Apart from the major feasts for the Virgin described in Chapter 2, there were several times, daily or weekly, when the monks of Saint-Denis venerated Mary by the end of the fourteenth century. One occasion was the daily commemoration of Mary during Lauds and Vespers. These services are first documented in the thirteenth-century ordinaries from Saint-Denis (F:Pm 526; F:Pn, lat. 976), although they undoubtedly existed before this time. A second commemoration for Mary was the

[220] On the later modifications to Saint-Denis, see Bruzelius, *St-Denis*, 15–32.

daily singing of the Ant. *Salve Regina* after Compline, a practice established as a result of the finding of the Holy Nail in the thirteenth century, described in Chapter 2. Another Marian service was the weekly Office of Mary on Saturdays, a complete cycle of Hours and Mass, which Abbot Suger had reinstituted in the mid-twelfth century, and which likewise had probably been celebrated much earlier. The earliest witness of the Saturday Mass for Mary is found in the ninth-century sacramentaries F:Pn, lat. 2290 and F:LA 118.[221] Both the Mass and Hours for this ceremony are found in the later missals and ordinaries from the abbey. It is not clear where the Saturday Mass was performed—perhaps at Hilduin's altar in the ninth century or at one of the Marian altars in the chevet of the Gothic church beginning in the twelfth century (see Pl. 3)—but any of these locations would certainly have been appropriate. Yet another occasion was the daily Mass for the Virgin, which was officially introduced into the liturgy of the abbey in the late fourteenth century. Just as the seven Masses for Mary and All Saints in the ninth-century portion of the sacramentary F:R(m), A. 566 were probably intended for Hilduin's chapel, so the daily Lady Mass was celebrated at the altar of Notre Dame *La Blanche*, located in the north transept (see Pl. 4). It was instituted at Saint-Denis by Blanche (d. 1392), daughter of Charles IV:

> The *Missa De Beata* which is said [*se dit*] everyday at six in the morning in the church of the royal abbey of Saint-Denis-en-France was founded in the fourteenth century by the Princess Blanche de France . . . This Princess . . . founded in the chapel of Notre Dame *La Blanche*, so called because of her, a Mass which should be said every day in this chapel where this Princess is buried along with other Princes and other Princesses of her family. Apart from this Mass which should be said every day both for her and for her family, we execute her anniversary annually on the 7th February [8 February in Saint-Denis calendar]. This Princess gave the abbey of Saint-Denis the land of Muneville le Bingard in the diocese of Coutance in Normandy.[222]

The chapel was named *La Blanche* because it contained a statue of Mary carved in white marble, the gift of Queen Jeanne d'Évreux in 1340.[223]

[221] F:Pn, lat. 2290, fo. 135; F:LA 118, fo. 207ᵛ.

[222] 'La Messe *De Beata* qui se dit tous les jours à six heure [*sic*] du matin dans l'Église de l'Abbaye Royale de Saint Denis en france a étée fondée dans le quatorzieme siècle par La Princesse Blanche De france . . . Cette Princesse . . . fonda dans la chapelle de notre Dame *La Blanche* ainsi nommée à cause d'elle une Messe qui se doit se dire chacque jour dans cette chapelle où cette Princesse est inhumée avec d'autres Princes, et d'autres Princesses de sa famille. Indépendamment de cette Messe qui doit etre dite chacque jour tant pour elle que sa famille, on fait tous les Ans son Anniversaire le sept du Mois de fevrier. C'est cette Princesse qui a donnée à l'Abbaye de S. Denis la terre de Muneville le Bingard, Diocese de Coutance en Basse Normandie'; F:Pan, L 836, No. 5 (18th-c. copy).

[223] Félibien, *Histoire*, 533.

An examination of these services and documents relating to them for traces of special music for the Virgin—polyphonic antiphons, motets, Mass—reveals no hint of the kind of polyphony that proliferated in the late Middle Ages in many other churches. In fact, it is not even clear that Blanche's foundation was for a sung Mass. One kind of monophonic music at Saint-Denis, on the other hand, may have been specially intended for these Marian Masses. The sequences for the Virgin in F:Pn, lat. 1107 and in GB:Lva 1346–1891 (Table 3.9) that are not assigned to particular feasts were probably used in the Saturday or perhaps in the daily Lady Mass.

Chaplaincies

The daily Mass for Mary, along with other celebrations in the chapels of the church, constitutes an important type of endowed observance in the abbey. The first known foundation at Saint-Denis was Abbot Hilduin's Office in the chapel at the eastern end of the crypt, discussed earlier. The royal endowments for anniversary services, such as Charles V's establishment in the chapel of John the Baptist (see Pl. 4), have likewise been treated in Chapter 2. Other endowments in the chapels of Saint-Denis were no doubt made between the ninth and thirteenth centuries, but only from the thirteenth century on do we find evidence of services celebrated regularly in places other than the choir of Saint-Denis. The evidence comes in the form of the records of the chaplaincies that were instituted in the various chapels and altars of Saint-Denis. Chaplaincies were set up through endowments, often made by lay persons from outside the community and consisting of sums of money earmarked for the recitation of a Mass (or Masses) on a specified day (or days). Sometimes the founder reserved the right to name the chaplain(s) who would carry out the foundation, as in the endowment of 1209 discussed below. An altar could receive more than one establishment; in fact, a number of the altars in the church became the sites of multiple chaplaincies. Once again, there is no evidence that any of the Masses that resulted from these foundations entailed polyphony or any other specially composed music. When the documents specify the type of service to be performed, they almost always stipulate what was probably a spoken Mass (*submissa voce*).

The records of the chaplaincies of Saint-Denis are found in the *Comptes de la Commanderie* of the abbey. The first known chaplaincy was founded in 1209 at the altar of Saint Hippolytus,[224] then located in the middle of the nave, but moved in 1236 to the first chapel west of the

[224] Ibid. 217.

north transept (see Pl. 4). By the end of the thirteenth century, there were at least eight chaplaincies in the church. The wording of the establishments names either the persons who founded the chaplaincies or the altar at which the foundations were made, and sometimes there is a mixture of both types of information, as in this list from 1281–2:

For the support [*pro beneficio*] of [the chaplaincy of] Alabuhorde . . .
For the support of [the chaplaincy of] Balduinus Carpentarius . . .
For the support of [the chaplaincy of] Count [Alphonse] of Poitiers . . .
For the support of [the chaplaincy of] Saint Nicholas. . .[225]
For the support of [the chaplaincy of] Saint Demetrius [subdedicatee at altar of Hilary of Mende] . . .
For the support of [the chaplaincy of] the wife of Johannes de Mitriaco . . .
For the support of [the chaplaincy of] Saint Clement [chapel probably located in north-east corner of cloister] . . .
For the support of [the chaplaincy of] Saint Hipploytus [chapel located on north side of church, Pl. 4].[226]

The presence of Saint Demetrius on this list probably solves the mystery of how his feast entered the liturgy of Saint-Denis between 1234 and 1259, as discussed in Chapter 2. There is no record of veneration of Demetrius at Saint-Denis before this time, and we can suggest that the endowment instituting the chaplaincy for this saint caused the monks to add his festival to the ritual. This was one important way in which new feasts entered local liturgies in the late Middle Ages.

The number of chaplaincies at Saint-Denis continued to grow throughout the fourteenth century. In 1411 there were some 24 chaplaincies in the church, several of which were founded at the new fourteenth-century altars of Saints Vincent, Nicholas, Mary Magdalene, and Lawrence:

One chaplaincy at altar of Saint Vincent under the lectern, founded by Queen Margaret (20 *livres parisienses*).
Two chaplaincies at altar of Saint Nicholas under the lectern, one founded by Thomas Crasset, another by Queen Margaret (20 *livres parisienses*).
Two chaplaincies at altar of Mary Magdalene [*north side of nave, Pl. 4*], one founded by Mary de Mitriaco, another by Robert Fullon.

[225] Suger mentions a chapel dedicated to Saint Nicholas in the west façade of the church, but Crosby is uncertain as to how long this chapel continued in use; see Panofsky, *Suger*, 45, 151; Crosby, *Abbey*, 159–60. By the mid-13th c. Nicholas was a subdedicatee at the altar of Hilary of Mende in the chevet (Table 4.1), but it is still possible that his chaplaincy was established in the west façade and was later moved to the nave (see below).

[226] F:Pan, LL 1240, fo. 14^{v}. The subsequent list of foundations from the 15th c. will show that there were often several chaplaincies at a single altar. It is impossible to determine whether or not this is the case in this late 13th-c. document. The precise locations of a number of the chaplaincies mentioned in this document (e.g. Alabuhorde) are clear from the 15th-c. document (below).

Three chaplaincies at altar of Saint Lawrence [north side of nave, Pl. 4], one called Saint Clarus' chaplaincy and held by Lord Master Stephen who is in charge at Gisors, second founded by Count [Alphonse] of Poitiers (16 *livres*), third founded by Guillelmus Leber.

Three chaplaincies at altar of Saint Bartholomew,[227] one founded by Simon the Wise, second founded by Alabuhorde, third founded by Balduinus Carpentarius.

One chaplaincy at altar of Saint Sanctinus [= John Baptist and Charles V chapel, Pl. 4].

One chaplaincy at altar of Saint Andrew [possibly at Peregrinus' altar, where Andrew was subdedicatee, Pl. 4], founded by the Count of Augus.

Four chaplaincies at altar *de Passu* [possibly in the chapel of Saint Clement], one called Saint Clement's chaplaincy and founded by Matthew Bellehomme, second founded by Queen Margaret (20 *livres*), third founded by King Philip V (40 *livres*), fourth was called the 'Capella picta'.

Two chaplaincies at altar of Saint Hippolytus [north side of nave, Pl. 4], one called Saint Hippolytus' chaplaincy, the other called Saint Vincent and Nicholas's chaplaincy.

One chaplaincy at altar of Saint Demetrius [possibly at Hilary of Mende's altar, where Demetrius was subdedicatee, Pl. 4].

Four chaplaincies at altar of Saint Sanctinus [= John Baptist and Charles V chapel, Pl. 4], one founded by Petronilla de Chambliaco, second founded by Mary de Mitriaco, third founded by King Philip V, fourth founded by Johannes Augier, tailor and citizen of Paris.[228]

This list provides new information on the location of an altar to Saint Vincent. In the thirteenth century Vincent was probably venerated in the chapel of Saint Cucuphas in the chevet (see Pl. 3) where he was a subdedicatee, as noted earlier. The cult of Vincent, which was exceptionally strong at this time, evidently continued to increase to the point where he was assigned his own altar, and Félibien notes that the chapels of Saints Vincent and Nicholas had been 'transférez aux autels de la nef'[229]. The location of the altars of Saints Vincent and Nicholas 'under the lectern' (*lectrinum*) presumably means the lectern or pulpit on the rood screen, that is the *lectrinum in pulpito*.[230] The Vincent and Nicholas altars would therefore probably have stood just to the west of the screen on the north side of the church.

[227] Like the chapel of Saint Nicholas, mentioned in n. 225, the chapel of Saint Bartholomew was located in the west façade of Suger's church, and Panofsky believes that it may have shared its location with the altar of Saint Nicholas; *Suger*, 99, 133–5, 151–3; Crosby, *Abbey*, 159–60. The fact that Bartholomew's altar is the site of a chaplaincy in this 15th-c. document suggests either that it was still in use in this location, or that the chaplaincy was located at Cucuphas' altar in the chevet, where Bartholomew was a subdedicatee (Table 4.1).

[228] Paraphrased from Félibien's edn. in *Histoire*, *PJ*, pt. ii, pp. ccxx–ccxxi. This document likewise shows that the abbey also kept records of a number of chaplaincies that were founded in other churches in the town.

[229] *Histoire*, 533.

[230] See Harrison, *Britain*, 52.

The foregoing discussion shows that important aspects of the ritual and music of Saint-Denis did reflect the succession of rebuildings of the abbey and the philosophy of the monks. Hilduin's addition of a chapel to the east end of the Carolingian church inaugurated the celebration of services outside the choir of Saint-Denis, and subsequent endowments, both royal and otherwise, filled virtually all the altars of Saint-Denis with celebrations by the end of the Middle Ages. Hand-in-hand with the reconstructions of the twelfth, thirteenth, and fourteenth centuries came significant enhancements of the ritual which included votive services for the Virgin and for Saint Denis, new liturgical books, numerous feasts, processions, and a confraternity for Saint Denis. The music for the Benedicamus Domino and Ite Missa Est for Saints Vincent and Benedict complements the stained-glass windows for these saints.

The philosophy of the abbey is apparent in two Offices for Saint Denis, which deliberately connect Saint Denis and the Areopagite figures, in the Areopagitist Hy. *Celi cives* and the Seq. *Salve pater*, *Ave pater gallie*, and *Doctorem egregium*, in the compilation of the Greek Mass, and perhaps even in the emphasis that the monks placed on melismas rather than on texted or polyphonic forms of music. The political overtones of this philosophy are likewise clear in the use of perpetual psalmody in the seventh century for the souls of dead kings, in the preservation of the Gallican vestiges in the late medieval ritual which nurtured the royal–monastic partnership, and in the anniversaries for kings. There can be little doubt that through the ages, artistic, architectural, and political implications were purposefully and inextricably woven into the liturgical fabric of Saint-Denis.

5

Performance Practices, Musicians, and Liturgists

Charged with the burials of kings and the yearly commemoration of these events, the monks of Saint-Denis paid close attention to the solemnity of the royal services as early as the twelfth century. The feastdays for the patron saint likewise varied in level of cult from *annuale* to duplex, and the community showed concern for the performance of its worship when it enhanced the ceremony of older celebrations, created new ranks of feasts, and added festivals to the liturgy in the thirteenth and fourteenth centuries. The monks were no less solicitous about the execution of their plainsong, and they clearly aimed for quality in singing, as the rubrics *bene cantans* ('singing well') and *honeste intonans* ('intoning properly') throughout the ordinaries of the abbey attest.[1] In addition, they carefully assigned many of the performing ensembles which sang the Divine Office. Although neither customary nor ceremonial from Saint-Denis exists,[2] the ordinaries, histories, and archival documents provide details on many aspects of performance practice in the abbey. The picture that emerges, at least for the execution of certain chants, suggests that Dom Doublet's seemingly partisan extolling of the Divine Service in the abbey in the seventeenth century was perhaps little exaggerated—the splendour of the festivals may in fact have approached the level which he considered to be nowhere in France more striking than at Saint-Denis.[3]

SINGING DUTIES

The number of persons at Saint-Denis varied from around 200 in 1297 to as few as 37 in the tumultuous year of the Huguenot invasion in 1567.[4] For Suger's abbacy (1122–51), Giles Constable names the

[1] See e.g. F:Pm 526, fos. 10, 12, 16ᵛ, 17, 53, 57ᵛ, 106ᵛ; F:Pn, lat. 976, fo. 30ᵛ, etc.

[2] Although F:Pan, L 863, No. 10 is called a *cérémonial*, it was copied from a 14th-c. ordinary. It does, however, give some information that would normally be found in a ceremonial.

[3] Doublet, *Histoire*, 353.

[4] The following figures are taken for the most part from primary sources cited in Constable, 'Administration', 25, and his n. 158; Raugel, 'Saint-Denis', col. 1248; Félibien, *Histoire*, 339: 150 monks in the 9th c., 180 under Philip Augustus (reg. 1180–1223), 200 in 1294, 132 under Charles VI (reg. 1380–1422), 70 in 1418, and 37 in 1567.

officers of the monastery, who also figure in the later ordinaries and necrologies: abbot, prior, subprior, *precentor* (cantor), infirmarian, treasurer, sacrist, chancellor, cellarer, almoner.[5] The relative ranks of these persons seem to be indicated by the order in which they witnessed charters in the twelfth century, as given above. Other employees of the community included the chamberlain, *coenator*, notary, doctor, provost, and cartographer.[6] As far as we know, Saint-Denis never laid down *consuetudines* which doubtless would have spelled out the specific duties of these officers and other members of the community with regard to the performance of the Divine Office. But the information in the three ordinaries, combined with that from other monastic establishments, helps sort out who assisted in the services of the abbey.

The ordinaries reveal the musical priority of the participants, which differs from the administrative priority of the officers just listed. In terms of singing assignments, the cantor (also called *archicantor* or *precentor*) was clearly the most important. Next in line were various numbers of singers (*cantores*) from an informal pool of monks with decently good voices, including those chosen weekly to act as *hebdomadarius*.[7] After these came the chief officer of the monastery, the abbot. Beneath the abbot were the *priores*, monks of particularly high seniority, followed by others of a little less seniority (*seniores*, *antiquiores*, *antiqui*). The next persons in the musical hierarchy were the *sacerdotes*, a level that encompasses the aforementioned abbot and senior monks, all of whom who were probably priests. The musical assignments made to the *sacerdotes* distinguish between these senior and the more junior monks. Finally came the youths in the choir-stalls (*juvenes de stallo*), youths on the floor of the choir (*juvenes de raya*), and the boys (*pueri*). Four *minores*, probably young novices of the monastery, are mentioned once in the ordinaries in the singing of the solo portions of the second alleluia on Pentecost.[8]

The choir was no doubt arranged in three rows on the left and right stalls of the lower choir in the church, with the senior monks on the upper and back row, the more junior monks and the *juvenes de stallo* on the lower row, and the *juvenes de raya* and the boys on the floor.

[5] Constable, 'Administration', 25. After the sacrist (*capicerius*), Constable lists a 'chanter', but this person is probably the cantor of the monastery (*cantor*), synonymous with *precentor*.

[6] Ibid.

[7] On the Office of *hebdomadarius* in medieval England, see Harrison, *Britain*, 51–2; other references to the *hebdomadarius* can be found in Fassler, 'Cantor', 40–7; and in Davril, *Floriacenses*, 13 and *passim*. The *hebdomadarius* in the ordinaries of Saint-Denis, as in the works just mentioned, would normally have been chosen from among the most capable singers; he was not one of the other types of official who rotated on a weekly basis (*hebdomadarius sacerdos*, *hebdomadarius subdiaconus*, etc.) and who are routinely mentioned in medieval ordinaries and customaries.

[8] F:Pm 526, fo. 74. On the *minores*, see Du Cange, *Glossarium*, v. 402, s.v. 'Minores'.

Whereas all three ordinaries witness the functions of these singers, F:Pan, L 863, No. 10 more often names them by their office or status, while the two thirteenth-century books (F:Pm 526 and F:Pn, lat. 976) normally provide only the numbers of singers.[9]

The Cantor and his Associates

The cantor of Saint-Denis is designated by several different names. Archival sources of the twelfth and thirteenth centuries frequently call him *precentor* (Table 5.1, below), and the thirteenth- and fourteenth-century ordinaries write *archicantor*, evidently synonymous with *precentor*. Necrological documents from the fourteenth to sixteenth centuries clarify the terminology by differentiating between the cantor of the monastery, whom they now call *cantor* rather than *precentor* or *archicantor*, and the next official down, the *succentor* (*subcantor*, *soubz chantre*). They likewise refer to the *tercius cantor*. The nature of their positions at Saint-Denis can be gleaned from the references in the thirteenth- and fourteenth-century ordinaries, as described below.

The ordinaries mention the cantor (*precentor*/*archicantor*) in two places, both of which are found in the Mass for Easter Day. The *archicantor* and two of his colleagues, holding the staves that are the sign of their office, intone the introit,[10] and the *archicantor* alone begins the sequence.[11] This *archicantor* is probably also the person intended in the ordinaries when the word *cantor* appears in the singular in the context of *annuale* feasts other than Easter. On Christmas, Assumption, and the feast of Saint Denis, he and six others sing the solo parts of the pre-eminent twelfth responsory at Matins,[12] and he joins as many as four soloists on the final ninth responsory on the anniversaries of Philip IV, Philip Augustus, Abbot Peter, and those which are celebrated similarly.[13] During the major procession after Terce on Christmas, the cantor (*precentor*/*archicantor*) intones the processional Ant. *O beata infancia*, and he chants the solo portions of the processional Resp. *Styrps jesse* and *Verbum caro*.[14] He likewise begins the Kyrie at the principal Mass at Christmas, and he intones the antiphons to the Magnificat at Vespers and to the Benedictus at Lauds on many

[9] At Matins on Dagobert's anniversary, for instance, F:Pan, L 863, No. 10 writes 'sextum [responsorium] a *quinque prioribus* in cappis' (fo. 137ᵛ). On the same feast: 'Resp. *Libera me domine* a *quinque* in cappis' (F:Pm 526, fo. 100; F:Pn, lat. 976, fo. 71). Since the 3 ordinaries almost invariably agree on numbers of performers and on their ranks, it is likely that the extra details found in F:Pan, L 863, No. 10 on certain feasts apply to the 13th-c. sources as well.

[10] See the discussion of the tropes to the introit on Easter in Ch. 3.

[11] F:Pm 526, fos. 57–57ᵛ; F:Pn, lat. 976, fo. 30ᵛ.

[12] F:Pan, L 863, No. 10, p. 2.

[13] Ibid. fos. 135ᵛ, 139, 140.

[14] F:Pm 526, fo. 16; F:Pan, L 863, No. 10, p. 23.

anniversaries. In addition, he initiates the first psalmodic antiphon at Vespers on *annuale* feasts, whereas at Lauds on *annuale* feasts, at Matins on anniversaries, and at Vespers on lesser occasions, the *hebdomadarius* usually intones the first antiphon to the psalms at Vespers. One *hebdomadarius* also serves as soloist for the fourth responsory at Matins on the Vigils of Christmas and Pentecost, and two *hebdomadarii* intone the responsory after the chapter reading as well as the closing chant *Requiescant in pace* during the Little Hours on Dagobert's anniversary.[15]

It is not clear from the ordinaries whether or not the cantor (*precentor/archicantor*) sings at Mass on high feasts lower than *annuale* rank. On most duplex feasts, the ordinaries call for three *cantores* as soloists for the introit. One of these is perhaps the *succentor*, although these *cantores* might also have been three singers recognized as particularly capable. Two of the three may have acted as *rectores chori* of the left and right sides of the choir. Most other feasts of twelve lessons and higher call for one or two *cantores* in the choir to begin the introit at Mass. On some minor twelve-lesson feasts, it was possible to cut corners by designating *hebdomadarii* to serve as *rectores chori*. This latter arrangement is certainly the case at the first and second Masses on Christmas Day (before the principal Mass), at Mass on certain Vigils and feasts during Lent, on a few simple twelve-lesson celebrations, and on most anniversaries as described in F:Pan, L 863, No. 10, where one or two *hebdomadarii* rule the choir.[16]

In medieval establishments the cantor (*precentor/archicantor*) customarily selected the variable musical items of the Mass and Offices, and the thirteenth-century ordinaries from Saint-Denis use the word *cantor* in these instances no doubt to refer to him. The cantor (*precentor/archicantor*) gave the starting pitch to the person chosen to intone the antiphon before the gospel and other important pieces,[17] appointed the *priores* who initiated the antiphons to the psalms at First Vespers on the highest feasts,[18] selected the sequence for the day,[19] and decided who would take particular, designated roles in services and

[15] F:Pm 526, fo. 138; F:Pan, L 863, No. 10, p. 23.

[16] Fos. 136, 136^{v}, 139.

[17] At Mass on Easter Day: 'transmittat cantor quemdam bene cantantem in capicio ante martyres qui honeste ante evangelium intonet antiphonam *Crucem sanctam subiit*'; F:Pm 526, fo. 57^{v}; F:Pn, lat. 976, fo. 30^{v}.

[18] 'Cantor incipiat primam antiphonam *Justorum anime* . . . Alie antiphone incipiantur a prioribus cui [*sic*] jusserit'; F:Pm 526, fo. 180; F:Pn, lat. 976, fo. 133^{v}.

[19] Ayzac, *Histoire*, i. 263. The table of sequences at Saint-Denis (see Table 3.9) demonstrates that there was some fluctuation from one MS to another in the choice of these chants, particularly in the 13th c.

processions,[20] no doubt publishing these assignments in the *tabula*.[21] If his other musical and ceremonial duties mirrored those of the cantor in Cluniac houses of the eleventh century, he likewise served as musical prompter during the Mass and Offices, corrected the performances of others, and had charge of the production and upkeep of books in the scriptorium and library.[22] The *hebdomadarius* also had some authority at Saint-Denis, for it was he who chose the *priores* who intoned the last four psalmodic antiphons at Lauds on the highest feasts.[23]

Later sources from the abbey indicate that there was a major shift in the duties of the official cantor (*precentor/archicantor*) of the monastery. Between the thirteenth and sixteenth centuries, the cantor of Saint-Denis sometimes performed routine, non-liturgical business. He also served occasionally as a diplomat or wrote chronicles, as we will see. By the end of the Middle Ages, the *succentor* seems to have taken over the most important musical functions at Saint-Denis.[24]

The Abbot and the Priores

The abbot (*abbas*), along with four of the most senior monks (*priores*), chanted the solo portions of the eighth responsory at Matins on the *annuale* feasts of Christmas[25] and Saint Denis,[26] and he also intoned the antiphon to the Benedictus at Lauds on Christmas and on Easter.[27] He likewise sang the V. *Viderunt omnes* in the nave of the church during the procession after Terce on Christmas.[28] Because of his senior rank, the abbot headed the procession to the altar at Mass on the highest feasts. This seems to have been the extent of his participation as soloist in the musical aspects of celebrations at Saint-Denis, and it is clear that

[20] The ordinaries record that the *cantor* chose the special ensemble which sang the tropes to the introit at Christmas and Easter (see Ch. 3), that he selected the soloist for the 2nd responsory at Matins on the 3rd Sunday in Advent (F:Pm 526, fo. 10), and that he chose the *priores* who intoned the antiphons at First Vespers on the feast of Saint Denis (F:Pm 526, fo. 180; F:Pn, lat. 976, fo. 133[v]). He no doubt made many other assignments which are simply taken for granted in the ordinaries.

[21] On the *tabula*, see Harrison, *Britain*, 52.

[22] See Fassler's description of the *armarius/cantor*, as discussed in the customary of Bernard of Cluny (1067); 'Cantor', 48–9. The *Règlement des offices claustraux* of Saint-Denis (F:Pan, LL 1180, fo. 19[v]) from the 15th c. likewise identifies the maintenance of books as the principal duty of the cantor; see also Nebbiai-Dalla Guarda, *Bibliothèque*, 70.

[23] On Christmas: 'Prima Ant. *Quem vidistis* quam incipiat ebdomadarius, reliquas antiphonas incipiant priores quibus jusserit ipse'; F:Pm 526, fo. 15[v].

[24] Such was also the case at the cathedral of Saint-Lambert in Liège in the 15th and 16th cs., where the *succentor* directed musical activities, while the cantor (*grand chantre*), no longer serving as a musician, acted as administrative director; Quitin, 'Maîtres', 9.

[25] F:Pm 526, fo. 15; F:Pan, L 863, No. 10, p. 2.

[26] F:Pm 526, fo. 180[v]; F:Pn, lat. 976, fo. 134; F:Pan, L 863, No. 10, fo. 124[v].

[27] F:Pm 526, fos. 15, 56[v].

[28] Ibid. fo. 16[v]; F:Pan, L 863, No. 10, p. 23.

his involvement was a consequence of his rank rather than of his musical expertise.

Apart from the function of the *priores* at Matins on Christmas, three, four, or five *priores* served as soloists for the sixth responsory at Matins on the anniversaries of Queen Margaret,[29] King Philip IV,[30] and King Dagobert, respectively.[31] Four *priores* in habits chanted the eighth responsory on the Octave of Saint Denis.[32] An unspecified number of *priores* likewise initiated the second, third, and fourth antiphons of First Vespers on Christmas,[33] the feast of Saint-Denis,[34] and Dagobert's anniversary;[35] and they chanted the last four and sometimes all five antiphons at Lauds on feasts where they did not sing the Matins antiphons.[36] Only on *annuale* feasts did the *priores* begin the antiphons both of Lauds and of Matins.[37]

Other Senior Monks

Next in descending order of dignity in singing assignments were the monks of slightly less seniority than the *priores* just mentioned: the *seniores*,[38] *antiquiores*, or *antiqui*.[39] On Dagobert's anniversary the *antiqui* played an active role at Matins, during which time three of them served as soloists for the fifth and eighth responsories. In similar fashion, the seventh and tenth responsories on Christmas were chanted by three and two *antiqui*, respectively. For the more important eleventh responsory, three somewhat more senior monks, called *antiquiores*, were chosen.[40] Earlier, at Vespers, one of four *antiquiores* in the choir was appointed to the first psalmodic antiphon, and the remaining three chanted the subsequent psalms. All four *antiquiores* executed the solo parts of the responsory after the chapter reading.[41] A like number of *antiqui* likewise chanted the sequence, perhaps antiphonally in groups of two, during Dagobert's Mass.[42] The pre-eminence of the *priores* over the *seniores* (*antiqui*, *antiquiores*) is evident in the performance of all but the first antiphon at Matins by *priores* on Dagobert's feast and by

[29] F:Pan, L 863, No. 10, fo. 136.

[30] Ibid. fo. 135^{v}.

[31] Ibid. fo. 137^{v}.

[32] F:Pm 526, fo. 183^{v}; F:Pn, lat. 976, fo. 137.

[33] F:Pm 526, fo. 14^{v}.

[34] Ibid. fo. 180; F:Pn, lat. 976, fo. 133^{v}; F:Pan, L 863, No. 10, fo. 124.

[35] F:Pan, L 863, No. 10, fo. 137.

[36] On the Vigils of Christmas and of Saint-Denis, the *hebdomadarius* intoned the first antiphon of Lauds, and the *priores* began the rest; F:Pm 526, fos. 14, 180^{v}; F:Pn, lat. 976, fo. 134; F:Pan, L 863, No. 10, fo. 124^{v}.

[37] F:Pm 526, fo. 9^{v}.

[38] Term used in the 13th-c. ordinaries F:Pm 526 and F:Pn, lat. 976.

[39] Terms used in the 14th-c. ordinary F:Pan, L 863, No. 10.

[40] See the discussion of Matins of Dagobert's feast, as compared with Christmas, in Ch. 2.

[41] F:Pan, L 863, No. 10, fos. 137^{r-v}

[42] Ibid. fo. 138.

the *seniores* on the slightly less elaborate anniversary of Philip Augustus.[43]

Monk-Priests

The next category in the array of soloists at Saint-Denis, the monk-priests (*sacerdotes*), overlaps the ones already mentioned. This order normally included the abbot and senior monks (*priores*, *seniores*, *antiquiores*, *antiqui*), and the word *sacerdotes* thus seems to be used to distinguish between those monks who were priests and those who had not yet attained this level. As many as four *sacerdotes* were assigned to the solo sections of the Vespers responsory on the anniversary of Charles the Bald,[44] but sometimes two *sacerdotes* shared this honour with two youths.[45] At Matins four *sacerdotes* held pride of place on the final responsory of the first nocturn on Christmas and on Dagobert's anniversary,[46] whereas three and two *sacerdotes*, respectively, chanted this same item on the less ornate anniversaries of Philip IV[47] and Queen Margaret,[48] and on the other anniversaries for which these are the prototypes. At Mass three *sacerdotes* served as soloists for the gradual on Dagobert's anniversary in the fourteenth century,[49] whereas four *sacerdotes* chanted this piece in the thirteenth century.[50] The same number of *sacerdotes* likewise sang the sequence (Tr. *De profundis*) on the anniversaries of Philip IV,[51] Abbot Peter,[52] and Abbot Yves,[53] and on those that were ordered in like manner. On Dagobert's more elaborate anniversary, the word *antiqui*, rather than *sacerdotes*, is used to designate the soloists for the *De profundis* at Mass.

Youths

At the lower end of the hierarchy of performers at Saint-Denis were the youths (*juvenes*), and beneath them the boys (*pueri*).[54] The youths

[43] F:Pn, lat. 976, fo. 107.

[44] Ibid. fo. 141.

[45] Ibid. fo. 135ᵛ (anniversary of Philip IV and those conducted in similar fashion).

[46] See the comparison of Matins of Dagobert's feast with Christmas in Ch. 2.

[47] F:Pan, L 863, No. 10, fo. 135ᵛ. 3 *sacerdotes* likewise performed the 3rd responsory on the anniversary of Philip Augustus (fo. 140).

[48] Ibid. fo. 136.

[49] Ibid. fo. 138.

[50] F:Pm 526, fo. 100ᵛ; F:Pn, lat. 976, fo. 71ᵛ. Neither MS specifies the soloists as *sacerdotes*, but the use of the word in F:Pan, L 863, No. 10 on the same feast suggests that it was also intended in the 13th-c. ordinaries.

[51] F:Pan, L 863, No. 10, fo. 136.

[52] Ibid. fo. 139.

[53] Ibid.

[54] The ordinaries consistently differentiate *pueri* and *juvenes*. See e.g. F:Pan, L 863, No. 10, which calls for both boys and youths to wear white copes, or albs, at the daybreak Mass on Easter: 'Ad hanc missam pueri et juvenes omnes debent esse in albis' (p. 23).

and boys were apparently educated in the abbey,[55] and many of them no doubt became novices. The *juvenes* were boys whose voices had changed; the younger *pueri* had unbroken voices. The *juvenes* were further subdivided into *juvenes de stallo* who sat in the choir-stalls, and the *juvenes de raya*[56] who sat in benches on the floor. Two *juvenes de stallo* joined with two *sacerdotes* to chant the solo parts of the Vespers responsory on Philip IV's anniversary and on those based on it.[57] At Matins two youths in the choir stalls served as soloists for the ninth responsory of Christmas, and for the corresponding seventh responsory on the anniversaries of Dagobert, Philip IV, and Philip Augustus, and for other services that referred back to these.[58] A single *juvenis de stallo* functioned likewise on the seventh responsory of the anniversary of Queen Margaret and of others that mirrored hers.[59]

The *juvenes de raya* were lower not only in physical placement in the church but also in dignity with respect to musical assignments. Theirs were the relatively less important third and fifth responsories at Matins of Christmas, as well as the fourth responsory on the anniversaries of the kings named above and of like observances.[60] One *juvenis de raya* chanted the fourth responsory on Margaret's anniversary and on those which hark back to it.[61] Two *juvenes de raya* ruled the choir from the seats on the floor at the morning Mass on the simplest anniversaries, all of which were patterned after the celebration for Abbot Yves. From this same location, they likewise executed the solo parts of the introit and the gradual.[62]

Boys

The boys (*pueri*) usually performed in pairs. They chanted the solo parts of the second responsory at Matins on Christmas, on the feasts of

[55] Two *magistri*, one for the boys and another for the youths, were paid for their services throughout the 13th and 14th cs. Evidently the instruction the boys received included the knowledge of singing, as Donatella Nebbiai-Dalla Guarda has shown in the discovery of payments to a *magister puerorum de cantu* in 1287–8 (F:Pan, LL 1240, fo. 63, as cited in Nebbiai-Dalla Guarda, *Bibliothèque*, 28). See also her 'Documents pour l'histoire de la bibliothèque' for a full listing of disbursements to the *magister puerorum* and the *magister juvenum*; ibid. 336–57. That these 2 Offices continued in the 15th and 16th cs. is clear from the necrology from Saint-Denis, F:Pan, LL 1320, which records the deaths of 9 *magistri puerorum* and 2 *magistri juvenum* between 1421 and the 1590s (see the edn. of this necrology in Samaran, 'Études', 56–81, Nos. 314, 468, 515, 533, 547, 559, 571, 628, 637, 387, 618).

[56] The word *raya* means 'line' or 'order'; see Du Cange, *Glossarium*, s.v. 'Reia' (French = Raïe).

[57] F:Pan, L 863, No. 10, fo. 135ᵛ.

[58] Ibid. 10, fos. 135ᵛ, 137ᵛ, 140. See also the comparison of Matins of Dagobert's feast with Christmas in Ch. 2.

[59] Ibid. fo. 136.

[60] Ibid. fos. 135ᵛ, 137ᵛ, 140. See also the comparison of Matins of Dagobert's feast with Christmas in Ch. 2.

[61] See n. 59 above.

[62] F:Pan, L 863, No. 10, fo. 139.

the three kings already named, and on services which drew from these;[63] and they sang the responsory at First Vespers and Lauds on the Vigils of Christmas[64] and Saint Denis,[65] and at Lauds on the twelve-lesson feasts of the Decollation of John the Baptist (29 August)[66] and of Matthew (21 September).[67] The versicles of all Offices, including the ornate Benedicamus Domino[68] on feasts of duplex rank and higher, were almost always assigned to two *pueri*.[69]

On some occasions one boy performed alone. A single boy, for example, chanted the second responsory at Matins of Queen Margaret and on anniversaries derived from hers,[70] and in general on all feasts of twelve lessons, except during the third week in Advent, when a soloist chosen by the cantor performed this piece.[71] On feasts of three lessons, a boy began the antiphon to the psalms at First Vespers, unless the day was shared with a twelve-lesson festival, in which case the *hebdomadarius* took his place.[72] One boy dressed in a white garment, or alb, performed the solo parts of the gradual and alleluia at Mass on ferial days.[73] Apparently the boys had their own internal hierarchy, according to which one boy served as soloist for the week. At Matins on ferial days the boy who had just finished his term as soloist (*puer hebdomadarius de alia ebdomada*) chanted the short reading of the first nocturn, while the current *puer hebdomadarius* executed the versicle which followed the responsory.[74]

SPECIAL ASPECTS OF PERFORMANCE OF THE MASS AND HOURS

The ordinaries of Saint-Denis distinguish grades of feasts in several ways. The numbers of singers on important items are the rubrics most consistently given, and, for higher festivals, there is also evidence about the locations of performers in the church, the use of special chants, incense, processions and other actions, and the kinds of vestment worn by the major participants. Taken together, these elements clearly differentiate one level of celebration from another. The ordinaries show

[63] See n. 58 above.

[64] F:Pm 526, fo. 13^{v}.

[65] Ibid. fos. 179^{r-v}; F:Pn, lat. 976, fos. 132^{v}–133; F:Pan, L 863, No. 10, fos. 123^{v}–124.

[66] F:Pm 526, fo. 164; F:Pn, lat. 976, fo. 121^{v}.

[67] F:Pm 526, fo. 172^{v}; F:Pn, lat. 976, fo. 127^{v} (where the word *pueris* is erased).

[68] See the section on the *Benedicamus* above; also Robertson, '*Benedicamus*', 7.

[69] One exception comes on First Vespers of the Vigil of Christmas, where the versicle following the hymn was performed by 1 boy; F:Pm 526, fo. 47.

[70] F:Pan, L 863, No. 10, fo. 136.

[71] F:Pm 526, fo. 10.

[72] Ibid. fo. 78; F:Pn, lat. 976, fos. 47^{r-v}.

[73] F:Pm 526, fo. 79^{v}; F:Pn, lat. 976. fos. 48^{v}–49.

[74] F:Pm 526, fo. 78^{v}; F:Pn, lat. 976, fo. 47^{v}.

further that fine shades of variation existed even among observances of the same rank. Indeed, enough information has survived to give a fairly detailed picture of the performance of the Mass and Offices at Saint-Denis. The following discussion treats the principal services, after which a brief comparison of the number of soloists on responsorial chants in these ceremonies with evidence found in other places will show that the celebrations at Saint-Denis in the thirteenth and fourteenth centuries were often as elaborate in this respect as those of the greatest churches in the West.

First Vespers

Vespers on *annuale* feasts was conducted with considerable pomp. On Christmas Day,[75] for example, all participants dressed in albs. Three *cantores* in festive copes stood in the choir.[76] One of these *cantores* intoned the first of the four antiphons to the psalms; the others were begun by *priores*. After the reading of the lesson, four soloists in copes chanted the solo portions of the prolix responsory. The final portion of the responsory, the *repetendum*, was repeated by the choir both after the verse and after the Gloria Patri. The community sang the antiphon to the Magnificat three times. On *semiannuale* and duplex feasts at Saint-Denis, the Vespers responsory was likewise chanted by four singers, vested usually in copes and on a few occasions in habits.[77] All *semiannuale* services and duplex celebrations of saints with relics in the church featured three *cantores* in the choir at Vespers.[78] The main difference between these two grades of celebration of Vespers is the number of times the Magnificat antiphon was intoned: three times on *semiannuale* celebrations, and twice on duplex festivals.[79] On festivals of all the ranks named so far, two thurifers with their incense vessels

[75] F:Pm 526, fos. 14^{v}–17.

[76] Rubrics for the feast of Saint Denis specify red copes; F:Pm 526, fo. 180; F:Pn, lat. 976, fo. 133^{v}. F:Pn, lat. 976 (fo. 159) stipulates the use of 3 *cantores* in the choir not only on *annuale* feasts but also on the celebrations that were designated as *semiannuale* in the 14th c., on the festivals of Saints Stephen (26 Dec.) and Innocents (28 Dec.), on the feasts of saints whose relics were in the church, and on the anniversaries of Abbot Suger (12, 14 Jan.), King Dagobert (19 Jan.), Philip Augustus (14 July), Robert II (20 July), Louis VI (2 Aug.), and Charles the Bald (6 Oct.), on All Souls Day (2 Nov.) and on the general anniversary of relatives and benefactors of members of the community, which took place after the feast of the Relics (Sunday after Ascension) some time in May or early June (F:Pan, L 863, No. 10, fo. 139^{v}).

[77] See the service for Hilary of Mende; F:Pn, lat. 976, fos. 139^{v}, 113^{v}, 114^{v}.

[78] See n. 76 above.

[79] Even though the 13th-c. ordinaries label both *semiannuale* and duplex feasts as duplex, they nonetheless distinguish different levels of services according to the number of times this antiphon is chanted. The festivals in which the piece was sung 3 times are those called *semiannuale* by the 14th c. On the practice of repeating the Magnificat antiphon, see Huglo, *Livres*, 24.

were sometimes present. In addition, prosulas and proper melismas for the concluding versicle Benedicamus Domino are often specified.[80]

Semiduplex feasts, along with celebrations in which only the fourth Matins responsory was duplex, stipulate that the Vespers responsory be sung by two or sometimes only one soloist, usually the *hebdomadarius*.[81] The antiphon to the Magnificat was probably chanted once on feasts of these ranks. Simplex feasts of twelve lessons rarely have special rubrics. One mark of distinction between many services of this rank and higher from feasts of three lessons and simple commemorations was the presence of a procession to the chevet at the end of Vespers.

Matins

The service of Matins on *annuale* feasts, treated in Chapter 2 in the discussion of King Dagobert's anniversary, is noteworthy because of both the numbers of performers and their placement in the church. The invitatory psalm (Venite) was sung by four soloists in copes who stood between the principal altar and the matutinal altar (*inter duo altaria*).[82] These singers then returned to the choir to perform the solo portions of the first responsory. The second, third, fifth, sixth, ninth, and tenth responsories were executed by two singers apiece, while the seventh and eleventh responsories—the penultimate chants in the second and third nocturns, respectively—were chanted by three soloists wearing habits. The climactic fourth, eighth, and twelfth responsories were sung by four, five, and seven singers, respectively, and these soloists performed in the order described for Matins for King Dagobert (see Table 2.2). There are small variations in the ranks of the persons called upon to chant the eighth responsory on *annuale* feasts, and this distinction serves to differentiate the level of solemnity of one festival from another. On the feasts of Christmas and Saint Denis, for instance, the solo portions of the eighth responsory were performed by the abbot and four others in copes, identified as four *priores* on the feast of Saint Denis.[83] At Pentecost, however, five *priores* in copes executed the chant. The participation of the abbot in the two former services is one feature that demonstrates the slight pre-eminence of these festivals over Pentecost.

[80] See the discussion of the prosulas and the Benedicamus Domino in Ch. 3.

[81] Service for Peter's Chains (1 Aug.); F:Pm 526, fo. 153; F:Pn, lat. 976, fo. 113.

[82] The placement of soloists in this special position between the 2 altars was reserved for 9 feasts at Saint-Denis by the mid-13th c.: Christmas, Saint John (26 Dec.), Dagobert's anniversary (19 Jan.), the Dedication of the Church (24 Feb.), Easter, Pentecost, Saints Peter and Paul (29 June), Assumption (15 Aug.), and Saint Denis (9 Oct.); F:Pn, lat. 976, fos. 158^{v}–9.

[83] F:Pan, L 863, No. 10, fo. 124^{v}.

When only three responsories were executed at Matins on Easter Day, during Easter week, and at Pentecost, they were performed by four, five, and seven soloists in copes. On Easter, the Gloria Patri was sung after the verses of all three responsories, and the *repetendum* was used after both the verse and the doxology.[84] This lengthened responsorial form was used only for the third responsory of Pentecost.[85] The six *annuale* celebrations at Saint-Denis, along with the anniversaries of Dagobert and Philip Augustus, had major censings at the end of each Nocturn.

On *semiannuale* and duplex festivals, four singers executed the Venite, just as on *annuale* feasts. But only on the *semiannuale* Feasts of Saint John (27 December) and of Peter and Paul (29 June) did they stand *inter duo altaria*.[86] Two of these soloists then remained in the choir to perform one or more of the responsories. Three soloists sang the fourth responsory, four performed the eighth, and five executed the twelfth. The solo parts of the remaining responsories were chanted by two singers apiece.[87] As at First Vespers, two thurifers were sometimes present on feasts of all of these grades. At least in the twelfth century, the festivals of Stephen, John, Innocents, and the Nativity of Mary incorporated prosulas (see Table 3.5), and many other responsories used untexted melismatic tropes (see Table 3.4).

The formula for semiduplex and lesser feasts of twelve lessons called for fewer personnel. Only two soloists in copes chanted the Venite. The fourth, eighth, and twelfth responsories were executed by two, three, and four soloists, respectively.[88] A procession to one of the altars in the chevet occurred on some festivals of twelve lessons and higher.

There is very little information on the performance of the antiphons for Matins. It seems that the first antiphon was sometimes begun by the *hebdomadarius* and the rest by the *priores* on the highest feasts, while the senior monks, as mentioned earlier, intoned all but the first antiphon on anniversaries other than Dagobert's.[89] The Vigils of *annuale* celebrations describe the execution of other Matins chants somewhat more carefully. The two soloists for the Venite were vested in white garments, or albs. The fourth responsory was chanted by a single *hebdomadarius*, and the twelfth responsory by a *cantor*. It is unclear whether or not this latter soloist is the cantor (*precentor/archicantor*) or

[84] F:Pm 526, fo. 56^{v}; F:Pn, lat. 976, fo. 29^{v}. This usage was also observed in 2 other festivals: the feast of the Invention of the Holy Nail (F:Pm 526, fo. 60), which was celebrated on Friday after Easter; and on Annunciation when it fell during Easter week.

[85] F:Pm 526, fo. 73^{v}.

[86] F:Pn, lat. 976, fos. 158^{v}–159.

[87] F:Pm 526, fos. 17^{r-v} (feast of Stephen, 26 Dec.).

[88] F:Pm 526, fo. 101 (feast of Fabian and Sebastian, 20 Jan.).

[89] F:Pm 526, fo. 9^{v}. See the discussion of the duties of the *priores* above.

some other soloist. The *repetendum* of the twelfth and occasionally the fourth responsory was sung after both the verse and the Gloria Patri.

Lauds

Lauds includes several musical items that call for varying numbers of singers: the five antiphons for the psalms, the responsory after the chapter reading, and the antiphon to the Benedictus. On *annuale*, *semiannuale*, and duplex feasts, the performance of the psalmodic antiphons is similar to that of First Vespers: the first was intoned by the *hebdomadarius*, and the remaining four by *priores*. While the ordinaries do not say whether the *hebdomadarius* carries out this function on feasts of lesser rank, it is clear that the *priores* initiated at least the last four antiphons on almost all feasts. The solo portions of the responsory were chanted by four in the choir on *annuale* feasts, and by two soloists, sometimes boys, on all other festivals. On Christmas and Easter, the abbot or *hebdomadarius* standing in the choir began the antiphon to the Benedictus, and it was sung three times. Directions for some duplex feasts call for this chant to be sung twice, as was customary for the Magnificat antiphon of First Vespers. Pairs of thurifers and a proper melody for the closing chant Benedicamus Domino are sometimes mentioned on services of duplex rank and higher. On celebrations of at least twelve lessons, Lauds often concluded with a procession to an *oratorium* in the chevet.

High Mass

A hallmark of *annuale* and some *semiannuale* festivals at Saint-Denis was a procession after Terce and before to High Mass through the church and sometimes the cloister. After the procession on these and many important duplex feasts, three *cantores* intoned the introit.[90] Often these *cantores* stood in the choir, but on feasts of saints of whom major relics lay in the church,[91] High Mass and sometimes Terce on days other than Sunday were celebrated in their chapels in the thirteenth century.[92] In the fourteenth century and no doubt thereafter, Vespers,

[90] The Saint-Denis sources do not state exactly which part of the introit was performed by the soloists, and this issue is in fact unclear in other medieval sources as well (see Hughes, *Manuscripts*, 35; Robertson, 'Review', 351–2).

[91] F:Pan, L 863, No. 10 (p. 3) identifies these saints as Eustace (2 Nov.), Firminus (25 Sept.), Osmanna (9 Sept.), the Eleven Thousand Virgins (21 Oct.), Maurice (22 Sept.), the Innocents (28 Dec.), Peregrinus (16 May), Patroclus (31 Jan.), Hilary of Poitiers (14 Jan.), Cucuphas (25 July), Eugene (15 Nov.), Hilary of Mende (25 Oct.), and Romanus (24 Nov.). The other lesser relics are listed in Ch. 2, n. 49.

[92] 'Notandum est quod utraque missa fiet de festo sanctorum quorum corpora in beati dyonisii ecclesia requiescunt, missa matutinalis cantetur ad maius altare de martyre. Magna missa ad

Terce, and High Mass were normally sung at these stational locations.[93] Two *cantores* ruled the choir on other duplex feasts, and one *cantor* on festivals of lesser rank and on most Vigils and Octaves, as we have already seen. During the introit, those designated to take part in the procession to the principal altar formed their line. They included the abbot, seven monks in the order of seven deacons and subdeacons on *annuale* and most *semiannuale* celebrations, five deacons and subdeacons on duplex festivals, and three deacons and subdeacons on lesser occasions. The solo portions of the gradual were often performed by three soloists on feasts of duplex level and higher, whereas two generally chanted this item on festivals lower than duplex. Four soloists were assigned to the verse of the alleluia on occasions of at least duplex rank, and three sang the chant at other times. One boy in an alb performed the solo parts of the gradual and alleluia on ferial days.

Apart from the numbers of participants for the various chants and actions, the ordinaries note the presence of special musical and ceremonial features at Mass. On *annuale* and *semiannuale* feasts, an antiphon was sung before the gospel, and tropes to the introit, offertory, and communion appeared on Christmas and Easter. Sequences were common on feasts of at least duplex rank in the thirteenth century, and on virtually all twelve-lesson celebrations in the fourteenth century. The Requiem Mass for Kings Dagobert, Philip Augustus, and Robert II and for Abbot Suger called for incense at the tombs of these sovereigns from the beginning of the gospel to the end of the offertory. High Mass frequently closed with a proper, melismatic Ite Missa Est on ceremonies of duplex level and higher.[94]

Prime, Little Hours, and Second Vespers

Only the description of Dagobert's anniversary in the fourteenth century ordinary F:Pan, L 863, No. 10 provides information about the performance of Prime and the Little Hours (Terce, Sext, None). The instructions call for two soloists apiece on the responsory, the versicles, and the final chant *Requiescant in pace*, as noted in Chapter 2. Since Dagobert's festival mirrors the *annuale* celebrations in many ways, it is possible that these stipulations for the Lesser Hours apply to the five or six principal feasts as well. Second Vespers of *annuale* feasts was performed almost exactly like First Vespers: three *cantores* in copes

oratorium ipsius et sint omnes in cappis'; F:Pm 526, fo. 105^{v}. Also, on the feast of Saint Eugene (15 Nov.): 'Missa matutinalis de sancto Eugenio ad maius altare . . . Et eant in capicio et ibi cantetur tercia et missa si dominica non fuerit'; ibid. fo. 193^{v}; see also F:Pn, lat. 976, fos. 75, 148.

93 F:Pan, L 863, No. 10, p. 3.

94 See the discussion of these items in Ch. 3.

stood in the choir, all vested in albs, a *cantor* initiated the first antiphon to the psalms, four soloists chanted the great responsory,[95] and the Magnificat antiphon was sung three times. The main difference between First and Second Vespers on *annuale* feasts was that the *repetendum* of the responsory was omitted from the latter service. When Second Vespers occurred on *semiannuale* and duplex feasts, the directions rarely specify anything but the number of soloists (four) on the responsory. The feast of All Saints (1 November) further stipulates that the Magnificat antiphon should be sung only once.[96] A proper Benedicamus Domino was employed on some celebrations of duplex rank and higher.

Comparisons with Other Institutions: The Responsorial Chants

In addition to the aspects of performance practice at Saint-Denis discussed above, many other factors would have to be taken into account before a full assessment could be made of the extent to which the Divine Office at Saint-Denis was more or less elaborate than that of other places. The monks' apparent disregard for liturgical polyphony already seems to place the abbey at a disadvantage, in comparison with Notre Dame of Paris and other institutions which cultivated organum and the motet. We saw in Chapter 4, however, that Saint-Denis may well have had specific reasons for preserving its monophonic tradition. Within the confines of the performance of monophony, therefore, it is instructive to look briefly at the execution of plainchant in other medieval institutions—even at the risk of treating regular and secular institutions as if they were alike—to begin to see how Saint-Denis compared in terms of the aspects of the singing plainchant that are treated here.[97]

The rubrics for the execution of responsorial chants of the *annuale* feasts of Saint-Denis, which are the instructions most consistently found in other ordinaries and customaries, serve as convenient points of comparison. The use of four soloists on the great responsory at Vespers was evidently the largest force employed in cathedrals and monasteries

[95] Only 2 soloists, described as 'singing well', are mentioned at Christmas; F:Pm 526, fo. 17.

[96] F:Pm 526, fo. 189^v; F:Pn, lat. 976, fo. 142.

[97] The sampling of ordinaries and customaries surveyed here includes the 22 documents consulted in Oury, 'Vêpres'; idem, 'Matines'; the study of English usage in Harrison, *Britain*; the 10th-c. *Regularis Concordia* from England (ed. Symons *et al.*, *Regularis*); the 10th-c. customary of Einsiedeln (Wegener, *Redactio*); the early 11th-c. epistle of Abbot Aelfric to the monks of Eynsham (Nocent *et al.*, *Aelfrici*); several Cluniac customaries of the 10th–12th cs. (Grünewald *et al.*, *Wirzeburgensis*; Vasaturo *et al.*, *Vallumbrosana*); the customary of Bec from the 12th to 14th cs. (Dickson, *Consuetudines*); the 14th-c. ordinary of Exeter (Dalton, *Ordinale*); and the 14th- and 15th-c. ordinary of Saint Mary's abbey at York (Abbess of Stanbrook, *Ordinal*). Citations come from descriptions of the performance of Christmas.

in the twelfth to fourteenth centuries, during which time the usual number was one to four.[98] The twelfth-century Cluniac customary from Vallumbrosa prescribes only three soloists,[99] and this slightly smaller ensemble seems to be typical of the other services, too, in sources prior to the thirteenth century. The later ordinaries from Exeter and from Saint Mary's abbey at York assign four to the Vespers responsory, as at Saint-Denis.[100]

The numbers of performers on the final responsory in each Nocturn at Matins on the highest feasts at Saint-Denis (four, five, or seven singers) exceed those in many other institutions,[101] where the norm was two to three soloists in the first and second Nocturns, and two to four in the third.[102] The sources from the tenth to twelfth centuries call for two soloists on the final responsory of the first Nocturn.[103] Exeter assigns only three, three, and four singers on these final chants,[104] and the custom elsewhere in England generally specifies two to five soloists.[105]

For High Mass the eleventh-century Cluniac customary from Würzburg assigns two soloists each to the gradual and the alleluia,[106] whereas the normal usage at Saint-Denis in the thirteenth century was three and four, respectively, on these chants. But the performance of this service at Saint-Denis was not always as lavish as that in some late medieval houses: the customary of Bec required six on the solo portions of the gradual and eight on the alleluia,[107] and Saint Mary's at York assigned three to the gradual and six on the alleluia.[108] Similarly, the versicle Benedicamus Domino was executed by as many as six soloists in some traditions.[109]

In most respects, the execution of the responsorial chants of the six *annuale* ceremonies at Saint-Denis seems to have been similar to those of the most venerable institutions in the West in the late Middle Ages. When the magnificent anniversary for Dagobert at Saint-Denis is also taken into consideration, the number of feasts solemnized at this high level increases. Add to these the substantial number of elaborate *semiannuale* and duplex celebrations of the abbey, along with the

[98] See Oury, 'Vêpres', 230.

[99] Vasaturo *et al.*, *Vallumbrosana*, 327.

[100] Dalton, *Ordinale*, i. 61; Abbess of Stanbrook, *Ordinal*, ii. 179; see also Harrison, *Britain*, 107.

[101] Oury, 'Matines', 160–1.

[102] Oury lists only 4 priests on the 9th responsory at the cathedral of Paris (ibid.), but Wright suggests that there might be as many as 6 for the processional responsory before High Mass on certain *annuale* feasts; *Notre Dame*, 342.

[103] Symons *et al.*, *Regularis*, 98; Nocent *et al.*, *Aelfrici*, 160; Wegener, *Redactio*, 243; Vasaturo *et al.*, *Vallumbrosana*, 327 (this last document specifies 2 or 3 soloists on the 4th, 8th, and 12th responsories).

[104] Dalton, *Ordinale*, i. 65–6.

[105] Harrison, *Britain*, 106–7.

[106] Grünewald, *Wirzeburgensis*, 290.

[107] Dickson, *Consuetudines*, 97.

[108] Abbess of Stanbrook, *Ordinal*, ii. 190.

[109] Robertson, '*Benedicamus*', 8.

annivesaries solemnized at duplex level, and we can conclude that the performance of the responsorial chants in the abbey merited at least a goodly part of the praise that Dom Doublet, the seventeenth-century historian of the abbey mentioned at the beginning of this chapter, so liberally extended.

INSTRUMENTAL MUSIC: THE ORGAN

Practically the only references to instruments at Saint-Denis are found in descriptions of the various festivities which took place there on account of its privileged status as royal abbey. The services for the crowning of queens at Saint-Denis from the late fifteenth century on were often accompanied by instrumentalists from the king's *musique de chambre*, but the monks evidently had no role in this music-making. Indeed, the only instruments known to have existed at Saint-Denis were a series of organs.

Little information survives about how the organ at Saint-Denis may have functioned in the Divine Service. In some houses the organ was played in extra-liturgical ceremonies in the twelfth century and on feast-days by the end of the thirteenth century. The use of the instrument in *alternatim* performance with singers probably began in the late fifteenth century,[110] and Saint-Denis may well have followed this series of dates. Likewise, when the instrument first appeared in the church is not known, but Raugel speculates that it may have been as early as the tenth century.[111] Its location in the church is also unclear. Passing references to it are found in 1244, when the organ was apparently heard in alternation with two choirs during services sung for the recovery of Louis IX,[112] and in 1410, when the organ was played for the visiting Duke of Guienne.[113] A monk named Gabriel Chollet gave a new organ to Saint-Denis some time before his death on 1 October 1510, and the instrument was placed inside the west façade.[114] This organ was replaced by another shortly thereafter, the gift of Jean Carlier.[115] Raugel notes repairs to the organ by Jehan Boullay in 1510, and he names Jehan Bastillet and Jehan du Mailly as organists between 1506

[110] Williams, 'Organ', 859–62.

[111] Raugel, 'Saint-Denis', col. 1248; see esp. the bibliog. cited in his col. 1249; also Ayzac, *Histoire*, i. 265. Many monastic churches in the West had organs by the 11th c.; Williams, 'Organ', 859–62.

[112] Reported in Ayzac, *Histoire*, i. 571–2.

[113] Félibien, *Histoire*, 324.

[114] 'Die mercurii, prima mensis octobris, anno Domini millesimo quingentesimo decimo obiit frater Gabriel Chollet, jubileo suo peracto pro quo dedit organa in fronte ecclesie posita'; F:Pan, LL 1320, fo. 41 (pub. in Samaran, 'Études', 66, No. 473; see also his discussion on pp. 39–40).

[115] Ibid. 40.

and 1517.[116] Marc Harbot was organist between 1532 and 1533.[117] The organ given by Jean Brocard in 1699 was long considered the best in France,[118] and in the eighteenth century the abbey was an important centre of organ building.[119]

MUSICIANS AND LITURGISTS

From time to time, sources from Saint-Denis bear witness to the accomplishments of musicians and liturgists who were famous both in and beyond the monastery. The names of these persons are found in the incipits and explicits of the works they wrote, in the attributions of their compositions, and, in one rare instance, in a chronicle which describes the official cantor of Saint-Denis actually singing. The entries are tantalizingly brief, however, and the archival references never show the cantor as a performer, but rather as signatory to a charter or as overseer of the purchase or sale of property. Moreover, these sources provide only a skeletal list of names of the persons who filled the office of cantor from the twelfth to the fourteenth centuries, although they do yield a more complete roster of cantors, *succentores*, and *tercii cantores* for the fifteenth and sixteenth centuries (Table 5.1).

In fact, the official cantor of Saint-Denis took on more and more extramusical responsibilities in the late Middle Ages and Renaissance, as mentioned earlier. Cantor Thomas, for example, served as legate of Louis IX in 1253,[120] and Cantors Michael Pintoin and Jean Chartier wrote official histories of Charles VI and Charles VII, respectively, in the late fourteenth and fifteenth centuries (Table 5.1).[121] Another person, probably the *succentor*, seems to have assumed a large part of the cantor's former role, but even as late as the fifteenth century the cantor of Saint-Denis still performed one of his customary duties as curator of books.[122]

No less important are the other musicians, both sacred and secular, liturgists, and students of music theory who once lived in the abbey. From these categories the works of a singing teacher, an abbot, an

[116] Raugel, 'Saint-Denis', col. 1248.

[117] F:Pan, LL 1302, fo. 63; document trans. in Nebbiai-Dalla Guarda, *Bibliothèque*, 356.

[118] Samaran, 'Études', 40, where further bibliog. is cited.

[119] Raugel, 'Saint-Denis', cols. 1248–9.

[120] See Berger, '*Chronicon*', 292.

[121] On Michael Pintoin, recently identified as the chronicler known as *le Religieux de Saint-Denis*, see Grévy-Pons and Ornato, 'Auteur'; and on Jean Chartier, see Ayzac, *Histoire*, i. 278; Spiegel, *Chronicle*, 124–5.

[122] The 15th-c. cartulary F:Pan, LL 1180 (*Règlement des offices claustraux*) states: 'Le chantre doit soutenir les livres du couvent' (fo. 19ᵛ); also cited in Nebbiai-Dalla Guarda, *Bibliothèque*, 82.

TABLE 5.1. *Cantors,* Succentores, *and* Tercii Cantores *of Saint-Denis*

Date of mention	Name	Designation	Source of mention
Cantors			
1125	Vivianus	*Cantor*	Lecoy de la Marche, *Œuvres*, 322
1137 and 1138	Bernardus	*Praecentor*	Ibid. 340, 343, 348. This may be the same Bernardus designated as *cantor* in the 13th-c. necrology of Saint-Denis, 18 Feb. (Molinier, *Obituaires*, i/1. 310).
1152/1153	Guillelmus?	*Praecentor*	Constable, 'Administration', 25, and n. 164[a]
1185	Girardus	*Cantor*, monk, priest	F:Pan, LL 1163, pp. 6–7; also listed in 13th-c. necrology, 10 Apr. (Molinier, *Obituaires* i/1. 314)
1239	G. (= Guillelmus?)	*Cantor*	See pp. 330–1 below.
1253	Thomas	*Cantor*	See p. 322 above.
before *c.*1261[b]	Hugo	*Cantor*, monk	Listed in 12th-c. necrology, 11 Feb. (Molinier, *Obituaires* i/1. 309)
before *c.*1261	Godefredus	*Praecentor*, monk	Listed in 13th-c. necrology, 17 Feb. (ibid. i/1. 310)
1260	Johannes	*Cantor*	F:Pan, LL 1163, p. 11
1277	Odo	*Frater*, *cantor*	F:Pan, LL 1163, pp. 44–5
13th c.	Vincentius	*Cantor*	I:Rvat, Reg. lat. 550, fo. 1, as cited in Nebbiai-Dalla Guarda, *Bibliothèque*, 70.
1390, d. before 1407	Guillaume de Roquemont	*Cantor*	F:Pan, LL 1163, p. iii; F:Pan, LL 1320,[c] fo. 8 (Samaran, 'Études', 52, No. 208)

Date of mention	Name	Designation	Source of mention
d. 16 Feb. 1420	Michael Pintoin	*Cantor*	See p. 322 above; F:Pan, LL 1320, fo. 10 (Samaran, 'Etudes', 47, 56, No. 312).
d. 1 Nov. 1441	Hugo Panis	*Praecentor, cantor*	F:Pan, LL 1320, fo. 11^{v} (Samaran, 'Études', 58, No. 359)
*c.*1440	Jean Chartier	*Cantor*	See p. 322 above; also Ayzac, *Histoire*, i. 275–8
3. 19 Feb. 1463	Jean Chartier	*Frater, cantor*	F:Pan, LL 1320, fo. 12^{v} (Samaran, 'Études', 46, 60, No. 393)
d. 31 May 1468	Johannes Jaloux	*Frater, cantor*[d]	F:Pan, LL 1320, fo. 13 (Samaran, Études', 60, No. 402)
d. 7 July 1483	Nicholaus Bare	*Frater, cantor*	F:Pan, LL 1320, fo. 14 (Samaran, 'Études', 62, No. 426)
d. 7 Nov. 1506	Johannes de Guidencourt, alias Haulberjon	*Frater, cantor*[e]	F:Pan, LL 1320, fo. 41 (Samaran, 'Études', 65, No. 467)
d. between 1542 and 1548	Johannes Haubergeon	*Frater, cantor*	F:Pan, LL 1320, fo. 44^{v} (Samaran, 'Études', 70, No. 530)
*c.*1528	Jean Chambellan	*Cantor*	Ayzac, *Histoire*, i. 278
d. 12 Apr. 1567	Jean Chambellan	*Frater, praefectus*[f]	F:Pan, LL 1320, fo. 47 (Samaran, 'Études', 73, No. 576; Félibien, *Histoire*, 578).
d. 27 Aug. 1575	Petrus Pichonnat	*Frater, cantor, praecentor*	F:Pan, LL 1320, fo. 48 (Samaran, 'Études', 75, No. 592); Ayzac, *Histoire*, i. 279
d. 14 Jan. 1581	Anthonius Bouchart	*Frater, cantor*	F:Pan, LL 1320, fo. 50^{v} (Samaran, 'Études', 77, No. 602)

1589	Henricus Godefroy	*Grand commandeur*	Ayzac, *Histoire*, i. 223, reports that he led a group of monks from Saint-Denis to Notre Dame in Paris, where they sang Mass and Solemn Vespers during the revolt in which Henri III fled to Navarre.
d. 1590	Henricus Godefroy	*Frater, cantor, praeceptor huius coenobii et doctor theologus*	F:Pan, LL 1320, fo. 51^{v} (Samaran, 'Études', 80, No. 625); Ayzac, *Histoire*, i. 279
d. 2 Apr. 1636	Augustinus de Valles	*Frater, praecentor, praeeptor seu commendator et tertius prior*	F:Pan, LL 1320, fo. 5 (Samaran, 'Études', 86, No. 671)
Succentores			
d. 14 Aug. 1447	Johannes Theodori	*Subcantor*	F:Pan, LL 1320, fo. 13 (Samaran, 'Études', 60, No. 399)
d. between 1517 and 1519	Nicolas Gasnier	*Soubz chantre*	F:Pan, LL 1320, fo. 42 (Samaran, 'Études', 67, No. 490)
d. 1570	Loys de Meaulx	*Frater, soubz chantre, soubs maistre, subprior, praefectus*	F:Pan, LL 1320, fos. 42, 53 (Samaran, 'Études', 67, 82, Nos. [644], 645)
d. 10 Apr. 1641	Loys Vyon	*Frater, sobz chantre, commendator, praepositus* of Garenna	F:Pan, LL 1320, fos. 42, 5 (Samaran, 'Études', 67, 87, Nos. [678], 679)

Date of mention	Name	Designation	Source of mention
Tercii cantores[g]			
d. 3 June 1474	Jehan Dorton	*Frere, tercius cantor*	F:Pan, LL 1320, fos. 13^{v}, 42 (Samaran, 'Études', 61, 67, Nos. [406], 407)
1 Oct. 1510	Gabriel Chollet	*Frere*	F:Pan, LL 1320, fos. 41, 42 (Samaran, 'Études', 66, 67, Nos. [472], 473)
d. between 1517 and 1519	Jaques Macy	*Frere*	F:Pan, LL 1320, fo. 42 (Samaran, 'Études', 67, No. 486)
d. between 1517 and 1519	Denys Charpentier	*Frere*	F:Pan, LL 1320, fo. 42 (Samaran, 'Études', 67, No. 487)
d. 18 July 1522	Pierre Courtiller	*Frere*	F:Pan, LL 1320, fo. 42 (Samaran, 'Études', 67, 68, Nos. [493], 494)
d. 1522	Jehan Martin	*Frere, subprior*	F:Pan, LL 1320, fos. 42, 42^{v} (Samaran, 'Études', 67, 68, Nos. [504], 505)
d. 19 Nov. 1538	Loys de May	*Frere, quartus prior*	F:Pan, LL 1320, fos. 42, 43 (Samaran, 'Études', 67, 69, Nos. [509], 510)
d. 3 July 1540	Matheus de Murdac	*Submagister puerorum, tercius cantor*	F:Pan, LL 1320, fo. 43 (Samaran, 'Études', 69, No. 515)
d. 1 Apr. 1588	Johannes Berthinus	*Tercius cantor*	F:Pan, LL 1320, fo. 51^{v}

[a] Constable relates that Suger's secretary William (Guillelmus) of Saint-Denis addressed a letter in this year to Precentor William and to several other officials, all called William. He suggests that the repeated use of this name may be rhetorical, rather than coincidental.

[b] Approximate date of necrology in which this and the following entry is found; ed. Molinier, *Obituaires*, i/1. 306–34; also Félibien, *Histoire*, *PJ*, pt. ii, pp. ccvii–ccxix. Félibien believed this document to date shortly after 1254; ibid. p. ccxix. The original MS no longer exists, hence it is impossible to distinguish layers of entries to try to refine the dates of Hugo and Godefredus.

[c] Necrology, 14th–17th cs. (see Samaran, 'Études', 27–100).

[d] This entry, along with Johannes de Guidencourt below, uses only the designation *cantor*, rather than *cantor istius ecclesie*, which appears with all other cantors' names in F:Pan, LL 1320.

[e] See n. *d* above.

[f] In this source, Johannes Chambellan is called *praefectus*, not *cantor*, a reference perhaps to the office he held toward the end of his life.

[g] The following names are designated as *tercii cantores* in a title which heads F:Pan, LL 1320, fo. 42.

anonymous monk-trouvère, and two theorists have survived. The following pages will bring together what is known about their achievements, and will broaden our notion of the kinds of music that were perhaps written and heard at Saint-Denis.

Magister Teutgarius

The powerful Abbot Fulrad (750–84) served simultaneously as archchaplain (*archicapellanus*) of the royal chapel. His responsibilities involved the general direction of the court clerics, but the instruction of singing in the chapel was left to trained musicians. One such specialist in the early ninth century was the cleric Vandelmarus, who had learned his art at Saint-Denis. Hincmar of Reims, a former monk of the abbey, reports to Emperor Charles the Bald that Vandelmarus was teaching singing to the clerics of the royal chapel some time before 854, most likely during Hilduin's tenure as abbot of Saint-Denis (814–41). Hincmar's letter further explains that Vandelmarus had acquired his musical skill in the abbey chiefly from a certain Teutgarius, whom Hincmar calls *magister*, and who was probably the singing teacher of the young boys of the monastery.[123] The necrologies of Saint-Denis seem to support the existence of Teutgarius: his name is included in the ninth-century list of names of deceased monks found in F:LA 118,[124] and a 'Tetgarius' is inscribed on 6 October in the thirteenth-century necrology.[125]

While these scanty details are all we have about Vandelmarus and Teutgarius, the fact that Vandelmarus was evidently trained at Saint-Denis and then served in the secular royal chapel is significant in the light of the early liturgical dependency of the abbey on the cathedral of Paris. His association with both places recalls the connections between Saint-Denis and Paris which continued well into the ninth century. At the same time, Teutgarius' role as mentor to such as Vandelmarus who went on to a career in the prestigious royal institution implies that the levels both of the musical education and presumably also of the performance of plainchant at Saint-Denis were high at this time.

123 'Quapropter a familiari suo [Charles the Bald] Bodone Clerico domni et nutritoris mei Hilduini Abbatis sacri palatii Clericorum summi, quemdam Clericum ipsius Bodonis propinquum, nomine Wandelmarum, qui cantilenam optime a Teugario magistro in sancti Dionysii Monasterio didicet, ad erudiendos Clericos suos obtinuit'; Mabillon, *Veterum*, i. 60; *PL*, cxxvi. 154; see also Félibien, *Histoire*, 84–5; Ayzac, *Histoire*, i. 264–5; Nebbiai-Dalla Guarda, *Bibliothèque*, 27. The training of young monks at Saint-Denis is discussed in ibid. 27–9.

124 F:LA 118, fo. 74^{v}; published in Wilmart, 'Frères', 241–57; and in Oexle, *Forschungen*, 28 (No. 103). Although the origin of the gradual of Laon F:LA 118 at Saint-Denis is questioned in this study, the list of *Nomina defunctorum fratrum nostrorum* on fo. 74^{v} is contained in the sacramentary portion, which clearly comes from the abbey.

125 Molinier, *Obituaires*, I/1. 328.

Abbot Hilduin (814–41), Liturgist

For Abbot Hilduin the liturgy proved a tool by which to propagate the theory that Saint Denis was in fact the famous Dionysius the Areopagite. From all accounts, it was probably he who around 835 composed the Hy. *Celi cives*, which portrays Saint Denis in terms that confuse his identity with the Areopagite and Pseudo-Areopagite, as discussed in Chapter 4. The success of Hilduin's propaganda was evidently more important to him than credit for the composition of the hymn, for he attributed it to Eugene of Toledo, thereby giving it the venerability that only age could bestow.

The hymn formed part of Hilduin's new Office for Saint Denis, which he offered to Louis the Pious around 835. In this service he continued his design to remake Saint Denis into the Areopagite, while at the same trying to conform the work to the monastic *cursus* as outlined by Saint Benedict. Precisely how Hilduin did this is difficult to deduce, owing to the lack of extant testimony for any Office for Saint Denis prior to Hilduin's version. Presumably, the first Office for Saint Denis was a Gallican Office composed in the fifth or sixth century from a Merovingian passion for the saint, probably the *Passio sanctorum martyrum Dionisii*,[126] mentioned in Chapter 1. This service would have been sung until the Carolingian reform of the mid-eighth century banned such usages. By the middle of the eighth century, a 'modern' Roman Office for Saint Denis, issued in the wake of the Carolingian liturgical reform in which the abbey played a role, may well have replaced the Gallican one. Since Saint-Denis still had close ties with the cathedral of Paris up until this time, it is reasonable to assume that both the Gallican and the eighth-century Roman Offices would have been modelled on the cathedral type. Indeed, during the organizational crisis of the early ninth century the erstwhile canons of Saint-Denis would certainly have preferred this kind of service to a monastic one. Hilduin seems to have been familiar not only with the current, Romanized Office but also with its Gallican predecessor, for when Louis the Pious asked Hilduin for a new Office, Hilduin stated in his response that he had resurrected the Gallican version on account of its graphic, eye-witness description of the martyrdoms of Saint Denis, Rusticus, and Eleutherius.[127] Then, in order to bring the Office into line with the Roman *sensus proprii*, he says he made certain changes, without giving details about the exact nature of these modifications. From this information it would appear that the abbot did not compose an office *ex nihilo*. Rather, he probably replaced some of the exuberant Gallican

[126] See Krusch, *Passio*.

[127] *Epistolae*, MGH, *Karolini Aevi*, iii. 330–1, chs. 5–7.

texts and chants from the oldest Office with more acceptable Roman versions (or remodelled them along these lines), creating a new Office around 835.[128]

Traces of this process may linger in the only notated version of Hilduin's Office, found in the twelfth-century antiphoner from Saint-Denis F:Pn, lat. 17296 (fos. 227–231ᵛ). The first responsory from the Matins service, *Post passionem*, is followed by two verses, both set to the text *Quicum imminere*.[129] The second version is much more elaborate than the first and includes a lengthy melisma on the syllable *-cum* (see Table 3.4). Apart from the melisma, a note-for-note comparison of the two chants shows that the second statement of *Quicum imminere* is the more ornate, and it appears less 'orthodox Roman' in its winding melodic configuration. It is possible that this second verse is in fact a remnant of the old Gallican music for Saint-Denis, which Hilduin revised in the ninth century. Later books from the abbey, such as F:Pn, lat. 17296, retain the chant as an alternative to the Romanized form to be sung on the feast of Saint Denis (9 October), with the simpler verse serving the Octave of the saint (16 October).

Finally, to model the renovated Office after the Benedictine plan, Hilduin probably composed three or more additional antiphons, lessons, and responsories, bringing the total number to at least twelve of each.[130] In sum, the abbot accomplished several things in his Hy. *Celi cives* and Office for Saint Denis: he followed the dictates of the Carolingian reform by structuring most of the music of this Office according to the Roman model; he appeased the adherents to the monastic reforms of Benedict of Aniane by making the service

[128] Hilduin's nebulous description of his reworking of the Gallican text is more or less corroborated by the concrete evidence that his extant Office provides. The Office, as described in Ch. 4, comes in large part from the *vita* (*Post beatam*; *PL*, cvi. 23–50) that Hilduin composed. But this *vita* was itself based on the Merovingian *Passio sanctorum martyrum Dionisii* (Krusch, *Passio*; see Levillain, 'Études' [1921], 36–40), and many of the chants in Hilduin's Office are likewise taken from texts common both to the *vita* and to the *Passio*. It is therefore reasonable to conclude that Hilduin compiled his Office for Saint Denis from both a Gallican and a contemporaneous source, just as his letter to Louis seems to suggest.

[129] See the discussion of this piece (with transcription) in Walters [Robertson], 'Reconstruction', 217–21.

[130] Examples of the Office for Saint Denis are almost as varied as the large number of MSS which transmit them, and a thorough study of both texts and music for this Office, well beyond the scope of the present work, is needed before further conclusions can be drawn. Such an investigation would have to take into account the multitudinous versions of the Office for Saint Denis (both secular and monastic) which appear in MSS of other houses beginning in the 9th c. There is e.g. an Ant. *Et facta est*, notated in neumes in the 9th-c. MS Augsburg, Ordinariats-bibliothek, MS 1, fo. 84 (I am indebted to Michel Huglo for providing me with a copy of this antiphon) which matches the 5th antiphon for Lauds found in the Office for Saint Denis in F:Pn, lat. 17296, fo. 232. The most consistent selection and ordering of pieces, however, is found in the Saint-Denis sources themselves, and it is likely that the Office that Hilduin disseminated has best been preserved in these books.

thoroughly Benedictine; and he injected traces of the Areopagitist identity of Saint Denis into his Office and hymn for all to see and hear.

King Robert II (996–1031), Composer?

Members of the royal houses of France attended services at Saint-Denis from time to time, and King Robert II (the Pious) came often on the feast-day of Saint Hippolytus (13 August). He is said to have participated enthusiastically in this celebration, standing in the choir next to the cantor and assisting in leading the singing.[131] No doubt this account of Robert's involvement in the Divine Office was embellished over time, and this is also true of the legends about his abilities as a composer. Some 15 chants, among them the Resp. *O constancia* for Saint Denis,[132] were once attributed to him. In all probability, though, Robert's record of accomplishment in this field was highly exaggerated, and it is likely that the list of chants rumoured to have been penned by him, including *O constancia*, is by and large apocryphal.[133]

Cantor William (Guillelmus)

The arrival of the Crown of Thorns from Constantinople in Paris in 1239 was hailed in a magnificent procession. King, monks, clerics, and lay persons alike accompanied the sacred relic from the outskirts of the city to the place prepared for its keeping in the Sainte-Chapelle.[134] Louis IX led the assembly, and the chroniclers report that Guillelmus, cantor of Saint-Denis, amazed the entire company with his singing:

> Guillelmus was at this time cantor of Saint-Denis. As special *precentor* [cantor] among the rest of the cantors, he began all the chants in extraordinary fashion [during the procession] from the Bois de Vincennes all the way to the Church of the Blessed Virgin [Notre Dame]. Particularly, he intoned the [Ant.] *Ave regina celorum* in the nave of Notre Dame so forcefully that all those who heard it were astonished.[135]

[131] Félibien, *Histoire*, 120; Duchesne, *Scriptores*, iv. 146–7.

[132] F:Pn, lat. 17296, fos. 205^{r-v}, 221, 242^{v} (Hesbert, *CAO*, vol. ii, Nos. 105, 111, 115); GB:Ob, Can. Lit. 192, fo. 407^{v}.

[133] For the list and discussion of Robert's supposed compositions, see *PM*, x. 25–6; also Huglo, *Tonaires*, 91–2, n. 2.

[134] The Reception of the Crown is described in many sources, among them the roughly contemporary *Chronicon* of Guillaume of Nangis (Géraud, *Chronique*, i. 191).

[135] 'Gwillelmus vero cantor tunc temporis ecclesie Beati Dyonisii a Vicenis usque ad dictam ecclesiam Beate Virginis omnes cantus tanquam inter ceteros cantores specialis precentor mirabiliter inchoavit, maxime in navi ecclesie Beate Virginis *Ave regina celorum* intonans ita alte quod omnes stupefacti sunt audientes'; I:Rvat, Reg. 309, fo. 53^{v} (pub. in Berger, '*Chronicon*', 291). One might suspect that this chronicle from Saint-Denis is biased in its assessment of Guillelmus' abilities. But other contemporaneous historians relate the event, particularly

This is the sole reference to Guillelmus' musical prowess, but it seems his talents were not only vocal. In a document from the year of the Reception of the Crown (1239), 'G. cantor ecclesie beati dyonisi' is named as agent in the acquisition of a piece of land.[136] Even though his name is not spelled out, the initial 'G.' suggests that this cantor may in fact be Cantor Guillelmus.

The Monk of Saint-Denis: Secular and Para-Liturgical Composer?

Evidence from around 1230 suggests that secular music was composed at Saint-Denis. The French *chansonnier* F:Pn, franç. 844 (*Le Manuscrit du Roi*) contains three love complaints which are attributed to 'the monk of Saint-Denis' (*li moines de saint denis*).[137] The first *chanson*, *En non Dieu, c'est la rage*, also appears as the *superius* of a motet on the tenor *Ferens pondera* in the polyphonic sources W_2,[138] *Mo*,[139] and *D*,[140] although no composer is named. If the anonymous monk of Saint-Denis wrote this work, it is one of only two extant examples of polyphony possibly written in, or by a member of, the monastery (see Appendix E). The monk's two other songs, *Amors m'a assise rente* and *D'amors me doit sovenir*, survive only as monophonic *chansons*.[141] Beck notes that all three pieces are musically and textually similar, and that the rubric designating *li moines de saint denis* was written at the beginning of each song. For these reasons he accepts their

Guillaume of Nangis in his life of Louis IX (Daunou, *Ludovici*, 326), and Guillaume's work is based on the highly authoritative F:Pn, lat. 5925, a mid-13th-c. compilation of Latin chronicles (see Spiegel, *Chronicle*, 68–71.) In view of the corroboration of the story from other coeval sources, the version in I:Rvat, Reg. 309 can be considered quite reliable. (I am grateful to Gabrielle Spiegel for her assistance with the different versions of this passage.) The modern historian Félicie d'Ayzac gives a much embellished account of the event, based on a MS that she says was cited by Doublet; Ayzac, *Histoire*, i. 273–5; see also Doublet, *Histoire*, 1241.

136 F:Pan, LL 1159, p. 12.

137 See the treatment of these pieces and of the anonymous monk-trouvère in Beck, *Manuscrit*, ii. 74–5; and the facsimile edns. of the songs in ibid. i, fos. 168[r–v]. *En non Dieu* is likewise found in the Noailles chansonnier F:Pn, franç. 12615, fo. 61[v] (see Gennrich, 'Trouvèrelieder', 22–3).

138 D:W 1206 (Helmst. 1099), fo. 227 (ed. in Dittmer, *Wolfenbüttel*).

139 F:MO, H 196, fo. 234 (ed. in Rokseth, *Polyphonies*; and in Tischler *et al.*, *Montpellier*, iii. 5 [No. 183], with trans. of text in ibid. iv. 67 [No. 183]); see also Van der Werf, *Directory*, 45, No. 271.

140 GB:Ob, Douce 308, fo. 258 (text only). The piece is ed. in Tischler, *Motets*, ii. 1057–8 (No. 167), with commentary in ibid. 151. For further bibliog., see idem, *Style*, iii, No. 167; Gennrich, *Bibliographie*, 272 (No. 271); Spanke, *Bibliographie*, No. 33. Beck analyses the motet from the viewpoint of the derivation of the *superius* from the Alle. Ver. *Dulce lignum* and its coupling with the tenor taken from the section *ferens pondera* of the alleluia; Beck, *Manuscrit*, ii. 74–5. See also Reaney, *Manuscripts*: No. 253 in *W2*; No. 171 in *Mo*.

141 *Amours*: F:Pn, franç. 844, fo. 168; F:Pn, franç. 12615, fo. 80; CH:BEsu 389, fo. 93. *D'Amour*: F:Pn, franç. 844, fo. 168; F:Pn, franç. 12615, fos. 84, 77. See Spanke, *Bibliographie*, Nos. 751 and 1468.

assignment to the anonymous monk of Saint-Denis,[142] and suggests that this anonymous monk-trouvère was active before and around 1230, during which period *En non Dieu* is cited in the *Roman de la Violette*.[143] The only known musician at Saint-Denis around the time of composition of these profane songs is the aforementioned Cantor William, but no documents support the connection of him with *li moines de saint denis*.

The appearance of secular compositions at Saint-Denis is not surprising in the light of the monks' non-liturgical activities as chroniclers of the lives of their royal patrons. Even the language of the songs, moreover, was not foreign to the thirteenth-century historians from the abbey. The early decades witnessed the birth of vernacular historiography in France, and, although Latin remained the official language of the regnal histories that emerged from Saint-Denis, the monks' works were translated almost as soon they were written into the vernacular prose that was so dear to the aristocracy.[144]

Apart from purely secular music, examples of para-liturgical music in honour of the Holy Nail at Saint-Denis existed in Paris around this time. The presence of this sacred relic inspired two *conductus* which are included in the Florence manuscript: the two-voice *Clavus pungens*[145] and the monophonic *Clavis clavo retunditur*,[146] both of which, Thomas Payne has convincingly shown, commemorate the miraculous finding of the Nail in 1233.[147] Ignoring the possibility that

[142] Beck, *Manuscrit*, ii. 74. The table of contents of F:Pn, franç. 844 places *Amors m'a assise rente* and *D'amors me doit souvenir* together among the works of Guiot de Dijon (see ibid. [9]), but the ascription of these pieces to the monk of Saint-Denis and their grouping together in the body of the MS points to the authorship of all 3 by the monk-trouvère. In F:Pn, franç. 12615, only *En non dieu* is attributed to the monk of Saint-Denis, while *Amours* is credited to 'the chaplain of Laon', and *D'Amour* is given anonymously.

[143] Beck, *Manuscrit*, ii. 74.

[144] Spiegel, *Chronicle*, 72–89; idem, '*Pseudo-Turpin*'. The 12th-c. satirical *chanson de geste* about the voyage of Charlemagne to the Orient, *Le Pèlerinage de Charlemagne*, was once considered as the work of a member of the convent, mostly on the basis of passing references to Saint-Denis in the work (Bates, 'Charlemagne', 21; Adler, '*Pèlerinage*', 550–61). If this attribution to Saint-Denis is correct, the composition of sung, secular poetry at Saint-Denis is witnessed several decades earlier than the evidence of the 3 trouvère songs. Later scholars, on the other hand, have ventured only that the poem originated in France (Burgess and Cobby, *Pilgrimage*, 2) or in Anglo-Norman territory (Aebischer, *Voyage*, 26; Carmody, *Pèlerinage*, 86–7), and they point out that the irreverent treatment of royalty in the *Pèlerinage* runs counter to Sandionysian ideology in the 12th c. (corr. with Gabrielle Spiegel). The *Pèlerinage* survived until the late 19th c. in a single MS, which was lost around 1879. The most recent edn. and English trans. of the work, based on earlier renderings, is Burgess and Cobby, *Pilgrimage* (see pp. 17–18, where all previous edns. and trans. are listed).

[145] I:Fl, Pluteo 29.1; published in Dittmer, *Florence*, fos. 358–359^{v} (see Reaney, *Manuscripts*, No. 793); also found in 1 voice only in the early 14th-c. *Roman de Fauvel* (Aubry, *Fauvel*, fo. 5); text edited in Dreves, *Cantiones*, *AH*, xxi, 22–3.

[146] Dittmer, *Florence*, fos. 437^{r-v}; text ed. in Dreves, *Cantiones*, 169.

[147] The forthcoming work of Thomas Payne is cited in the following n.; see also Falck, *Conductus*, 111.

these pieces may emanate from Saint-Denis, scholars have generally credited Philip, Chancellor of Paris (d. 1236), with composition of the latter,[148] based on his alleged authorship of a saga about the Nail, now lost.[149] Philip was certainly no stranger to Saint-Denis, having delivered sermons in the abbey over a period of years.[150] But Philip's loyalties were to the cathedral of Paris, and this church had vied with Saint-Denis since the twelfth century over their respective claims to the relics of the Passion.[151] It seems just as likely, therefore, that the monks of Saint-Denis themselves would wish to glorify the finding of the Nail by composing texts, and perhaps also music, in memory of the event.

In fact, the community had more than motive to create the *conductus Clavis clavo retunditur* and *Clavus pungens*; they had both the opportunity and the capacity to do so. We saw earlier that the abbey commemorated the finding of the Nail by instituting both a new feast (the Invention of the Holy Nail) and the contrafact Resp. *Clavus refulgens*. They were likewise no strangers to musical composition. Although no *conductus* from Saint-Denis are extant, the monks wrote music and texts for rhymed prosulas and sequences in the twelfth and thirteenth centuries, as shown in Chapters 3 and 4. And whereas the existence of Philip's account of the loss of the Nail has never been firmly established, a detailed, contemporaneous report by a monk of Saint-Denis does survive.[152] This version of the story is more than an official record of the event, it was designed to edify the reader and at the same time to promote the fame of Saint-Denis.[153] At one point the monk, momentarily attributing his remarks to 'a certain wise man' (*quidam sapiens*), sermonizes about the meaning of the loss of the Nail in language that evokes the text of *Clavis clavo retunditur*.[154] The similarities between the 'wise man's' words and those of *Clavis clavo* leave little doubt that they were composed by one and the same person. While Aubry speculates that the *sapiens* is Philip the Chancellor, it is at least equally possible that the monk is referring rhetorically or allusively

[148] Aubry speculates that Philip wrote *Clavus clavo retunditur* ('Chant', 430–4), and Falck adds that the presence of the piece in the Florence MS among other works of Philip supports this assumption (*Conductus*, 111; see also his bibliog. on both *conductus*, pp. 190–1). In his study of the works of Philip the Chancellor, Payne cites the arguments of these authors and opts for Philip's authorship of *Clavus pungens*, noting that it likewise comes between 2 works attributed to the Chancellor in *F*. He points out that both poems are quite similar both in structure and in language, but this only suggests that they may have been written by the same person.

[149] See Félibien, *Histoire*, 228.

[150] On the sermons, given on feasts of the Dedication of the Church (24 Feb.), see Schneyer, *Repertorium*, Nos. 155, 156, 159, 161.

[151] See Perdrizet, *Calendrier*, 199–200.

[152] Edited in Aubry, 'Clou'.

[153] See Aubry's introd. to the text in ibid. (1906), 185–92, 286–9.

[154] Ibid. (1907), 176–7.

to himself or to another member of the convent.[155] Whatever the case, this *sapiens* probably penned both *Clavis clavo* and *Clavus pungens*. Of the two musicians who flourished at Saint-Denis during this period, we have just seen that the anonymous *moine de saint denis* was a composer. This monk-trouvère, and perhaps Cantor William as well, should at the very least rival Philip the Chancellor as the 'in-house' candidates for authorship of *Clavis clavo* and *Clavus pungens*.

Guido, Theorist

A ninth-century copy of Boethius' *De Institutione Musica* (F:Pn, lat. 7199[156]) in the library of Saint-Denis suggests that the monks had some interest in the study of music theory, and two works by persons connected with the abbey attest to the community's enthusiasm for this topic: the *Tractatus de Tonis* of Guido and the *Tractatus de Musica* of Petrus de Sancto Dionysio. The sole copy of Guido's treatise is found in the manuscript GB:Lbm, Harl. 281.[157] The explicit describes him as a monk of Saint-Denis,[158] but particulars of his life are not known, since he cannot be distinguished among the numerous Guidos in the thirteenth- and fourteenth-century necrologies of the abbey.[159] His treatise consists in two parts, theoretical and practical, and Huglo dates it between about 1299 and 1318.[160] The work is a disquisition on plainchant, ignoring the new theories of mensural music that had recently been codified by Franco of Cologne and others. This is not surprising, in view of the fact that the abbey of Saint-Denis seems to have composed little, if any, polyphonic music. Instead, Guido borrows from the writings on monophony of such authorities as Boethius, Guido of Arezzo, and Petrus de Cruce, and from a lost portion of the treatise on plainchant by Johannes de Garlandia.[161]

[155] Witness the examples of anonymous composers/authors at Saint-Denis both in the case of the 3 French *chansons* attributed to *li moines de saint denis*, and in the present instance, in which an unnamed monk of the abbey composed the account of the Nail. It is not surprising that the monks would have been reluctant to claim authorship for other compositions as well, and a monk-author might easily have adopted the epithet *sapiens* simply to add weight to his admonitory words.

[156] See Nebbiai-Dalla Guarda, *Bibliothèque*, 105, 217.

[157] Fos. 54^v–93^v [58^v–96^v]; see *Catalogue of the Harleian Manuscripts*, i. 104.

[158] 'Explicit tractus de tonis a fatre [*sic*] guidone monacho monasterii sancti dionysii in francia compilatus', (GB:Lbm, Harl. 281, fo. 93^v [96^v]; quotation written in a hand different from the rest of the treatise).

[159] See e.g. the many Guidos recorded in the 3 necrologies of the period: (1) a lost 13th-c. necrology, ed. in Félibien, *Histoire*, *PJ*, pt. ii, pp. ccvii–ccxix; and in Molinier, *Obituaires*, I/1. 306–34; (2) a 14th-c. obituary list, ed. in ibid. 338–42; and (3) a list of anniversaries that were celebrated in 1325, ed. in ibid. 336–8. See also Huglo, 'Guy', 859.

[160] Ibid.; idem, *Tonaires*, 336–8, and *passim*.

[161] Sources for the treatise are listed in ibid; and the lost work of Johannes de Garlandia is discussed in Baltzer, 'Johannes', 662. The *Micrologus* of Guido of Arezzo and the *Tractatus de*

In general, Guido draws his musical examples from the antiphoner and gradual of the abbey.[162] He isolates and characterizes the 'usage of Saint-Denis' (*secundum usum nostrum* or *apud nos*) in describing the application of the first *differentia* of the first mode,[163] the use of simple and solemn methods of intoning antiphons,[164] and *musica ficta*.[165] Guido, moreover, shows his familiarity with the musical practices of the cathedrals of Notre Dame of Paris and of Amiens through reference to the treatises of Johannes de Garlandia and Petrus de Cruce just mentioned. In particular, he tries to distinguish the customs of Saint-Denis from those of the other two churches in his comparison of the Gloria Patri[166] and the Venite[167] at Saint-Denis and Amiens, and of the Venite at Saint-Denis and Notre Dame.[168] He likewise treats the use of neumas, or melismas, as ornaments to antiphons and sequences.[169]

Petrus de Sancto Dionysio, Theorist

If Guido completely ignored the latest developments in music, Petrus de Sancto Dionysio seems to have been fully abreast of the current trends. His *Tractatus de Musica* draws heavily on the mensural treatise *Notitia Artis Musicae* of Johannes de Muris.[170] Petrus' work apparently post-dates by a short period the *Notitia*, which was written in 1321.[171] The explicit of the *Tractatus* calls the author 'frater Petrus de Sancto Dionysio',[172] and this may be the same Petrus who once owned the manuscript F:Pn, lat. 8454.[173] The first part of the treatise, derived from the first book of Johannes' *Notitia*, is strikingly similar to the corresponding portion of the treatise of Anonymous VI from the third volume of Edmond Coussemaker's theorists.[174] Michels therefore believes that Petrus is Anonymous VI, who wrote in the area of Paris in

tonis of Petrus de Cruce are also contained in GB:Lbm, Harl. 281: Guido, fos. 1–12; Petrus, fos. 48ᵛ–54.

162 'Sciendum est igitur quod quantum colligere potui ex *nostro* antiphonario et gradali'; ibid. fo. 76 [80]. Guido cites 2 alleluia verses, *Dyonisi pater alme* (fo. 86ᵛ [90ᵛ]) and *Magne pater Dyonisi* (fo. 88 [92]), which are not found in the extant missals of Saint-Denis.

163 Fo. 76ᵛ [80ᵛ].

164 Fos. 83ᵛ [87ᵛ]; 91ᵛ [94ᵛ].

165 Fo. 85 [89].

166 Fo. 78ᵛ [82ᵛ].

167 Fos. 92ʳ⁻ᵛ [95ʳ⁻ᵛ].

168 Fos. 80 [84]; 84ᵛ [88ᵛ]; 92ʳ⁻ᵛ [95ʳ⁻ᵛ].

169 See the discussion of the sequences, Venite, Gloria patri, and neumas in Ch. 3. Further analysis of Guido's interesting treatise, which deserves to be edited in full, is beyond the scope of the present work.

170 See the edn. and brief commentary on these 2 works in Michels, *Johannis*.

171 Ibid. 39.

172 'Explicit ars cantus fratris Petri de Sancto Dionysio, quam scripsit dominus Johannes Franciscus Praeottonus de Papia'; ibid. 166.

173 The name 'Petrus de Sancto Dionysio' is written on fo. 1 of this 12th- or 13th-c. book of medical and other miscellaneous tracts.

174 See Coussemaker, *Scriptorum*, iii. 398–403.

the fourteenth century,[175] and this identification is supported by the explicit of Anonymous VI's work which seems to imply that the author was a 'Frater Petrus'.[176]

As a monk of Saint-Denis and a contemporary of Johannes de Muris, Petrus could easily have come into contact with the master in the course of his education, for the abbey of Saint-Denis sponsored a *collège* in Paris from the thirteenth to the seventeenth centuries.[177] In this school, a few young monks were trained in grammar, philosophy, theology, and canon law, and they also enjoyed close association with the University of Paris, where Johannes taught. Petrus may well have been among those chosen to attend the *Collège de Saint-Denis*. Here he might have learned the new mensural techniques of Johannes de Muris, which required sophisticated means of notating the rhythm of polyphonic music. But in spite of his advanced knowledge, there is no evidence that Petrus ever imparted any of the new musical philosophy to his comrades at Saint-Denis. The monastery apparently cultivated little if any polyphony, and it is likely that Petrus' connection with the abbey, at least with respect to his musical avocation, was in name only.[178]

175 Michels, *Johannis*, 38–40.

176 'Explicit explicite quod erat implicite. Versus: *F*ons *at*rox *er*ia *pe*dalis *tr*uncus *us*ya. Primi dant nomen benefactoris et omen'; Coussemaker, *Scriptorum*, iii. 403 (see Gushee, 'Anonymous', 445; Fischer, 'Theoretikerhandschrift', 29).

177 On the *collège*, see Nebbiai-Dalla Guarda, 'Collège', 461–9.

178 Because Petrus' treatise probably does not represent the musical practice of the abbey, it is not treated here.

6

Liturgical Sources from Saint-Denis

INTRODUCTION

The overview of liturgy and music at Saint-Denis in Chapter 1 comes largely from historical texts relating to the abbey, and the study of feasts, ceremony, and music in Chapters 2–5 draws largely on the service-books that preserve the ritual. The present chapter deals more closely with these books. All volumes now known to have been used, or suspected of having been used in the Divine Office at Saint-Denis up to 1550 are treated here, including those which were probably copied elsewhere and then adapted for use in the abbey (F:Pn, grec. 375; F:Pn, lat. 103; F:Pn, lat. 9387; F:Pn, n.a.l. 305; F:Pn, n.a.l. 306). Also surveyed here are sources that were intended for private use but which contain calendars that clearly portray the liturgy of the abbey (e.g. Chapel Hill Psalter; F:Pn, lat. 1072).

Thirty-one books of thirteen different types have survived: an antiphoner, a collection of readings for the day Hours, two breviaries, four evangeliaries, two graduals, one book of hours, three lectionaries, six missals, three ordinaries, one pontifical, one psalter, two psalter/hymnals, and four sacramentaries (see Appendix C). Although the number and variety of extant liturgical sources is impressive by any standards, at least three important kinds of manuscript—troper, processioner, and customary—are not officially represented at Saint-Denis.[1] The lack of a customary is probably the most serious lacuna. Not only would a customary have outlined the duties of the participants in the Divine Service in detail, it would have provided more information about the special aspects of the ritual than appears in the ordinaries. Without the witness of a customary, for example, we cannot be absolutely certain that polyphony was not improvised on certain occasions at Saint-Denis. Fortunately, the three ordinaries of Saint-Denis (F:Pm 526; F:Pn, lat. 976; and F:Pan, L 863, No. 10) in part fill the gap. Outstanding in the wealth of detail that they offer, the ordinaries incorporate not only the text incipits of tropes, sequences, Benedicamus Domino, Ite Missa Est, invitatory antiphons, hymns, antiphons before the gospel, and other musical items; they also contain abundant information on processions, performance practice, liturgical

[1] Part of a processioner is extant: F:Pn, n.a.l. 306, a pontifical from Rouen which was modified for use in the major processions at Saint-Denis in the 14th c. (see the discussion below).

objects, and other aspects of the ritual. They focus with remarkable precision on the period, from 1234 to around 1364, in which they were written, painting an intimate portrait of the state of the liturgy during this time. The earliest ordinary (F:Pm 526) probably has implications for the twelfth century as well. The music of many tropes and processional pieces is likewise embedded in the twelfth-century antiphoner F:Pn, lat. 17296 and in the later missals F:Pn, lat. 1107 and GB:Lva 1346–1891. Taken together, the surviving musical sources, coupled with the ordinaries, permit at least partial reconstruction of the troper and processioner of the abbey.

Just as the types of source are numerous, so the period of time covered by these 31 codices is eight centuries, from shortly after 700 to 1550 (see Appendix B). The distribution of books in a given era, however, is not always even. The thirteenth century is especially well represented, with a quarter of all sources dating from this time. Seventeen manuscripts precede the year 1200, while only six come after 1300. This lack of liturgical evidence from the period between 1364 and 1550 is not catastrophic, however, since the later manuscripts F:Pn, lat. 1072 and F:Pn, Rés. B. 5209 almost invariably confirm the liturgical information given in the fourteenth-century missal (GB:Lva 1346–1891), breviary (GB:Ob, Can. Lit. 192), and ordinary (F:Pan, L 863, No. 10), showing that little change occurred from the end of the Middle Ages until the mid-sixteenth century. Historical sources from the abbey help interpret the earliest liturgical books, and archival documents shed light on the later periods. With all this evidence at hand, it is possible to trace the broad outlines of the ritual of the monastery from the Merovingian era up to the mid-sixteenth century.

Thirty-one books, as just noted, are identified in this chapter as having been used at Saint-Denis at one time or another. But by what criteria has this list been established—that is, what characterizes 'the liturgical usage' of Saint-Denis? The most telling feature is the gallery of saints singled out for special devotion in the calendar (if one is included), formularies, litanies, and Canon of the Mass of these sources. Saint Denis and his companions must be present, and a number of the saints whose relics the church housed at a given time should likewise figure prominently. These saints fall into two categories: the ones for whom the abbey possessed major relics and to whom chapels in the chevet or elsewhere in the church were often dedicated,[2] and other, more fragmentary relics.[3] The latter group includes saints too widely observed to be called 'particular' to Saint-Denis: James, Stephen, Vincent, John the Baptist, and others. These names, even in

[2] Designated by * in App. A.

[3] Designated by † in App. A. Saints in both categories are also named in Ch. 2, n. 49.

conjunction with Saint Denis, do not prove that a book was used in the abbey. Rather, it is saints in the former category (Firminus, Osmanna, Cucuphas, Hilary of Mende, and others described in Chapter 2) that help secure the assignment of a source to Saint-Denis. Some manuscripts likewise contain the names of abbots, benefactors, and other persons associated with the abbey in prayers and obituary lists. Similarly, the series of alleluias for Sundays during Easter season and after Pentecost in the missals and graduals can witness to the origin or destination of a source for Saint-Denis. In addition, the ordering of responsories for Matins of the Office of the Dead, the number of different services for the Dead, and the comparison of responsories for Advent and Holy Week can help single out a manuscript from Saint-Denis. One or all of these distinguishing characteristics may exist in a manuscript;[4] in fact, the strength of the attribution of a source to the monastery normally rests on the degree to which these features are present.

Other factors can further support the assignment of a manuscript to Saint-Denis, when it is already founded on the elements of liturgical usage mentioned above. Books with musical notation, for instance, may incorporate neumes which are characteristic of the scriptorium of the abbey. Likewise, one or more shelf-marks of the library of Saint-Denis are found in four liturgical books (F:Pm 384; F:Pn, lat. 103; F:Pn, lat. 256; I:Rvat, Reg. lat. 257),[5] and the eighteenth-century *ex libris* of the Saint-Denis library appears in F:Pm 414. These indicators were normally written on one of the first folios of a manuscript, and they would doubtless appear in more sources, were it not for the fact that the initial leaf was in many instances separated from the rest of the book. The presence of the shelf-mark, in any event, does not establish the liturgical usage of Saint-Denis, nor does it show that a book was even written for the monastery. It proves only that a manuscript was housed in the Saint-Denis library at a certain time.

Indeed, books with shelf-marks from Saint-Denis did not always remain in the abbey. The dispersal of the monastic library by the Huguenots in the sixteenth century caused some liturgical manuscripts to come into the hands of such well-known collectors as Nicolas Lefèvre, Jacques-Auguste de Thou, Antoine Loisel, Claude Joly, and Jean-Baptiste Colbert, one or more of whom who are mentioned in F:Pm 384; F:Pn, grec. 375; F:Pn, lat. 103; F:Pn, lat. 256; F:Pn, lat.

[4] These and other ways of identifying the usage of MSS are discussed in Leroquais, *Sacramentaires*, vol. i, pp. xix–xxxii; idem, *Bréviaires*, vol. i, pp. lxxvii–lxxxii; Möller, 'Research', 8.

[5] The shelf-marks, consisting of distinctive symbols from the 13th, 14th, and 15th cs., are described and reproduced in Nebbiai-Dalla Guarda, *Bibliothèque*, 72–121, and pls. i, ii, iv; see also Delisle, *Cabinet*, i. 203–4.

976; F:Pn, lat. 1072; F:Pn, lat. 2290; and I:Rvat, Reg. lat. 257.[6] But like the shelf-marks, the names of these bibliophiles account for the whereabouts of a manuscript only at the time the entries were made. The use of a manuscript in the ritual of Saint-Denis has to be demonstrated from internal features.

What follows, then, is a catalogue of the liturgical manuscripts containing the 'tell-tale' Sandionysian features just described.[7] The nature of the connection of each source to Saint-Denis and the musical and liturgical peculiarities of the books are summarized. Chapter 7 describes the codices erroneously attributed to the abbey on the basis of usage, decoration, script, or some combination of these elements. The information given in these two chapters should make it possible to identify sources from Saint-Denis which may come to light in the future. Preceding the catalogue in Chapters 6, three brief essays covering topics common to a number of manuscripts discuss: (1) the musical notation of Saint-Denis, (2) the history of the sacramentaries, and (3) the dating of the thirteenth-century books. The sources in Chapters 6 and 7 are arranged alphabetically by manuscript siglum, and include secondary literature, listed chronologically.[8] When an author is cited more than once in the bibliography of a manuscript, this is indicated by a number appearing in parentheses after his name.[9] Codicological information is given in cases where such data are not available elsewhere and where it helps explain how a volume was compiled. The nomenclature of the books surveyed here follows the system recently outlined by Andrew Hughes,[10] except for the sacra-

[6] See the discussion of these collectors in Nebbiai-Dalla Guarda, *Bibliothèque*, 130–41, as well as her brief descriptions of the MSS mentioned here.

[7] Apart from the MSS treated here, Nebbiai-Dalla Guarda includes in her list of liturgical MSS from Saint-Denis 2 fragments of Offices for Saint Denis: an 11th-c. secular Office in F:Pn, lat. 656 (fo. 78), and a table of chants for a monastic Office in F:Pn, lat. 2395 (fo. 1), which comes from Saint-Germain of Auxerre (see Nebbiai-Dalla Guarda, *Bibliothèque*, 314–15). Because these Offices are not of the usage of the abbey, they are omitted here. Nebbiai-Dalla Guarda does not take into account 4 sources which are described here: the Chapel Hill psalter, the ordinary F:Pan, L 863, No. 10, the breviary F:Pn, Rés. B. 5209, and the collection of readings for the day Hours I:VEcap LXXXVIII. Another book belonging to the abbey, NL:Lu, BPL 98, includes a 12th-c. list of readings for meal-times from Saint-Denis on fo. 1; see Schmitz, 'Soir'; Nebbiai-Dalla Guarda, *Bibliothèque*, 188, 331–2, and *passim*; idem, 'Listes', 281–3. This source is not treated here.

[8] Among the books treated in the present study are important codices which have inspired a myriad of writings (e.g. D:Mbs, Clm. 14000; F:Pn, lat. 1152; I:Rvat, Reg. lat. 316). Since it not possible to list all the secondary literature, I have concentrated generally on the more recent bibliog., citing the most significant older works, as well as bibliographies of the sources where they exist. Nebbiai-Dalla Guarda traces the later provenance of many of the sources treated here, as noted in each of her descriptions.

[9] E.g. 'Huglo (2)' in the Bibliography corresponds to a reference in the text: 'Huglo (2) demonstrates that . . .'.

[10] Hughes, *Manuscripts*, Nos. 627–8, draws on the method of classification proposed in Fiala and Irtenkauf, 'Versuch'. For other discussions of the contents of medieval liturgical sources, see Gy, 'Typologie', 11–20; Steiner, 'Liturgy', 85.

mentary and missal, for which Bourque's and Vogel's subcategories 'augmented sacramentary' and 'factitious plenary missal' are used.[11]

The Musical Notation of Saint-Denis

The library of Saint-Denis was one of the richest in Western Christendom,[12] yet ironically the inner workings of the scriptorium and even the location of the room itself are unclear.[13] As early as the eighth century the monks were evidently active in the scriptorium, but it has proved impossible to identify enough characteristic features of the various writing styles clearly to define the style of the scriptorium of Saint-Denis for any one period.[14] Jean Vezin's observations on the ninth-century scriptorium centre instead on marks of punctuation, for example a distinctive question mark with two points which appears in such sources as the sacramentary F:Pn, lat. 256 and the collection of readings for the Day Hours in I:VEcap LXXXVIII.[15] Likewise, Harvey Stahl has begun to define a twelfth-century style of painting in the abbey through his study of the illuminations of the lectionary F:Pn, grec. 375, the antiphoner F:Pn, lat. 17296 (Pls. 13 and 14), the gradual F:Pm 384 (Pl. 9), and other non-liturgical sources.[16]

Details of the operations of the scriptorium in fact remain sketchy until the thirteenth century, from which time records of payments to scribes have survived.[17] Evidently not all copying was done at Saint-Denis, however, for the archives from the 1280s and 1290s show that liturgical books were purchased outside the abbey. Fourteenth-century documents record payments evidently to other ateliers for the addition of musical notation, correction, illumination, stretching of parchment, and ruling of codices.[18] Thus it is not surprising that art-historical evidence likewise suggests that the two thirteenth-century missals from Saint-Denis F:Pm 414 and F:Pn, lat. 1107 were decorated by Parisian artists.[19] On the other hand, it is clear that at least some books were

[11] Bourque, *Sacramentaires*; Vogel, *Liturgy*, 106.

[12] An exhaustive study of the library has recently been published in Nebbiai-Dalla Guarda, *Bibliothèque*.

[13] See the discussion of the scriptorium in ibid. 65–71; also the earlier study in Lesne, *Scriptoria*, 205–14, 591–4. Recent scholarship on books produced at Saint-Denis includes the bibliog. listed in Stahl, 'Problem', n. 1; the passing mentions in Bischoff, *Paläographie*, 107, 157, 160, 197, 225, 268; and the works cited in n. 15 below.

[14] Nebbiai-Dalla Guarda, *Bibliothèque*, 70–1.

[15] See Vezin, 'Point', 184, 188; Meersseman, *Capitules*, 10–1. Vezin has led the recent research into the 9th-c. scriptorium, clarifying the relations between the ateliers of Saint-Denis and Reims (idem, 'Hincmar'; idem, 'Reims'), and pointing out some peculiarities in the manner of book production at Saint-Denis (idem, 'Faute'); see also idem, 'Observations'. Another recent study of books produced at Saint-Denis during this period is Duval, 'Travail'.

[16] Stahl, 'Painting'.

[17] Nebbiai-Dalla Guarda, *Bibliothèque*, 65–7.

[18] Ibid. 67, and her nn. 253, 254.

[19] Branner, *Painting*, 89, 90, 130–2, 136, 224, 238.

produced at Saint-Denis until the end of the fourteenth century, and older codices continued to be maintained there up to the sixteenth century.[20]

Because the style of handwriting in sources copied at Saint-Denis contains few unique features, it is important to try to identify particularities of musical notation which might help define a 'house style'. The early, neumed sources are naturally more likely to possess special characteristics than the books notated on four staff lines, since square notation is generally less distinctive than neumatic. Solange Corbin classifies the neumatic notation of the abbey as a branch of the French school, and names four manuscripts which she considers representative of its notational style: F:Pm 384 (Pl. 9); F:Pn, lat. 9436 (Pl. 11); I:Rvat, Reg. lat. 255 (Pl. 7); and Vendôme, Bibl. Mun. 17C (Pl. 12).[21] We will see that F:Pn, lat. 9436 probably does not belong in this category, for although this augmented sacramentary reflects the usage of Saint-Denis, the layout, the decoration, and the contents strongly suggest that it was copied at Saint-Vaast of Arras, and Denis Escudier's study of the notation of F:Pn, lat. 9436 points either to Saint-Vaast as place of copying or to the presence of a notator from this scriptorium at Saint-Denis. Similarly, no direct evidence suggests that Vendôme, Bibl. Mun. 17C (Pl. 12) was copied in the abbey. But the notation of the manuscript, written probably for a dependency of Saint-Denis, is similar to that of the Saint-Denis antiphoner F:Pn, lat. 17296 (Pls. 13 and 14), and hence the two sources can be usefully compared.

Neumes from the eleventh century are found in six manuscripts known to have been in the library of Saint-Denis at one time or another. These sources, named in Table 6.1, date from the ninth to the mid-eleventh centuries.[22] The mere fact that these books were kept in the library, of course, does not prove that their neumes were written at Saint-Denis. The New Testament manuscript F:Pn, lat. 250 (Pl. 5), for instance, was copied in Tours. Since the book contains only the fifteenth-century shelf-mark of the library of Saint-Denis,[23] it could have been acquired by the monks at almost any time between the ninth

[20] Nebbiai-Dalla Guarda, *Bibliothèque*, 69, and the archival documents which are transcribed in ibid. 336–57. Both the production and maintenance of books were the responsibility of the cantor, as discussed in Ch. 5.

[21] Corbin, *Neumen*, 3.122–3. For further discussion of the musical notation of specific MSS from Saint-Denis, see Hesbert, *Graduel*, pp. xxx–xxxi (for F:Pm 384); and Udovich, 'Modality', 86–102 (for F:Pn, lat. 17296). On the French school in general, see Corbin, 'Notations', 141–2; Suñol, *Introduction*, 230–82; and the bibliogs. given in these works.

[22] Table 6.1 is compiled from the MSS cited in Nebbiai-Dalla Guarda's section of sources clearly from Saint-Denis ('Provenance attestée'); *Bibliothèque*, 187–233. Facsimiles of the musical notation from these and other MSS from Saint-Denis are given in the Pls. 5–20, as well as in the literature listed in App. D.

[23] Nebbiai-Dalla Guarda, *Bibliothèque*, 203.

TABLE 6.1. *Manuscripts from the Saint-Denis Library Containing Neumatic Notation from the Eleventh Century*[a]

MS	Pl. No.	Author/type of MS	Location of neumes	Date of MS
F:Pn, lat. 250	1	New Testament	Fo. 13^{v}	9th c.
F:Pn, lat. 1647A	2	Cyprian and other authors	Fo. 262	9th c.
I:Rvat, Reg. lat. 255	3	Isidore and other authors	Fos. 79^{v}, 191[b]	9th c.[c]
F:Pn, n.a.l. 305	4	Evangeliary	Fo. 7	10th c.
F:Pm 384	5	Gradual	Throughout, also uses significative letters (fos. 50, 160^{r-v})	Early and mid-11th c.
F:Pn, lat. 103	6	Psalter/hymnal	Fo. 154^{v}	mid-11th c.

[a] For bibliog. on F:Pn, lat. 250, lat. 1647A, and I:Rvat, Reg. lat. 255, see the discussions of each MS in Nebbiai-Dalla Guarda, *Bibliothèque*.
[b] Facsimile of fo. 191 in Bannister, *Monumenti*, pl. 46a.
[c] Corbin dates the neumes around 1000; *Neumen*, 3.123.

and fifteenth centuries. The music on fo. 13^{v} may therefore have been added in Tours, although these neumes seem closer to those of the gradual of Saint-Denis F:Pm 384 (Pl. 9) than to the ninth-/tenth-century sacramentary of Tours, F:TO 184 (1017).[24] Similarly, the earliest Sandionysian shelf-mark in F:Pn, lat. 1647A (Pl. 6) is from the thirteenth century.[25] I:Rvat, Reg. lat. 255, on the other hand, was clearly present in the monastery in the eleventh century, as witnessed in the notes on fos. 1 and 109^{v}: *Hic est liber sancti dionisii*.[26] There is good reason, then, to believe that at least some of the neumes in this manuscript may have been written at Saint-Denis. F:Pn, lat. 103 (Pl. 10) likewise was in use at Saint-Denis by the mid-eleventh century, at which time the musical notation was written on fo. 154^{v}.

Ironically, none of these manuscripts was intended to have music; rather, notation was added later to a single item or folio.[27] The eleventh-century gradual F:Pm 384 is the first extant source notated throughout, and the attribution of this manuscript to Saint-Denis is secure.[28] The neumes in this book, therefore, are the most probable representatives of the neumatic notation of the abbey. Since the musical fragments in F:Pn, lat. 103; F:Pn, n.a.l. 305 (Pl. 8) and to a slightly lesser degree F:Pn, lat. 250 and F:Pn, lat. 1647A, resemble the notation used in F:Pm 384, these four books may be examined along with F:Pm 384 as the most reliable examples of the notation of Saint-Denis.[29]

In general, the neumatic notations of F:Pm 384; F:Pn, lat. 103; F:Pn, lat. 250, and F:Pn, lat. 1647A are typical of other houses within the sphere of influence of the French style, but a few seemingly

[24] Facsimile in *PM*, iii. pl. 181 (= fo. 64). The hook of the *virga* in F:TO 184 is on the right, while in F:Pn, lat. 250 and F:Pm 384 it is on the left. Similarly, the *punctum* in F:TO 184 is a flat lozenge, whereas in F:Pn, lat. 250 and F:Pm 384 it resembles a circular point.

[25] Nebbiai-Dalla Guarda, *Bibliothèque*, 207; Walters [Robertson], 'Reconstruction', 227–8.

[26] Nebbiai-Dalla Guarda, *Bibliothèque*, 229; Wilmart, *Codices*, ii. 19; Bannister, *Monumenti*, 84.

[27] Indeed, F:Pn, lat. 1647A and I:Rvat, Reg. lat. 255 are not even liturgical books, strictly speaking, although the latter contains scattered Offices and other music added in the 11th c. See the discussion of musical notation in non-liturgical books in Escudier, 'Notations'.

[28] On F:Pm 384 see below. For published facsimiles of the neumes in F:Pm 384, see App. D.

[29] Denis Escudier has recently outlined 2 criteria for the study of the neumatic notation from a given place and time: the origin of the MSS under consideration must be firmly established, and there should be enough different examples to constitute a plausible corpus of sources from which conclusions can reasonably be drawn ('L'étude de la notation pratiquée dans un scriptorium à une époque déterminée ne peut se faire qu'à partir de témoins dont l'origine est sûrement localisée (cela va de soi), et suffisamment étendus pour constituer un inventaire sémiologique complet'); 'Notations', 43. The gradual F:Pm 384 meets the 1st condition, but the attributions of the other sources in Table 6.1 to Saint-Denis are sometimes less firm, and the number of sources with musical notation similar to F:Pm 384 is rather small. Hence the conclusions drawn from this brief study of the neumatic notation of Saint-Denis must be viewed in the light of the fact that the evidence from the abbey is less complete and less compelling than that for other houses from which more musical sources from the 11th c. survive.

individual features are distinguishable. The axis of notation in French sources is normally vertical, but the Saint-Denis notators consistently wrote music with a slight rightward lean. Like other notations of the French school, the neumatic style at Saint-Denis includes a sharply pointed *clivis* and *torculus*, and a *virga* with a small hook on the left side.[30] In these respects, the neumes of Saint-Denis are quite similar to those of Saint-Vaast of Arras (Pl. 11) and of Fécamp in Normandy, as Corbin has already shown.[31] But Saint-Denis varies from these places in using both a wider angle in the formation of the *climacus*—usually 45° or slightly more—and sometimes an inward swing on the descending arm of the *clivis*.

These two small details of the eleventh-century notation of Saint-Denis are clear in comparison with the neumes from Saint-Vaast, as exemplified in F:Pn, lat. 9436 (Pl. 11). Denis Escudier considers that the type of notation in this volume emanated from the scriptorium of Saint-Vaast during its 'classic period', which extended from about 1000 to around 1075,[32] and that a scribe from Saint-Vaast may therefore have influenced the writing of the book at Saint-Denis.[33] Escudier shows that both the *virga* and neumes composed of *virgae* are normally absolutely vertical at Saint-Vaast, except when a *punctum* climbs to a *virga*, in which case an inclined *virga*, pointing in the direction of the vocal line, is occasionally used.[34] Both the *clivis* and the *climacus* are written with an angle of less than 45°.[35] The slight rightward slant of the neumes in F:Pm 384 (Pl. 9); F:Pn, lat. 103 (Pl. 10); F:Pn, n.a.l. 305 (Pl. 8); and F:Pn, lat. 1647A (Pl. 6), in contrast, is missing from F:Pn, lat. 9436 (Pl. 11). The neumes in F:Pn, lat. 250 (Pl. 5), on the other hand, are more or less vertical, as in F:Pn, lat. 9436. Saint-Denis most often uses *virgae* with hooks, while the *virgae* in F:Pn, lat. 9436 are written as straight lines. The descending dots of the *climacus* are placed consistently higher at Saint-Denis than in F:Pn, lat. 9436. These features of the notation of F:Pn, lat. 9436, along with other liturgical affinities to Saint-Vaast which will be explored later, all suggest that manuscript was strongly affected both by the notation and by the ritual of Saint-Vaast of Arras and may well have been written there.[36]

It is difficult to say whether the French notations in I:Rvat, Reg. lat. 255 (lower halves of fos. 79^{v} [Pl. 7] and 191) come from Saint-Denis.

[30] Corbin, 'Notations', xiii, 141–2.

[31] Idem, *Neumen*, 3.122.

[32] Escudier, 'Scriptorium', 78–81.

[33] Idem. 'Notation', 112–13.

[34] Ibid. 108–15. The author refers to this phenomenon of showing directionality in melodies as 'graphie évolutive'.

[35] Escudier, 'Scriptorium', 81.

[36] Cf. Corbin, *Neumen*, 3.122–3, who offers F:Pn, lat. 9436 as an example of Saint-Denis notation, considering that the scriptorium of the abbey was influenced by the notation of Saint-Vaast. She does not, however, take into account the non-musical signs of Saint-Vaast provenance in F:Pn, lat. 9436, which are discussed below.

In many respects, these neumes differ from those of F:Pm 384 and the other presumed Sandionysian notations. The generally 'neat' appearance of the examples from Saint-Denis is missing from I:Rvat, Reg. lat. 255, fo. 191, and the antiphons for Saint Germanus of Auxerre which are notated here are not found in any Sandionysian source. On fo. 79^{v} (Pl. 7), the slant of the neumes seems too far to the right, and the *torculus* has a curved instead of a straight back. On the other hand, the axis of notation on fo. 191 is like that of the manuscripts from Saint-Denis, and the formations of most neumes are comparable in many respects to those of the abbey. Moreover, the two responsories notated on fo. 79^{v}, *O constantia martyrum* and *O martyrum gemma*, also form part of the Saint-Denis repertory. Since I:Rvat, Reg. lat. 255 is known to have been in the Saint-Denis library in the eleventh century, we may conjecture that the notation occurred there. If this is the case, the two examples from this book are clearly less representative of the 'formal' style of the monastery.

One further peculiarity of the neumatic notation of F:Pm 384 is noteworthy. This gradual contains a few examples of significative letters, signs which clarify pitch or rhythm.[37] The symbol *st* on fo. 50, which indicates 'ascend' and 'drag out' (*sursum*, *trahere*), is the only one written in the original hand of F:Pm 384. Five other signs are found in the rhymed Office for Saint Denis on fos. 160–161^{v},[38] copied in a hand different from and slightly later than the body of the manuscript. Significative letters are commonly found in the notation of Saint-Gall, but they are not unheard of in other neumatic scripts. They are relatively rare in French notation, however, and their presence in F:Pm 384 may be a peculiarity of the scriptorium of the abbey, or it may simply indicate that the rhymed Office of Saint Denis was notated by someone who was versed in these letters. Only a larger sampling of neumatic sources written in the abbey than we have would help settle this question.

The eleventh-century notation of Saint-Denis is largely non-diastematic, as the figures show. By the mid-twelfth century, the musical scribes clarified the question of pitch considerably by using neumes on dry-point staves, as found in F:Pn, lat. 17296 (Pls. 13 and 14). The characteristic notational axis of Saint-Denis is still apparent in this manuscript, but in other ways most of the antiphoner (fos. 2–322^{v}) diverges markedly from the earlier sources. The differences are understandable because the 'neumes' in F:Pn, lat. 17296 are actually well on the way to being square shapes. The *punctum* in F:Pn, lat. 17296 is

[37] See Corbin, 'Notations', 132; see also Corbin and Bernard, *Répertoire*, ii. 17.

[38] Ibid.; however, the authors list only 4. The 5 symbols are: fo. 160, l. 13, *r* on *mox*; fo. 160^{v}, l. 1, *m* on *Dyonisius*; l. 2, *r* on *haberi*; l. 6, *m* on *Chrustum*; l. 10, *m* on *patriae*.

almost square, as are the descending notes in the *climacus*. A 'hook' still appears on the left side of the *virga*, but it is larger than in the eleventh century and nearly square. The *pes* has two note-heads on the left side, both about equal in size and practically square. The *porrectus*, too, uses a square note at the end. The *scandicus* is, for all purposes, a square form, with the two ascending dots replaced by the type of *pes* just described. Only the *clivis* and *torculus* retain the characteristically neumatic point at the top, instead of a square note. F:Pn, lat. 17296 also uses ligatures of up to four notes.

The neumes in a comparable book from a dependency of Saint-Denis, Vendôme, Bibl. Mun. 17C (Pl. 12), are likewise diastematic, but they are written without staves. The major difference between the notations in Vendôme, Bibl. Mun. 17C and F:Pn, lat. 17296 (Pls. 13 and 14) is the *scandicus*, which has its neumatic shape with two *puncta* in Vendôme. Bibl. Mun. 17C, but which appears virtually in square form in F:Pn, lat. 17296. The hook on the *virga* and the top note of the *pes* in Vendôme, Bibl. Mun. 17C are less prominent and more circular than in F:Pn, lat. 17296, and the *clivis* and *torculus* in Vendôme. Bibl. Mun. 17C are rounder at the summit. These distinctions do not prove that Vendôme, Bibl. Mun. 17C was notated at Saint-Denis, nor do they establish the contrary. They simply suggest that the neumes and probably the entire manuscript pre-date F:Pn, lat. 17296, which was probably copied between 1140 and 1150. In terms of notation, this mid-twelfth-century date for F:Pn, lat. 17296 is supported by comparison with several other twelfth-century sources, especially the antiphoners from Nevers (F:Pn, n.a.l. 1236) and from Sens (F:Pn, n.a.l. 1535), both of which look later. The neumes of F:Pn, lat. 17296 closely resemble the notation of the Parisian missal F:Psg 93,[39] which probably dates from about the same time.

Whereas the neumes help distinguish the earlier manuscripts copied at Saint-Denis from those of other houses, the square notation in books from the thirteenth and fourteenth centuries is not sufficiently distinctive to serve this function. The number of manuscripts with square notation, moreover, is not large enough to form a reliable corpus for study, for square notation on staff lines appears in only three notated missals: F:Pn, lat. 1107 (Pls. 17, 18) from the thirteenth century, and F:Pn, lat. 10505 (Pl. 19) and GB:Lva 1346–1891 (Pl. 20) from the fourteenth century.[40] From their contents, it is clear that these sources were produced for the abbey from exemplars of Saint-Denis usage, but we cannot be certain that they were actually written in the scriptorium,

[39] Facsimile in Corbin and Bernard, *Répertoire*, i, pl. iii (for discussion, see ibid. 25).

[40] There are also a few minuscule samples of square notation in the unnotated missal F:Pm 414 (see Pls. 15 and 16).

since manuscripts from this time were often purchased or commissioned from ateliers outside Saint-Denis. If the missals did not come from Saint-Denis itself, the decoration of the volumes indicates that they were copied in the area of Paris. Another hint of Parisian origin is the lack of the *custos*, the sign placed at the end of a line to identify the initial pitch of the next staff. This curious omission, first called for by Franciscan notators, was widely adopted in monastery and cathedral alike in the region of the Île-de-France in the thirteenth and fourteenth centuries.[41] The missing *custos* helps establish that F:Pn, lat. 1107, F:Pn, lat. 10505, and GB:Lva 1346–1891 were produced in the region of Paris, but it certainly does not show that they were notated at Saint-Denis. Clearly, the eleventh-century neumes of Saint-Denis, with their distinctive axis and characteristic formations of the *climacus* and *clivis*, prove more useful in identifying other liturgical manuscripts from the abbey.

Sacramentaries

The eleven manuscripts surveyed here which consist all or in part of sacramentaries (see Appendix C) vary as widely in type as they do in place of origin. The beginnings of the sacramentary have been the subject of much recent enquiry, and its main lines of development are slowly being unravelled. Drawing from these studies, the following paragraphs offer a brief overview of the evolution of the sacramentary, so that the volumes discussed in Chapters 6 and 7 can more properly be situated.[42]

The sacramentary contains the prayers of the Mass, and it was a forerunner of the missal, a later book which includes all that was necessary for the celebration of Mass—prayers, readings, texts, and sometimes music of chants.[43] During the sixth century, liturgical formulas, heretofore improvised, were written in individual fascicles or small books (*libelli missarum*). These collations consisted of a few items

[41] Huglo provides the text of this Franciscan ordinance in his 'Règlement', 124–31. The author notes the lack of the *custos* in F:Pn, lat. 1107 and GB:Lva 1346–1891, but he does not mention F:Pn, lat. 10505, which likewise omits the sign.

[42] The following summary gives only a general picture of the history of these sources, which is substantially more complex and interrelated than represented here. Abundant literature exists on this subject, and it is constantly being augmented and revised in current liturgical studies. A recent treatment of the sacramentaries, with extensive bibliography, is Storey and Rasmussen's revised edition of Vogel, *Liturgy*, 31–106. The best discussion of the Gregorian sacramentary is found in Deshusses, *Sacramentaire*, i. 50–80; ii. 19–30; iii. 60–92; and idem, 'Sacramentaires', which are current to the early 1980s. More recent refinements of Deshusses's work and that of Chavasse for the Gelasian sacramentary (see n. 50 below) are mentioned in the bibliography following each sacramentary discussed here.

[43] For a concise outline of the evolution of the missal, see Huglo, *Livres*, 120–6.

for a certain festival, usually destined for use in one particular church. The first large compilation of such formulas dates from the sixth century, and the sole surviving representative of this book was copied in the early seventh century. Mistakenly called the 'Leonine sacramentary' (I:VEcap LXXXV[44]), this document is not actually a sacramentary at all, but simply a collection of *libelli missarum*.[45]

The sacramentary book (*liber sacramentorum*) itself developed along two main, though not entirely distinct, lines prior to the eighth century: (1) the Gregorian sacramentary, representing the liturgy of the pope; and (2) the Gelasian sacramentary, which portrays in part the usage of the titular or presbyteral churches in Rome (later, the parish churches), and in part some presbyteral practices mixed with papal influences. The Gregorian sacramentary, which emerged formally in the first part of the seventh century, soon separated into three branches. The central branch was revised in the late seventh and early eighth centuries, resulting in the book known as the *Hadrianum* (e.g. F:CA 164[46]) in honour of Pope Hadrian I, who sent a copy of it to Charlemagne between 784 and 791. When this sacramentary reached the Frankish kingdom, it gradually supplanted native Gallican books such as I:Rvat, Reg. lat. 257 (*Missale Francorum*), which show little trace of Roman influence.[47]

Not long after its arrival, the Franks corrected and augmented the *Hadrianum* with a supplement, which helped adapt the book for use in Gaul. This new section, composed between 810 and 815, was the work of Benedict of Aniane (*c*.746–821), Louis the Pious's principal agent of liturgical reform.[48] Both I:Rvat, Reg. lat. 337 and F:Pn, lat. 2292, discussed in Chapter 7, embody the *Hadrianum* complemented with Benedict's additions. The newly expanded Gregorian sacramentary was again reworked, and different stages of this twice-revised book can be seen in four manuscripts treated in Chapters 6 and 7: I:Rvat, Ott. lat. 313; F:Pn, lat. 2290; F:Psg 111; and F:Pn, lat. 2291. Other changes to the *Hadrianum* were the work of the Carolingian liturgist, Alcuin of York (d. 804), who between 796 and 804 composed a series of votive Masses for the ferial days along with some Masses for the

[44] Ed. in Mohlberg, *Sacramentarium*.

[45] See the recent analysis of the contents of the Leonine collection in Chavasse, 'Léonien'; and on *libelli* in general, see Huglo, *Livres*, 64–75.

[46] Deshusses uses mainly this MS in his reconstruction of the Gregorian sacramentary; Deshusses, *Sacramentaire* (MS A).

[47] I:Rvat, Reg. lat. 257 is one of a family of 'Gallican' sacramentaries, the best representative of which is I:Rvat, Reg. lat. 317, ed. in Mohlberg, *Gothicum*. See the list of Gallican sacramentaries in Vogel, *Liturgy*, 108.

[48] Deshusses was first to show that Benedict of Aniane compiled the additional material; see Deshusses, '"Supplément"'; also the discussion in idem, *Sacramentaire*, i. 64–7; ii. 23–4; iii. 66–75; and in Vogel, *Liturgy*, 85–92.

common of saints and for the festivals of All Saints, Benedict and Scholastica, Martin, and others. Some of these services appear in F:Pn, lat. 2290 and in other sacramentaries.[49]

The Gelasian[50] is the second principal sacramentary line, descended from a hybrid Roman model[51] which prominently displayed the liturgical customs of the titular or presbyteral churches of Rome and at the same time incorporated certain Gregorian, though not thoroughly papal, traits. This Gelasian compilation appeared in Rome in the second half of the seventh century, and it was evidently used alongside the Gregorian variety (i. e. the forerunner of the *Hadrianum*) during the seventh and early eighth centuries. The Gelasian sacramentary of Rome, meanwhile, was transported into Gaul at the end of the seventh century. Here the book was augmented slightly to conform to Gallican usage. I:Rvat, Reg. lat. 316, evidently written in the nunnery of Chelles in the region of Paris around 750, is a Gallicanized version of the Gelasian sacramentary, and Chavasse terms it 'Gelasian supplemented in Gaul'.[52] A few years after it was copied, however, I:Rvat, Reg. lat. 316 was eclipsed by the new 'Gelasian of the eighth century' (e.g. F:Pn, lat. 12048;[53] CH:SGs 348[54]), which was principally a combination of (1) the type I:Rvat, Reg. lat. 316, and (2) the third Gregorian variety which had broken away from the *Hadrianum* line in the seventh century. This 'Gelasian of the eighth century' was used by Benedict of Aniane to amplify the *Hadrianum*, and it served in this way as the intermediary between books containing the liturgy of the Roman suburban churches and those displaying the ritual of the pope.

The sacramentary was further altered over the course of the ninth to eleventh centuries to meet the needs of individual churches. Of the manuscripts treated, three sources from this period (F:LA 118; F:R[m], A. 566; F:Pn, lat. 9436) show many of the diverse influences

[49] On Alcuin's contributions, see Deshusses, *Sacramentaire*, i. 64–6; ii. 25–6; iii. 75–8. One source that contains his *Officia per ferias* is the 9th-c. codex F:Pn, lat. 1153, a book which was in the Saint-Denis library from the 16th c. The MS contains neither the 13th- nor the 15th-c. marks of the library, however, and it is therefore impossible to say whether or not it was used in the monastery in the 9th c. (see Nebbiai-Dalla Guarda, *Bibliothèque*, 134, 299). The litanies (fos. 12^{r-v}, 79^{v}–80^{v}) do contain Saint Denis, but they omit others whose relics the abbey possessed, and include many other saints not particular to the monastery. For this reason F:Pn, lat. 1153 is not taken into consideration in this study. A text which has been wrongly attributed to Alcuin, the *Expositio missae* (incipit *Primum in ordine*), is found in Einsiedeln, Stiftsbibliothek 110, a MS copied at Einsiedeln in the 11th c. from a now lost Saint-Denis source (Nebbiai-Dalla Guarda, *Bibliothèque*, 59–60, 320). Since this book was not used in the abbey, it is likewise omitted here.

[50] See the discussion of the Gelasian sacramentary in Chavasse, *Gélasien*, esp. 525–604, 679–92; also Deshusses, *Sacramentaire*, i. 56–60; iii. 79–83.

[51] Deshusses's 'Type II' (see the literature cited in the preceding n.).

[52] Chavasse, *Gélasien*, 690.

[53] Ed. in Dumas, *Liber*.

[54] Ed. in Mohlberg, *Gelasianum*. See the list of other surviving examples of the 8th-c. Gelasian in Vogel, *Liturgy*, 70–3; and the recent study of this sacramentary type in Chavasse, '*Gélasiens*'.

which later affected the supplemented and revised *Hadrianum*. F:LA 118 and F:Pn, lat. 9436 also bear witness to the development of the sacramentary into the plenary missal. F:LA 118 is a factitious plenary missal, that is, a separate gradual and lectionary bound together with a sacramentary. This book clearly illustrates the early attempts at physically combining the three books which constitute the missal. F:Pn, lat. 9436, on the other hand, is an augmented sacramentary, composed of a sacramentary integrated formulary by formulary with a gradual. At the same time, F:Pn, lat. 9436 illustrates ways in which the Gelasian sacramentary of the eighth century was mingled with the *Hadrianum*: the Mass for Rogation Wednesday after Pentecost contains the marginal indication *Ordo secundum [sacramentarium] Gelasium* (Pl. 11), which refers to the eighth-century Gelasian; while the corresponding Mass in September adds the rubric *Secundum [sacramentarium] Gregorium* (fo. 63^{v}), recalling the formulas of the *Hadrianum*.

Dating the Thirteenth-Century Manuscripts

Datable events of purely local significance are often valuable aids for determining the dates of the manuscripts of a particular establishment. At Saint-Denis, several happenings in the thirteenth century provide a framework for dating a number of liturgical books and their calendars with some precision (Table 6.2). At the same time, these events establish a *terminus ad quem* for the twelfth-century books (F:Pn, lat. 17296; F:Pn, lat. 16820; F:Pn, n.a.l. 306; F:Pn, n.a.l. 307), which contain none of the items listed in the Table, and a *terminus a quo* around 1296/7 for the fourteenth-century sources, which include the feast of Saint Louis in the original hand (e.g. GB:Lva 1346–1891; GB:Ob, Can. Lit. 192; F:Pan, L 863, No. 10).

The relative chronology of the manuscripts is clear from Table 6.2. Critical for dating these sources is the time of addition of three festivals to the ritual of the abbey: Dionysius of Corinth (8 April) in 1216, Bernard of Clairvaux (23 August) in 1241, and Sanctinus and Antoninus (19 October) in 1259. It is reasonable to assume that the three documents which provide these dates, described in Chapter 2, likewise mark the approximate beginning of the observance of these services in the monastery. Unlike the widely publicized decrees which called for veneration of Saint Louis and for the institution of the feast of Corpus Christi, obeyed at different times by different houses, the documents for Dionysius of Corinth, Bernard of Clairvaux, and Sanctinus and Antoninus pertain only to Saint-Denis and have no bearing on the liturgies of other places. Since there is no previous indication of formal cults for these saints in the ritual of Saint-Denis prior to the dates given

TABLE 6.2 *Dating the Late Twelfth- and Thirteenth-Century Liturgical Manuscripts from Saint-Denis*

Date	Event	N-t	CH-c	M1-t	M1-c	M2-t	M2-c	N4-t	N4-c	N5-t	N5-c	C-t	C-c
1216	**Relics of Dionysius of Corinth acquired**			2	1	1	1	1	1	1	1	1	1
1228	**Death of Francis of Assisi (feast on 4 Oct.)**						1	1	1	1	1	1	1
1233	**Invention of the Holy Nail**					1							
1234 (17 Jan.)	**Count Philip of Boulogne buried at Saint-Denis**					1	1	1	1				1
1236 (2 Feb.)	**Relics of Hippolytus moved from centre of nave to first chapel west of north transept**					2		1					
Between 1234 and 1259	Adoption of feast of Ursula and Eleven Thousand Virgins (21 Oct.)		2			2	1	1	1	1	1	1	1

Between 1234 and 1259	Adoption of feast of Demetrius (17 Oct.).	2	I	I	I	I	I	I
1241	**Abbot Eudes establishes feast of Bernard of Clairvaux (23 Aug.)**	2	I	I	I	I	I	I
1259	**Relics of Sanctinus and Antoninus acquired**		2	I	I	I	I	I
1270	**Death of Louis IX**							I
1271 (21? Aug.)	**Death of Alphonse of Poitou**			2?				I
1271? (5 Nov.)	**Death of Margaret of Brabant**			2				
1296/1297	**Adoption of feast of Saint Louis (25 Aug.)**				2		2	

Abbreviations: I: Feast or event written in original hand. 2: Feast or event written in later hand. Blank space: Feast or event not given. Bold print: Event firmly dated. t: Text. c: Calendar.

Manuscript sigla (as in App. A): Ch: Chapel Hill, Univ. Lib., Rare Book Coll. 11. M1: F:Pm 414. M2: F:Pm 526. N4: F:Pn, lat. 976. N5: F:Pn, lat. 1107. C: I:Rc 603.

in these records, they are our best evidence for the time of entry of these feasts into the liturgy.[55]

Other feasts and events in the abbey can also be dated with some certainty. The burial of Count Philip of Boulogne at Saint-Denis (17 January 1234), the death of Alphonse of Poitou (21? August 1271), and the death of Margaret of Brabant (5 November 1270/1) all set chronological points of reference for the books which contain necrological notices. The transfer of Hippolytus' relics on 2 February 1236, recorded in both versions of the *Chronicon Sancti Dionysii ad Cyclos Paschales*,[56] is crucial for dating the texts of the two ordinaries (F:Pm 526; F:Pn, lat. 976), since F:Pm 526 witnesses the event only in the second hand (fo. 112^v), whereas F:Pn, lat. 976 acknowledges it in the original hand (fo. 80^v). Finally, the death of Louis IX in 1270 and the adoption of his feast at Saint-Denis, probably in 1296/7, help establish the dates of the missals F:Pn, lat. 1107 and I:Rc 603.

From Table 6.2 we can therefore draw several conclusions. The Chapel Hill psalter, which seems to date from the early thirteenth century on the basis of its decoration, omits Dionysius of Corinth and thus falls just before 1216. The text of F:Pm 526 was written between the burial-day of Count Philip on 17 January 1234, entered in the first hand of the manuscript, and the Translation of Hippolytus on 2 February 1236. The calendar of F:Pm 526 was copied between 17 January 1234 and 1241, the year of the establishment of the feast of Bernard of Clairvaux, which is an addition. The temporal variance of text and calendar of F:Pm 526 is confirmed by the presence of the twelve-lesson festival of Saint Francis (4 October) in the original hand of the calendar, and by his complete absence from the body of the manuscript. Similarly, the calendar includes the feast of the Eleven Thousand Virgins (21 October) in the first hand, while the text adds this observance on fo. 185.[57]

[55] Leroquais uses the same methodology of tracing the history of local translations of saints to construct his chronologies of feasts adopted in various churches; see *Bréviaires*, i. pp. xcvi–cxviii; also Walters [Robertson], 'Reconstruction', 192–5.

[56] Pub. in Berger, '*Chronicon*', 281, 290 (original MS, I:Rvat 309, fos. 32, 53^v). See the discussion of this passage in Walters [Robertson], 'Reconstruction', 192, n. 20.

[57] Both these feasts are important 12-lesson services which entered the liturgy of Saint-Denis in the 13th c., and their presence in the calendar of F:Pm 526 and absence from the text of this book is a significant discrepancy, one which argues that calendar and text were copied at different times. On the other hand, a number of other purely martyrological mentions in the calendar (named in Foley, 'Ordinary', ii. 56, n. 68)—all of them feasts of only 3 lessons or Commemorations—have no bearing on the celebrations which actually took place in the church, and these offer no evidence of the time of copying of either calendar or text. Kurzeja similarly distinguishes carefully between the proper liturgy found in the calendar of a MS and the more general martyrological mentions which likewise are inscribed there (*Liber*, 59). On the difference between calendar and martyrology, see Ch. 2.

The dates of the calendar and text of F:Pn, lat. 976 are derived in similar fashion. Bernard of Clairvaux appears in the original hand of the text of F:Pn, lat. 976, and Sanctinus and Antoninus are written in a later hand. Thus the text of F:Pn, lat. 976 was copied between 1241 and 1259, and historical circumstances further suggest that Abbot Matthew of Vendôme (1258–70) had the book written around 1258. Since the calendar of F:Pn, lat. 976 contains Sanctinus and Antoninus in the first hand and Margaret of Brabant in a later hand, it probably dates between 1259 and ?1271.[58] If, however, the obituary notice for Alphonse of Poitou (26 August, d. 21? August 1271) was entered by the original scribe of the calendar, then the calendar dates between 21 August 1271 and the death-day of Margaret on 5 November 1271.[59]

The earlier dates of the two subsequent missals F:Pn, lat. 1107 and I:Rc 603 are more or less certain. The text and calendar of F:Pn, lat. 1107 are coeval, and the *terminus a quo* of the manuscript is 1259 because the feast of Sanctinus and Antoninus is written in the first hand of both. The later date is technically around 1296 or 1297, the time at which the feast of Saint Louis (25 August), an addition to F:Pn, lat. 1107, was first celebrated at Saint-Denis. The illuminations in the volume are much earlier, however, and evidently were done during the abbacy of Matthew of Vendôme (1258–86), who probably also ordered the copying of F:Pn, lat. 976. The calendar of I:Rc 603, which is contemporaneous with the text, contains an obituary notice for Alphonse of Poitou in the first hand and hence dates from after 1271. The addition of the feast of Saint Louis to the manuscript suggests a later date of *c.*1296 or 1297, but the decoration of the missal resembles that of F:Pn, lat. 1107 and argues for a date not long after 1271.

The missal F:Pm 414 is the most difficult to situate chronologically. The manuscript contains additions from the fourteenth century, and these have to be separated from the original, thirteenth-century portion of the text, which was written apparently at or very near the same time as the calendar. Robert Branner, studying both the illuminations and the contents of the calendar, places the codex in the group which he

[58] Margaret was the daughter of Louis IX and the first wife of Duke John I of Brabant. According to the calendar of F:Pn, lat. 976, she died on 5 Nov. I have not found confirmation of the precise day of her death in any other source, and F:Pn, lat. 976 hence appears to make a contribution to her biography. There is apparently also some question as to the year itself, for Anselm writes 'environ 1271' (Anselm, *Histoire*, i. 87). Margaret is thought to have married John of Brabant in 1269, only to die in childbirth shortly thereafter (ibid.). It is possible, then, that she died in 1270, in which case the *terminus ad quem* of the calendar of F:Pn, lat. 976 would change accordingly.

[59] Because the entry for Alphonse is partly erased, it is impossible to say whether it is by the original or a later scribe. In either case, there is little (if any) difference between the hand that wrote it and the first hand of the calendar, which suggests that the calendar was in fact copied around the time of Alphonse's death in 1271.

names the '*Vie de Saint-Denis* Atelier', and he dates the book 'before about 1228'.[60] His estimation is based on the calendar, from which he notes the absence of Abbot Peter of Auteuil (d. 1229) and of Saint Francis of Assisi (d. 1228). Branner's reliance on the death of Saint Francis, is unwise, however, for this feast provides only a loose guide for establishing dates. The time of the first observance of Francis' feast-day (4 October) varied from house to house, in the same way that the date of the adoption of the feast of Saint Louis fluctuated from one place to another. At Saint-Denis, for example, the celebration of Francis evidently did not begin until some time between 1234 and 1241, as Table 6.2 shows. Hence the *terminus ad quem* of the calendar and original portion of F:Pm 414 probably falls around 1234/5.

The earlier limit for the copying of F:Pm 414 is suggested by the presence of Saint Dionysius of Corinth (8 April) in the original hand of the calendar. Whereas the calendar of F:Pm 414 must then post-date his translation in 1216, the text of the manuscript contains his Mass as an addition. Moreover, the feast is out of order in F:Pm 414, falling before Saint Benedict (21 March) on fo. 146, instead of between the observances for Saint Ambrose (4 April) and Saints Tiburtius *et al.* (14 April) on fo. 149^{v}. There are several possible explanations for this odd arrangement: either the omission of the feast of Dionysius from the body of F:Pm 414 was simply an oversight, and his presence in the calendar reflects the correct date of the manuscript (i. e. after 1216), or the calendar slightly pre-dates the text of the missal, or this discrepancy between text and calendar demonstrates that F:Pm 414 was copied precisely around 1216, just at the time the Mass for Dionysius was being incorporated into the liturgy. Whatever the case, the contents of F:Pm 414 suggest that the original portion of the codex and probably the calendar as well were both produced between about 1216 and 1235.

CATALOGUE OF LITURGICAL SOURCES FROM SAINT-DENIS

1. Chapel Hill, Univ. Lib., Rare Book Coll. 11: Chapel Hill, University Library, Rare Book Collection 11

Psalter, copied shortly before 1216 (probably between 1210 and 1215). Vellum. I + 171 + I folios. 196 × 142 mm.

Bibliography: Sotheby, *Catalogue*, 55 (No. 294); Faye and Bond, *Supplement*, 415; Lansing, 'Perspective', 22–3; Brown, 'Psalter'; Gerson and Robertson, 'Psalter'.

[60] Branner, *Painting*, 89, 90, 224.

The Chapel Hill psalter is the latest of the three extant psalters from Saint-Denis (see Appendix C). The text of psalms in this manuscript is the version commonly known as Gallican,[61] and the book is a liturgical psalter containing eight sections. This eightfold division corresponds to the arrangement of the psalms for the seven weekdays at Matins, with the eighth section reserved for the psalms of Vespers.[62] Each division in the psalter is introduced by a historiated initial. The other parts of the manuscript contain a calendar (fos. 1–6ᵛ), the canticles (fos. 143–154ᵛ), the Athanasian Creed (fos. 154ᵛ–156ᵛ), the litany (fos. 156ᵛ–159ᵛ), and the Office for the Dead (fos. 160–170ᵛ).

The origin of the psalter at Saint-Denis is established first by the calendar. This section of the book clearly depicts the liturgy of Saint-Denis as it existed in the first 15 years of the thirteenth century, before the Translation of the relics of Dionysius of Corinth to the abbey in 1216. The entries of the important feasts of Saint-Denis are written in blue letters, sometimes with gold initials, and the letters of the name 'Dionysius' on 9 October are spaced conspicuously far apart. The litany likewise includes the names of Saints Denis, Rusticus, and Eleutherius twice, and other saints, many of whose relics were in the church, are also listed: Cucuphas, Maurice, Innocent, Vincent, Hippolytus, Eustace, Eugene, Peregrinus, Patroclus, Firminus, Hilary of Mende, Hilary of Poitiers, Romanus, Benedict, Osmanna. The Chapel Hill psalter is the first extant manuscript from the abbey which contains royal obits or anniversaries of important persons in the calendar, and Brown notes that six of these are present: Abbot Suger (14 January), Dagobert (19 January), Robert II (20 July), Louis VI (2 August), Charles the Bald (6 October), and Queen Constance (7 October). She likewise calls attention to the special prayer to Saints Denis, Rusticus, and Eleutherius on fo. 171, and to the misplaced folios in the thirteenth gathering, which can be reordered as 95, 96, 98, 99, 100, 101, 97, 102.

Two candidates seem the most likely choices for recipient of this book: Abbot Henry Troon (reg. 1204–21) or a member of the royal household, perhaps King Philip Augustus (1185–1223). The endings of many nouns and pronouns in the prayers are singular, with plural alternatives written above the words. The use of singular inflections suggests that the book may have been intended originally for a lay

[61] Despite its name, this psalter is 'Gallican' only by reason of its popularity in Gaul in the late 8th and 9th cs. There were 3 translations of the Bible in the late 4th c.: the 1st from the Greek Septuagint in 384, the 2nd by Saint Jerome from the *Hexapla* in 389 (Vulgate version), and the 3rd also by Jerome from the Hebrew in 393. The psalter was translated only in the 1st and 2nd of these efforts, and the Gallican psalter comes from the 2nd translation. This version, in spite of its shortcomings due to corruptions retained from earlier psalters, dominated the Middle Ages; see Leroquais, *Psautiers*, vol. i. pp. xxii–xxxiii; Hughes, *Manuscripts*, No. 873.

[62] Ibid. No. 874.

person, or at least for one person, rather than for the entire community. The decorated initials and the use of gold suggest the highest-ranking person in the abbey, Abbot Henry Troon, but they may also hint at a royal connection. The reigning king, Philip Augustus, visited Saint-Denis often, and he demonstrated his predilection for the abbey in numerous ways, not least of which was his gift of important relics to the monastery in 1205, as discussed in Chapter 2.

The contents of the psalter provide arguments for both these persons as possible recipient of the manuscript, the most persuasive being for Philip Augustus. Psalters for use in a Benedictine monastery usually include the *Te decet laus* after the *Te deum* (fos. 152–3), along with canticles for the different seasons of the year in place of the psalms of the third nocturn of Matins. Because none of these items is present in the Chapel Hill psalter, the connection with the Benedictine abbot of Saint-Denis Henry Troon seems weak. Indeed, the royal obits in the calendar, mentioned above, may point instead to Philip Augustus or to one of his family. But the series of responsories for the Office of the Dead at the end of the book appears to argue against connection with the king. These responsories do not comprise the distinctively royal list that the monks of Saint-Denis fashioned in the twelfth century, but rather the standard series that is also found in the fourteenth- to sixteenth-century books from Saint-Denis and in numerous other houses, as described in Chapter 3. Since, however, the psalter would have been presented to King Philip Augustus during his lifetime, it would not necessarily have employed the royal series of responsories for the Office of the Dead. It may have been meant instead for Philip's private use during his visits to Saint-Denis. In sum, the possible links between this book and Philip Augustus or one of his relatives seem stronger than those with Henry Troon.

How and when the psalter left Saint-Denis is not known. None of the characteristic shelf-marks of the library is present. Five non-Dionysian feasts are added to the calendar in a fourteenth- or fifteenth-century hand (Gereon, Translation of Augustine, Dedication of Church of Andrew, Judocus, Nicasius), and these seem to have been written by someone familiar with an English or possibly northern French liturgy. It is even possible that the psalter actually received these additions in England, since the Saint-Denis missal GB:Lva 1346–1891 and breviary GB:Ob, Can. Lit. 192 were transported to England, possibly in the late fifteenth century. But the seventeenth- or eighteenth-century mark of provenance found on fo. 1 ('. . . ye de S. Denis en Franca') suggests that the psalter remained in the abbey. By the nineteenth or twentieth century, however, the psalter was definitely in England, where

Sotheby's obtained it from G. C. Willoughby.[63] Burton Emmett bought the book at a Sotheby's auction on 16 April 1929, and it was sold to the University of North Carolina Library from Emmett's estate in 1951.

2. *F:LA 118: Laon, Bibliothèque Municipale 118*

Unnotated gradual, sacramentary, and lectionary; late ninth and early tenth century; sacramentary and lectionary of the usage of Saint-Denis, gradual of the usage of Saint-Denis and Laon.

Parchment. 249 folios. 257 × 227 mm.

Bibliography: *Catalogue général*, i. 100–1; Leroquais, *Sacramentaires*, i. 64–8; Wilmart, 'Frères'; Lesne, *Scriptoria*, 592; Huglo (1), 'Mélodie', 34; *PM*, xvi. 36; *GR* (MS *DEN* 5); Bourque, *Sacramentaires*, ii. 314; Huglo (2), 'Chants', 75, 78; Barré and Deschusses, 'Recherche', 32; Gamber, *CLLA*, ii. 414–15, 484–5, 508–9; Huglo (3), *Tonaires*, 91–102; Dikmans, 'Obituaires', 644, n. 186; Oexle, *Forschungen*, 27–31; Lemaître, *Répertoire*, 596; Atkinson (1), '*O Amnos*', 10; Atkinson (2), 'Entstehung', 121; Jeffery, 'Sources', 319; Nebbiai-Dalla Guarda, *Bibliothèque*, 33, 308, 313, 318; Rasmussen, 'Liturgy', 41.

Bourque describes F:LA 118 as a 'factitious missal' (*missel factice*), because it contains the three main components normally associated with the missal (unnotated gradual, sacramentary, lectionary), all of them simply bound together. The binding was carelessly done, and the misplaced folios and gatherings, reordered in Leroquais's description, create numerous lacunae. It appears that two contemporaneous hands wrote the gradual,[64] while a third hand copied the sacramentary and lectionary, except fos. 165–168ᵛ and 224–49, which may have been taken from another codex.

Gamber dated the sections of F:LA 118 separately, assigning the gradual to the second half of the ninth century and the sacramentary and lectionary to the tenth century. These approximations are reasonable, and the date of the gradual is supported by the fact that the script and format of this part of the manuscript closely resemble that of the sacramentary of Senlis, F:Psg 111, which was probably copied at Saint-Denis between 877 and 882. The binding of F:LA 118 as well as the responsories for the Office of the Dead, added on fos. 149–150ᵛ, show

[63] I am indebted to Nicole Morfin of the Bibliothèque Nationale for supplying me with this information.

[64] Scribe A: fos. 1–10ᵛ, 12–12ᵛ, 15–15ᵛ; brown ink, red rubrics, brown and red initials. Scribe B: fos. 11–11ᵛ, 13–14ᵛ, 222–223ᵛ; brown ink, orange rubrics, brown and orange initials. Leroquais says that these are the same hand, but the formations of letters differ, and the colours used for the rubrics and initials likewise vary.

that the book was in the Cistercian abbey of Vauclair near Laon by the thirteenth century.

The origin and usage of F:LA 118 have been universally ascribed to Saint-Denis, and the sacramentary portion contains the familiar signs which justify this assessment. The votive Masses for ferial days in the sacramentary contain precisely the same formularies given in F:Pn, lat. 2290. These include the *Missa specialium sanctorum* (fo. 35), which names seven saints whose relics were at Saint-Denis: Denis, Rusticus, Eleutherius, Hippolytus, Cucuphas, Innocent, and Hilary of Poitiers. Similarly, Wilmart and Oexle published a list of names from fo. 74^{v}, which incorporates several abbots of Saint-Denis, among them Abbot Hilduin (814–41). Besides the Sandionysian elements, there are additions relative to Saint-Germain-des-Prés on fo. 232^{v}. These insertions probably date from the time when Saint-Germain was under the joint care of the abbot of Saint-Denis in the ninth and tenth centuries. The lectionary was written in the same hand as the sacramentary and hence probably comes from Saint-Denis as well.

If the destination of the sacramentary and lectionary of F:LA 118 for Saint-Denis is clear, the usage of the gradual presents a more confused picture, one which heretofore has not been recognized. The gradual was copied at a different time from the sacramentary and lectionary, and hence does not necessarily agree with the other two books in content. Leroquais claims that the liturgy embodied in the gradual is that of Saint-Denis, aside from 'a few variants'. These differences include the selection of chants for various Masses, particularly the offertories, which have verses in F:LA 118.[65] Even more critical, however, are the feasts contained in the book. The gradual includes a Mass for Saint Martina (1 January; fo. 3),[66] a third-century virgin and martyr of Rome whose cult was uncommon in western Gaul and unknown to Saint-Denis.[67] Since Martina seems to have enjoyed brief

[65] F:LA 118 (fo. 2) gives the Offer. *In virtute tua* for Saint Stephen, while the later Saint-Denis sources (except F:Pn, lat. 9436, which was possibly copied at Saint-Vaast of Arras) employ *Posuisti domine*.

[66] On Saint Martina, see *AASS*, Jan., i. 11 ff. Although she was inscribed in martyrologies on 1 Jan., her feast was often celebrated on 30 Jan. (*VSB*, i, 614–15).

[67] No extant calendar of the abbey contains her name (see App. A). Of the MSS inventoried by Leroquais, Saint Martina on 1 Jan. is named in 4, 3 of which emanated from Rome or northern Italy: F:Pn, lat. 755, a lectionary from the second half of the 13th c. for the winter months from the papal chapel (Leroquais, *Bréviaires*, i. 369); Paris, Musée Jacquemart-André, MS 22 (1078), a 15th-c. (2nd half) Roman missal (ibid. 425); and F:Pn, lat. 15030, a 14th-/15th-c. book of daytime offices from the Benedictine monastery of Saint-Sixtus in Piacenza (ibid. 378, 380). Martina's appearance in F:Pn, lat. 15030 is due to the translation of her relics to Saint-Sixtus, a feast celebrated on 28 May (*AASS*, Janu. i. 11). A 15th-c. missal of the hermits of Saint Augustine mentions her in the calendar (Leroquais, *Bréviaires*, i. 420), and a Saint Martina on 2 Jan. is named in the calendar of F:Pn, lat. 2298, a 12th-/13th-c. missal of Saint-Gervais-de-Fos, located in the diocese of Arles.

popularity in a type of Carolingian lectionary that was disseminated from Aix-la-Chapelle,[68] it may be that the incorporation of her feast into F:LA 118 is a vestige of Roman service-books, the liturgy of which was propagated from Metz during the second half of the eighth century. In any event, the presence of Saint Martina in the gradual bespeaks a non-Dionysian—and seemingly east Frankish—influence on the contents of the manuscript.

In similar fashion, the list of alleluias for the Sundays after Pentecost in F:LA 118 (fos. 14^{v}, 222–223^{v}) includes several verses which do not appear in the 'standard' list from Saint-Denis. The series in F:LA 118, like the one from Saint-Denis, forms part of the group of alleluia lists that begin with the Alle. Ver. *In te domine speravi* (Ps. 30). Comparison of the two series reveals the differences shown in Table 6.3. The verses for Sundays III–V in the Saint-Denis series are displaced ahead by one week in F:LA 118, and those for Sundays XV and XVI at Saint-Denis are listed two weeks earlier in F:LA 118. Furthermore, the Saint-Denis list gives the Ver. *Preoccupemus faciem* (Sunday III), *Dominus regnavit* (XIII), *Jubilate deo* (XIV), and *Replebimur in bonis* (XXI), while F:LA 118 does not. The Laon list, in turn, has three verses that are foreign to Saint-Denis: Ver. *Domine in virtute* (III), *Confitebor tibi* (XV) and *Lauda anima mea* (XVI). All three verses appear in the alleluia list from Metz, preserved in F:MZ 10, where they were sung on Sundays XXI, XII and VII, respectively (Table 6.4).

These verses likewise are found in the alleluia list of Laon itself. This series, preserved in the tenth-century gradual F:LA 239 and in the thirteenth-century missal F:LA 234, is a numerically ordered series, beginning with the Ver. *Deus judex justus* (Ps. 7) and continuing in ascending order according to the Book of Psalms. F:LA 239 and F:LA 234 assign the Ver. *Domine in virtute* to Sunday IV, *Confitebor tibi* to Sundays XXII–XXIV, and *Lauda anima* to Sunday XXV (Table 6.4).

Although the alleluia series in F:LA 118 begins with *In te domine* instead of with *Deus judex*, the order of the three non-Dionysian verses in F:LA 118 follows more rigorously the arrangement found in the series emanating from Laon than the one which represents the usage of Metz (F:MZ 10). It is possible, then, that the alleluia list of F:LA 118 represents a mixture of the usages of Saint-Denis with those of Laon. Furthermore, the three non-Dionysian verses common to all three lists may have been disseminated from Metz (e.g. a forerunner of F:MZ 10)—probably during or after the Carolingian reform—to Laon (e.g. a forerunner of F:LA 239; F:LA 234) and thence to the gradual of Saint-

[68] Frere, *Kalendar*, 74.

TABLE 6.3. *Alleluias for the Sundays after Pentecost at Saint-Denis and in the Gradual of F:LA 118*

Sunday	Psalm	Saint-Denis[a]	Psalm	F:LA 118
I	30	*In te domine speravi*		–
II	17	*Diligam te*		–
III	94	*Venite exultemus*	20	*Domine in virtute*
	94	*Preoccupemus faciem*		n.g.
IV	104	*Confitemini domino*	94	*Venite exultemus*
V	113	*Qui timent dominum*	104	*Confitemini domino*
VI	89	*Domine refugium*	113	*Qui timent dominum*
VII	46	*Omnes gentes*		–
VIII	94	*Quoniam deus magnus*		–
IX	146	*Qui sanat*		–
X	121	*Letatus sum*		–
XI	107	*Paratum cor meum*		–
XII	80	*Exultate deo*		–
XIII	92	*Dominus regnavit*	87	*Domine deus*
XIV	99	*Jubilate deo*	116	*Laudate dominum*
XV	87	*Domine deus*	137	*Confitebor tibi*
XVI	116	*Laudate dominum*	145	*Lauda anima mea*
XVII	7	*Deus judex*		–
XVIII	147	*Qui posuit*		–
XIX	58	*Eripe me*		–
XX	77	*Attendite popule*		–
XXI	64	*Te decet hymnus*		–
	64	*Replebimur in bonis*		n.g.
XXII	129	*De profundis*		–
XXIII	117	*Dextera dei*		–

Abbreviations: –: Same alleluia. n.g.: Alleluia not given.

[a] List compiled from F:Pn, lat. 9436; F:Pn, lat. 1107; F:Pn, lat. 10505; GB:Lva 1346–1891.

Denis/Laon (e.g. F:LA 118) in the late ninth century. Occasions for such cross-influence between Laon and Saint-Denis will be explored presently.

In spite of these indications, it might be objected that the presence of Saint Martina and the alleluia list in F:LA 118 simply represent an earlier stage of the liturgy of Saint-Denis, one which perhaps was modified or in some measure standardized under the influence of Cluny in the tenth and eleventh centuries. Two factors argue against this assumption. First, the ninth-century calendar of Saint-Denis is known through the two manuscripts F:Psg 111 and F:Pn, lat. 2290 (see Appendix A), and neither of these early calendars records the name of

Saint Martina (1 January). Second, while the *antiphonale missarum* of F:LA 118 contains the feast of Saint Denis (9 October, fo. 14), it does not include the Vigil (8 October), a festival which is documented in the abbey from Merovingian times and which is also found in the ninth-century sacramentary F:Pn, lat. 2290.[69] This is a serious omission, for any number of churches might have celebrated the *natale* of the favoured saint of the monarchy, while the commemoration of the Vigil is rarer and suggests a house with closer ties to the abbey. The cathedral of Paris, for example, under whose jurisdiction the basilica of Saint-Denis stood in the Merovingian era, celebrated the Vigil as well as the *natale* of Saint Denis. No extant service book of the usage of Saint-Denis omits the Vigil, and its absence from F:LA 118, coupled with the abnormal alleluia list and the appearance of Saint Martina, calls the usage of the gradual of this manuscript into question.

The later provenance of F:LA 118 in the region of Laon suggests that the mingling of liturgies which is apparent in the gradual occurred in the region of Laon. The monks of Saint-Denis took refuge in and around Reims and Laon on at least two occasions in the late ninth century. Moreover, the non-Dionysian verses in the alleluia list cited above are characteristic of the liturgy of Laon.[70] Since there is no evidence that F:LA 118 ever formed part of the library of Saint-Denis in Paris, it is conceivable that the composite manuscript was fashioned instead in Laon in the late ninth or early tenth century. The compilers would have joined a newly written sacramentary and lectionary from Saint-Denis with a slightly older gradual of mixed usage that had served the monks perhaps during their exile in Consevreux near Laon in 876. Indeed, there were dealings between Saint-Denis and Saint-Vincent of Laon in the ninth and tenth centuries. Charles the Bald commissioned a monk of Saint-Denis to reform Saint-Vincent in 851,[71] and a spiritual association between the two abbeys was established somewhat later, around 989.[72] Whatever house in Laon may have been the precise origin of the non-Dionysian elements in F:LA 118, the manuscript is significant, for it shows that the monks of Saint-Denis evidently made liturgical concessions to their temporary hosts during sojourns away from their home in Paris. In view of the evidence given here, the catalogue descriptions of F:LA 118 which call the manuscript a source from

[69] Fo. 14 of F:LA 118 begins with the Mass for Saint Mark (7 Oct.) and follows directly with that of the *natale* of Saint Denis, omitting the Vigil.

[70] One of the alleluia lists from Reims begins with the Ver. *In te domine speravi*, but the 3 verses common to F:LA 118, F:LA 239, and F:LA 234, and the series from Metz, apparently were not used at Reims.

[71] Mabillon, *Annales*, iii. 11–12; *GC*, ix. 567; see also Poupardin, 'Cartulaire', 174; Contreni, *School*, 13.

[72] Poupardin, 'Cartulaire', 192; also Félibien, *Histoire*, *PJ*, pt. i, No. cvii.

Table 6.4. *Alleluias for Sundays after Pentecost at Metz (F:MZ 10), in F:LA 118, and at Laon (F:LA 239)*

Sunday	Psalm	F:MZ 10	Psalm	F:LA 118	Psalm	F:LA 239
I	30	*In te domine*		Same	7	*Deus judex*
II	146	*Qui sanat*	17	*Diligam te*	17	*Diligam te*
III	113	*Qui timent*	20	*Domine in virtute*	18	*Celi enarrant*
IV	7	*Deux judex*	94	*Venite exultemus*	20	*Domine in virtute*
V	89	*Domine refugium*	104	*Confitemini*	30	*In te domine*
VI	104	*Confitemini*	113	*Qui timent*		(Erased)
VII	145	*Lauda anima*	46	*Omnes gentes*	64	*Te decet*
VIII	17	*Diligam te*	116	*Quoniam deus*	77	*Attendite*
IX	94	*Quoniam deus*	146	*Qui sanat*	80	*Exultate deo*
X	129	*De profundis*	121	*Letatus sum*	87	*Domine deus*
XI	87	*Domine deus*	107	*Paratum cor*	89	*Domine refugium*
XII	137	*Confitebor tibi*	92	*Dominus regnavit*	94	*Venite exultemus*
XIII	124	*Qui confidunt*	87	*Domine deus*	94	*Quoniam deus*
XIV	77	*Attendite*	116	*Laudate dominum*	104	*Confitemini*

XV	107	*Paratum cor*	137	*Confitebor tibi*	107	*Paratum cor*
XVI	116	*Laudate dominum*	145	*Lauda anima*	110	*Redemptionem*
XVII	147	*Qui posuit*	7	*Deus judex*	113	*Qui timent*
XVIII	121	*Letatus sum*	147	*Qui posuit*	116	*Laudate dominum*
XIX	110	*Redemptionem*	58	*Eripe me*		(Not given)
XX	89	*Domine refugium*	77	*Attendite popule*	117	*Dextera dei*
XXI	20	*Domine in vir.*	64	*Te decet*	129	*De profundis*
XXII	117	*Dextera domini*	*129*	*De profundis*	137	*Confitebor*
XXIII		*Propitius esto*	117	*Dextera dei*	(137	*Confitebor*)
XXIV					137	*Confitebor*
XXV					145	*Lauda anima*

[a] F:LA 239 is published in facsimile edn. in *PM*, x. The alleluia list given here is gathered from the alleluia incipits found in the formularies for the Sundays after Pentecost in the body of the gradual. Another slightly different series appears with musical notation later in the MS, on fos. 87–8ᵛ. The only real difference between the 2 lists is on Sunday VI, which is assigned the Alle. Ver. *Omnes gentes* in the 2nd series, whereas the incipit is erased in the text of the MS. In addition, the 2nd list gives the Ver. *Quoniam deus* on Sunday XIX. This 2nd list breaks off 4 or 5 Sundays from the end, due to the loss of the last fo. The list in the 13th-c. missal F:LA 234 preserves almost exactly the one found in the earlier gradual F:LA 239. The verse *Eripe me* (Ps. 58) is given on Sunday VI, and *Quoniam* appears on Sunday XIX. The folios that should contain this alleluia for the 15th and 16th Sundays are missing from F:LA 234. The contemporaneous 13th-c. ordinary from Laon, F:LA 215, gives *Paratum cor* (fo. 170ᵛ, Sunday XV) and *Redemptionem* (fo. 172, Sunday XVI), which are also the verses given in F:LA 239.

Saint-Denis should be revised as follows: F:LA 118 is an unnotated gradual from the late ninth century of the combined usage of Saint-Denis and Laon, coupled with an early tenth-century sacramentary and lectionary of the use of Saint-Denis.

Apart from the points that have been raised with regard to the origins of F:LA 118, the manuscript contains several noteworthy textual features relating to music. The communions have *versus ad repetendum*, and the tonal designations for both introits and communions are given in the margin of the gradual. F:LA 118, together with F:Pn, lat. 12050 and the Mont-Renaud manuscript, are the sources which Huglo (3) compiled in his 'tonary of Corbie-Saint-Denis'. But new evidence presented here on the origins of F:LA 118 and of the Mont-Renaud source suggests that Huglo's tonary is probably in fact characteristic of the rather more limited area of Corbie–Laon, although the Saint-Denis monks may well have used it when in residence there. Huglo (3) demonstrates in addition that this tonary also resembles a version of the Carolingian tonary that emanated from Metz, a noteworthy coincidence in view of the deviant alleluia verses in F:LA 118. Another distinctive aspect of F:LA 118 is the evangelic Comm. *Oportet te* (fo. 35), which includes the ending *in aeternum*, found only in a few French manuscripts.

As in F:Pn, lat. 2290, vestiges of the early *missa graeca* in the West also appear in F:LA 118. Atkinson (1, 2) has noted the Latin text of the Gloria in Excelsis in the sacramentary portion of the manuscript (fo. 156^{v}), followed by an incomplete version of the Greek counterpart *Doxa in ipistis* which is transcribed in Latin characters. Fo. 16, also part of the sacramentary, contains the Greek Gloria Patri. The gradual of F:LA 118 is a newly discovered source for the text of the Cherubic hymn, or *Cheroubikon* (fo. 223^{v}), as discussed in Chapter 4.

3. F:Pan, L863, No. 10: Paris, Archives Nationales, L863, No. 10

Ordinary, mid-eighteenth century, *c.*1760. Abridged from a fourteenth-century ordinary, written between 1350 and 1364.
Paper. 92 folios. 202 × 160 mm.

Bibliography: Martimort, *Documentation*, 544; Walters [Robertson], 'Reconstruction', 205–31; Foley, 'Ordinary', ii. 65–72, 425–49; Rasmussen, 'Liturgy', 42; Robertson, '*Benedicamus*', 7, 16, 34–6, 56.

The latest surviving ordinary from Saint-Denis, F:Pan, L 863, No. 10, was written in the eighteenth century, but it represents the mid-fourteenth-century liturgical usage of the monastery. The first 54 folios of F:Pan, L 863, No. 10 are paginated, pp. 1–106. One unnumbered page comes between pp. 34 and 35; it is misplaced and should follow

p. 36: 34, 35, 36, 34a, 34b, 37. Beginning with fo. 104, which comes after p. 106, the subsequent 38 leaves are foliated: fos. 104–141^{v}. Blank pages and folios occur throughout the text (pp. 9–12, 72, 74–5, 81, 102–6, fos. 105^{v}, 108–111^{v}), and the flyleaves are blank except for the appearance of the shelf-mark of the Archives Nationales on fo. I at the beginning and on fo. VI verso at the end. The book is covered with a modern binding (end of the nineteenth century) in burgundy and black. Printed on the spine are the words 'Cérémonial de l'abbaye de Saint-Denis/Extrait, copie du XVIIIe s'.

Evidence of authorship and provenance is established by: (1) p. 1, top: 'Extrait de l'ancien Cérémonial de St. Denis en France écrit sous le Roi Jean, et qui étoit enchaîné dans le choeur, pour y avoir recours en cas de besoin'; (2) p. 1, top quarter and throughout the manuscript: 'Archives du Royaume, Sect. Hist.'; (3) p. 1, bottom: 'l'auteur de cet Extrait est D. Dégré, chantre et Tresorier de St. Denis en 1760' (written in the same hand as No. 1 above). From these indications, it appears that the manuscript was copied around 1760 by Dom Dégré, and was kept in the library of Saint-Denis until the French Revolution, when it came into the Archives Nationales. The text was written in the same cursive hand (light-brown ink), presumably that of Dom Dégré, from beginning to end.

According to the statement at the top of p. 1, the exemplar of F:Pan, L 863, No. 10 was made between 1350 and 1364, during the reign of King John II. The latest anniversary in the manuscript for Abbot Guido of Châtres (21 February, d. 1350) supports these dates, and hence the manuscript may be considered to represent mid-fourteenth-century practice. The contents of F:Pan, L 863, No. 10 are constantly truncated in terms of both rubrics and textual incipits, and its format differs substantially from that of the two earlier ordinaries (F:Pm 526; F:Pn, lat. 976). Because it is a ceremonial, F:Pan, L 863, No. 10 gives details of the actions, manner of dress and locations of the various services, while usually reducing the cues for musical selections to abbreviations followed by ellipses, e.g. 'Resp . . . ' or 'V . . . ' Hence the book is useful for the study of such features as the itineraries of mid-fourteenth-century processions at Saint-Denis, although the names of introits, responsories, versicles, and other items have to be supplied by comparison with the contemporaneous missal (GB:Lva 1346–1891) and breviary (GB:Ob, Can. Lit. 192). Rubrics for the weekly commemoration of Saint Denis on Thursdays are given on pp. 1–8, and the manuscript occasionally designates tropes, sequences, hymns, antiphons *ante evangelium*, and melodies for the Benedicamus Domino and Ite Missa Est.

There are two large lacunae in the text of F:Pan, L 863, No. 10:

between the feasts of Assumption (25 March, fo. 100) and Saint Landericus (10 June, fo. 104), and between Saints Peter and Paul (29 June, fo. 107ᵛ) and Peter's Chains (1 August, fo. 112). The blank folios mentioned earlier cause other services to be omitted, but otherwise F:Pan, L 863, No. 10 reaffirms the roster of feasts given in the two thirteenth-century ordinaries (F:Pm 526; F:Pn, lat. 976) and contains several later added services. The new feasts in F:Pan, L 863, No. 10 are for Saint Jonas (12 August), the feast and Octave of Saint Louis (25 August, 1 September), the celebration of the victory of Philip IV at Mons on 22 August 1304 in a morning Mass on the Octave of Assumption (22 August), Saint Taurinus (20 October), and Corpus Christi. The series of anniversaries at the end of the manuscript (fos. 135ᵛ–141ᵛ) contains 41 services, the greatest number in any extant book from the abbey.[73] The anniversaries (Table 6.5) are arranged according to the liturgical calendar, beginning with Philip IV (29 November), and ending with Queen Blanche (27 November).

4. *F:Pm 384: Paris, Bibliothèque Mazarine 384 (748)*

Gradual and unnotated list of chants for an antiphoner, early eleventh century (Pl. 9).

Parchment. 192 leaves (pagination, pp. 1–35; then foliation, fos. 36–209).[74] 268 × 164 mm.

Bibliography: Molinier, *Mazarine*, i. 140–1; Gastoué, 'Origines' (1902/3), 169; Suñol, *Introduction*, pl. C, No. 11A; Brou, 'Chants', 148; Handschin, 'Tropaires', 32; Beyssac, 'Mont-Renaud', 134–49; Gay, 'Formulaires', 85; *GR* (MS *DEN* 1); Hourlier and Huglo, 'Notation', 215; Cardine, 'Preuves', 50; Huglo (1), 'Chants', 74, 79; Corbin and Bernard, *Répertoire*, ii. 17–21, 184–5; Hesbert, *CAO*, v, vi (MS 779); Huglo (2), 'Débuts', 105–6; Stäblein, *Schriftbild*, 13; Corbin, *Neumen*, 3.1222–3.1223; Huglo (3), 'Origines', 48; 'Sources', 615; Hiley, 'Traditions', 15; Hesbert, *Graduel* (facsimile edn. of the gradual portion of F:Pm 384); Huglo (4), 'Review' (1982); Steiner, 'Traditions', 133; Walters [Robertson], 'Reconstruction', 226–7; Nebbiai-Dalla Guarda, *Bibliothèque*, 34, 106, 141, 194, 237, 273, 287, 382; Rasmussen, 'Liturgy', 41; Stahl, 'Problem', 172, 180, n. 56; Colette, 'Sémiologie', 125; Huglo (5), 'Remarques'.

The palaeographic details and contents of F:Pm 384 are outlined by Corbin and Bernard, and more recently in Hesbert's facsimile of the gradual portion. The original, early eleventh-century layer of the book

[73] The services are treated in some detail in Ch. 2, and death-dates are given in the Notes to the Calendar in App. A.

[74] Actualy, 2 different systems of numbering are in use at the beginning of the volume, as explained in Hesbert, *Graduel*, xii. In his facsimile edn. of the MS, Hesbert attempts to simplify matters by employing pagination throughout.

TABLE 6.5. *Anniversaries Contained in the Third Ordinary from Saint-Denis (F:Pan, L 863, No. 10)*

Fo.	Date	Name
135v	29 Nov.	Philip IV
136	23 Dec.	Queen Margaret of Provence
136v	30	Abbot Giles
137	3 Jan.	Philip V
	10	Queen Mary
	12/14	Abbot Suger
	18	Count Philip
	19	King Dagobert
138v	28	Queen Isabel
	1 Feb.	Charles IV
	7	Abbot Peter of Auteuil
139	14	Abbot Yves
	19	Abbot Adam
	21	Abbot Guido of Châtres
139v	4 Mar.	Abbot William of Macouris
	11	Abbot Renaud Giffart
	29	Pope Martin IV
	1 Apr.	Archbishop Peter of Cosenza
	18	Abbot Hugh of Milan
	19/29	Cardinal William of Braye
	5 May	Abbot Eudes Clément
		In anniversario parentum, fratrum, familiarum et benefactorum nostrorum
	5 June	Louis X
140	17	Princess Blanche
	14 July	King Philip Augustus
140v	16	Pope Innocent III
	20	Robert II
	29	Abbot William of Gap
	30	Cardinal John Cholet
	2 Aug.	Louis VI
	4	Louis III and Henry I
141	27	Count Alphonse of Poitou
	26 Sept.	Abbot Matthew of Vendôme
	5 Oct.	Philip III
	6	King Charles the Bald
	7	Queen Constance of Castille
141v	26	Abbot Hugh Foucault
	30	Abbots Hilduin, Eudes of Deuil, Eudes Taverny
	3 Nov.	All Souls Day
	7	Louis VIII
	27	Queen Blanche of Castille

contains two main sections: a gradual and a list of textual incipits for the chants of the Office. A table of readings for the Mass, clearly for use at Saint-Denis, was written on blank folios (158^{v}–159^{v}, 161^{v}–162^{v}, 208^{r-v}) probably in the late twelfth century. Other additions seem to have been made nearer the time of writing of the gradual portion, perhaps in the mid-eleventh century: a rhymed, notated Office for Saint Denis not otherwise found in sources from the abbey (fos. 160–161^{v}, see Pl. 9), a group of notated processional antiphons (fos. 201–3), and a list of verbal incipits for other antiphons and responsories for penitential days, followed by the litanies (fos. 204^{v}–207^{v}).

Several peculiarities of the content of F:Pm 384 indicate that the original portion of the volume was copied toward the beginning of the eleventh century, probably before the augmented sacramentary F:Pn, lat. 9436 was written around 1050. Like other early sacramentaries, the *sanctorale* of F:Pm 384 is integrated with the *temporale*, whereas F:Pn, lat. 9436 separates these two cycles entirely. In the litanies of F:Pm 384, moreover, the name of Saint Vedast is added twice in a later hand (fos. 205, 206^{v}). Since F:Pn, lat. 9436 appears to have been produced in or influenced by the scriptorium of Saint-Vaast of Arras, it is likely that the entries of Saint Vedast in F:Pm 384 were made around the time that the association between the abbeys of Saint-Denis and Saint-Vaast was established—clearly after F:Pm 384 was copied. Hesbert points out other vestiges of older tradition in F:Pm 384: the omission of Masses for the Saturdays before the first Sunday in Lent and before Palm Sunday, and the use of responsories instead of alleluias on Saturday of the week of Pentecost.

F:Pm 384 is the earliest known manuscript to include the Mass for the Octave of Saint Denis. The emphasis on the saint throughout the text, the presence of material for Saints Peregrinus, Cucuphas, Maurice, and Hilary of Mende, and the alleluia list of F:Pm 384 indicate that the manuscript was copied and notated in the abbey. The appearance of the fifteenth-century shelf-mark (fo. 1) demonstrates that the book remained in the library of Saint-Denis until this time, although by the seventeenth century F:Pm 384 was in the library of the cathedral of Paris, as demonstrated by the mark on fo. 103.

The processional antiphons mentioned above are not the only pieces of this type given in F:Pm 384. A displaced gathering near the beginning of the manuscript includes the prolix antiphons for the processions of Christmas, Lent, Easter, Pentecost, Saints Peter and Paul, and rogation days. The pages of this gathering are out of order and should be arranged thus: 17, 18, 21–8, 19, 20. These processional antiphons normally came at the ends of the old graduals and antiphoners, and the gathering in which they appear in F:Pm 384 was in fact mistakenly bound out of order, interrupting the series of Masses for the Christmas season. Several of these chants are remnants of the great processional antiphons which were employed in the Gallican rite.

Corbin and Bernard, as well as Hesbert, have pointed out many peculiar features in the gradual of F:Pm 384, notably the lack of Masses for All Saints and for Saint Martin. They also note the presence of the Kyrie *Qui passurus* for the three holy days before Easter (*Triduum Sacrum*). This chant, described in Chapter 4, was a Gallican *Preces* sung after the Benedictus at Lauds and thus normally preserved in antiphoners. The offertories contained in F:Pm 384 all include verses, one of which, the *Cheroubikon* (*Qui cherubim mystice*, fo. 153), is a vestige both of the Byzantine and the Gallican liturgies and was sung at Saint-Denis in the later Greek Mass of the abbey. The alleluia list for the Sundays after Pentecost in F:Pm 384 contains one alleluia that is not otherwise found in books from the monastery, *Adorabo ad templum*, for the nineteenth Sunday. Huglo (3) has pointed out a unique melodic formation in F:Pm 384 in the Comm. *Video celos* for Saint Stephen (fo. 9). In this chant, the final word *faciunt* contains a florid melismatic trope on the syllable *fa*-, not yet found in any other source, as noted in Chapter 3.

Another noteworthy aspect of F:Pm 384 is the feast of the Dedication of the Church. This service is recorded on 24 February in extant calendars from Saint-Denis as early as the ninth century. Yet no text of any surviving liturgical manuscript preserves the Dedication on this date before the end of the twelfth century. The mid-eleventh-century sacramentary F:Pn, lat. 9436 (fos. 120–121ᵛ) and the twelfth-century antiphoner F:Pn, lat. 17296 (fos. 287–9ᵛ; Hesbert, *CAO*, ii. No. 127a), along with the antiphonary portion of F:Pm 384 (fo. 196ᵛ), all place this service after the *commune sanctorum*. The table of readings which was interpolated on blank folios of F:Pm 384 in the late twelfth or perhaps early thirteenth century is in fact one of the earliest sources from Saint-Denis to put the Dedication on its proper day (24 February, fo. 159), and all subsequent manuscripts do likewise. The gradual of F:Pm 384, however, is old-fashioned in this respect. Here a Mass 'In dedicatione aecclesiae' is entered between the services for Saints Nereus and Pudentiana, that is, between 12 and 19 May (fo. 108ᵛ). This date is a vestige of earlier Roman books which placed a standard dedication feast on 13 May.[75]

[75] See Frere, *Kalendar*, 105. The inscription of the Dedication in F:Pm 384 is characteristic of other feasts of the *temporale*, not the *sanctorale*. That is, the headings of the services of the *sanctorale* are invariably provided with dates, e.g. '*iiii id. maii*' for Saint Nereus (fo. 108; Hesbert, *Graduel*, 81), while the Dedication bears only the rubric '*In dedicatione aecclesiae*', which is the practice employed for the titles of feasts of the *temporale*.

5. *F:Pm 414: Paris, Bibliothèque Mazarine 414 (735)*

Unnotated missal (summer months only), thirteenth century (original portion copied between about 1216 and 1235), with interpolations from the fourteenth century (Pls. 15 and 16).

Parchment. 344 folios. 285 × 210 mm.

Bibliography: Molinier, *Mazarine*, i. 162; Leroquais, *Sacramentaires*, ii. 73; Corbin and Bernard, *Repertoire*, ii. 121; Samaran and Marichal, *Catalogue*, i. 239; Branner, *Painting*, 89, 90, 224; Lemaître, *Répertoire*, 599; Nebbiai-Dalla Guarda, *Bibliothèque*, 70, 163–4, 176, 195, 259, 273, 288, 369; Rasmussen, 'Liturgy', 42.

This missal, more than any other source that survives from Saint-Denis, clearly illustrates the liturgical expansion that took place in the thirteenth and fourteenth centuries. Copied probably between 1216 and 1235, the text of F:Pm 414 was later revised to update the book for use in the fourteenth century. The modifications are easily discernible: the change in colour of ink from black in the earlier portions to brown in the fourteenth-century sections, the absence of ruling lines in the folios containing material that was added later, and the presence of two styles of decoration, the earlier of which Branner places in his '*Vie de Saint Denis* atelier'. The transformation of the volume is not limited to the insertion of integral portions of text: the fourteenth-century hand often altered individual items within the original folios of the codex.

The newer sections of F:Pm 414, catalogued only in part by Leroquais and by Samaran and Marichal, reflect many of the later additions to the liturgy of Saint-Denis.

Fos. 51^{v}–57: The material for the ember days of the week of Pentecost incorporates the alleluias given in the mid-fourteenth-century missal GB:Lva 1346–1891 (fos. 183–7), rather than those provided in the thirteenth-century missal F:Pn, lat. 1107 (fos. 175–177^{v}).

Fos. 61–66^{v} include the feast of Corpus Christi (fos. 65–7), which is added to F:Pn, lat. 1107 (fos. 283–284^{v}).

Fos. 127–135^{v}: Abbot Matthew of Vendôme (d. 1286) is listed in the *Missa pro uno defuncto* (fo. 131).

Fos. 140–146^{v} contain a Mass for Dionysius of Corinth (fos. 146–146^{v}), whose relics were translated to Saint-Denis in 1216.

Fos. 213–217^{v} incorporate the morning Mass in celebration of the victory of Philip IV at Mons (1304), the feast of Saint Bernard of Clairvaux (23 August) which was established at Saint-Denis in 1241, and the feast and Octave of Saint Louis (canonized in 1297).

Fos. 239–240^{v} include Saint Francis of Assisi (4 October), whose cult was instituted in the abbey between 1234 and 1241.

Fos. 244–248^{v} add Masses for Saints Demetrius (17 October),

Sanctinus and Antoninus (19 October), Taurinus (20 October), and the Eleven Thousand Virgins (21 October). All but Taurinus were implanted in the liturgy between 1234 and 1259, and Taurinus was inserted in the fourteenth century. In addition, the Octave of Saint Denis contains the musical and textual incipits for the Greek Gloria (*Doxa*) and Credo (*Pisteuo*) of the Greek Mass (Pls. 15 and 16).

Fos. 253^{r-v} contain a Mass for Saint Marcellus, who was venerated in the abbey after 1234.

Fos. 259^{v}–267 present material under the rubric *Hic sequuntur quae supra deficiunt* ('Here follow those things that are missing above') which is meant to be added to the contents of feasts given elsewhere in the manuscript. These changes usually involve the replacement of a piece from the *commune sanctorum* with another selection from the *commune*, and these substitutions regularly agree with the chants, prayers, and readings listed in the fourteenth-century missal GB:Lva 1346–1891. Furthermore, the feast of Saint Osmanna on fo. 265^{v} is placed on 9 September, the day on which she was commemorated at Saint-Denis after about 1234. The calendar of F:Pm 414, on the other hand, places her festival on 16 August (Appendix A, MS M1).

Fos. 313^{v}–331: The votive Masses provided in this section correspond more closely to GB:Lva 1346–1891 (fos. 342^{v}–352) than to F:Pn, lat. 1107 (fos. 320^{v}–324).

Fos. 342–344^{v} modify the *Missa pro pace* in similar fashion, so that the service is comparable to the formulary preserved in the late thirteenth-century missal I:Rc 603 (fos. 270^{v}–271) and the fourteenth-century GB:Lva 1346–1891 (fo. 356).

Although the manuscript is almost entirely unnotated, square notaion is provided for the prefaces (fos. 136–139^{v}) and for the incipits of the Greek Gloria (*Doxa en ipsistis*) and Credo (*Pisteuo ys ena theon*) of the Greek Mass for the Octave of Saint Denis (fos. 245^{r-v}; Pls. 15 and 16). Nebbiai-Dalla Guarda suggests that F:Pm 414 is one of a handful of liturgical manuscripts described in the catalogue of the Saint-Denis library F:Pa 6494, compiled during the French Revolution. If this identification is correct, the presence of the missal at Saint-Denis is thus established until the end of the eighteenth century, at which time it came into the Bibliothèque Mazarine.

6. *F:Pm 526: Paris, Bibliothèque Mazarine, MS 526 (744)*

Ordinary, copied between 1234 and 1236. Calendar of F:Pm 526 in a different hand,[76] copied between 1234 and 1241.

[76] In addition to the liturgical differences cited earlier, the formations of many letters vary between text and calendar of F:Pm 526, notably capitals D, E, and S.

Parchment. 195 folios. 230 × 161 mm.

Bibliography: Molinier (1), *Mazarine*, i. 211; Molinier (2), *Obituaires*, i. 334–5; Omont, 'Messe', 180; Wilmart, 'Anniversaires', 30; Bourque, *Sacramentaires*, ii. 341–2; Samaran and Marichal, *Catalogue*, i. 245; Huglo, 'Chants', 76; Martimort, *Documentation*, 543–5; Lemaître, *Répertoire*, 598; Walters [Robertson], 'Reconstruction', 191–231; Bruzelius, *St-Denis*, 200–1; Nebbiai-Dalla Guarda, *Bibliothèque*, 34, 70, 148, 160, 166, 175–6, 195, 205, 242, 273, 288; Foley, 'Ordinary' (edn. of F:Pm 526[77] and commentary); Payne, 'Associa', 249; Rasmussen, 'Liturgy', 42–4; Stahl, 'Problem', 176, n. 18; Robertson, '*Benedicamus*', 7, 16, 27, 34–7, 56.

F:Pm 526 is the earliest extant ordinary from Saint-Denis. The manuscript encompasses services from the beginning of Advent in the *temporale* to the feast of Saint Catherine (25 November) in the *sanctorale*, during which the text breaks off. There are lacunae between fos. 192^{v} and 193 (9–12 November) and between fos. 194^{v} and 195 (20–4 November). The book was composed during the first years of the thirteenth-century reconstruction of Saint-Denis (1231–81) and witnesses the early phases of that endeavour in terms both of the festivals celebrated in the 1230s and of the architecture of the church, as discussed in Chapter 4.

F:Pm 526 is the only manuscript from Saint-Denis that contains the feast commemorating the Finding of the Holy Nail in 1233 (*In invencione sacri clavi*, fos. 60^{r-v}). The tropes, sequences, hymns, antiphons *ante evangelium*, invitatory antiphons, and melodies for the Benedicamus Domino and Ite Missa Est which were sung in the abbey are named in the rubrics for many services. Detailed information on processions and on performance practice of the Mass and Office appear throughout the manuscript. The first complete description of the Greek Mass for the Octave of Saint Denis (16 October) is found on fo. 184.

The ordinary likewise provides directions for the weekly services of commemoration for Saint Denis on Thursdays, for the Virgin on Saturdays, and for the variations in these observances during various times of the year (fos. 9, 10, 11^{v}, etc.), as outlined by Abbot Suger in the twelfth century. To some extent, in fact, the contents of F:Pm 526 may mirror the liturgical practice in Suger's church, as Rasmussen has suggested. Most of the music contained in F:Pn, lat. 17296, probably copied under Suger, is still named in F:Pm 526. Suger no doubt regularized the custom of processing to individual altars as part of his revolutionary new plan for radiating chapels at Saint-Denis, and these

[77] Foley's dissertation became available to me only after I had finished my own work on F:Pm 526, including the numerous passages from this MS quoted throughout the present study. Since my own system of abbreviations was already in place, I have not drawn on his edn.

processions were still used in the thirteenth century. He also described in detail the consecration of 21 *oratoria* in the church in 1144, and F:Pm 526 as well as the later ordinaries show that these altars were likewise employed in the thirteenth century, albeit sometimes with different designations. At the same time, however, it is clear that certain liturgical changes were made after Suger's time, particularly in the performance practice of services such as the royal anniversaries, as discussed in Chapter 2.

7. *F:Pn, grec. 375: Paris, Bibliothèque Nationale, grec. 375*

Greek lectionary for the Mass, eleventh century, copied in 1021 by Byzantine? monk-priest Helie, adapted for use at Saint-Denis in the twelfth and thirteenth centuries.
Parchment. 195 folios. 237 × 163 mm.

Bibliography: Delisle, *Cabinet*, i. 201; Omont (1), *Inventaire*, i. 39; Omont (2), 'Messe', 182; Lake and Lake, *Manuscripts*, 12, pl. 256; Lesne, *Scriptoria*, 209; Weiss, 'Studio', 428; Huglo, 'Chants', 80; Nebbiai-Dalla Guarda, *Bibliothèque*, 34, 133, 136, 314, 318; Stahl, 'Problem', 165–7.

Given the interest in all things Greek at Saint-Denis, it is not surprising to find a Greek manuscript among the survivors of the liturgy of the abbey. The colophon, published by Lake, reveals that F:Pn, grec. 375 was written in 1021 by a monk-priest named Helie, and the manuscript seems to have been in use at Saint-Denis by the twelfth century. The readings for the Mass naturally appear in Greek, but there are often marginal cues in Latin which were perhaps added at Saint-Denis.

F:Pn, grec. 375 is approximately coeval with the gradual of Saint-Denis F:Pm 384, the earliest source which documents the feast of the Octave of Saint Denis (16 October), a service which was later sung in Greek. It is noteworthy that the epistle and gospel for this festival, *Stans paulus in medio* (fos. 56, 153, 194^{v}) and *Videns jhesus christus turbas* (fo. 154), are among the lessons later incorporated into F:Pn, grec. 375, probably at Saint-Denis. Huglo notes that the texts of these readings on fos. 56 and 154 were written in the twelfth or thirteenth centuries; those on fos. 153 and 194^{v} also appear to be later additions. Fragments of the two brief sentences which were sung before the gospel at Mass are also added in Latin and Greek on fo. 193^{v}: '[Dominus vobiscum. Et cum] spiritu tuo' = 'tato nematoso', and 'gloria tibi domine' = 'doxa sy kirie'.

8. F:Pn, lat. 103: Paris, Bibliothèque Nationale, lat. 103

Psalter, early eleventh-century, adapted for use at Saint-Denis by mid-eleventh century. Hymnal added by mid-eleventh century (Pl. 10). Parchment. 166 folios (= fos. 1–41 + another folio numbered 41 + fos. 42–165). 283 × 215 mm.

Bibliography: Bibliothèque Nationale (1), *Catalogue*, i. 39; Mearns, *Hymnaries*; Rand, 'Traces', 430, n. 1; Leroquais, *Psautiers*, vol. i, pp. xlv–xlvi; ii, 30–2; Bibliothèque Nationale (2), *Manuscrits* (1954), 85–6; Schapiro, 'Drawings', 346, n. 80; Descandres, 'Manuscrits', 14; Szövérffy, *Hymnendichtung*, 150, 154; Gamber, *CLLA*, ii. 586; Nebbiai-Dalla Guarda, *Bibliothèque*, 80, 85, 131, 134, 203, 241, 263, 275, 287, 379; Rasmussen, 'Liturgy', 41.

The original portion of F:Pn, lat. 103 (fos. 1–141^{v}) is a Gallican psalter, divided into five sections according to the order of the Book of Psalms.[78] A prominent feature of F:Pn, lat. 103 is the critical marks that are characteristic of this translation of the psalter. Each psalm is followed by a collect, a vestige of the early Divine Service when the Office consisted largely of the recitation of psalms and orations.[79]

The psalter contains the canticles for the third nocturn of Matins (fos. 162–5), added to the original text by the mid-eleventh century. Thus F:Pn, lat. 103 was adapted by this time presumably for use in a Benedictine establishment. The calendar and the hymnal (fos. 142–161^{v}), likewise both added by the mid-eleventh century, suggest that this Benedictine house was Saint-Denis. Leroquais distinguishes a number of different hands in these sections of the manuscript. The original text of the calendar (fos. 143–145^{v}), written in light-brown ink, is not sufficiently telling to attribute it to Saint-Denis. Rather, the various layers of later additions to the calendar, penned mostly in dark-brown, conform to the usage of the abbey.[80] Some of the added feasts, such as the Detection of Saint Denis (9 June) and Saint Clarus (4 November), seem to have entered the liturgy later in the eleventh or twelfth century, and the calendar of F:Pn, lat. 103 is one of the first witnesses of these celebrations.

[78] Fos. 1–37 = Ps. 1–40; fos. 38–61 = Ps. 41–71; fos. 62–79 = Ps. 72–88; fos. 79^{v}–95 = Ps. 89–105; fos. 95–129 = Ps. 106–50. The oldest psalters, called 'biblical psalters', are divided in this way; Leroquais, *Psautiers*, pp. xliv–xlvi. On the Gallican psalter, see n. 61 above.

[79] Long after these collects had lost their liturgical usefulness, they continued to be included in some psalters. The prayers contained in F:Pn, lat. 103 embody the widely employed Roman series (Leroquais, *Psautiers*, vol. i, pp. xliv–xlvii; Masai, 'Review', 293–5).

[80] Refer to App. A, which differentiates the original scribe of the calendar and the later hands as a group, but does not distinguish the different later hands. Another feature which separates the early hand of the calendar from the later ones is the use of the abbreviation '*mr.*' for 'martyr' by the former, and '*mar.*' by the latter.

The hand that copied the hymnal (fos. 146–161ᵛ) is roughly coeval with the original portion of the calendar, and it probably dates from around the second quarter of the eleventh century. Proper hymns from the Gallican rite for Saints Cucuphas, Hippolytus, and Denis are included here, as discussed in Chapters 3 and 4. The presence of these hymns for three saints whose relics were in the abbey, along with the additions to the calendar, support the attribution of the entire manuscript to Saint-Denis, although it may not have been written in the abbey, but rather adapted early on for use there. The hymnal is unnotated, except for *Veni creator spiritus* (fo. 154ᵛ; see Pl. 10). A final feature of F:Pn, lat. 103 that confirms its presence at Saint-Denis in the later Middle Ages is the appearance of the thirteenth-century shelf-mark of the library of Saint-Denis on fo. 5.

9. F:Pn, lat. 256: Paris, Bibliothèque Nationale, lat. 256

Evangeliary, early eighth century, probably copied at Saint-Denis, usage (from ninth century at least) Saint-Denis.
Parchment. 467 folios. 335 × 230 mm.

Bibliography: Delisle, *Cabinet*, i. 201–3; iii, 215–16; Berger, *Vulgate*, 91, 355, 402; Morin, 'Lectionnaire', 439; Lowe, *CLA*, v. 3; vi, p. xxvi; Klauser, *Capitulare*, xxxiii; Lesne, *Scriptoria*, 37, 592; Bibliothèque Nationale (1), *Catalogue*, i. 94; Salmon, 'Texte'; Bibliothèque Nationale (2), *Manuscrits* (1954), 6–7; Combaluzier, 'Fragments'; Gamber, *CLLA*, i. 177; Sicard (1), 'Messe'; Sicard (2), *Liturgie* (MS *D*); Vezin, 'Point', 184, 188; Nebbiai-Dalla Guarda, *Bibliothèque*, 92, 103, 134, 203, 241, 259, 275, 287, 380; Rasmussen, 'Liturgy', 41; Stahl, 'Problem', 176, n. 18; Vogel, *Liturgy*, 326.

Vezin has recently suggested that F:Pn, lat. 256 was copied at Saint-Denis, on the basis of the presence of a question mark with two points on some added folios (fos. 169–77), a form that he shows was characteristic of the ninth-century scriptorium of the abbey. The fifteenth-century shelf-mark of the library of Saint-Denis (fo. 1) demonstrates that the manuscript was housed in the abbey as late as this. Although these indications witness the whereabouts of F:Pn, lat. 256 only from the ninth up to the fifteenth centuries, it is entirely possible that the manuscript was both written at Saint-Denis in the eighth century and was used there as a source of gospel readings during the celebration of the Gallican Mass.

10. F:Pn, lat. 846: Paris, Bibliothèque Nationale, lat. 846

Unnotated missal (incomplete), thirteenth century, *c.*1240.
Parchment. 93 folios. 267 × 175 mm.

Bibliography: Bibliothèque Nationale, *Catalogue*, i. 297; Leroquais, *Sacramentaires*, ii. 140; Walters [Robertson], 'Reconstruction', 191; Nebbiai-Dalla Guarda, *Bibliothèque*, 314, 319; Rasmussen, 'Liturgy', 42.

F:Pn, lat. 846 is an incomplete missal, and the contents of the book alone offer little evidence about the precise time of copying. The decoration and style of writing, however, are characteristic of the second quarter of the thirteenth century (*c*.1240),[81] and it appears that at least seven different hands were at work: scribe A = fos. 1–1^v, B = 2–9^v, C = 10–47, D = 48^v (fo. 49 is blank), E = 49^v, F = 50–91^v, G = 92–93^v. The format and order of material in fact suggest that the volume was not produced as an integral book, but rather was pieced together, perhaps from different sources. Fo. 1, which was added later, contains the Mass for the feast of Circumcision. Services for a number of Sundays beginning with Advent I follow on fos. 2–9^v, although the major festivals of the *temporale* are missing.[82] Each formulary includes only the three prayers of the Mass: oration, secret, and post-communion. This initial portion of the manuscript may have been added to complement the ensuing section, which contains the principal feasts of the *temporale* (scribe C, fos. 10–47). Here the services often incorporate the texts of the musical selections as well. Two Marian feasts of the *sanctorale*, Purification (fo. 16^v) and Annunciation (fo. 18^v), are found between Epiphany and Holy Saturday. The *officium* for the Octave of Christmas (fo. 13^v) bears the title *Commemoratio beate Marie*, which is a vestige of much older Roman service-books.[83]

The highly abbreviated *sanctorale* includes Saints John the Baptist (fo. 29^v), Peter and Paul (fo. 31^v), Assumption (fo. 33^v), Nativity of Mary (fo. 36), Saint Denis (fo. 38), All Saints (fo. 40^v), Saint Andrew (fo. 43), and the Illation of Benedict (fo. 44^v). Folios 47^v–48 were left blank, and part of a service for Saint Nicholas occurs on fo. 48^v. It is likely that this leaf was added from an outside source, since it includes the text of the Alle. *Tumba sancti Nicholai*, a chant not found in the extant missals of the abbey, where the Alle. *Sancte Nicholae qui in celis* is given instead. The canon and votive services follow (fos. 49^v–76^v), as well as Masses for Saints Mary Magdalene, Eustace, Martin, and Eugene. The common of saints (fos. 81–91^v) and the rituals for

[81] I am grateful to Patricia Stirnemann of the Bibliothèque Nationale for her opinion of the date of this MS, based on the style of the filigree decoration.

[82] Among the feasts absent from this section (= scribe B) are Christmas, Stephen, John, and Innocents, all of which appear later in the book. A physical break occurs after the service for Palm Sunday on fo. 8, and fo. 8^v was left blank. Fo. 9 begins with the 21st Sunday after Trinity.

[83] See Frere, *Kalendar*, 80.

the blessing of the salt and water (scribe G, fos. 92–93^{v}) conclude the manuscript.

The evidence for the origin of the codex at Saint-Denis comes in the emphasis on the titular saint. The names of Saint Denis and his companions are inscribed in red in the orations for the feast of Saint Denis (fos. 38–40), and these saints are the only ones accorded devotional services (fos. 61–2) in the collection of votive Masses near the end of the manuscript.

11. F:Pn, lat. 976: Paris, Bibliothèque Nationale, lat. 976

Ordinary, copied between 1241 and 1259, probably *c.* 1258. Calendar of F:Pn, lat. 976 in a different hand,[84] copied between 1259 and ?1271. Parchment. 161 folios. 260 × 175 mm.

Bibliography: Delisle, 'Peintures', 448, 463–6; Omont, 'Messe', 179–80; Schmitz, 'Table'; Bibliothèque Nationale, *Catalogue*, i. 347–8; Leclercq, 'Grecque', col. 1583; Weiss, 'Studio', 434; *GR*, ii. 195; Bourque, *Sacramentaires*, ii. 341–2; Huglo, 'Chants', 76; Martimort, *Documentation*, 543–5; Walters [Robertson], 'Reconstruction', 191–231; Bruzelius, *St-Denis*, 200–1; Nebbiai-Dalla Guarda (1), *Bibliothèque*, 34, 39, 70, 130, 131, 134, 195, 205, 242, 257, 275, 288, 290, 332–6; Foley, 'Ordinary', ii. 49–64, 425–49; Nebbiai-Dalla Guarda (2), 'Listes', 299–301; Rasmussen, 'Liturgy', 42; Robertson, '*Benedicamus*', 7, 16, 27, 34–7, 56.

F:Pn, lat. 976, the second extant ordinary from Saint-Denis, serves in many respects as an updated revision of the earlier ordinary (F:Pm 526). Although F:Pn, lat. 976 follows the format and often the exact wording of F:Pm 526, it reflects the changes that were made both to the liturgy and to the architecture of the church during the thirteenth-century reconstruction (1231–81), as described in Chapter 4. One scribe seems to have written the text of F:Pn, lat. 976. The calendar, copied some time after the rest of the manuscript, occupies a much larger writing space on each folio, and is found in a separate gathering between the *temporale* and *sanctorale*. It may have been added to the volume after the initial folios, which probably included the original calendar, were detached.

Because several folios from the beginning of the book are missing, F:Pn, lat. 976 lacks the directions for Advent, Christmas, and the feasts of Stephen, John, and Innocents. The first rubric is for Sunday within the octave of Christmas (fo. 1). At the end, the manuscript breaks off at the beginning of what would no doubt have been a lengthy section of anniversaries. Only the service for Abbot Suger is given in full, while

[84] In addition to the differences in content, noted earlier, the formations of many letters vary between text and calendar of F:Pn, lat. 976, notably B, E, and S.

the anniversary for Count Philip of Boulogne is interrupted on the final folio (161^{v}). Moreover, the description of the feast of the Detection of Saint Denis (9 June) on fo. 95^{v} indicates that a small lectionary once ended the codex: 'Quere lectiones in parvo lectionario in fine.' Apart from these gaps, F:Pn, lat. 976 provides a complete picture of the feasts and ceremonies that were celebrated in the abbey around the middle of the thirteenth century.

Like the earlier ordinary F:Pm 526, F:Pn, lat. 976 contains rubrics for the weekly services of commemoration for Saint Denis on Thursdays and for the Virgin on Saturdays. The tropes, sequences, hymns, antiphons *ante evangelium*, invitatory antiphons, and melodies for the Benedicamus Domino and Ite Missa Est that were sung in the abbey are named in the directions for many feasts. The second complete description of the Greek Mass for the Octave of Saint Denis (16 October) is contained in fos. 137–137^{v}, and a list of altars that were consecrated in the church beginning in 1218 is found in a section of liturgical miscellany toward the end of the volume (fos. 157–8; see Table 4.1). In addition to the record of the altar consecrations, this final part of the manuscript includes lists of: alleluias for Sundays between Easter and Pentecost (fo. 158^{v}), feasts on which the invitatory psalm (Venite) was sung in the special place between the main altar and the matutinal altar (*inter duo altaria*, fos. 158^{v}–159), festivals on which three cantors were to stand in the choir to lead the singing (fo. 159), days on which an antiphon was sung before the gospel (*antiphona ante evangelium*, fo. 159), and readings for meal-times (fo. 159–61).[85] F:Pn, lat. 976 was probably written around 1258 at the beginning of the abbacy of Matthew of Vendôme (1258–86), who directed the final phases of the thirteenth-century reconstruction.

12. F:Pn, lat. 1072: Paris, Bibliothèque Nationale, lat. 1072

Book of hours, copied between 1474 and 1493.
Parchment. 240 folios. 170 × 118 mm.
Bibliography: Bibliothèque Nationale, *Catalogue*, i. 388; Samaran, *Jean*, 11–127; Leroquais, *Heures*, ii. 49–52; Marinis, *Legatura*, ii. 105; Samaran and Marichal, *Catalogue*, ii. 462; Hesbert, *CAO*, vol. ii, p. xv; Nebbiai-Dalla Guarda, *Bibliothèque*, 206, 242, 252, 276, 288; Rasmussen, 'Liturgy', 42.

F:Pn, lat. 1072 is a book of hours, a manuscript intended for the devotional use of an individual, and as such would not have been employed in the daily ritual of Saint-Denis. Nevertheless, the calendar, the litany, the Little Office of the Virgin, and the Office for the Dead

[85] The readings are listed in Nebbiai-Dalla Guarda, *Bibliothèque*, 332–6.

duplicate these same features of other manuscripts from Saint-Denis. And since F:Pn, lat. 1072 is the only source, albeit paraliturgical, that is extant from the two centuries which separate the two latest liturgical books from the abbey, the breviaries GB:Ob, Can. Lit. 192 (copied in 1350) and F:Pn, Rés. B. 5209 (printed in 1550), it seems appropriate to include this F:Pn, lat. 1072 in this discussion of books which were actually used in the celebration of the Divine Office in the abbey.

Fos. 176 and 194 of F:Pn, lat. 1072 contain the coat of arms of Jean de Bilhères, who was abbot of Saint-Denis from 1474 until his elevation to the rank of cardinal in 1493. The manuscript was undoubtedly copied between these dates.[86] The calendar at the beginning of the volume occupies a separate gathering (fos. 1–12^{v}) but is contemporaneous with the rest of the manuscript. Along with the calendar, both the suffrages of saints (fos. 125^{v}–140) and the litany (fos. 184^{v}–193) establish the usage of F:Pn, lat. 1072 through their inclusion of saints who were specially venerated at Saint-Denis. The Little Office of the Virgin, which forms a sizeable portion of the manuscript (fos. 51–104), is presented exactly as it is found in the breviaries GB:Ob, Can. Lit. 192 (fos. 257–262^{v}) and F:Pn, Rés. B. 5209. The liturgy of Saint-Denis distinguished between ordinary and solemn anniversaries in its use of distinct Offices for the Dead. Two of these services are provided in F:Pn, lat. 1072 (fos. 194–237).

13. F:Pn, lat. 1107: Paris, Bibliothèque Nationale, lat. 1107

Notated missal, thirteenth century, copied after 1259 and before about 1275 (Pls. 17 and 18).
Vellum. 6 (numbered I–VI) + 401 folios (fos. 1–177 + 177 *bis* + 178–400). 225 × 140 mm.
Bibliography: Misset and Weale, *Analecta*, i. 357–68; Molinier, *Obituaires*, i. 334–5; Aubry, *Motets*, iii. 83; Leroquais, *Sacramentaires*, ii. 140–2; Wilmart, 'Anniversaires', 30; Bibliothèque Nationale (1), *Catalogue*, i. 404; Samaran, 'Manuscrits', 325–6; Weisbein, '"Laudes"', 19; Stäblein, 'Gallikanische', cols. 1307–8; Bibliothèque Nationale (2), *Manuscrits* (1955), 20–1; Gay, 'Formulaires', 85; *GR* (MS *DEN* 2); Huglo (1), 'Chants', 76, 78, 80; Huglo (2), 'Règlement', 130; Stäblein, *Schriftbild*, 13; Branner, *Painting*, 130–2, 136, 238; Lemaître, *Répertoire*, 598–9; Hiley (1), 'Traditions', 15; Hiley (2), 'Observations', 70–2, 74; Walters [Robertson], 'Reconstruction', 191–231; Hiley (3), 'Ordinary', 3, 7, 9, 44, 58, 59, 62, 66, 68, 74, 80, 84, 86, 88, 89, 97, 98, 99, 109, 115, 117, 121; Nebbiai-Dalla Guarda, *Bibliothèque*, 314, 319;

[86] Leroquais, *Heures*, i. 52; Samaran and Marichal, *Catalogue*, ii. 462. Unfortunately, the will of this prelate, which might have listed F:Pn, lat. 1072 among his possessions, has never been found (Samaran, *Jean*, 67). Jean died in Rome in 1499 and is named in the calendar of F:Pn, Rés. B. 5209 (see App. A, 6 Sept.).

Rasmussen, 'Liturgy', 42; Colette, 'Sémiologie', 125; Robertson, '*Benedicamus*', 14–27, 31, 33, 43, 44, 52; Huglo (3), 'Remarques'.

F:Pn, lat. 1107 is one of the first surviving examples of the liturgy of Saint-Denis, as it was enhanced by additions of the mid-thirteenth century. The original texts of both the calendar and the body of the manuscript include all the feasts that were adopted during the early phases of the reconstruction of the church between the 1230s and the 1250s: Saints Francis (4 October), Bernard of Clairvaux (23 August), Ursula and the Eleven Thousand Virgins (21 October), Demetrius (17 October), and Sanctinus and Antoninus (19 October). By contrast, F:Pn, lat. 1107 pre-dates the incorporation of the celebrations for Corpus Christi, Saint Louis (25 August), and the Conception of the Virgin (8 December), all of which are later additions to the manuscript (fos. 283^{v}–25). For several reasons, F:Pn, lat. 1107 seems slightly earlier than the missal I:Rc 603, which was copied after 1271. I:Rc 603, along with the fourteenth-century missals F:Pn, lat. 10505 and GB:Lva 1346–1891, calls for the proper Comm. *Mitte manum tuam* for the feast of Saint Thomas (21 December), while F:Pn, lat. 1107 employs *Vos qui secuti* from the *commune*. In terms of illumination, Branner places F:Pn, lat. 1107 in his 'Cholet group' of manuscripts from the atelier of the Sainte-Chapelle, whose characteristic features appear to have developed in the 1260s. Taken together, these ceremonial and decorative indications suggest that F:Pn, lat. 1107 was written between 1259, the year of the translation of the relics of Sanctinus and Antoninus, and *c.*1275. It is likely that Abbot Matthew of Vendôme (1258–86) commissioned this beautifully illustrated book, probably as a replacement for an older missal which lacked the newly adopted feasts.

The original text of F:Pn, lat. 1107 omits three services which appear in the calendar, as well as in the later missals I:Rc 603 and GB:Lva 1346–1891: Saint Landericus (10 June), the Octave of Saint Benedict (18 July), and the Consecration of the Altar (28 July). Like the later missals, however, F:Pn, lat. 1107 contains an alleluia peculiar to Parisian usage, *Herodes iratus* (fo. 24) for the feast of Holy Innocents (28 December), which Aubry mentions in his discussion of the chant segment *In Bethleem*, a melody frequently used as the tenor voice in thirteenth-century motets.

Beyond the usual presentation of feasts in the *temporale* and *sanctorale*, F:Pn, lat. 1107 is the only musical source from Saint-Denis which includes the music for the Tropes *Ab increpatione* and *Laus, honor, virtus* for the Offertory and Communion for Easter (fos. 145–145^{v}; see Pl. 17 and Ex. 3.15). The end of the missal contains:

Fos. 340–92: a fully notated sequentiary, which includes an antiphon before the gospel for the anniversary of King Dagobert, the Gallican Ant. *Salvator omnium deus* (fo. 348^{v});
Fos. 392^{v}–395^{v}: the *Kyriale*;
Fos. 395^{v}–396^{v}: 25 melodies for the Benedicamus Domino;
Fos. 396^{v}–397: 16 melodies for the Ite Missa Est (see Pl. 18);
Fos. 397–399: votive material for the Virgin, including three antiphons (*Ave gratia plena dei genitrix*, *Adorna thalamum tuum syon*, *Responsum accepit symeon*), the Hy. *Virginis marie laudes intonant*, a Gloria with the trope *Spiritus et alme*, the rhymed Offer. *Preter rerum ordinem parit*, the Offer. *Recordare virgo mater* with its prosula *Ab hac familia tua*, and an Agnus Dei with the trope *Gloriosa spes rerum*.

Samaran notes that the recto and verso of the final folio of the volume (fos. 400^{r-v}), added in the fifteenth century, demonstrate a codicological innovation of this period: the 'imposition' of eight sides of text—four each on the front and back of a single, larger folio. This method produces the desired order of four folios (eight sides) after the larger page has been folded and cut. The eight sides are an extract from a fifteenth-century book of hours in the making, and they contain an Office for Corpus Christi and part of the Hours for Saint Catherine. The script is remarkably similar to that of the Hours of Saint-Denis, F:Pn, lat. 1072.

14. F:Pn, lat. 2290: Paris, Bibliothèque Nationale, lat. 2290

Ninth-century sacramentary, probably copied between 878 and 886 at Saint-Amand for use at Saint-Denis.
Parchment. 182 folios. 282 × 221 mm.

Bibliography: Delisle (1), *Cabinet*, i. 201; Delisle (2), *Sacramentaires*, 102–4, 324–5, 388–9; Molinier, *Obituaires*, 1025; Leroquais (1), *Sacramentaires*, i. 19–21; Leroquais (2), *Bréviaires*, vol. i, p. lxxxix; Hesbert, *AMS*, p. xxiii; Lesne, *Scriptoria*, 209, 395, 592; Bibliothèque Nationale (1), *Catalogue*, ii. 390–1; Boutemy (1), 'Foyer', 757, 759–60, 764–5, 767–9; Boutemy (2), 'Style', 261–4; Handschin, 'Neumenschrift', 89; Huglo (1), 'Mélodie', 33; Bibliothèque Nationale (2), *Manuscrits* (1954), 31; Gamber (1), *Sakramentartypen*, 140; Bourque, *Sacramentaires*, ii. 54; Samaran and Marichal, *Catalogue*, ii. 474; Coens, 'Litanies', 133; Gaiffier, 'Légende', 349, n. 5; Grégoire, 'Prières', 58; Gros, 'Ordo', 342, 352–3; Huglo (2), 'Chants', 75–6; Nocent, 'Fragment', 754; Barré and Deshusses, 'Recherche', 22, 32; Gamber (2), *CLLA*, ii. 356; Mütherich, 'Scriptorium', 211–12; Sicard (1), 'Messe'; Deshusses (1), *Sacramentaire* (MS R); Deshusses (2), 'Messes', 12 and *passim*; Deshusses (3), 'Chronologie', 230–7; Gastaldelli, *Traduzione*, 56–76; Martimort, *Documentation*, 99; Sicard (2), *Liturgie* (MS *Den*); Lemaître, *Répertoire*, 596; Mazal, 'Spuren', 160–3; Atkinson (1), '*O Amnos*', 12, 27–8;

Atkinson (2), 'Entstehung', 123, 127–31, 136–44; Nebbiai-Dalla Guarda, *Bibliothèque*, 33, 131, 135, 315, 318; Rasmussen, 'Liturgy', 41; Kaczynski, *Greek*, 103; Atkinson (3), '*Doxa*', 82, 84, 89, 90, 92, 93, 97, 99, 102, 105.

The destination and usage of F:Pn, lat. 2290 are clearly Saint-Denis, and yet the manuscript was not copied in the abbey. It was commissioned instead from the scriptorium of Saint-Amand, an atelier renowned for its production of splendid codices in the second half of the ninth century, as Boutemy (1, 2) first recognized. Deshusses (3) has recently shown that six other sacramentaries originated at Saint-Amand during this period, and these sources all embody the ritual of Saint-Amand. F:Pn, lat. 2290, however, clearly was intended for Saint-Denis. The initial folios (1–6ᵛ) contain the calendar of the abbey, which incorporates all the feasts of the patron, the names of the other saints who were particularly honoured at Saint-Denis, and even the record of the Translation of relics into the abbey on 22 August (see Appendix A, MS N1). The Vigil and feast of Saint Denis (8, 9 October, fo. 85) are included, along with a *Missa in veneratione sanctorum martyrum Dyonisii, Rustici et Eleutherii*, which is added on fo. 93ᵛ. The names of these three saints are likewise written in the margin beside the preface entitled *In natale plurimorum martyrum* (fo. 92ᵛ), and the section of votive Masses contains a *Missa specialium sanctorum* (fo. 129ᵛ), which lists not only Denis and his two companions but also the highly regarded Saints Hippolytus, Cucuphas, Innocent, Hilary of Poitiers, and Hilary of Mende.

If the destination of F:Pn, lat. 2290 for Saint-Denis is obvious, the precise date of its copying is difficult to deduce. Deshusses (1) shows that the manuscript is a Gregorian sacramentary, complemented by a supplement which borrows from material composed by Benedict of Aniane, along with other sources. Deshusses (1, 2, 3) likewise notes the presence of elements which set F:Pn, lat. 2290 apart from the other six manuscripts from Saint-Amand, notably a series of votive Masses apportioned among the seven ferial days, which include services composed by the aforementioned Alcuin of York (fos. 121–39ᵛ). This series of Masses is replicated in the Saint-Denis sacramentary F:LA 118 (fos. 192ᵛ–207ᵛ). F:Pn, lat. 2290, moreover, is the only sacramentary from Saint-Amand which begins with a calendar. Because of the unique design of F:Pn, lat. 2290, Deshusses concludes that the abbey of Saint-Denis, in ordering a sacramentary from Saint-Amand, would have furnished this northern scriptorium with its own liturgical documents. This explains on the one hand the ceremonial variants in F:Pn, lat. 2290 and on the other hand the fact that all the sources issuing from Saint-Amand still share the same characteristic styles of decoration and script. Deshusses (3) estimates the time of origin of F:Pn, lat. 2290 around 867, a date which coincides with the accession of Charles the Bald as lay abbot of Saint-Denis (867–77), and he suggests that the sacramentary was a gift to the abbey in commemoration of this momentous occasion.

It is possible, however, that F:Pn, lat. 2290 was copied slightly later than Deshusses has conjectured. Among the liturgical records that the Sandionysians would have forwarded to Saint-Amand for reference in the production of this manuscript was the current calendar of Saint-Denis. During this period, it was apparently the policy of the abbey to derive its calendars from the martyrology of Saint Jerome, for two such documents from Saint-Denis have survived in the manuscripts F:Psg 111 and F:Pn, lat. 2290 with almost identical wording and content. F:Psg 111 can be dated between 877 and 882, and its calendar was copied at the same time as the rest of the manuscript. A small number of entries in the original hand of the calendar of F:Pn, lat. 2290 do not appear at all in F:Psg 111 (Saints Ignatius, Vedast and Amandus, Peter's Chair, Matthew, Regulus, Richarius, Memmius, Translation of Richarius), and these hint that the calendar and coeval text of F:Pn, lat. 2290 are slightly newer than F:Psg 111.

A later date for F:Pn, lat. 2290 between 878 and 886, first suggested by Boutemy (1), does not preclude the royal influence that Deshusses believes prompted the production of the manuscript, for its presence was still felt at Saint-Denis even after the death of Charles the Bald in 877. Charles' successor to the abbacy in the following year, Gozlin, retained this post until he became bishop of Paris in 884. Formerly arch-chaplain of the royal court, Gozlin's curriculum vitae also included the joint abbacy of Saint-Germain-des-Prés by 867 and of Saint-Amand itself beginning in 871.[87] According to Deshusses's (3) dating of the sacramentaries from this scriptorium, Gozlin would have supervised the copying of at least the two latest volumes, F:Pn, lat. 2291 and S:Sk, A 136, and hence would have become thoroughly familiar with the style of this workshop. Upon adding to his responsibilities the direction of Saint-Denis in 878, Gozlin himself may have ordered a sacramentary for the abbey,[88] one which would naturally have included the most recent calendar of this house. Perhaps he intended to enrich the legacy of magnificent manuscripts that Charles the Bald had willed to Saint-Denis with a sacramentary written and decorated in the magisterial style of Saint-Amand.[89] Gozlin's simultaneous stewardship

[87] *GC*, vii. cols. 428–30; iii, col. 258. McKitterick reports that Gozlin took control of the abbey of Saint-Amand in 870; 'Library', 42.

[88] Boutemy (1) in fact speculated that F:Pn, lat. 2290 was copied under Gozlin's abbacy, but without citing the evidence which results from my dating of the calendar and MS.

[89] Charles bequeathed his library to his 2 sons and to his 2 favourite monasteries, Saint-Denis and Sainte-Marie-de-Compiègne in 877; McKitterick, 'Library', 28. His second Bible (F:Pn, lat.

of Saint-Germain-des-Prés would explain the addition of names relative to this monastery on fo. 129^{v}.

Deshusses's (3) exclusion of F:Pn, lat. 2290 from the group of six other manuscripts from Saint-Amand helps account for the orthographical and textual peculiarities which Atkinson (2) has noted in the Greek Gloria (*Doxa*), Sanctus (*Agios*), and Agnus Dei (*O amnos*) on fos. 7^{v}–8^{v} of the manuscript. Atkinson (1, 2, 3) shows that F:Pn, lat. 2290 is an important source for the earliest Greek Mass at Saint-Denis, since the manuscript contains the oldest surviving example of *O amnos*, gives the best reading of the *Doxa*, and is the only eighth- or ninth-century source to include Greek versions for all four chants of the ordinary of the Mass. Curiously, however, the texts of *Agios* and of *O amnos* are characteristic of east Frankish, not west Frankish, sources. Moreover, the spellings of words in the *Doxa* do not match those found in the three sacramentaries of Saint-Amand that contain this piece.

While the chants of the *missa graeca* in F:Pn, lat. 2290 thus support the theory that the abbey of Saint-Denis sent the scriptorium of Saint-Amand exemplars of its own liturgical practice, the presence of east Frankish spellings in these pieces raises the issue of how these texts came to be handed down in a Saint-Denis manuscript, which presumably would have upheld the western usage. Several answers are possible. The sojourns of the monks in the region of Reims and Laon during the Norman invasions of the second half of the ninth century brought them at least physically closer to the eastern dividing line, and one other contemporaneous Sandionysian liturgical source, F:LA 118, contains elements which seem to suggest east Frankish influence, as noted earlier. On another front, the library of Saint-Denis may have included books dating from the period in which Atkinson (1) has placed the composition of *O amnos* (827–35), a time which preceded the first decisive split in the east and west Frankish chant traditions around 843.[90] Indeed, the orthographical irregularities evident in the manuscript tradition of this and other portions of the Greek Mass mirror the same types of error that are found in the translations of the works of Pseudo-Dionysius the Areopagite and of the *akathistos* hymn, both of which were probably done at Saint-Denis under the direction of Abbot Hilduin (814–41).[91] Whatever the precise explanation for the appearance of the eastern version of the *missa graeca* in F:Pn, lat. 2290, its presence is significant for one final reason: this compilation of the ordinary of the Mass is the only surviving witness—albeit the texts only—of the ninth-century *ordinarium* which was sung in the abbey.

2), which was also inherited by Saint-Denis, was copied at Saint-Amand during Gozlin's term of tenure there; ibid. 42, 46.

[90] Huglo, 'Antiphoner', 483.

[91] See Huglo, 'Acathiste', 54–9.

15. F:Pn, lat. 9387: Paris, Bibliothèque Nationale, lat. 9387

Evangeliary, ninth century (first quarter), copied in north-eastern France, later provenance Saint-Denis.
Parchment. 250 folios. 280 × 190 mm.
Bibliography: Delisle, *Cabinet*, i. 206–7; ii. 3; Omont, 'Messe', 182–3; Goldschmidt, *Elfenbeiskulpturen*, i. 21; Lesne, *Scriptoria*, 393, 474, 592; Weiss, 'Studio', 428; Bibliothèque Nationale, *Manuscrits* (1954), 38–9; *Charlemagne*, 284, 287–8; Huglo, 'Chants', 80; Mütherich 'Buchmalerei', 40, n. 150; Montesquiou-Fezensac and Gaborit-Chopin, *Trésor*, i. 193; ii. 256–7; iii. 86–7; Nebbiai-Dalla Guarda, *Bibliothèque*, 34, 157, 219, 241, 280, 287; Stahl, 'Problem', 177, n. 25.

While F:Pn, lat. 9387 is known to have been at Saint-Denis from the fourteenth century until the French Revolution, the place of its copying in the early ninth century has never been firmly established. The catalogue of the Bibliothèque Nationale notes features of the manuscript which recall the court school of Charlemagne, which centred around Aix-la-Chapelle. Wherever it originated, F:Pn, lat. 9387 was in use at Saint-Denis at least by the fourteenth century, at which time the monks added the epistles and gospels in Greek for Christmas (fo. 153), the Dedication of the Church (fo. 154^{v}), Easter (fo. 155^{v}), Pentecost (fo. 156), and Saint Denis (fo. 157^{v}). The reading of the lessons first in Greek and then in Latin on these feast-days corresponds to the rubrics of the mid-fourteenth-century ordinary F:Pan, L 863, No. 10 (pp. 53, 65, 96, fo. 124^{v}). Huglo has noted that the signs placed above these Greek texts are imitations of the phonetic notation used in Byzantine lectionaries. Montesquiou-Fezensac and Gaborit-Chopin document the presence of F:Pn, lat. 9387 in the *trésor* of Saint-Denis until 1791.

16. F:Pn, lat. 9436: Paris, Bibliothèque Nationale, lat. 9436

Augmented sacramentary (sacramentary and gradual), mid-eleventh century (Pl. 11).
Parchment. 165 folios. 310 × 230 mm.
Bibliography: Delisle (1), *Cabinet*, i. 206–7; Delisle (2), *Sacramentaires*, 289–92; Bouchot, *Reliures*, 24; Omont, 'Messe', 178–9; Leclercq, 'Grecque', cols. 1581–2; Leroquais, *Sacramentaires*, i. 142–4; Wilmart, 'Manuel', 286, 291, 295; Handschin, 'Neumenschrift', 83; Huglo (1), 'Mélodie', 33; Weiss, 'Studio', 428, n. 13; Hourlier, 'Review', 222–3, n. 1; Bibliothèque Nationale, *Manuscrits* (1954), 86; Schulten, 'Büchmalerei', 66–70, 86–90; *GR* (MS *DEN* 4); Bourque, *Sacramentaires*, ii. 63, 335; Oury, 'Messes', 82, 84; Grégoire, 'Prières', 60–1; Huglo (2), 'Chants', 74–8; Salmon, 'Livrets', 229; Escudier (1), 'Scriptorium', 81; Montesquiou-Fezensac and Gaborit-Chopin, *Trésor*, i. 172; iii. 70–2; Samaran and Marichal, *Catalogue*, iii. 628; Corbin,

Neumen, 3.123; Planchart, *Tropes*, i. 61; Martimort, *Documentation*, 99; 'Sources', 616; Atkinson (1), '*O Amnos*', 12; Hiley, 'Traditions', 15; Atkinson (2), 'Entstehung', 123, 127–9, 143; Nebbiai-Dalla Guarda, *Bibliothèque*, 219, 222, 259, 280, 287; Rasmussen, 'Liturgy', 41; Stahl, 'Problem', 167; 175, n. 8; 178, n. 36; Escudier (2), 'Notations'; Atkinson (3), '*Doxa*', 89, 90, 92.

Scholars have given various names to F:Pn, lat. 9436: Delisle (2) calls it 'sacramentaire ou missel', Leroquais a 'missel', Escudier (1, 2) a 'sacramentaire'. The differences in terminology are understandable, for the volume, with its spectacular jewelled cover, dates from the period of transition during which distinct books for the Mass—sacramentary, gradual, and lectionary—were gradually being fused into a single, composite source, the notated missal. F:Pn, lat. 9436 contains the two former components, and Bourque and Vogel adopt the designation 'augmented sacramentary'.[92] In each formulary, the elements of the sacramentary and gradual are blended together, unlike F:LA 118, which simply binds three separate books.

The decorative prominence given to the feast of Saint Denis both in the calendar and in the body of the manuscript led Delisle and Leroquais to assume that the codex was produced for the abbey. To be sure, the text of F:Pn, lat. 9436 incorporates the feasts which most readily support this identification: the Invention (22 April), Vigil (8 October), *natale* (9 October), and Octave (16 October) of Saint Denis, as well as Masses for the days within this Octave. The observances for several saints whose relics lay in the church are likewise present, notably Peregrinus (16 May), Cucuphas (25 July), and Hilary of Mende (25 October). The list of alleluias for Sundays after Pentecost is also the one traditionally sung in the abbey.

But although the usage of Saint-Denis should be secured by these features, scholars have recently called into question the origin of F:Pn, lat. 9436 in the abbey on several counts. Schulten first recognized that the calendar of the manuscript is laden with non-Dionysian saints (see Appendix A, MS N2). The majority of these names point to the region of Arras: Saint Vedast (6 February), his Translation (1 October), Saints Venditian (11 March), Amatus (19 October), Ragnulfus (9 November), and Autbert (13 December). The feast of Saint Vedast is written in gold capitals, that of Saint Denis in gold minuscules. Moreover, the Parisian Saints Landericus (10 June) and Clodoaldus (7 September) are added in a slightly later hand. Schulten concludes from this, and from his study of the decoration of the volume, that F:Pn, lat. 9436 was written at Saint-Vaast of Arras for use at Saint-

[92] Although Vogel does not specifically mention F:Pn, lat. 9436, he does use the term 'augmented sacramentary' to describe the type of book exemplified by this MS; *Liturgy*, 106.

Denis. Escudier (1, 2) corroborates this finding in his study of the neumatic notation of F:Pn, lat. 9436, which he shows to be characteristic of Saint-Vaast.

In addition to the calendar, the text of F:Pn, lat. 9436 betrays several non-Dionysian features. A Mass for Saints Sabinian and friends on 31 December (fo. 13) is not otherwise found in the liturgy of Saint-Denis.[93] Likewise, the Vigil of Saint Benedict (20 March, fo. 81^{v}) was not observed in the abbey. The rubric for the Invention of Saint Denis (22 April) mistakenly reads *transl[atio]* (fo. 83), a noteworthy slip in light of Abbot Hilduin's unsuccessful attempt to alter the title of this event in the ninth century, as described in Chapter 1. The feast of Saint Martial is commemorated on the day of his *natale* (30 June) in F:Pn, lat. 9436, whereas the other sources from Saint-Denis celebrate only the Octave (7 July).

In spite of these discrepancies, however, the hallmarks of the Saint-Denis liturgy—the alleluia list and the emphasis on Saint Denis and on other saints particular to the abbey—are decisive in terms of the usage of F:Pn, lat. 9436, and the sacramentary should clearly be counted among the sources of the monastery. The history of F:Pn, lat. 9436 is probably similar to that of the ninth-century sacramentary F:Pn, lat. 2290: the book was apparently made *for* Saint-Denis but was written and notated either *at* Saint-Vaast or by scribes trained in this scriptorium. As in F:Pn, lat. 2290, the copyists of F:Pn, lat. 9436 incorporated the proper liturgy of Saint-Denis in the manuscript, but they also included palaeographic signs and other vestiges of its probable place of origin, Saint-Vaast.

The peculiar arrangement of the large divisions of F:Pn, lat. 9436 likewise deserves mention. The two basic sections of the manuscript (*temporale* and *sanctorale*) are ordered in such a way that all saints' feasts are placed in the *sanctorale*, including Stephen (26 December), John (27 December), and Innocents (28 December), whose services normally appear in the *temporale*. Moreover, the *temporale* begins with the Vigil of Christmas (fo. 18) instead of with Advent, relegating the four Sundays of Advent to the end of the cycle (fos. 67–70). The Mass for Transfiguration (6 August) is entered out of order between the *temporale* and the *sanctorale* (fo. 70^{v}), suggesting that the feast was something of an afterthought. This service, in addition, includes readings which are not otherwise provided in the manuscript. The presence of the Transfiguration in F:Pn, lat. 9436 is significant, for

93 The Benedictine authors of *VSB* (xii. 820) are mistaken in their claim that this feast was celebrated at Saint-Denis. They may have based this statement on the presence of the service in F:Pn, lat. 9436; nevertheless, the observance is not contained in any other calendar or MS of the abbey that is known to me.

although this feast began to be commemorated in the West in the tenth century,[94] its presence in the calendar and text of F:Pn, lat. 9436 marks its first appearance in the extant manuscripts from Saint-Denis. The script and decoration of this folio appear to be the same as the rest of the *temporale*, and it is possible that the feast was left out of the *sanctorale* simply as an oversight. It appears that F:Pn, lat. 9436, unlike the Mont-Renaud manuscript, was intended from the start to receive musical notation. Although the music sometimes continues into the margin or is omitted altogether from certain chants, the syllables of words are spaced widely enough to accommodate neumes.

As in the gradual F:Pm 384, the offertories in F:Pn, lat. 9436 have verses. The choice of these chants agrees in most instances with F:Pm 384, but F:Pn, lat. 9436 calls for the Gallican chant *Elegerunt apostoli* as offertory for the feast of Saint Stephen (fo. 72), while F:Pm 384 gives the Offer. *Posuisti domine*. The Mass for the Invention of the Cross contains the Offer. *Protege domine* in both sources; however, F:Pn, lat. 9436 employs the Ver. *Salus omnium*.[95] Two different verses, *In conspectu tuo* and *Salvator mundi*, are indicated in F:Pm 384.[96]

F:Pn, lat. 9436 witnesses the use of the first Greek Mass at Saint-Denis and foreshadows the later *missa greca* for the Octave of Saint Denis (16 October). Atkinson (2) has shown that the Greek Gloria (*Doxa*) which formed part of the early Greek Mass is transmitted both in F:Pn, lat. 9436 (fo. 1^{v}) and in F:Pn, lat. 2290 in a form which is curiously characteristic of the east Frankish sources. The Greek Credo (*Pisteuo*) is also present on fo. 2. F:Pn, lat. 9436 is, moreover, a newly discovered source for the Offer. Ver. *Qui cherubim mystice* (fo. 58^{v}, see Pl. 11), which is the Latin version of the Byzantine hymn of the Cherubim (*Cheroubikon*), sung as the offertory in the later Greek Mass, as noted in Chapter 4.

Leroquais, Schulten and Samaran have all dated F:Pn, lat. 9436 to the mid-eleventh century, and the liturgical contents of the manuscript support this estimation. The Masses for the Saturdays after Ash Wednesday and before Palm Sunday, which were added after 950,[97] are given in F:Pn, lat. 9436, but are omitted from the early eleventh-century gradual F:Pm 384. This would seem to indicate that the contents of F:Pn, lat. 9436 are more fully developed, and hence that it is later than F:Pm 384. Other 'modern' features of the organization of F:Pn, lat. 9436 include the use of alleluias instead of tracts on Saturday

[94] *CE*, xv. 19.

[95] Fo. 84^{v}. This verse is listed neither in Ott, *Offertoriale*, nor in any of the sources indexed in Bryden and Hughes, *Index*.

[96] Fo. 107 (also Hesbert, *Graduel*, 179). Both verses are found in the gradual of Saint-Yrieix (*PM*, xiii. 175), and *Salvator mundi* is likewise given in Ott, *Offertoriale*, 170.

[97] See Apel, *Chant*, 56–9, 68.

during the week after Pentecost, and the placement of the feast of Trinity on the Octave of Pentecost. F:Pm 384 again clings to older usage in these respects.

The abbey of Saint-Denis kept this magnificent sacramentary in its possession for more than 700 years. Montesquiou-Fezensac and Gaborit-Chopin have identified F:Pn, lat. 9436 in the earliest inventory of the abbey's treasures in 1505, and it appears in subsequent lists until the outset of the French Revolution. Probably because of the extraordinary quality of the jewelled binding, the manuscript was transferred to the Cabinet des Médailles in 1791.

17. F:Pn, lat. 10505: Paris, Bibliothèque Nationale, lat. 10505

Notated missal (incomplete), first quarter of fourteenth century (Pl. 19).
Parchment. 137 folios. 235 × 153 mm.
Bibliography: Leroquais, *Sacramentaires*, ii. 292; Beyssac, 'Mont-Renaud', 134; *GR* (MS *DEN* 3); Samaran and Marichal, *Catalogue*, iii. 730; Huglo (1), 'Chants', 78, 80; Nocent, 'Fragment', 760–1; Nebbiai-Dalla Guarda, *Bibliothèque*, 316, 319; Rasmussen, 'Liturgy', 42; Huglo (2), 'Remarques'.

The presence of the feast of Corpus Christi in the original hand of F:Pn, lat. 10505 (fos. 89^{v}–91) places this missal in the fourteenth century, but the incomplete *sanctorale*, which ends with the feast of Saint Simeon (5 January), and the absence of a calendar make further precisions on the basis of content impossible. The decoration of the book, however, is characteristic of the first quarter of the fourteenth century.[98] There are lacunas in the text, beginning: (1) on Monday of the second Sunday in Lent (between fos. 36^{v} and 37), (2) on the first Sunday following the Octave of Easter (between fos. 77^{v} and 78), and (3) on Pentecost (between fos. 86^{v} and 87).

No feasts for Saint Denis are included in the surviving portion of F:Pn, lat. 10505, and hence the destination of the book would seem to be in doubt. Indeed, so little of the *sanctorale* is present that confirmation of the origin of F:Pn, lat. 10505 comes from the series of alleluias for the Sundays after Pentecost—this list is manifestly the one found in all other graduals and missals of Saint-Denis. Although F:Pn, lat. 10505 does not contain a sequentiary, the textual incipits of sequences are added in the margins or blank spaces of many services.

[98] I am grateful to François Avril of the Bibliothèque Nationale for his assistance with the dating of this MS on the basis of its initials and filigree decoration.

18. F:Pn, lat. 16820: Paris, Bibliothèque Nationale, lat. 16820

Summer lectionary for the Office (March to September only), shortly after *c.*1150.
Parchment. 180 folios. 304 × 245 mm.
Bibliography: Delisle, *Inventaire*, 11; Étaix, 'Épreuves', 272–3; Nebbiai-Dalla Guarda, *Bibliothèque*, 316, 319; Stahl, 'Problem', 177, n. 23; 178, n. 40; Robertson, 'Transmission', 506–7.

The text of F:Pn, lat. 16820 contains the twelve readings for Matins for feasts of the summer *sanctorale* of Saint-Denis. The services provided for are those which have the rank of twelve lessons and higher in the later sources from the abbey. The main body of the lectionary begins with Annunciation (fo. 3, 25 March) and concludes with Saint Firminus (fo. 173^{v}, 25 September). The first two folios, which are not part of the original text, contain readings for Saint Barnabas (11 June) and an incomplete series for John the Baptist (24 June), and both are followed by lacunas.

In many instances, texts of the responsories sung at Matins follow each lesson. The presence of responsories in F:Pn, lat. 16820 is fortuitous since so few twelfth-century liturgical sources from Saint-Denis have survived. In most cases these pieces, their verses, and the services to which they are attached correspond to the earlier antiphoner F:Pn, lat. 17296.[99] At the same time, F:Pn, lat. 16820 also lists the lections for the twelve-lesson services that did not have proper music in the liturgy of the abbey and hence are not included in F:Pn, lat. 17296. F:Pn, lat. 16820 thus clarifies in part the roster of festivals at Saint-Denis and the level of their cult for a period from which no calendar is extant.

The feast of Saint Philibert (20 August) illustrates the way in which F:Pn, lat. 16820 provides details that are not otherwise known, for F:Pn, lat. 16820 implies that this festival was once celebrated with twelve lessons (fos. 125^{v}–128^{v}), while the later sources give only three lessons (see Appendix A). The lectionary likewise verifies that twelve-lesson services were sung for the feasts between March and September for saints whose relics were kept in the abbey: Invention of Denis (fo. 10^{v}, 22 April), Philip (fo. 15^{v}, 1 May), Commemoration of Hippolytus (fo. 23^{v}, 12 May), Peregrinus (fo. 26, 16 May), Detection

[99] One exception is the feast of Peter and Paul (29 June), in which F:Pn, lat. 16820 adds a 13th responsory. While the 1st 11 responsories are identical in both sources (F:Pn, lat. 16820, fos. 51–55^{v}; F:Pn, lat. 17296, fo. 177–179^{v}, also Hesbert, *CAO*, vol. ii, No. 101a), F:Pn, lat. 16820 gives the Ver. *Tu es inquit* for the 12th Resp. *Quodcumque ligaveris* (Ver. *Et ego dico* in F:Pn, lat. 17296), and then adds a supernumerary Resp. *Cornelius centurio*, Ver. *Cum orasset*, which is the Vespers responsory in F:Pn, lat. 17296.

of Denis (fo. 36, 9 June), John the Baptist (fos. 2, 46^{v}, 24 June), Peter and Paul (fo. 51, 29 June), Cucuphas (fo. 85^{v}, 25 July), Hippolytus (fo. 113^{v}, 13 August), Osmanna (fo. 122, 16 August), Maurice (fo. 168, 22 September), and Firminus (fo. 173^{v}, 25 September).

Because the lectionary includes only services for March to September, it does not incorporate the feast of Saint Denis himself (9 October). Perhaps the lack of this information led Delisle to assign F:Pn, lat. 16820 to Saint-Corneille of Compiègne, relying on the mark of provenance found on fo. 1: 'S. Cornelii Compend. Congr. S. Mauri.' This ex-libris is written by the hand that inscribed the same words into the antiphoner F:Pn, lat. 17296 (fo. 2).[100] Unlike the antiphoner, however, F:Pn, lat. 16820 was never adapted to the use of Saint-Corneille, since not even the feast of the patrons Corneille and Cyprian (14 September) was inserted.[101]

At least two principal scribes copied the lectionary: a hand identified by light-brown ink wrote the original text, while later interpolations of entire folios are penned in black ink (fos. 11–16^{v}, 22^{r-v}, 41^{r-v}, 48^{r-v}, 148–151^{v}). A few rubrics in the original section were also replaced by a later hand, for instance, the beginning of the rubric for the feast of the Detection of Saint Denis (fo. 36): 'Lc in detectione' (later hand) 'sancti dyonisii' (original rubricator). The presence of the feast of Mary Magdalene (22 July) in the original hand of F:Pn, lat. 16820 (fo. 80) suggests that the manuscript post-dates the antiphoner F:Pn, lat. 17296, which contains this festival as an addition (fos. 348^{v}–51). F:Pn, lat. 17296 was probably in use by 1150, and Stahl suggests that F:Pn, lat. 16820 was produced shortly after this date, perhaps in the 1160s.

19. F:Pn, lat. 17296: Paris, Bibliothèque Nationale, lat. 17296

Twelfth-century antiphoner, probably copied between 1140 and 1150 (Pls. 13 and 14).

Parchment. 355 folios. 220 × 145 mm.

Bibliography: Delisle, *Inventaire*, 499; Hesbert (1), 'Office', 404; Handschin, 'Neumenschrift', 92; Huglo (1), 'Office', 194–202; Brou, 'Antienne', 217–21; Marosszéki, *Origines*, 167; Lambot, 'Canis'; Combe, 'Réforme', 219; Hesbert (2), *CAO*, vol. ii, pp. xi-xv (also inventories F:Pn, lat. 17296 [MS D]), vols. v, vi (MS 796); Le Roux, 'Guillaume', i, 381; Arlt, *Festoffizium*, ii. 204, 219–20, 228, 256; Steiner (1), 'Responsories', 172; Hofmann-Brandt, 'Die Tropen', i. 11; ii, Nos. 114, 182, 282, 369, 372, 374, 426, 558; Huglo (2), *Tonaires*, 319; Bautier, *Odorannus*, 63, 182, 194; Bastiaensen, 'Antienne', 391–4; Steiner

[100] For further discussion of the provenance of F:Pn, lat. 16820, see Robertson, 'Transmission', 506–7.

[101] It is highly unlikely, therefore, that F:Pn, lat. 16820 was copied at Saint-Denis for Saint-Corneille, as Stahl has suggested; 'Problem', 178, n. 40 (see also Étaix, 'Épreuves', 272, n. 2).

(2), 'Melismas', 111–15, 122–3; Kelly (1), 'Elaboration', 464–5, 471–2; Samaran and Marichal, *Catalogue*, iii. 745; Huglo (3), 'Débuts', 101–4; Stäblein, *Schriftbild*, 13, 116, 122, 156, 182, 216; 'Sources', 625; Udovich (1), 'Antiphons'; Steiner (3), 'Antiphons', 4–7; Steiner (4), 'Traditions', 133–7; Udovich (2), 'Modality' (study of differentiae in F:Pn, lat. 17296); Walters [Robertson], 'Reconstruction', 206–38; Nebbiai-Dalla Guarda, *Bibliothèque*, 34, 316, 319; Crocker, 'Antiphons' (study of Matins antiphons in numerical Offices of F:Pn, lat. 17296); Meersseman, *Capitules*, 13; Rasmussen, 'Liturgy', 42; Stahl, 'Problem', 166; 172–3; 181, n. 68; Steiner (5), 'Repertory', 178; Robertson (1), '*Benedicamus*', 17–28, 30, 52; Huglo (4), 'Remarques'; Huglo (5), *Livres*, 95; Kelly (2), 'Neuma', 5, 6, 8, 24; Robertson (2), 'Transmission'.

The antiphoner F:Pn, lat. 17296 is one of the most valuable French sources of melodies for the chants of the Office. The contents of the book, inventoried by Hesbert (2), are nearly complete, and the diastematic notation of the music is exceptionally legible. Apart from the melodies for hundreds of antiphons and responsories, important musical aspects of F:Pn, lat. 17296 include the implied tonary found in the ending formulas (differentiae) of the psalms. The differentiae are placed in the margins of the manuscript alongside the majority of antiphons. A series of melodies for the Gloria Patri and for the Benedicamus Domino are given in the middle of the proper Office for John the Baptist (fos. 170–1). Music for the invitatory antiphon appears throughout the book, and an incomplete collection of five tones for the invitatory psalm (Venite) is found on fos. 346–8. Both texted and untexted responsory tropes appear in F:Pn, lat. 17296, and, like several other notated sources from Saint-Denis, the antiphoner contains a substantial number of Gallican remnants, including antiphons that were sung before the gospel at Mass and processional antiphons. The manuscript is the earliest witness to the special series of responsories for the Office of the Dead, rubricated in honour of King Dagobert and subsequently used on royal anniversaries.

The physical aspects of the manuscript are important to note, since they help explain the few lacunas and additions that are present in F:Pn, lat. 17296. The original first folio, which would have contained the service of First Vespers for the first Sunday in Advent, was lost. It was replaced, probably in the thirteenth century, by a folio which includes four Marian responsories and antiphons and the Inv. Ant. *Ecce venit rex* for the first Sunday in Advent. In addition, it seems from the numbering which was added to the lower right-hand corners of the recto sides of the initial folios of many gatherings that another gathering, perhaps containing a calendar, once headed the book. The first visible numeral *4* on fo. 17 begins what is now the *third* gathering;

similarly, the final number *47* on fo. 352 marks the start of the *46th* gathering. Most gatherings consist of four bifolios or eight folios (e.g. fos. 1–8, 9–16, 17–24). Gatherings 26, 29, 30, 38, 42, 45, and 46 are irregular.[102] Gatherings 24 (fos. 185–92) and 25 (fos. 193–200) were reversed; this occurred prior to the numbering of gatherings and folios, which run consecutively throughout the manuscript. The foliation was apparently made after the loss of the initial gathering, since the first folio is numbered 1 instead of 9. It is clear that the pages of the antiphoner were originally somewhat wider, since many of the differentiae found in the margins of the manuscript are trimmed (e.g. fo. 327^{v}), and since most of the prickings have disappeared.

The ruling of folios was done with a dry-point. The double bounding lines in each outer margin often enclose the differentiae of antiphons, and a single bounding line appears on the inner margin of each leaf. The staves are fashioned from four dry-point lines, while the text is written on a fifth line lying below the staff. Each text-line falls just above the next four-line staff, creating the appearance that the subsequent staff consists of five lines. In certain parts of the manuscript, brown ink was later used to draw over the dry-point staff-lines, doubtless to assist in the reading of the notation: fos. 37^{v}, 135^{v}–136, 137–175^{v}, 177–202, 209–14, 221^{v}–231^{v}, 264^{v}–273, 286^{v}–290, 330^{v}–337 (top), 337^{v} (top). Red ink was employed for this purpose on fos. 176–176^{v}, 202^{v}–203 (top), 340^{v}, 343–345^{v}. Folios containing later additions use red (fos. 1^{r-v}, 352–355^{v}) or brown (fos. 1^{v}, 346–51) for staff-lines, but without an earlier layer of dry-point lines. Normally, 13 lines of music and text occur on each page, but 15 lines are found in gathering 2 (fos. 9–16^{v}) and 11 lines on fo. 1.

The lacunas and additions in F:Pn, lat. 17296 are best understood in the context of the irregular gatherings described above. The missing bifolio in gathering 30, which stood between fos. 231^{v}–232 and 233^{v}–234, once included the final responsories for the Office of Saint Denis and the conclusion to the service of his Octave. A lost folio between 327^{v} and 328 (gathering 42) interrupts the Office of the Dead between its antiphons and responsories. Gathering 45 (fos. 346–351^{v}) consists of material which was added mostly at later times: a collection of invitatory tones (fos. 346–348), some of which are incomplete because of a lacuna between fos. 347^{v} and 348, and a proper Office for Mary Magdalene (fos. 348^{v}–351). The final gathering (No. 46, fos. 352–355^{v}), also an addition, includes part of a proper Office for Saints Corneille and Cyprian, which begins abruptly in the middle of the antiphons for the psalms at Matins, along with the antiphons and five

[102] These nos. are in each case 1 less than those which appear in the MS, since, as mentioned earlier, an initial gathering which was probably lost is assumed.

responsories from the proper service for Saint Pantaleon (fos. 354^{v}–355^{v}).

Several hands were involved in the production of the main, twelfth-century body of F:Pn, lat. 17296 (fos. 2–348). The scribes and decorators worked roughly contemporaneously, as is suggested from the homogeneous style of the initials. In addition, the changes in scribe and notator are often independent of the gathering structure, except in gatherings 32 and 33 (fos. 244–59), which are clearly written by one scribe in a hand that is distinct from the rest of the manuscript. The musical notation in these two gatherings was done by the notator of the previous and subsequent sections, and hence they are clearly coeval at least with the notation of the volume. Sometimes the texts of the marginal differentiae seem to have been copied by the hand which wrote the words of the chants on that leaf; in other cases, the differentiae were inscribed slightly later. One hand added a significant number of differentiae throughout the manuscript on fos. 69^{v} (bottom), 144^{v} (middle), 166 (bottom), 166^{v} (top), etc.

The texts of chants were written before music was added, and some pieces were left unnotated. The notation throughout most of the manuscript (fos. 2–322^{v}) is French and shows the transition from neumes to square shapes. One or possibly two hands, influenced by the notational style of Metz, wrote the music of fos. 323–347^{v} at or around the time the rest of the manuscript was copied.[103] Musical notation from other periods is evident in the rest of the antiphoner, and these notations suggest a chronological order for the additions to the manuscript. The melodies for the Venite on fos. 346–347^{v} were notated by the Messine scribe mentioned above, and these chants, if not contemporaneous with the main body of F:Pn, lat. 17296, were added at an early date. The Office of Mary Magdalene (fos. 348^{v}–351) is written in French neumes dating probably from the late twelfth or early thirteenth century. The Marian antiphons and responsories (fos. 1^{r-v}) as well as the Offices of Saints Corneille, Cyprian, and Pantaleon (fos. 352–355^{v}) employ a type of thirteenth-century notation which Corbin and Bernard call 'joined points' ('points liés');[104] this notation is also found elsewhere in the manuscript to fill in chants whose music was originally omitted (fo. 7, etc.). The most recent notations, found on fos. 1^{v} (bottom), 176^{r-v}, 348, and 350^{v}, are close to actual square shapes and probably date from the late thirteenth or early fourteenth century.[105]

[103] A facsimile of one of the Messine fos. (fos. 340^{v}–341) is given in Stäblein, *Schriftbild*, 157, no. 40. The axis of the notation is that of Metz, and the *punctum*, as well as the *podatus* with notes on opposite sides, are especially characteristic of this region.

[104] See Corbin and Bernard, *Répertoire*, i. pl. xvii.

[105] This notation is named 'little joined squares' ('petits carrés liés') in ibid. pls. xviii ff.

The palaeographic details just mentioned assist in determining the date, origin, and later provenance of F:Pn, lat. 17296. Because the musical notation of the body of the manuscript is less developed than that of other twelfth-century notated sources (see the foregoing discussion of the notation of Saint-Denis), the antiphoner probably falls in the first half of the century. A *terminus a quo* is established by the contents of the volume, specifically, the Office of the Dead for kings, headed by the rubric 'In natali dagoberti regis' (fos. 327–30). Since this service was instituted by Abbot Adam (reg. 1094?–1122) probably in 1108, we can assume that the antiphoner post-dates this year. Other indications circumscribe the date even more closely. Adam's successor Abbot Suger (1122–51) continued and indeed expanded his predecessor's liturgical activities, enhancing the Divine Office significantly in the 1130s, as described in Chapter 4. The full solemnity of these heightened ceremonies would have been realized only in the new church, which was consecrated in 1144. In terms of decoration, too, F:Pn, lat. 17296 appears to lie between 1140 and 1150,[106] and it is then reasonable to posit that the antiphoner was penned during this decade to provide for the liturgical needs of the new church building. A similar case occurred in the thirteenth century, when the rebuilding of Saint-Denis necessitated the rewriting of the earliest ordinary of the abbey, F:Pm 526, resulting in the second ordinary F:Pn, lat. 976 and missal F:Pn, lat. 1107.

The markings on flyleaf V ('Volume de 355 Feuillets . . . 22 Decembre 1869') and on fo. 2 ('S[ancti] Cornelii Compend[iensis], Congr[egationis] S[ancti] Mauri') show that the antiphoner passed from Saint-Denis to Saint-Corneille of Compiègne. The same scribe also added the indication from fo. 2 to the Saint-Denis lectionary F:Pn, lat. 16820, a book likewise transferred to Saint-Corneille. The marking on flyleaf V is similar to the description given at the beginning of the thirteenth-century gradual of Saint Corneille F:Pn, lat. 17329, written in the same nineteenth-century hand: 'Volume de 256 feuillets . . . 27 Décembre 1869'. The approximate time at which F:Pn, lat. 17296 arrived at Saint-Corneille is clear from the notation of the added sections. The proper Offices for Saints Corneille, Cyprian, and Pantaleon (fos. 352–355^{v}) were doubtless incorporated at Saint-Corneille, since in the liturgy of Saint-Denis these services are simple commemorations without proper texts. The notation of these folios dates from the thirteenth century, hence it appears that the book was in the possession of Saint-Corneille by this time, no more than 150 years after its copying, and the marking

[106] I am grateful to François Avril and Patricia Stirnemann of the Bibliothèque Nationale for their assistance in the dating of this MS on the basis of decoration. Harvey Stahl dates the antiphoner slightly later, placing it in the 1150s; 'Problem', 172, 174.

on flyleaf V demonstrates that F:Pn, lat. 17296 was housed there along with the Saint-Corneille gradual F:Pn, lat. 17329 in the nineteenth century. Presumably, then, F:Pn, lat. 17296 remained at Saint-Corneille from some time in the thirteenth century until it came to what is now the Bibliothèque Nationale.

There are two possible explanations for the presence of the antiphoner at Saint-Corneille. The liturgical dependence of Saint-Corneille on Saint-Denis is apparent in the similarities between the books for the Mass and Office from these two houses.[107] Perhaps F:Pn, lat. 17296 was offered to Saint-Corneille as an exemplar for the production of new antiphoners. The second explanation is a corollary to this. We saw in Chapter 2 that a systematic reduction in the number of proper chants from many saints' Offices occurred at Saint-Denis, beginning in the mid-thirteenth century. F:Pn, lat. 17296, dating from the previous century, contains complete proper Offices for Saints Cucuphas (fos. 193^{v}–198^{v}), Maurice (fos. 216^{v}–222), and Hilary of Mende (fos. 234–238), and these were among the ones simplified and standardized in the later books. It is possible, therefore, that F:Pn, lat. 17296 was simply outdated at Saint-Denis in the thirteenth century. The thirteenth-century ordinaries F:Pm 526 and F:Pn, lat. 976 witness to the gradual abandonment of the proper chants for Cucuphas, Maurice, and Hilary, while the mid-fourteenth-century breviary GB:Ob, Can. Lit. 192 shows the results of this process, listing proper responsories only in the final positions in each nocturn. This implies that similar changes would have been made in any contemporaneous antiphoner or notated breviary of the abbey, examples of which have not survived. If F:Pn, lat. 17296 was no longer usable at Saint-Denis in the thirteenth century, the monks might have decided to send it to Saint-Corneille.

Hesbert (2) has shown that the original destination of F:Pn, lat. 17296 for Saint-Denis is clear from the proper Offices that it contains. Not only are the Invention (fos. 152^{r-v}), Vigil (fos. 226–7), *natale* (fos. 227–232^{v}) and Octave (fos. 232^{v}–233^{v}) of Saint Denis included, but the proper services for saints whose cults were particular to the abbey are also present. Furthermore, there is evidence that the ordering of the antiphoner was based on the eleventh-century antiphonary list from Saint-Denis in F:Pm 384. The table of readings for the Mass added to F:Pm 384 in the late twelfth century suggests that the book was still in use even after F:Pn, lat. 17296 was copied, and that it could therefore have been employed for the production of the antiphoner. The antiphonary list in F:Pm 384 consists of textual incipits for the Office chants, written near the end of the eleventh-century portion of the manuscript (fos. 163–199^{v}). Designed perhaps as a guide for the

[107] See Robertson, 'Transmission'.

copying of new antiphoners, the antiphonary list in F:Pm 384 has certain peculiarities which are preserved in F:Pn, lat. 17296.[108] The placement of Saint Lucy's feast in the two books is especially telling. Both F:Pm 384 and F:Pn, lat. 17296 mistakenly locate the service between the first and second Sundays in Advent, whereas the date of her feast, 13 December, invariably falls after the second or third Sunday in Advent. The two manuscripts likewise include a curious conflation of the *natale* (21 March) and the Translation (11 July) of Saint Benedict, which is described in Chapters 2 and 4. Both sources place the responsories for the weeks between Epiphany and Septuagesima at the ends of the volumes, following the series of histories. Even the illuminated initials for Easter, studied by Harvey Stahl, indicate the possible dependence of F:Pn, lat. 17296 on F:Pm 384. Stahl has proposed that the artist for the letter *A(ngelus)* in F:Pn, lat. 17296 (fo. 136^{v}) may have derived his inspiration directly from the initial *R(essurexi)* in F:Pm 384 (fo. 95^{v}).

In addition to these individual similarities, F:Pn, lat. 17296 and F:Pm 384 resemble one another in overall organization. The *sanctorale* is integrated with the *temporale* in both sources, and their ordering of Offices is by and large the same, except, of course, for the appearance of the newer Office of Saint Nicholas only in F:Pn, lat. 17296 (fos. 261–264^{v}). The two volumes also share a peculiarity of format within the individual Offices: the twelve antiphons are grouped separately from the twelve responsories, instead of being combined into nocturns, as Hesbert (2) notes is more often the case. In spite of this large-scale agreement, however, F:Pn, lat. 17296 sometimes diverges from F:Pm 384 in its choice of individual antiphons, responsories, or verses, and F:Pm 384 seems to contain more pieces than F:Pn, lat. 17296. The reason for this is probably that the antiphonary list in F:Pm 384 served as a kind of catalogue or compendium of chant titles for celebrations. From this source the compilers of a new antiphoner such as F:Pn, lat. 17296 would select the desired number of pieces, keeping the order presented in F:Pm 384. But a notated book would necessarily have been on hand as well, to provide the music for the antiphoner. The few differences between F:Pm 384 and F:Pn, lat. 17296 perhaps stem from this interposed source (or sources).

20. *F:Pn, n.a.l. 305: Paris, Bibliothèque Nationale, n.a.l. 305*

Evangeliary, tenth century, provenance in thirteenth (perhaps) and fifteenth centuries Saint-Denis (Pl. 8).

[108] Hesbert (2) notes some of these unusual features in F:Pn, lat. 17296, but without relating them to F:Pm 384.

Parchment. 158 folios. 212 × 142 mm.
Bibliography: Delisle, *Acquisitions*, 236; Klauser, *Capitulare*, p. lxii; Bibliothèque Nationale, *Manuscrits* (1954), 33; Montesquiou-Fezensac and Gaborit-Chopin, *Trésor*, i. 47, 192; ii. 255; iii. 84–5; Nebbiai-Dalla Guarda, *Bibliothèque*, 222, 241, 256, 281, 287; Rasmussen, 'Liturgy', 41; Stahl, 'Problem', 175, n. 8.

Although the scriptorium that produced F:Pn, n.a.l. 305 has not yet been determined, the Bibliothèque Nationale notes that the style of this tenth-century evangeliary is characteristic of northern France. The addition of some orations and versicles for the feasts of Saint Denis and Saint Eugene (fos. 45–6) suggests that the book may have been at Saint-Denis as early as the thirteenth century, and perhaps before. By the fifteenth century F:Pn, n.a.l. 305 was clearly in use in the abbey, for the oath of abbots of Saint-Denis is present: 'Juramentum abbatis sancti Dyonisi in francia: Vous jures que vous garderes les honorables observances anciennes' (fos. 46^{r-v}). Subsequent inventories of the *trésor* of the abbey, reviewed by Montesquiou-Fezensac and Gaborit-Chopin, document the presence of the manuscript at Saint-Denis until the French Revolution.

21. F:Pn, n.a.l. 306: Paris, Bibliothèque Nationale, n.a.l. 306

Pontifical, mid-twelfth century, usage of Rouen, adapted for processional use at Saint-Denis in the fourteenth century.
Parchment. 244 folios (A + B + fos. 1–242). 237 × 168 mm.
Bibliography: Delisle, *Acquisitions*, 500–1; Leroquais, *Pontificaux*, ii. 220–9; Samaran and Marichal, *Catalogue*, iv/1. 317. Montesquiou-Fezensac and Gaborit-Chopin, *Trésor*, i. 47, 187; ii. 245–7; Jackson, '*Manuscrits*', 80–1; Nebbiai-Dalla Guarda, *Bibliothèque*, 223, 262, 281, 288; Rasmussen, 'Liturgy', 42.

The abbey of Saint-Denis acquired F:Pn, n.a.l. 306 from the cathedral of Rouen in the fourteenth century. At that time the monks added two separate gatherings (fos. 214–215^{v}, fos. 216–238^{v}) which include the rubrics, versicles, and orations for the portion of the major processions of the abbey which took place in the chevet of the church. Montesquiou-Fezensac and Gaborit-Chopin have shown that the manuscript remained at Saint-Denis until the French Revolution.

22. F:Pn, n.a.l. 307: Paris, Bibliothèque Nationale, n.a.l. 307

Lectionary for the Mass, twelfth century.
Parchment. 130 folios (fos. 1–19 + one unnumbered folio after fo. 19 + 20–128 + one unnumbered folio after fo. 128). 199 × 130 mm.

Bibliography: Delisle, *Acquisitions*, 238; Klauser, *Capitulare*, p. cxix; Montesquiou-Fezensac and Gaborit-Chopin, *Trésor*, i. 173; ii. 211–12; iii. 72–3; Samaran and Marichal, *Catalogue*, iv/1. 365; Nebbiai-Dalla Guarda, *Bibliothèque*, 223, 241, 281; Rasmussen, 'Liturgy', 42; Stahl, 'Problem', 175, n. 8; 177, n. 23.

The liturgical usage of Saint-Denis is clear in F:Pn, n.a.l. 307, as Delisle and Montesquiou-Fezensac and Gaborit-Chopin have noted: the marks of provenance on fos. 1 and 4, the feasts for which readings are provided, and the appearance of the volume in inventories of the treasury of the abbey from 1505 until the nineteenth century. The lections include the epistle *Stans Paulus in medio*, which is a slightly later addition to the beginning of the volume (fo. 4). This lesson deals with Saint Paul's convert and disciple Dionysius the Areopagite, whom the monks of Saint-Denis had associated with their patron since the ninth century. The community added this reading to the formulary for the feast of Saint Denis (9 October) and for the Greek Mass on the Octave (16 October) some time after F:Pn, n.a.l. 307 was copied, probably in the late twelfth century.

F:Pn, n.a.l. 307 contains both the epistles and the gospels for the Mass. The format of the book resembles that of the twelfth-century antiphoner F:Pn, lat. 17296 in integrating the *sanctorale* with the *temporale* (fos. 1–110^{v}). The *commune sanctorum* begins on fo. 111, readings for the Dedication of the Church are found on fo. 122, and a series of votive Masses starts on fo. 122^{v}.

23. F:Pn, n.a.l. 1420: Paris, Bibliothèque Nationale, n.a.l. 1420

Evangeliary, early thirteenth century with additions from the fourteenth and eighteenth century.
Parchment. 128 folios (fos. 1–28 + 28 *bis* + 29–127). 280 × 200 mm.
Bibliography: Bibliothèque Nationale, *Inventaire*, i. 118^{v} [98]; Héron de Villefosse, 'Manuscrits', 253; Delisle, *Acquisitions*, 238; Klauser, *Capitulare*, p. cviii; Montesquiou-Fezensac and Gaborit-Chopin, *Trésor*, ii. 202–8; iii. 69–70; Nebbiai-Dalla Guarda, *Bibliothèque*, 224, 241, 281, 288; Rasmussen, 'Liturgy', 42; Stahl, 'Problem', 175, n. 8.

The spectacular original binding of this manuscript became a casualty of the French Revolution in 1794, when the jewel-studded cover was melted down and replaced with a plain one. The manuscript was then incorporated into the Bibliothèque Nationale.[109] In spite of this ignominious fate, the volume enjoyed great prominence in the fifteenth

[109] Montesquiou-Fezensac and Gaborit-Chopin, *Trésor*, iii. 69–70, and pl. 54 (drawing taken from Félibien, *Histoire*, unnumbered page following p. 542, pl. iv, no. AA).

century, when it was evidently carried on a special cushion by the subdeacon during the solemn processions of Saint-Denis.[110]

The original thirteenth-century text contains the cycle of gospels for the feasts of the *temporale* (fos. 3–80^{v}) and the *sanctorale* (fos. 81–103^{v}; feast of Saint Denis = fo. 97). A curious feature of this section is the systematic elimination of the word 'dominus' from the ubiquitous abbreviation 'dominus ih'c' (= 'Dominus Jesus Christus') through barring or erasure. The thirteenth-century sources for the readings of the Mass from Saint-Denis (e.g. F:Pn, lat. 1107) normally omit the word 'dominus' altogether, but it seems to be more common, though not uniformly so, in books from other houses. It is possible, therefore, that one of the models for this book was a non-Dionysian source which used the abbreviation. The 'correction' of this abbreviation in F:Pn, n.a.l. 1420 may have happened when the fourteenth-century portion of the manuscript was added (fos. 104–125^{v}). This more recent section consists of readings for Christmas, the Dedication of the Church, Maundy Thursday, and Easter.

Fos. 126–7 were written in the eighteenth century, and the latter folio contains two musical settings of the Ite Missa Est on the melismas *Omni prosequenda* and *Alma redemptoris mater* for use on *annuale* and *semiannuale* feasts (see Ex. 3.16). It is noteworthy that the practice of singing the Ite in florid chant, a tradition established at Saint-Denis before the middle of the thirteenth century, apparently continued there until the Revolution.

24. F:Pn, Rés. B. 5209: Paris, Bibliothèque Nationale, Rés. B. 5209, and B. 5209 bis.

Unnotated breviary, printed in Paris in 1550.
Paper. 424 folios (not numbered consecutively). 138 × 92 mm.
Bibliography: Félibien, *Histoire*, 394; Alès, *Description*, 430–2; Andoyer, 'Bréviaire'; Levillain, 'Office'; Bohatta, *Bibliographie*, 91–2; Lemaître, *Répertoire*, 600.

The breviaries designated by the two shelf-marks F:Pn, Rés. B. 5209 and F:Pn, Rés. B. 5209 *bis* are the most recent books treated in this study, apart from F:Pan, L 863, No. 10, which was copied in the eighteenth century but represents mid-fourteenth-century practice. Printed for the first time in 1550, the breviary of the abbey was thus standardized under Abbot Louis, cardinal of Bourbon. While the number of copies produced in 1550 is not known, it is clear that only a

[110] Montesquiou-Fezensac and Gaborit-Chopin, *Trésor*, iii. 69–70; and ii. 202–8, which lists the inventories in which the MS it cited.

handful have survived. The Bibliothèque Nationale now possesses three examples, one with the shelf-mark B. 5209 and two others with the number B. 5209 *bis*. Lemaître gives a partial listing of exemplars that exist elsewhere. The pillage of Saint-Denis by the Huguenots only 17 years later no doubt caused the loss and scattering of many copies, while others would have become obsolete after the Maurists imposed their rule in 1633. There are several minor differences between B. 5209 and the two books marked B. 5209 *bis* in the arrangement of sections. The *Preparationes missae*, for example, come at the end of B. 5209 *bis*, whereas they fall between the *temporale* and *sanctorale* in B. 5209.

Félibien, referring to the printing of this breviary almost two centuries later, related that with the help of F:Pn, Rés. B. 5209 the monks of Saint-Denis were finally able to recite the Office with uniformity, whether in or out of the monastery. Andoyer has noted that the small dimensions of the book indicate that it was not meant for use in the choir. All the material necessary for the performance of the Offices is of course present, and the contents of this printed breviary mirror those of its manuscript predecessor from the mid-fourteenth century, GB:Ob, Can. Lit. 192. The similarity in content of these two sources in fact attests to the long-term stability of the liturgy of Saint-Denis, which was firmly fixed by around 1350. While the calendar of F:Pn, Rés. B. 5209 contains fewer obits than the fourteenth- and fifteenth-century manuscripts, several entries are recent and appear in no other source (see Appendix A, source N7). The two Offices for the Dead, one for regular use and the other for solemn anniversaries, likewise agree with those which were sung at Saint-Denis from the fourteenth century on.

25. F:Psg 1186: Paris, Bibliothèque Sainte-Geneviève 1186

Psalter, tenth century, with additions, including an unnotated hymnal from the eleventh century.
Parchment. 224 folios. 232 × 191 mm.
Bibliography: Kohler, *Manuscrits*, i. 548–53; Gastoué, 'Origines' (1903/4), 13–15; Mearns, *Hymnaries, passim*; Leroquais, *Psautiers*, ii. 148–52; Corbin and Bernard, *Répertoire*, i. 37; Nebbiai-Dalla Guarda, *Bibliothèque*, 42, 316, 318; Rasmussen, 'Liturgy', 41.

The tenth-century portion of F:Psg 1186 is a biblical psalter in five sections, containing the Gallican text of the Psalms like the other psalter-hymnal from Saint-Denis F:Pn, lat. 103. Musical incipits for the antiphons and differentiae of the ferial Office were added in the margins of the original text of F:Psg 1186, and these demonstrate that the psalter was adapted for use on ordinary days.[111] An unnotated hymnal (fos. 196^{v}–221) including some Gallican remnants was joined to the psalter in the eleventh century, while hymns for the common of saints and for Saint Nicholas were appended to the hymnal in the twelfth century. Two folios in F:Psg 1186 are misplaced: fos. 17^{r-v} should follow fo. 22^{v}, and fos. 199^{r-v} should follow fo. 195^{v}. A lacuna of one folio occurs between fos. 62^{v} and 63.

The signs of origin and later provenance in F:Psg 1186 are less convincing than in F:Pn, lat. 103. Leroquais first deduced the destination of F:Psg 1186 for a Benedictine house through examination of the names of the saints listed in the litanies (tenth century), through the composition of the hymnal (eleventh century), and through the presence of canticles for the third nocturn of the monastic Office of Matins (eleventh century). He then attributed the volume to Saint-Denis on the basis of its emphasis on the Parisian Saints Denis, Germanus of Paris, and Geneviève.

It is true that Saints Denis, Rusticus, and Eleutherius are listed in both series of litanies (fos. 70^{v}, 179^{v}); moreover, the text of Abbot Hilduin's hymn to Saint Denis, *Celi cives adplaudite*, is given (fos. 216^{r-v}). Likewise, the presence of Germanus of Paris in the litany may well recall the years during which Saint-Denis and Saint-Germain-des-Prés shared the same abbot and consequently must have experienced some mingling of their liturgies. On the other hand, the litanies of F:Psg 1186 do not include Saints Cucuphas, Hilary of Mende, and others whose relics the abbey had long cherished. One of the orations (fo. 162^{v}), furthermore, employs feminine inflections, implying perhaps that F:Psg 1186 was once used in a house of nuns. Finally, the added neumes, mentioned above and identified by Corbin and Bernard as French, are not like the ones found in F:Pm 384 and in F:Pn, lat. 103, both thought to have been written at Saint-Denis. In spite of these objections, sheer process of elimination led Leroquais to propose Saint-Denis as the likeliest place of origin, and at least sometime usage, of F:Psg 1186, and there seems no overwhelming reason to contest this assessment.

If F:Psg 1186 was made for Saint-Denis, the psalter portion was either taken at some time to England or was used by a person with interests in this area. Leroquais notes ten English saints (Lawrence, Mellitus, Justus, Honorius, Paulinus, another Mellitus, Deusdedit,

[111] See Corbin and Bernard, *Répertoire*, i. 37, and pl. viii. The beginnings and ends of antiphons were often eliminated during the blocking of the volume. The incipits are found on the following fos.: 36^{v}, 38, 39^{v}, 41, 44, 46^{v}, 50, 55, 58, 59, 61, 63, 65^{v}, 67, 69, 71, 74, 77^{v}, 80^{v}, 83^{v}, 86^{v}, 88, 94, 96^{v}, 98, 100, 102, 103^{v}, 112, 113^{v}, 115, 116, 118^{v}, 122^{v}, 127^{v}, 130. This music cannot be compared with Saint-Denis usage, since the antiphons for the ferial Office are absent from the only surviving notated antiphoner from the abbey, F:Pn, lat. 17296.

Theodore, Liuthard, and Adrian) in the second litany (fo. 180), and he believes that these names were incorporated shortly after the psalter was copied in the tenth century. Many of these saints were seventh- and eighth-century archbishops of Canterbury and abbots of the abbey of Saints-Peter-and-Paul of Canterbury. Relations between Saint-Denis and several religious houses in England (for example Deerhurst and Bury St Edmund's) are apparent in the tenth and eleventh centuries, although there is no evidence of a special connection with Canterbury itself.

26. F:R(m), A. 566: Rouen, Bibliothèque Municipale, A. 566[112]

Fragments of sacramentaries, ninth, tenth, and eleventh centuries. Parchment. 32 folios. 170 × 130 mm.

Bibliography: Delisle, *Sacramentaires*, 292–6; Omont, *Catalogue*, i. 53, Leroquais, *Sacramentaires*, i. 144–5; Bourque, *Sacramentaires*, ii. 51; Nebbiai-Dalla Guarda, *Bibliothèque*, 317, 318; Rasmussen, 'Liturgy', 42; Palazzo, '"Libellus"'.

The small dimensions of F:R(m), A. 566 led Delisle to suggest that the manuscript was put together in the eleventh century from three fragments, and that it was used by itinerant priests or monks. The three distinct layers are (1) a section of seven Masses in honour of the Virgin and of all the saints (fos. 1–8^v), written in the late ninth century, (2) the services for the principal feasts of the *sanctorale* for November and December (fos. 9–12) in a late tenth-century hand, and (3) a series of votive Masses, the canon of the Mass, and the feast of Saint Michael (fos. 12–32), all in eleventh-century script. Delisle attributed the manuscript to Saint-Denis on the basis of the names listed in the canon, which include nine saints who were specially regarded in the abbey: Denis, Rusticus, Eleutherius, Cucuphas, Hippolytus, Innocent, Hilary, Eustace, Romanus (fos. 17^v–18). Palazzo has recently suggested that the ninth-century portion was made for Saint-Denis in the scriptorium of Saint-Amand.

Delisle's assessment of the provenance of F:R(m), A. 566 is based on the eleventh-century part of the book only. But it is possible to suggest connections of the earlier portion of F:R(m), A. 566 with Saint-Denis as well. Around 832, Abbot Hilduin (814–41) called for the continuous performance of the Divine Office in the chapel which he had added to

[112] Leroquais and others cite this source as 'Bibliothèque municipale de Rouen, ms. 275 (A. 566)'; Leroquais, *Sacramentaires*, i. 144. The no. '275', however, is the number of the notice for this MS, as given in the catalogue of the library of Rouen (Omont, *Catalogue*, i. 53). The actual shelf-mark for the volume itself is 'A. 566'. Bourque likewise lists the number as 'ms 275 (olim A. 566)'; *Sacramentaires*, ii. 51. I am indebted to Christian Nicaise of the Bibliothèque Municipale of Rouen for his assistance on this point.

the eastern end of the church, as described in Chapter 4. This new structure was dedicated to Mary and to all the saints. So, too, are the seven Masses which apparently form a unit in the ninth-century portion of F:R(m), A. 566.[113] Moreover, this section of the manuscript was just the type of small *libellus* that might have been used in Hilduin's chapel. Perhaps this oldest part of the manuscript was commissioned from Saint-Amand for employment in the new oratory in the ninth century and later became part of the composite volume F:R(m), A. 566. When the manuscript came into the area of Rouen is not known, but Nebbiai-Dalla Guarda traces its provenance from the sixteenth century onwards in that region.

27. *GB:Lva 1346–1891: London, Victoria and Albert Museum 1346–1891*

Notated missal, mid-fourteenth century, probably copied between 22 February and 22 August 1350 (Pl. 20).
Vellum. 448 folios (fos. 1–439 + 9 added fos., numbered 1–9). 232 × 170 mm.
Bibliography: Misset and Weale, *Analecta*, ii. 530–41; Laborde, *Manuscrits*, 207, 232, n. 5; Wilmart, 'Anniversaires', 22–31; Victoria and Albert Museum Library, *Catalogue*, ii (pp. unnumbered); White, *Birth*, 222–3; Huglo (1), 'Chants', 79–80; Huglo (2), 'Règlement', 130; Pächt and Alexander, *Manuscripts*, ii. 47; Ker, *Manuscripts*, i. 387; Avril (1), 'Chef-d'œuvre', 112–14; Schmidt, 'Datierung', 57; Avril (2), *Enluminure*, 25, 35–6, 80–3; Lemaître, *Répertoire*, 600; *Fastes*, 321–2 (No. 273); Winter, '*Heures*', 805; Byrne, 'Drawing', 71–4; Walters [Robertson], 'Reconstruction', 205–32; Nebbiai-Dalla Guarda, *Bibliothèque*, 313, 319; Rasmussen, 'Liturgy', 42; Huglo (3), 'Remarques'.

Wilmart dates this missal in the first half of 1350 on the basis of the obits listed in the calendar. The latest necrological notice is for Abbot Guido of Châtres (d. 22 February 1350), and since King Philip VI, who died on 22 August of the same year, is not mentioned, Wilmart concludes that GB:Lva 1346–1891 was copied during this period of six months. His estimation of the date, although an argument *ex silentio*, is probably correct, for the death-days of every king from Robert II (d. 20 July 1031) to Philip's immediate predecessor, Charles IV (d. 1 February 1328), are recorded in the calendar.

[113] These services appear in the 1st layer of the MS, as described above. The Masses are presented as follows: the prayers and readings are given (fos. 1–7^{v}) for each service under the rubrics '*Missa in honore dei genetricis et omnium sanctorum*' (= Mass No. 1), '*Alia missa*' (= No. 2) . . . '*Alia missa*' (= No. 7). On fos. 8^{r-v} the textual incipits for the introit, gradual, offertory, and communion are provided under the rubrics '*Officia ad praedictas missas*' (= No. 1), '*Item alia*' (= No. 2) . . . '*Item alia*' (= No. 7).

The text of GB:Lva 1346–1891 includes all the feasts adopted at Saint-Denis in the fourteenth century, and its contents represent the final stage of liturgical growth of the monastery. In general, the missal is more specific than its thirteenth-century counterpart F:Pn, lat. 1107. It often gives in considerable detail the contents of such three-lesson feasts as Saint Sulpicius (17 January; fo. 247), which is omitted from the text of F:Pn, lat. 1107. Curiously, the Mass for Saint Silvester appears both in the *temporale* (fo. 39^{v}) and in the *sanctorale* (fo. 235^{v}) of GB:Lva 1346–1891 with one and the same formulary. The votive service *Pro familiaribus* (fos. 252^{v}–253^{v}) corresponds to the *Missa pro amico* in F:Pn, lat. 1107 (fos. 327–328), except that the Offer. *Populum humilem* is given with the first of its verses *Clamor meus* in GB:Lva 1346–1891. Like F:Pn, lat. 1107, GB:Lva 1346–1891 contains a *Kyriale* (fos. 364–369^{v}) and a sequentiary (fos. 370–430^{v}), and the latter is apparently the sole surviving testimony of several new sequence texts which were probably written at Saint-Denis in the fourteenth century: *Christo regi glorie* for Saint Hilary of Poitiers, *Laudemus omnes* for Saint Hippolytus, and *Ave pater gallie* for Saint Denis (Table 4.5). The sequentiary of GB:Lva 1346–1891 also incorporates four antiphons to be sung before the gospel on Christmas (*Verbum caro*), Easter (*Crucem sanctam*[114]), Pentecost (*Hodie completi sunt*), and Saint-Denis (*O beate Dyonisi*; see Pl. 20).

Although GB:Lva 1346–1891 clearly contains the liturgy of Saint-Denis, it evidently was not copied in the abbey. Avril (2) shows that the sumptuous illuminations in the manuscript are characteristic of a new naturalist style cultivated in Parisian ateliers under the patronage of King John (1350–64), and he suggests that the book was presented to the abbey by a member of the royal household. Much of the later provenance of the volume, including how and when the manuscript was transported across the Channel, is unclear prior to the eighteenth century. The English binding of the missal, which dates from this time, demonstrates that the book was no longer in the abbey. The nine folios added at the end of the volume contain an *Ordo ad catechuminum faciendum* from a book belonging to Ferry de Clugny (d. 1483), who served as bishop of Tournai before his elevation to cardinal in 1480. This suggests that the missal may yet have been in French-speaking territory in the late fifteenth century, passing into English hands in the early sixteenth century, during which period Henry VIII controlled Tournai. The Victoria and Albert Museum Library acquired the missal in 1891 from the sale of the collection of W. Horatio Crawford.

[114] Walters [Robertson], 'Reconstruction', fig. 2.

28. GB:Ob, Can. Lit. 192: Oxford, Bodleian Library, Can. Lit. 192 (19309)

Unnotated breviary, mid-fourteenth century, copied perhaps between 22 February and 22 August 1350 as companion book to the notated missal GB:Lva 1346–1891.

Parchment. 556 folios. 250 × 175 mm.

Bibliography: Madan, *Catalogue*, iv. 354; Frere, *Bibliotheca*, i. 36; Van Dijk, *Handlist*, ii/2. 244; Pächt and Alexander, *Manuscripts*, ii. 47; Hesbert, *CAO*, vol. v, vi (MS 755); Nebbiai-Dalla Guarda, *Bibliothèque*, 176, 313, 319.

The calendar of GB:Ob, Can. Lit. 192, which is almost an exact replica of the one found in the notated missal GB:Lva 1346–1891,[115] includes the same obits which were used to date GB:Lva 1346–1891 in the first half of 1350. The similarity of these calendars and the comparable decoration and contents of the two texts led Pächt and Alexander to suspect that GB:Ob, Can. Lit. 192 was conceived as a companion volume for the notated missal. Like the missal, GB:Ob, Can. Lit. 192 incorporates all the festivals which were celebrated at Saint-Denis at the end of the Middle Ages and which continued to be solemnized there at least up to the mid-sixteenth century. The breviary preserves many of the texts of antiphons and responsories which are found in the twelfth-century antiphoner F:Pn, lat. 17296. It differs markedly from F:Pn, lat. 17296, however, in the Offices for Saints Cucuphas, Maurice, and Hilary of Mende, for the earlier antiphoner transmits the old proper Offices for these saints, while GB:Ob, Can. Lit. 192 replaces them largely with selections from the *commune sanctorum*. The breviary includes some of the texts of hymns which were sung during the Offices in the abbey. Likewise, the two characteristic series of responsories for the ordinary and solemn services for the dead at Saint-Denis are present (fos. 538–540). The manuscript is somewhat disappointing, however, in its lack of rubrics relating to performance practice.

GB:Ob, Can. Lit. 192 contains all the components normally associated with breviaries, but in an unusual order, with the calendar following the *temporale* rather than placed at the beginning of the manuscript. On the surface, this arrangement suggests that the volume deviates from the standard layout of French sources, in which the calendar is normally placed first.[116] But the calendar is found in a separate gathering of ten folios (Frere's 'gathering r', fos. 189–198^{v}), and it could easily have been moved when the book was bound in its present form. If the binding took place in England, the ordering of

[115] The 2 small differences are listed in the introd. to App. A, 20 and 21 Nov.

[116] Hughes, *Manuscripts*, No. 890.

sections with the calendar placed second would be perfectly normal. Hence it is likely that GB:Ob, Can. Lit. 192 was written in France, and that the gatherings were reshuffled in England when the manuscript was rebound. Although there is no palaeographical evidence to suggest when the book was transported to England, it may have come with its presumed companion missal GB:Lva 1346–1891.

29. I:Rc 603: Rome, Biblioteca Casanatense 603 (B. IV. 25)

Unnotated missal, copied between 1271 and *c.*1297, probably *c.*1271. Parchment. 284 folios. 245 × 170 mm.

Bibliography: Ebner, *Missale*, 155; Molinier, *Obituaires*, i. 334–5; Wilmart, 'Anniversaires', 30; Dikmans, 'Obituaires' 640, n. 174; Saitta-Revignas, *Catalogo*, vi. 73; Lemaître, *Répertoire*, 599; Walters [Robertson], 'Reconstruction', 191; Nebbiai-Dalla Guarda, *Bibliothèque*, 317, 319; Rasmussen, 'Liturgy', 42; Huglo, 'Remarques'.

In the catalogue of the Casanatense Library, Saitta-Revignas describes the physical aspects of this manuscript, its later provenance, and states that the date of copying is after 1270, because the death of Louis IX—here called 'King Louis' rather than 'Saint Louis'—is written in the original hand of the calendar. This estimation should be amended, however, to 'after 1271'. The latest obit in the first hand of the calendar, copied at the same time as the body of the manuscript, is not that of Louis, but rather of his brother Alphonse of Poitou (d. 21? August 1271). Saitta-Revignas also suggests a *terminus ad quem* of 1297, on the basis of the addition of the feast of Saint Louis (25 August, fos. 179, 223), and this date is supported by the fact that the monks of Saint-Denis began to refer to Louis IX as 'Saint' Louis between 1296 and 1297 and probably instigated the observance of his feast at this time. Like the notated missal F:Pn, lat. 1107, I:Rc 603 contains all feasts that had been added to the liturgy of the monastery by 1259 and none of the changes of rank that occurred in the fourteenth century. Furthermore, the style of the decoration resembles that of F:Pn, lat. 1107, which belongs to Branner's 'Cholet group' from the Sainte-Chapelle atelier, a style which flourished during the third quarter of the thirteenth century.[117] Hence it is likely that I:Rc 603 was written shortly after 1271.

The usage of this missal at Saint-Denis is established through its calendar and contents, which exemplify the liturgical practice of the abbey in the second half of the thirteenth century. The feast of Thomas of Canterbury (29 December) appears both in the *temporale* (fo. 23)

[117] Branner, *Painting*, 130–2. The author speculates that the stylistic changes which define the MSS of this circle may have taken place in the 1260s.

and in the *sanctorale* (fo. 180), with the same formulary from the *commune sanctorum*, except for the choice of gospel reading. Certain additions to I:Rc 603 show that the book was probably used in the divine celebration more often than its copyists had foreseen: the texts of musical items for the Sundays after Pentecost are written out in the lower margins of fos. 149–74, expanding on what were originally only incipits in the body of the manuscript.

30. I:Rvat, Reg. lat. 257: Rome, Biblioteca Apostolica Vaticana, Reg. lat. 257

Sacramentary, first half of or mid-eighth century, copied in the area of Poitiers or of Paris–Corbie–Soissons, later provenance Saint-Denis. Parchment. 150 folios. 232 × 146 mm.

Bibliography: Delisle, *Sacramentaires*, 71–3; Wilmart (1), 'Psautier'; Lowe, *CLA*, i. 103; Lesne, *Scriptoria*, 37, 592; Wilmart (2), *Codices*, ii. 22–4; Mohlberg *et al.*, *Francorum* (edn. of I:Rvat, Reg. lat. 257); Bourque, *Sacramentaires*, ii. 395–6; Gamber (1), *Sakramentartypen*, 61; Dekkers, *Clavis*, 437; Gamber (2), *CLLA*, i. 231–2; Biblioteca Vaticana, *Centenario*, 13–14; Kleinheyer, 'Studien', 96; McKitterick, 'Scriptoria', 193, 194; Chavasse, 'Oraisons', 43, 46, 54, 61–4; Nebbiai-Dalla Guarda, *Bibliothèque*, 80, 85, 101, 106, 138, 229, 259, 283, 287, 379, 382; Vogel, *Liturgy*, 108.

I:Rvat, Reg. lat. 257 is commonly known as the *Missale Francorum*, because of its Gallican heritage and because it contains a Mass 'pro regibus [Francorum]'. A recent catalogue from the Vatican Library attributes the copying of I:Rvat, Reg. lat. 257 'perhaps to Corbie or Saint-Denis'. Neither the Masses nor the saints listed in the canon of this Gallican book, however, suggest that it was written at or for the abbey; in fact, the liturgical evidence is insufficient to propose any assignment of origin. Mohlberg believes that I:Rvat, Reg. lat. 257 was copied around Poitiers during the first half of the eighth century, while Gamber (2) opts for the region of Paris–Corbie–Soissons in the mid-eighth century on the basis of the handwriting and decoration.

Whatever its beginnings may have been, the manuscript was later acquired by Saint-Denis, as demonstrated by the presence of the characteristic thirteenth- and fifteenth-century shelf-marks of the library of the abbey on fo. 1. Even if I:Rvat, Reg. lat. 257 came into the library of Saint-Denis at an early date, however, there is very little chance that the manuscript was much used in the celebration of the Divine Office. The new books from Rome which made great headway in Gaul in the eighth century rendered the Gallican text of I:Rvat, Reg. lat. 257 obsolete soon after it was written.

31. I:VEcap LXXXVIII: Verona, Biblioteca Capitolare (Cattedrale) LXXXVIII

Collection of readings for the day Hours, mid-ninth century (*c*.850), copied at Saint-Denis, later provenance Verona.
Parchment. iii + 80 + ii folios. 148 × 116 mm.
Bibliography: Ongaro, 'Cultura', 34–5, 50–1, 57–8, 61, 74; Venturini, *Vita*, 116; Turrini (1), *Biblioteca*, 21–6; Turrini (2), *Indice*, 12, 27, 40; Meersseman (1), *L'Orazionale*, 72; Borders, 'Verona', i. 233–43; ii. 455–7, 485–90; Meersseman (2), *Capitules* (edn. of I:VEcap LXXXVIII); Zivelonghi and Adami, *Codici*, 93.

Meersseman's (2) recent edition and study of I:VEcap LXXXVIII, once thought to have been a Veronese source, now attribute the book to Saint-Denis. The main portion of the volume (fos. 9–75^{v}) contains (1) the short readings that were heard after the psalms of the canonical Hours, (2) the texts for the proper Office for Saint Cucuphas (fos. 76–9), and (3) a number of shorter poetic texts (fos. 57–64^{v}, 80). A separate gathering (fos. 1–8^{v}), which Meersseman believes probably comes from Verona, was added to the beginning of this manuscript possibly in the seventeenth century. Two factors were especially important in Meersseman's determination that I:VEcap LXXXVIII was copied for Saint-Denis. First, the book contains a proper Office for Cucuphas, who was specially venerated at Saint-Denis. This Office mirrors exactly the one found in the eleventh-century antiphonary list from Saint-Denis F:Pm 384 (fos. 185^{v}–186) and in the twelfth-century antiphoner F:Pn, lat. 17296 (fos. 193^{v}–198^{v}) except for the reversal of the order of two responsories for Matins.[118] Second, the text in numerous places uses the question mark with two points that Jean Vezin has shown was characteristic of the ninth-century scriptorium of Saint-Denis.

Because the rubrics in I:VEcap LXXXVIII do not specify the Hours to which the readings in the manuscript were assigned, it is impossible to determine with complete assurance the precise times at which they were used. Meersseman's (2) study addresses this question in his comparison of the texts in I:VEcap LXXXVIII with those of other sources whose rubrics are more specific. We likewise do not know how or when the manuscript came into the Veronese library, although Borders mentions that Ilduinus and Ratherius, two tenth-century Benedictine French prelates who later became bishops at Verona, might have had something to do with the codex. In spite of its nebulous

[118] F:Pm 384 and F:Pn, lat. 17296 have *Jussit tyrannus* and *Domine jhesu christi* as 4th and 5th responsories, respectively, whereas I:VEcap LXXXVIII has them as 5th and 4th, respectively. This is not a serious discrepancy and can be explained by the difference in time of the 3 sources.

history, I:VEcap LXXXVIII is an important source for the early liturgy of Saint-Denis on two counts: it is the earliest extant manuscript for the Office and one of only three books for the Office (along with F:Psg 1186 and the antiphonary list in F:Pm 384) prior to the twelfth century; and it is the earliest liturgical source to contain the proper Office for Saint Cucuphas.

7

Liturgical Sources of Questionable Attribution

INTRODUCTION

From the first years of modern manuscript research, scholars have from time to time ascribed sources to Saint-Denis, only to have their views later called into question. Both the political importance of the abbey and the approximate periods of flowering of the scriptorium were recognized early on, and these prompted numerous attributions. More recent refinements in Sandionysian scholarship have brought about some adjustments in our thinking about these liturgical codices. The manuscripts that were actually used in the daily celebration of the Divine Office in the abbey can now be identified with greater precision.

The list of extant service books from Saint-Denis is in fact shorter than it once was. Excluded from it are a number of ninth- and tenth-century manuscripts, the liturgical implications of which are equivocal at best. Often in the past it was the style of decoration or the handwriting that led scholars to think of Saint-Denis as the place of origin of certain volumes. The presence, likewise, of one or more of the distinctive shelf-marks of the library of the abbey sometimes unduly influenced the assignment of a book to the scriptorium, when it may simply have been acquired by the monks at one time or another. In sum, the distinction between place of origin and place of destination of a codex has not always been carefully made, and mistaken attributions continue in the modern literature.

Of the thirteen sources surveyed below, a little more than half are sacramentaries from the eighth and ninth centuries. We have seen that the contents of this book evolved rapidly at this time, and no two surviving examples are exactly alike. Hence it is often difficult to determine the liturgical usage of sacramentaries, doubly so because details of the performance of the Mass and Offices in a house are much less certain at this time than for later periods. The need for practicality in these books outweighed the marks of individuality that might relate them to particular places. Indeed, monastic practices were in some respects undifferentiated until the eleventh century, and, as is apparent in the Mont-Renaud source, they often remained intertwined with the usages of the secular cathedrals on which the abbeys originally depended.

For sources produced from the eleventh century onwards, the determination of use is simpler. This is to be expected, since the features that distinguish the usages of different houses appeared more and more systematically in all genres of manuscript after this time. Yet even some later volumes have been wrongly evaluated with regard to origin, destination, or usage. For this reason, it seems appropriate to treat the sources whose attribution to Saint-Denis is in some way questionable, in order to try to clarify the connections of these books with the abbey. The manuscripts are grouped here according to category of relationship with Saint-Denis—if it exists at all—beginning with sources written at Saint-Denis for employment in other houses and ending with those which have been assigned to the abbey but clearly were never used there. Within each subdivision, the books are ordered alphabetically by library.

CATALOGUE OF LITURGICAL SOURCES OF QUESTIONABLE ATTRIBUTION

MANUSCRIPT WRITTEN AT SAINT-DENIS

32. F:Psg 111: Paris, Bibliothèque Sainte-Geneviève 111 (BB 20)

Unnotated gradual followed by a sacramentary, ninth century (copied probably at Saint-Denis between 877 and 882), usage of the cathedral of Senlis.

Bibliography: Delisle, *Sacramentaires*, 143–6, 313–24, 363–6, 371; Kohler, *Catalogue*, i. 68–71; Leroquais, *Sacramentaires*, i. 32–5; Hesbert, *AMS*, pp. xxiii–xxiv (inventory of F:Psg 111 [MS S]; Amiet, 'Prologue', 188; Beyssac, 'Mont-Renaud', 133–4; *GR* (MS *DEN* 7); Bourque, *Sacramentaires*, ii. 31–2; Samaran and Marichal, *Catalogue*, i. 323; Canal, 'Elementos', 291; Gamber, *CLLA*, ii. 352–3, 505; Deshusses, *Sacramentaire* (MS X); De Clerck, '"*Prière*"', 278–9; Huglo (1), 'Gallican', 116; Jeffery, 'Sources', 319; Nebbiai-Dalla Guarda, *Bibliothèque*, 316, 318; Vogel, *Liturgy*, 360; Huglo (2), 'Remarques'.

Delisle dated F:Psg 111 and recognized the signs of its destination for Senlis. Most of these indications are later additions: the name of bishop of Senlis Saint Sanctinus in the calendar (7 January), a tenth- and eleventh-century list of later prelates of this diocese (fo. 34), and references to persons or events pertaining to the cathedral (fos. II, III). But the name of reigning bishop of Senlis, Hadebertus (reg. after 871), is inscribed in the litany (fo. 24^{v}) in the original hand of the volume, and it is clear, therefore, that the book was in fact intended for use at Senlis.

The calendar of F:Psg 111, on the other hand, places the copying of the manuscript in the scriptorium of Saint-Denis (see Appendix A, MS G). Many entries support this estimation: the Vigil and feast of the patron saint (8, 9 October), the feast of the Dedication of the Church of Saint-Denis (24 February)—rather than that of the cathedral of Senlis (16 June)—the Invention of Saint Denis (22 April), the Consecration of the Altar (28 July), the Translation of the relics of Hilary, Innocent, and Peregrinus to the abbey (22 August), and the commemorations of several saints whose relics the abbey possessed (16 May, 25 July, 25 September, 25 October, etc.). The favoured saints of Senlis that one would expect to find in a book written in this city are by and large absent.[1] Furthermore, the calendar of F:Psg 111 is almost exactly duplicated in the late ninth-century sacramentary from Saint-Denis F:Pn, lat. 2290. Presumably the cathedral of Senlis commissioned F:Psg 111 from the abbey, perhaps shortly after the monks had resumed work in the scriptorium after their return from Consevreux in 876.

The calendar of F:Psg 111 includes important information on the celebration of the Divine Office at Saint-Denis, serving as a kind of directory of services, as noted in Chapter 2. For most feasts, an abbreviation in the right margin indicates the type of observance which apparently was to be held on that day. Delisle has interpreted these abbreviations as follows: '*pl. mis.*' = full Mass, '*pl. of.*' = full Office, '*mis. in gl.*' = Mass from a text of the eighth-century Gelasian sacramentary, '*com.*' = Mass or Office from the common of saints, '*com. et evgl.*' = Mass or Office from the common of saints with some of the lessons at Matins taken from gospel texts, and '*pl. of. et evangl.*' = full Office with some of the lessons at Matins taken from gospel texts. The abbreviations are in the original hand of the calendar and hence were written at Saint-Denis along with the rest of the manuscript. Comparison of these liturgical indications with the books for the Mass and Office from Saint-Denis shows that the abbreviations appear to refer to the daily ritual as it was performed in the abbey rather than at Senlis. The majority of feasts marked 'full Mass' in F:Psg 111 are found in the sacramentary from Saint-Denis F:Pn, lat. 2290. The entries marked 'full Office' correspond to festivals which probably were originally 'full', possibly nine-lesson Offices in the abbey, and which were later celebrated with twelve lessons and responsories at Matins. Included in this

[1] The calendar of F:Pn, lat. 1031, a late 13th- and early 14th-c. summer breviary from Senlis, contains the following 9-lesson feasts which are not present in F:Psg 111: the Translation of Richarius (30 Mar.), Mary of Egypt (2 Apr.), Saint Prothasia (20 May), the Dedication of the Church (16 June) and its Octave (23 June), Saint Leonorius (1 July), Saint Arnulf (18 July), Saint Frambaldus (16 Aug.), Saint Fiacre (30 Aug.), Saint Vigor (3 Nov.), Saint Maxentia (20 Nov.), Queen Oda (21 Nov.), Saints Fuscian *et al.* (11 Dec.).

category of 'full Office' are feasts of singular importance at Saint-Denis, notably the Dedication of the Church (24 February) and Saint Peregrinus (16 May), neither of which were observed at Senlis. The abbreviations in the calendar of F:Psg 111 thus are doubly significant with respect to the history of the Divine Office at Saint-Denis. Not only do they confirm the Sandionysian feasts known from contemporaneous books of the Mass from the ninth century, but they likewise provide early evidence of the shape of the antiphoner and breviary of the abbey, whose first extant witness is the eleventh-century antiphonary list in F:Pm 384.

The alleluia list of F:Psg 111 for the Sundays after Pentecost, like the series from Saint-Denis, begins with the Ver. *In te domine speravi*, and Beyssac shows that the two lists are alike. Two verses in F:Psg 111, *Adorabo* (Sunday XIX) and *Redemptionem* (Sunday XXII), do not appear in the Saint-Denis list after the mid-eleventh century (see Table 3.1). Huglo (2) demonstrates that they are found in several other houses whose series likewise begin with the Ver. *In te domine speravi*: Winchester, Bury St Edmunds, Corbie, and Reims.

Like F:LA 118, the unnotated gradual of F:Psg 111 includes the verses of offertories as well as the psalms and *versus ad repetendum* for communions. Immediately before the sacramentary begins, a Mass for Saint Denis (fo. 30^{v}) is added in a tenth- or eleventh-century hand. Apart from mentions of the saint in the calendar, this is the only appearance of Saint Denis in the manuscript. As to the type of sacramentary represented by F:Psg 111, Deshusses notes that the book contains many rearrangements and additions, such that the text of the *Hadrianum* is hardly distinguishable. The principal features of the supplement of Benedict of Aniane are nevertheless recognizable.

THE COURT SCHOOL OF CHARLES THE BALD

The three sources listed in this category are from the group of deluxe manuscripts that art historians ascribe to the court school of Charles the Bald on the basis of their decoration. Although the name 'court school' implies that the style was clearly associated with the reign of Charles the Bald (840–77), the precise location of the workshop that produced these books is not known, and it is generally agreed that its scribes and illuminators may in fact have been itinerant, rather than attached to a single institution. In the past, scholars have frequently mentioned the areas of Saint-Denis/Reims and Saint-Denis/Corbie as possible candidates for the origin of sources now assigned to this school. Three copyists, Ingobertus, Liuthard, and Berenger, are associated with this style, and the last two assisted in the copying and illumination of two sources described below: D:Mbs, Clm. 14000 and F:Pn, lat. 1152.[2]

33. D:Mbs, Clm. 14000: Munich, Bayerische Staatsbibliothek, Clm. 14000

Evangeliary, copied in 870 by Liuthard and Berenger in the court school of Charles the Bald, later provenance Saint-Emmeram of Ratisbon.

Bibliography: Delisle, *Cabinet*, i. 6; Goldschmidt, *Elfenbeiskulpturen*, i. 5; Leidinger, *Codex* (facsimile edn. of D:Mbs, Clm. 14000); Klauser, *Capitulare*, p. lv; Lesne, *Scriptoria*, 211–12, 591; Honburger, 'Schule', 425; Bischoff (1), 'Hofbibliothek'; Hubert *et al.*, *Empire*, 351; Bischoff (2), *Schreibschulen*, i. 225; ii. 15, 241; Mütherich and Gaedhe, *Painting*, 15–17, 27, pls. 35–8; Vandersall, 'Relationship', 201 and *passim*; Brubaker, 'Codex'; Guilmain, 'Illumination', 106; Köhler and Mütherich, *Hofschule*, 175–98; Dutton and Jeauneau, 'Verses' (includes survey of earlier literature on D:Mbs, Clm. 14000); Calkins (1), *Books*, 119–45, 293; Calkins (2), *Programs*, 33–8, 63–7, 104–5, figs. 56–63; Nebbiai-Dalla Guarda, *Bibliothèque*, 73, 323; Crosby, *Abbey*, 95; McKitterick, *Carolingians*, 148.

The sumptuous D:Mbs, Clm. 14000, also known as the *Codex Aureus*, was copied in 870 by two brothers, Liuthard and Berenger, and it bears a dedicatory preface to King Charles the Bald. Three aspects of this gospel book suggest that it may have been written at Saint-Denis: the magnificence of its decoration, the facts that Liuthard was a monk of Saint-Denis and that F:Pn, lat. 1152 likewise is attributed to him, and the lay abbacy of Charles at Saint-Denis during this period. Mütherich and Gaedhe and Köhler and Mütherich, however, emphasize that the connection with Saint-Denis remains hypothetical and that the physical characteristics of D:Mbs, Clm. 14000 and F:Pn, lat. 1152 are reminiscent of the style of the court school of Charles the Bald. Wherever D:Mbs, Clm. 14000 may have originated, political events caused the codex to be taken from Frankish territory. Leidinger relates that King Eudes of France (888–98) may have offered the volume to King Arnoul of Germany (887–99), who in turn presented it to the monks of Saint-Emmeram of Ratisbon. This convent reminded Saint-Denis of its possession of the manuscript on the occasion of the famous eleventh-century controversy between Saint-Denis and Saint-Emmeram over the relics of Saint Denis, which gave rise to the feast of the Detection of Saint Denis (9 June).

[2] For recent discussions of the court school, see Mütherich and Gaedhe, *Painting*, 15–17; Vandersall, 'Relationship', 201; Dutton and Jeauneau, 'Verses', 77 (and the studies cited in their n. 14); Crosby, *Abbey*, 95.

34. F:Pn, lat. 1141: Paris, Bibliothèque Nationale, lat. 1141

Fragment of a sacramentary, ninth century (*c*.870), copied in the court school of Charles the Bald, later provenance Metz.

Bibliography: Delisle, *Sacramentaires*, 146–8; Leroquais, *Sacramentaires*, i. 35–6; Friend, 'Manuscripts', 63–70; Bibliothèque Nationale (1), *Catalogue*, i. 417; Bibliothèque Nationale (2), *Manuscrits* (1954), 27–8, No. 53; Honburger, *Schule*, 425; Bourque, *Sacramentaires*, ii. 53; Gamber, *CLLA*, ii. 357–8; Hubert *et al.*, *Empire*, 351; Deshman, 'Servant', 400; Mütherich, *Sakramentar* (facsimile edn. of F:Pn, lat. 1141); Mütherich and Gaedhe, *Painting*, 27, pls. 32–4; Vandersall, 'Relationship', 201; Köhler and Mütherich, *Hofschule*, 165; Calkins, *Books*, 177–9, 298; Nebbiai-Dalla Guarda, *Bibliothèque*, 73, 324; Crosby, *Abbey*, 95.

The similarity of the decoration of F:Pn, lat. 1141 to F:Pn, lat. 2292 led Friend to posit Saint-Denis as the scriptorium that produced this de luxe manuscript. Too few folios remain, however, to permit a determination of origin on liturgical grounds, and the handwriting is likewise equivocal. Earlier writers, such as Honburger, Bourque, Gamber, and Hubert, attributed the script to Corbie or to the 'school' of Corbie–Saint-Denis, but Mütherich, Gaedhe, and Köhler have more recently suggested that the handwriting is characteristic of manuscripts associated with the court school of Charles the Bald. The codex was later presented to the cathedral of Metz.

35. F:Pn, lat. 1152: Paris, Bibliothèque Nationale, lat. 1152

Psalter, ninth century (between *c*.842 and 869), copied by Liuthard for King Charles the Bald in the court school.

Bibliography: Delisle (1), *Cabinet*, i. 6, 449, 479; iii, 320–1; Delisle (2), 'Mystère', 2; 'Les Rois', 657–8; Berger, *Vulgate*, 404; Burn, *Creed*, 2, 4–6; Goldschmidt, *Elfenbeiskulpturen*, i. 24; *DACL*, xii/2, cols. 1981–8; Lesne, *Scriptoria*, 211; Bibliothèque Nationale (1), *Catalogue*, i. 420; Leroquais, *Psautiers*, vol. i, p. cvii; ii. 67–70; Bibliothèque Nationale (2), *Manuscrits* (1954), 27, No. 52; Honburger, 'Schule', 425; Samaran and Marichal, *Catalogue*, ii. 59; Coens, 'Litanies', 298–300; Gamber, *CLLA*, ii. 585; Hubert *et al.*, *Empire*, 351; Huglo, 'Review' (1969), 227; Corbin, 'Jeu', 51–2; Seebass, *Musikdarstellung*, i. 182; Bischoff, *Schreibschulen*, i. 225; Mütherich and Gaedhe, *Painting*, 15; Deshman, 'Servant' , 404; Vandersall, 'Relationship', 201; McKitterick, 'Library', 37; Köhler and Mütherich, *Hofschule*, 132–43; Dutton and Jeauneau, 'Verses', 102; Nebbiai-Dalla Guarda, *Bibliothèque*, 73, 325; Rasmussen, 'Liturgy', 41; Crosby, *Abbey*, 95; McKitterick (2), *Carolingians*, 148, 157, 268–9.

The reasons for assigning the magnificent psalter of Charles the Bald (F:Pn, lat. 1152) to Saint-Denis are mentioned above in the discussion of D:Mbs, Clm. 14000. Hubert and Honburger assigned the script and decoration of the book to the 'school' of Corbie–Saint-Denis, and other possible connections to Saint-Denis include the names found in the litany (fos. 170–171ᵛ, published by Leroquais), which incorporate saints whose relics were present in the abbey: Denis, Rusticus, Eleutherius, Hippolytus, Fiminus, Eustace, Cucuphas, Peregrinus, and Hilary. Mütherich, Gaedhe, and Köhler, however, have noted that these features are characteristic of the court school of Charles the Bald, and they date the manuscript approximately between 842 and 869. In addition, the copyist of F:Pn, lat. 1152, Liuthard, was a monk of Saint-Denis.[3] Leroquais shows that the illuminations and inscriptions in the manuscript prove that it was intended as a book of private devotion for Charles the Bald. Hence, no one in the community at Saint-Denis probably ever actually used F:Pn, lat. 1152, and for this reason the book is not treated in Chapter 6. It is possible, however, that the psalter was often present or perhaps was even kept in the abbey. Charles the Bald was lay abbot of Saint-Denis after 867, and he may well have consulted the manuscript during his frequent visits there.

Like the Chapel Hill psalter, F:Pn, lat. 103 and F:Psg 1186, the text of F:Pn, lat. 1152 is a Gallican psalter complete with the editorial symbols that Jerome and his predecessor Origen used to distinguish omissions and additions made to the original Hebrew text of the psalms by the translators of the Septuagint.[4] Versicles, lessons, and responsories for each day of the ferial Office are provided after Pss. 25, 37, 51, 67, 79, 96, and 108.

In 869, Charles the Bald offered F:Pn, lat. 1152 as a gift to the Cathedral of Metz, possibly, as McKitterick suggests, in conjunction with his coronation as king of Lorraine in that year. The psalter was still in the possession of the canons of Metz in the seventeenth century, and it was no doubt in this region that a fragment of the liturgical drama *The Magi Kings*, notated in Messine neumes, was incorporated as a flyleaf (fo. 173ᵛ) in the eleventh century.[5]

36. F:Pn, lat. 2292: Paris, Bibliothèque Nationale, lat. 2292

Sacramentary, copied shortly before 876, origin court school of Charles the Bald, later provenance Nonantola.

[3] On the copyist/poet Liuthard, see Chevalier, Bio-*Bibliographie*, ii, col. 2844. It is possible that he is the 'Leotardus' or 'Leutardus' whose name is inscribed in the 9th-c. list of monks of the abbey, preserved in F: LA 118, fo. 74ᵛ (published in Wilmart, 'Frères', 247; and in Oexle, *Forschungen*, 28, Nos. 89, 125 [see also his unnumbered 5th pl.]).

[4] Leroquais mistakenly states that the use of these 'astérisques et obèles' is discontinued after the 5th psalm.

[5] See Delisle, 'Mystère'; 'Rois'; Corbin, 'Jeu', 51–2.

Bibliography: Delisle, *Sacramentaires*, 126–8; Leroquais, *Sacramentaires*, i. 28–30; Friend, 'Manuscripts', 60–3; Bibliothèque Nationale, *Catalogue*, ii. 392; Brou, 'Sacramentaire'; Bourque, *Sacramentaires*, ii. 15–16; Samaran and Marichal, *Catalogue*, ii. 530; Gamber, *CLLA*, ii. 357; Deshusses, *Sacramentaire* (MS N); Martimort, *Documentation*, 92; Passalacqua, *Codici*, 29; Köhler and Mütherich, *Hofschule*, 199; Nebbiai-Dalla Guarda, *Bibliothèque*, 315, 318; Rasmussen, 'Liturgy', 41.

Friend assigned F:Pn, lat. 2292, along with F:Pn, lat. 1141, to the scriptorium of Saint-Denis on the basis of its decoration. He also noted the close connection between the monastery and King Charles the Bald, who was lay abbot after 865, and who might have caused this beautiful manuscript to be copied. Liturgical evidence does not support the attribution to Saint-Denis, however, and Gamber and Köhler ascribe F:Pn, lat. 2292 instead to the court school of Charles the Bald. With respect to the later provenance of the book, Delisle points out a note on fo. 6^{v}, which explains that John, bishop of Arezzo and envoy to Charles, offered the manuscript to the Italian abbey of Nonantola, where it was later adapted to the usage of this house through the addition of Masses for the saints especially honoured there. John's mission to France took place in 876, and Samaran and Marichal place the date of F:Pn, lat. 2292 just before this time. Deshusses likewise estimates that the sacramentary was copied in the third quarter of the ninth century, and he shows that F:Pn, lat. 2292 represents the type *Hadrianum* complemented by the supplement of Benedict of Aniane, and containing certain peculiarities which demonstrate a mixture of other influences.

MANUSCRIPTS FORMERLY ASSIGNED TO SAINT-DENIS

37. I:Rvat, Ott. lat. 313: Rome, Biblioteca Apostolica Vaticana, Ott. lat. 313

Sacramentary, mid-ninth century, northern France, adapted to usage of Notre Dame of Paris.

Bibliography: Delisle, *Sacramentaires*, 149–50; Wilson, *Gregorian* (older edn. of the Gregorian sacramentary, using I:Rvat, Ott. lat. 313 for variant readings); Bishop, *Liturgica*, 64; Rand, *Survey*, 173; Handschin, 'Neumenschrift', 89; *GR* (MS *DEN* 6); Bourque, *Sacramentaires*, ii. 27–8; Canal, 'Elementos', 290; Gamber, *CLLA*, ii. 350–1; Mütherich, 'Scriptorium', 211; Salmon, *Manuscrits*, vol. i. No. 460; ii. No. 17; iii. No. 52, 184; Deshusses (1), *Sacramentaire* (MS P); Oexle, *Forschungen*, 82–90 (bibliog. on I:Rvat, Ott. lat. 313, p. 82, n. 337); Sicard, *Liturgie* (MS *Alk*); Deshusses (2), 'Anciens', 294; Biblioteca Vaticana, *Centenario*, 63; *NGD*, xiii. 346; Vogüé and Neufville, 'Pères', 132; Jeffery, 'Sources', 320; Dykmans, 'Préface',

63; Nebbiai-Dalla Guarda, *Bibliothèque*, 327–8; Vogel, *Liturgy*, 90; Huglo, *Livres*, 121; Saxer, 'Observations', 31–3, 34; Wright, *Notre Dame*, 62–6.

I:Rvat, Ott. lat. 313 was long thought to be the purest example of the Gregorian sacramentary (*Hadrianum*) with the supplement of Benedict of Aniane. Deshusses (1), however, has recently pointed to a number of variants whose origins are difficult to trace, and considers the book to be a text of the *Hadrianum* augmented by Benedict and further corrected from the other types of Gregorian manuscript. The origin of I:Rvat, Ott. lat. 313 has been repeatedly misstated. A recent catalogue of the Vatican Library assigns I:Rvat, Ott. lat. 313 to the abbey of Saint-Martin of Tours or Saint-Denis, and the provenance of the manuscript is listed as 'Saint-Denis' in *The New Grove Dictionary*. Liturgical evidence does not support the attribution of this sacramentary to the abbey, and Mütherich notes that the palaeography and decoration suggest its relationship to the ninth-century scriptorium of Saint-Germain-des-Prés. If I:Rvat, Ott. lat. 313 did originate there, some liturgical influence from Saint-Denis is possible, since the two houses had close ties in the ninth century, when abbots of Saint-Denis often served as abbots of Saint-Germain.

Delisle and Wilson show that the sacramentary seems to have been moved soon after it was copied, for the saints designated at the end of the canon of the Mass and the lists of names added to the codex suggest that it was probably used at Notre Dame of Paris. Oexle's further study of these names shows that the manuscript must have been in service at Notre Dame between 849 and 851. He concludes that I:Rvat, Ott. lat. 313 was copied slightly before this time, although Saxer has recently chosen a late year, 855.

38. I:Rvat, Reg. lat. 316: Rome, Biblioteca Apostolica Vaticana, Reg. lat. 316; and F:Pn, lat. 7193: Paris, Bibliothèque Nationale, lat. 7193 (fos. 41–56ᵛ)

Sacramentary, mid-eighth century, copied probably at Chelles, destination possibly Saint-Denis.

Bibliography: Delisle, *Sacramentaires*, 66–8; Wilson, *Gelasian*; Bishop, *Liturgica*, 43; Duchesne, *Origines*, 124–5; Gastoué, 'Origines' (1902/3), 142, 156; Zimmermann, *Miniaturen*, 78–84; Lowe (1), 'Vatican'; Lowe (2), *Papers*, i. 217–20; Frere, *Kalendar*, 36; Lowe (3), *CLA*, i. 31, 43a; Wilmart, *Codices*, ii. 200–4; Bourque, *Sacramentaires* i, 173–80 (bibliog. on I:Rvat, Reg. lat. 316 up to 1940); Schmidt, 'Bibliographia' (bibliog. on I:Rvat, Reg. lat. 316 to 1953), 731–3; Bischoff, 'Nonnenhandschriften'; Chavasse (1), *Gélasien* (bibliog. on I:Rvat, Reg. lat. 316 to 1958); Dekkers, *Clavis*, 424–5; Martimort, 'Recherches', 32–6; Gamber, *CLLA*, i. 301–3; Deshusses (2),

Sacramentaire, i. 51, 81; iii. 81; Montessus, 'Sacramentaires', 274; Michelini Tocci, *Gelasianum* (facsimile edn. of I:Rvat, Reg. lat. 316); Moreton (1), *Gelasian*; Moreton (2), 'Festival'; Ziegler, 'Sacramentarium'; De Clerck, '*Prière*', 125; Chavasse (2), 'Sermonnaire', 265, 280; Sicard, *Liturgie* (MS *V*); Chavasse (3), 'Homilaire', 211, 214, 225; Kleinheyer, 'Studien', 96; Atkinson (1), '*O Amnos*', 12; Eizenhöfer, 'Beobachtungen'; McKitterick, 'Scriptoria', 189–92, 194, 195; Mohlberg *et al.*, *Liber* (edn. of I:Rvat, Reg. lat. 316 and F:Pn, lat. 7193); Atkinson (2), 'Entstehung', 124, 127, 136; Deshusses (2), 'Sacramentaires', 28; Chavasse (4), 'Oraisons', 33, and *passim*; Chavasse (5), '*Gélasiens*' (MS V); Janini, 'Oraciones'; Nebbiai-Dalla Guarda, *Bibliothèque*, 328; Vogel, *Liturgy*, 31, 64–70, 165; Atkinson (3), '*Doxa*', 83, 86, 92; Chavasse (6), 'Aménagements', 75–8; Wright, *Notre Dame*, 64.

As early as the seventeenth century, I:Rvat, Reg. lat. 316 was recognized as one of the most illustrious survivors from the ranks of early liturgical codices. The major portion of the manuscript is contained in the volume belonging to the Regina Collection in the Vatican Library in Rome. The two final gatherings, detached some time before 1651, were discovered by Lowe (1) in a manuscript now in Paris, F:Pn, lat. 7193. Theologians and liturgists alike have since scrutinized this sacramentary to determine its connections with Rome and with Gaul, as well as its role in the development of the other types of sacramentary. Antoine Chavasse's (1) monumental study of the contents of the manuscript defined the category to which it belongs: he terms it 'Gelasian supplemented in Gaul'.

Yet no amount of study—liturgical, palaeographical, or art historical—has been able to unearth incontrovertible evidence regarding the origin of I:Rvat, Reg. lat. 316 itself. Indeed, such findings about books of this period are rare, since so few of them contain features that substantiate an attribution to one house rather than another. Authors in the nineteenth and early twentieth centuries suggested Saint-Denis because of the presence of the partially erased names '[dionysii, rustici] et eleutherii' in the canon of the Mass (fo. 180), and the precedence given them over the other French saints that are listed. A connection with the abbey solely on this basis is unlikely, however, for Saint Denis was well known in north-eastern France by this time. At best, the inclusion of Rusticus and Eleutherius delimits the region of copying to the Île-de-France, where the association of the three saints as a unit was just gaining popularity. Wilmart conjectured the scriptorium of Corbie, but Lowe (3) cited the handwriting of a portion of the manuscript as evidence against this house.

It was Bernhard Bischoff who offered the most plausible theory when he proposed the convent of Chelles as centre for the copying of a number of manuscripts, among them I:Rvat, Reg. lat. 316. Lying only

19 km. to the east of Paris, this Benedictine abbey had boasted a close rapport with both French and Anglo-Saxon ruling houses since its foundation by Queen Bathildis in the middle of the seventh century.[6] Its status with respect to the Carolingian throne was only enhanced toward the end of the eighth century under the leadership of Abbess Giselle (b. 757), daughter of Pepin the Short and sister of Charlemagne.[7] The production of codices in this convent is documented from her reign, and Ziegler dates the earliest surviving sources from this scriptorium in the 740s. Bischoff identifies a type of script known as 'nun-minuscule', which seems to have originated at Chelles and which is evident in I:Rvat, Reg. lat. 316.

If the reasons for assigning I:Rvat, Reg. lat. 316 to the scriptorium of Chelles are well founded, the evidence that may point to Saint-Denis as the destination of the manuscript is somewhat less compelling. The codex was written and decorated with an eye to the aesthetic. A single hand appears to have executed most of the text, and the ornamentation is likewise colourful and artistically unified. There are few corrections, and Wilmart mentions only one addition (fos. 195^{r-v}) from the ninth century. The manuscript is in fact preserved in remarkably fine condition, almost devoid of signs of wear from the period immediately following its compilation, dated by Zimmermann to around 750 and more recently by Ziegler to 740–50. This is not surprising, for at the time I:Rvat, Reg. lat. 316 was written, sacramentaries of this type ('Gelasian supplemented in Gaul') were being superseded in Gaul by the 'Gelasian of the eighth century'. The book probably received little actual use.

What reasons might have existed, then, for the production of a splendid but virtually superannuated codex (I:Rvat, Reg. lat. 316) in the Île-de-France around the middle of the eighth century? While the answer will probably never be known, the evidence of a growing interest in liturgical matters at Saint-Denis at precisely this time may shed some light on the question. During Pope Stephen's sojourn in the abbey in 754, he was surrounded by retainers not only from the papal *Schola*, but also from the suburban churches in which the liturgy of the Gelasian sacramentary type developed. One can fairly assume that the celebration of the Divine Service received special attention in the abbey during the pope's extended stay. On the eve of the Carolingian reform, this attention probably consisted of displays of Roman and native Gallican practice. No doubt the cantors from the outlying churches of Rome would have taken particular interest in the Gallicanized form that

[6] In addition to Bischoff's article, see *GC*, vii, cols. 558–60.

[7] Giselle granted certain dependencies to Saint-Denis in 799; see Félibien, *Histoire*, 63, and his *PJ*, vol. i, No. lxv.

the Gelasian liturgy had recently assumed in Gaul ('Gelasian supplemented in Gaul'). And while Metz was the principal centre for the diffusion of the Roman rite in Gaul, the witness of papal and royal patronage of Saint-Denis at this time suggests that the abbey likewise occupied a privileged place with regard to the liturgy, at least in the region of Paris. It was Abbot Fulrad of Saint-Denis whose ambassadorship had prepared the way for the installation of the Carolingian line; indeed, the very act of unction had taken place at Saint-Denis in 754. Shortly thereafter Pope Stephen reputedly fell ill and was miraculously healed in the abbey.

These factors illustrate the political prominence of Saint-Denis at the moment I:Rvat, Reg. lat. 316 was copied. But the manuscript itself adds something further. Because I:Rvat, Reg. lat. 316 appears to have had little wear, it might have been intended as a presentation or display copy, one produced in the most renowned scriptorium in the area, Chelles. That is, the sacramentary may have been written not so much for use as in order to enshrine a current but quickly dying liturgy.[8] In this case, the destination of I:Rvat, Reg. lat. 316 would have been a house that had an interest in such a liturgico-historical document. Given the importance of Saint-Denis in Paris at this time, it is plausible that the abbey was the recipient of this splendid book. If this is the case, a hypothesis for the destination of I:Rvat, Reg. lat. 316 (Saint-Denis) can be added to Bischoff's and Ziegler's theory for the origin (Chelles) of the manuscript.

39. I:Rvat, Reg. lat. 337: Rome, Biblioteca Apostolica Vaticana, Reg. lat. 337

Sacramentary, ninth century (first/second quarter, perhaps 835–8), copied at Lyon.

Bibliography: Wilson, *Gregorian* (older edn. of the Gregorian sacramentary based primarily on I:Rvat, Reg. lat. 337); Bishop, *Liturgica*, 64; Wilmart, *Codices*, ii. 255–7; Amiet, 'Prologue', 196; Bourque, *Sacramentaires*, ii. 16; Canal, 'Elementos', 290; Gamber, *CLLA*, ii. 343–4; Deshusses (1), *Sacramentaire* (MS L); Sicard, *Liturgie* (manuscript *Alg*); Heiming, 'Benedictiones', 122; Deshusses (2), 'Sacramentaires', 42; Nebbiai-Dalla Guarda, *Bibliothèque*, 328; Vogel, *Liturgy*, 91; Saxer, 'Observations', 33–4.

Deshusses shows that the sacramentary I:Rvat, Reg. lat. 337 contains the text of the *Hadrianum*, complemented by a rearranged version of the supplement of Benedict of Aniane. Wilmart thought that the book

[8] Vogel evidently believes that MSS were always copied for 'the actual conduct of worship' (*Liturgy*, 62), but Hucke offers a contrasting view in his explanation of the phenomenon of writing down Old Roman chant in the 11th c. as a means of preserving a waning ritual ('View', 466).

came from Saint-Denis or from Reims, and Amiet likewise suggested Saint-Denis as place of origin because of the similarities between I:Rvat, Reg. lat. 337 and two other sources which he likewise attributed to the scriptorium of the abbey: F:Pn, lat. 2290 and F:Pn, lat. 2292. There is no liturgical evidence to support the attribution to Saint-Denis, however, and Gamber proposes the area of Lyon on palaeographical grounds. Saxer has recently dated I:Rvat, Reg. lat. 337 between 835 and 838.

40. *Paris, Private Collection, Manuscript of Mont-Renaud*

Gradual and antiphoner, tenth century, origin and usage probably Corbie or one of its dependencies.

Bibliography: *PM*, xvi (facsimile edn. of the Mont-Renaud manuscript); Beyssac, 'Mont-Renaud'; *GR* (MS ELI); Huglo (1), 'Chants', 74, n. 2; Jonsson, *Historia*, 77–82, 113–14; Arlt, *Festoffizium*, i. 72, 74, 103; ii. 197–8, 201, 204, 210, 213, 215, 217, 219, 222–4, 227, 229–32, 255; Huglo (2), *Tonaires*, 91–102; Hesbert, *CAO*, vols. v, vi (MSS 326, 728); Corbin, *Neumen*, 3.120; Planchart, *Tropes*, i. 61; Steiner, 'Chant', 245; 'Sources', 612–13; Hiley, 'Traditions', 15; Nebbiai-Dalla Guarda, *Bibliothèque*, 317, 318; Colette, 'Sémiologie', 125; Kelly, 'Neuma', 2.

The place of origin and date of this gradual and antiphoner have been contested ever since the monks of Solesmes published a facsimile edition of the codex in the first series of *Paléographie Musicale* in 1955. Now in private ownership, the volume has taken the name of the site on which it was discovered in 1874, the Château of Mont-Renaud near Noyon in north-eastern France. In their introduction to the facsimile, the editors discussed the destination and date of copying of the Mont-Renaud manuscript at length. Their results, though conjectural in some respects, point to the area in which the source had been found, the monastery of Saint-Éloi of Noyon. This conclusion is based largely on additions to the Mont-Renaud manuscript, particularly to the names entered in the litany. The liturgy, they suggest, represents the usage of Corbie, whence the monks who populated Saint-Éloi could easily have come. As to the date of the manuscript, the scholars of Solesmes suggest that the text was written in the mid-tenth century, with musical notation added about 50 years later and from time to time thereafter.

In his review of the edition that appeared in 1957, Beyssac took issue with the monks of Solesmes over both the date and the provenance of the Mont-Renaud manuscript. The manuscript contains the Resp. *O Constancia* which was written, as he believed, by King Robert II ('the Pious') after his marriage to Constance of Arles in 1006. Citing also the style of certain initials and the presence of alleluias that he attributed to a later period, Beyssac dated the volume to the first part of the eleventh century. He studied the contents of the manuscript in two sections, gradual first and then antiphoner. In the former, he pointed out various similarities to the liturgies of Noyon, Corbie, Amiens, Saint-Denis, and elsewhere, and he concluded that the usage of Saint-Denis was nearest that of the Mont-Renaud manuscript. Beyssac outlined three points that he claimed argue most decisively in favour of assigning the Mont-Renaud manuscript to Saint-Denis. He noted first that the alleluia list for the Sundays after Pentecost differs from that of the eleventh-century gradual of Saint-Denis F:Pm 384 on one Sunday only. Secondly, he stated that the neumes added on fos. 120^{v}–121 of the Mont-Renaud manuscript were written by the same scribe who notated the mid-eleventh-century augmented sacramentary of Saint-Denis F:Pn, lat. 9436. And finally, Beyssac claimed that the melodies of four of the five Lenten communions drawn from the gospels show the same characteristic variants in the Mont-Renaud manuscript as in the eleventh-century gradual of Saint-Denis F:Pm 384.[9] Beyssac concluded by taking the monks of Solesmes to task for not having consulted the twelfth-century antiphoner of Saint-Denis F:Pn, lat. 17296 in their study of the Mont-Renaud manuscript.[10] In the fourth volume of their subsequently published *Graduel romain*, the monks of Solesmes seem to cede to Beyssac on the date of the book, placing it at the beginning of the eleventh century,[11] but they still recognize musical differences between the sources from Saint-Denis and the Mont-Renaud manuscript.[12]

Huglo (2) criticized Beyssac's attribution and dating in his study of the modal designations found in the margins of the Mont-Renaud manuscript. The tonary implied by these indications belongs to the group which Huglo calls 'the tonary of Corbie–Saint-Denis'. Huglo also points out that King Robert's supposed career as a composer is now considered largely legendary, and that the script and style of decoration of the manuscript are in fact characteristic of the first half or middle of the tenth century. The usage of the codex he tentatively ascribes to Corbie. More recently, Corbin reiterates Huglo's opinion in her study of the neumatic notation of books from Corbie, and Hesbert concludes that the origin of some of the additions to the manuscript was Noyon.[13]

[9] Both the melodies and the texts of these communions based on the gospels (rather than on the psalms) tend to vary rather inexplicably from one MS to another; see Beyssac, 'Mont-Renaud', 138; Huglo, *Livres*, 103.

[10] 'Je m'étonne que les éditeurs n'aient pas pensé à consulter ce ms. [F:Pn, lat. 17296], puisqu'ils citent pour le Graduel une collection de livres de Saint-Denis, et ne citent pas une seule fois, pour l'Antiphonaire, le 17296 qu'ils semblent ignorer'; Beyssac, 'Mont-Renaud', 150.

[11] *GR*, iv/1, 290.

[12] *GR*, iv/2, 39.

[13] Specifically, Hesbert notes that the responsories of several monastic Offices in the antiphoner portion were later numbered from I to IX in the margins, which suggests that the book was

The origin of the Mont-Renaud manuscript presents several puzzles. The antiphoner is hybrid in nature, containing both secular and monastic Offices, and the sometimes indistinguishable layers of additions of text and neumes offer at best conflicting evidence. Because the antiphoner contains two kinds of Office, we can not rule out a priori either a cathedral or a monastery as place of origin. Indeed, recent studies have emphasized the dual nature of the liturgies of the Benedictine monasteries before and even after the Cluniac reform. Hence, the presence of both nine- and twelve-lesson Offices in the Mont-Renaud manuscript is not surprising in a source from this era.

If the types of Office in the antiphoner do not shed light on the origin of the book, the overall content of the manuscript does. The original text of the Mont-Renaud manuscript includes proper Offices for four saints who were venerated in a specific region of France: Quintinus (31 October), Eligius (1 December), Fuscian *et al.* (11 December), and Nicasius (14 December).[14] These saints are particular to the area of Corbie, Reims, Amiens, and Noyon, but not to Saint-Denis. The calendar of Saint-Denis includes only the first two (Appendix A): Quintinus with three lessons, and Eligius with a twelve-lesson Office drawn entirely from the common of saints. Fuscian and Nicasius were not commemorated in the abbey at all, and none of these saints had proper chants in the liturgy of the monastery. The basic content of the antiphoner thus argues strongly against Saint-Denis as place of origin of the Mont-Renaud manuscript.

These proper services point instead to Corbie and Noyon. The Office for Saint Quintinus in the Mont-Renaud manuscript (fo. 106^{v}) is exactly like the one found in the printed summer breviary from Noyon, F:Pn, Rés., Vélins 1614.[15] Similarly, the incomplete Office for Saint Eligius in the Mont-Renaud manuscript (fo. 112) contains precisely the same items as the twelfth-century breviary-missal from Corbie F:Pn, lat. 11522 (fo. 198). Moreover, the Office for Saint Fuscian in the Mont-Renaud manuscript (fo. 113) has nine responsories for Matins, but only three of them are notated. These three responsories (*Gloriosi*

adapted for use in a secular church. Analysing the orders of the responsories designated by the marginal numeration, Hesbert concludes that they represent the usage of Noyon; *CAO*, v. 353, 479.

[14] See the table in Beyssac, 'Mont-Renaud', 143–5. On the Office of Saint Fuscian in this MS, see Jonsson, *Historia*, 77–114.

[15] *Breviarium secundum usum insignis ecclesie Noviomensis . . . Impressum vero impensis honesti viri Petri Attaingnant*, publ. by Pierre Attaingnant in 1525 (see Bohatta, *Bibliographie*, 231). Evidently, the selection of chants for Quintinus' Office was not derived from Saint Quentin, for there are differences between the readings in the Mont-Renaud and Noyon sources, on the one hand, and those in the 16th-c. breviary from Saint Quentin, F:Pn, Rés., Vélins 2859–2860 (see Bohatta, *Bibliographie*, 249).

martyres, *Ambigere debet*, and *Hodie martyr*) are the same three found in the printed winter breviary from Noyon, F:Pn, Rés., Vélins 1615.[16] Likewise, the Office for Saint Nicasius in the Mont-Renaud manuscript (fo. 114ᵛ) follows exactly the service for Nicasius in F:Pn, Rés., Vélins 1615. None of these services is found in sources from Saint-Denis.

Drawn back now to the area of Corbie and Noyon, we must re-examine the alleluia list for the Sundays after Pentecost. Like other early graduals, the Mont-Renaud manuscript contains two series of alleluias: one that is actually incorporated into the Masses for these weeks, and another at the end of the book (fos. 46–7). While Beyssac shows that the first series varies from the one given in the Saint-Denis gradual F:Pm 384 in only one instance, he fails to realize that the series in F:Pm 384 is not entirely representative of the abbey (Table 7.1). What is more, he apparently ignores the fact that there are no discrepancies at all between the Mont-Renaud manuscript and the breviary-missal from Corbie F:Pn, lat. 11522 (Table 7.1).[17] Although Beyssac himself first systematically employed this methodology of comparing alleluia lists, which he terms 'pièce maîtresse de notre instrument d'identification',[18] in this instance he seems to have overlooked the evidence that it supplies. The alleluia list of the Mont-Renaud antiphoner points first and foremost to the region of Corbie as place of origin of the manuscript.

Recent studies of the notation of the augmented sacramentary from Saint-Denis F:Pn, lat. 9436 likewise controvert Beyssac's attribution of the Mont-Renaud manuscript to the abbey. Beyssac claims that the notation in F:Pn, lat. 9436 is identical to that of the added neumes on fos. 120ᵛ–121 of the Mont-Renaud manuscript. While it is clear that F:Pn, lat. 9436 was written *for* Saint-Denis, Escudier has recently shown that the manuscript was in all likelihood notated either in the scriptorium of Saint-Vaast of Arras or under the direction of a scribe from this centre.[19] The neumes, then, which Beyssac cites as characteristic of Saint-Denis come not from the abbey at all, but from Arras.

As for the communions based on the gospels in Lent, Beyssac alleges a close agreement between the Mont-Renaud manuscript and F:Pm 384, but he offers no proof of this. When readings of the Comm. *Lutum fecit*, sung on Wednesday after the fourth Sunday in Lent, are compared in sources from Mont-Renaud, Corbie (F:Pn, lat. 18010), Noyon (GB:Lbm, Eg. 857), and Saint-Denis (F:Pm 384; F:Pn, lat.

[16] *Breviarium secundum usum insignis ecclesie Noviomensis . . . Rothomagi Impressum*, pub. in Rouen in 1515 (see Bohatta, *Bibliographie*, 231).

[17] Beyssac, 'Mont-Renaud', 133–5. It is also noteworthy that the alleluia list of F:Pm 384 is slightly irregular, and that the 'true' Saint-Denis series contains not 1 but 2 verses that are at odds with the Mont-Renaud MS (see the discussion of the alleluia list of Saint-Denis in Ch. 3).

[18] Beyssac, 'Mont-Renaud', 148.

[19] Escudier, 'Scriptorium', 81.

Ex. 7.1. *Transmission of Communion* Lutum fecit *in the Manuscript of Mont-Renaud, compared to Corbie, Noyon, and Saint Denis*

9436 and F:Pn, lat. 1107), a picture of the transmission of the piece emerges (Ex. 7.1): (1) *pes* in Mont-Renaud manuscript, Corbie and Noyon; *virga* in sources from Saint-Denis; (2) *virga* in Mont-Renaud, Corbie and Noyon; *punctum* in Saint-Denis; (3) *virga* in Mont-Renaud along with either Corbie or Noyon; *pes* in remaining sources; (4) *virga* in Mont-Renaud, Corbie, Noyon, and the Saint-Denis manuscript with notation from Arras (F:Pn, lat. 9436); *punctum* in other Saint-Denis source (F:Pm 384); (5) *climacus* with two 'tails' in Mont-Renaud and Corbie; points in Noyon and Saint-Denis; (6) *cephalicus* in Mont-Renaud and Corbie; *virga* in Noyon and Saint-Denis; (7) Mont-Renaud differs in notational custom from the other four manuscripts; (8) Mont-Renaud agrees in notational custom with Noyon and Saint-Denis; Corbie differs.

This analysis leads to a conclusion that differs significantly from Beyssac's. Points 1 and 6 suggest actual melodic variations between Mont-Renaud, Corbie, and Noyon (point 1 only) on the one hand and Saint-Denis on the other. Points 2, 3, and 5 demonstrate notational conventions that likewise distinguish Mont-Renaud, Corbie, and Noyon from Saint-Denis. At point 4, F:Pn, lat. 9436 (*not* Saint-Denis notation) agrees with Mont-Renaud, Corbie, and Noyon. Point 7, at which Mont-Renaud deviates notationally from all the other sources,

TABLE 7.1. *Alleluias for Sundays after Pentecost at Saint-Denis and Corbie, compared with the Mont-Renaud Manuscript*

Sunday	Psalm	Saint-Denis[a]	Psalm	Corbie[b]	Psalm	Mont-Renaud[c]
I	30	*In te domine speravi*		–	–	–
II	17	*Diligam te*		–		
III	94	*Venite exultemus*		(lacuna)[d]	94	*Venite*
	94	*Preoccupemus faciem*		(lacuna)	94	*Preoccupemus*
IV	104	*Confitemini domino*		–		–
V	113	*Qui timent dominum*		–		–
VI	89	*Domine refugium*		–		–
VII	46	*Omnes gentes*		–		–
VIII	94	*Quoniam deus magnus*		–		–
IX	146	*Qui sanat*		–		–
X	121	*Letatus sum*		–		–
XI	107	*Paratum cor meum*		–		–
XII	80	*Exultate deo*		–		–
XIII	92	*Dominus regnavit*		–		–
XIV	99	*Jubilate deo*		–		–
XV	87	*Domine deus*		–		–

XVI	116	*Laudate dominum*		–		–
XVII	7	*Deus judex*		–		–
XVIII	147	*Qui posuit*		–		–
XIX	137	*Adorabo ad templum*[e]		–[f]		–
	58	*Eripe me*[g]		n.g.		n.g.
XX	77	*Attendite popule*	110	*Redemptionem misit*	110	*Redemptionem*
XXI	64	*Te decet hymnus*		–		–
	64	*Replebimur in bonis*		–		–
XXII	129	*De profundis*		–		–
XXIII	117	*Dextera domini*		n.g.[h]	117	*Dextera domini*

Abbreviations: –: Same alleluia. n.g.: Not given.

[a] List compiled from F:Pm 384; F:Pn, lat. 9436; F:Pn, lat. 1107; F:Pn, lat. 10505; and GB:Lva 1346–1891.

[b] List compiled from F:Pn, lat. 11522.

[c] List compiled from the Mass formularies for the Sundays after Pentecost in the Mont-Renaud MS, fos. 37v–43.

[d] The 12th-c. gradual from Corbie F:Pn, lat. 18010 contains the Ver. *Venite exultemus* and *Preoccupemus faciem* on this Sunday, and it is therefore likely that F:Pn, lat. 11522 once included these verses as well.

[e] Given only in F:Pm 384.

[f] Ver. *Qui confidunt* given in Corbie gradual F:Pn, lat. 18010.

[g] Given in all MSS from Saint-Denis.

[h] Ver. *Dextera dei* given in F:Pn, lat. 18010.

are non-conclusive. Only at point 8 does the notation of Mont-Renaud differ from that of Corbie. The same types of variation, yielding similar results, occur in the comparison of the other evangelic communions.[20] Of the manuscripts cited, the transmission of *Lutum fecit* in the Mont-Renaud manuscript resembles that of the gradual of Saint-Denis F:Pm 384 least; it corresponds only slightly more closely to the augmented sacramentary of Saint-Denis F:Pn, lat. 9436, which contains notation of Arras; it adheres more faithfully to the gradual of Noyon GB:Lbm, Eg. 857; and it follows closely the gradual of Corbie F:Pn, lat. 18010.

Although the antiphoner of the Mont-Renaud manuscript contains some proper Offices which are foreign to the Saint-Denis liturgy, its version of the Office for the patron saint (fo. 104) bears a striking resemblance to the that of the antiphoner F:Pn, lat. 17296. The presence of this Office in the Mont-Renaud manuscript, however, does not substantiate the claim that the manuscript hails from Saint-Denis. Rather, the service simply suggests that there was some connection between the abbey and the place of origin of the Mont-Renaud manuscript at the time the manuscript was copied. Interaction among the monasteries in northern France during the ninth to eleventh centuries was commonplace. Scriptoria tended to flourish in one region for extended periods, and outlying houses frequently received their books from the centre currently in operation, as is clear from the origins of F:Pn, lat. 2290 and F:Pn, lat. 9436. Abbots of Saint-Denis in the ninth and tenth centuries governed several monasteries at once, and their divided allegiances undoubtedly contributed to the mingling of usages that makes it difficult for us to determine the provenance of so many early codices. Likewise, the ever-present threat of Norman invasion caused the monks of Saint-Denis on several occasions to live for extended periods in other areas. An exchange of liturgical ideas and practices, as reflected in the gradual of F: LA 118, is not surprising under these circumstances.

Indeed, reciprocal influence between Corbie and Saint-Denis is evident in the early centuries. Queen Bathildis, wife of Clovis II, was instrumental both in the foundation of the monastery of Saint-Pierre of Corbie and in the introduction of a monastic rule in the basilica of Saint-Denis in the mid-seventh century.[21] On 28 July 667, the church at Corbie was dedicated to both Saint Peter and Saint Paul, although only

[20] One of these communions, *Oportet te* for the Saturday after the 2nd Sunday in Lent, stands apart in the Mont-Renaud MS from the other sources because it adds the phrase *in aeternum*. This ending is also found in a few other French sources, such as F:LA 118 (see Ch. 6).

[21] Krusch, *Balthildis*, 490–1.

Peter was subsequently retained as the common designation.[22] The day of this ceremony is recorded in the ninth-century calendar of Corbie, USSR:Lsc, Q v I 56,[23] which also reports the reception of some relics of Saint Denis at Corbie on 15 July ('Exceptio reliquiarum sci. Dionysii cum sociis suis'). The history of the consecration of the main altar at Saint-Denis is all too similar—this altar was also dedicated to Saints Peter and Paul, and even on the same day: 28 July. The event was thought to have been fabricated by Abbot Hilduin (814–41) of Saint-Denis, but it is possible that Hilduin chose both the patrons (Peter and Paul) and the day (28 July) in order to acknowledge or promote a rapport between Saint-Denis and Corbie. Indeed, the relationship between these two houses is known to us in other ways: books passed between them,[24] and their alleluia lists are nearly identical (see Table 7.1). Whatever other connections might exist, one can safely say that the Office for Saint Denis in the Mont-Renaud manuscript and other reminiscences of Saint-Denis usage in this book simply attest to the longevity of the association between Saint-Denis and Corbie. They do not suggest that the Mont-Renaud manuscript comes from Saint-Denis.

The purpose of this reassessment of Beyssac's appraisal of the Mont-Renaud manuscript is not to assign the origin of the manuscript unequivocally to Corbie or to Noyon. The issues involved are complicated by the layers of additions to the book which indicate that it later belonged to another religious house or even houses. These aspects are difficult to confront in scholarly fashion, especially since the manuscript is accessible only in facsimile edition.[25] But given the available evidence, it is reasonable to conclude that the Mont-Renaud manuscript did not emanate from the abbey of Saint-Denis. The fundamental methodologies for determining provenance, applied to the earliest layer of text of the manuscript and, in the case of the notation, to later additions, point to an area to the north of Paris. It is more likely that the Mont-Renaud manuscript was written at Corbie or in an establishment dependent on or liturgically closely connected with it, such as Saint-Éloi of Noyon. Thus the hypothesis originally proposed by the monks of Solesmes is probably closer to the truth.[26] Although the manuscript

[22] 'Tres ab initio pro temporum illorum more in asceterio Corbeiensi erectae sunt basilicae. Praecipua Ss. Petro et Paulo dedicata V calendas Augusti anno Chlotarii regis VII, jam, quod et alibi passim, solo fere sancti Petri nomine censetur'; *GC*, x, col. 1263.

[23] 'Corbeia, Dedicatio sci. Petri.' The entire calendar is pub. in Staerk, *Manuscrits*, i. 205–13.

[24] See Nebbiai-Dalla Guarda, *Bibliothèque*, 304, 309.

[25] The current owners of the MS have chosen to remain anonymous.

[26] Here I correct Beyssac's postscript (see above, n. 10) to point out that the monks of Solesmes did indeed know of the existence of the 12th-c. antiphoner from Saint-Denis F:Pn, lat. 17296—it is cited in their introd. to the edn. (*PM*, xvi, n. 3). No doubt they were well aware of the overall

does contain traces of Saint-Denis usage both in its gradual and antiphoner, we would expect to find such similarities in the service-books of any of a number of houses loosely associated with the abbey. Taken in sum, the ties linking the Mont-Renaud manuscript to Saint-Denis are much weaker than those connecting it to Corbie. For this reason, the manuscript is not treated as a Saint-Denis source in the present study.

41. F:Pn, lat. 2291: Paris, Bibliothèque Nationale, lat. 2291

Sacramentary, copied *c.*875–6 at Saint-Amand, adapted to the use of Saint-Germain-des-Prés.

Bibliography: Delisle (1), *Cabinet*, i. 201; iii. 266–7; Delisle (2), *Sacramentaires*, 148–9; Delisle (3), 'Vatican', 485; Leroquais, *Sacramentaires*, i. 58; Lesne, *Scriptoria*, 592; Huglo, 'Mélodie', 33; Bibliothèque Nationale, *Catalogue*, ii. 392; Boutemy, 'Foyer', 765; Handschin, 'Neumenschrift', 73–7, 87–9, and *passim*; *GR* (MS *SAM* 2); Bourque, *Sacramentaires*, ii. 53; Samaran and Marichal, *Catalogue*, ii. 474; Gamber, *CLLA*, ii. 413–14; Deshusses (1), *Sacramentaire*, i. 46; ii and iii (MS T3); Deshusses (2), 'Messes', 12 and *passim*; Stäblein, *Schriftbild*, 29; Deshusses (3), 'Chronologie', 236; Deshusses (4), 'Anciens', 289–90; Deshusses (5), 'Encore'; Vezin, 'Point', 182; Atkinson (1), '*O Amnos*', 12; Atkinson (2), 'Entstehung', 123, 129, 136; Jeffery, 'Sources', 318, 321; Nebbiai-Dalla Guarda, *Bibliothèque*, 325–6; Rasmussen, 'Liturgy', 41; Vogel, *Liturgy*, 229; Huglo, *Livres*, 120; Atkinson (3), '*Doxa*', 89, 90, 92, 93.

Delisle (2) assigned F:Pn, lat. 2291 to the abbey of Saint-Amand because of the invocation of Amandus in the *Libera nos*, and Gamber noted that his name, now erased, once stood in the canon of the Mass. Additions to the manuscript, however, show that it did not remain at Saint-Amand. The names of some Parisian bishops interpolated on fos. 1–7^{v} indicate that the manuscript was subsequently used in the area of Paris. Delisle (2), Lesne, and Gamber suggested that F:Pn, lat. 2291 later came to Saint-Denis, basing their estimation on the appearance of the names of Abbots Gozlin (fo. 6^{v}, reg. after 878–84) and Suger (fo. 21, reg. 1121–51). But Gozlin held multiple abbacies, serving also as abbot of Saint-Amand and of Saint-Germain-des-Prés before he became bishop of Paris in 884. And the name of a figure as prominent as Abbot Suger could easily appear in a book belonging to any Parisian house in the twelfth century. Scholars therefore concluded that the later provenance of F:Pn, lat. 2291 was either Saint-Denis or Saint-

similarity in content between F:Pm 384 and F:Pn, lat. 17296, and chose, logically, to make the majority of their comparisons with the MS that is much closer in age to the Mont-Renaud MS, i.e. the 11th-c. F:Pm 384.

Germain; but the choice between these two places was difficult, on account of the absence of distinguishing features. There is no evidence that the sacramentary was ever housed in the Saint-Denis library, and Boutemy and Deshusses (3) finally opted for Saint-Germain. Deshusses (5) recently redated the manuscript between 875 and 876.

The texts and partial notation for the Gloria and Credo in Greek are given in F:Pn, lat. 2291 (fo. 16), as documented by Atkinson (1, 2). Deshusses (1) shows that the text of the manuscript contains the basic elements of the Gregorian sacramentary, but in a form too developed for inclusion in his edition of the book. F:Pn, lat. 2291 also includes the supplement of Benedict of Aniane, along with additions from Gelasian books of the eighth century.

MANUSCRIPT FROM A DEPENDENCY OF SAINT-DENIS

42. Vendôme, Bibl. Mun. 17C: Vendôme, Bibliothèque Municipale 17C

Notated breviary (winter months only), early twelfth century, usage of a secular church dependent on Saint-Denis (Pl. 12).

Bibliography: Molinier and Omont, *Catalogue*, iii. 399; Leroquais, *Bréviaires*, iv. 291–3; Le Roux, 'Répons', 147 and *passim*; Hesbert, *CAO*, vols. v, vi (MS 571); Corbin, *Neumen*, 3.123; Hofmann-Brandt, 'Die Tropen', ii, Nos. 202, 206, 218, 346, 558; Rasmussen, 'Liturgy', 42.

Leroquais shows that Vendôme, Bibl. Mun. 17C was destined for a secular establishment through his analysis of the services of Matins, which contain nine lessons and responsories. He assigns the breviary to a parish church under the control of Saint-Denis because the names of saints particular to the abbey appear in the litany and calendar. Although the litany (fo. 247ᵛ) does contain the names of twelve of the fifteen major relics the abbey possessed in the eleventh century (Denis and companions, Maurice, Hippolytus, Eustace, Eugene, Peregrinus, Firminus, Hilary [of Poitiers], Hilary [of Mende], Romanus), it omits the names of three important relics (Cucuphas, Patroclus and Osmanna), all of which were present at Saint-Denis by the time Vendôme, Bibl. Mun. 17C was copied. The calendar, moreover, lists numerous festivals which were not observed in the abbey (see Appendix A, MS V1), and it includes only the months of December to March, a period during which only one Dionysian feast, the Dedication of the Church (24 February), occurs.

Although Saint-Denis had numerous dependent churches throughout its history,[27] Leroquais was unable to discover the place of origin or

[27] See Félibien, *Histoire*, *PJ*, vol. ii, No. ix.

use of Vendôme, Bibl. Mun. 17C for a variety of reasons. The non-Dionysian saints in the calendar were too widely cultivated to point to a particular area, and the total lack of information for eight months of the year further complicates the task. Several saints named in the breviary were specially venerated in areas south of Paris: Viventius (13 January), Bonitus (15 January), Leobard of Tours (18 January), Leobinus (14 March). Some were honoured in Parisian churches other than Saint-Denis: Phara (7 December), Speussipus *et al.* (17 January), Metranus (31 January), Severinus (11 February). Still others were particular to regions north of Paris: Macarius of Egypt (15 January), Ansbert (9 February). Likewise, the description of the feast of Holy Innocents (28 December) in the calendar includes the number of children slaughtered, and this precision indicates the use of a martyrology from a region outside the Île-de-France (see Appendix A, p. 461, 28 December). In the end, Leroquais tentatively suggested that Vendôme, Bibl. Mun. 17C comes from a church in Paris, basing his estimation mainly on the presence of the characteristic Parisian responsories for the three days before Easter (*Triduum Sacrum*) and on the possibility that the Bishop of Paris William of Auvergne (1228–48) once owned the manuscript. Further support for a Parisian origin for Vendôme, Bibl. Mun. 17C comes in the neumatic notation of the breviary, which is clearly French and which, moreover, resembles that of the twelfth-century antiphoner from Saint-Denis F:Pn, lat. 17296, as noted in Chapter 6.

At least one musico-liturgical difference between Vendôme, Bibl. Mun. 17C and F:Pn, lat. 17296 further demonstrates the dissimilarity between the breviary and books from Saint-Denis. Three famous responsory prosulas for the Christmas Resp. *Descendit de celis* (*Fac deus munda*, *Familiam custodi christe*, and *Facinora nostra*) are given in Vendôme, Bibl. Mun. 17C (see Pl. 12). Only the melodies of these tropes appear in F:Pn, lat. 17296 in the form of the neuma triplex, and there is no evidence that these popular texts were sung at Saint-Denis.

ERRONEOUS ATTRIBUTIONS TO SAINT-DENIS

43. I:Rc 1695: Rome, Biblioteca Casanatense 1695

Notated Missal, end of twelfth or beginnning of thirteenth century, usage of Notre Dame of Paris.

Bibliography: Ebner, *Missale*, 159–61; *GR*, ii. 121.

Ebner ascribes this missal 'either to Paris or to Saint-Denis', choosing Saint-Denis because the feast of the Invention of the patron saint

(22 April) appears in the text. The sequence of alleluias for Easter Week and for the Sundays after Pentecost, however, follows the series in use at Notre Dame, not Saint-Denis. And the mere presence of the Invention in I:Rc 1695 is insufficient to attribute the book to the abbey, for this festival was not particular to Saint-Denis. Along with the *natale* (9 October) and Vigil of Saint Denis, the Invention was celebrated in the cathedral of Notre Dame, as demonstrated in the thirteenth-century Parisian calendar contained in F:Pn, lat. 5185cc. Other observances more particular to Saint-Denis, such as the Dedication of the Church (24 February), the Detection of Saint Denis (9 June), and the Consecration of the Altar (28 July) are missing both from the calendar and from the text of I:Rc 1695. For this reason, the monks of Solesmes in *Le Graduel romain* assign I:Rc 1695 to the diocese of Paris.

44. Sheffield, Ruskin Museum (olim Reading, University Library, Ruskin Collection of the Guild of Saint-George, R. 3549), fourteenth-century missal (presently housed in the Graves Art Gallery in Sheffield, property of the Guild of Saint George, R. 3549).

Notated missal, fourteenth century (second quarter), usage of Notre Dame of Paris.

Bibliography: Delisle, *Recherches*, i. 158; Dearden, 'Ruskin'; Bibliothèque Nationale, *Librairie*, 66–7; Nebbiai-Dalla Guarda, *Bibliothèque*, 327.

Dearden speculates that this missal was copied at Saint-Denis, presumably on the basis of its beautiful decoration. He offers no proof for his conjecture, however, and even if the book were written in the abbey, its contents argue against Sandionysian usage. The shelf-marks of the Saint-Denis library are not present, and the feast of the Detection of Saint Denis (9 June) is lacking. Similarly, the calendar contains no obituary notices, a hallmark of Saint-Denis calendars from the fourteenth century.

In all likelihood the missal was used in the cathedral of Paris, as noted in the catalogue of the Bibliothèque Nationale. The calendar rankings *iii* and *ix* immediately indicate a secular rather than monastic house. The liturgy in the text of the missal is that of Notre Dame, and the observances are comparable to those found in the thirteenth-century Parisian calendar F:Pn, lat. 5185cc. Even the inscription of Saint Eugene (15 November) in the calendar demonstrates Parisian usage. Here he is called *martyr*, a customary designation in sources from the cathedral, rather than *episcopus et martyr*, which distinguishes him at Saint-Denis. The alleluias for Easter season and for the Sundays after Pentecost are also of the usage of the cathedral, and the processional directives for Palm Sunday explicitly name the *Ecclesia beate marie* as points of origin and return of the itinerary.[28] A peculiarity of the book is the absence of a separate sequentiary; the fully notated sequences are integrated into the body of the text.

[28] Fos. 107–10. Further mention of Notre Dame is found on fos. 180, 441v.

Conclusion

Throughout this study, the liturgical manuscripts have been the point of departure for the discussion of ritual and music at Saint-Denis, and it is appropriate to take a final look at the books themselves. The analysis of the sources in Chapters 6 and 7 provides more than a catalogue of liturgical codices used at Saint-Denis. The provenances of F:LA 118 and of the Mont-Renaud manuscript can now be stated with greater assurance, and the tonaries found in these sources are more correctly assigned to the region of Corbie–Laon. Circumstantial cases have been made for the presence of the old Gelasian sacramentary I:Rvat, Reg. lat. 316 at Saint-Denis on the brink of the Carolingian reform, and for the use of *Ordo Romanus XLI* at the dedication of the abbey; and a plausible use for the sacramentary F:R(m), A. 566 in the ninth-century church at Saint-Denis has been proposed. Unusual aspects of the ordering of the twelfth-century antiphoner F:Pn, lat. 17296 have been shown to hark back to the eleventh-century gradual/antiphonary list in F:Pm 384. Important new sources for the Greek Mass at Saint-Denis are uncovered in F:LA 118, in F:Pn, lat. 9436, and F:Pm 414, and our notion of the content of this service has been revised. The dates of the ninth-century sacramentary F:Pn, lat. 2290 and of all the late twelfth- and thirteenth-century manuscripts have been refined to an unprecedented degree.

In addition to palaeographical findings, the distinctive aspects of the music and ritual of Saint-Denis are now apparent. The troper of the abbey that has been reconstructed here reveals a number of pieces seemingly unique to the monastery. A surprisingly large number of new sequence texts clearly emanated from Saint-Denis in the thirteenth century, and the melody of *Salve pater dyonisi* was evidently composed, or at least compiled from other Parisian melodies, by the monks. The vestiges of these repertories which have survived in the later sources suggest that Saint-Denis was perhaps a significant centre of trope and sequence production in the tenth and eleventh centuries. An important series of melodies for the Benedicamus Domino and Ite Missa Est illuminates the whole tradition of preserving and recreating these tunes. In addition, the identification of the Ite *Joseph* as a segment of a Marian chant accounts for its tremendous popularity throughout Europe, and for the number of polyphonic compositions based on this tune. At least one monk of Saint-Denis was active in the composition of secular *chansons*.

While the examination of the manuscripts offers these and other tangible results, the liturgy that they preserve raises other important questions. How did a pointedly conservative musical tradition, one that paid little attention to the latest musical styles of the twelfth and thirteenth centuries, serve a church that is so commonly known for its innovations in architecture? And what lasting influence did the musico-liturgical tradition of Saint-Denis have? Glimpses into the first issue have come in each chapter. The novel aspects of the Gothic church at Saint-Denis were not independent displays of a revolutionary architecture; they were physically attached to and in some ways limited by the remains of the previous buildings. When Suger remodelled the western and eastern ends of the church in the twelfth century, he did so in a way that caused them to line up with the Carolingian nave.[1] Clearly, he revered the building that (legend had it) was built by King Dagobert and consecrated by Christ himself in the seventh century,[2] and he wanted his new edifice to underscore these features. The abbot even wrote about the reconstruction in a style that was decidedly old-fashioned.[3] Similarly, the thirteenth-century church incorporated Suger's twelfth-century chevet into a structure whose new transept and nave made it an early and striking example of the Rayonnant Gothic style.[4] It is not surprising, therefore, that insofar as the church at Saint-Denis was a model of architectural innovation, the liturgy, complete with its old melismatic tropes and Gallican remnants, served like the vestiges of the previous buildings as part of its solid foundation, another palpable link to the past.

As conservative as the medieval liturgy of Saint-Denis was, it was far from immutable. The ritual grew unchecked until the end of the Middle Ages, and newly added compositions and services focused with ever greater precision on Saint Denis and on the other saints who were particular to the abbey, on the royalty who patronized it, and on the architectural, artistic, and philosophical aspects of the church. In the seventh century, the monks briefly honoured the monarchs buried in the abbey with the practice of perpetual psalmody. Abbot Hilduin composed a hymn and Office for Saint Denis in the ninth century which asserted the false identification of the saint with Dionysius the Areopagite and the philosopher Pseudo-Dionysius, and a similar piece of medieval agitprop, a short-lived eleventh-century rhymed Office for Saint Denis, must also have originated in the monastery. The hymn

[1] See Crosby, *Abbey*, 280–2; Simson, *Cathedral*, 101, 132.

[2] See Doublet, *Histoire*, 165 ff.; Simson, *Cathedral*, 137.

[3] See Hanning, 'Style'.

[4] See Bruzelius, *St-Denis*, 161.

and Offices were doubly significant because they presented the Areopagite connection in liturgical form, the 'fundamental context'[5] for Pseudo-Dionysius. In the twelfth century, Abbot Suger continued this trend, emphasizing what he thought was Pseudo-Dionysian philosophy anew in liturgical texts and music, raising the levels of feasts, and instituting or re-establishing new services. In so doing, he caused the liturgy, not simply his 'costly vessels and other decorations',[6] to enhance the beauty of the new architecture. But just as Suger's church, unfinished when he died in 1151, had introduced only some elements of the Gothic style, so the ritual that he touched had further to go.

Not until the thirteenth century did Abbots Eudes Clément, Matthew of Vendôme, and others shoulder the project which led to the completion of the building. To complement the new church, they had new liturgical books copied, and the contents of these sources helped perfect the artistic, musical, and philosophical programme that Suger had begun. Not only did the monks of the thirteenth century have the stained glass for Vincent and Benedict to admire from afar; they could now do so in front of the windows themselves, and while chanting the distinctive Benedicamus and Ite music from the liturgies for these saints in the stational services that were sung in the chapels in which the windows were probably located. Not only did new sequences and added processions to the radiating chapels honour the saints especially venerated at Saint-Denis; their greater numbers highlighted these jewels in the tiara of Suger's chevet. Not only could the community claim that their patron was Dionysius the Areopagite in a hymn; they could now sing his praises in sequences composed in his honour, and in a Mass in the Greek tongue that they supposed to be his. Not only did vestiges of Gallican chant enhance the more solemn ceremonies; on another level they stressed the fixity of the alliance between abbey and monarchs. Indeed, not until the music and ritual interacted with the other elements to this degree was the church at Saint-Denis finally complete, and this unique mixture of the musical, the ceremonial, the visual, and the philosophical was the important legacy of the thirteenth century. Consequently, little change to the Mass and Office occurred after about 1350, although the fourteenth and fifteenth centuries saw the establishment of a daily Mass for Mary, and of a number of other endowed services.

In such a church, therefore, there was evidently no need for polyphony, for a sublime 'harmony' already existed in the uniting of music with the elements just mentioned. Apart from a pair of para-liturgical pieces possibly composed at Saint-Denis in the thirteenth century, the

[5] Louth, *Denys*, 30. [6] Crosby, *Abbey*, 287.

polyphonic movement of the twelfth and thirteenth centuries which penetrated neighbouring institutions, in Paris and elsewhere, that were allied with the universities and major cathedrals seems to have been disregarded in the abbey. The archival sources from Saint-Denis appear to corroborate this view. Whereas these sources attest the presence of a confraternity for Saint Denis, a daily Lady Mass and foundations by numerous royal persons, they make no mention of the kinds of special music for these occasions that existed in other places. And if improvised polyphony was used, the Sandionysian customary that might have documented the practice has not survived.

Instead, the monks preferred to maintain ties with the past by preserving their plainchant, and versions of it which may well pre-date the Carolingian reform of the mid-eighth century. Perhaps, in place of polyphony, they ornamented their music with neumas, and by cultivating mainly the earliest, melismatic form of trope. Furthermore, they employed long, mostly textless passages of chant in their Benedicamus Domino and Ite Missa Est, eschewing the troped and multi-voiced settings of these pieces in favour of music that was more wordless and hence 'transparent' in the Pseudo-Dionysian or at least neo-Platonic sense. Besides infusing their liturgy with Pseudo-Dionysian reminders, the monks sang old Gallican vestiges in the Mass and Office on important feast-days to stress their venerability, and they jealously guarded these and other ancient traditions in the face of the pressures that must have been exerted on them during the Cluniac reform.

Along with this substantial liturgical growth, however, the richness of the ritual waned somewhat in the late Middle Ages.[7] The Sandionysians dropped many proper antiphons and responsories from the oldest Offices and replaced them with selections from the *commune sanctorum*. Perhaps this was a result of the community's increasing dependence on written sources. Some special services enjoyed relatively short lives. The rhymed Office for Saint Denis seems to have flourished only in the eleventh century, and the Office for Saint Cucuphas, sung only once a year and no doubt burdensome to remember, was remodelled with chants from the *commune*. In like fashion, the number and variety of the chants for the invitatory, Benedicamus Domino, and Ite Missa Est diminished as certain ones were specified for entire categories of saints in the late thirteenth and fourteenth centuries. In spite of these tendencies, some aspects of the liturgy resisted standardization. The series of responsories for the special Office of the Dead for royalty

[7] Another possible indication that polyphony was not used in the Divine Office in the late Middle Ages is Félibien's account of the visit of a certain prelate to Saint-Denis in 1493. He mentions that on this occasion the Office was sung in the normal manner, that is, by heart and without books; *Histoire*, 368.

persisted at least until the sixteenth century. And a conscious inflation of the ritual caused the creation both of new ranks of feasts and of new sequences for Mass.

Although reluctant to follow the latest musical trends, the monks developed a performance practice which, at least for the responsorial chants of the highest feasts, seems as elaborate as that of the grandest churches in France by the thirteenth centuy. Such celebrations took place not only on Christmas, Easter, and other *annuale* days; they were heard, for example, when the lost Nail of the Passion was found in 1233, and particularly on the anniversaries of some of the kings who were buried in the church. The liturgical equation of king with saint was further enhanced by the use of a special Gallican antiphon before the gospel at the Requiem Mass. The monks' full-scale effort to ingratiate themselves with the Crown through political and literary means was thus substantially reinforced by the level of ceremony that kings were accorded.

Clearly, the outstanding element of the liturgy of Saint-Denis was its exceptional relationship to the church in which it was enacted.[8] At the same time, this ritual was not an isolated usage. Interaction between Saint-Denis and other houses in England and northern France—Corbie, Noyon, Reims, Laon, Saint-Germain-des-Prés, Saint-Amand, Saint-Vaast—is documented not only in historical sources, but also in similarities in alleluia lists, in musical readings in the gradual, and in styles of manuscript writing, musical notation and decoration. The ancient chant tradition which the gradual F:Pm 384 preserves is also seen in sources from many of the places just named, and the late medieval liturgy of Saint-Denis (e.g. F:Pn, lat. 1107; F:Pn, lat. 10505; GB:Lva 1346–1891) was in part derived from Parisian tradition, a dependence that is especially clear in the sequences and tropes. Even the most individual repertories of the abbey, the melodies for the Benedicamus Domino and Ite Missa Est, had less extensive counterparts in other places. What is unique about the Sandionysian liturgy, however, is the way in which its elements were put together—a combination that fitted perfectly the architecture, history, and philosophy of this singularly important chuch. In the light of all this, it is understandable that, with the exception of the direct influence that the ritual exerted in the abbey of Saint-Corneille of Compiègne, it seems to have had little direct impact outside the walls of the monastery.

At its height in the Middle Ages, Saint-Denis boasted famous

[8] In the realm of architecture, Radding and Clark have shown that the architect of Abbot Suger's church made an important break with the past when he likewise conceived the various different elements of the building not separately, but rather as interacting one with another; 'Abélard'.

musicians and liturgists. Two renowned teachers of singing, Teutgarius and Vandelmarus, were connected with the abbey in the ninth century. Abbots Hilduin, Suger, William of Gap, Eudes Clément, and Matthew of Vendôme successively raised the level of cult of the Divine Office, and they likewise caused new feasts and royal services to be added, and oversaw the composition of proper tropes and sequences and the compilation of the Greek Mass. The cantor William, the theorists Guido and Petrus and even a monk-trouvère left their marks on music of the thirteenth and early fourteenth centuries as well.

Toward the end of the monastic era, by the mid-fourteenth century, the liturgy at Saint-Denis assumed what would be its final form. Musical leadership in the Middle Ages passed from monastery to cathedral and thence to court and private chapel. Saint-Denis was out of step with the avant-garde, of course, for the old rites were performed in the abbey right through the fifteenth and sixteenth centuries—this era which music historians have termed the Renaissance was completely ignored at Saint-Denis. In 1567, the year of the birth of the great opera composer Claudio Monteverdi, Huguenot marauders made off with many of the plainchant manuscripts and printed books that enshrined the time-honoured ritual of the abbey. Only a few decades later, reformers from Saint-Maur restructured the liturgy of Saint-Denis.

In spite of these upheavals, Benedictine monks continued to celebrate the Divine Service in the abbey until the French Revolution. Following the last Office of Compline at Saint-Denis on 14 September 1792,[9] the abbey was completely secularized, declared a parish church, and provided with a new clergy of priests. The revolutionaries who descended on Saint-Denis in these riotous years no doubt dashed liturgical manuscripts along with the heads of the monarchs that they wrested from the magnificent *tombeaux* of kings.[10] Happily a few books were spared, among them the beautifully decorated eleventh-century sacramentary F:Pn, lat. 9436, which had been moved to the Cabinet des Médailles in 1791. Anachronistic though it was in terms of the musical mainstream of the eighteenth century, this manuscript stood as a monument to the best of times, an age when ritual and music in the church at Saint-Denis embodied one of the most remarkable liturgical practices in all of France.

[9] Regarding the final Office, the organist of Saint-Denis, Ferdinand Albert Gautier, in an eye-witness account, comments: 'ainsi ont fini les Bénédictins à l'abbaye de Saint-Denis'; F:Pn, franç. 11681, p. 98.

[10] A monk of Saint-Denis recorded the day-by-day extraction of royal bodies from the tombs from 12 to 25 Oct. 1793; see Guilhermy, *Monographie*, 55–83.

APPENDIX A.
The Calendar of Saint-Denis

INTRODUCTION

Fourteen examples of the calendar of Saint-Denis are currently known, and these range in date from the end of the 9th c. to 1550. These documents are collated in Table A.1 below, along with the calendars of 3 MSS (F:Pn, lat. 9436; F:Pn, lat. 103; Vendôme, Bibl. Mun. 17C) which contain a number of non-Dionysian feasts. These entries occupy a separate column in Table A.1. The obituaries celebrated in the abbey are written in brackets in the column that lists the Saint-Denis feasts. Notes about necrological mentions and other curiosities of the calendar are arranged by date in the notes to the calendar (pp. 456–61). The once-only entries of anniversaries in the calendars of F:Psg 111, F:Pn, lat. 2290, and F:ML 81 which did not result in longstanding services have been removed.[1]

Descriptions of the sources cited here are found elsewhere, with the exception of two bibles whose calendars are pertinent to this study:

M3 (F:ML81): Moulins, Bibliothèque Municipale, MS81[2]

Bible (end of 13th c.) with calendar of Saint-Denis usage inserted on fos. 311–16. The inclusion of Alphonse of Poitou on 26 Aug. (d. 1271) in the original hand and of Matthew of Vendôme on 26 Sept. (d. 1286) as an addition determine the dates of the calendar between 1271 and 1286. Several obits are incorrectly placed (e.g. Queen Isabel on 23 instead of 28 Jan.). Ranks of feasts are not given.

B1 (GB:Ob, Auct. D. 5. 17): Oxford, Bodleian Library, MS Auct. D. 5. 17 (1848)[3]

Bible (end of 13th c.) with calendar, probably of Saint-Denis usage, added at the beginning of the 14th c. on fos. 601–3^{v}.[4] The calendar contains a small number of non-Dionysian feasts (e.g. Appolonia, 9 Feb.). A new hand begins in July; from here on, the ranks of feasts are occasionally entered.[5]

[1] The names of deceased monks from the calendar of F:Pn, lat. 2290 are published in Molinier, *Obituaires*, i/2. 1025.

[2] On this MS, see Lemaître, *Répertoire*, 599; Nebbiai-Dalla Guarda, *Bibliothèque*, 295.

[3] See Van Dijk, *Handlist*, iii. 113; Nebbiai-Dalla Guarda, *Bibliothèque*, 295.

[4] Since the majority of obits are written in a different hand from the rest of the calendar, it is impossible to determine the precise date of the MS. The entries nevertheless include most of the changes that occurred at Saint-Denis in the late 13th and 14th cs.

[5] The symbols for the degrees of feasts (iii, xii) resemble those in use in the 13th c., an

The calendars of F:Pm 526 and F:Pn, lat. 976 employ the symbols 'iii' and 'xii' in the ranking of feasts. Where more specific information, such as 'fiat duplex festum', appears in the texts of these MSS, it is included in Appendix A. Astronomical data, dominical letters, and other distinguishing features of the various ages of calendars have been omitted.[6]

ALPHABETICAL LIST OF FEASTS AND OBITS IN THE SAINT-DENIS CALENDAR

Feast/Obit	*Date*
ABDON, SENNEN	30 July
Adam	19 Feb.
ADRIAN	8 Sept.
AGAPITUS	18 Aug.
AGATHA	5 Feb.
AGNES	21 Jan.
AGNES (second)	28 Jan.
Aichardus	15 Sept.
Aigulphus	3 Sept.
Alban	22 June
Albinus	1 Mar.
Aldegund	30 Jan.
ALEXANDER	3, 4 May
Alexander	26 Feb.
Alexander	21 Sept.
All Souls	2, 3 Nov., 2 Dec.
Alphonse of Poitou	26, 27 Aug.
Amatus	19 Oct.
Ambrose	4 Apr.
Amos	31 Mar.
Anastasia	25 Dec.
ANDREW	30 Nov.
Anianus	17, 19 Nov.
ANNUNCIATION	25 Mar.
Ansbert	9 Feb.
Antoninus	2 Sept.
Antony	17 Jan.
Apollinaris	23 July
Appollonia	9 Feb.
Arnulf	18 July
Arnulf	16 Aug.
Ascension	5 May

indication that the change to the level of greater specificity that is evident in the mid-14th-c. calendars (GB:Lva 1346–1891 and GB:Ob, Can. Lit. 192) had not yet taken place.

[6] For a discussion of these items, see Hughes, *Manuscripts*, nos. 1000–4.

Feast/Obit	*Date*
ASSUMPTION	15 Aug.
Athanasius	2 May
AUGUSTINE	28 Aug.
Augustine of Canterbury	26 May
Austregisilius	15 Feb.
Austregisilius	20 May
Autbert	13 Dec.
Avitus	17 June
Babilas	24 Jan.
Babolenus	7 Dec.
Barbara	4 Dec.
Barnabas	11 June
BARTHOLOMEW	24 Aug.
BASIL	12 June
Basil	1 Jan.
Basil	12 Feb.
Bathildis	30 Jan.
Benedict	21 Mar.
Bernard of Clairvaux	23 Aug.
Bertinus	5 Sept.
Blaise	3 Feb.
Blaise	15 Feb.
Blanche	8 Feb.
Blanche	4 Oct.
Blanche	27 Nov.
Boniface	5 June
Bonitus	15 Jan.
Brice	13 Nov.
Brigid	1 Feb.
CALLISTUS	14 Oct.
Carilefus	1 July
Cassian	5 Aug.
Cassius, Victorinus	16 May
Catherine	25 Nov.
CECELIA	22 Nov.
CHAIR OF PETER	22 Feb.
Charles IV	30 Jan., 1 Feb.
Charles V	15 Sept.
Charles the Bald	6 Oct.
Christina	24 July
CHRISTMAS	25 Dec.
Christopher	25, 26, 27 July
Chrodegang	3 Sept.
Chrysanthus	1 Dec.
Chrysanthus, Daria	25 Oct.

Feast/Obit	*Date*
CHRYSOGONUS	24 Nov.
Circumcision	1 Jan.
Clarus	4 Nov.
Claudius, Nicostratus	7 July
*CLEMENT**	23 Nov.
Clodoaldus, Evortius	7 Sept.
Columba	31 Dec.
Columbanus	21 Nov.
Commemoration of Hippolytus*	12 May
COMMEMORATION OF PAUL	30 June
Conception of John Baptist	24 Sept.
Conception of Mary	8 Dec.
Consecration of Altar	28 July
Constance	6, 7 Oct.
CONVERSION OF PAUL	25 Jan.
CORNEILLE, CYPRIAN	13, 14 Sept.
COSMAS, DAMIAN	27 Sept.
Crispin, Crispinian	25, 26 Oct.
Cucuphas*	25 July
Cyprian, Justina	26, 28 Sept.
CYRIACUS	7, 8 Aug.
Cyriacus	4 May
Cyriacus, Julitta	16 June
Dagobert	19 Jan.
DAMASUS	11 Dec.
Daniel	21 July
Daria	1 Dec.
David	29 Dec.
DECOLLATION OF JOHN BAPTIST	29 Aug.
Dedication of Church	23, 24 Feb.
Dedication of Church of Andrew	6 Nov.
DEDICATION OF CHURCH OF SAINT MICHAEL	29 Sept.
Demetrius	17 Oct.
Denis*, Rusticus*, Eleutherius*	9 Oct.
Desiderius	11 Feb.
Detection of Denis*	9 June
Dionysius of Corinth*	8 Apr.
Donatian, Rogatian	24 May
DONATUS	6, 7 Aug.
Dorothy	13 Feb.
Easter	27 Mar.
Edmund	20 Nov.
Eleven Thousand Virgins*	21 Oct.
Eligius	1 Dec.
EMERENTIANA (MACARIUS)	23 Jan.

Feast/Obit	*Date*
EPIPHANY	6 Jan.
Eudes Clément	5 May
Eugene*	15 Nov.
Eugenia	25 Dec.
Eulalia	10 Dec.
EUPHEMIA	13 Apr.
EUPHEMIA, *LUCY*, *GEMINIAN*	16 Sept.
EUSEBIUS	14 Aug.
Eusebius	20, 21 June
Eustace*	2 Nov.
Eutropius	30 Apr.
EXALTATION OF HOLY CROSS	14 Sept.
FABIAN, *SEBASTIAN*	20 Jan.
Faith	6 Oct.
Faro	27, 28, 29 Oct.
Fausta, Evilasius	20 Sept.
FELICITY	23 Nov.
Felix	1 Aug.
FELIX, *ADAUCTUS*	30 Aug.
FELIX, Remigius	14 Jan.
FELIX, *SIMPLICIUS*	29 July
Firminus*	25 Sept.
Florentius	26 Oct.
Forty Soldiers	8, 9, 11 Mar.
FOUR CROWNED MARTYRS	8 Nov.
Francis	3, 4 Oct.
Gaugericus	11 Aug.
Genesius	25 Aug.
Geneviève	3, 5 Jan.
GEORGE	23 Apr.
Geremarus	20 May
Geremarus	24 Sept.
Gereon	10 Oct.
Germanus	29 Apr.
Germanus	28 May
Germanus of Auxerre	31 July
Gertrude	17 Mar.
GERVASE, *PROTASE*	19 June
Giles	30 Dec.
Giles, Lupus	1 Sept.
GORDIAN, *EPIMACHUS*	10 May
GORGONIUS, Dorotheus	9, 10 Sept.
Gratian	23 Oct.
GREGORY	12 Mar.
Guido	28 Apr.

Feast/Obit	*Date*
Guido of Châtres	21 Feb.
Henry Troon	22 Oct.
Herbert	24 Apr.
Hermagoras, Fortunatus	12 July
HERMES, Julian	28 Aug.
Hilarion	21 Oct.
Hilary of Mende*	25 Oct.
Hilary of Poitiers*	13, 14 Jan.
Hilduin, Eudes of Deuil, Eudes Taverny	30 Oct.
*HIPPOLYTUS**	13 Aug.
Honorina	27 Feb.
Hubert	3 Nov.
Hugh	19, 20 Mar.
Hugh	10 Apr.
Hugh Foucault	26 Oct.
Hugh of Milan	18 Apr.
Hunegund	25 Aug.
Ignatius	1 Feb.
Illation of Benedict	4 Dec.
Innocent III	9, 16 July
*INNOCENTS**	28 Dec.
Invention of Denis*	22 Apr.
Invention of Head of John Baptist	24 Feb.
INVENTION OF HOLY CROSS	3 May
Invention of Stephen†	3 Aug.
Isabel	23, 28 Jan.
Isabel	3 Oct.
JAMES	25, 26 July
Jeanne	6 Feb.
Jehan Rogier	22 Mar.
JEROME	30 Sept.
Job, Hippolytus	10 May
JOHN	27 Dec.
JOHN AT LATIN GATE	6 May
JOHN BAPTIST†	24 June
John II	7 May
John Cholet	30 July
John Chrysostom	27 Jan.
John of Nevers	5 Aug.
John of Villiers	6 Sept.
John Pastourel	3 Mar.
JOHN, *PAUL*	26 June
Jonas	12 Aug.
Joseph	19 Mar.
Judocus	13 Dec.

Feast/Obit	*Date*
Julian	27 Jan.
Julian	27 Feb.
JULIANA	16 Feb.
Justin	4 Aug.
Justus	2 Sept.
Lambert	17 Sept.
Landericus	10 June
LAWRENCE	10 Aug.
LEO	11 Apr.
LEO	28 June
Leobard	18 Jan.
Leobinus	14 Mar.
Leodegarius	3 Oct.
Leonard	6 Nov.
Leutfrid	21 June
Lewina	23 July
Linus	26 Nov.
Liphardus	3 June
Lomer	19 Jan.
Louis III, Henry I	4 Aug.
Louis VI	2 Aug.
Louis VIII	6, 7, 8 Nov.
Louis IX	25, 26 Aug.
Louis X	5 June
Louis of Estampes	30 May
Lucian	16 Oct.
Lucian of Antioch	7 Jan.
Lucian of Beauvais	8 Jan.
LUCY	13 Dec.
LUKE	18 Oct.
Macarius	15 Jan.
Machabees	1 Aug.
Maglorius	24 Oct.
MAGNUS	19 Aug.
Majolus	11 May
Malo	15 Nov.
Mamertus, Majolus	11 May
Mansuetus	3 Sept.
MARCELLINUS, PETER	1, 2 June
MARCELLUS	16 Jan.
Marcellus	4 Sept.
Marcellus	1, 5 Nov.
MARCELLUS, APULEIUS	7 Oct.
Margaret	15 May
Margaret	19, 20 July

Feast/Obit	*Date*
Margaret	5 Nov.
Margaret	23 Dec.
Marianus, Pelagius	3 Nov.
MARIUS, MARTHA	19 Jan.
MARK	7 Oct.
Mark	25 Apr.
MARK, MARCELLIAN	18 June
Martial	30 June
MARTIN	11 Nov.
Martin IV	28, 29 Mar.
MARY AD MARTYRES	13 May
Mary Magdalene	22 July
Mary of Egypt	1, 2 Apr.
MATTHEW	21 Sept.
Matthew of Vendôme	25, 26 Sept.
Matthias	24, 25 Feb.
Maurice*	22 Sept.
Maurilius	13 Sept.
Maurus	15 Jan.
Maximinus	29 May
Maximinus	15 Dec.
Medard, Gildard	8 June
Medericus	29 Aug.
Melanus	6 Nov.
Mellonius	22 Oct.
Memmius	5 Aug.
MENNAS	11 Nov.
Metranus	31 Jan.
NATIVITY OF MARY	8 Sept.
Nazarius, Celsus	28 July
NEREUS, ACHILLEUS, *PANCRAS*	11, 12 May
Nicasius	14 Dec.
Nicholas	6 Dec.
Nicodemus, Gamaliel, Abibas	3 Aug.
NICOMEDES	1 June
NICOMEDES	15 Sept.
Octave of All Saints	7, 8 Nov.
OCTAVE OF ANDREW	7 Dec.
Octave of Assumption	22 Aug.
Octave of Benedict	18 July
OCTAVE OF CHRISTMAS	1 Jan.
Octave of Denis	16 Oct.
OCTAVE OF EPIPHANY	12, 13 Jan.
Octave of Eustace	9 Nov.
Octave of Innocents	4 Jan.

Feast/Obit	*Date*
Octave of John	3 Jan.
Octave of John Baptist	1 July
OCTAVE OF LAWRENCE	17 Aug.
Octave of Martial	7 July
Octave of Martin	18 Nov.
Octave of Mary's Nativity	15 Sept.
Octave of Maurice	28 Sept.
OCTAVE OF PETER, PAUL	6 July
Octave of Saint Louis	31 Aug.
Octave of Stephen	2 Jan.
Octave of Thomas of Canterbury	4 Jan.
Odo of Massay	7 June
Omer	9 Sept.
Ordination of Constantius	16 June
Ordination of Gregory	29 Mar.
Osmanna*	16 Aug., 9 Sept.
Oswald	5 Aug.
Ouen	24, 26 Aug.
Pantaleon	28 July
Patrick	17 Mar.
Patroclus*	31 Jan.
Paul	9, 10 Jan.
Paulinus	22, 23 June
Paulinus	31 Aug.
Pentecost	15 May
Peregrinus*	16 May
PERPETUA, FELICITAS	7 Mar.
Peter	1 Apr.
Peter	25 Nov.
Peter of Auteuil	7 Feb., 11 Aug.
PETER†, *PAUL*	29 June
PETER'S CHAINS	1 Aug.
Petronilla	31 May
Phara	7 Dec.
Philibert	20 Aug.
Philip III	5 Oct.
Philip IV	29 Nov.
Philip Augustus	13, 14 July
Philip V	3 Jan.
Philip VI	11 Aug.
Philip of Boulogne	18 Jan.
Philip of Gamaches	29 Jan.
PHILIP†, *JAMES*†	1 May
Phocas	5 Mar.
Phocas	14 July

Feast/Obit	*Date*
Polycarp	26 Jan.
Polychronius	17 Feb.
PRAEJECTUS	25 Jan.
Praxedes	21 July
PRIMUS, FELICIAN	9 June
PRISCA	18 Jan.
PRISCUS	1 Sept.
Privatus	21 Aug.
PROCESSUS, MARTINIAN	2 July
PROTUS, HYACINTH	11 Sept.
Pudentiana	19 May
PURIFICATION	2 Feb.
QUINTINUS	31 Oct.
Regulus	30, 31 Mar.
Regulus	24 Apr.
Remaclus	3 Sept.
Renaud Giffart	11 Mar.
Richarius	26 Apr.
Robert II	20 July
Romanus	28 Feb.
Romanus	9 Aug.
Romanus of Blaye*	24 Nov.
RUFUS	27 Aug.
SABINA	29 Aug.
Sabinian	24 Jan.
Sabinian	29 Jan.
Samson of Brittany	28 July
Sanctinus	7 Jan.
Sanctinus*, Antoninus*	19 Oct.
SATURNINUS	29 Nov.
Scholastica	10, 11 Feb.
Sequanus	19 Sept.
Sergius, Bacchus	7 Oct.
SEVEN BROTHERS	10 July
Severinus	11 Feb.
Severinus	23 Nov.
Severinus, Romanus	23 Oct.
SILVESTER	31 Dec.
Silvinus	15 Feb.
Simeon	4 Jan.
Simeon Senex†	8 Oct.
Simeon Stylites	5 Jan.
SIMON, JUDE	28 Oct.
SIMPLICIUS	29 July
Sisinius	29 Nov.

Feast/Obit	*Date*
SIXTUS, *FELICISSIMUS*, *AGAPITUS*	5, 6 Aug.
SOTERIS	10 Feb.
Speussipus *et al.*	17 Jan.
STEPHEN	2 Aug.
STEPHEN†	26 Dec.
Suger	12, 14 Jan.
Sulpicius	17 Jan.
Taurinus	20 Oct.
Ten Thousand Martyrs	22 June
Thecla	23 Sept.
Theobald	1 July
Theodocia	3 Apr.
Theodora	1 Apr.
THEODORE	9, 10 Nov.
Theodota	2 Aug.
THOMAS	21 Dec.
Thomas Boucel	21, 23 Feb.
Thomas of Canterbury	29 Dec.
TIBERTIUS, *VALERIAN*, MAXIMUS	14 Apr.
TIBURTIUS	11 Aug.
Timothy	24 Jan.
Timothy, Apollinaris	23 Aug.
TIMOTHY, Symphorian	22 Aug.
Transfiguration	6 Aug.
Translation and Ordination of Martin	4 July
Translation of Anianus	14 June
Translation of Augustine	11 Oct.
TRANSLATION OF BENEDICT	11 July
Translation of Clare	17 July
Translation of Eligius	25 June
Translation of Germanus	25 July
Translation of Nicholas	9 May
Translation of Probatius	1 June
Translation of Richarius	9 Oct.
Translation of Thomas	3 July
Translations of Hilary*, Innocent*, Peregrinus*	22 Aug.
Translations of Remigius, Germanus, Vedast	1 Oct.
Translations of Remigius, Germanus, Vedast	2 Oct.
URBAN	24, 25 May
VALENTINE	13, 14 Feb.
Valentine, bishop of Terni	14 Feb.
Valerius	29 Jan.
Valerius, Rufinus	14 June
Vedast, Amandus	6 Feb.
Venditian	11 Mar.

Feast/Obit	*Date*
Victor	20 Apr.
Victor	21 July
Victor, Corona	14 May
Victoricus, Fuscian, Gentian	11 Dec.
Vigil of All Saints	31 Oct.
VIGIL OF ANDREW	29 Nov.
VIGIL OF ASSUMPTION	14 Aug.
VIGIL OF CECELIA	21 Nov.
Vigil of Christmas	24 Dec.
Vigil of Dedication	23 Feb.
Vigil of Denis	8 Oct.
VIGIL OF EPIPHANY	5 Jan.
VIGIL OF JOHN BAPTIST	23 June
VIGIL OF LAWRENCE	9 Aug.
VIGIL OF MATTHEW	20 Sept.
VIGIL OF PETER, PAUL	28 June
VIGIL OF SIMON, JUDE	27 Oct.
VINCENT†	22 Jan.
VITALIS	14 Feb.
VITALIS	28 Apr.
Vitalis, Agricola	27 Nov.
VITUS, MODESTUS, CRESCENTIA	15 June
Viventius	13 Jan.
Walaburga	1 May
Walaricus	1 Apr.
Walaricus	12 Dec.
Wandrille	22 July
William Guillemere	23 Jan.
William of Gap	19, 29 July
William of Macouris	4 Mar.
Winoc	6 Nov.
Wulmar	20 July
Yves	7, 14 Feb.
Zachary	10 June

NOTES TO THE CALENDAR[7]

January

3 King Philip V: d. 3 Jan. 1322 (Wilmart, 'Anniversaires', 25).

4 F:Pm 526: commemoration for Thomas (fo. 97), but no mention in calendar.

[7] 'Abbot' here refers to abbots of Saint-Denis, and 'king' to kings of France, unless otherwise stated.

8 GB:Ob, Auct. D. 5. 17: mistakenly reads 'Juliani cum sociis suis'.

12, 14 Abbot Suger: d. 13 Jan. 1151 (Benton, 'Life', 3).

12, 13 Octave of Epiphany: 4th, 8th, and 12th responsories are duplex in the texts of F:Pm 526 and F:Pn, lat. 976.

18 Philip Hurepel, count of Boulogne: d. 1233, buried at Saint-Denis on 17 Jan. 1234 (Wilmart, 'Anniversaires', 25; Foley, 'Ordinary', vol. i, p. xx).

19 King Dagobert: d. 639 (Wilmart, 'Anniversaires', 25). The rank given in F:Pn, lat. 1107 (ix) probably refers to the number of lessons in the service of Matins on Dagobert's anniversary.

22 F:Pn, lat. 976: 'duplex' given on fo. 72v; 'xii' in later hand in calendar.

23 Macarius: omitted from all calendars after Vendôme, Bibl. Mun. 17C.

23 Queen Isabel of Aragon: see 28 Jan.

23 William Guillemere: prior of Argenteuil, d. 1479 (Molinier, *Obituaires*, i/1. 338; Samaran, 'Études', 61, No. 413); document recording foundation of his anniversary is F:Pan, L 836, No. 16.

25 F:Pn, lat. 103: names illegible from Praejectus to end of month.

26 F:Pn, lat. 976: ranks in calendar illegible from Polycarp to end of month. (They are supplied from text of MS.)

28 Queen Isabel of Aragon: wife of Philip III, d. 28 Jan. 1271 (Wilmart, 'Anniversaires', 25).

29 Abbot Philip of Gamaches: d. 1463 (Samaran, 'Études', 60, No. 392), anniversary established in 1464 (Molinier, *Obituaires*, i/1. 338).

30 King Charles IV: d. 1 Feb. 1328 (Wilmart, 'Anniversaires', 25).

February

1 King Charles IV: see 30 Jan.

6 Queen Jeanne of Bourbon: wife of Charles V, d. 6 Feb. 1378 (Delachenal, *Histoire*, v, 120).

7 Abbot Peter of Auteuil: d. 6 Feb. 1229 (Wilmart, 'Anniversaires', 25).

7 Abbot Yves: see 14 Feb.

8 Blanche, duchess of Orléans: d. 1392 (Molinier, *Obituaires*, i/1. 338).

14 Both the Gregorian saint Valentine and the bishop of Terni are thought to have died *c*. 270, and there is some speculation that these 2 men should be identified as 1 (*VSB*, ii. 322–5).

14 Abbot Yves: d. 14 Feb. 1173 or perhaps 1172? (Wilmart, 'Anniversaires', 25).

19 Abbot Adam: d. 19 Feb. 1123 (ibid.).

21 Abbot Guido of Châtres: d. 22 Feb. 1350 (ibid.).

21, 23 Thomas Boucel: death date unknown (Molinier, *Obituaires*, i/1. 339).

23 F:Pn, lat. 103: names illegible from Dedication to end of month.

March

1 F:Pm 526: calendar omits Saint Albinus, but the text provides him with a feast of 3 lessons (fo. 113v).

3 John Pastourel: d. *c*.1395 (Molinier, *Obituaires*, i/1. 339).
4 Abbot William of Macouris: d. 4 Mar. 1253 or 1254 (Wilmart, 'Anniversaires', 25).
11 Abbot Renaud Giffart: d. 10 Mar. 1304 (ibid.; document recording foundation of his anniversary is F:Pan, L 836 No. 10).
19, 20 Cardinal Hugh: Molinier, *Obituaires*, i/1. 335; but this notice lists Hugh as abbot. To date I have been unable to find information about him.
22 Jean Roger (also known as Jehan Rogier): priest of Beauvais and canon at Saint-Paul's, founded his own anniversary on 3 May 1502; see F:Pan LL 1194, pp. 21–2; Levillain, 'Office', 60; Molinier, *Obituaires*, 1/2. 875.
27 F:Psg 111: indication '*pl. of.*' is not present for this feast, probably because it was customary to sing a shortened form of Matins with only 3 responsories on Easter (see Huglo, 'Office', 191–203).
27 F:Pn, lat. 103: names illegible from Easter to end of month.
27 F:Pn, lat. 976: ranks in calendar illegible from Easter to end of month. (They are supplied from text of MS.)
28, 29 Pope Martin IV: d. 28 Mar. 1285 (Wilmart, 'Anniversaires', 26).
30 F:Pm 526: calendar has xii lessons, but text has iii (fo. 116^{v}).

April

1 Archbishop Peter of Cosenza: formerly a monk of Saint-Denis, d. early Apr., probably in 1290 (see Félibien, *Histoire*, 260; Molinier, *Obituaires*, i/1. 339; Eubel, *Hierarchia*, i. 220).
10 Abbot Hugh: see 18 Apr.
18 Abbot Hugh of Milan: d. 11 (18?) Apr. 1204 (Wilmart, 'Anniversaires', 26).
24 Herbert de Monte: preceptor of *Artenne* (Artannes-sur-Thouet); see Molinier, *Obituaires*, i/1. 340.
28 Abbot Guido of Monceaux: d. 1398 (ibid.; Samaran, 'Études', 52, No. 195).

May

5 Abbot Eudes Clément: d. 5 May 1247 (Wilmart, 'Anniversaires', 26); document recording foundation of his anniversary is F:Pan, L 836, No. 8 (copy in F:Pan, LL 1157, pp. 85–7).
7 King John II: d. 7 May 1364.
12 F:Pm 414: the name of Hippolytus is noticeably separate from the others.
16 F:Pn, lat. 976: calendar has xii lessons, but rubrics in text are like those of other duplex feasts for saints with relics in the abbey (fos. 92^{v}–93).
28 F:Pm 526: ranks in calendar omitted from Germanus to end of month. (They are supplied from text of MS.)
28 F:Pn, lat. 976: ranks in calendar illegible from Germanus to end of month. (They are supplied from text of MS.)
30 Count Louis of Estampes: d. 1400 (Molinier, *Obituaires*, i/1. 340); document recording foundation of his anniversary is F:Pan, L 836, No. 12.

June

3 F:Pn, lat. 976: name virtually erased.
5 King Louis X: d. 5 June 1316 (Wilmart, 'Anniversaires', 26).
22 GB:Ob, Auct. D. 5. 17: mistakenly reads 'decem milia virg.'.
22, 26 F:Pm 526: ranks in calendar have been changed to xii on these days. Text of MS gives iii lessons with provisions for a 3rd nocturn if feast falls on Sunday (fos. 136, 138^{r-v}).
30 F:Pn, lat. 9436: the only MS actually to incorporate the feast of Saint Martial on this day in its text (fos. 90^{v}–91). The other sources, while noting Martial on 30 June in their calendars, place his feast on the Octave (7 July) in the texts.

July

7 F:Pm 526: name of Martial given on 30 June, but rank and description of feast given on the Octave (see above, 30 June).
9 Innocent: see below, 16 July.
13, 14 King Philip Augustus: d. 14 July 1223 (Wilmart, 'Anniversaires', 26).
13 F:Pn, lat. 1107: name of Philip almost erased.
13 F:Pn, lat. 976: rank of Phocas given 1 day early.
16 Pope Innocent III: d. 16 July 1216 (Wilmart, 'Anniversaires', 26).
19 Abbot William of Gap: see 29 July.
20 King Robert II ('the Pious'): d. 20 July 1031 (Wilmart, 'Anniversaires', 26).
20 F:Pn, lat. 1107: name of Robert virtually erased.
23 F:Pm 526: rank given in calendar (iii) is almost erased, but xii is given in text (fo. 149).
29 Abbot William of Gap: death date unknown, but he became abbot in 1173 (Wilmart, 'Anniversaires', 26).
30 F:Pn, lat. 976: ranks in calendar illegible from Abdon to end of month. (They are supplied from text of MS).
30 Cardinal John Cholet: d. 2 Aug. 1292 (Wilmart, 'Anniversaires', 26); document recording foundation of his anniversary is F:Pan, L 836, No. 9.

August

2 King Louis VI: d. 1 Aug. 1137 (ibid.).
4 King Louis III, King Henry I: Louis was buried at Saint-Denis on 5 Aug. 882, Henry died Aug. 1060 (ibid.).
5 Count John of Nevers: d. 1270 (Molinier, *Obituaires*, i/1. 335).
11 King Philip VI: d. 22 Aug. 1350.
11 Peter of Auteuil: see 7 Feb.
17 The Octave of Lawrence was reduced from 12 to 3 lessons before being dropped in the 14th c.
25, 26 King Louis IX (canonized in 1297 as Saint Louis): d. 25 Aug. 1270.

The calendar of I:Rc 603 calls him 'king': '*ludovici regis qui obiit apud carthaginem*'.

26, 27 Alphonse, Count of Poitou and Toulouse: d. 21? Aug. 1271 (Wilmart, 'Anniversaires', 27).

September

6 Abbot John of Villiers, cardinal of Lombès: became abbot in 1474 (Eubel, *Hierarchia*, ii. 179); d. in Rome, 6 Aug. 1499 (Samaran, 'Études', 64, No. 446). His anniversary was celebrated 1 month later, on 6 Sept., no doubt because of the feast of Transfiguration on 6 Aug.

7 F:Pn, lat. 9436: Evortius written in original hand, Clodoaldus in later hand.

9 F:Pn, lat. 2290: mistakenly reads 'Georgii' instead of 'Gorgonii'.

15 King Charles V: d. 15 Sept. 1380.

25, 26 Abbot Matthew of Vendôme: d. 25 Sept. 1286 (Wilmart, 'Anniversaires', 27).

26 F:Pn, lat. 976: ranks in calendar illegible from Cyprian to end of month. (They are supplied from text of MS.)

27 F:Pm 526: rank in calendar erased; xii lessons added in text (fo. 175).

28 F:Pm 526: both name and rank of Octave of Maurice almost erased.

October

1 F:Psg 111: Vedast added in later hand.

3 Queen Isabel of Bavières: wife of Charles VI, d. 30 Sept. 1435; document recording foundation of her anniversary is F:Pan, L 836, No. 14.

4 Queen Blanche of Navarre: wife of Philip VI, d. 1398 (Molinier, *Obituaires*, i/1. 341).

5 King Philip III: d. 5 Oct. 1285 (Wilmart, 'Anniversaires', 27).

6 King Charles the Bald: d. 6 Oct. 877 (ibid.).

6, 7 Queen Constance of Castille: 2nd wife of Louis VII, d. 4 Oct. 1160 (ibid.).

16 F:Pn, lat. 976: name of Lucian almost erased.

21 F:Pm 526: Eleven Thousand Virgins given in calendar but added to text in the margin.

22 Abbot Henry Troon: d. 22 Oct. 1221 (Wilmart, 'Anniversaires', 27).

23 F:Pn, lat. 9436: Severinus written in original hand, Romanus in later hand.

23 F:Pm 526, F:Pn, lat. 976; I:Rc 603, F:ML 81: add name of Gratian to Severinus and Romanus.

26 Abbot Hugh Foucault: d. 22 (26?) Oct. 1197 (Wilmart, 'Anniversaires', 27).

30 Abbots Hilduin, Eudes of Deuil, Eudes Taverny: Hilduin d. 22 Nov. 842?, Eudes of Deuil d. *c.*1162, Eudes Taverny d. *c.*1169 (ibid.).

31 F:Pn, lat. 976: Vigil almost erased.

November

5 Princess Margaret: daughter of Louis IX, 1st wife of Duke John I of Brabant; Margaret d. 5? Nov. *c.*1271; see Ch. 6, n. 58.

6, 7, 8 King Louis VIII: d. 8 Nov. 1226 (Wilmart, 'Anniversaires', 27).

15 F:Psg 111, F:Pn, lat. 2290: Eugene = *martyris*. F:Pn, lat. 9436: Eugene = *episcopi* (added in later hand). All other calendars: Eugene = *episcopi et martyris*.

20, 21 GB:Lva 1346–1891: Edmund's feast not ranked. 3 lessons originally given for Columbanus but changed to xii. The 'xii' was probably intended for Edmund.

27 Queen Blanche of Castille: wife of Louis VIII, d. 1 Dec. 1252 (Wilmart, 'Anniversaires', 27).

29 F:Pn, lat. 976: ranks in calendar illegible from Saturninus to end of month. (They are supplied from text of MS.)

29 King Philip IV: d. 29 Nov. 1314 (Wilmart, 'Anniversaires', 27).

December

7 F:Pn, lat. 103: Andrew given in original hand and again in later hand.

23 Queen Margaret of Provence: wife of Louis IX, d. 20 Dec. 1295 (Wilmart, 'Anniversaires', 27).

25 F:Pn, lat. 976: names partially erased from 25 to 29 Dec.

28 Vendôme, Bibl. Mun. 17C: includes the number of Holy Innocents ('Bethleem passio sanctorum Innocentum centa quadraginta quatuor milia'), which is also recorded in the martyrology of Usuard from Haguenau (*VSB*, xi. 742).

30 Abbot Giles: d. 30 Dec. 1325 (Wilmart, 'Anniversaires', 27); document recording foundation of his anniversary is F:Pan, L 836, No. 11.

Table A.1. *The Calendar of Saint-Denis*

Symbols and Abbreviations

ALL CAPITALS AND ITALICS Gregorian feast.
ALL CAPITALS Gelasian feast. (The list of Gregorian and Gelasian feasts has been compiled from Leroquais, *Bréviaires*, vol. i, pp. cxxx–cxxxii.
1 Name of feast written in original hand of calendar.
2 Name of feast written in later hand.
- Feast present, with exactly the same information as the entry to the left (blank spaces not counted).
blank space feast not listed in the calendar.
X Name of feast erased or barred from calendar.
* Major relics of saint in the abbey.
† Lesser relics of saint in the abbey.
() feast listed in calendar of F:Pm 526 or F:Pn, lat. 976, but not in body of MS.

Ranks and Descriptions of feasts

po *Plenum officium*. (These first 6 descriptions of services are found only in F:Psg 111).
pm *Plena missa*.
c *Commune*.
mg *Missa in Gelasii*.
ce *Commune et evangelium*.
e *Evangelium*.
iii, xii Rank of feast written in original hand.
III, XII Rank of feast written in later hand.
a *Annuale*.
p *Principale*.
sa *Semiannuale*.
d Duplex, written in original hand.
D Duplex, written in later hand.
sd Semiduplex.
d-4 12-lesson feast in which the 4th responsory at Matins is duplex.
m Commemoration.

Manuscript Sigla

B1 GB:Ob, Auct. D. 5. 17.
B2 GB:Ob, Can. Lit. 192.
C I:Rc 603.
CH Chapel Hill, Univ. Lib., Rare Book Coll. 11.
G F:Psg 111.
M1 F:Pm 414.
M2 F:Pm 526.
M3 F:ML 81.
N1 F:Pn, lat. 2290.
N2 F:Pn, lat. 9436.
N3 F:Pn, lat. 103.
N4 F:Pn, lat. 976.
N5 F:Pn, lat. 1107.
N6 F:Pn, lat. 1072.
N7 F:Pn, Rés. B. 5209.
V1 Vendôme, Bibl. Mun. 17C.
V2 GB:Lva 1346–1891.

Saint-Denis calendar: feasts [obits]		Other feasts	Century																
			9		11		12	13							14			15	16
			(Quarter of century) or dates																
			(3–4) MSS		(3–4)		(1)	(1)		1234–71			(4)			1350		(4)	1550
			G	N1	N2	N3	V1	CH	M1	M2	N4	N5	C	M3	B1	V2	B2	N6	N7
January																			
1	*OCTAVE OF CHRISTMAS*		1 po	1	*X*	1	–	–	–	1 xii	–	1	1 xii	1	–	1 d	–	1 xii	1 d
	Circumcision		1	–	–	–		–	–	–	–	–	–	–	–	–	–	–	–
		Basil				1													
2	Octave of Stephen							–	1	1 xii	–	–	–	1	–	1 xii	–	–	–
3	Geneviève, Octave of John		1 po	1	–	–	–	–	–	1 xii	–		–	1					
	Octave of John											1			–	1 xii	–	–	–
	[Philip V]														2	1	–	–	–
4	Octave of Innocents							1	–		1 xii	–	–	1	–	1 xii	–	–	–
	Octave of Thomas of Canterbury											*X*							
	Octaves of Thomas, Innocents									1 xii									
		Simeon				1	–												
5	VIGIL OF EPIPHANY					1			–							–	–	–	
	Simeon Stylites		1	–	–			–	–	1 iii	–	1	1 iii	1		1 m	–	–	–
	Geneviève											1			–	1 xii	–	–	–

	Saint-Denis calendar: feasts [obits]	Other feasts	Century																
			9 (Quarter of century) or dates		11		12	13							14			15	16
			(3–4) MSS		(3–4)		(1)	(1)		1234–71			(4)			1350		(4)	1550
			G	N1	N2	N3	V1	CH	M1	M2	N4	N5	C	M3	B1	V2	B2	N6	N7
January (*contd.*)																			
6	*EPIPHANY*		1	1	X	2	1	–	–	1	–	1	–	1	–	1	–	–	–
			po							d		xii				sa			
7		Sanctinus	2																
		Lucian of Antioch					1												
8	Lucian of Beauvais		1	–	–	–	–	–	–	1	–	–	–	1	–	1	–	–	–
										xii						xii			
9		Paul				1													
10	Paul		1		1			–		(1)	(1)	1	–	1					
			c							iii		iii							
11																			
12	OCTAVE OF EPIPHANY									1		1							
										d–4		xii							
	[Suger]														2	1	–	–	–
13	OCTAVE OF EPIPHANY		1	–	–		–	–	–		–		–	–	–	1	–	–	–
																sd			
	Hilary of Poitiers*		1	1	–	–	–	–	–	1	–	1	–	1	–				
			po							d		xii							
		Viventius					1												
14	*FELIX*, Remigius		1	1	–	–	–	–	–	1	–	–	–	1	–	1	–	–	–
			pm							iii						m			
	Hilary of Poitiers*															1	–	–	–
																d			
14	[Suger]							–	1	–	–	–	–	–					

15	Maurus				1	–	–	–	–	1	–	–	–	1	–	1	–	–	–
										xii						xii			
		Macarius					1												
		Bonitus					1												
16	*MARCELLUS*		1	1	–	–	–	–	–	1	–	–	–	1	–	1	–	–	–
			pm							iii						iii			
17	Sulpicius		1	–		–	–	–	–	1	–	–	–	1	–	1	–	–	–
										iii						iii			
		Antony			1	–	–												
		Speussipus *et al.*					1												
18	*PRISCA*		1	1	–	–	–	–	–	1	–	–	–	1	–	1	–	–	–
			c							iii						iii			
	[Philip of Boulogne									1	–		–	–	2	1	–	–	–
		Leobard					1												
19	MARIUS, MARTHA		1				1												
			pm																
	Lomer				2	1	–	–	–	1	–	1	1	1	–	1	–	–	–
										iii			iii			iii			
	[Dagobert]								1	1	–	1	1	–	2	1	–	–	–
										d		ix							
20	*FABIAN, SEBASTIAN*		1	1	–	–	–	–	–	1	–	1	1	1	–	1	–	–	–
			mg							xii			xii			sd			
21	*AGNES*		1	1	–	–	–	–	–	1	–	–	–	1	–	1	–	–	–
			po							xii						xii			
22	*VINCENT*†		1	1	–	–	–	–	–	1	–	1	–	1	–	1	–	–	–
			po							d		xii				d			
23	EMERENTIANA, (MACARIUS)		1		1	–	–	–	–	1	–	–	–	1	–	1	–	–	–
			pm							iii						iii			
	[Isabel]													1					
	[William Guillemere]																		1
24	Babilas		1	1	2		1	–	–	1	–	–	–	1	–	1	–	–	–
			mg							iii						iii			
		Sabinian			1														
		Timothy				1	–												

	Saint-Denis calendar: feasts [obits]	Other feasts	Century																
			9 (Quarter of century) or dates		11		12	13							14			15	16
			(3–4) MSS		(3–4)		(1)	(1)		1234–71			(4)			1350		(4)	1550
			G	N1	N2	N3	V1	CH	M1	M2	N4	N5	C	M3	B1	V2	B2	N6	N7
January (*contd.*)																			
25	CONVERSION OF PAUL		1	1	–	–	–	–	–	1	–	–	1	–	–	1	–	–	–
			mg							xii						sd			
	PRAEJECTUS		1	–	–		–	–	–	1	–	1	–	–		1	–	–	–
										m						m			
26	Polycarp		1	–	–			–	–	1	–	–	–	1	–	1	–	1	1
										iii						iii			iii
27		John Chrysostom			1		–												
	Julian				2		1	–	–	1	–	–	–	1	–	1	–	–	–
										xii						xii			
28	*AGNES* (second)		1	1	–		–	–	–	1	–	–	–	1	–	1	–	–	–
			pm							iii									
	[Isabel]															1	–	–	–
29		Valerius			1														
		Sabinian					1												
	[Philip of Gamaches]																		1
30	Bathildis				1		–	*X*	1	1	–	–	–	1	–	1	–	–	–
										iii						iii			
		Aldegund			1		–												
	[Charles IV]															1	–	–	–
31	Patroclus*							1	–	1	1	1	–	1	–	1	–	–	–
										D	d	xii				d			
		Metranus					1												

February

Day	Feast	Other feast																	
1	Ignatius															1 iii	–	–	–
	Brigid		1 c													1 m	–	–	–
	Ignatius, Brigid			1	–	–	–	–	–	1 iii	–	1	–	–	–				
	[Charles IV]														2				
2	*PURIFICATION*		1 po	1	–	–	–	–	–	1 xii	–	–	–	1	–	1 sa	–	–	–
3	Blaise				1	–	2	1	1 *XII*	1 xii	–	–	–	1	–	1 xii	–	–	–
5	*AGATHA*		1 po	1	–	–	–	–	1 XII	1 xii	–	–	–	1	–	1 xii	–	–	–
6	Vedast, Amandus		2	1	–	–	–	–	1 XII	1 xii	–	–	–	1	–	1 xii	–	–	–
	[Jeanne]																		1
7	[Peter of Auteuil]								2	1	–		–		2	1	–	–	–
	[Yves]													1					
8	[Blanche]																		1
9		Ansbert					1												
		Appollonia													1				
10		SOTERIS			2	1	–												
	Scholastica		1		–	–	–	–	1 XII	1 xii	–	–	–	1	–	1 xii	–	–	–
11	Scholastica			1															
		Severinus					1												
		Desiderius				1	–												
12		Basil			1														
13	*VALENTINE*		1 pm																
		Dorothy					1												
14	*VALENTINE*			1	–	–		–	1 III	1 iii	–	–	–	1	–	1 iii	–	–	–
	VITALIS		1	–		–	–												
	Valentine, bishop of Terni		1	–															
	[Yves]								2		1		–		2	1	–	–	

	Saint-Denis calendar: feasts [obits]	Other feasts	Century																
			9 (Quarter of century) or dates		11		12	13							14			15	16
			(3–4) MSS		(3–4)		(1)	(1)		1234–71			(4)			1350		(4)	1550
			G	N1	N2	N3	V1	CH	M1	M2	N4	N5	C	M3	B1	V2	B2	N6	N7
February (*contd.*)																			
15	Silvinus		1	1		–	–	–	1	1	–	–	–	1	–	1	–	–	–
			c						III	iii						iii			
		Austregisilius			1														
		Blaise			1														
16	JULIANA		1	1	–		–	–	1	1	–	–	–	1	–	1	–	–	–
			mg						III	iii						iii			
17		Polychronius			2														
19	[Adam]								2		1		–		2	1	–	–	
21	[Guido of Châtres]										2					1	–	–	
	[Thomas Boucel]												1						
22	CHAIR OF PETER			1	–	–	–	–	1	1	–	1	–	1	–	1	–	–	–
									XII	d–4		xii				sd			
23	Vigil of Dedication															1	–	–	
	Dedication of Church											1							
												xii							
	[Thomas Boucel]									1									
24	Dedication of Church		1	1	–		–	–	–	1	–		1	–	–	1	–	–	–
			po							d						a			
	Matthias			1	–		–	–	–	1	–		1	–					
										xii									
	Invention of Head of John Baptist			1															

25	Matthias														1	1	1	–	–
																sd	d		
26		Alexander			1														
27	Honorina									(1)	(–)	–	1	–	–				
										iii									
		Julian			1														
28		Romanus			1														
March																			
1	Albinus		1	1	–	–	–	–	–		1	1	1	1					
			c							iii	iii		iii						
3	[John Pastourel]																		1
4	[William of Macouris]										1	–	–	–	2	1	–	–	–
5		Phocas				2													
7	PERPETUA, FELICITAS		1	1	–	2	1	–	–	1	–	–	–	1	–				
			mg							iii									
8		Forty Soldiers				2													
9	Forty Soldiers		1	1															
			c																
11		Venditian			1														
		Forty Soldiers			2														
	[Renaud Giffart]										2				–	1	–	–	–
12	*GREGORY*		1	1	–	–	–	–	–	1	–	–	–	1	–	1	–	–	–
			po							xii						d			
14		Leobinus					1												
17		Gertrude			1														
		Patrick				2													
19		Joseph				2													
	[Hugh]									2				1					
20	[Hugh]													*X*					
21	Benedict, *natale*		1	1	–	–	–	–	–	1	1	1	–	1	–	1	–	–	–
			po							xii	d	xii				d			
22	[Jean Roger]																		1
25	*ANNUNCIATION*		1	1	–	–	–	–	–	1	–	–	–	1	–	1	–	–	–
			po							xii						sa			
27	Easter		1	–	–		–	–	–	1	–	1	–		1	1	–	–	–
										p						a			

	Saint-Denis calendar: feasts [obits]	Other feasts	Century																
			9 (Quarter of century) or dates		11		12	13							14			15	16
			(3–4) MSS		(3–4)		(1)	(1)		1234–71			(4)			1350		(4)	1550
			G	N1	N2	N3	V1	CH	M1	M2	N4	N5	C	M3	B1	V2	B2	N6	N7
March (*contd.*)																			
28	[Martin IV]																		1
29		Ordination of Gregory			1														
	[Martin IV]										2				–	1	–	–	
30	Regulus			1	2			1		1	–	1	1	1	X				
										iii				iii					
31	Regulus								1					X					
		Amos			1														
April																			
1	Mary of Egypt							1											
		Walaricus				2													
		Theodora			1														
	[Peter]														2				1
2	Mary of Egypt				1					(1)	(–)	1	1		1				
										iii			iii						
3	Theodocia		1	1		2													
			c																
4	Ambrose		1	1	–	–		–	–	1	–	–	–	1	–	1	–	–	–
			c							xii						d			
8	Dionysius of Corinth*								1	1	1	1	–	1	–	1	–	–	–
										D	d	xii				d			
9																			
10	[Hugh]														2				
11	LEO				1	2									1				

13	EUPHEMIA		1	1	–	2								1				
			mg															
14	*TIBURTIUS*,		1	1	–	–	–	–	1	–	–	–	1	–	1	–	–	–
	VALERIAN,		pm						iii						iii			
	MAXIMUS																	
18	[Hugh of Milan]									1		–	–	2	1	–	–	
20		Victor				2												
22	Invention of		1	1	–	2	1	–	1	–	1	–	1	–	1	–	–	–
	Denis*		pm						d		xii				sa			
23	*GEORGE*		1	1	–	–	–	–	1	–	–	–	1	–	1	–	–	–
			pm						iii						iii			
24	[Herbert]										1							
	Regulus													2	1	–	–	–
															iii			
25	Mark		1	1	–	–	–	–	1	–	–	–	1	–	1	–	–	–
			pm						xii						d			
26	Richarius			1	–													
28	*VITALIS*		1	1	–	–	–	–	1	–	–	–	1	–	1	–	–	–
			pm						iii						iii			
	[Guido]																	1
29		Germanus			1													
30	Eutropius													1	1	–	–	–
															iii			
May																		
1	*PHILIP*†,		1	1	–	–	–	–	1	–	1	–	1	–	1	–	–	–
	JAMES†		po						d		xii				d			
	Walaburga								(1)	(1)		1						
										iii								
2	Athanasius		1	1	–		–	–	1	–	–	–	1	–	1	–	–	–
			c						iii						iii			
3	INVENTION		1	1	*X*	1	–	–	1	–	–	1	–	–	1	–	–	1
	OF HOLY		po						xii						d			sd
	CROSS																	
	ALEXANDER		1	–		–	–	–	1	–	1	–	–	–	1	–	–	–
									m						m			
4		*ALEXANDER*			1													
		Cyriacus				2												

	Saint-Denis calendar: feasts [obits]	Other feasts	Century																
			9 (Quarter of century) or dates		11		12	13							14			15	16
			(3–4) MSS		(3–4)		(1)	(1)		1234–71			(4)			1350		(4)	1550
			G	N1	N2	N3	V1	CH	M1	M2	N4	N5	C	M3	B1	V2	B2	N6	N7
May (*contd.*)																			
5	Ascension				*X*					1 d	–	1				1 sa	–	–	–
	[Eudes Clément]									2	1	–	–	–	2	1	–	–	–
6	*JOHN AT LATIN GATE*				1	–		–	–	1 XII	1 xii	–	–	1	–	1 xii	–	–	–
7	[John II]																		1
9		Translation of Nicholas													1				
10	*GORDIAN, EPIMACHUS*		1 pm	1	–	–		–	–	1 iii	–	–	–	1	–	1 iii	–	1 m	1 iii
		Job, Hippolytus			1														
11	NEREUS, ACHILLEUS, *PANCRAS*			1															
		Majolus			1	–													
	Mamertus			2															
	Mamertus, Majolus							1	–	1 xii	–	–	–	1	–	1 xii	–	–	–
12	NEREUS, ACHILLEUS, *PANCRAS*		1 pm		1	–													
	Commemoration of Hippolytus*				2														
	Hippolytus*, NEREUS, ACHILLEUS, *PANCRAS*							1	–	1 xii	–	–	–	1	–	1 xii	–	–	–

13		*MARY AD MARTYRES*			1	–												
14		Victor, Corona				2												
15	Pentecost								1 p	–					1 a	–	–	–
	[Margaret]																	1
16	Peregrinus*		1 po	1	*X*	2	1	–	1 D	1 xii	–	–	1	–	1 d	–	–	–
		Cassius, Victorinus				1												
19	Pudentiana				1	–	–	–	1 iii	–	–	–	1	–	1 iii	–	–	–
20		Geremarus			2													
	Austregisilius					2	1	–	1 iii	–	–	–	1	–	1 iii	–	–	–
24	*URBAN*			1														
	Donatian, Rogatian				1	2	1	–	1 iii	–	–	–	1	–	1 iii	–	–	–
25	*URBAN*		1 pm		1	–	–	–	1 iii	–	–	–	1	–	1 iii	–	–	–
26		Augustine of Canterbury			1									–				
28	Germanus		1 po	1	–	–	–	–	1 xii	–	–	–	1	–	1 xii	–	–	–
29	Maximinus		1		1	2	1	–	1 iii	–	–	–	1	–	1 iii	–	–	–
30	[Louis of Estampes]																	1
31	Petronilla		1 ce	1	–	2	1	–	1 iii	–	–	–	1	–	1 iii	–	–	–
June																		
1	*NICOMEDES*				1	–	–	–	1 iii	–	–	–	1	–	1 iii	–	–	–
	MARCELLINUS, PETER			1														
	Translation of Probatius			2														

	Saint-Denis calendar: feasts [obits]	Other feasts	Century																
			9 (Quarter of century) or dates		11		12	13							14			15	16
			(3–4) MSS		(3–4)		(1)	(1)		1234–71			(4)			1350		(4)	1550
			G	N1	N2	N3	V1	CH	M1	M2	N4	N5	C	M3	B1	V2	B2	N6	N7
June (*contd.*)																			
2	*MARCELLINUS, PETER*		1 pm		1	–		–	–	1 xii	–	–	–	1	–	1 xii	–	–	–
3	Liphardus					2				(1)	(–)	1		–					
5	Boniface		1 c	1	–	2		1	–	1 iii	–	–	–	1	–	1 iii	–	–	–
	Louis X										2					1	–	–	
7		Odo of Massay				2													
8	Medard		1 po	1															
	Medard, Gildard				1	–		–	–	1 xii	–	–	–	1	–	1 xii	–	–	–
9	PRIMUS, FELICIAN		1 pm	1	–	–		–	–	1 m	–		–		1	1 m	–	–	–
	Detection of Denis*					2		1	–	1 d–4	–	1 xii	1	–	–	1 d	–	–	1 xii
10	Landericus				2	–		1	–	1 xii	–	–	1	–	–	1 xii	–	–	–
		Zachary			1														
11	Barnabas		1 c	1	–	–		–	–	1 xii	–	–	–	1	2	1 d	–	–	–
12	BASIL		1 pm	1	–	2		1	–	1 iii	–	–	–	1	–	1 iii	–	–	–
14	Valerius, Rufinus		1 c	1	2	–		1	–	1 iii	–	–	–	1	–	1 iii	–	–	–
		Translation of Anianus				2													

15	VITUS, MODESTUS, CRESCENTIA		1 po mg	1	–	2	1	–	1 iii	–	1	1 iii	1	–	1 iii	–	–	–
16	Cyriacus, Julitta				1	–	–	–	1 iii	–	–	–	1	–	1 iii	–	–	–
		Ordination of Constantius	2															
17	Avitus		1 c	1	–	2	1	–	1 iii	–	1	1 iii	1	–	1 iii	–	–	–
18	*MARK,* *MARCELLIAN*		1 pm	1	–	–	–	–	1 iii	–	–	–	1	–	1 iii	–	–	–
19	*GERVASE,* *PROTASE*		1 pm	1	–	–	–		1 xii	–	–	–	1	–	1 xii	–	–	–
20		Eusebius			1													
21	Eusebius		1 c	1		2	1	–	1 iii	–	–	–	1	–	1 iii	–	–	–
		Leutfrid			2													
22	Ten Thousand Martyrs						1	–	1 XII	1 xii	–	–	1	–	1 xii	–	–	–
	Paulinus				2	2	1	–	–	–	–	–						
		Alban			1													
23	*VIGIL OF JOHN* *BAPTIST*		1 pm	1	–	–	–	–	–	–	–	–	–	–	–	–	–	–
	Paulinus														1 iii	–	–	–
24	*JOHN* *BAPTIST*†		1 po	1	*X*	1	–	–	1 d	–	1 xii	–	1	–	1 d	–	–	–
25		Translation of Eligius		2														
26	*JOHN, PAUL*		1 pm	1	–	–	–	–	1 XII	1 xii	–	–	1	–	1 xii	–	–	–
28	*LEO*		1 pm	1	–		–	–	1 iii	–	–	–	1		1 m	–	–	–
	VIGIL OF *PETER, PAUL*		1	–	–	–	*X*	1	–	–	–	–	–	–	–	–	–	–
29	*PETER, PAUL*†		1 po	1	*X*	1	–	–	1 d	–	1 xii	–	1	–	1 sa	–	–	–

	Saint-Denis calendar: feasts [obits]	Other feasts	Century																
			9 (Quarter of century) or dates		11		12	13							14			15	16
			(3–4) MSS		(3–4)		(1)	(1)		1234–71			(4)			1350		(4)	1550
			G	N1	N2	N3	V1	CH	M1	M2	N4	N5	C	M3	B1	V2	B2	N6	N7
June (*contd.*)																			
30	*COMMEMORATION OF PAUL*				1	–		–	–	1 d–4	–	1 xii	–	1	–	1 d	–	–	–
	Martial				1	–			–	–	2				1				
July																			
1	Octave of John Baptist				1			–	–	1 xii	–	–	–	1	–	1 xii	–	–	–
	Theobald							1		(1)	(–)		1						
	Carilefus		1 c	1															
2	*PROCESSUS, MARTINIAN*		1 pm	1	–	–		–	–	1 iii	–	–	–	1	–	1 m	–	–	–
3		Translation of Thomas			1														
4	Translation and Ordination of Martin			2	1	–		–	–	1 xii	–	–	–	1	–	1 xii	–	–	–
5																			
6	*OCTAVE OF PETER, PAUL*		1 pm	1	–	–		–		1 xii	–	–	–	1	–	1 xii	–	–	–
7	Octave of Martial							1		xii	1 xii	–	–	1	–	1 xii	–	–	–
	Claudius, Nicostratus			2															

9	[Innocent III]												1					
10	*SEVEN BROTHERS*		1 pm	1	–	2	1	–	1 iii	–	–	–	1	–	1 iii	–	–	–
11	TRANSLATION OF BENEDICT		1 c	1	–	–	–	–	1 xii	1 d	1 xii	–	1	–	1 d	–	–	–
12	Hermagoras, Fortunatus		1 c	1	2	–	1	–	1 iii	–	–	–	1	–	1 m	–	–	–
13	[Philip Augustus]									iii	2							
14	Phocas		1 c	1	2	–	1	–	1 iii	1	1 iii	1	–	–	1 m	–	–	–
	[Philip Augustus]								1	–		–	–	2	1	–	–	–
16	[Innocent III]								1	–		–	–	2	1	–	–	–
17	Translation of Clare								(1)	(–)			1	–				
18	Octave of Benedict						1	–	1 xii	–	–	–	1	2	1 xii	–	–	–
	Arnulf				2	1	–	–	1 m	–	1	–	–	–	1 m	–	–	–
19	Margaret					2	X		1 iii	–	1 xii	1	–					
	[William of Gap]												1					
20	Margaret						2	1						2	1 iii	–	–	–
		Wulmar			1													
	[Robert II]						1		–	1 d	2	1	–	2	1	–	–	–
21	Praxedes		1 iii	1	–	–	–	–	1 iii	–	–	1	–	–	1 iii	– –	– –	– –
	Victor			2														
		Daniel			1													
22	Mary Magdalene				1	2	1	–	1 d	–	1 xii	1	–	2	1 d	–	–	–
	Wandrille		1	–	–	2	1	–	1 m	–	1	–	–	–	1 m	–	–	–

Saint-Denis calendar: feasts [obits]	Other feasts	Century																
		9 (Quarter of century) or dates		11		12	13							14			15	16
		(3–4) MSS		(3–4)		(1)	(1)		1234–71			(4)			1350		(4)	1550
		G	N1	N2	N3	V1	CH	M1	M2	N4	N5	C	M3	B1	V2	B2	N6	N7
July (*contd.*)																		
23 Apollinaris		1 pm	1	—	—		—	—	1 xii	—	—	1	—	—	1 xii	—	—	1 iii
	Lewina			1														
24 Christina		1 c	1	—	—		—	—	1 xii	—	—	—	1	—	1 xii	—	—	—
25 JAMES		1	—	—	—		—	—	1 xii	1 d	1	—	—					
Cucuphas*		1 po	1	—	—		—		1 d	—	1	—	—	—	1 d	—	—	—
Christopher			2	1	—		—	—	1 iii	—	1	—	—	—	1 m	—	—	—
Translation of Germanus			2															
26 JAMES														1 xii	1 d	—	—	—
Christopher		1	—															
27 Christopher														1 iii	—	—	—	—
28 Consecration of Altar		1 po	1		2		1	—	1 xii	—	—	—	1	—	1 sd	—	—	—
Pantaleon		1	—	—	—		—	—	1 m	—	1	—	—	—	1 m	—	—	—
Nazarius, Celsus		1	—	—														
Samson of Brittanay			2		1													

29	*FELIX, SIMPLICIUS*				I	–	–	–	I iii	–	–	I	–	–	I iii	–	–	–
	SIMPLICIUS		I pm	I														
	[William of Gap]									I		–		2	I	–	–	
30	*ABDON, SENNEN*		I pm	I	–	–	–	–	I iii	–	–	I	–	–	I iii	–	–	–
	[John Cholet]													2	I	–	–	–
31	Germanus of Auxerre		I c	I	–	–	–	–	I xii	–	–	–	I	–	I xii	–	–	–
August																		
I	*PETER'S CHAINS*				I	–	–	–	I xii	–	–	–	I	–	I sd	–	–	–
	Machabees		I	–	–		–	–	I m	–	I	–	–	–	I m	–	–	–
	Felix		I	–														
2	*STEPHEN*		I	–	–	–	–	–	I iii	–	–	I	–	–	I iii	–	–	–
	Theodota		I	–														
	[Louis VI]						I		–	–	–	–	–	2	I	–	–	–
3	Invention of Stephen†		I pm	I	–	–	I	–	I xii	–	–	I	–	–	I sd	–	–	–
	Nicodemus, Gamaliel, Abibas				I				(I)	(–)		I						
4	Justin		I	–	2	–	I	–	I iii	–	–	I	–	–	I iii	–	–	–
	[Louis III, Henry I]									I		–	–	2	I	–	–	
5	Memmius			I	–	2	I	–	I iii	–	–	I	–	–	I iii	–	–	–
	Oswald				2				I	–								
	[John of Nevers]											I						
		Cassian			I													

Saint-Denis calendar: feasts [obits]	Other feasts	Century																
		9 (Quarter of century) or dates		11		12	13							14			15	16
		(3–4) MSS		(3–4)		(1)	(1)		1234–71			(4)			1350		(4)	1550
		G	N1	N2	N3	V1	CH	M1	M2	N4	N5	C	M3	B1	V2	B2	N6	N7
August (*contd.*)																		
5 *SIXTUS, FELICISSIMUS, AGAPITUS*		1 pm																
6 *SIXTUS, FELICISSIMUS, AGAPITUS*			1	–	–		–	–	1 m	–	1	1 m	1	–	1 m	1 iii	1 m	–
Transfiguration				1			–	–	1 xii	–	–	1 XII	–	2	1 xii	–	–	–
	DONATUS	1 c																
7 DONATUS			1	–	–		–	–	1 iii	–	–	1	–	–	1 iii	–	–	–
	CYRIACUS	1 pm																
8 *CYRIACUS*			1	–	–		–	–	1 iii	–	–	1	–	–	1 iii	–	–	–
9 *VIGIL OF LAWRENCE*		1 pm	1	–	–			–	–	–	–	–	–	–	–	–	–	–
Romanus				1			–	–	1 iii	–	–	1	–	–	1 iii	–	–	–
10 *LAWRENCE*		1 po	1	–	–		–	–	1 d–4	–	– xii	–	1	1 xii	1 d	–	–	–

11	*TIBURTIUS*	1 pm	1	–	–	–	–	1 iii	–	–	–	1	1	– iii	–	–	–
	Gaugericus	1	–	–													
	[Philip VI]																1
	[Peter of Auteuil]											1					
12	Jonas									2 iii			1 iii	–	–	–	–
13	*HIPPOLYTUS**	1 po	1	–	–	–	–	1 d	–	1 xii	–	1	1 xii	1 d	–	–	–
14	*EUSEBIUS*	1 pm	1	–		–	–	1 iii		–							
	VIGIL OF ASSUMPTION				1		–	–	–	–	–	–	–	–	–	–	–
15	*ASSUMPTION*	1 po	1	–	–	–	–	1 p	–	1 xii	–	1	1 xii	1 a	–	–	–
16	Arnulf	1	–	–		–		–	1 iii		1	–					
	Osmanna*			2		1	–										
17	OCTAVE OF LAWRENCE	1 pm	1	–	–	–	–	(1) xii	(1) iii		1	–					
18	*AGAPITUS*	1 pm	1	–	–	–		(1) iii	(–)	1	–	–					
19	MAGNUS	1 mg	1	–	2	1		(1) iii	(–)	1	–	–					
20	Philibert	1 c	1	–	–	–		(1) iii	(–)	1	–	–					
21	Privatus	1 c	1	2	–	1		(1) iii	(–)	1	–	–					
22	*TIMOTHY*, Symphorian	1	–	–	–	–	–	(–)	–	1	–	–					
	Octave of Assumption			1		–	–	1 xii	–	–	1	–	1 xii	1 d	–	–	–
	Translations: Hilary*, Innocent*, Peregrinus*	1 po	1														

Saint-Denis calendar: feasts [obits]		Other feasts	Century																
			9 (Quarter of century) or dates		11		12	13							14			15	16
			(3–4) MSS		(3–4)		(1)	(1)		1234–71			(4)			1350		(4)	1550
			G	N1	N2	N3	V1	CH	M1	M2	N4	N5	C	M3	B1	V2	B2	N6	N7
August (*contd.*)																			
23	Timothy, Apollinaris				1			–		–			–	–					
23	Bernard of Clairvaux									2	1 d–4	1 xii	–	1	1 xii	1 d	–	–	–
24	BARTH-OLOMEW		1 po	1	–	–		–	–	1 xii	1 d	1 xii	1	–	–	1 d	–	–	–
	Ouen		1	–		X		1	–	1 xii	–	1	–	–					
25	Saint Louis												1		1 xii	1 d	–	–	–
		Hunegund			1														
		Genesius			2														
26	Ouen														1 xii	–	–	–	–
	[Alphonse of Poitou]										1		–	–					
	Saint Louis													1					
27	RUFUS		1 c	1	–	2		1	–	1 iii	–	–	–	1	–	1 m	–	–	–
	[Alphonse of Poitou]														2	1	–	–	–
28	*HERMES*		1	–	–														
	AUGUSTINE		1 pm	1	–	–		–	–	1 xii	–	–	1	–	–	1 d	–	–	–
	HERMES, Julian					1		–	–	1 m	–	1	1 m	1	–	1 m	–	–	–

29	DECOLLATION OF JOHN BAPTIST		1 po	1	–	–	–	–	1 xii	–	–	–	1	1 xii	1 sd	–	–	–
	SABINA		1 c	1	–	–	–	–	1 m	–	1		–		1 m	–	–	–
	Medericus		1	–														
30	*FELIX, ADAUCTUS*		1	–	–	–	–	–	1 iii	–	–	–	1	–	1 m	–	–	–
31	Paulinus		1	–	–	–	–	–	1 iii	–	–	–	1	–	1 m	–	–	–
	Octave of Saint Louis													1	1 xii	–	–	–
September																		
1	PRISCUS		1 mg	1	–	–	–	–	1 iii	–	1	–	–		1 m	–	–	–
	Giles				2	–												
	Giles, Lupus						1	–	1 xii	–	–	–	1	–	1 xii	–	–	–
2		Justus			1													
		Antoninus			1	–												
3		Chrodegang		2														
		Remaclus			1													
		Mansuetus				2												
		Aigulphus				2												
4	Marcellus		1 c	1		–	–	–	1 iii	–	–	–	1	–	1 iii	–	–	–
5	Bertinus				1	2	1	–	1 iii	–	–	–	1	–	1 iii	–	–	–
6	[John of Villiers]																1	
7	Clodoaldus, Evortius		1 po	1	–	–	–	–	1 xii	–	–	1	–	–	1 xii	–	–	–
8	*NATIVITY OF MARY*		1 po	1	–	–	–	–	1 d	–	1 xii	–	1	1 xii	1 sa	–	–	–
	ADRIAN		1	–	–	–	–	–	1 m	–	1	–	–		1 m	–	–	–

Saint-Denis calendar: feasts [obits]	Other feasts	Century 9 (Quarter of century) or dates (3–4) MSS		11 (3–4)		12 (1)	13 (1)		 1234–71			 (4)		14	 1350		15 (4)	16 1550
		G	N1	N2	N3	V1	CH	M1	M2	N4	N5	C	M3	B1	V2	B2	N6	N7
September (*contd.*)																		
9 GORGONIUS		1 pm	1	—	—		—	—										
GORGONIUS, Dorotheus									2 xii	1 xii								
Osmanna*									2	1 xii	—	1	—	1 xii	1 d	—	—	—
	Omer			1														
10 GORGONIUS											1 xii	1	—	1 xii	—	—	—	—
11 *PROTUS, HYACINTH*		1 pm	1	—	2		1	—	1 iii	—	—	—	1	—	1 m	—	—	—
13 Maurilius				2	1		—	—	1 iii	—	—	—	1	—	1 m	—	—	—
	CORNEILLE, CYPRIAN			1														
14 *EXALTATION OF HOLY CROSS*		1 po	1		—		—	—	1 xii	—	—	—	1	—	1 d	—	—	—
CORNEILLE, CYPRIAN		1	—		—		—	—	1 m	—	1	—	—	—	1 m	—	—	—
15 *NICOMEDES*		1 pm	1	—	—		—	—	1 m	—	1 iii	—	1	—	1 m	—	—	—
Octave of Mary									1 xii					1	1 xii	—	—	—
[Charles V]																		1
	Aichardus			1														

16	EUPHEMIA, *LUCY, GEMINIAN*		1 pm	1					1 iii				1		1 m			1 iii
17	Lambert		1 c	1	–	–	–	–	1 iii	–	–	–	1	–	1 iii	–	–	–
19		Sequanus			1													
20	VIGIL OF MATTHEW		1	–		–	–	–	–	–	–	–	–		–	–	–	–
	Fausta, Evilasius		1	–	2		1	–	1 iii	–	–	–	1	1	1 iii	1	– iii	–
21	MATTHEW		1 po	1	–	–	–	–	1 xii	–	–	–	1	1	1 xii	– d	–	–
	Alexander		1	–														
22	Maurice*		1 po	1	–	–	–	–	1 d	–	1 xii	–	1	1 xii	1 d	–	–	–
23	Thecla		1 c	1	–	–	–	–	1 iii	–	–	–	1	1 iii	–	–	–	–
24	Geremarus					1	–	–	1 iii	–	–	–	1	1 iii	–	–	–	–
		Conception of John Baptist			1													
25	Firminus*		1 c	1	–	2	1	–	1 D	1 d	1 xii	–	1	1 xii	1 d	–	–	–
	[Matthew of Vendôme]											2						
26	Cyprian, Justina				1	–	–	–	1 iii	–	–	–	1	–	1 iii	–	–	–
	[Matthew of Vendôme]									2				–	1	–	–	–
27	*COSMAS, DAMIAN*		1 pm	–	–	–	–	–	1 XII	1 xii	1 iii	–	1	–	1 xii	–	–	–
28	Cyprian, Justina		1	–														
	Octave of Maurice						1	–	1 xii									
29	*DEDICATION OF CHURCH SAINT MICHAEL*		1 po	1	–	–	*X*	1	1 d	–	1 xii	–	1	–	1 d	–	–	–
30	JEROME		1 po	1	–	–	–	–	1 xii	–	–	–	1	–	1 d	–	–	–

	Saint-Denis calendar: feasts [obits]	Other feasts	Century																
			9 (Quarter of century) or dates		11		12	13							14			15	16
			(3–4) MSS		(3–4)		(1)	(1)		1234–71			(4)			1350		(4)	1550
			G	N1	N2	N3	V1	CH	M1	M2	N4	N5	C	M3	B1	V2	B2	N6	N7
October																			
1	Translation of Remigius		1 po	1												1 xii	–	–	–
	Translations: Remigius, Germanus, Vedast							1											
2	Translations: Remigius, Germanus, Vedast				1				–	1 xii	–	–	–	1	–				
		Translations: Remigius, Germanus				1													
	Translations: Germanus, Vedast															1 m	–	–	–
	[Isabel]																		1
	Leodegarius		1 c	1	–	–		–	–	1 xii	–	–	–	1	–	1 xii	–	–	–
3	Francis											1 xii							
4	Francis									(1) xii	1 xii		–•	1	–	1 xii	–	–	–
	[Blanche]																		1

5	[Philip III]									2				–	1	–	–	–
6	Faith						1	–	1 iii	–	–	–	1	–	1 iii	–	–	–
	[Charles the Bald]						1		–	1 d	1		–	2	1	–		–
	[Constance]											1						
7	*MARK*		1 pm	1	–	–	–	–	1 iii	–	–	–	1	–	1 iii	–	–	–
	MARCELLUS, APULEIUS		1	–	–													
		Sergius, Bacchus				1												
	[Constance]						1		–	–	–		–		–	–	–	
8	Vigil of Denis		1 pm	1	–		–	–	1 iii	1	1 iii			1	–	–	–	–
		Simeon Senex†			2													
9	Denis,* Rusticus*, Eleutherius*		1 po	1	–	–	–	–	1 p	–	1 xii	–	1	1 xii	1 a	–	–	–
	Translation of Richarius			1														
10		Gereon					2											
11		Translation of Augustine					2											
14	*CALLISTUS*		1 c	1	–	–	–	–	(1) iii	(–)	1	1 iii	1					
16	Octave of Denis				1		–	–	–	–	1 xii	1	–	1 xii	1 sa	–	–	–
	Lucian					2			1	–		–						
17	Demetrius								(2) XII	1 d–4	1	–	–	1 xii	1 d	–	–	–
18	LUKE		1 pm	1	–	2	1	–	1 xii	–	–	1	–	1 xii	1 d	–	–	–
19	Sanctinus*, Antoninus*									2 XII	1 xii	–	1	–	1 xii	–	–	–
		Amatus			1													
20	Taurinus													1 iii	–	–	–	–

Saint-Denis calendar: feasts [obits]	Other feasts	Century																
		9 (Quarter of century) or dates		11		12	13							14			15	16
		(3–4) MSS		(3–4)		(1)	(1)		1234–71			(4)			1350		(4)	1550
		G	N1	N2	N3	V1	CH	M1	M2	N4	N5	C	M3	B1	V2	B2	N6	N7
October (*contd.*)																		
21 Eleven Thousand Virgins*							2		(1) xii	1 d	1 xii	–	1	–	1 d	–	–	–
	Hilarion			1														
22 Mellonius				2	–		1	–	1 iii	–	–	1	–	–	1 iii	–	–	–
[Henry Troon]									2	1	–	–	–	2	1	–	–	–
23 Severinus, Romanus				1			–	–	1 iii	–	–	1	–	–	1 iii	–	–	–
Gratian							1		(1)	(–)		1	–					
24 Maglorius				2	1		–	–	1 xii	–	–	–	1	–	1 xii	–	–	–
25 Hilary of Mende*		1 po e	1	–			–	–	1 D	1 d	1 xii	–	1	–	1 d	–	–	–
Crispin, Crispinian		1	–	–	–		–	–	1 iii	–		1 m	1					
Chrysanthus, Daria		1	–															
26 Florentius		1	–	2	–													
Crispin, Crispinian														1	1 iii	–	–	–
[Hugh Foucault]										1		–		2	1	–	–	
27 VIGIL OF SIMON, JUDE		1 mg	1	–	–		–	–	1 xii	1	–	–			–	–	–	
Faro											1 [illegible]							

28	SIMON, JUDE		1 po	1	–	–	–	–	1 xii	–	–	–	1	–	1 d	–	–	–
	Faro		1	–		–	–	–	1 iii	–		1	–					
29	Faro													1 iii	–	–	–	–
30	[Hilduin, Eudes of Deuil, Eudes Taverny]									1		–	–	–	–	–	–	
31	QUINTINUS		1 c	1	–		–	–	1 iii	–	–	–	1	1 iii	–	–	–	–
	Vigil of All Saints		1	–	–	–	–	–	–	–	–	–		–	–	–	–	–
November																		
1	All Saints		1 po	1	–	–	–	–	1 d	–	1 xii	–	1	–	1 sa	–	–	–
	Marcellus								1			–						
2	Eustace*		1 ce	1	–	–	–	–	1 d	–	1 xii	–	1	–	1 d	–	–	–
	All Souls																	1
3	All Souls									1 iii	1	–	–	–	1 d	–	–	
		Hubert			1													
		Marianus, Pelagius			2													
4	Clarus					2	1	–	1 xii	–	–	–	1	–	1 xii	–	–	–
5	Marcellus									1 xii	–	1	–	–	1 xii	–	–	–
	[Margaret]									2								
6	Leonard						1	–	(1) iii	–	1	1 iii	1					
		Dedication of Church of Andrew					2											
		Winoc			1													
		Melanus				2												
	[Louis VIII]													2				

Saint-Denis calendar: feasts [obits]	Other feasts	Century																
		9 (Quarter of century) or dates		11		12	13							14			15	16
		(3–4) MSS		(3–4)		(1)	(1)		1234–71			(4)			1350		(4)	1550
		G	N1	N2	N3	V1	CH	M1	M2	N4	N5	C	M3	B1	V2	B2	N6	N7
November (*contd.*)																		
7 Octave of All Saints [Louis VIII]									(1) xii	1 xii 2		1 xii	1		1	–	–	
8 *FOUR CROWNED MARTYRS*		1 pm	1	–	–		–	–	(–)	–	1	1 iii	–					
Octave of All Saints [Louis VIII]								1	(–)	1 XII	1 xii	–	–	1	1 xii	–	–	–
9 *THEODORE*		1 pm	1		–		–	–	(–)	1 iii	1	1 xii	1					
	THEODORE, Ragnulfus			1														
Octave of Eustace								1	(1) xii	1 xii	–			1	1 xii	–	–	–
10 *THEODORE*														1	1 iii	–	–	–
11 *MARTIN*		1 po	1	–	–		–	–	(1) xii	1 d–4	1 xii	–	1	–	1 d	–	–	–
MENNAS		1	–	–	–		–	–	(–)	1 m	1	–		–	1 m	–	–	–
13 Brice		1 c	1	–	–		–	–	1 xii	–	–	–	1	–	1 xii	–	–	–
15 Eugene*		1	–	–			–		1 d	–	1 xii	–	1	–	1 d	–	–	–
	Malo				1													

17	Anianus		1 c	1	–		–	–	1 iii	–	–	–	1					
		Anianus, Gregory				1												
18	Octave of Martin				1		–	–	1 xii	–	–	–	1	–	–	1 xii	–	–
19	Anianus													1	1 iii	–	–	–
20	Edmund					2	1	–	(–) xii	1 xii	–	–	1	–	1	1 xii	–	–
21	VIGIL OF CECELIA		1 pm	1														
	Columbanus				2	1	–	–	(1) iii	1 iii	–	–	1	–	1 xii	1 iii	–	–
22	*CECELIA*		1 po	1	–	–	–	–	(1) xii	1 xii	–	–	1	–	1 xii	–	–	–
23	*CLEMENT**		1 po	1	–	–	–	–	(1) xii	1 d	1 xii	–	1	1 xii	1 d	–	–	–
	FELICITY		1	–	2	1		–	(–)	1 m	1	–	–		1 m	–	–	–
23	Severinus		1	–														
24	*CHRYSOGONUS*		1 pm	1	–	–	–	–	1 m	–	1	–	–		1 m	–	–	–
	Romanus of Blaye*				1	2	1	–	1 D	1 d	1 xii	–	1	–	1 d	–	–	–
25	Catherine						1	2	1 xii	–	–	–	1	–	1 sd	–	–	–
		Peter				2												
26		Linus			1	2												
27		Vitalis, Agricola				2												
	[Blanche]									1		–		–	–	–	–	
29	*SATURNINUS*		1 c	1	–	–	–	–	(1) iii	1 iii	–	–	1	–	1 iii	–	–	–
	VIGIL OF ANDREW		1		–	–	–	–	(–)	–	1	–	–		–	–	–	–
		Sisinius			2													
	[Philip IV]													2	1	–	–	
30	*ANDREW*		1 po	1	–	–	*X*	–	(1) xii	1 d	1 xii	–	1	–	1 d	–	–	–

	Saint-Denis calendar: feasts [obits]	Other feasts	Century																
			9 (Quarter of century) or dates		11		12	13							14			15	16
			(3–4) MSS		(3–4)		(1)	(1)		1234–71			(4)			1350		(4)	1550
			G	N1	N2	N3	V1	CH	M1	M2	N4	N5	C	M3	B1	V2	B2	N6	N7
December																			
1	Eligius		1 c	1	–	–	–	–	–	(1) xii	1 xii	–	–	1	1 xii	–	–	–	–
		Chrysanthus, Daria				1													
2	All Souls							–				X							
4	Illation of Benedict				1	–		–		(1) xii	1 xii	–	–	1	1 xii	–	–	–	–
	Barbara									(1)	–	–	–	–					
6	Nicholas				1	–	–	–	–	(1) xii	1 d	1 xii	–	1	–	1 d	–	–	–
7	OCTAVE OF ANDREW				1	–		–	–	(1) xii	1 xii	–	–	1	1 xii	–	–	–	–
		Babolenus				1													
		Phara					1												
8	Conception of Mary						2	–		(1)	–				1 xii	1 sa	–	–	–
10	Eulalia		1 c	1	2	–	1	–	–	(1) iii	1 iii	–	–	1	–	1 m	–	–	–
11	DAMASUS		1 mg	1	–	2	1	–	–	(1) iii	1 iii	–	–	1	–	1 m	–	–	–
		Victoricus, Fuscian, Gentian			1														
12	Walaricus				1		–	–	–	(1) iii	1 iii	–	–	1	–	1 m	–	–	–

13	*LUCY*		1 pm	1	–	–	–	–	–	(1) xii	1 xii	–	–	1	1 xii	–	–	–	–
		Judocus						2											
		Autbert			1														
14		Nicasius			1			2											
15	Maximinus		1 c	1	2	1	–	–	–	(1) xii	1 xii	–	–	1	1 xii	–	–	–	–
21	THOMAS		1 po	1	–	–	–	–	–	(1) xii	1 xii	–	–	1	–	1 d	–	–	–
23	[Margaret]														1	–	–	–	
24	Vigil of Christmas		1 pm	1	–	–	–	–	–	–	(–)	1 iii	–	1	–	–	1 iii	1	–
25	*CHRISTMAS*		1 po	1	–	–	–	–	–	1 p	(1)	–	1 xii	1	–	1 a	–	–	–
	Anastasia		1	–		–	–		–	1 m	(1)		1 xii	1		1 m	–	–	–
	Eugenia		1	–			–												
26	*STEPHEN*†		1 po	1	–	–	–	–	–	1 d	(–)	1 xii	–	1	–	1 d	–	–	–
27	*JOHN*		1 po	1	–	–	–	–	–	1 d	(–)	1 xii	–	1		1 sa	–	–	–
28	*INNOCENTS**		1 po	1	–	–	–	–	–	1 xii	(–)	–	–	1	1 xii	1 d	–	–	–
29	Thomas of Canterbury							1		(1) xii	(–)	–	–	1	1 xii	–	–	–	–
		David			2														
30	[Giles]														1	–	–	–	–
31	*SILVESTER*		1 pm	–	–	–	–	–	–	1 xii	–	–	–	1	1 xii	–	–	–	–
	Columba		1	–		–	–		–	(–)	–	1	–	–					

APPENDIX B.

Chronology of Liturgical Sources from Saint-Denis

Date	*Manuscript*
700	
	F:Pn, lat. 256
	I:Rvat, Reg. lat. 257
750	
800	
	F:Pn, lat. 9387
850	I:VEcap LXXXVIII
878	
	F:Pn, lat. 2290
	F:LA 118 (gradual)
	F:R(m), A. 566 (see below)
900	
	F:LA 118 (sacramentary, lectionary)
	F:Psg 1186 (psalter)
950	F:Pn, n.a.l. 305
	F:R(m), A. 566 (see above and below)
1000	
	F:Pm 384
	F:Psg 1186 (hymnal)
	F:Pn, lat. 103 (psalter)
	F:R(m), A. 566 (see above)
1022	F:Pn, grec. 375
1050	F:Pn, lat. 9436
	F:Pn, lat. 103 (hymnal)
1100	
1140	
	F:Pn, lat. 17296
1150	
	F:Pn, lat. 16820

Date	*Manuscript*
	F:Pn, n.a.l. 306
	F:Pn, n.a.l. 307
1200	
	F:Pn, n.a.l. 1420 (see below)
1210	
	Chapel Hill, Univ. Lib., Rare Book Coll. 11
1216	
	F:Pm 414
1234	
	F:Pm 526
1236	
1240	F:Pn, lat. 846
1250	
	F:Pn, lat. 976
1259	
	F:Pn, lat. 1107
1271	
	I:Rc 603
1300	
	F:Pn, n.a.l. 1420 (see above)
	F:Pn, lat. 10505
1350	GB:Lva 1346–1891
	GB:Ob, Can. Lit. 192
	model for F:Pan, L 863, No. 10 (see below)
1364	
1400	
1450	

Date	*Manuscript*	*Date*	*Manuscript*
1474	F:Pn, lat. 1072	1650	
1493		1700	
1500		1750	
1550	F:Pn, Rés. B. 5209	1760	F:Pan, L 863, No. 10 (see above)
1600			

APPENDIX C.

Liturgical Manuscripts by Genre

SOURCES FROM SAINT-DENIS (DESCRIBED IN CHAPTER 6)

Antiphoner

F:Pn, lat. 17296: Paris, Bibliothèque Nationale, lat. 17296

Breviary—unnotated

F:Pn, Rés. B. 5209: Paris, Bibliothèque Nationale, Rés. B. 5209, and B. 5209 *bis*
GB:Ob, Can. Lit. 192: Oxford, Bodleian Library, Can. Lit. 192 (19309)

Evangeliary

F:Pn, lat. 256: Paris, Bibliothèque Nationale, lat. 256
F:Pn, lat. 9387: Paris, Bibliothèque Nationale, lat. 9387
F:Pn, n.a.l. 305: Paris, Bibliothèque Nationale, n.a.l. 305
F:Pn, n.a.l. 1420: Paris, Bibliothèque Nationale, n.a.l. 1420

Gradual

F:Pm 384: Paris, Bibliothèque Mazarine 384 (748)

Gradual/Sacramentary/Lectionary

F:LA 118: Laon, Bibliothèque Municipale 118

Hours (Book of)

F:Pn, lat. 1072: Paris, Bibliothèque Nationale, lat. 1072

Lectionary for the Mass

F:Pn, grec. 375: Paris, Bibliothèque Nationale, grec. 375
F:Pn, n.a.l. 307: Paris, Bibliothèque Nationale, n.a.l. 307

Lectionary for the Office

F:Pn, lat. 16820: Paris, Bibliothèque Nationale, lat. 16820

Missal—notated

F:Pn, lat. 1107: Paris, Bibliothèque Nationale, lat. 1107
F:Pn, lt. 10505: Paris, Bibliothèque Nationale, lat. 10505
GB:Lva 1346–1891: London, Victoria and Albert Museum 1346–1891

Missal—unnotated

F:Pm 414: Paris, Bibliothèque Mazarine 414 (735)
F:Pn, lat. 846: Paris, Bibliothèque Nationale, lat. 846
I:Rc 603: Rome, Biblioteca Casanatense 603 (B. IV. 25)

Ordinary

F:Pan, L 863, No. 10: Paris, Archives Nationales, L 863, No. 10
F:Pm 526: Paris, Bibliothèque Mazarine, MS 526 (744)
F:Pn, lat. 976: Paris, Bibliothèque Nationale, lat. 976.

Pontifical

F:Pn, n.a.l. 306: Paris, Bibliothèque Nationale, n.a.l. 306

Psalter

Chapel Hill, Univ. Lib., Rare Book Coll. 11: Chapel Hill, University Library, Rare Book Collection 11

Psalter/Hymnal

F:Pn, lat. 103: Paris, Bibliothèque Nationale, lat. 103
F:Psg 1186: Paris, Bibliothèque Sainte-Geneviève 1186

Readings for the day Hours

I:VEcap LXXXVIII: Verona, Biblioteca Capitolare (Cattedrale) LXXXVIII

Sacramentary

F:Pn, lat. 2290: Paris, Bibliothèque Nationale, lat. 2290
F:R(m), A. 566: Rouen, Bibliothèque Municipale, A. 566
I:Rvat, Reg. lat. 257: Rome, Biblioteca Apostolica Vaticana, Reg. lat. 257

Sacramentary/Gradual (augmented sacramentary)

F:Pn, lat. 9436: Paris, Bibliothèque Nationale, lat. 9436

SOURCES DESCRIBED IN CHAPTER 7

Breviary—notated

Vendôme, Bibl. Mun. 17C: Vendôme, Bibliothèque Municipale 17C

Evangeliary

D:Mbs, Clm. 14000: Munich, Bayerische Staatsbibliothek, Clm. 14000

Gradual/Antiphoner

Paris, Private Collection, Manuscript of Mont-Renaud

Missal—notated

I:Rc 1695: Rome, Biblioteca Casanatense 1695
Sheffield, Ruskin Museum (*olim* Reading, University Library, Ruskin Collection of the Guild of Saint-George, R. 3549)

Psalter

F:Pn, lat. 1152: Paris, Bibliothèque Nationale, lat. 1152

Sacramentary

F:Pn, lat. 1141: Paris, Bibliothèque Nationale, lat. 1141
F:Pn, lat. 2292: Paris, Bibliothèque Nationale, lat. 2292
I:Rvat, Ott. lat. 313: Rome, Biblioteca Apostolica Vaticana, Ott. 313
I:Rvat, Reg. lat. 316: Rome, Biblioteca Apostolica Vaticana, Reg. lat. 316; and F:Pn, lat. 7193: Paris, Bibliothèque Nationale, lat. 7193 (fos. 41–56^{v})
I:Rvat, Reg. lat. 337: Rome, Biblioteca Apostolica Vaticana, Reg. lat. 337
F:Pn, lat. 2291: Paris, Bibliothèque Nationale, lat. 2291

Sacramentary/Gradual

F:Psg 111: Paris, Bibliothèque Sainte-Geneviève 111 (BB 20)

APPENDIX D.

Published Fascimiles of Musical Notation

Manuscript	*Folio*	*Published source*
I. SAINT-DENIS NOTATIONS		
A. *Neumatic notation*		
F:Pm 384	5	Huglo, 'Débuts', pl. 2
	10	*PM* (1st ser.), iii, pl. 186
	10	*PM* (1st ser.), iii, pl. 186
	48	Corbin, *Neumen*, pl. 41
	95^{v}	Huglo, *Musicologie*, pl. x
	95^{v}	Stahl, 'Painting', Fig. 19
	133, 134^{v}	Corbin and Bernard, *Répertoire*, ii, pl. 1
	153	Huglo, 'Chants', pl. following p. 78
	158, 160^{v}	Corbin and Bernard, *Répertoire*, ii, pl. 2
	Entire gradual	Hesbert, *Graduel*
B. *Neumatic and transitional notation on dry-point lines*		
F:Pn, lat. 17296	41^{v}	Steiner, 'Melismas', fig. 5
	51^{v}	Hesbert, *CAO*, ii, pl. ix
	73^{v}	Stahl, 'Problem', fig. 4
	136^{v}–7	Stäblein, *Schriftbild*, pl. 39
	171	Robertson, '*Benedicamus*', fig. 2
	340^{v}–1	Stäblein, *Schriftbild*, pl. 40
C. *Square notation on stafflines*		
F:Pn, lat. 1107	19^{v}	Branner, *Painting*, fig. 386 Parrish, *Notation*, pl. viii
	144^{v}	Huglo, *Musicologie*, pl. xi
	348^{v}	Stäblein, 'Gallikanische', cols. 1307–8
GB:Lva 1346–1891	34	Byrne, 'Drawing', pl. 4
	34	*Fastes*, 321 (No. 273)
	256^{v}	Avril, *Enluminure*, pl. 21 Laborde, *Manuscrits*, pl. x
	376	Walters [Robertson], 'Reconstruction', fig. 2

Manuscript	*Folio*	*Published source*
II. NEUMATIC NOTATIONS OF THE MONT-RENAUD MANUSCRIPT AND OF F:Pn, lat. 9436		
Mont-Renaud MS	Entire MS	*PM*, xvi
F:Pn, lat. 9436	2	Huglo, *Musicologie*, pl. vii
	20	Schulten, 'Buchmalrei', fig. 35
	41 [42]	*PM*, xvi, near end of vol.
	56v	Schulten, 'Buchmalerei', fig. 37
	127v	Parrish, *Notation*, pl. iii

APPENDIX E.

Music and Texts Composed at Saint-Denis

	Discussed in	*Example*
I. *Music and text from Saint-Denis*		
French *chanson En non Dieu, c'est la rage*	Ch. 5	
French *chanson Amors m'a assise rente*	Ch. 5	
French *chanson D'amors me doit sovenir*	Ch. 5	
Office for Saint Denis (up to late 9th c.)	Ch. 1, Ch. 5	
Prosula *Christo nato de virgine*	Ch. 3	3.1
Prosula *Hebraeorum gens*	Ch. 3	3.1
Prosula *Inter hec frendet*	Ch. 3	3.1
Rhymed Office for Saint Denis (11th c.)	Ch. 4	Pl. 9
Seq. *Salve pater Dionysi*	Ch. 4	4.3
II. *Text only from Saint-Denis*		
Gloria Patri *Gloria deo patro magno*	Ch. 3	3.3
Hy. *Celi cives*	Ch. 4	
Kyrie Trope *O christe precamur*	Ch. 3	
Prosula *Et intellectus johannem*	Ch. 3	
Prosula *Hodie processit regina*	Ch. 3	
Prosula *Judicabunt innocentes*	Ch. 3	3.2
Prosula *Justus johannes*	Ch. 3	3.2, Pl. 13
Prosula *Justus virginitate*	Chs. 3, 4	3.2, Pl. 13
Prosula *Non vos quos eligi*	Chs. 3, 4	
Resp. *Clavus refulgens*	Ch. 2	
Seq. *Ave lux insignis*	Ch. 4	
Seq. *Ave pater gallie*	Ch. 4	
Seq. *Christo regi glorie*	Ch. 4	
Seq. *Doctorem egregium*	Ch. 4	
Seq. *Gaude plebs Autrica*	Ch. 4	
Seq. *Laudemus omnes dominum in sanctis gloriosum*	Ch. 4	
Seq. *Letabundus exultet fidelis coetus*	Ch. 4	
Seq. *Plebs fidelis jubila*	Ch. 4	
Seq. *Psallat cum tripudio*	Ch. 4	

	Discussed in	*Example*
III. *Music and text possibly from Saint-Denis*		
Ant. *Benedicat nos deus pater*	Ch. 4	4.1
Ant. *Salvator omnium deus peccatorum*	Ch. 4	Walters [Robertson], 'Reconstruction', ex. 1
French motet *En non Dieu, c'est la rage*	Ch. 5	
Monophonic *conductus Clavis clavo retunditur*	Ch. 5	
Polyphonic *conductus Clavus pungens*	Ch. 5	

BIBLIOGRAPHY

Abbess of Stanbrook (Laurentia McLachlan) and Tolhurst, J. (eds.), *The Ordinal and Customary of the Abbey of Saint Mary York*, 3 vols., HBS 73, 75, 84 (London, 1936–51).

Acta Sanctorum, 67 vols. (Antwerp, 1643–1902).

Adler, A., '*Pèlerinage de Charlemagne* in a New Light on Saint-Denis', *Speculum* 22 (1947), 550–61.

Aebischer, P., *Le Voyage de Charlemagne à Jérusalem et à Constantinople*, Textes littéraires français (Geneva, 1965).

Aimoin, *Libri quinque de gestis Francorum* (Paris, 1602).

Alès, A., *Description des livres de liturgie imprimés aux XVe et XVIe siècles faisant partie de la bibliothèque de S.A.R. Mgr Charles-Louis de Bourbon* (Paris, 1878).

Allard, G.-H., *Jean Scot écrivain: Actes du IVe colloque international, Montréal, 28 août–2 septembre 1983*, Cahiers d'études médiévales, Cahier spécial, 1 (Montreal and Paris, 1986).

Amiet, R., 'Le Prologue *Hucusque* et la table des *Capitula* du supplément d'Alcuin au sacramentaire grégorien', *Scriptorium* 7 (1953), 177–209.

Analecta Hymnica Medii Aevi, 55 vols. (Leipzig, 1888–1922).

Anderson, G., 'Newly Identified Tenor Chants in the Notre Dame Repertory', *ML* 50 (1969), 158–71.

Andoyer, R. P., 'Le Bréviaire de Saint-Denis-en-France', *RM* 1 (1905), 139–57, 195–210.

Andrieu, M., *Les Ordines romani du haut moyen âge*, 5 vols. (Louvain, 1931–61).

Anglès, H., 'Latin Chant before St. Gregory', *NOHM* ii: *Early Medieval Music up to 1300*, ed. A. Hughes (London, 1954).

Anselm de Saint-Marie, *Histoire généalogique et chronologique de la maison royale de France et des grands officiers de la couronne*, 3rd edn., 9 vols. (New York, 1967).

Apel, W., *Gregorian Chant* (Bloomington, Ind., 1958).

Les Archives nationales: Etat général des fonds, 4 vols. (Paris, 1978).

Arlt, W., *Ein Festoffizium des Mittelalters aus Beauvais in seiner liturgischen und musikalischen Bedeutung*, 2 vols. (Cologne, 1970).

Atkinson, C. M., '*O Amnos Tu Theu*: The Greek Agnus Dei in the Roman Liturgy from the Eighth to the Eleventh Century', *Kirchenmusikalisches Jahrbuch* 65 (1981), 7–30.

——, The *Doxa*, the *Pisteuo*, and the *ellinici fratres*: Some Anomalies in the Transmission of the Chants of the "Missa graeca"', *JM* 7 (1989), 81–106.

——, 'The Earliest Agnus Dei Melody and its Tropes', *JAMS* 30 (1977), 1–19.

——, 'Zur Entstehung und Überlieferung der "Missa graeca"', *Archiv für Musikwissenschaft* 39 (1982), 113–45.

Atsma, H., and Vezin, J., 'Le Dossier suspect des possessions de Saint-Denis en Angleterre revisité (VIIIe–IXe siècles)', *Fälschungen im Mittelalter: Internationaler Kongress der Monumenta Germaniae Historica, München. 16.–19. September 1986*, 5 vols., Monumenta Germaniae Historica Schriften 33/1 (Hanover, 1988), iv. 211–36.

Aubry, P., *Cent Motets du XIIIe siècle*, 3 vols. (Paris, 1908).

——, 'Comment fut perdu et retrouvé le saint clou de l'abbaye de Saint-Denys', *RM* 2 (1906), 185–92, 286–300; 3 (1907), 43–50, 147–82.

——, *Le Roman de Fauvel* (Paris, 1907).

——, 'Un Chant historique latin du XIIIe siècle: Le saint clou de Saint-Denys (1223)', *Le Mercure Musicale* 1 (1905), 423–34.

Avril, F., *L'Enluminure à la cour de France au XIVe siècle* (New York, 1978).

——, 'Un Chef-d'œuvre de l'enluminure sous le règne de Jean le Bon, la Bible moralisée, manuscrit français 167 de la Bibliothèque nationale', *Monuments et mémoires de la Fondation Eugène Piot* 58 (1972), 95–125.

Ayzac, F. d', *Histore de l'abbaye de Saint-Denis en France*, 2 vols. (Paris, 1860–61).

Bailey, T., *The Processions of Sarum and the Western Church* (Toronto, 1971).

Baldwin, J., *The Government of Philip Augustus: Foundations of French Royal Power in the Middle Ages* (Berkeley, Calif., 1986).

Baltzer, R., 'Another Look at a Composite Office and its History: The Feast of *Susceptio Reliquiarum* in Medieval Paris', *PRMA* 113 (1988), 1–27.

——, 'Johannes de Garlandia', *NGD* ix. 662–4.

Bannister, H. (ed.), *Monumenti Vaticani di paleografia musicale latina*, Codices e Vaticanis selecti phototypice expressi 12 (Leipzig, 1913).

—— (ed.), *Sequentiae Ineditae, Liturgische Prosen des Mittelalters*, *AH*, xl (Leipzig, 1902).

Barbet, J., *Johannis Scoti Eriugena Expositiones in Ierarchiam Coelestem*, CC, Continuatio Mediaevalis 31 (Turnholt, 1975).

Barclay, B., 'The Medieval Repertory of Polyphonic Untroped "Benedicamus Domino" Settings', 2 vols. (Ph.D. diss., Univ. of California at Los Angeles, 1977).

Barré, H., and Deshusses, J., 'À la Recherche du missel d'Alcuin', EL 82 (1968), 22–45.

Barroux, M., *Les Fêtes royales de Saint-Denis en mai 1389* (Paris, 1936).

Barroux, R., 'L'Anniversaire de la mort de Dagobert à Saint-Denis au XIIe siècle, charte inédité de l'abbé Adam', *Bulletin philologique et historique (1942–3), 131–51.*

Bastgen, H. (ed.), Libri Carolini, MGH, *Legum*, Sectio iii, *Concilia* ii, Supplementum (Hanover, 1895).

Bastiaensen, A., 'L'Antienne "Genuit puerpera regem": Adaptation liturgique d'un passage du "Paschale Carmen" de Sedulius', *RB* 83 (1973), 388–97.

Bates, R. C., 'Le Pèlerinage de Charlemagne: A Baroque Epic', *Yale Romanic Studies* 18 (1941), 1–47.

Bäumer, S., *Histoire du bréviaire*, trans. Reginald Biron, 2 vols. (Paris, 1905).

Bautier, R., Giles, M., Duchez, M. E., and Huglo, M. (eds.), *Odorannus de Sens Opera Omnia* (Paris, 1972).

Bautier, R., and Labory, G. (trans. and eds.), *Helgaud de Fleury: Vie de Robert le Pieux*, Sources d'histoire médiévale 1 (Paris, 1965).

Baxter, J. H., *An Old St. Andrews Music Book* (London, 1931).

Beaune, C., *Naissance de la nation France*, Bibliothèque des histoires (Paris, 1985).

Beck, J., and Beck, L., *Le Manuscrit du roi*, 2 vols., Corpus Cantilenarum Medii Aevi, 1st ser., Les Chansonniers des Troubadours et des Trouvères 2 (Philadelphia, 1938).

Bellaguet, M. L. (eds.), *Chronique du religieux de Saint-Denys*, 6 vols. (Paris, 1839–52).

Benedictine Monks of St Augustine's Abbey, Ramsgate (eds.), *The Book of Saints: A Dictionary of Servants of God Canonized by the Catholic Church*, 4th edn. (New York, 1947); 5th edn. (London, 1966).

Bennett, P., 'Le *Pèlerinage de Charlemagne*: le sens de l'aventure', *Essor et fortune de la chanson de geste dans l'Europe et l'Orient latin*, 2 vols. (Modena, 1984), ii. 475–87.

Benson, R., and Constable, G. (eds.,), *Renaissance and Renewal in the Twelfth Century* (Cambridge, Mass., 1982).

Benton, J., 'Introduction: Suger's Life and Personality', *Abbot Suger and Saint-Denis*, ed. P. Gerson (New York, 1986), 3–15.

Berger, E., 'Annales de Saint-Denis généralement connues sous le titre de *Chronicon Sancti Dionysii ad Cyclos Paschales*', *BEC* 40 (1879), 261–95.

Berger, S., *Histoire de la Vulgate* (Nancy, 1893).

Besse, J. M., *Les Moines de l'ancienne France* (Paris, 1906).

Besson, M., *Monasterium Acaunense: Etudes critiques sur les origines de St-Maurice en Valais* (Fribourg, 1913).

Beyssac, G., 'Le Graduel-antiphonaire du Mont-Renaud', *RdM* 40 (1957), 131–50.

Biblioteca Vaticana, *XV Centenario della Nascita di S. Benedetto (480–1980): Catalogo della Mostra* (Vatican, 1980).

Bibliothèque Nationale, *Catalogue général des manuscrits latins*, 6 vols. (Paris, 1939–75).

——, *Inventaire des nouvelles acquisitions latines*, 2 vols. (n.d., n.p.).

——, *La Librairie de Charles V* (Paris, 1968).

——, *Les Manuscrits à peintures en France du VIIe au XIIe siècle*, 2nd edn. (Paris, 1954).

——, *Les Manuscrits à peintures en France du XIIe au XVIe siècle* (Paris, 1955).

Bischoff, B., 'Die Hofbibliothek unter Ludwig dem Frommen', *Karl der Grosse: Lebenswerk und Nachleben*, ii: *Das Geistige Leben* (Düsseldorf, 1965), 42–62.

——, 'Die Kölner Nonnehandschriften und das Skriptorium von Chelles', *Forschungen zur Kunstgeschichte und christliche Archäologie* 3 (Wiesbaden, 1957), 395–411.

——, *Die Südostdeutschen Schreibschulen und Bibliotheken in der Karolinger-*

zeit, 3rd edn., 2 vols.; i: *Die Bayrischen Diözesen*; ii: *Die Vorwiegend Österreicheschen Diözessen* (Wiesbaden, 1974–80).
——, 'Eine Beschreibung der Basilika von Saint-Denis aus dem Jahre 799', *Kunstchronik* 34/3 (1981), 97–103.
——, *Paläographie des römischen Altertums und des abendländischen Mittelalters*, 2nd edn., Grundlagen der Germanistik 24, ed. H. Moser and H. Steinecke (Berlin, 1986).
Bishop, E., *Liturgica Historica: Papers in the Liturgy and Religious Life of the Western Church* (Oxford, 1918).
Bjork, D., 'The Kyrie Trope', *JAMS* 33 (1980), 1–41.
Björkvall, G., Iversen, G., and Jonsson, R. (eds.), CT iii: *Tropes du propre de la messe, 2. Cycle de Pâques*, SLS 25 (Stockholm, 1982).
Blum, P., and Crosby, S., 'Le Portail central de la façade occidentale de Saint-Denis', *Bulletin monumental* 131 (1973), 209–16.
Blume, C. (ed.), *Hymnodia Gotica, Die Mozarabischen Hymnen des alt-spanischen Ritus*, *AH* xxvii (Leipzig, 1897).
——, *Sequentiae Ineditae, Liturgische Prosen des Mittelalters*, *AH* xxxiv, xxxvii, xxxix, xlii, xliv (Leipzig, 1900–4).
——, *Thesauri Hymnoligici Hymnarium, Die Hymnen des Thesaurus Hymnologicus H. A. Daniels*, *AH* li (Leipzig, 1908).
——, *Thesauri Hymnologici Prosarium, Liturgische Prosen zweiter Epoche auf Feste der Heiligen*, *AH* lv (Leipzig, 1922).
—— and Bannister, H. (eds.), *Thesauri Hymnologici Prosarium, Liturgische Prosen des Übergangstiles und der zweiten Epoche*, *AH* liv (Leipzig, 1915).
—— and ——, *Thesauri Hymnologici Prosarium, Liturgische Prosen erster Epoche*, *AH* liii (Leipzig, 1911).
—— and ——, *Tropi Graduales, Tropen des Missale im Mittelalter*, ii: *Tropen zum Ordinarium Missae*, *AH* lxvii (Leipzig, 1905).
Boe, J., 'Gloria A and the Roman Easter Vigil Ordinary', *MD* 36 (1982 [1985]), 5–37.
Bohatta, H., *Bibliographie der Breviere, 1501–1850* (Leipzig, 1937).
Bonniwell, W., *A History of the Dominican Liturgy* (New York, 1944).
Borders, J., 'The Cathedral of Verona as a Musical Center in the Middle Ages; Its History, Manuscripts, and Liturgical Practice', 2 vols. (Ph.D. diss., Univ. of Chicago, 1983).
——, 'The Northern Italian Antiphons *ante evangelium* and the Gallican Connection', *The Journal of Musicological Research* 8 (1988), 1–53.
Bordier, E., *Des Reliques de Saint Edmond roi et martyr* (Paris, 1971).
Boretius, A. (ed.), *Capitularia regum Francorum*, 2 vols., *MGH*, *Legum*, Sectio III (Berlin, 1883).
Bosse, D., *Untersuchungen einstimmiger mittelalterlicher Melodien zum Gloria in excelsis Deo*, Foschungsbeiträge zur Musikwissenschaft 2 (Regensburg, 1955).
Bouchot, H., *Les Reliures d'art à la Bibliothèque Nationale* (Paris, 1988).
Bourque, E., *Étude sur les sacramentaires romains*, 2 vols., Studi di Antichità Christiana 20, 25 (Rome, 1948–58).

Boussel, P., *Des Reliques et de leur bon usage* (Paris, 1971).

Boutemy, A. 'Le Style franco-saxon, style de Saint-Amand', *Scriptorium* 3 (1949), 261–4.

——, 'Quel fut le foyer du style franco-saxon', *Annales du congrès archéologique et historique de Tournai* (1949), 749–73.

Branner, R., *The Manuscript Painting in Paris during the Reign of Saint Louis* (Berkeley, Calif., 1977).

Brenet, M., *Les Musiciens de la Sainte-Chapelle du palais* (Paris, 1910).

Brou, L., 'L'Antienne "Dignum namque est": sa source littéraire', *SE* 4 (1952), 217–25.

——, 'Le Sacramentaire de Nonantola', EL 64 (1950), 274–82.

——, 'Les Chants en langue grecque dans les liturgies latines', *SE* 1 (1948), 165–80.

Brouette, É., 'Bathildis, St.', *NCE* ii. 164.

Brown, E. A. R., 'The Ceremonial of Royal Succession in Capetian France', *Speculum* 55 (1980), 266–93.

—— and Cothren, M. W., 'The Twelfth-Century Crusading Window of the Abbey of Saint-Denis: "Praeteritorum enim recordatio futurorum est exhibitio"', *JWCI* 49 (1986), 1–40.

Brown, J. H., 'A Thirteenth Century St.-Denis Psalter: MS. 11 in the Rare Book Collection of Louis Round Wilson Library, University of North Carolina at Chapel Hill' (Master's thesis, Univ. of North Carolina at Chapel Hill, 1976).

Brubaker, L., 'Codex Aureus', *DMA* iii. 474.

Bruckner, A., and Marichal, R. (eds.), *Chartae Latinae Antiquiores: Facsimile edition of the Latin Charters Prior to the Ninth Century*, xiii, xiv, xv, xvii, xviii, xix: *France*, ii, iii, v, vi, vii, ed. H. Atsma and J. Vezin (Zurich, 1981, 1982, 1986, 1984, 1985, 1987).

Bruzelius, C., *The 13th-Century Church at St-Denis*, Yale Publications in the History of Art 33 (New Haven, Conn., 1985).

Bryden. J. R., and Hughes, D. G., *An Index of Gregorian Chant*, 2 vols. (Cambridge, 1969).

Buchner, M. 'Das Vizepapsttum des Abtes von St. Denis', *Quellen-fälschungen aus dem Gebiete der Geschichte*, 3 vols. (Paderborn, 1928).

Bukofzer, M., 'Changing Aspects of Medieval and Renaissance Music', *MQ* 44 (1958), 1–18.

Burgess, G., and Cobby, A., *The Pilgrimage of Charlemagne (Le Pèlerinage de Charlemagne) and Aucassin and Nicolette (Aucassin et Nicolette)*, Garland Library of Medieval Literature 47, ser. A (New York and London, 1988).

Burn, A., *The Athanasian Creed and its Early Commentaries*, Texts and Studies 4/7 (Cambridge, 1896).

Butler, C., *Benedictine Monachism* (London, 1919).

Byrne, D., 'A 14th-Century French Drawing in Berlin and the *Livre du Voir-Dit* of Guillaume de Machaut', *Zeitschrift für Kunstgeschichte* 47 (1984), 70–81.

Cabaniss, A. (trans.), *The Emperor's Monk: Contemporary Life of Benedict of Aniane by Ardo* (Ilfracombe, Devon, 1979).

'Calendar, Christian', *CE* iii. 158–68.

Calkins, R., *Illuminated Books of the Middle Ages* (Ithaca, NY, 1983).

——, *Programs of Medieval Illumination*, Franklin D. Murphy Lecture 5 (Lawrence, Kan., 1984).

Campbell, T. (ed. and trans.), *Dionysius the Pseudo-Areopagite: The Ecclesiastical Hierarchy* (Washington, DC, 1981).

Canal, J., 'Elementos Marianos en la antigua liturgia romana', *Ephemerides Mariologicae* 16 (1966), 289–318.

Cappuyns, M., *Jean Scot Erigène: sa vie, son œuvre, sa pensée*, Universitas Catholica Lovaniensis, Dissertationes ad gradum magistri in Facultate Theologica consequendum conscriptae, series ii, Tomus 26 (Louvain, 1933).

Cardine, E., 'Preuves paléographiques du principe des "coupures" dans les neumes', *EG* 4 (1961), 43–54.

Carmody, F., *Le Pèlerinage de Charlemagne: Sources et parallèles* (Darien, Conn., 1967).

Carolus-Barré, L., 'Pillage et dispersion de la bibliothèque de l'abbaye de Saint-Denis, 1er octobre–10 novembre 1567', *BEC* 138 (1980), 97–101.

Carpe, W., 'The *Vita Canonica* in the *Regula Canonicorum* of Chrodegang of Metz' (Ph.D. diss., Univ. of Chicago, 1975).

Castets, M., '*Iter Hierosolymitanum* ou Voyage de Charlemagne à Jérusalem et à Constantinople: Texte latin d'après le ms. de Montpellier', *Revue des langues romanes*, 4th ser., 36 (1892), 417–74.

Catalogue général des manuscrits des bibliothèques publiques des départements, 7 vols. (Paris, 1849–85).

Catalogue of Additions to the Manuscripts of the British Museum in the Years 1876–1881 (London, 1882).

Catalogue of the Harleian Manuscripts in the British Museum, 4 vols. (London, 1808–12).

'Catalogus Codicum Hagiographicorum Latinorum Bibliothecae Publicae Rotomagensis', *Analecta Bollandiana* 23 (1904), 129–275.

Catholic Encylopedia, The, 15 vols. (New York, 1907–12).

Caviness, M., 'Suger's Glass at Saint-Denis: The State of Research', *Abbot Suger and Saint-Denis*, ed. P. Gerson (New York, 1986), 257–72.

Charlemagne, œuvre, rayonnement et survivances (Düsseldorf, 1965).

Chavasse, A., 'Aménagements liturgiques, à Rome, au VIIe et au VIIIe siècle', *RB* 99 (1989), 75–102.

——, *Le Sacramentaire dans le groupe dit "gélasiens du VIIIe siècle": Étude des procédés de confection et synoptique nouveau modèle*, 2 vols., Instrumenta Patristica, 14A and 14B (Steenbrugis, 1984).

——, 'Le Sacramentaire, dit Léonien, conservé par le Veronensis LXXXV (80)', *SE* 27 (1984), 151–90.

——, *Le Sacramentaire gélasien* (Paris, 958).

——, 'Le Sermonnaire Vatican du VIIe siècle', *SE* 23 (1978–9), 225–89.

——, 'Les Oraisons pour les dimanches ordinaires: vers une organisation préétablie, premières tentatives, premières collections', *RB* 93 (1983), 31–70, 177–244.

——, 'Un Homilaire liturgique romain du VIe siècle', *RB* 90 (1980), 194–233.

Chevalier, U. (ed.), *Ordinaires de l'église cathédrale de Laon*, Bibliothèque Liturgique 6 (Paris, 1897).

——, *Répertoire des sources historiques de moyen âge: Bio-Bibliographie* 2 vols. (Paris, 1905).

——, *Répertoire des sources historiques du moyen âge: Topo-Bibliographie*, 2 vols. (Montbéliard, 1903).

——, *Repertorium Hymnologicum*, 6 vols. (Louvain, 1892–1912, Brussels, 1920–21).

Chew, G., 'Doxology', *NGD* v. 599–600.

Clarke, H. B., and Brennan, M. (eds.), *Columbanus and Merovingian Monasticism*, BAR International Series 113 (Oxford, 1981).

Clément, J. M., *Lexique des anciennes règles monastiques occidentales*, 2 vols., Instrumenta Patristica 7A (Steenbrugis, 1978).

Coens, M., 'Anciens litanies des saints', *Recueil d'études bollandiennes*, Subsidia hagiographica 37 (Brussels, 1963), 129–322.

Colette, M. N., 'La Sémiologie comme voie d'accès à la connaissance de l'interprétation au moyen âge', *Musicologie médiévale: Notations et séquences*, ed. M. Huglo (Paris, 1987), 121–8.

Combaluzier, F., 'Fragments de messe "pro defuncto"', EL 69 (1955), 31–5.

Combe, P., 'La Réforme du chant et des livres de chante grégorien à l'abbaye de Solesmes (1833–1883)', *EG* 6 (1963), 185–234.

Constable, G., 'Suger's Monastic Administration', *Abbot Suger and Saint-Denis*, ed. P. Gerson (New York, 1986), 17–32.

Contamine, P., 'L'Oriflamme de Saint-Denis aux XIVe et XVe siècles: Étude de symbolique religieuse et royale', *Annales de l'est* 3, 5th ser. (1973), 179–244.

Contreni, J., *The Cathedral School of Laon from 850 to 930: Its Manuscripts and Masters*, MBMRF 29 (Munich, 1978).

Corbin, S., *Die Neumen*, *Palaeographie der Musik*, I/3 (Cologne, 1977).

——, 'Neumatic Notations', *NGD* xiii. 128–44.

——, 'Un Jeu liturgique d'Hérode: Manuscrit Paris, Bibliothèque Mazarine, 1712 (1316)', *Mittellateinisches Jahrbuch* 8 (1973), 43–52.

—— and Bernard, M. (eds.), *Répertoire de manuscrits médiévaux contenant des notations musicales*, 3 vols.; i: *Bibliothèque Sainte-Geneviève: Paris* by M. Bernard (Paris, 1965); ii: *Bibliothèque Mazarine: Paris* by M. Bernard (Paris, 1966); iii: *Bibliothèques parisiennes Arsenal, Nationale (Musique), Universitaire, École des Beaux-Arts et Fonds Privés* by M. Bernard (Paris, 1974).

Cothren, M., 'The Infancy of Christ Window from the Abbey St.-Denis: A Reconsideration of its Design and Iconography', *Art Bulletin* 68 (1986), 398–420.

Cottineau, L. H., *Répertoire topo-bibliographique des abbayes et prieurés*, 3 vols. (Mâcon, 1939).

Coussemaker, E. de, *Scriptorum de Musica Medii Aevi*, 4 vols. (Paris, 1931).

Cowdrey, H. E. J., *The Cluniacs and the Gregorian Reform* (Oxford, 1970).
Crichton, J. D., 'The Divine Office, 3. The Office in the West: The Early Middle Ages', *The Study of Liturgy*, ed. C. Jones, G. Wainwright, and E. Yarnold (New York, 1978), 369–78.
——, 'The Divine Office, 4. The Office in the West: The Later Middle Ages', *The Study of Liturgy*, ed. C. Jones, G. Wainwright, and E. Yarnold (New York, 1978), 378–82.
Crocker, R., 'Matins Antiphons at St. Denis', *JAMS* 39 (1986), 441–90.
Crosby, S. M., 'Abbot Suger's Program for his New Abbey Church', *Monasticism and the Arts*, ed. T. Verdon (Syracuse, NY, 1984), 189–206.
——, *L'Abbaye royale de Saint-Denis* (Paris, 1953).
——, *Supplementary Drawings to the Royal Abbey of Saint-Denis from its Beginnings to the Death of Suger, 475–1151* (New Haven, Conn., 1987).
——, *The Royal Abbey of Saint-Denis from its Beginnings to the Death of Suger, 475–1151*, ed. and completed by P. Blum, Yale Publications in the History of Art 37 (New Haven, Conn., 1987).
—— and Hayward, J., Little, C. T., and Wixom, W. D., *The Royal Abbey of Saint-Denis in the Time of Abbot Suger (1122–1151)* (New York, 1981).
Cross, F. L. (ed.), *The Oxford Dictionary of the Christian Church*, 2nd edn. (London, 1974).
Dalton, J., *Ordinale Exon*, 4 vols., HBS 37, 38, 63, 79 (London, 1909–40).
Daunou, P. C. F. (ed.), *Vita Sancti Ludovici Regis Franciae*, Recueil des historiens des Gaules et de la France xx (Paris, 1840), 310–465.
Davril, A. (ed.), *Consuetudines Floriacenses Saeculi Tertii Decimi*, CCM 9 (Siegburg, 1976).
Dearden, J. S., 'John Ruskin, the Collector: With a Catalogue of the Illuminated and Other Manuscripts formerly in his Collection', *The Library: Transactions of the Bibliographical Society* 21, 5th ser. (1966), 124–54.
De Clerck, P., *La 'Prière Universelle' dans les liturgies latines anciennes: Témoinages patristiques et textes liturgiques*, LQF 62 (Münster, 1977).
De Clercq, C. (ed.), *Concilia Galliae A. 511–A. 695*, CC, Series Latina 148A (Turnholt, 1963).
Dekkers, E., *Clavis Patrum latinorum*, 2nd edn., *SE* 3 (Steenbrugge, 1961).
Delaborde, H.-F., 'Le Procès du chef de Saint Denis en 1410', *Mémoires de la société de l'histoire de Paris et e l'Île-de-France* 11 (1884), 297–409.
——, *Œuvres de Rigord et de Guillaume le Breton, historiens de Philippe-Auguste*, 2 vols. (Paris, 1882–5).
Dellachenal, R., *Histoire de Charles V*, 5 vols. (Paris, 1909–31).
Delalande, D., *Le Graduel des prêcheurs* (Paris, 1949).
Delisle, L., *Inventaire des manuscrits latins conservés à la Bibliothèque Nationale sous les numéros 16719–18613* (Paris, 1871).
——, *Le Cabinet des manuscrits de la Bibliothèque impériale (nationale)*, 4 vols. (Paris, 1868–81).
——, 'Le Mystère des rois mages dans la cathédrale de Nevers', *Romania* 4 (1875), 1–6.
——, *Manuscrits latins et français ajoutés aux fonds des nouvelles acquisitions pendant les années 1875–1891* (Paris, 1891).

——, *Mémoire sur d'anciens sacramentaires*, Mémoires de l'Institut Nationale de France, Académie des Inscriptions et Belles-Lettres 32 (Paris, 1886).
——, 'Notice sur un livre à peintures exécuté en 1250 dans l'abbaye de Saint-Denis', *BEC* 38 (1877), 444–76.
——, 'Notice sur vingt manuscrits du Vatican', *BEC* 37 (1876), 471–527.
——, *Recherches sur la librairie de Charles V*, 3 vols. (Paris, 1907).
Descandres, Y., 'Les Manuscrits décorés au XIe siècle à Saint-Germain-des-Prés par Ingelard', *Scriptorium* 9 (1955), 3–16.
Deshman, R., 'The Exalted Servant: The Ruler Theology of the Prayerbook of Charles the Bald', *Viator* 11 (1980), 385–417.
Deshusses,, J., 'Chronologie des grands sacramentaires de St. Amand', *RB* 87 (1977), 230–7.
——, 'Encore les sacramentaires de Saint-Amand', *RB* 89 (1979), 310–12.
——, *Le Sacramentaire grégorien: Ses principales formes d'après les plus anciens manuscrits*, 3 vols., SF 16, 24, 28 (Fribourg, 1971, 1979, 1982).
——, 'Le "Supplément" au sacramentaire grégorien: Alcuin ou s. Benoît d'Aniane?', *AfL* 9 (1965), 48–71.
——, 'Les Anciens sacramentaires de Tours', *RB* 89 (1979), 281–302.
——, 'Les Messes d'Alcuin', *AfL* 14 (1972), 1–41.
——, 'Les Sacramentaires: État actuel de la recherche', *AfL* 24 (1982), 19–46.
Devisse, J., *Hincmar, archévêque de Reims (845–882)*, 3 vols. (Geneva, 1975–6).
Dickson, M. (ed.), *Consuetudines Beccenses*, CCM 4 (Siegburg, 1967).
Dictionary of the Middle Ages, ed. J. Strayer, 12 vols. (New York, 1982–8).
Dictionnaire d'archéologie chrétienne et de liturgie, 15 vols. (Paris, 1924–53).
Dictionnaire d'histoire et de géographie ecclésiastiques, 17 vols. (Paris, 1912).
Die Musik in Geschichte und Gegenwart, ed. F. Blume, 14 vols. (Kassel, 1949–51).
Dikmans, M., 'Les Obituaires romains, une définition suivie d'une vue d'ensemble', *SM* 19 (1978), 591–652.
Dinter, P. (ed.), *Liber Tramitis aevi Odilonis Abbatis*, CCM 10 (Siegburg, 1980).
Dittmer, L. (ed.), *Facsimile Reproduction of the Manuscript Florence, Biblioteca Mediceo–Laurenziana, Pluteo 29.1*, PMMM 10, 11 (Brooklyn, NY, 1966).
——, *Facsimile Reproduction of the Manuscript Wolfenbüttel, Herzog-August-Bibliothek, 1206 (Helmst. 1099)*, PMMM 2 (Brooklyn, NY, 1960).
——, *Worcester Add. 68, Westminster Abbey 33327, Madrid, Bibl. Nac. 192: Facsimile, Introduction, Index and Transcriptions*, PMMM 5 (Brooklyn, NY, 1959).
Donatus, *Regula ad Virgines*, *PL* lxxxvii, 273–98.
Doublet, J., *Histoire d l'abbaye de S. Denys en France* (Paris, 1625).
Dreves, G. (ed.), *Cantiones et Moteti, Lieder und Motetten des Mittelalters*, *AH* xxi (Leipzig, 1895).
——, *Hymni Inediti, Liturgische Hymnen des Mittelalters, AH* xi, xii, xix (Leipzig, 1891–5).

——, *Hymnographi Latini*, *AH* l (Leipzig, 1907).
——, *Prosarium Lemovicense*, *AH* vii (Leipzig, 1889).
——, *Sequentiae Ineditae, Liturgische Prosen des Mittealters*, *AH* viii–x (Leipzig, 1890–1).
Drinkwater, J. F., *Roman Gaul: The Three Provinces, 58 BC–AD 260* (Ithaca, NY, and New York, 1983).
Dronke, P. (ed), *A History of Twelfth-Century Western Philosophy* (Cambridge, 1988).
Dubois, J., *Histoire monastique en France au XIIe siècle*, repr. edn. (London, 1982).
——, *Le Martyrologe d'Usuard: Texte et commentaire* (Brussels, 1965).
——, *Les Martyrologes du moyen âge latin*, Typologie des sources du moyen âge occidental 26 (Brepols, 1978).
——, 'Saint Eugène de Deuil', *RB* 70 (1960), 83–100.
—— and Beaumont-Maillet, L., *Sainte-Geneviève de Paris* (Paris, 1982).
Dubruel, M., *Moines et religieuses d'Alsace, Fulrad, abbé de Saint-Denis* (Colmar, 1902).
Du Cange, *Glossarium Mediae et Infimae Latinitatis*, 10 vols. (Paris, 1842–6).
Duchesne, F., *Historiae Francorum Scriptores*, 5 vols. (Paris, 1636–49).
Duchesne, L., *Fastes épiscopaux de l'ancienne Gaule*, 2nd edn., 2 vols. (Paris, 1907).
——, *Le Liber Pontificalis: Texte, introduction et commentaire*, 3 vols. (Paris, 1886–92, repr. edn. 1981).
——, *Origines du culte chrétien, étude sur la liturgie latine avant Charlemagne* (Paris, 1889).
Dumas, A., and Deshusses, J. (eds.), *Liber Sacramentorum Gellonensis*, 2 vols., CC, Series Latina 159 and 159A (Turnhout, 1981).
Durand, G., *Ordinaire de l'église Notre-Dame Cathédrale d'Amiens par Raoul de Rouvroy (1291)*, Mémoires de la société des antiquaires de Picardie, Documents inédits concernant la province 22 (Amiens and Paris, 1934).
Dutton, P., and Jeauneau, E., 'The Verses of the "Codex Aureus" of Saint-Emmeram', *SM* 24 (1983), 75–110.
Duval, Y.-M., 'Un Triple travail de copie effectué à Saint-Denis au IXe siècle et sa diffusion à travers l'Europe carolingienne et médiévale', *Scriptorium* 38 (1984), 3–49, 181–210.
Dyer, J., 'Monastic Psalmody of the Middle Ages', *RB* 99 (1989), 41–74.
Dykmans, M., 'La Préface du pontifical de Ferry de Clugny envoyée à Mabillon d'après un manuscrit de la Reine Christine de Suède', *Scriptorium* 38 (1984), 63–70.
Eberle, L. (trans.), *The Rule of the Master*, introduction by Adalbert de Vogüé (Kalamazoo, 1977).
Ebner, A., *Quellen und Forschungen zur Geschichte und Kunstgeschichte des Missale Romanum im Mittelalter* (Fribourg, 1896).
Eifrig, W., 'The Ite Missa Est Melodies of Paris, Bibliothèque Nationale, lat.

1107: A Medieval Chant Hit-parade', paper presented at the International Congress on Medieval Studies (Kalamazoo, 1984).

Eisenhöfer, L., 'Paläographisch–kodikologische Beobachtungen am Vatikanischen Faksimile des Alten Gelasianums', *AfL* 23 (1981), 176–82.

Eisenhöfer, L., and Lechner, J., *The Liturgy of the Roman Rite*, trans. A. J. and E. F. Peeler (New York, 1961).

Elvert, C., *Clavis Voluminum CCM VII/1–3*, CCM 7/4 (Siegburg, 1986).

Epistolae Variorum, MGH, *Epistolarum* v/1, *Karolini Aevi*, iii (Berlin, 1898).

Erlande-Brandenburg, A., *Le Roi est Mort: Etude sur les funérailles, les sépultures et les tombeaux des rois de France jusqu' à la fin du XIIIe siècle* (Geneva, 1975).

Escudier, D., 'Des Notations musicales dans les manuscrits non liturgiques antérieurs au XIIe siècle', *BEC* 129 (1971), 27–48.

——, 'La Notation musicale de Saint-Vaast: Étude d'une particularité graphique', *Musicologie médiévale: Notations et séquences*, ed. M. Huglo (Paris, 1987), 107–20.

——, 'Le Scriptorium de St. Vaast d'Arras des origines au XIIe siècle: Contribution à l'étude des notations neumatiques du nord de la France', *Positions des thèses de l'École de Chartes* (1970), 75–82.

Étaix, R., 'Les Épreuves du juste: Nouveau sermon de saint Césaire d'Arles', *Rue des études augustiniennes* 24 (1978), 272–7.

Eubel, C., *Hierarchia Catholica Medii Aevi*, 7 vols. (Regensburg, 1913).

Ewig, E., 'Saint Chrodegang et la réforme de l'église franque', *Saint Chrodegang: Communications présentées au colloque tenu à Metz à l'occasion du douzième centenaire de sa mort* (Metz, 1967), 25–53.

Falck, R., *The Notre Dame Conductus: A Study of the Repertory*, MuS 33 (Henryville, Pa., 1981).

Fassler, M., 'Musical Exegesis in the Sequences of Adam and the Canons of St. Victor' (Ph.D. diss., Cornell Univ., 1983).

——, 'The Office of the Cantor in Early Western Monastic Rules and Customaries: A Preliminary Investigation', *EMH* 5 (1985), 29–51.

——, 'The Role of the Parisian Sequence in the Evolution of Notre-Dame Polyphony', *Speculum* 62 (1987), 345–74.

——, 'Who Was Adam of St. Victor? The Evidence of the Sequence Manuscripts', *JAMS* 37 (1984), 233–69.

Les Fastes du gothique: Le siècle de Charles V (Paris, 1981).

Faye, C. U., and Bond, W. H., *Supplement to the Census of Medieval and Renaissance Manuscripts in the United States and Canada* (New York, 1962).

Félibien, M., *Histoire de l'abbaye royale de Saint-Denis en France* Paris, 1706).

Fiala, V., and Irtenkauf, W., 'Vesuch einer liturgischen Nomenklature', *Zur Katalogisierung mittelalterlicher und neuerer Handschriften*, Zeitschrift für Bibliothekswesen und Bibliographie Sonderheft (Frankfurt, 1963), 105–37.

Fischer, K. von, 'Eine wiederaufgefundene Theoretikerhandschrift des späten 14. Jahrhunderts', *Schweizer Beiträge zur Musikwissenschaft* 1, 3rd ser. (1972), 23–33.

Fleckenstein, J., *Die Hofkapelle der Deutschen Könige*, Schriften der Monumenta Germaniae Historica 16/1 (Stuttgart, 1959).

——, 'Fulrad von Saint-Denis und der fränkische Ausgriff in den süddeutschen Raum', *Studien und Vorarbeiten zur Geschichte des grossfränkishen und frühdeutschen Adels*, Forschungen zur Oberrheinischen Landesgeschichte 4 (Fribourg, 1957).

Foley, E., 'Paris, Bibliothèque Mazarine 526, The First Ordinary of the Royal Abbey of St.-Denis in France: An Edition and Commentary', 2 vols. (Ph.D. diss., Univ. of Notre Dame, 1986).

Folz, R., 'La Sainteté de Louis IX d'après les textes liturgiques de sa féte', *Revue d'histoire de l'église de France* 57 (1971), 31–45.

——, 'Pierre le Vénérable et la liturgie', *Pierre Abélard, Pierre le Vénérable, les courants philosophiques, littéraires et artistiques en occident au milieu du XIIe siècle* (Paris, 1975).

——, *The Coronation of Charlemagne: 25 December 800*, trans. J. E. Anderson (London, 1974).

——, 'Tradition hagiographique et culte de sainte Bathilde, reine des Francs', *Comptes rendus des séances de l'Académie des Inscriptions et Belles-Lettres* (1975), 369–83.

Fontaine, J. (trans.), *Sulpice Sévére: Vie de saint Martin*, 3 vols., SC 133–5 (Paris, 1967–9).

Foreville, R., 'La Diffusion du culte de Thomas Becket dans la France de l'ouest avant la fin du XIIe siècle', *Cahiers de civilisation médiévale* 19 (1976), 347–69.

Formigé, J., *L'Abbaye royale de Saint-Denis: Recherches nouvelles* (Paris, 1960).

Forney, K., 'Music, Ritual and Patronage at the Church of Our Lady, Antwerp', *EMH* (1987), 1–51.

Fortescue, A., *The Ceremonies of the Roman Rite*, 8th edn. (London, 1948).

Frere, W. H., *Bibliotheca Musico-Liturgica: A descriptive handlist of the Musical and Latin-Liturgical Manuscripts of the Middle Ages*, 2 vols., The Plainsong and Mediaeval Society (London, 1901–32).

——, *Introduction to the Sarum Antiphonal*, repr. edn. (London, 1927).

——, *Studies in Early Roman Liturgy*, i: *The Kalendar*, Alcuin Club Collections 28 (London, 1930).

——, *The Use of Sarum*, 2 vols. (Cambridge, 1898–1901).

Friend, A. M., 'Two Manuscripts of the School of Saint-Denis', *Speculum* 1 (1926), 59–70.

——, 'Le Lieu de destination et de provenance du "Compendiensis"', *Ut Mens concordet voci, Festschrift Eugene Cardine zum 75. Geburtstag* (Sankt Ottilien, 1980), 338–53.

——, *Les Origines de prime*, Bibliotheca Ephemerides Liturgicae 19 (Rome, 1946).

——, 'The Critical Edition of the Roman Gradual by the Monks of Solesmes', *JPMMS* 1 (1978), 81–97.

Fry, T. (ed.), *The Rule of St. Benedict in Latin and English with Notes* (Collegeville, Minn., 1981).

Gage, J., 'Gothic Glass: Two Aspects of a Dionysian Aesthetic', *Art History* 5 (1982), 36–58.

Gaiffier, B. de, 'La Légende de St. Eugène de Tolède martyr à Deuil près de Paris', *Analecta Bollandiana* 83 (1965), 329–49.

Gallia Christiana in provincias ecclesiasticas distributa, 16 vols. (Paris, 1715–1865).

Gamber, K., *Codices liturgici latini antiquiores*, 2nd edn., 2 pts. (Fribourg, 1968).

——, *Ordo Antiquus Gallicanus: Der gallikanische Messritus des 6. Jahrhunderts*, Textus Patristici et Liturgici 3 (Regensburg, 1965).

——, *Sakramentartypen: Versuch einer Gruppierung der Handschriften und Fragmente bis zur Jahrtausendwende*, Texte und Arbeiten 49–50 (Beuron, 1958).

Gams, P. B. (ed.), *Series Episcoporum Ecclesiae Catholicae* (Ratisbon, 1873).

Gastaldelli, F., *La Traduzione del "De divinis Nominibus" dello pseudo-Dionigi nel commento di Guillelmo Da Lucca (+ 1178)* (Salesianum, 1977).

Gastoué, A., 'Le Chant gallican', *RCG* (1937), 101–6, 131–3, 167–76; (1938), 5–12, 57–62, 76–80, 107–12, 146–51, 171–6; (1939), 7–12, 44–6.

——, 'Les Origines du chant liturgique dans l'église de Paris', *RCG* (1902/3), 102–7, 140–6, 155–61, 169–74, 187–8; (1903/4), 13–15, 31–3, 36–9, 70–4, 89–92, 107–10, 120–3, 178–83, 209–12.

Gauthier, M.-M., 'Reliques des Saints Innocents et châsse limousine au trésor de Saint-Denis', *Gesta* 5 (1976), 293–302.

Gay, C., 'Formulaires anciens pour la messe des défunts', *EG* 2 (1957), 83–129.

Gennrich, F. (ed.), *Bibliographie der Altesten Französischen und Lateinischen Motteten*, Summa Musicae Medii Aevi 2 (Darmstadt, 1957).

——, 'Trouvèrelieder und Motettenrepertoire', *Zeitschrift für Musikwissenschaft* 9 (1926), 8–39.

Géraud, H. (ed.), *Chronique latine de Guillaume de Nangis de 1113 à 1300*, 2 vols., Société de l'histoire de France 29 (Paris, 1843).

Gerson, P. (ed.), *Abbot Suger and Saint-Denis* (New York, 1986).

——, 'Suger as Iconographer: The Central Portal of the West Facade of Saint-Denis', *Abbot Suger and Saint-Denis*, ed. P. Gerson (New York, 1986), 183–98.

——, 'The West Facade of Saint-Denis', (Ph.D. diss., Columbia Univ., 1970).

—— and Robertson, A., 'A Thirteenth-Century Psalter from Saint-Denis Rediscovered: Chapel Hill, University Library, Rare Book Collection, MS 11', forthcoming in *Scriptorium*.

Giesey, R., *The Royal Funeral Ceremony in Renaissance France*, Travaux d'humanisme et de renaissance 37 (Geneva, 1960).

Gindele, C., 'Der "Alleluiaticus": Ein elementares Kennzeichen vorbenediktinischer Psalmodie', *Studien und Mitteilungen zur Geschichte des benediktinischen Ordens und seiner Zweige* 78 (1967), 310–21.

——, 'Die gallikanischen "Laus perennis"-Klöster und ihr "Ordo officii"', *RB* 49 (1959), 32–48.

——, 'Die Römische und monastische Überlieferung im Ordo Officii der Regel St. Benedikts', *Commentationes in Regulam S. Benedicti*, Studia Anselmiana 42 (Rome, 1957).

——, 'Doppelchor und Psalmvortrag im Frühmittelalter', *Die Musikforschung* 6 (1953), 296–300.

Giry, A., Prou, M., and Tessier, G. (eds.), *Recueil des actes de Charles II, le Chauve, roi de France*, 3 vols., Chartes et diplômes relatifs à l'histoire de France 8–10 (Paris, 1943–55).

Gneuss, H., *Hymnar und Hymnen im Englischen Mittelalter* (Tübingen, 1968).

Godefroy, T., *Le Cérémonial de France* (Paris, 1619).

——, *Le Cérémonial françois* 2 vols. (Paris, 1649).

Goldschmidt, A., *Die Elfenbeiskulpturen aus der Zeit der karolingischen und sächischen Kaiser*, 4 vols. (Berlin, 1914–26).

Le Graduel romain: Édition critique, 2 vols., ii: *Les Sources* (Solesmes, 1957), iv/1, *Le Texte neumatique: Le groupement des manuscrits*, iv/2, *Le Texte neumatique: Les relations généalogiques des manuscrits* (Solesmes, 1962).

Graesse, J. G. T., Benedict, F., and Plechl, H. (eds.), *Orbis Latinus: Lexikon Lateinischer geographischer Namen des Mittelalters und der Neuzeit*, 3rd edn., 3 vols. (Brunswick, 1972).

Grégoire, R., 'Benedetto di Aniane nella riforma monastica carolingia', *SM* 26 (1985), 573–610.

——, 'Prières liturgiques médiévales en l'honneur de saint Benoît, de Sainte Scolastique et de Saint Maur', *Analecta Monastica: Textes et études sur la vie des moines au moyen âge*, 7th ser., Studia Anselmiana 54 (Rome, 1965), 1–85.

Gregory, T., 'The Platonic Inheritance', *A History of Twelfth-Century Western Philosophy*, ed. P. Dronke (Cambridge, 1988), 54–80.

Grévy-Pons, N., and Ornato, E., 'Qui est l'auteur de la chronique latine de Charles VI, dite du Religieux de Saint-Denis?', *BEC* 134 (1976), 85–102.

Griffe, Élie, *La Gaule chrétienne à l'époque romaine*, 2nd edn., 2 vols. (Paris, 1964–6).

Grisbrooke, W. J., 'The Divine Office, 2. The Formative Period: Cathedral and Monastic Offices', *The Study of Liturgy*, ed. C. Jones, G. Wainright, and E. Yarnold (New York, 1978), 358–69.

Grodecki, L. *Les Vitraux de Saint-Denis: Etude sur le virtrail au XIIe siècle*, Corpus Vitrearum Medii Aevi, France, Etudes 1 (Paris, 1976).

——, 'The Style of the Stained-Glass Windows of Saint-Denis, *Abbot Suger and Saint-Denis*, ed. P. Gerson (New York, 1986), 273–81.

—— and Brisac, C., *Gothic Stained Glass, 1200–1300* (Ithaca, NY, 1985).

Gros, M., 'El Ordo romano-hispanico de Narbona para la consagracion de iglesias', *Hispania Sacra* 19 (1966), 321–401.

Grünewald, R., Hallinger, K., and Elvert, C. (eds.), *Consuetudines Cluniacensium Antiquiores Cum Redactionibus Derivatis* 4: *Redactio Wirzeburgensis*, CCM 7/2 (Siegburg, 1983).
Guérard, B., *Cartulaire de l'église Notre-Dame de Paris*, 4 vols., Collection des cartulaires de France 4–7 (Paris, 1850).
Guilhermy, F., *Monographie de l'église royale de Saint-Denis, tombeaux et figures historiques* (Paris, 1848).
Guilmain, J., 'MS Illumination, European', *DMA* viii. 105–10.
Gushee, L., 'Anonymous Theoretical Writings', *NGD* i. 441–6.
Gy, P.-M., 'L'Office du Corpus Christi et S. Thomas d'Aquin, état d'une recherche', *Revue des sciences philosophiques et théologiques* 64 (1980), 491–507; 66 (1982), 81–6.
——, 'Typologie et ecclésiologie des livres liturgiques médiévaux', *La Maison Dieu* 121 (1975), 7–21.
Hallinger, K. (ed.), *Consuetudines Benedictinae Variae*, CCM 6 (Siegburg, 1975).
—— (ed.), *Initia Consuetudinis Benedictinae: Consuetudines saeculi octavi et noni*, CCM 1 (Siegburg, 1963).
——, Wegener, M., and Elvert, C. (eds.), *Consuetudines Cluniacensium Antiquiores Cum Redactionibus Derivatis 1. Cluniacensium Antiquiorum Redactiones Principales*, CCM 7/2 (Siegburg, 1983).
Handschin, J., 'Bis zur Wende des Mittelalters', *Schweizer Musikbuch*, ed. W. Schuh (Zurich, 1939), i. 11–53.
——, 'Eine alte Neumenschrift', *AM* 22 (1950), 69–97.
——, 'Sur quelques tropaires grecs traduits en latin', *Annales musicologiques* 2 (1954), 27–60.
——, 'Trope, Sequence, and Conductus', *Early Medieval Music up to 1300*, ed. A. Hughes, NOHM ii (London, 1954), 128–74.
Hanning, R., 'Suger's Literary Style and Vision', *Abbot Suger and Saint-Denis*, ed. P. Gerson (New York, 1986), 145–50.
Hanssens, J. M. (ed.), *Amalarii episcopi opera liturgica omnia*, 3 vols., SeT 138–40 (Rome, 1948–50).
Harbinson, D., *Petrus de Cruce Ambianensi: Tractatus de Tonis*, Corpus Scriptorum de Musica 29 (Rome, 1976).
Haren, M., *Medieval Thought: The Western Intellectual Tradition from Antiquity to the Thirteenth Century* (New York, 1985).
Harrison, F. L., 'Benedicamus, Conductus, Carol: A Newly-Discovered Source', *AM* 37 (1965), 35–48.
——, *Music in Medieval Britain*, 2nd edn. (London, 1963).
——, Sanders, E., and Lefferts, P. (eds.), PMFC, xvi: *English Music for Mass and Offices (I)* (Monaco, 1983).
Havet, J., 'Questions mérovingiennes, V: Les Origines de Saint-Denis', *BEC* 51 (1890), 1–62, 43–4.
Heiming, O., 'Die Benedictiones Episcopales des Sacramentarium Gelasianum Phillips', *AfL* 22 (1980), 118–23.
Heinzelmann, M., *Translationsberichte und andere Quellen des Reliquien-*

skultes, Typologie des sources du moyen-âge occidental 33 (Turnhout, 1979).

Heller, J., and Waitz, G. (eds.), *Flodoardi Historia Remensis Ecclesiae*, MGH, *Scriptorum* xii (Hanover, 1881), 405–599.

Héron de Villefosse, R., 'Manuscrits provenant de l'abbaye de Saint-Denis au Musée du Louvre', *Comptes rendus de la Société Française de Numismatique et d'Archéologie* 5 (1874), 248–55.

Herrgott, M. (ed.), *Vetus disciplina monastica: Ordo cluniacensis Bernardi monachi* (Paris, 1726), 133–364.

Herrmann-Mascard, N., *Les Reliques des saints: Formation coutumière d'un droit* (Paris, 1975).

Hesbert, R.-J. (ed.), *Antiphonale Missarum Sextuplex* (Brussels, 1935).

——, *Corpus Antiphonalium Officii*, 6 vols., Rerum ecclesiasticarum documenta, Series major, Fontes vii–xii (Rome, 1963, 1965, 1968, 1970, 1975, 1979).

——, *Le Graduel de St. Denis: Manuscrit 384 de la Bibliothèque Mazarine de Paris*, Monumenta Musicae Sacrae 5 (Paris, 1981).

——, *Le Prosaire de la Sainte-Chapelle: Manuscrit du chapitre de Saint-Nicholas de Bari (vers 1250)*, Monumenta musicae sacrae 1 (Mâcon, 1952).

——, 'Les Matines de Pâques dans la tradition monastique', *Studia Monastica* 24 (1982), 311–48.

——, 'L'Office de la commémoraison des Défunts à Saint-Benoît-sur-Loire au XIIIe siècle', *Miscellanea Liturgica in Honorem L. Cuniberti Mohlberg*, 2 vols., EL 23 (Rome, 1949), ii. 393–421.

——, 'The Sarum Antiphoner: Its Sources and Influence', *JPMMS* 3 (1980), 49–55.

Hilduin, *Arepoagitica, sive Sancti Dionysii Vita*, *PL*, cvi, 13–50.

Hiley, D., 'Benedicamus Domino and Ite Missa Est Melodies at St. Denis and St. Corneille de Compiègne: Some Preliminary Notes', paper presented at the symposium 'Das Ereignis, "Notre-Dame"', Herzog August Bibliothek (Wolfenbüttel, April 1985).

——, 'Further Observations on W_1: The Ordinary of Mass Chants and the Sequences', *JPMMS* 4 (1981), 67–80.

——, 'Neuma', *NGD* xiii. 123–5.

——, 'Ordinary of Mass Chants in English, North French and Sicilian Manuscripts', *JPMMS* 9/1–2 (1986), 1–128.

——, 'The Norman Chant Traditions: Normandy, Britain, Sicily', *PRMA* 107 (1980–1), 1–33.

Hofmann-Brandt, H., 'Die Tropen zu den Responsorien des Officiums', 2 vols. (Ph.D. diss., Friedrich-Alexander-Universität, 1971).

Hofmeister, A. (ed.), *Translationis et Inventionis Sancti Dionysii Ratisponensis Historia Antiquior*, MGH, *Scriptorum* 30/2/1 (Leipzig, 1934), 823–37.

Holman, H.-J., 'Melismatic Tropes in the Responsories for Matins', *JAMS* 16 (1963), 35–46.

Holweck, F. G., *Calendrarium liturgicum festorum Dei et Dei Matris Mariae* (Westminster, Md., 1925).

Honburger, O., 'Eine Spätkarolingische Schule von Vorbie', *Karolingische und Ottonische Kunst* (Wiesbaden, 1957).

Hope, E. M., 'The Medieval Western Rites', *The Study of Liturgy*, ed. C. Jones, G. Wainwright, and E. Yarnold (New York, 1978), 220–40.

Hoppin, R., '*Exultantes Collaudemus*: A Sequence for Saint Hylarion', *Aspects of Medieval and Renaissance Music*, ed. J. LaRue, repr. edn. (New York, 1978).

——, *Medieval Music* (New York, 1978).

Horrent, J., *Le Pèlerinage de Charlemagne: Essai d'explication littéraire avec des notes de critique textuelle*, Bibliothèque de la Faculté de Philosophie et Lettres de l'Université de Liège 158 (Paris, 1961).

Hourlier, J., 'Review of Smits van Waesberghe, *De musico-paedagogice et theoretico Guidone Aretino (Florence, 1953)*', *EG* 2 (1957), 221–4.

——, 'Saint Odilon et la fête des morts', *RG* 28 (1949), 208–12.

—— and Huglo, M., 'Notation paléofranque', *EG* 2 (1957), 212–19.

Hubert, J., Porcher, J., and Volbach, W. F., *L'Empire carolingien* (Paris, 1968).

Hucke, H., 'Gregory the Great', *NGD* vii. 699.

—— 'Toward a New View of Gregorian Chant', *JAMS* 33 (1980), 437–67.

Hughes, A., *Medieval Manuscripts for Mass and Office: A Guide to their Organization and Terminlogy* (Toronto, 1982).

——, 'Modal Order and Disorder in the Rhymed Office', *MD* 37 (1983), 29–52.

——, 'Research Report: Late Medieval Rhymed Offices', *JPMMS* 8 (1985), 33–49.

Huglo, M., 'Antiphoner', *NGD* i. 482–90.

——, 'Aux Origines des tropes d'interpolation: Le trope méloforme d'introït', *RdM* 64 (1978), 5–54.

——, 'Gallican Rite, Music of the', *NGD* vii. 113–25.

——, 'Guy de Saint-Denis', *NGD* vii. 859.

——, 'La Mélodie grecque du gloria in excelsis', *RG* 29 (1950), 30–40.

——, 'L'Ancienne version latine de l'hymne acathiste', *Le Muséon* 64 (1951), 27–61.

——, 'Les Antiennes de la procession des reliques: Vestiges de chant "Vieux-Romain" dans le pontifical', *RG* 31 (1952), 136–9.

——, 'Les Chants de la *missa greca* de Saint-Denis', *Essays Presented to Egon Wellesz* (Oxford, 1966), 74–83.

——, 'Les Débuts de la polyphonie à Paris: Les premiers *organa* parisiens', *Forum musicologicum* 3 (Bern, 1975), 117–63.

——, 'Les Listes alléluiatiques dans les témoins du graduel grégorien', *Speculum Musicae Artis, Festgabe für Heinrich Husmann zum 60. Geburtstag* (Munich, 1970), 219–27.

——, *Les Livres du chant liturgique*, Typologie des sources du moyen âge occidental 52 (Brepols, 1988).

——, *Les Tonaires: Inventaire, analyse, comparaison*, Publications de la Société Française de Musicologie, 3rd ser., No. 2 (Paris, 1971).

——, 'L'Office du dimanche de Pâques dans les monastères bénédictins', *RG* 30 (1951), 191–203.

—— (ed.), *Musicologie médiévale: Notations et séquences*, Actes de la Table Ronde cu CNRS à l'Institut de Recherche et d'Histoire des Textes, 6–7 septembre 1982 (Paris, 1987).

——, 'Origine de la mélodie du Credo "authentique" de la Vaticane', *RG* 30 (1951), 68–78.

——, 'Processional', *NGD* xv. 278–81.

——, 'Règlement du XIIIe siècle pour la transcription des livres notés', *Festschrift Bruno Stäblein zum 70. Geburtstag* (Kassel, 1967), 121–33.

——, 'Remarques sur les listes d'alleluias et de répons du tropaire de Winchester', forthcoming in *JPMMS*.

——, 'Review of *Le Graduel de Saint-Denis* (by Dom R.-J. Hesbert)', *Scriptorium* 36/2 (1982), 337–8.

——, 'Review of *Liturgischen Handschriften der Hessischen Landes- und Hochshulbibliothek Darmstadt*', *BEC* 127 (1969), 227.

——, 'St. Denis', *NGD* xvi. 385–6.

Husmann, H., 'Notre-Dame und Saint-Victor: Repertoire-Studien zur Geschichte der gereimten Prosen', *AM* 36 (1964), 98–123, 191–221.

Huvelin, P., 'Essai historique sur le droit des marchés et des foires', Thèse de la Faculté de Droit de Paris (Paris, 1897).

Iversen, G. (ed.), CT iv: *Tropes de l'Agnus Dei*, SLS 27 (Uppsala, 1980).

Jackson, R., 'Les Manuscrits des "ordines" de couronnement de la bibliothèque de Charles V roi de France', *Le Moyen-Âge* 82 (1976), 67–88.

——, *Vive le roi!: A History of the French Coronation from Charles V to Charles X* (Chapel Hill, NC, and London, 1984).

Jaffe, P. (ed.), *Regesta pontificum romanorum ab Condita Ecclesia ad Annum Post Christum Natum MCXCVIII*, 2 vols. (Leipzig, 1885–8).

James, E., *The Origins of France from Clovis to the Capetians, 500–1000* (New York, 1982).

Jammers, E., *Die Essener Neumenhandschriften der Landes- und Stadt-Bibliothek Düsseldorf* (Ratingen, 1952).

Janini, J., 'Las Oraciones visigóticas de los formularios penitenciales del Reginensis 316', *Hispania Sacra: Revista de historia ecclésiastica* 27 (1985), 191–204.

Jeauneau, E., 'Pierre Abélard à Saint-Denis', *Abélard en son temps*, ed. J. Jolivet (Paris, 1981), 161–73.

Jeffery, P., 'The Oldest Sources of the *Graduale*: A Preliminary Checklist of MSS Copied before about 900 AD', *JM* 2 (1983), 316–21.

Jones, C., Wainwright, G., and Yarnold, E. (eds.), *The Study of Liturgy* (New York, 1978).

Jonsson, R., CT i: *Tropes du propre de la messe 1. Cycle de Noël*, SLS 21 (Stockholm, 1975).

——, *Historia: Etudes sur la genèse des offices versifiés*, SLS 15 (Stockholm, 1968).

Jungmann, J. A., *The Early Liturgy of the Time of Gregory the Great*, trans. F. Brunner (Notre Dame, Ind., 1959).

——, *The Mass of the Roman Rite: Its Origins and Development*, trans. F. Brunner, 2 vols. (New York, 1951–5).

Juvénal des Ursins, J., *Histoire de Charles VI*, ed. T. Godefroy (Paris, 1653).

Kaczynski, B., *Greek in the Carolingian Age: The St. Gall Manuscripts*, Speculum Anniversary Monographs 13 (Cambridge, Mass., 1988).

Kapsner, O. L., *A Benedictine Bibliography*, 2nd edn., 2 vols. (Collegeville, Minn., 1962).

——, *A Benedictine Bibliography, First Supplement* (Collegeville, Minn., 1982).

Kasch, E., *Das Liturgische Vokabular der Frühen Lateinischen Mönchsregeln* (Hildesheim, 1974).

Keitel, E., 'The So-Called Cyclic Mass of Guillaume de Machaut', *MQ* 68 (1982), 307–23.

Kelly, T. F., 'Melisma and Prosula: The Performance of Responsory Tropes', *Liturgische Tropen: Referate zweier Colloquien des* Corpus Troporum *in München (1983) und Canterbury (1984)*, MBMRF, ed. G. Silagi (Munich, 1985), 163–80.

——, 'Melodic Elaboration in Responsory Melismas', *JAMS* 27 (1974), 461–74.

——, 'Neuma Triplex', *AM* 60 (1988), 1–30.

——, 'New Music from Old: The Structuring of Responsory Prosas', *JAMS* 30 (1977), 366–90.

Ker, N. R., *Medieval Manuscripts in British Libraries*, 3 vols. (Oxford, 1969, 1977, 1983).

Kidson, P., 'Panofsky, Suger and St-Denis', *JWCI* 50 (1987), 1–17.

Klauser, T., *A Short History of the Western Liturgy: An Account and Some Reflections*, trans. J. Halliburton, 2nd edn. (Oxford, 1979).

——, *Das Römische Capitulare Evangeliorum: Texte und Untersuchungen zu seiner ältesten Geschichte*, Liturgiegeschichtliche Quellen und Forschungen 28 (Münster, 1935).

——, 'Die liturgischen Austauschbeziehungen zwischen der römischen und der fränkisch-deutschen Kirche vom achten bis zum elften Jahrhundert', *Historisches Jahrbuch* 53 (1933), 169–89.

Kleinheyer, B., 'Studien zur Nichtrömische-Westlichen Ordinationsliturgie', *AfL* 22 (1980), 93–107.

Knowles, D., and Hadcock, R. N., *Medieval Religious Houses: England and Wales* (London, 1971).

——, *The Monastic Order in England: A History of its Development from the Times of St. Dunstan to the Fourth Lateran Council, 940–1216* (Cambridge, 1950).

Kohler, C., *Catalogue des manuscrits de la Bibliothèque Sainte-Geneviève*, 2 vols. (Paris, 1896).

Köhler, W., and Mütherich, F. (eds.), *Die Hofschule Karls des Kahlen*, vol. V of *Die Karolingischen Miniaturen* (Berlin, 1982).

Köpke, R., *Anonymi Ratisbonensis Translatio S. Dionysii Areopagitae*, MGH, *Scriptorum* 11 (Hanover, 1854), 343–75.

Kraus, A., *Die Translatio S. Dionysii Areopagitae von St. Emmeram in Regensburg*, Bayerische Akademie der Wissenschaften, Philosophisch-Historische Klasse, Sitzungsberichte, Jahrgang 1972, Heft 4 (Munich, 1972).

——, 'Saint-Denis und Regensburg: Zu den Motiven und zur Wirkung hochmittelalterlicher Fälschungen', *Fälschungen im Mittelalter: Internationaler Kongress der Monumenta Germaniae Historica, München. 16.–19. September 1986*, 5 vols., Monumenta Germaniae Historica Schriften 33/1 (Hanover, 1988), iii. 535–49.

Krusch, B. (ed.), *Chronicarum quae dicuntur Fredegarii Scholastici libri IV cum Continuationibus*, MGH, *SS. Rer. Mer.* ii. 1–193 (Hanover, 1888).

——, *Gesta Dagoberti I. Regis Francorum*, MGH, *SS. Rer. Mer.* ii. 396–425 (Hanover, 1888).

——, *Gregorii episcopi Turonensis de cursu stellarum ratio, qualiter ad officium implendum debeat observari*. MGH, *SS. Rer. Mer.* i. 854–72 (Hanover, 1885).

——, *Gregorii Turonensis historia Francorum*, MGH, *SS. Rer. Mer.* i/1, Editio altera (Hanover, 1951).

——, *Liber Historiae Francorum*, MGH, *SS. Rer. Mer.* ii. 215–328 (Hanover, 1888).

——, *Passio sanctorum martyrum Dionisii, Rustici et Eleutherii*, MGH, *Auct. Ant.* iv/2. 101–5 (Berlin, 1885).

——, 'Über die Gesta Dagoberti', *Forschungen zur Deutschen Geschichte* 26 (1886), 163–91.

——, *Vita Eligii Episcopi Noviomagensis*, MGH, *SS. Rer. Mer.* iv. 634–761 (Hanover and Leipzig, 1902).

——, *Vita Genovesae Virginis Parisiensis*, MGH, *SS. Rer. Mer.* iii. 215–38 (Hanover, 1896).

——, *Vita Sanctae Balthildis*, MGH, *SS. Rer. Mer.* ii. 475–508 (Hanover, 1888).

Kurzeja, A. (ed.), *Der Älteste Liber Ordinarius der Trierer Domkirche (London, Brit. Mus., Harley 2958, Anfang 14. Jh.): ein Beitrag zur Liturgiegeschichte der deutschen Ortskirchen*. LQF 52 (Münster, 1970).

Laborde, A. de, *Les Manuscrits à peintures de la Cité de Dieu de saint Augustin*, 3 vols. (Paris, 1909).

Lafond, J., 'The Stained Glass Decoration of Lincoln Cathedral in the Thirteenth Century', *Archaeological Journal* 103 (1946), 119–56.

Lake, K., and Lake, S. (eds.), *Dated Greek Miniscule Manuscripts to the Year 1200*, iv: *Manuscripts in Paris*, pt. 1, Monumenta Palaeographica Vetera, 1st ser. (Boston, 1935).

Lambot, C., 'Canis Decoratus Angelicis', *RB* 64 (1954), 132–6.

Landwehr-Melnicki, M., *Das einstimmige Kyrie des lateinischen Mittelalters*, Forschungsbeiträge zur Musikwissenschaft 1 (Regensburg, 1955).

Lansing, E. 'A Perspective on the Manuscripts in the Rare Book Collection',

The Bookmark: Friends of the University of North Carolina Library 44 (1974), 16–37.

Latouche, R., *Caesar to Charlemagne: The Beginnings of France*, trans. J. Nicholson (London, 1968).

Lawrence, C. H., *Medieval Monasticism: Forms of Religious Life in Western Europe in the Middle Ages* (London and New York, 1984).

Lebel, G., *Catalogue des actes de l'abbaye de Saint-Denis relatifs à la Province ecclésiastique de Sens de 1151 à 1346* (Paris, 1935).

——, *Histoire administrative, économique et financière de l'abbaye de Saint-Denis etudiée spécialement dans la Province ecclésiastique de Sens, de 1151 à 1346* (Paris, 1935).

Leclercq, H., 'Denis, Abbaye de Saint-', *DACL* iv/1, cols. 588–642.

——, 'Grecque (Messe) de l'abbaye de Saint-Denis', *DACL* vi/2, cols. 1581–6.

Leclercq, J., 'L'Office de la transfiguration de Pierre le Vénérable', *Pierre le Vénérable* (St Wandrille, 1946).

Lecoy de la Marche, A. (ed.), *Œuvres complètes de Suger* (Paris, 1867).

'Lectionary', *NGD* x. 595.

Lefferts, P., and Bent, M. (compilers), 'New Sources of English Thirteenth- and Fourteenth-Century Polyphony', *EMH* 2 (1982), 273–362.

Leidinger, G. (ed.), *Der Codex Aureus der Bayerischen Staatsbibliothek in München (Munich, 1925).*

Lemaître, J.-L., Répertoire des documents nécrologiques français, 2 vols., Recueil des historiens de la France, Obituaires 7, 8 (Paris, 1980).

Leroquais, V., *Les Bréviaires manuscrits des bibliothèques publiques de France*, 6 vols. (Paris, 1934).

——, *Les Livres d'heures manuscrits de la Bibliothèque nationale*, 3 vols. (Paris, 1927).

——, *Les Pontificaux manuscrits des bibliothèques publiques de France*, 3 vols. (Paris, 1937).

——, *Les Psautiers manuscrits latins des bibliothèques publiques de France*, 2 vols. (Mâcon, 1940–1).

——, *Les Sacramentaires et les missels manuscrits des bibliothèques publiques de France*, 4 vols. (Paris, 1924).

Le Roux, R., 'Guillaume de Volpiano: Son cursus liturgique au Mt. St. Michel et dans les abbayes normandes', *Millénaire monastique du Mt.-St. Michel*, 4 vols. (Paris, 1966), i. 417–72.

——, 'Les Répons "De Psalmis" pour les matines de l'épiphanie à la septuagésime selon les cursus romain et monastique', *EG* 6 (1963), 39–148.

'Les Rois mages, fragment d'un drame liturgique du XIe siècle,' *BEC* 34 (1873), 657–8.

Lesne, E., *Les Livres, scriptoria et bibliothèques du commencement du VIIIe à la fin du XIe siècle*, Histoire de la propriété écclésiastique en France 4 (Lille, 1938).

Levavasseur, F., *Saint-Denis à travers l'histoire* (n.p., n.d.).

Levillain, L., 'Essai sur les origines du Lendit', *Revue historique* 155 (1927), 241–76.

——, 'Études sur l'abbaye de Saint-Denis à l'époque mérovingienne', *BEC* 82 (1921), 5–116; 85 (1925), 5–99; 87 (1926), 20–97, 245–346; 91 (1930), 5–65, 264–300.

——, *Examen critique des chartes mérovingiennes et carolingiennes de Corbie*, Mémoires et documents publiés par la Société de l'École de Chartes 5 (Paris, 1902).

——, 'Les Plus anciennes églises abbatiales de Saint-Denis', *Mémoires de la Société de l'histoire de Paris et de l'Île-de-France* 36 (1909), 41–68.

——, 'L'Office divin dans l'abbaye de Saint-Denis: Le Calendrier de 1550', *RM* 1 (1905), 54–72.

Levy, K., 'A Hymn for Thursday in Holy Week', *JAMS* 16 (1963), 127–75.

——, 'Charlemagne's Archetype of Gregorian Chant,' *JAMS* 40 (1987), 1–30.

——, '*Lux de luce*: The Origin of an Italian Sequence', *MQ* 57 (1971), 40–61.

——, 'The Byzantine Sanctus and its Modal Tradition in East and West', *Annales Musicologiques*, 6 (1963), 7–67.

——, 'Toledo, Rome and the Legacy of Gaul', *EMH* 4 (1984), 49–99.

Liber Usualis missae et officii (Rome, 1904).

Lillich, M., 'Monastic Stained Glass: Patronage and Style', *Monasticism and the Arts*, ed. T. Verdon (Syracuse, NY, 1984), 207–54.

Loenertz, R., 'Le Légende parisienne de S. Denys l'Aréopagite, sa genèse et son premier témoin', *Analecta Bollandiana* 69 (1951), 217–37.

Louth, A., *Denys the Areopagite*, Outstanding Christian Thinkers (Wilton, Conn., 1989).

Lowe, E. A. (ed.), *Codices Latini Antiquiores: A Palaeographic Guide to Latin Manuscripts prior to the Ninth Century*, 12 vols. (Oxford, 1934–71).

——, *Palaeographical Papers, 1907–1965*, ed. L. Bieler, 2 vols. (Oxford, 1972).

——, 'The Vatican Manuscript of the Gelasian Sacramentary and its Supplement at Paris', *JTS* 27 (1926), 357–74.

Ludwig, F., *Repertorium Organorum Recentioris et Motetorum Vetustissimi Stili*, 2 vols., MuS 7, 17, 26 (repr., ed. Luther Dittmer, New York, 1964).

Luibheid, C., and Rorem, P. (trans.), *Pseudo-Dionysius: The Complete Works*, Classics of Western Spirituality (Mahwah, NJ, 1987).

Luscombe, D., 'Denis the Pseudo-Areopagite in the Middle Ages from Hilduin to Lorenzo Valla', *Fälschungen im Mittelalter: Internationaler Kongress der Monumenta Germaniae Historica, München. 16.–19. September 1986*, 5 vols., Monumenta Germainiae Historica Schriften 33/1 (Hanover, 1988), i. 133–52.

Lütolf, M., *Analecta Hymnica: Register*, 3 vols. (Berne and Munich, 1978).

Maassen, F. (ed.), *Concilia Aevi merovingici*, MGH, *Legum*, Sectio iii, *Concilia* i (Hanover, 1893).

Mabillon, J. (ed.), *Acta Sanctorum Ordinis Sancti Benedicti*, 9 vols. (Lyons–Paris, 1668–1701).

———, *Annales Ordinis Sancti Benedicti*, 6 vols. (Lucae, 1739–45).

——, *De cursu gallicano disquisitio*, *PL* lxxii, 381–416.

——, *De liturgica gallicana libri tres*, *PL* lxxii, 99–382.

——, *Œuvres posthumes*, 3 vols. (Paris, 1724).

——, *Veterum analectorum*, 4 vols. (Paris, 1675–85).

Madan, F., *A Summary Catalogue of Western Manuscripts in the Bodleian library at Oxford*, 5 vols. (Oxford, 1895–1922).

Malnory, A., *Quid Luxovienses monachi, discipuli sancti Columbani, ad regulam monasteriorum atque ad communem Ecclesiae profectum contuleunt* (Paris, 1894).

Mansi, J. (ed.), *Sacrorum Conciliorum Nova Amplissima Collectio* 53 vols. (Venice, 1758–98, repr. edn., Graz. 1960).

Marcusson, O. (ed.), CT ii: *Prosules de la messe*, 1: *Tropes de l'alleluia*, SLS 22 (Uppsala, 1976).

Marinis, T. de, *La Legatura artistica in Italia nei secoli XVe, XVI*, 3 vols. (Florence, 1960).

Marosszéki, S. R., *Les Origines du chant cistercien: Recherches sur les réformes du plain-chant cistercien au XIIe siècle*, Analecta Sacri ordinis cisterciensis 8/1–2 (Rome, 1952).

Martène, E., *De Antiquis monachorum ritibus libri quinque* (Lyon, 1690).

——, *Thesaurus novum anecdotorum*, 5 vols. (Paris, 1717).

——, *Veterum scriptorum et monumentorum historicorum, dogmaticorum, moralium, amplissima collectio*, 9 vols. (Paris, 1724–33).

——, *Voyage littéraire de deux religieux bénédictins de la congrégation de Saint-Maur* (Paris, 1717).

Martimort, A. G., *La Documentation liturgique de Dom Edmond Martèn: Étude codicologique*, SeT 279 (Vatican, 1978).

——, *L'Église en prière: Introduction à la liturgie*, I: *Principes de la liturgie*, 3rd edn. (Paris, 1983).

——, 'Recherches récentes sur les sacramentaires', *Bulletin de littérature ecclésiastique* 63 (162), 28–40.

Masai, F., 'La "Vita patrum iurensium" et les débuts du monachisme à Saint-Maurice d'Agaune', *Festschrift Bernhard Bischoff zu seinem 65. Geburtstag* (Stuttgart, 1971), 43–69.

——, 'Review of *The Psalter Collects*, ed. with Introduction by Dom L. Brou from papers of Dom A. Wilmart, HBS 83 (London, 1949)', *Scriptorium* 6 (1952), 295.

Mathiesen, T., 'The Office of the New Feast of Corpus Christi in the *Regimen Animarum* at Brigham Young University', *JM* 2 (1983), 13–44.

Mazal, O., 'Spuren einer "Missa graeca" in Benediktinerstift Kremsmünster', *Biblos* 29 (1980), 159–65.

McKinnon, J., 'Representations of the Mass in Medieval and Renaissance Art', *JAMS* 31 (1978), 21–52.

McKitterick, R., 'Charles the Bald (823–877) and his Library: The Patronage of Learning', *English Historical Review* 95 (1980), 28–47.

——, *The Carolingians and the Written Word* (Cambridge, 1989).

——, *The Frankish Church and the Carolingian Reforms, 789–895*, Royal Historical Society Studies in History (London, 1977).

——, *The Frankish Kingdoms under the Carolingians, 751–987* (London and New York, 1983).

——, 'The Scriptoria of Merovingian Gaul: A Survey of the Evidence', *Columbanus and Merovingian Monasticism*, ed. H. B. Clarke and M. Brennan, BAR International Series 113 (Oxford, 1981), 173–207.

Mearns, J., *Early Latin Hymnaries* (Cambridge, 1913).

Meersseman, G., *Les Capitules du diurnal de Saint-Denis (Cod. Verona Cap. LXXXVIII, Saec. IX)*, SF 30 (Fribourg, 1986).

——, Adda, E., and Deshusses, J., *L'Orazionale dell'Archdiacono Pacifico e il Carpsum del Cantore Stefano: Studi e Testi sulla Liturgia del Duomo di Verona del IX all' XI secolo*, SF 21 (Fribourg, 1974).

Melnicki, *Kyrie*: see Landwehr-Melnicki.

Mershman, F., 'All Souls' Day', *CE* i. 315–16.

Michelini Tocci, L. (ed.), *Sacramentarium Gelasianum: e codice vaticano reginensi latino 316 vertente anno sacro MCMLXXV*, 2 vols. (Vatican, 1975).

Michels, U. (ed.), *Johannis de Muris Notitia Artis Musicae et Compendium Musicae Practicae, Petrus de Sancto Dionysio Tractatus de Musica*, Corpus Scriptorum de Musica 17, gen. ed. G. Reaney (Rome, 1972).

Misset, E., and Aubry, P., *Les Proses d'Adam de Saint-Victor* (Paris, 1900).

—— and Weale, W. (eds.), *Analecta Liturgica*, ii: *Thesaurus Hymnologicus*, 3 vols. (London, 1892–1901).

Mohlberg, L. (ed.), *Das Fränkische Sacramentarium Gelasianum in alamannischer Überlieferung*, 3rd edn. (Münster, 1971).

——, *Missale Gothicum: Das Gallikanische Sakramentar (Cod. Vatican. Regin. Lat. 317) des VII.–VIII. Jahrhunderts*, 2 vols. (Augsburg, 1929).

——, Eizenhöfer, L., and Siffrin, P. (eds.), *Liber Sacramentorum Romanae Aeclesiae Ordinis Anni Circuli*, 3rd edn., RED, Series Major, Fontes iv (Rome, 1981).

——, ——, and ——, *Missale Francorum*, RED, Series Major, Fontes ii (Rome, 1957).

——, ——, and ——, *Sacramentarium Veronense*, 3rd edn., RED, Series Major, Fontes i (Rome, 1978).

Molinier, A., *Catalogue des manuscrits de la Bibliothèque Mazarine*, 4 vols. (Paris, 1885).

——, *Obituaires de la Province de Sens,* i: *Diocèses de Sens et de Paris*, 2 vols. (Paris, 1902).

—— and Omont, H. (eds.), *Catalogue général des manuscrits des bibliothèques publiques de France, Départements* iii (Paris, 185).

Möller, H., 'Research on the Antiphoner: Problems and Perspectives', *JPMMS* 10 (1987), 1–14.

Montesquiou-Fezensac, B. de, and Gaborit-Chopin, D., *Le Trésor de Saint-Denis. Inventaire de 1634*, 3 vols. (Paris, 1973–7).

Montessus, T. de, 'Sacramentaires carolingiens à l'abbaye de Chelles', *Scriptorium* 28 (1974), 274.

Moran, D., *The Philosophy of John Scottus Eruigena: A Study of Idealism in the Middle Ages* (Cambridge, 1989).

Moreton, B., 'A Patronal Festival? St. Prajectus and the Eighth-Century Sacramentary', *JTS* 27 (1976), 370–80.

——, *The Eighth-Century Gelasian Sacramentary: A Study in Tradition*, OTM 8 (London, 1976).

Mortin, G., 'Fragments inédits et jusqu'à présent uniques d'antiphonaire gallican', *RB* 22 (1905), 327–56.

——, 'Le Lectionnaire de l'église de Paris au VIIe siècle', *RB* 10 (1893), 438–41.

Moyse, G., 'Monachisme et règlementation monastique en Gaule avant Benoît d'Aniane', *Sous la règle de saint Benoît: Structures monastiques et sociétés en France du moyen-âge à l'époque moderne*, École Pratique des Hautes Études, IVe Section, Sciences historiques et philologiques v, Hautes Études médiévales et modernes 47 (Geneva and Paris, 1982), 3–19.

Mühlbacher, E. (ed.), *Die Urkunden Pippins, Karlmanns und Karls des Grossen*, MGH, *Diplomatum Karolinorum*, 3 vols. (Hanover, 1906).

Mütherich, F., 'Die Buchmalerei am Hofe Karls des Grossen', *Karl der Grosse*, iii: *Karolingische Kunst* (Düsseldorf, 1966).

——, 'Communication à la société des antiquaires de France, séance du 27 novembre 1968: Le Scriptorium de Saint-Germain-des-Prés au IXe siècle', *Bulletin de la Société nationale des Antiquaires de France* (1968), 210–2.

—— (ed.), *Sakramentar von Metz: Fragment MS. latin 1141, Bibliothèque Nationale, Paris* (Graz, 1972).

—— and Gaedhe, J., *Carolingian Painting* (New York, 1976).

Neale, J., *A History of the Holy Eastern Church*, 5 vols. (London, 1847–73, repr. edn., New York, 1976).

Nebbiai-Dalla Guarda, D., *La Bibliothèque de l'abbaye de Saint-Denis en France du IXe au XVIIIe siècle* (Paris, 1985).

—— 'Le Collège de Paris de l'abbaye de Saint-Denis-en-France', *Sous la règle de saint Benoît, Structures monastiques et sociétés en France du moyen-âge à l'époque moderne*, École Pratique des Hautes Études, IVe Section, Sciences historiques et philologiques v, Hautes Études médiévales et modernes 47 (Geneva and Paris, 1982), 461–88.

——, 'Les Listes médiévales de lectures monastiques: Contribution à la connaissance des anciennes bibliothèques bénédictines', *RB* 96 (1986), 271–326.

Netzer, H., *L'Introduction de la messe romaine en France sous les Carolingiens* (Paris, 1910).

New Catholic Encyclopedia, The, ed. W. McDonald, 15 vols. (New York, 1967).

New Grove Dictionary of Music and Musicians, The, ed. S. Sadie, 20 vols. (London, 1980).

New Grove Dictionary of Musical Instruments, The, ed. S. Sadie, 3 vols. (London, 1980).

New Oxford History of Music, 10 vols. (London, 1954–74).

Nocent, A., 'Un Fragment du sacramentaire de Sens au Xe siècle: La Liturgie baptismale de la province ecclésiastique de Sens dans les manuscrits du

IXe au XVIe siècles', *Miscellanea Liturgica in onore di Sua Eminenza Il Cardinale Giacomo Lercaro* ii (Paris, 1967), 649–794.
——, Hallinger, K., and Elvert, C. (eds.), *Consuetudinum Saeculi X/XI/XII: Monumenta Non-Cluniacensia,* 3: *Aelfrici Abbatis Epistula ad Monachos Egneshamnenses Directa*, CCM 7/3 (Siegburg, 1984).
Oexle, O. G., *Forshungen zu monastischen und geistlichen Gemeinschaften im westfränkischen Bereich*, Münstersche Mittelalter Schriften 31 (Munich, 1978).
O'Meara, J. J., *Eriugena* (Oxford, 1988).
Omont, H. (ed.), *Catalogue général des manuscrits des bibliothèques publiques de France, Départements* 1–2 (Rouen and Paris, 1886).
——, *Inventaire sommaire des manuscrits grecs de la Bibliothèque Nationale*, 3 vols. (Paris, 1886–98).
——, 'La Messe grecque de Saint-Denys au moyen-âge', *Études d'histoire du moyen-âge dédiées à Gabriel Monod* 1 (Paris, 1896).
Ongaro, G., 'Cultura e Scuola calligrafica veronese del secolo X', *Memorie del Reale Istituto veneto di Scienze, Lettere ed Arti* 29/7 (Venice, 1925).
Ott, C. (ed.), *Offertoriale sive versus offertoriorum cantus Gregoriani* (Paris, 1935).
Oury, G., 'La Structure cérémonielle des vêpres solennelles dans quelques anciennes liturgies françaises', *EG* 13 (1972), 225–36.
——, 'Les Matines solennelles aux grandes fêtes dans les anciennes églises françaises', *EG* 12 (1971), 155–62.
——, 'Les Messes de Saint Martin dans les sacramentaires gallicans, romano-francs et milannais', *EG* 5 (1962), 73–97.
Pächt, O., and Alexander, J., *Illuminated Manuscripts in the Bodleian Library Oxford*, 3 vols. (Oxford, 1966–73).
Palazzo, É., 'Un "Libellus Missae" du scriptorium de Saint-Amand pour Saint-Denis: son intérêt pour la typologie des manuscrits lituriques', *RB* 99 (1988), 286–92.
Paléographie Musicale, 1st ser., 19 vols. (Solesmes, 1889–1974); 2nd ser., 2 vols. (Solesmes, 1900–24).
Panofsky, E. (ed.), *Abbot Suger on the Abbey Church of St.-Denis and its Art Treasures*, 2nd edn., ed. G. Panofsky-Soergel (Princeton, NJ, 1979).
Pardessus, J.-M., and Bréquiny, L. G. O. (eds.), *Diplomata, chartae, epistolae, leges aliaque instrumenta ad res Gallo-Francicas spectantia*, 2 vols. (Paris, 1843–9).
Parisot, J., 'Les Chorévêques', *Revue de l'Orient chrétien* 6 (1901), 157–71, 419–43.
Parker, J. H., *The Hierarchies of Dionysius the Areopagite* (London, 1894).
Parrish, C., *The Notation of Medieval Music* (New York, 1957,. repr. 1978).
Passalacqua, R. (ed.), *I Codici liturgici miniati dugenteschi nell'Archivio Capitolare del Duomo di Arezzo* (Florence, 1980).
Payne, T., 'Associa tecum in patria: A Newly Identified Organum Trope by Philip the Chancellor', *JAMS* 39 (1986), 233–54.
Perdrizet, P., *Le Calendrier parisien à la fin du moyen âge d'après le bréviaire*

et les livres d'heures, Publications de la Faculté des Lettres de l'Université de Strasbourg 63 (Paris, 1933).

Pertz, G. H. (ed.), *Annales Laurissenses Minores*, MGH, *Scriptorum* i. 112–3 (Hanover, 1826).

——, *Annales Mettenses*, MGH, *Scriptorum* i. 314–36 (Hanover, 1826).

——, *Chronicon Moissiacense*, MGH, *Scriptorum* i. 280–313 (Hanover, 1826).

Pfaff, R., *New Liturgical Feasts in Later Medieval England*, OTM 1 (Oxford, 1970).

Picherit, J.-L., *The Journey of Charlemagne to Jerusalem and Constantinople (Le Voyage de Charlemagne à Jérusalem et à Constantinople)* (Birmingham, Ala., 1984).

Planchart, A., *The Repertory of Tropes at Winchester*, 2 vols. (Princeton, NJ, 1977).

Pothier, J., '*Alleluia V. Justus germinabit* avec tropes', *RCG* 11 (1897), 169–73.

Poupardin, R., 'Cartulaire de Saint-Vincent de Laon', *Mémoires de la société de l'histoire de Paris et de l'Île-de-France* 29 (1902), 173–267.

Prinz, F., 'Columbanus, the Frankish Nobility and the Territories East of the Rhine', *Columbanus and Merovingian Monasticism*, ed. H. B. Clarke and M. Brennan, BAR Interantional Series 113 (Oxford, 1981), 73–87.

——, *Frühes Mönchtum in Frankenreich: Kultur und Gesellschaft in Gallien, den Rheinlanden und Bayern am Beispiel der monastischen Entwicklung (4. bis 8. Jahrhundert)* (Munich and Vienna, 1965).

Processionale monasticum ad usum congregationis gallicae (Solesmes, 1893).

Prunières, H., 'La Musique de la chambre et de l'écurie sous le règne de François Ier, 1516–1547', *L'Année musicale* 1 (1911), 215–51.

Quentin, H., *Les Martyrologes historiques du moyen âge* (Paris, 1908).

Quitin, J., 'Les Maîtres de chant de la cathédrale St. Lambert, à Liège aux XVe et XVIe siècles', *Revue belge de musicologie* 8 (1954), 5–18.

Raby, F. J. E., *A History of Christian–Latin Poetry from the Beginnings to the Close of the Middle Ages*, 2nd edn. (Oxford, 1953).

Radding, C., and Clark, W., 'Abélard et le bâtisseur de Saint-Denis: Études parallèles d'histoire des disciplines', *Annales: Economies, sociétés, civilisations* 6 (1988), 1263–90.

Rand, E. K., *A Survey of the Manuscripts of Tours* (Cambridge, 1929).

——, 'Traces de piqûres dans quelques manuscrits du haut moyen âge', *Comptes rendus de l'Académie des Inscriptions et Belles Lettres* (1939), 411–31.

Randel, D. (ed.), *The New Harvard Dictionary of Music* (Cambridge, Mass., 1986).

Rasmussen, N. K., 'The Liturgy at Saint-Denis: A Preliminary Study', *Abbot Suger and Saint-Denis: A Symposium*, ed. P. Gerson (New York, 1986), 41–8.

Ratcliff, E. C. (ed.), *Expositio Antiquae Liturgiae Gallicanae*, HBS 98 (London, 1971).

Raugel, F., 'Saint-Denis', trans. A. Frese, *MGG* xi, cols. 1246–9.

Raynaud, G., *Bibliographie des chansonniers français des XIIIe et XIVe siècles*, 2 vols. (Paris, 1884, repr. Osnabrück, 1971).

Reaney, G. (ed.), *Manuscripts of Polyphonic Music, 11th–Early 14th Century*, *RISM* B IV[1] (Munich, 1966).

Reiffenberg, Baron de (ed.), *Chronique rimée de Philippe Mouskes*, 2 vols., Collection des chroniques belges (Brussels, 1836–8).

Renaudin, A., 'Deux antiphonaires de Saint-Maur', *EG* 13, (1972), 53–150.

'Responsory', *NGD* xv. 759–63.

Reymond, M., 'La Charte de Saint Sigismond pour Saint-Maurice d'Agaune 515', *Zeitschrift für Schweizerische Geschichte* 6 (1926), 1–60.

Riché, P., 'Columbanus, his Followers and the Merovingian Church', *Columbanus and Merovingian Monasticism*, ed. H. B. Clarke and M. Brennan, BAR International Series 113 (Oxford, 1981), 59–72.

Robertson, A. W.: see also Walters [Robertson], Anne.

——, '*Benedicamus Domino*: The Unwritten Tradition', *JAMS* 40 (1988), 1–62.

——, 'Review of *Medieval Manuscripts for Mass and Office: A Guide to their Organization and Terminology* by Andrew Hughes', *JM* 4 (1985–6), 350–4.

——, 'The Transmission of Music and Liturgy from Saint-Denis to Saint-Corneille of Compiègne', *Trasmissione e recezione delle forme di cultura musicale*, Atti del XIV Congresso della Società Internazionale di Musicologia, Bologna, 27 augusto–1° settembre 1987, III. Free Papers (Bologna, 1990), 505–14.

Roederer, C. D., 'Eleventh-Century Aquitanian Chant-Studies relating to a Local Repertory of Processional Antiphons', 2 vols. (Ph.D. diss., Yale Univ., 1971).

Rokseth, Y., *Polyphonies du XIIIe siècle: Le Manuscrit H196 de la Faculté de médecine de Montpellier*, 4 vols. (Paris, 1935–9).

Roques, R. (ed.), *Jean Scot Erigène et l'histoire de la philosophie*, Colloques internationaux du Centre National de la Recherche Scientifique 561 (Paris, 1977).

——, *L'Univers dionysien: Structure hiérarchique du monde selon le Pseudo-Denys* (Paris, 1954; repr. Paris, 1983).

Rorem, P., *Biblical and Liturgical Symbols within the Pseudo-Dionysian Synthesis*, Studies and Texts 71 (Toronto, 1984).

Rosenwein, B., *Rhinoceros Bound: Cluny in the Tenth Century* (Philadelphia, 1982).

Ruysschaert, J., 'La Bibliothèque du cardinal de Tournai Ferry de Clugny à la Vaticane', *Horae Tornacenses 1171–1971* (Tournai, 1971), 131–41.

Sackur, E., *Die Cluniacenser*, 2 vols. (Halle, 1892–4).

Saillot, J., *Les Seize quartiers des reines et impératrices françaises* (Angers, 1977).

Saint Chrodegang: Communications présentées au colloque tenu à Metz à l'occasion du douzième centenaire de sa mort (Metz, 1967).

Sainte-Beuve, Dom de, 'Un ancien Répons de l'office des morts', *RG* 8 (1923), 12–15, 81–8.

Saitta-Revignas, A. (ed.), *Catalogo dei Manoscritti della Biblioteca Casanatense*, 6 vols. (Rome, 1949–78).

Salmon, P., 'Le Texte biblique de l'évangéliaire de Saint-Denis', *Miscellanea Mercati* i (Rome, 1946), 103–6.

——, *Les Manuscrits liturgiques de la Bibliothèque Vaticane*, 5 vols., SeT 251, 253, 260, 267, 270 (Vatican, 1968–72).

——, 'Livrets de prières de l'époque carolingienne', *RB* 86 (1976), 218–34.

——, *L'Office divin au moyen âge: Histoire de la formation du bréviaire du IXe au XVIe siècle*, Lex Orandi 43 (Paris, 1967).

Samaran, C., 'Études sandionysiennes, i: Notes sur la bibliothèque de l'abbaye de Saint-Denis au XVe siècle', *BEC* 104 (1943), 5–26, 'ii: Un Nécrologe inédit de l'abbaye de Saint-Denis', *BEC* 104 (1943), 27–100.

——, *Jean de Bilhères: Lagraulas, cardinal de Saint-Denis*, Bibliothèque de XVe siècle 26 (Paris, 1921).

——, 'Manuscrits "imposés" à la manière typographique', *Mélanges en hommage à la mémoire de Fr. Martroye* (Paris, 1940).

—— and Marichal, R. (eds.), *Catalogue des manuscrits en écriture latine portant des indications de date, de lieu ou de copiste*, 7 vols. (Paris, 1959, 1962, 1974, 1981, 1965, 1968, 1984).

Sanders, E., *English Music of the Thirteenth and Early Fourteenth Centuries*, PMFC xiv (Monaco, 1979).

Sandon, N. (ed.), *The Use of Salisbury: The Ordinary of the Mass* (Newton, Abbott, Devon, 1984).

Saxer, V., *Le Culte de Marie Madeleine en occident des origines à la fin du moyen âge* (Paris, 1959).

——, 'Observations codicologiques et liturgiques sur trois sacramentaires grégoriens de la première moitié du IXe siècle: Paris Latin 2812, Vatican Ottoboni Latin 313 et Reginensis Latin 337', *Mélanges de l'école française de Rome: Moyen âge–Temps modernes, Paris–Rome*, 97 (1985), 23–43.

Schapiro, M., 'Two Romanesque Drawings in Auxerre and Some Iconographic Problems', *Studies in Art and Literature for Belle da Costa Greene*, ed. D. Miner (Princeton, NJ, 1954).

Schildbach, M., *Das einstimmige Agnus Dei und seine handschriftliche Überlieferung vom 10. bis zum 16. Jahrundert* (Ph.D. diss., Univ. of Erlangen, 1967).

Schlager, K., 'Eine Melodie zum griechischen *Credo*', *AM* 56 (1984), 221–34.

——, *Thematischer Katalog der ältesten Alleluia-Melodien* (Munich, 1965).

—— and Wohnhaas, T., 'Spuren Bamberger Choralgeschichte in Fragmenten mit Notation aus dem Staatsarchiv Bamberg', *Historischer Verein für die Pflege der Geschichte des ehemaligen Fürstbistums Bamberg* 119 (Bamberg, 1983), 33–8.

Schmidt, G., 'Zur Datierung des "kleiner" Bargello-Diptychons und der Verkundigungstafel in Cleveland', *Études d'art offertes à Charles Sterling* (Paris, 1975), 47–63.

Schmidt, H., 'De Sacramentariis romanis, Bibliographia cum notitiis', *Gregorianum* 34 (1953), 713–33.

Schmitz, P., 'Les Lectures de table à l'abbaye de Saint-Denis vers la fin du moyen-âge', *RB* 42 (1930), 163–7.

——, 'Les Lectures du soir à l'abbaye de Saint-Denis au XIIe siècle', *RB* 44 (1932), 147–9.

Schneyer, J., *Repertorium der lateinischen Sermones des Mittelalters für die Zeit 1150–1350*, Beiträge zur Geschichte der Philosophie und Theologie des Mittelalters 43/4 (Münster Westfalen, 1972).

Schramm, P., *Der König von Frankreich: Das Wesen der Monarchie vom 9. zum 16. Jahrhundert*, 2nd edn., 2 vols. (Weimar, 1960).

Schueller, H., *The Idea of Music: An Introduction to Musical Aesthetics in Antiquity and the Middle Ages*, Early Drama, Art, and Music Monograph Series 9 (Kalamazoo, 1988).

Schuh, W. (ed.), *Schweizer Musikbuch*, 2 vols. (Zurich, 1939).

Schulten, S., 'Die Buchmalerei des 11. Jahrhunderts im Kloster St. Vaast in Arras', *Münchener Jahrbuch der Bildenden Kunst* 7 (1956), 49–90.

Seebass, T., *Musikdarstellung und Psalterillustration*, 2 vols. (Berne, 1973).

Semmler, J., 'Die Beschlüsse des Aachener Konzils im Jahre 816', *ZfK* 74 (1963), 15–82.

——, 'Reichsidee und kirchliche Gesetzgebung bei Ludwig dem Frommen', *ZfK* 71 (1960), 37–65.

Sicard, D., *La Liturgie de la mort dans l'église latine des origines à la réforme carolingienne*, LQF 63 (Münster, 1978).

——, 'La Messe aux obsèques', *Concilium* 32 (1968), 43–8.

Sigebert de Gemblous, *Chronicon* (Antwerp, 1608).

Simson, O. von, *The Gothic Cathedral: Origins of Gothic Architecture and the Medieval Concept of Order*, 3rd edn., Bollingen series 48 (Princeton, NJ, 1988).

Smith, N., 'Some Exceptional Clausulae of the Florence Manuscript', *ML* 54 (1973), 405–14.

——, The *Clausulae* of the Notre Dame School: A Repertorial Study', 3 vols. (Ph.D. diss., Yale Univ., 1967).

Sotheby and Co., *Catalogue of Valuable Printed Books and Illuminated Manuscripts* (London, 1929).

'Sources', *NGD* xvii. 590–702.

Spanke, H., *G. Raynauds Bibliographie des Altfranzösischen Liedes* (Leyden, 1980).

Spätling, L., and Dinter, P. (eds.), *Consuetudines Fructuarienses: Sanblasianae*, CCM 12/1–2 (Siegburg, 1985).

Spiegel, G. M., 'History as Enlightenment: Suger and the *Mos Anagogicus*', *Abbot Suger and Saint-Denis*, ed. P. Gerson (New York, 1986), 151–8.

——, *Pseudo-Turpin*, the Crisis of the Aristocracy and the Beginnings of Vernacular Historiography in France', *Journal of Medieval History* 12 (1986), 207–23.

——, *The Chronicle Tradition of Saint-Denis: A Survey* (Brookline, Mass., and Leyden, 1978).

Stäblein, B., 'Gallikanische Liturgie', *MGG* iv, cols. 1299–1325.

—— (ed.), *Hymnen, Die mittelalterlichen Hymnenmelodien des Abendlandes*, Monumenta Monodica Medii Aevi 1 (Regensburg, 1956).

—— (ed.), *Schriftbild der Einstimmigen Musik*, Musikgeschichte in Bildern, iii: *Musik des Mittelalters und der Renaissance*, Lfg. 4 (Leipzig, 1975).

—— 'Tropus', *MGG* xiii, cols. 797–826.

Staerk, A., *Les Manuscrits latins du Ve au XIIIe siècle conservés à la bibliothèque impériale de Saint-Pétersbourg*, 2 vols. (Snt Petersburg, 1910, repr. New York, 1976).

Stahl, H., 'The Problem of Manuscript Painting at Saint-Denis During the Abbacy of Suger', *Abbot Suger and Saint-Denis*, ed. P. Gerson (New York, 1986), 163–82.

Steiner, R., 'Antiphons for the Benedicite at Lauds', *JPMMS* 7 (1984), 1–17.

——, 'Hymn, II. Monophonic Latin', *NGD* viii. 838–41.

——, 'Invitatory', *NGD* ix. 286–9.

——, 'Liturgy and Liturgical Books', *NGD* xi. 84–8.

——, 'Local and Regional Traditions of the Invitatory Chant', *Studia Musicologica: Academiae Scientiarum Hungaricae* 27, ed. J. Ujfalussy (Budapest, 1985), 131–8.

——, Prosula', *NGD* xv. 310–12.

——, 'Reconstructing the Repertory of Invitatory Tones and their Uses at Cluny in the late 11th Century', *Musicologie médiévale: Notations et séquences*, ed. M. Huglo (Paris, 1987), 175–82.

——, 'Some Melismas for Office Responsories', *JAMS* 26 (1973), 108–31.

——, 'The Gregorian Chant Melismas of Christmas Matins', *Essays on Music for Charles Warren Fox* (Rochester, NY, 1979).

——, 'The Music for a Cluny Office of Saint-Benedict', *Monasticism and the Arts*, ed. T. Verdon (Syracuse, NY, 1984), 81–114.

——, 'The Prosulae of the MS Paris, Bibliothèque Nationale, f. lat. 1118', *JAMS* 22 (1969), 367–93.

——, 'The Responsories and Prosa for St. Stephen's Day at Salisbury', *MQ* 56 (1970), 162–82.

——, 'Tones for the Palm Sunday Invitatory', *JM* 3 (1984), 142–56.

——, 'Trope', *NGD* xix. 172–87.

Stevens, J., *Words and Music in the Middle Ages: Song, Narrative, Dance and Drama, 1050–1350*, Cambridge Studies in Music (Cambridge, 1986).

Stoclet, A., 'La *Descriptio Basilicae Sancti Dyonisii*: Premiers commentaires', *Journal des Savants* (1980), 103–17.

Strohm, R., *Music in Late Medieval Bruges*, Oxford Monographs on Music (Oxford, 1985).

Summers, W., *English Fourteenth-Century Polyphony: Facsimile Edition of Sources Notated in Score*, München Editionen zur Musikgeschichte 4 (Tutzing, 1983).

Suñol, G., *Introduction à la Paléographie musicale Grégorienne* (Paris, 1935).

Symons, T., Spath, S., Wegener, M., and Hallinger, K. (eds.), *Consuetudinum Saeculi X/XI/XII: Monumenta Non-Cluniacensia, 2: Regularis Concordia Anglicae Nationis*, CCM 7/3 (Siegburg, 1984).

Szövérffy, J., *A Concise History of Medieval Latin Hymnody: Religious Lyrics between Antiquity and Humanism*, Medieval Classics, Texts and Studies 19 (Leyden, 1985).

——, *Die Annalen der Lateinischen Hymnendichtung: Ein Handbuch,* I: *Die lateinischen Hymnen bis zum Ende des 11. Jahrhunderts* (Berlin, 1964).

Taft, R., 'Quaestiones Disputatae in the History of the Liturgy of the Hours: The Origins of Nocturns, Matins, Prime', *Worship* 58 (1984), 130–58.

Tardif, J., *Monuments Historiques: Cartons des Rois* (Paris, 1866).

Thannabaur, P. J., *Das einstimmiger Sanctus der römischen Messe in der handschriftlichen Überlieferung des 11. bis 16. Jahrhunderts*, Erlanger Arbeiten zur Musikwissenschaft 1 (Munich, 1962).

Théry, G., 'Contribution à l'histoire de l'aréopagitisme au IXe siècle', *Le Moyen âge* 34 (1923), 111–53.

——, *Études dionysiennes*, i: *Hilduin, traducteur de Denys*, ii: *Hilduin, traducteur de Denys, édition de sa traduction*, Études de philisophie médiévale 16, 19 (Paris, 1932–7).

Theurillat, J. M., 'L'Abbaye de Saint-Maurice d'Agaune des origines à la réforme canoniale (515–830)', *Vallesia* 9 (1954), 1–128.

Thorpe, L. (trans.), *Einhard and Notker the Stammerer: Two Lives of Charlemagne* (Baltimore, 1969).

——, *Gregory of Tours: The History of the Franks* (London, 1974).

Tischler, H., *The Earliest Motets (to Circa 1270): A Complete Comparative Edition*, 3 vols. (New Haven, Conn., 1982).

—— (ed.), *The Style and Evolution of the Earliest Motets (to Circa 1270)*, 3 vols., MuS 40/1–3 (Henryville, Pa., 1985).

——, Stakel, S., and Relihew, J. (eds.), *The Montpellier Codex*, 4 pts., Recent Researches in the Music of the Middle Ages and Early Renaissance 2–8 (Madison, Wis., 1978–85).

Tolhurst, J. (ed.), *The Monastic Breviary of Hyde Abbey, Winchester*, 6 vols., HBS 69, 70, 71, 76, 78, 80 (London, 1932–42).

Tomasello, A., 'Ritual, Tradition, and Polyphony at the Court of Rome', *JM* 4 (1985–86), 447–71.

Treitler, L., 'Homer and Gregory: The Transmission of Epic Poetry and Plainchant', *MQ* 60 (1974), 333–72.

Turner, D. H., *The Missal of the New Minster*, HBS 93 (London, 1962).

Turrini, G., *Biblioteca Capitolare di Verona* (Verona, 1948).

——, *Indice dei codici capitolari di Verona, redatto nel 1625 dal canonico A. Rezzani*, Testo critico rapportato al catalogo di A. Spagnolo (Verona, 1965).

Udovich, J., 'Modality, Office Antiphons, and Psalmody: The Musical Authority of the Twelfth-Century Antiphonal from St.-Denis' (Ph.D. diss., Univ. of North Carolina at Chapel Hill, 1985).

——, 'The Magnificat Antiphons for the Ferial Office', *JPMMS* 3 (1980), 1—25.

Valous, G. de, *Le Monachisme clunisien des origines au XVe siècle*, 2nd edn., 2 vols. (Paris, 1970).

Van Dam, R., *Leadership and Community in Late Antique Gaul* (Berkeley, Calif., 1985).

Vandersall, A., 'The Relationship of Sculptors and Painters in the Court School of Charles the Bald', *Gesta* 15 (1976), 201–10.

Van der Werf, H., *Integrated Directory of Organa, Clausulae, and Motets* (Rochester, NY, 1989).

Van Dijk, S. J., *Handlist of the Latin Liturgical Manuscripts in the Bodleian Library Oxford*, 7 vols., (n.p., 1957–60).

——, 'Papal Schola *versus* Charlemagne', *Organicae Voces: Festschrift Joseph Smits van Waesberghe* (Amsterdam, 1963), 21–30.

——, 'The Urban and Papal Rites in Seventh and Eighth-Century Rome', *SE* 12 (1961), 411–87.

Vasaturo, N., Hallinger, K., Wegener, M., and Elvert, C. (eds.), *Consuetudines Cluniacensium Antiquiores Cum Redactionibus Derivatis* 5: *Redactio Vallumbrosana*, CCM 7/2 (Siegburg, 1983).

Vauchez, A., *La Sainteté en occident aux derniers siècles du moyen-âge d'après les procès de canonisation et les documents hagiographiques*, Bibliothèque des écoles français d'Athènes et de Rome 241 (Rome, 1981).

Venturini, M., *Vita ed Attività dello 'Scriptorium' veronese nel secolo XI* (Verona, 1930).

Vezin, J., 'Hincmar de Reims et Saint-Denis', *Revue d'histoire des textes* 9 (1979), 289–98.

——, 'Le Point d'interrogation, un élément de datation et de localisation des manuscrits: L'Exemple de St. Denis au IXe siècle', *Scriptorium* 34 (1980), 181–96.

——, 'Les Manuscrits copiès à Saint-Denis en France pendant l'époque carolingienne', *Le Haut Moyen Âge en Île-de-France* (Paris, 1982), 273–87.

——, 'Observations sur l'origine des manuscrits légués par Dungal à Bobbio', *Paläographie 1981, Colloquium des Comité international de paléographie*, ed. G. Silagi, MBMRF 32 (Munich, 1982), 125–44.

——, 'Reims et Saint-Denis au IXe siècle: L'ancêtre du manuscrit 118 de la Bibliothèque Municipale de Reims', *RB* 94 (1984), 315–25.

Viard, J. (ed.), *Les Grandes Chroniques de France*, 10 vols. (Paris, 1922).

Victoria and Albert Museum Library, *Catalogue of Illuminated Manuscripts*, 2 vols. (London, 1957).

Vies des saints et des bienheureux selon l'ordre du calendrier avec l'histoire des fêtes par les Bénedictins de Paris, 13 vols. (Paris, 1935–59).

Villetard, H., *Office de Pierre de Corbeil (Office de la Circoncision) improprement appelé "Office des fous"*, Bibliothèque Musicologique 4 (Paris, 1907).

Vincent, A. J. H., 'Note sur la messe grecque qui se chantait autrefois à l'abbaye royale de St.-Denis, le jour octave de la fête patronale', *Revue archéologique* 9 (n.s., 1864), 268–81.

Vogel, C., 'Les Échanges liturgiques entre Rome et les pays francs jusqu'à

l'époque de Charlemagne', *Le Chiese nei regni dell'Europa occidentale*, Settimane de studio sull'alto medioevo 7 (Spoleto, 1960), 229–46.
——, *Medieval Liturgy: An Introduction to the Sources*, rev. and ed. W. G. Storey and N. K. Rasmussen (Washington, DC, 1986).
——, 'Saint Chrodegang et les débuts de la romanisation du culte en pays franc', *Saint Chrodegang: Communications présentées au colloque tenu à Metz à l'occasion du douzième centenaire de sa mort* (Metz, 1967), 91–109.
Vogüé, A. de, 'La Règle des Quatre Pères et les statuts de la Société des Douze Apôtres', *RB* 90 (1980), 132–4.
——, *La Règle du maître*, 3 vols., SC 105–7 (Paris, 1964–5).
—— and Neufville, J., *La Règle de Saint Benoît*, 7 vols. (Paris, 1971–7).
'Votive Mass, Votive Antiphon', *NGD* xx. 84.
Waddell, C., 'The Origin and Early Evolution of the Cistercian Antiphonary: Reflections on Two Cistercian Chant Reforms', *The Cistercian Spirit: A Symposium*, ed. M. B. Pennington (Spencer, Mass., 1970), 190–223.
——, *The Twelfth-Century Cistercian Hymnal*, 2 vols., Cistercian Liturgy Series 1–2 (Trappist, Ky., 1984).
Wagner, P., *Einführung in die gregorianischen Melodien*, 3 vols. (Leipzig, 1911–21).
Waitz, G. (ed.), *Ademari Historiarum Libri III*, MGH, *Scriptorum* iv (Hanover, 1841), 106–48.
—— (ed.), *Annales Bertiniani*, MGH, *Scriptores rerum germanicarum in usum scholarum* (Hanover, 1883).
Walafrid Strabo, *De ecclesiasticarum rerum exordiis et incrementis*, *PL* cxiv, 919–66.
Walker, G. S. (ed.), *Sancti Columbani Opera*, Scriptores latini Hiberniae 2 (Dublin, 1957).
Walpole, A. S., *Early Latin Hymns* (repr. Hildesheim, 1966).
Walters [Robertson], Anne; see also Robertson, Anne Walters.
——, 'Music and Liturgy at the Abbey of Saint-Denis (567–1567): A Survey of the Primary Sources' (Ph.D. diss., Yale Univ., 1984).
——, 'The Reconstruction of the Abbey-Church at St-Denis (1231–81): The Interplay of Music and Ceremony with Architecture and Politics', *EMH* 5 (1985), 187–238.
Waquet, H., *Vie de Louis le Gros*, Les Classiques de l'histoire de France au moyen âge 11 (Paris, 1929).
Weakland, R. G., 'The Performance of Ambrosian Chant in the 12th Century', *Aspects of Medieval and Renaissance Music: A Birthday Offering to Gustave Reese* (New York, 1966, repr. 1978), 856–66.
Wegener, M., Elvert, C., and Hallinger, K. (eds.), *Consuetudinum Saeculi X/XI/XII: Monumenta Non-Cluniacensia, 4. Redactio Sancti Emmerammi Dicta Einsidlensis*, CCM 7/3 (Siegburg, 1984).
Weisbein, N., 'Le "Laudes Crucis Attollamus" de Maître Hughes d'Orléans dit le Primat', *Revue du moyen âge latin* 3 (1947), 5–26.
Weiss, R., 'Lo Studio del greco all'abbazia de San Dioinigi durante il Medioevo', *Revista di Storia della Chiesa in Italia* 6 (1952), 426–38.

Wellesz, E., *A History of Byzantine Music and Hymnography*, 2nd edn. (Oxford, 1961).
——, *Eastern Elements in Western Chant: Studies in the Early History of Ecclesiastical Music* (Copenhagen, 1967).
Werminghoff, A. (ed.), *Concilia in Monasterio Sancti Dyonisii habita 829–830. 832*, MGH, *Legum*, Sectio iii, *Concilia*, ii: *Concilia Aevi Karolini* i/2 (Hanover and Leipzig, 1908), 783–94.
—— (ed.), *Concilium Attiniacense*, MGH, *Legum*, Sectio iii, *Concilia*, ii: *Concilia Aevi Karolini* i/1 (Hanover and Leipzig, 106), 72–3.
—— (ed.), *Concilium Parisiense A. 829*, MGH, *Legum*, Sectio iii, *Concilia*, ii: *Concilia Aevi Karolini* i/2 (Hanover and Leipzig, 1908), 605–80.
White, J., *The Birth and Rebirth of Pictorial Space* (London, 1957).
Wieland, G., *The Canterbury Hymnal*, Toronto Medieval Latin Texts 12 (Toronto, 1982).
Williams, P., 'Organ', *NGDMI* ii. 838–916.
Wilmart, A., *Codices Reginenses Latini*, 2 vols. (Vatican, 1945).
——, 'Le Manuel des prières de Saint Jean Gualbert', *RB* 48 (1936), 258–99.
——, 'Le Psautier de la Reine n. XI', *RB* 28 (1911), 369–76.
——, 'Les Anniversaires célébrés à St. Denis au milieu du XIVe siècle', *RM* 14 (1924), 22–31.
——, 'Les Frères défunts de St.-Denis au début du IXe siècle', *RM* 15 (1925), 241–57.
Wilson, H. A. (ed.), *The Gelasian Sacramentary: Liber Sacramentorum Romanae ecclesiae* (Oxford, 1894).
——, *The Gregorian Sacramentary Under Charles the Great*, HBS 49 (London, 1915).
Winter, P. M. de, 'The *Grandes Heures* of Philip the Bold, Duke of Burgundy: The Copyist Jean L'Avenant and His Patrons at the French Court', *Speculum* 57 (1982), 786–842.
Wood, I., 'A Prelude to Columbanus: The Monastic Achievement in the Burgundian Territories', *Columbanus and Merovingian Monasticism*, ed. H. B. Clarke and M. Brennan, BAR International Series 113 (Oxford, 1981), 3–32.
Wormald, F. (ed.), *English Kalendars after A.D. 1100* (London, 1939–46).
——, *English Kalendars before A.D. 1100* (London, 1934).
Wright, C., 'Leoninus, Poet and Musician', *JAMS* 39 (1986), 1–35.
——, *Music and Ceremony at Notre Dame of Paris, 500–1550*, Cambridge Studies in Music (Cambridge, 1989).
Ziegler, U., 'Das Sacramentarium Gelasianum Bibl. Vat. Reg. lat. 316 und die Schule von Chelles', *Archiv für Geschichte des Buchwesens* 16 (1976), 1–142.
Zimmermann, E., *Vorkarolingische Miniaturen* (Berlin, 1916).
Zinn, G., 'Suger, Theology, and the Pseudo-Dionysian Tradition', *Abbot Suger and Saint-Denis*, ed. P. Gerson (New York, 1986), 33–40.
Zivelonghi, G., and Adami, C., *I Codici Liturgici della cattedrale di Verona* (Verona, 1987).

INDEX OF MANUSCRIPT, ARCHIVAL, AND PRINTED SOURCES

Note: Numbers in bold type signal central discussion of manuscript found in Chapters 6 and 7.

MANUSCRIPTS

ARCHIVES

PRINTED SOURCES

GENERAL INDEX